SIR WILLIAM LAIRD CLOWES was born in 1865 and made his reputation as naval correspondent of *The Times* between 1890 and 1895. He was a member of the Navy League and involved in the agitation for greater naval resources, and his anonymous articles which appeared in the *Daily Graphic* in 1893 undoubtedly influenced the naval Estimates.

He wrote and compiled this seven-volume history of the Royal Navy between 1897 and 1903, involving a number of distinguished contemporary writers to assist him. From America he employed Captain Mahan, author of *The Influence of Sea Power upon History*, and Theodore Roosevelt who covered the history of the war with the United States. Sir Clements Markham, President of the Royal Geographical Society, dealt with the history of voyages and discoveries, and H W Wilson, author of *Battleships in Action*, described many of the minor naval operations.

Walter Lofts RA. G.

Types of the Old Navy.

Queen Victoria, in the "Fairy," leading the Baltic Fleet to Sea. 1854.

From the painting by Mulligan in possession of the Hon. Mrs Joseph Denman.

The Royal Navy

A History

From the Earliest Times to the Death of Queen Victoria

By

Sir Wm. Laird Clowes

Fellow of King's College, London; Gold Medallist U.S. Naval Institute;
Hon. Member of the Royal United Service Institution;
Assoc., Institute of Naval Architects

Assisted by

Sir Clements Markham, K.C.B., P.R.G.S.
Captain A. T. Mahan, U.S.N.
Mr. H. W. Wilson
Col. Theodore Roosevelt, President of the United States
etc.

VOL. VII.

CHATHAM PUBLISHING

LONDON

PUBLISHER'S NOTE
In the original edition the four photogravure plates and
twenty-five full-page illustrations faced the text pages
as listed on pages xiii–xiv. In this edition these
illustrations are collected at the back of the book
after page 584, in the order in which they
appeared in the first edition.

Published in 1997 by
Chatham Publishing,
1 & 2 Faulkner's Alley, Cowcross Street,
London EC1M 6DD

Chatham Publishing is an imprint of
Gerald Duckworth and Co Ltd

First published in 1903 by
Sampson Low, Marston and Company

ISBN 1 86176 016 7

A catalogue record for this book is available from the British Library

Printed and bound in Great Britain by Biddles Ltd, Guildford, Surrey

INTRODUCTION TO VOLUME VII.

THE present volume completes the History of the Royal Navy from the earliest times down to the date of the death of her late Majesty, Queen Victoria, at the beginning of the year 1901. Publication of the work, which, it was originally intended, should be finished in about three years and a half, counting from the summer of 1896, has unfortunately occupied instead a period of nearly seven years; and I fear that the unpremeditated delay in the appearance of volume after volume has been not only a disappointment to many people who have been good enough to take a lively interest in the progress of the work, but also a source of great additional expense to my most courteous and considerate publishers.

Begun at a time when I was in my usual good health, Volume I. was still in the rough when I was attacked by a malady, which, though its action is sometimes slow, seldom spares the life of its victim; and, in consequence, I was suddenly ordered away from England, where alone I could have prosecuted the work under conditions entirely favourable. Except during brief intervals, I had to remain abroad or in the Channel Islands until the autumn of 1902. These facts account for some part of the delay.

Another part is to be accounted for by a determination, arrived at about the year 1898, that the book should consist of a larger number of volumes than had been originally contemplated. The number first fixed upon had been five: it grew to six, and then to seven. I do not think that this extension of scope is, upon the whole, to be regretted, although undoubtedly it postponed the publication of the final volume for more than two years. It has enabled a more liberal allowance of space than otherwise would

have been available to be devoted to an account of the marvellous
material changes which revolutionised naval warfare in the last
half of the nineteenth century, and it afforded room for the inclusion of what, I trust, will be found to be a sufficiently full history
of the Navy's share in the important operations in South Africa
and China in the closing days of the Victorian era. The lamented
death of the great Queen, at the very threshold of a new century,
and immediately after success had been secured in China and
assured in South Africa, furnished me with a date obviously suitable, in every respect, at which to bring my task to a halt.

I do not wish to insist too strongly upon the disadvantages
under which, as I have explained, I laboured almost from the
commencement: but it is necessary that I should ask that any
unfavourable sentence which may be passed upon my work shall
be mitigated in consideration of the hostile circumstances in which
I have been obliged to perform it. I know, far better than anyone
who may be my critic, the numerous shortcomings of these seven
volumes. I know, too, how much fewer those shortcomings would
have been, if I had had good health instead of bad, throughout
these seven years. Excellent searchers, and other fellow-workers,
have aided me from the beginning to the utmost of their power;
yet I would have preferred to do for myself what they have done
for me; and, had I been in a position to do so, the results would
have been more satisfactory, certainly to myself, possibly also to
the reader; for it hardly needs saying that notes and documents
copied in one's own handwriting are less likely to be misunderstood, mis-transcribed in quotation, and misapplied, than notes and
documents copied in a score of different writings, not all of which
are equally legible. Nevertheless, thanks to the large revision
which most of the history of the events of the second half of the
last century has undergone at the kind hands of those who took
personal part in them, I have reason to hope that, upon the
whole, the contents of this volume are very trustworthy records
of the facts.

During the long and interesting period covered by this final
instalment of the work, Great Britain was engaged in no purely
maritime war of any importance. She was not called upon to
fight one considerable action in the open sea; and such bombardments as her ships were concerned in were far less serious matters
than the bombardment of Copenhagen, in 1801, or even the naval

attack upon Sebastopol in 1854. Yet at no period has the British Navy been more continuously engaged, or more widely employed, in small wars, and in those too soon forgotten police duties, which confer so many benefits upon the Empire, and often lack, nevertheless, any chronicler other than the officer who reports them dryly to the Admiralty. Some hundreds of these minor operations will be found described in the present volume; and few readers, I suspect, will fail to be surprised at the number of them. They give one a new idea of the wakefulness and ubiquity of the Empire's maritime forces. Here a rebel tribe is chastised; there a consul is protected and vindicated; elsewhere a slaver is captured and her cargo of slaves set at liberty; and much of this is done without the great public hearing a word about it at the time. The extent and usefulness of this quiet work of the Navy is one of the characteristics of the period under review.

Another is the frequency, previously unparalleled, with which the officers and men of the service, either with troops or alone, have been employed to do what should be purely landsmen's work, all over both hemispheres, sometimes fighting hundreds of miles from the sea. I venture to think that this employment of them has tended of late to become far too common. The naval officer and the bluejacket are expensive servants of His Majesty. They cannot be trained or replaced quickly, and they are entered and educated for another object. When a ship disembarks and sends up-country a large contingent of her people, and possibly also a number of her guns, she reduces her own usefulness, perhaps to vanishing point; and, on certain stations, it might be an extremely serious matter if, in the event of a large man-of-war being suddenly required to cope with an emergency, she could neither move nor fight. One can hardly resist the conclusion that if the army, regular and irregular, were formed, organised, armed, and stationed as it should be, the calls for the assistance of the Navy on shore would be fewer. It is, however, a subject for congratulation that the Navy, when thus summoned, has never failed to respond in the handsomest and noblest manner; and that, whether working single-handed or with the army, alike in New Zealand, in India, in the Soudan, in South Africa, and in China, it has gathered to itself fresh laurels. The Royal Marines, of course, are properly enough regarded as an amphibious corps; yet the manner in which, on at least one occasion, they were employed in South Africa suggests that those generals who recollected that the Marines are soldiers may have forgotten that they are also part of every efficient British man-of-war's complement. Even more than the seamen, if that be possible, have the Royal Marines added, since 1856, to their magnificent reputation.

Yet another characteristic of the period – and I greet it as a happy omen—is the increasing frequency with which the officers and bluejackets of the United States of America have found themselves ranged side by side with their cousins of the British Navy. In the Pei-ho, in Japan, in Central America, in the far North-West, on the Atlantic during the laying of the early cables, in Egypt, in Chile, in Samoa, and, more recently, in China, American seamen and marines have been the loyal comrades of British ones; nor, I believe, has any unpleasantness, jealousy, or friction ever arisen when men of both nations have served together, as has often happened, under the leadership and command of a single officer, British or American. The naval services of the two English-speaking nations have shown their trust in, and sympathy with, one another so repeatedly, and have so often cemented their good feeling with the shedding of blood and the sacrifice of gallant life, that one is entitled to hope that never in the future will the relations between them be less frank and cordial, and that the general body of the people of the two countries will soon learn to look towards one another as generously and confidently as the two navies do already. Britain and America, acting together, should always be able to ensure the peace of the world. Their action on opposite sides would be the greatest catastrophe that could possibly happen to the interests of civilisation, freedom, and progress.

To name here all those who have encouraged and assisted me in the final stage of my long task would be impossible. His most gracious Majesty has been pleased to show his personal interest in the undertaking by conferring upon me an honour which only his kindness could have deemed me deserving of. From Viscount Goschen, the late, and the Earl of Selborne, the present, First Lord of the Admiralty, I have received help for which I cannot too fully express my gratitude. To the Foreign Office also I am much indebted. The authorities of the British Museum Library, and the Library of the Patent Office, as usual, have given ready help to my assistants; and Sir William Howard Russell has facilitated their researches in certain directions by placing at their disposal, and allowing to be removed from his office, his own file of the *Army and Navy Gazette*.

To Mr. A. F. Yarrow, the well-known builder of fast small craft, I am deeply obliged for the personal interest which he has taken in the completion of the work, and for the sympathetic manner in which he has aided me.

To mention the naval officers who have furnished me with facts and suggestions would almost involve the transcription to these pages of the entire list of living and lately living flag-officers and captains. It has been my aim, whenever possible, to secure personal narratives, in the shape of letters, diaries, and private journals, wherewith to supplement the information, often very meagre and defective, contained in official despatches : and my efforts in that direction have brought me into correspondence, during the past ten years, with no fewer than 741 naval and Marine officers, who, nearly without exception, have taken much trouble on my behalf, and have generously placed at my disposal everything in their possession that could be of use to me. Many valuable facts relating to the work of the Royal Marines have been brought to my notice, thanks to the courtesy of the officers editing the *Globe and Laurel*, the admirable journal of that distinguished corps.

Of officers who, though not in the Navy, were associated intimately with duties in which the Navy was employed, no one showed me greater kindness, or took more pains to be of real service to me than the late General Sir Andrew Clarke.

To Miss E. M. Samson, who has again undertaken the difficult business of providing the index, I tender my grateful thanks. To my publishers, Messrs. Sampson Low, Marston & Co., Ltd., and, in particular to Mr. E. Marston and to his son, Mr. R. B. Marston, members of the Directorate, I owe more gratitude than I can express for the generous and cheerful way in which they have borne with the numerous disappointments and annoyances incidental to the association with them in a great and costly undertaking of one who too frequently has been incapable, for weeks at a time, of carrying out the letter of his agreements with them. The kindly allowances which Mr. R. B. Marston, with whom I chiefly corresponded, was ever willing to make, and the thoughtful way in which he ever considered my health rather than his convenience, will never be forgotten by me. If this History, as I hope it may, be welcomed as a chronicle of affairs which hitherto have never been chronicled together in a single work; if it aid, as I trust it will, in strengthening my countrymen for many a year to come in their determination that the British Navy shall be second to none in the world; and if, in the future, the long story which is told in it shall contribute aught to the encouragement of Britons who are inclined to despair, or to the ardour of those who believe in the glorious destinies of their race, then let the credit be given to the Messrs. Marston, but for whose patriotic co-operation it could not have been offered to the public.

WM. LAIRD CLOWES.

April, 1903.

CONTENTS.

VOLUME VII.

ERRATA.

Page 8, col. 1, line 18, *for* Balfour *read* Balfour (2).
,, 8, ,, 2, ,, 3, *for* John *read* James.
,, 87, ,, 2, ,, 39, *for* Farquhar *read* Farquhar (2).
,, 103, line 6 from bottom, *for* Abercrombie Brown *read* Abercrombie Otto Brown.
,, 217, ,, 5 from bottom, *for* Edge *read* Edye.
,, 221, ,, 38, *for* Rutherfold *read* Rutherford.
,, 238, ,, 4, *for* Cresswell *read* Creswell.
,, 246, ,, 6, *for* Alexander *read* Victor Alexander.
,, 246, ,, 8, *for* Valentia *read* Valencia.
,, 292, ,, 17, *for* Sir Edmund *read* Sir John Edmund.
,, 297, ,, 2 from bottom, *for* Balfour *read* Balfour (2).
,, 298 n.[2] *for* Henry Boys *read* Henry Boys (2).
,, 299, line 6 from bottom, *for* Sir Edmund *read* Sir John Edmund.
,, 324, last col. line 22, *for* S. John *read* St. George.
,, 324, line 13, *for* Balfour *read* Balfour (2).
,, 336, line 14, *for* Balfour *read* Balfour (2).
,, 336, ,, 21, *for* Herbert *read* Hubert.
,, 396, ,, 2 from bottom, *after* Pigeon *insert* Lieut.
,, 401, ,, 9 from bottom, *for* Parrayon and McCann *read* McCann and Parrayon.
,, 428 n.[2] *for* Gore-Brown *read* Gore-Browne.
,, 429, line 14, *for* Campbell *read* Campbell (2).
,, 431, ,, 9, *for* Carnegie Codrington *read* Codrington Carnegie.
,, 493, ,, 14, *for* Ethelstone *read* Ethelston.
,, 508 n.[2] *for* Lieut. England *read* Lieut. George Plunkett England.
,, 527, line 9 from bottom, *for* Captain *read* Captains.
,, 557, ,, 9, *for* Captain James *read* Captain George James, etc.
,, 571, col. 1, line 26, *for* Nicolson *read* Nicholson.
,, 581, line 33, *for* Hawkworth *read* Hawksworth.

Publisher's note
The photogravure plates and twenty-five full-page illustrations listed below
appear in this edition at the back of the book, after page 584.

LIST OF ILLUSTRATIONS.

VOLUME VII.

—————

PHOTOGRAVURE PLATES.

FULL-PAGE ILLUSTRATIONS.

ILLUSTRATIONS IN THE TEXT.

NAVAL HISTORY.

CHAPTER XLVI.

CIVIL HISTORY OF THE ROYAL NAVY, 1857–1900.

Administrative Officials at the Admiralty and the Dockyards—Changes at the Admiralty—Division of Admiralty Work—The Navy Estimates—Alterations in the Active List—Admirals of the Fleet—Flag-Officers—Ensigns—The Navigating Branch—New Ranks—Retirement—Pay—Wages—Naval Reserves—Naval Architecture—Ironclads—Experimental Types—New factors in Naval Warfare—Armoured Cruisers—Unarmoured Cruisers—Gunboats—Torpedo-boats—Torpedo-boat Catchers—Destroyers—Miscellaneous Craft—Yachts—Mercantile Auxiliaries—Ordnance—The first Breech-loaders—Improved Muzzle-loaders—The later Breech-loaders—Quick-firing Guns—Small Arms—Machine-guns—Gunnery—Engines and Boilers—Screws—Turbines—Water-tube Boilers—Armour—Projectiles—Torpedoes—Torpedo-nets—Submarine Boats—Illumination—Electricity—Masts and Sails—Conning-towers—Signalling—Uniform—Health of the Navy—Training and Technical Education—The *Britannia*—Gunnery and Torpedo Schools—Training-ships—Technical Schools—Guardships—Royal United Service Institution—Miscellaneous Innovations—Orders and Medals—Naval Clubs—Influence of the British Navy on Foreign Services—Attachés—The Naval Intelligence Department—The Bluejacket—Sailors' Homes—Royal Naval Fund—Influence of popular Interest in the Navy—Naval Reviews—The Royal Naval Exhibition—The Navy League—The Navy Records Society—The Jubilee Reviews.

THE CRIMEA MEDAL.

THE succession of the more important administrative officers of the Royal Navy from 1857 to the end of the reign of Queen Victoria was as follows :—

FIRST LORDS OF THE ADMIRALTY.[1]

Rt. Hon. Sir Charles Wood, Bart., M.P.
Mar.   8, 1858. Rt. Hon. Sir John Somerset Pakington, Bart., M.P. (G.C.B. 1859).
June 28, 1859. Edward Adolphus, 12th Duke of Somerset, K.G.
July 13, 1866. Rt. Hon. Sir John Somerset Pakington, Bart., G.C.B., M.P.
Mar.   8, 1867. Rt. Hon. Henry Thomas Lowry Corry, M.P.
Dec. 18, 1868. Rt. Hon. Hugh Culling Eardley Childers, M.P.
Mar. 13, 1871. Rt. Hon. George Joachim Goschen, M.P.
Mar.   6, 1874. Rt. Hon. George Ward Hunt, M.P.
Aug. 15, 1877. Rt. Hon. William Henry Smith, M.P.
May 13, 1880. Thomas George, 1st Earl of Northbrook, G.C.S.I.
July   2, 1885. Rt. Hon. Lord George Francis Hamilton, M.P.
Feb. 16, 1886. George Frederick Samuel, 1st Marquess of Ripon, G.C.S.I.
Aug.   6, 1886. Rt. Hon. Lord George Francis Hamilton, M.P.
Aug. 23, 1892. John Poyntz, 5th Earl Spencer, K.G.
July   4, 1895. Rt. Hon. George Joachim Goschen, M.P.
Nov.   1900. William Waldegrave, 2nd Earl of Selborne.

SECRETARIES OF THE ADMIRALTY.

FIRST SECRETARY.

Ralph Bernal Osborne, M.P.
Mar.   9, 1858. Rt. Hon. Henry Thomas Lowry Corry, M.P.
June 30, 1859. Lord Clarence Edward Paget, C.B., M.P., R.-Adm. (V.-Adm. 1865).
Apr. 30, 1866. Hon. Thomas George Baring, M.P. (Lord Northbrook, 1866).
July 16, 1866. Lord Henry Charles George Gordon-Lennox, M.P.
Dec. 18, 1868. William Edward Baxter, M.P.

(*Title changed to that of Parliamentary Secretary,* 1870.)

SECOND SECRETARY.

Thomas Phinn.
May   7, 1857. William Govett Romaine, C.B.

June 29, 1869. Vernon Lushington, Q.C.

(*Title changed to that of Permanent Secretary,* 1870.)

PARLIAMENTARY SECRETARY.

Mar. 17, 1870. George John Shaw-Lefevre, M.P.
July 12, 1870. William Edward Baxter, M.P.
Mar.   6, 1874. Hon. Algernon Fulke Egerton, M.P.
May 15, 1880. Rt. Hon. George John Shaw-Lefevre, M.P.
Dec.   1, 1880. George Otto Trevelyan, M.P.
May 13, 1882. Henry Campbell-Bannerman, M.P.
Nov. 20, 1884. Sir Thomas Brassey, K.C.B., M.P.   [M.P.
July   3, 1885. Charles Thomson Ritchie,
Feb. 16, 1886. Rt. Hon. John Tomlinson Hibbert, M.P.   [M.P.
Aug.   6, 1886. Arthur Bower Forwood,

---

[1] For convenience of reference, the names of the Prime Ministers from 1857 to the end of 1900, with the dates of their accession to office, are appended : Feb. 10, 1855, Lord Palmerston ; Feb. 25, 1858, Earl of Derby; June 18, 1859, Lord Palmerston; Nov. 6, 1865, Earl Russell ; July 6, 1866, Earl of Derby ; Feb. 27, 1868, Mr. Disraeli; Dec. 9, 1868, Mr. Gladstone ; Feb. 21, 1874, Mr. Disraeli (Earl of Beaconsfield, 1876) ; Apr. 28, 1880, Mr. Gladstone ; June 24, 1885, Marquess of Salisbury ; Feb. 6, 1886, Mr. Gladstone; Aug. 3, 1886, Marquess of Salisbury; Aug. 18, 1892, Mr. Gladstone; Mar. 3, 1894, Earl of Rosebery ; July 2, 1895, Marquess of Salisbury (again 1900).

Aug. 24, 1892. Rt. Hon. Sir Ughtred James Kay - Shuttleworth, Bart., M.P.

July 4, 1895. William Grey Ellison-Macartney, M.P.

Nov. 1900. Hugh Oakeley Arnold-Forster, M.P.

PERMANENT SECRETARY.

(*This office was established in 1870, and abolished on Nov. 1, 1877. It was re-established in 1882, upon the abolition of the office of Naval Secretary.*)

July 12, 1870. Vernon Lushington, Q.C. (till Nov. 1877).

(*Office temporarily abolished, and duty done by the Naval Secretary.*)

May 8, 1882. Robert George Crookshank Hamilton.

May 15, 1882. Robert Hall (3), C.B., retd. v.-adm., (actg.), (died June 11, 1882).

June 13, 1882. George Tryon, C.B., Capt., R.N. (actg.).

May 3, 1883. George Tryon, C.B., Capt., R.N.

Apr. 2, 1884. Evan Macgregor, C.B. (K.C.B., 1892).

NAVAL SECRETARY.

May 8, 1872. Robert Hall (3), C.B., Capt., R.N. (later retd. r.-adm. and v.-adm.)

(*This office was abolished, May 8, 1882.*)

SURVEYOR OF THE NAVY.

Sir Baldwin Wake Walker (1), Bart., K.C.B., Capt., R.N. (R.-Adm. 1858).

(*This office became in 1860 that of Controller.*)

CONTROLLER OF THE NAVY.

1860. Sir Baldwin Wake Walker (1), Bart., K.C.B., R.-Adm.

Feb. 7, 1861. Robert Spencer Robinson,[1] R.-Adm.(V.-Adm.1866, K.C.B. 1868).

Feb. 14, 1871. Robert Hall (3),[1] C.B., Capt., R.N.

Apr. 29, 1872. William Houston Stewart, C.B., R.-Adm. (V.-Adm. 1876; K.C.B. 1877: Adm. 1881).

Dec. 1, 1881. Thomas Brandreth, R.-Adm.[1] (V.-Adm. 1884).

Nov. 28, 1885. William Graham, C.B., V.-Adm.[1] (K. C. B., 1887).

Aug. 6, 1888. John Ommanney Hopkins, R.-Adm.[1] (V.-Adm. 1891).

Feb. 2, 1892. John Arbuthnot Fisher, C.B., R.-Adm.[1] (K.C.B., 1894 : V.-Adm. 1896).

Aug. 24, 1897. Arthur Knyvet Wilson, C.B., V.C., R.-Adm.[1]

([1] *From Jan. 14, 1869, to Mar. 19, 1872, and again from April 18th, 1882, to the end of the century, the Controller was a Lord of the Admiralty.*)

CONTROLLER OF THE VICTUALLING.

Thomas T. Grant, F.R.S.[2]

May 10, 1858. Charles Richards, Paym., R.N.[2]

(*This title was changed in 1870 to that of Superintendent of Victualling Stores.*)

SUPERINTENDENT OF VICTUALLING STORES.

Apr. 1, 1870. Samuel Sayer Lewes.

(*This title was changed in 1878 to that of Director of Victualling.*)

DIRECTOR OF VICTUALLING.

Aug. 12, 1878. Samuel Sayer Lewes (Kt. 1886).

Feb. 1, 1886. Henry Francis Redhead Yorke (late R.N.), (C.B. 1897).

([2] *Also, from 1857 to 1862, Controller of the Transport Service.*)

DIRECTOR OF TRANSPORTS AND
PRISONERS OF WAR.

Feb. 21, 1855. William Drew.

(*In 1857 the duties of this office were
added to those of the Controller of
the Victualling; but the services were
again separated in 1862.*)

DIRECTOR OF TRANSPORTS.

Apr. 30, 1862. William Robert Mends,
C.B., Capt. R.N. (retd.
r.-adm. 1868; K.C.B.;
retd. v.-adm. 1874;
retd. ad., 1879; G.C.B.
1882).
Apr. 1, 1883. Sir Francis William Sullivan, K.C.B., C.M.G.,
R. - Adm. (V. - Adm.
1885).
Aug. 20, 1888. Harry Woodfall Brent,
Capt., R.N. (retd. 1889 ;
retd. r.-adm. 1890).
Aug. 20, 1896. Bouverie Francis Clark,
Capt., R.N. (retd. 1897 ;
retd. r.-adm., 1899.)

STOREKEEPER-GENERAL.

Hon. Robert Dundas.

(*Title changed in 1869 to that of
Superintendent of Stores.*)

SUPERINTENDENT OF STORES.

Apr. 13, 1869. Nelson Girdlestone.
Jan. 23, 1872. Coghlan McLean Hardy.

(*Title changed in 1876 to that of
Director of Stores.*)

DIRECTOR OF STORES.

1876. Coghlan McLean Hardy.
Apr. 1, 1889. William George Prout
Gilbert.
Apr. 1, 1895. Gordon William Miller.

HYDROGRAPHER.

John Washington, Capt.,
R.N.
Sept. 19, 1863. George Henry Richards,
Capt., R.N. (R.-Adm.
1870; C.B. 1871 ; retd.
r.-adm., Jan. 19, 1874).
Feb. 3, 1874. Frederick John O. Evans,
C.B., retd. capt., R.N.
(later K.C.B.)
Aug. 1, 1884. William James Lloyd
Wharton, Capt., R.N.
(retd. 1891; retd. r.-adm.
1895; C.B. 1895; K.C.B.,
1897).

CHIEF CONSTRUCTOR.

Isaac Watts (C.B. 1862).
July 9, 1863. Edward James Reed (C.B.,
1868, K.C.B., 1880).

*Resigned July 8, 1870,
whereupon the office was
left open until*

Aug. 17, 1872. Nathaniel Barnaby (C.B.,
1876 ; K.C.B., 1885.)

(*Title changed in 1875 to that of Director
of Naval Construction.*)

DIRECTOR OF NAVAL CONSTRUCTION.

1875. Nathaniel Barnaby.
Oct. 1, 1885. William Henry White.

(*Title of Assistant Controller added
Dec. 17, 1885.*)

ASSISTANT CONTROLLER AND DIRECTOR
OF NAVAL CONSTRUCTION.

Dec. 17, 1885. William Henry White
(C.B. 1891; K.C.B.
1895).

CHIEF ENGINEER AND INSPECTOR OF
STEAM MACHINERY.

Thomas Lloyd.
(*Title abolished, Feb. 4, 1869.*)

SURVEYOR OF FACTORIES AND WORK-
SHOPS AND CONSULTING ENGINEER.

Jan. 19, 1869. Andrew Murray.

(*Title abolished, Feb. 24, 1870.*)

ENGINEER-ASSISTANT.

Oct. 20, 1860. James Wright.

(*Title changed in 1872 to that of Engineer-
in-Chief.*)

ENGINEER-IN-CHIEF.

Aug. 17, 1872. James Wright (C.B. 1880).
May 1, 1887. Richard Sennett, Insp. of Mach., R.N.
May 6, 1889. Albert John Durston, Insp. of Mach., R.N. (Chf. Insp. of Mach. 1893; C.B.1895; K.C.B. 1897).

ACCOUNTANT-GENERAL OF THE NAVY.

Sir Richard Madox Bromley, K.C.B.
Apr. 1, 1863. James Beeby.
Oct. 31, 1872. Henry William Routledge Walker.
June 1, 1878. Robert George Crookshank Hamilton.
May 8, 1882. William Willis (Kt.1885).
June 1, 1885. Sir Gerald Fitzgerald, K.C.M.G.
Dec. 1, 1896. Richard Davis Awdry, C.B.

DIRECTOR-GENERAL OF THE MEDICAL
DEPARTMENT OF THE NAVY.

Sir John Liddell, M.D., F.R.S., R.N.
Jan. 21, 1864. Alexander Bryson, C.B., M.D., R.N.
Apr. 15, 1869. Alexander Armstrong, M.D., R.N. (K.C.B. 1874).

Feb. 1, 1880. John Watt Reid, M.D., R.N. (K.C.B. 1882).
Feb. 27, 1888. James Nicholas Dick, C.B., R.N. (K.C.B. 1895).
Apr. 1, 1898. Sir Henry Frederick Norbury, M.D., K.C.B., R.N.

COMPTROLLER-GENERAL OF THE
COAST GUARD.

Charles Eden, Commodore.
Aug. 3, 1859. Hastings Reginald Yelverton, C.B., Commodore.
Apr. 27, 1863. Alfred Phillipps Ryder, Commodore.
Apr. 9, 1866. John Walter Tarleton, C.B. (R.-Adm. 1868).

(*This office was abolished in 1869.*)

ADMIRAL SUPERINTENDENT OF NAVAL
RESERVES.

Jan. 1, 1875. Sir John Walter Tarleton, K.C.B., V.-Adm.
Nov. 13, 1876. Augustus Phillimore, R.-Adm. (V.-Adm. 1879).
Nov. 21, 1879. H.R.H. Alfred Ernest Albert, Duke of Edinburgh, K.G., etc., R.-Adm.
Nov. 23, 1882. Sir Anthony Hiley Hoskins, K.C.B., R.-Adm. (V.-Adm. 1885).
Sept. 6, 1885. John Kennedy Erskine Baird, R.-Adm. (V.-Adm. 1886).
Apr. 17, 1888. Sir George Tryon, K.C.B., R.-Adm. (V.-Adm. 1889).
Apr. 21, 1891. Robert O'Brien FitzRoy, C.B., R.-Adm.
Apr. 25, 1894. Edward Hobart Seymour, C.B., R.-Adm. (V.-Adm. 1895).
May 10, 1897. Compton Edward Domvile, V.-Adm. (K.C.B. 1898).
May 21, 1900. Sir Gerard Henry Uctred Noel, K.C.M.G., R.-Adm.

DIRECTOR OF NAVAL INTELLIGENCE.

Feb. 1, 1887. William Henry Hall, Capt., R.N.
Jan. 1, 1889. Cyprian Arthur George Bridge, Capt., R.N. (R.-Adm. 1892).
Sept. 1, 1894. Lewis Anthony Beaumont, Capt., R.N. (R.-Adm. 1897).
Mar. 20, 1899. Reginald Neville Custance, C.M.G., Capt., R.N. (R.-Adm. 1899).

SUPERINTENDENTS OF H.M. DOCKYARDS.

Chatham.

George Goldsmith, C.B., Capt., R.N.
Apr. 1, 1861. Edward Gennys Fanshawe, Capt., R.N.
Nov. 19, 1863. William Houston Stewart, C.B., Capt., R.N.
Dec. 1, 1868. William Charles Chamberlain, Capt., R.N.
Jan. 19, 1874. Charles Fellowes, C.B., Capt., R.N. (R.-Adm. 1876).
Feb. 3, 1879. Thomas Brandreth, R.-Adm.
Dec. 1, 1881. Georges Willes Watson, R.-Adm. (V.-Adm. 1886).
May 1, 1886. William Codrington, C.B., R.-Adm.
Nov. 1, 1887. Edward Kelly, R.-Adm.
Jan. 25, 1892. George Digby Morant, R.-Adm. (V.-Adm. 1895).
Sept. 2, 1895. Hilary Gustavus Andoe, C.B., R.-Adm.
Sept. 2, 1899. Swinton Colthurst Holland, R.-Adm.

Portsmouth.

William Fanshawe Martin, R.-Adm.
Feb. 25, 1858. Hon. George Grey (2), R.-Adm.
Feb. 19, 1863. George Elliot (4), R.-Adm.

July 1, 1865. George Greville Wellesley, C.B., R.-Adm.
July 1, 1869. Astley Cooper Key, C.B., R.-Adm.
Nov. 20, 1871. William Houston Stewart, C.B., R.-Adm.
Apr. 29, 1872. Sir Francis Leopold M'Clintock, R.-Adm.
Apr. 30, 1877. Hon. Fitzgerald Algernon Charles Foley, R-.Adm. (V.-Adm. 1881).
May 1, 1882. John Dobree M'Crea, R.-Adm.
Apr. 6, 1883. Frederick Anstruther Herbert, R.-Adm.
Nov. 1, 1886. John Ommanney Hopkins, R.-Adm.
Aug. 6, 1888. William Elrington Gordon, R.-Adm.
May 21, 1891. John Arbuthnot Fisher, C.B., R.-Adm.
Feb. 1, 1892. Charles George Fane, R.-Adm.
Feb. 1, 1896. Ernest Rice, R.-Adm. (V.-Adm. 1899).
Sept. 1, 1899. Pelham Aldrich, R.-Adm.

Devonport.

Feb. 19, 1855. Sir James Hanway Plumridge, K.C.B., R.-Adm.
Dec. 9, 1857. Sir Thomas Sabine Pasley, Bart., R.-Adm.
Nov. 28, 1862. Thomas Matthew Charles Symonds, C.B., R.-Adm.
May 9, 1866. Hon. James Robert Drummond, C.B., R.-Adm.
July 13, 1870. William Houston Stewart, C.B., R.-Adm.
Nov. 22, 1871. Sir William King Hall, K.C.B., R.-Adm.
Aug. 12, 1875. William Charles Chamberlain, R.-Adm.
May 1, 1876. George Ommanney Willes, C.B., R.-Adm.
Feb. 1, 1879. Charles Webley Hope, R.-Adm.
Feb. 23, 1880. Charles Thomas Curme, R.-Adm.
Feb. 23, 1885. John Crawford Wilson, R.-Adm. (died).
July 10, 1885. Henry Duncan Grant, C.B., R.-Adm. (V.-Adm. 1888).

Aug. 1, 1888. Sir Walter James Hunt-
Grubbe, K.C.B., R.-
Adm. (V.-Adm. 1890).
Aug. 4, 1891. Sir Robert Henry More-
Molyneux, K.C.B., R.-
Adm. (V.-Adm. 1894).
Aug. 7, 1894. Edmund John Church,
R.-Adm.
Nov. 3, 1896. Henry John Carr, R.-
Adm.
July 7, 1899. Thomas Sturges Jackson,
R.-Adm.

Woolwich (" Commod. in Charge ").

(Dec.31, 1853.) John Shepherd (2), Com-
mod. 2nd Cl.
Dec. 20, 1858. Hon. James Robert Drum-
mond, Commod., 2nd Cl.
June 29, 1861. Sir Frederick William
Erskine Nicholson, Bart.,
Commod., 2nd Cl.
Jan. 1, 1864. Hugh Dunlop, C.B., Com-
mod., 2nd Cl.
Apr. 9, 1866. William Edmonstone,C.B.,
Commod., 2nd Cl.

(*Dockyard closed* 1869.)

Deptford.

Horatio Thomas Austin,
C.B., Capt., R.N.
Dec. 12, 1857. Claude Henry Mason
Buckle, C.B., Capt.,
R.N.
Feb. 9, 1863. Henry Chads, Capt., R.N.
Apr. 10, 1866. Arthur Parry Eardley
Wilmot, C.B., Capt.,
R.N.

(*Dockyard closed,* 1869.)

Sheerness.

John Jervis Tucker, Capt.,
R.N.
Sept. 23, 1857. John Coghlan Fitzgerald,
Capt., R.N.
June 9, 1859. Rundle Burges Watson,
C.B., Capt., R.N.

July 3, 1860. Charles Wise, Capt., R.N.
Apr. 27, 1865. William King Hall, C.B.,
Capt., R.N.
Apr. 1, 1869. Hon. Arthur Auckland
Leopold Pedro Coch-
rane, C.B., Capt., R.N.
May 25, 1870. William Garnham Luard,
C.B., Capt., R.N.
Jan. 9, 1875. Hon. Fitzgerald Algernon
Charles Foley, Capt.,
R.N.
Jan. 9, 1877. Thomas Brandreth, Capt.,
R.N.
Jan. 4, 1879. Theodore Morton Jones,
Capt. R.N.
Jan. 1, 1883. John Ommanney Hopkins,
Capt., R.N.
Apr. 6, 1883. William Codrington, C.B..
Capt., R.N.
July 17, 1885. Henry Frederick Nichol-
sōn, C.B., Capt., R.N.
July 1, 1886. Sir Robert Henry More-
Molyneux,K.C.B.,Capt.,
R.N.
June 1, 1888. Charles George Fane,Capt.,
R.N.
Aug. 6, 1890. Richard Duckworth King,
Capt., R.N.
Jan. 25, 1892. Armand Temple Powlett,
Capt. R.N.
Jan. 1, 1894. John Fellowes, C.B.,
Capt., R.N.
Jan. 15, 1895. John Coke Burnell, Capt.,
R.N.
Jan. 11, 1898. Andrew Kennedy Bick-
ford, C.M.G., Capt.,
R.N.
June 28, 1899. Reginald Friend Hannam
Henderson, C.B., Capt.,
R.N.

Pembroke.

(May 22, 1854.) Robert Smart, K.H.,
Capt., R.N.
July 27, 1857. George Ramsay, C.B.,
Capt., R.N.
Sept. 1, 1862. William Loring, C.B.,
Capt., R.N.
Mar. 21, 1866. Robert Hall (3), C.B.,
Capt., R.N.
Mar. 22, 1871. William Armytage, Capt.,
R.N.

Jan. 22, 1872. Richard William Courtenay, Capt., R.N.

Mar. 15, 1875. Richard Vesey Hamilton, Capt., R.N.

Oct. 16, 1877. George Henry Parkin, Capt., R.N.

Oct. 15, 1882. Alfred John Chatfield, Capt., R.N.

Jan. 1, 1886. Edward Kelly, Capt., R.N.

June 22, 1887. George Digby Morant, Capt., R.N.

Jan. 7, 1889. Samuel Long, Capt., R.N.

Aug. 28, 1891. Walter Stewart, Capt., R.N.

Jan. 1, 1893. Charles Cooper Penrose FitzGerald, Capt., R.N.

Mar. 21, 1895. Charles John Balfour, Capt., R.N.

Oct. 4, 1896. Burges Watson, Capt., R.N.

Oct. 2, 1899. Charles James Barlow, D.S.O., Capt., R.N.

(*In* 1895 Capt. William Henry Hall, *appointed to succeed Capt. FitzGerald, died before he assumed office.*).

Gibraltar (" N.O. in Charge ").

Apr. 14, 1862. Erasmus Ommanney, Capt., R.N.

Jan. 1, 1865. James Charles Prevost, Capt., R.N.

Feb. 1, 1870. Augustus Phillimore, Capt., R.N.

Jan. 1, 1874. John Dobree M'Crea, Capt., R.N.

Jan. 16, 1878. William Henry Edye, Capt., R.N.

Jan. 10, 1881. Hon. Edmund Robert Fremantle, Capt., R.N.

Dec. 27, 1883. John Child Purvis (2), Capt., R.N.

Dec. 15, 1886. Henry Craven St. John, Capt., R.N.

Sept. 3, 1889. Claude Edward Buckle, Capt., R.N.

Jan. 7, 1892. Atwell Peregrine Macleod Lake, Capt., R.N.

Jan. 20, 1895. John Andrew Thomas Bruce, Capt., R.N.

Jan. 20, 1898. Charles Carter Drury, Capt., R.N.

Sept. 1, 1899. William Harvey Pigott, Capt., R.N.

Malta.

Hon. Sir Montagu Stopford, K.C.B., R.-Adm.

July 27, 1858. Henry John Codrington, C.B., R.-Adm.

Apr. 6, 1863. Horatio Thomas Austin, C.B., R.-Adm.

Nov. 26, 1864. Henry Kellett, C.B., R.-Adm.

May 25, 1868. Edward Gennys Fanshawe, R.-Adm.

June 6, 1870. Astley Cooper Key, C.B., R.-Adm.

Aug. 8, 1872. Sir Edward Augustus Inglefield, Kt., C.B., R.-Adm.

Dec. 22, 1875. Edward Bridges Rice, R.-Adm.

May 30, 1876. William Garnham Luard, C.B., R.-Adm (temp.).

Apr. 13, 1878. William Garnham Luard, C.B., R.-Adm.

July 18, 1879. John Dobree M'Crea, R.-Adm.

Mar. 24, 1882. William Graham, C.B., R.-Adm.

Mar. 25, 1885. Hon. William John Ward, R.-Adm.

May 4, 1887. Robert Gordon Douglas, R.-Adm.

Jan. 10, 1889. Alexander Buller, R.-Adm.

Jan. 12, 1892. Richard Edward Tracey, R.-Adm.

Jan. 20, 1894. Richard Duckworth King, R.-Adm.

Feb. 1, 1897. Rodney Maclaine Lloyd, C.B., R.-Adm.

Feb. 1, 1900. Burges Watson, R.-Adm.

Some of the changes in the administrative methods of the Admiralty may be traced in the foregoing. Under the rule of Mr. Childers it was felt that the position of the Controller, who had not then a seat at the Board, was anomalous and unsatisfactory; and, by an Order in Council of January 14th, 1869, the Board was accordingly reconstructed, as follows :—

THE OLD BOARD.	THE NEW BOARD.
The First Lord.	The First Lord.
Four Naval Lords.	The First Naval Lord.
The Civil Lord.	The Third Lord and Controller.
The First, or Parliamentary Secretary.	The Junior Naval Lord.
The Second, or Permanent Secretary.	The Civil Lord.
	The Parliamentary Secretary.
	The Permanent Secretary.

RT. HON. GEORGE JOACHIM, FIRST VISCOUNT GOSCHEN; FIRST LORD OF THE ADMIRALTY, 1871–74, 1895–1900.

(From a photograph by the London Stereoscopic Company.)

The Order, however, besides effecting this reconstruction, restricted each Lord to the peculiar business assigned to him, and so rendered meetings of the Board almost unnecessary. An embarrassment of affairs resulted. It was sought to reduce this by creating temporarily a " Chief of the Staff," by establishing the Contract and Purchase Department, and by transferring the offices of the Civil Departments from Somerset House to Whitehall and Spring

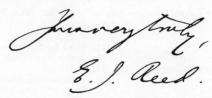

SIR EDWARD JAMES REED, K.C.B., F.R.S., CHIEF CONSTRUCTOR OF THE NAVY, 1863–1870.

Gardens. Under Mr. Goschen, a new Order in Council, of March 19th, 1872, made all the Lords directly responsible to the First Lord, appointed a Second Naval Lord, deprived the Controller of his seat, and added to the Board a Third, or Naval Secretary. But under Lord Northbrook, by Order in Council of March 10th, 1882, the Naval Secretary disappeared, the Permanent Secretary was revived, the Controller resumed his seat at the Board, and a non-parliamentary Civil Lord was given him as his assistant. This non-parliamentary Civil Lord [1] disappeared in 1885 ; and, at about the same time, the Accountant-General of the Navy was

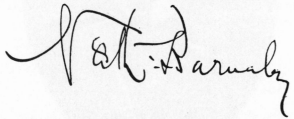

SIR NATHANIEL BARNABY, K.C.B., CHIEF CONSTRUCTOR OF THE NAVY.

ordered to act as deputy and assistant to the Parliamentary and Financial Secretary.[2] The Board as thereafter constituted consisted of :—

> The First Lord (salary £4500, with house).
> The First Sea Lord (salary £1500, with house, and naval pay).
> The Second Sea Lord (salary £1200, with naval pay).
> The Third Lord and Controller (salary £1700, with naval pay).
> The Junior Sea Lord (salary £1200).
> The Civil Lord (salary £1000).
> The Parliamentary and Financial Secretary (salary £2000).
> The Permanent Secretary (salary £2000).

---

[1] Mr. George Wightwick Rendel.   [2] O. in C. of Nov. 18, 1885.

The manner in which the business of the Board is divided, and the relationship of the various Lords and the Parliamentary Secretary to the subsidiary departments, is shown in the following table, which is adapted from Admiral Sir R. Vesey Hamilton's useful volume on ' Naval Administration ' (1896) :—

FIRST LORD.	PARLIA- MENTARY AND FINANCIAL SECRETARY.	Accountant-General. Director of Contracts (who is also under the particular Lord of the department for which purchases are made). All Departments (for questions of finance).	*Finance.*
	CIVIL LORD.	Director of Works. Accountant-General (for special questions affecting pay and allowances). Director of Greenwich Hospital.	*Works and Civil Personnel.*
	THIRD LORD AND CON- TROLLER.	Director of Naval Construction. Director of Dockyards. Engineer-in-Chief (for material). Director of Naval Ordnance (for material). Director of Stores (except for coals). Expense Accounts Branch.	*Material of the Fleet.*
	JUNIOR SEA LORD	Director of Transports. Director-General of the Medical Department. Director of Victualling. Director of Stores (for coals). Accountant-General (for allowances, table-money, etc.). Chaplain of the Fleet (for chaplains and naval instructors). Intelligence Department (for mobilization business affecting the above).	*Naval personnel organisation ; condition ; mobilisation ; stores ; coals; education ; manning ; surveying ; discipline.*
	SECOND SEA LORD.	Adm.-Supt. of Naval Reserves (for personnel). Engineer-in-Chief (for personnel). Chaplain of the Fleet (for naval schools). Manning the Navy. Intelligence Department (for mobilisation of the Fleet). D.A.G., Royal Marines.	
	FIRST SEA LORD.	Adm.-Supt. of Naval Reserves (for ships). Hydrographer. Director of Naval Ordnance (for training establishments for gunnery and torpedo). Intelligence Department. Discipline.	

The business of the Permanent Secretary is to superintend all correspondence in the name of the Board ; to prevent independent action by any department; to provide for the transmission and execution of orders ; and to keep unbroken the administrative machinery of the Admiralty.

The sums voted for the service of the Navy, and the numbers of seamen and Royal Marines authorised to be borne each from 1856–57 to 1900–01 inclusive were :—

Financial Year.[1]	Total Naval Supplies Granted.	Seamen and Boys Voted.	Royal Marines Voted.	Total Numbers Voted.	Total Numbers Actually Borne.
	£				
1856	16,568,614	60,000 (3 mos.) / 40,000 (9 mos.)	16,000	76,000 (3 mos.) / 56,000 (9 mos.)	60,659
1857	9,962,840	38,700 (3 mos.) / 40,700 (9 mos.)	15,000	53,700 (3 mos.) / 55,700 (9 mos.)	54,291
1858 [2]	9,878,859	44,380	15,000	59,380	
1859	11,775,718	47,400	15,000	62,400	
1860	11,836,100	66,100	18,000	84,100	
1861	12,640,588	59,000	18,000	77,000	
1862	11,794,305	56,850	18,000	74,850	
1863	10,736,032	57,000	18,000	75,000	
1864	10,708,651	53,000	18,000	71,000	
1865	10,392,224	52,000	17,000	69,000	
1866	10,434,735	51,450	16,400	67,850	
1867	10,978,253	52,912	16,400	69,312	
1868	11,157,290	52,070	14,700	66,770	
1869	9,996,641	49,000	14,000	63,000	
1870	9,370,530	47,000	14,000	61,000	
1871	9,789,956	47,000	14,000	61,000	
1872	9,532,149	47,000	14,000	61,000	
1873	9,899,725	46,000	14,000	60,000	
1874	10,440,105	46,000	14,000	60,000	
1875	10,825,194	46,000	14,000	60,000	
1876	11,288,872	46,000	14,000	60,000	
1877	10,971,829	46,000	14,000	60,000	
1878	12,129,901	46,000	14,000	60,000	
1879	10,586,894	45,800	13,000	58,800	
1880	10,566,935	45,800	13,000	58,800	
1881	10,945,919	45,100	13,000	58,100	
1882	10,483,901	45,100	12,400	57,500	
1883	10,899,500	44,850	12,400	57,250	
1884 [3]	11,185,770	44,550	12,400	56,950	
1885	12,694,900	45,564	12,770	58,334	
1886	13,270,100	48,500	12,900	61,400	
1887	12,476,800	49,600	12,900	62,500	62,072
1888 [4]	13,082,800	49,500	12,900	62,400	62,600
1889	13,685,100	51,400	14,000	65,400	63,598
1890	13,786,600	54,795	14,005	68,800	66,566
1891	14,215,100	56,995	14,005	71,000	68,805
1892 [5]	14,240,200	59,595	14,505	74,100	72,245
1893 [6]	14,240,100	61,695	15,005	76,700	75,207
1894	17,366,100	67,895	15,505	83,400	79,862
1895	18,701,000	73,345	15,505	88,850	84,569
1896	21,823,000	77,745	16,005	93,750	90,160
1897	22,338,000	83,045	17,005	100,050	92,322
1898	23,778,000	88,583	17,807	106,390	97,518
1899	26,594,500 [7]	92,350	18,290	110,640	104,239
1900	28,791,900	96,290	18,590	114,880	112,255

[1] The financial year began on April 1st of the year named, and ended on the following March 31st: thus, for 1856, read, from April 1st, 1856, to March 31st, 1857.

[2] In 1858 the Coast Guard was transferred from the Customs to the Admiralty.

[3] "Truth About the Navy" Agitation.

[4] City Agitation, followed by Naval Defence Act, 52 Vict. cap. 8, authorising special expenditure of £10,000,000 out of the Consolidated Fund in the seven years ending Mar. 31, 1896, and of £11,000,000 out of the Naval Votes for the five years ending Mar. 31, 1894 : all for building purposes. The £10,000,000 was in addition to the above.

[5] Supplementary Naval Defence Act of 1893.

[6] "Needs of the Navy" Agitation.

[7] Of this a sum of £863,279 was not expended.

During the changeful and progressive period under review, immense alterations, as might be expected, were made in the constitution of the active list of officers. For convenience of reference, the numbers of officers of the various ranks, both active and retired, included in the official lists for January, 1857, and January, 1901, respectively, are here given side by side :—

	Jan. 1857 (complete to Dec. 20, 1856).		Jan. 1901 (complete to Dec. 20, 1900).	
	Active.	Retired.	Active.	Retired.
Admirals of the Fleet . . .	..	..	4	5 [1]
Admirals	21	12	10	81
Vice-Admirals	29	21	21	42
Rear-Admirals	51	188	37	94
Captains	389	372	200	359
Commanders	542	489	303	432
Lieutenants	1,138	641	1,163 [2]	211
Masters [3]	336	143	..	57
Mates (later Sub-Lieuts.) . .	154	..	286 [4]	44
Second-Masters [5] . .	105	..	..	4
Engineer Officers . . .	123	..	916	441
Chaplains [6]	142	13	118	72
Naval Instructors [7] . . .	51	..	39	24
Medical Officers	618	387	400	244
Accountant Officers . . .	447	221	578	256
Royal Marine Officers . . .	481	344	473	309
Midshipmen	[8]	[8]	703	
Naval Cadets	[8]	[8]	32	
Staff-Captains [9]	[8]	[8]	14	
Staff-Commanders [10] . . .	[8]	[8]	22	27
Chief Gunners and Gunners. .	[8]	[8]	715	76 [11]
Chief Boatswains and Boatswains .	[8]	[8]	451	101 [11]
Chief Carpenters and Carpenters .	[8]	[8]	252	56
Artificer Engineers [12] . . .	[8]	[8]	99	
Head Schoolmasters . . .	[8]	[8]	15	
Head Wardmasters . . .	[8]	[8]	3	

[1] Including 2 Honorary Admirals of the Fleet.
[2] Including 139 Supplementary Lieutenants.
[3] Masters became Navigating-Lieutenants by O. in C. of June 26, 1867. No additions to special navigating list after 1883.
[4] Including 1 Supplementary Sub-Lieutenant.
[5] Second-Masters became Navigating-Sub-Lieutenants by O. in C. of June 26, 1867.
[6] Including the Chaplains who were also Naval Instructors.
[7] Naval Instructors only who were not also Chaplains.
[8] These ranks were either non-existent in 1857, or not then included in the Navy List.
[9] Rank of Staff-Captain (navigating officer) created July 1st, 1867.
[10] Rank of Staff-Commander (navigating officer) created June 11th, 1863.
[11] Some of these are Honorary Lieutenants under Os. in C. of Sept. 15, 1887, and Aug. 19, 1889.
[12] Rank of Artificer Engineer created Apl. 1st, 1898.

Although there was no Admiral of the Fleet at the beginning of 1857, the rank was in temporary abeyance only. Admiral of the Fleet Sir Thomas Byam Martin had died in October, 1854, leaving Admiral Thomas Le Marchant Gosselin at the head of the active list. Gosselin, though in the early part of his career he had been on full pay for twenty-nine years, had subsequently been on half-pay for no fewer than forty-five years in succession, and had never hoisted his flag. Moreover, he was eighty-nine years of age. He lived, nevertheless, until nearly the last days of 1857. Not until then was the officer next on the list, Admiral Sir Charles Ogle, Bart., promoted. Ogle had hoisted his flag more than once; and his claim to promotion, when his turn came, could hardly have been resisted. Nevertheless, be it noted, although Gosselin had not been promoted, he had not been passed over. While he lived he simply, as it were, blocked the way.

For many years after 1857 the flag-officer at the top of the list of Admirals always received promotion as a vacancy occurred; and in 1862 a second Admiral of the Fleet was appointed, a third being added in 1863. Three remained the extreme number until nearly the close of the century. In making the appointments, provided that the officer next on the list had served as a Commander-in-Chief, or had commanded at sea as a flag-officer for two years, seniority was never ignored until, in 1892, came the turn of Admiral Algernon Frederick Rous de Horsey, who had been Commander-in-Chief in the Pacific for nearly three years, and, in addition, had been senior officer in the Channel for about five months. On that occasion, her Majesty the Queen, exercising her right of selection, saw fit to pass over de Horsey, and to promote Sir John Edmund Commerell, whose name stood next on the active list. Thenceforward seniority, subject to the provisions above indicated, was not interfered with, except in the case of H.R.H. the Duke of Edinburgh,[1] until 1898, when Sir Frederick William Richards [2] was promoted as a fourth Admiral of the Fleet, although, at the time, he was not next on the list, but third on it. This promotion, however, differed from that of Commerell in that it was an extra one, and was not made to the permanent prejudice of any other officers; for when, in 1899, the turn came of the officer, Sir Nowell Salmon, who had all along stood first for promotion (assuming an establishment of only three Admirals of the Fleet), he was promoted.

It may be noted here that the rank of Honorary Admiral of the Fleet was first created in 1887 in favour of his present Majesty, then Prince of Wales, on the occasion of Queen Victoria's Jubilee, and that his Majesty, William II., German Emperor, was honoured with the like dignity in 1889.

On July 9th, 1864, an Order in Council discontinued the time-honoured classification which had previously subdivided the various ranks of flag-officers into those of the Red, the White, and the Blue

---

[1] O. in C. of Nov. 23, 1893.   [2] O. in C. of Nov. 29, 1898.

Squadrons respectively; and by an Admiralty circular of August 5th following it was directed that, for the future, all flag-officers should wear a white flag with a red Cross of St. George therein, with, in the case of Vice-Admirals, one red ball, and, in the case of Rear-Admirals, two red balls, in the upper part, near the staff. At the same time it was ordered that all Commodores should wear a white broad-pennant, with a red St. George's Cross therein; that all her Majesty's ships in commission should fly the White Ensign; that the Blue Ensign should be borne by vessels " in the service of any public office," and by ships commanded by officers of the Royal Naval Reserve,[1] and having a fourth part of the crew composed of reserve men ; and that the Red Ensign should continue to be flown by all other British vessels, with the exception of certain yachts, and craft authorised to bear distinguishing flags.

An Order in Council of June 26, 1867, transformed the then existing Masters into Navigating-Lieutenants; the Second Masters into Navigating-Sub-Lieutenants; the Masters' Assistants into Navigating-Midshipmen; and the Naval Cadets, 2nd Class, into Navigating-Cadets.

The title of Sub-Lieutenant was substituted for that of Mate in 1861.

The commissioned ranks of Chief Gunner, Chief Boatswain, and Chief Carpenter were created by an Admiralty Circular of July 25th, 1864.

It is impossible to say much here on the large subject of naval retirement. The chief Orders in Council which affected it during the period under review are those of :—

1860. Aug. 1.	1878. Jan. 15.	1895. June 29; July 16.
1864. July 9.	1879. Nov. 29.	1896. Mar. 6.
1865. Mar. 31.	1881. Nov. 29.	1897. Feb. 26 ; Aug. 3.
1866. Feb. 23; Mar. 24;	1882. Nov. 30.	1898. Nov. 29.
Aug. 9.	1887. July 12.	1900. Jan. 29; Mar. 3.
1870. Feb. 22.	1890. Mar. 21.	

The Order of November 29th, 1898, fixed the limit of strength of the active list, so far as certain ranks were concerned, at :—

Admirals of the Fleet. . .	3	Chief Gunners ⎫	
Admirals	12	Chief Boatswains ⎭ . . .	100
Vice-Admirals	22	Chief Carpenters	20
Rear-Admirals.	43	Gunners ⎫	
Captains	245	Boatswains ⎬	1,150
Commanders	360	Carpenters	240
Lieutenants	1,550		

[1] *See also* Circ. of Aug. 3, 1864.

and made provision for the rate at which the flag-officers', Captains', and Commanders' lists were to be increased annually. In several of the ranks at the end of the century (*see* Table on p. 13) the numbers fell far short of what they then should have been.

Under the regulations which remained in force at the end of 1900, Admirals of the Fleet were compulsorily retired at seventy; Admirals, at sixty-five (or seven years after last active service); Vice-Admirals at sixty-five (or seven years after last active service); Rear-Admirals at sixty (or seven years after last active service); Captains at fifty-five (or six years after last active service); Commanders at fifty (or five years after last active service); Lieutenants at forty-five (or four years after last active service); Chief Inspectors and Inspectors of Machinery at sixty (or seven years after last active service); Fleet Engineers, Staff Engineers, and Chief Engineers at fifty-five (or five years after last active service); Engineers at forty-five (or five years after last active service); Assistant Engineers at forty (or five years after last active service); Chaplains and Naval Instructors at sixty; Inspectors-General, and Deputy Inspectors-General of Hospitals at sixty; Fleet Surgeons, Staff Surgeons, and Surgeons at fifty-five; and Fleet Paymasters, Staff Paymasters and Paymasters at sixty.

All things considered, the pay of naval officers underwent singularly little alteration during the period. The good executive officer of 1857 was, relatively speaking, little more scientific than his predecessor of 1805. It was not necessary that he should know much about steam; the gunnery requirements of the day were simple; and hydraulics, electricity, Morse signalling, and torpedoes were unknown in the service. On the other hand, it was required of the good executive officer of 1900 that he should be not only a seaman and a gunner, but also something of an engineer, something of a physicist, something of a chemist, and much more. Yet his emoluments were hardly increased in proportion. Still more modestly were the emoluments of the Accountant branch added to. The most notable advances were in the pay of officers of the purely and avowedly scientific branches, the engineering and the medical. It is impracticable to give here a full statement of all such changes as were made; but the full pay received by officers of a few typical ranks and standings in 1857 and 1900 respectively is shown in the appended table :—

ANNUAL FULL PAY, WITH ALLOWANCES, ETC., OF CERTAIN NAVAL OFFICERS
IN 1857 AND 1900.

(Fractions of pounds omitted.)

—	1857.	1900.	Remarks.
	£	£	
Admiral of the Fleet	2,190 }3,285	2,190 }3,285 to	In 1900, in certain cir-
Table Money (to C. in Chief)	1,095	1,095 to 1,642} 3,832	cumstances, these
Admiral	1,825 }2,910	1,825 }2,910 to	officers also received
Table Money (to C. in Chief)	1,095	1,095 to 1,642} 3,467	from £250 to £500 as
Vice-Admiral	1,460 }2,555	1,460 }2,555 to	commutation in lieu
Table Money (to C. in Chief)	1,095	1,095 to 1,642} 3,102	of the retinue of
Rear-Admiral, or Commodore (1st Cl.)	1,095 }2,190	1,095 }2,180 to	servants which had
Table Money (to C. in Chief)	1,095	1,095 to 1,642} 2,737	been allowed in 1857.
Commodore (2nd Cl.) }	182 to 365	182 to 365	
Additional to pay as Captain }			
Captain	450 to 701	410 to 602	
Total, with Command Money		501 to 930	
Commander	301	365 to 456	
Lieutenant	182 to 200	182 to 346	
Mate, or Sub-Lieutenant	66	91 to 136	
			Less a deduction of £3 if receiving instruction.
Midshipman	31	31	Naval cadets in the
Naval Cadet	16	18	*Britannia* receive no pay.
Chief Gunner, Boatswain or Carpenter	..	182 to 237	
Gunner, Boatswain, Carpenter	86 to 124	100 to 182	
Chief Inspector of Machinery	..	730 to 784	
			£45 to £91 extra to senior engineer officers of flag-ships.
Fleet, Staff, or Chief Engineer	182 to 328	255 to 638	
Engineer	182	164 to 237	
Assistant Engineer	56 to 158	109 to 157	
Inspector General of Hospitals	574 to 766	1,003	
Deputy Inspector General of Hospitals	355	766	
Fleet and Staff Surgeon }	182 to 328	{ 383 to 693	
Surgeon, or Assistant-Surgeon }		209 to 282	
Fleet and Staff Paymaster, or Paymaster	249 to 600	255 to 693	
Assistant-Paymaster	91 to 155	91 to 255	
Clerk	73	73	
Assistant-Clerk	45	45	

The continuous service wages of Able Seamen (£28 17*s.* 11*d.*), Ordinary Seamen (£22 16*s.* 3*d.*), and First Class Boys (£10 12*s.* 11*d.*), fixed in 1853, were not altered ere the end of the century; but the introduction of extra pay for good conduct badges, for re-engagement, etc., and the creation of numerous new and specially paid ratings, gave the ambitious and capable seaman many opportunities of increasing his wages from time to time, and vastly ameliorated his financial prospects.

Up to 1859 the naval reserves of the country consisted of (*a*) Royal Marines quartered ashore; (*b*) the Coast Guard, which in the previous year had been transferred from the control of the Customs to that of the Admiralty; (*c*) the Royal Naval Coast Volunteers[1]; and (*d*) short service pensioners. In spite of the introduction of the Continuous Service System,[2] in 1853, and of the entry of seamen for ten years, considerable difficulty was still

[1] Raised 1853. They died out in 1873. [2] *See* Vol. VI. p. 207.

experienced in manning the fleet. For example, the *Diadem*, commissioned in August, 1857, could not complete her crew until January, 1858 ; the *Renown*, commissioned in November, 1857, was detained by lack of men for 172 days, and then sailed 62 short of her complement ; and the *Marlborough*, commissioned in February, 1858, was similarly delayed for 129 days.

To consider this unsatisfactory condition of affairs, and to make recommendations for its amelioration, a Royal Commission was appointed. It reported on February 19th, 1859, advocating, among other things, the maintenance of at least five large training-ships for the preparation of boys for the Navy ; the creation of larger reserves ; the better training of the reserves in gunnery ; improvements in the comforts and dietary of seamen ; modifications in the system of the payment of wages, and of allotments, etc., etc.

The first effect of the report was the issue, on April 27th, 1859, of an Admiralty Order, which slightly altered the scale of victualling [1] ; authorised the supply to all boys and men on joining of bed, blanket, and bedcover, free of charge ; gave continuous service men, on entering, and boys, on being rated as men, a free part kit, or money in lieu of it [2] ; and promised the gratuitous supply to ships commissioning of mess utensils, so soon as suitable ones could be found.

Other results which followed were the increase of the Royal Marines, and of the Coast Guard, the introduction of training-ships for boys, and the establishment of a corps of Royal Naval Volunteers, a force which ultimately developed into the Royal Naval Reserve, the earliest commissions to which, as such, were dated in February, 1862. Various regulations for the officers of this corps were subsequently embodied in Orders in Council dated respectively March 1st, 1864, October 15th, 1872, June 28th, 1880, and May 3rd, 1882. These were consolidated and revised by an Order of June 26th, 1886, which was further modified by Orders of February 7th, 1888, July 23rd, 1889, February 23rd, 1891, March 20th, 1891, May 9th, 1892, and May 16th, 1893. The whole regula-

---

[1] Allowance of biscuit per man per diem increased from 1 lb. to 1¼ lb., but savings' price per lb. reduced from 2*d*. to 1½*d*. Allowance of sugar per man per diem increased from 1¾ ozs. to 2 ozs. Extra allowance in middle or morning watch, at Captain's discretion, of ½ oz. of sugar, and ½ oz. of chocolate to men sick, or specially exposed.

[2] The uniform articles thus furnished, with the equivalents in money, were : Blue cloth jacket (No. 2 cloth), 17*s*. 8*d*. ; blue cloth trousers (No. 2 cloth), 11*s*. 7*d*. ; blue serge frock, 8*s*. 6*d*. ; duck frock, 2*s*. 9*d*. ; duck trousers, 2*s*. 7*d*. ; black silk handkerchief, 2*s*. 10*d*. ; and shoes, 6*s*. 7*d*.

tions were again consolidated and revised in 1896 ; when the number
of officers was fixed at 1800. An Order of June 29th, 1895, authorised the entry of 100 officers of the mercantile marine (nearly
all of whom were of the Royal Naval Reserve) as Supplementary
Officers of the Royal Navy in the ranks of Lieutenant and Sub-
Lieutenant, and provided for their full pay, half pay, and retirement.
An increase of this number was subsequently ordered. The total
strength of the Royal Naval Reserve at the end of the nineteenth
century was 28,700 officers and men. In addition, there were also
available as reserves 11,952 seamen and Royal Marine pensioners.
The whole number of officers and men, including the active list and
all reserves, at disposal for naval services was, nominally, 145,532.
A new force, the Royal Fleet Reserve, designed to consist of seamen
and Royal Marines who have been discharged with or without
pensions, and eventually to supersede the old seamen pensioner
reserve, was planned and decided upon in 1900 · but no men were
entered until later. In the same year also two important steps
were taken towards the creation of additional and more efficient
naval reserve forces in her Majesty's dominions beyond the seas.
New Zealand initiated the discussion among the Australasian
colonies of a project for the establishment of reserves both military
and naval ; and fifty Newfoundland fishermen belonging to the
naval reserve of the island were embarked in H.M.S. *Charybdis*,
Captain George Augustus Giffard, for a six months' training cruise
in the West Indies. Concerning the ordinary naval resources of
the colonies a few words will be said later.[1]

For nearly twenty years, towards the end of the century, yet
another naval reserve existed in the shape of the Royal Naval
Artillery Volunteers, which were raised under an Act of August 5th,
1873.[2] This body was intended to provide trained gunners for
service within the home seas, and consisted for the most part of
yacht-owners and professional men of good social standing. Its
headquarters and drill-ship (first the *Rainbow*, and later the *Frolic*)
was moored in the Thames, off Somerset House. Owing to regrettable misunderstandings, frictions and jealousies, the corps was
disbanded on April 1st, 1892. A few months before that date it had
included 66 officers and 1849 men.[3]

For several years after 1856 the construction of wooden men-

[1] See p. 77 and note.   [2] Modified in 1882 by the National Defence Act.
[3] Report of Sir G. Tryon's Committee, Apr. 7, 1891.

of-war,[1] of all classes, continued. The lessons of Kinburn, indeed, seemed to produce in England no tangible results whatsoever until the spring of 1859, when the first British sea-going armoured iron ship, the *Warrior*, was laid down at Blackwall. The armoured wooden floating batteries of the *Trusty* class, and the armoured iron floating batteries of the *Erebus* class,[2] built in 1854–56, remained, up to the *Warrior's* launch in December, 1860, the only ironclads belonging to her Majesty's fleet. Progress was at length forced upon the country by the action of France, which, suspending the completion of the original designs of four large and fast wooden screw ships which she had upon the stocks at Brest and Toulon, had begun to armour them, and to convert them from 90-gun vessels of the line to 36-gun frigates. One of these, the *Gloire*, was actually launched in November, 1859.

Great Britain also adapted as ironclads a certain number of fine wooden ships which were available for the purpose at the time when it became evident that the armoured vessel must be the battleship of the future. These adapted ships were the following :—

> *Royal Oak, Caledonia, Prince Consort*, and *Ocean*, originally designed and begun as wooden line-of-battleships of 91 guns, 3716 tons (old measurement), and 800 H.P. nom., but converted, in accordance with an Admiralty Order of May 14, 1861, to armour-plated ships of about 6400 tons displacement, and from 3700 to 4240 H.P.I. As adapted, they were full-rigged broadside ships, with iron armour of a maximum thickness of 4½ inches, carrying 24 6½-ton 7-in. muzzle-loaders. They had single screws, and an extreme speed of from 12 to 13 knots. All were launched in 1862 and 1863.
>
> *Royal Alfred*, originally designed and begun as a wooden line-of-battle ship of 91 guns, 3716 tons (old measurement), and 800 H.P. nom., but converted, in accordance with an Admiralty Order of June 5, 1861, to an armour-plated ship of 6720 tons' displacement, and 3434 H.P.I. As adapted, she was a full-rigged broadside ship, with iron armour of a maximum thickness of

---

[1] This sketch of the progress of Naval Architecture during the years 1857–1900 is mainly based upon the following authorities:—King, 'The Warships of Europe' (1878); Very, 'Navies of the World' (1880); Reed, 'Our Ironclad Ships' (1869); Brassey, 'The British Navy' (1882–83); White, 'A Manual of Naval ,Architecture' (1882); The Catalogue of the Museum at Greenwich, and the Collection of Ship Models there; Brassey, 'The Naval Annual' (1886–1901); Clowes, 'The Naval Pocket Book' (1896, etc.); Lloyd's 'Warships of the World' (annually); Busk, 'The Navies of the World' (1859); Armstrong, 'Torpedoes and Torpedo Vessels' (1896); Williams, 'The Steam Navy of England' (1893); and numerous articles and papers, especially in the *Transactions of the Institution of Naval Architects; The Year's Naval Progress* (Washington); the *Journal of the Royal United Service Institution;* the *Proceedings of the United States' Naval Institute* (Annapolis); the *Engineer;* and *Engineering.*

[2] See Vol. vi., p. 198.

6 inches, carrying 18 6½-ton 7-in. muzzle-loaders. She had a single screw, and a speed of 12·3 knots, and was launched in 1864.

Repulse, originally designed and begun as a wooden line-of-battle ship of 90 guns, 3074 tons (old measurement), and 800 H.P. nom., but converted, in accordance with an Admiralty Order of October 9, 1866, to an armour-plated ship of 6190 tons' displacement, and 3350 H.P.I. As adapted, she was a full-rigged broadside ship, with iron armour of a maximum thickness of 6 inches, carrying 12 8-in. 9-ton (but later 10 9-in. 12-ton) muzzle-loaders. She had a single screw, and a speed of about 12 knots, and was launched in 1868.

Favorite, originally designed and begun as a wooden corvette of 22 guns, but converted, according to designs by Mr. E. J. Reed and the Controller's Department, in 1862, to a rigged, armour-plated corvette of 3169 tons' displacement, and 1773 H.P.I., with iron armour of a maximum thickness of 4½ inches, carrying 10 8-in. 9-ton muzzle-loaders. She had a single screw, and a speed of 11·8 knots, and was launched in 1864.

Research, designed and begun as a wooden 17-gun sloop in 1861, but converted in 1862 to an armoured, rigged vessel, and launched in 1863. Displacement, 1680 tons; speed 10·3 knots; thickest armour 4½ inches; 4 7-in. 6½-ton muzzle-loaders.

The above, as converted, differed outwardly in no essential respects from their immediate predecessors, the wooden screw battleships and frigates. They were still fine specimens of the old picturesque style of naval architecture, and were fairly good craft under sail.

The only other wooden ship, the *Royal Sovereign*, which was converted to an ironclad for the British Navy received very different treatment. She was cut down, armoured all over, supplied merely with three light pole masts, and furnished with four armoured revolving turrets, which were placed on the upper deck in the middle line of the ship. Although herself of little practical use, she was a most important and significant craft, in that she embodied the first British admission of two novel principles which, many years afterwards, obtained universal acceptance; viz., that sail-power had ceased to be useful in vessels intended for heavy fighting; and that the main armament of every ship intended for heavy fighting should be protected as completely as possible, and should moreover be so mounted as to have as near an approach as might be to all-round fire. In addition, possessing a relatively low freeboard, the converted *Royal Sovereign* had the advantage of offering but a proportionately small target to an enemy. These features were all due to the advocacy of Captain Cowper Phipps Coles, R.N., C.B.

Royal Sovereign, originally launched in 1857 as a wooden line-of-battle ship of 131 guns, 3765 tons (old measurement), and 800 H.P. nom., was converted, in accordance with an Admiralty Order of April 3rd, 1862, to an armoured turret-ship of 4965 tons' displacement, and 800 H.P. nom. As adapted, she had iron armour of a maximum thickness of 5½ inches, and carried 5 9-in. 12-ton muzzle-loaders, one in each of her three aftermost turrets, and two in the foremost one. She had a single screw, and a speed of 11 knots, and was undocked in 1864.

It has been said that the iron-hulled armoured ship *Warrior* was laid down in the spring of 1859; yet it should be added here that, for several years later, the Admiralty seemed unable to make up its mind whether, after all, iron was or was not to be the building material of future heavy fighting ships. In that period of apparent

H.M.S. ' ROYAL SOVEREIGN.'

[Launched as a 131-gun ship of the line, 1857: converted to an ironclad turret-ship, at Portsmouth, 1862–64.]

doubt and hesitation it caused both iron-hulled and wooden-hulled armoured ships to be constructed. The wooden-hulled ones are briefly noted below :—

> *Lord Clyde* and *Lord Warden*, laid down in 1863, after designs by Mr. E. J. Reed, and the Controller's Department, as single-screw, wooden-hulled, armoured broadside ships of 7602 and 7839 tons' displacement, and 6034 and 6706 H.P.I. respectively ; each fully rigged, and ultimately carrying 18 6½-ton 7-in. muzzle-loaders. Speed, about 13·5 knots. Launched respectively in 1864 and 1865. Maximum thickness of iron armour 5½ inches.
>
> *Zealous*, laid down in October, 1859, after designs by the same, as a single-screw, wooden-hulled, armoured, broadside ship of 6102 tons' displacement, and 3623 H.P.I. ; rigged ; and ultimately carrying 20 6½-ton 7-in. muzzle-loaders. Speed, 11·7 knots. Launched in 1864. Maximum thickness of iron armour, 4½ inches.

Pallas (laid down 1863, launched 1865), a single-screw, wooden-hulled, rigged, armoured, broadside corvette, designed by Mr. E. J. Reed, and the Controller's Department. Displacement, 3661 tons; H.P.I., 3581; speed 13 knots; maximum thickness of armour 4½ inches; ultimate armament, 8 8-in. 9-ton muzzle-loaders.

Enterprise, laid down in 1862, after designs by the same, as a single-screw, wooden-hulled, rigged, armoured sloop of 993 tons' displacement, and 9·9 knots' speed, carrying 4 7-in. 6½ ton guns. Launched in 1864. Maximum thickness of iron armour, 4½ inches. In this case, although the hull was of wood the upper works were of iron.

Thus, from 1859 until 1866, the Admiralty still thought it worth while either to build wooden ironclads or to armour existing wooden hulls. From 1866, however, that idea was definitely abandoned, the Order for the conversion of the *Repulse* being the final symptom of official hesitation.

The rise of the iron-built, sea-going ironclad, and its development may now be studied without further interruption.

At first the traditions of the old wooden navy greatly influenced the designs of all new fighting-ships, and vessels continued to be built not only with heavy rigging and large sail-power, but also with their guns disposed, as previously, in broadside along the major parts of their length. The armoured ships, arranged in order of their launch, which were constructed on this principle were:—

CLASS 1.—BROADSIDE IRONCLAD.

Name.	Date of Launch.	Displace-ment in Tons.	H.P.I.	Speed.	Thickest Armour.	Heaviest Gun.[3]	No. of Guns.	Comple-ment.
				Knots.	In.			
Warrior [1]	1860	9,210	5,469	14·3	4·5	95 cwt. 68 pr.	40	635
Black Prince [1] . .	1861	9,210	5,772	13·6	4·5	95 cwt. 68 pr.	40	635
Defence [1]	1861	6,270	2,540	11·6	4·5	95 cwt. 68 pr.	22	450
Resistance [1] . . .	1861	6,270	2,430	11·8	4·5	6½ ton 7 in.	22	450
Hector	1862	6,710	3,256	12·3	4·5	7 in. B.	32	500
Valiant	1863	6,710	3,350	12·6	4·5	6½ ton 7 in.	24	500
Achilles [2]	1863	9,820	5,720	14·3	4·5	6½ ton 7 in.	20	705
Minotaur [2]. . . .	1863	10,690	5,772	14·3	5·5	7 in. B.	50	705
Agincourt [2] . . .	1865	10,690	6,870	15·4	5·5	12 ton 9 in.	26	705
Northumberland [2] .	1866	10,780	6,621	15·4	5·5	12 ton 9 in.	26	705

[1] Only central part armoured.   [2] End to end armour on water-line.

[3] As originally designed. The largest guns in all these cases, except where otherwise stated, were muzzle-loaders. The breech-loaders were of the early Armstrong screw type. See p. 44. They were soon superseded.

The next developments which were generally adopted were the confinement of the heavy armament of the ironclad vessel to a central battery, where it was mounted behind comparatively thick iron armour, and shut off fore and aft by armoured bulkheads; and the restriction of armour elsewhere to the neighbourhood of the water-line. The ships of this class, as successively launched, are

catalogued below. All were, as before, heavily rigged; and, as
regards general appearance, the old lines were preserved, except
that the ram bow,[1] which was not introduced in some of the earliest
ironclads, and which was adopted largely in consequence of the
advocacy of Admiral Sir George Rose Sartorius, had become a
regular feature.

CLASS 2.—CENTRAL BATTERY IRONCLADS.

Name.	Date of Launch.	Displacement in Tons.	H.P.I.	Speed.	Thickest Armour.[3]	Heaviest Gun.[4]		No. of Guns.	Complement.
				Knots.	In.	Ton.	In.		
Bellerophon . . .	1865	7,550	6,520	14	6·0	12	9	14	475
Penelope [1]	1867	4,470	4,700	12·7	6·0	12	9	10	350
Hercules	1868	8,680	7,840	13·8	9·0	18	10	14	600
Audacious [1] . . .	1869	6,010	4,830	12·8	8·0	12	9	10	450
Invincible [1] . . .	1869	6,010	4,830	14	8·0	12	9	10	450
Iron Duke [1] . . .	1870	6,010	3,526	13·6	8·0	12	9	10	450
Vanguard [1] . . .	1869	6,010	3,500	13·6	8·0	12	9	10	450
Sultan	1870	9,200	7,720	14·1	9·0	18	10	12	600
Swiftsure	1870	6,910	4,910	13 7	8·0	12	9	10	480
Triumph	1870	6,640	5,110	14	8·0	12	9	10	490
Alexandra [1] . . .	1875	9,490	8,610	14	12·0	25	11	12	670
Superb [2] . . .	1875	9,170	6,580	13·1	12·0	18	10	16	620
Belleisle [1] [2] . . .	1876	4,870	3,200	11·5	12·0	25	12	4	280
[Orion [1] [2]	1879	4,870	4,040	11.7	12·0	25	12	4	280

[1] Twin screws.   [2] Purchased in 1874: originally ordered for Turkey.   [3] Armour iron.
[4] All heavy guns were muzzle-loaders.

Each of the above had a complete water-line belt, with good
protection over the central battery. The *Alexandra* was the earliest
of the above to be provided with a substantial deck of steel in the
neighbourhood of the water-line; but it was not curved below the
water-line at its edges, and was not so arranged as to deflect
upwards any projectiles that might enter the vessel near the line of
flotation, and thus to protect the machinery. In her case this deck
was two inches thick. It was mainly designed as a protection
against plunging fire. Save for this belt, the entire hull of the
Alexandra, as of the other craft in the list, was of iron, neither
compound armour nor steel as a building material having yet come
into use.

Although, for the six years after 1859 the broadside-rigged ironclad, and for the ten or twelve years after 1865 the central-battery
rigged ironclad met, upon the whole, with most favour at the
Admiralty, it must not be supposed that these types of heavy
fighting ships were ever without competitors. Captain Cowper

---

[1] The popular and exaggerated estimate of the value of this was greatly increased
in 1875, when, on Sept. 2, the *Iron Duke*, in a fog off Wicklow, accidentally rammed
her sister ship, the *Vanguard*, which sank within an hour. As a matter of fact, the
ram has proved to be more dangerous in accident than formidable in action. *See*
Author's Lecture at R.U.S.I., Jan. 19, 1894.

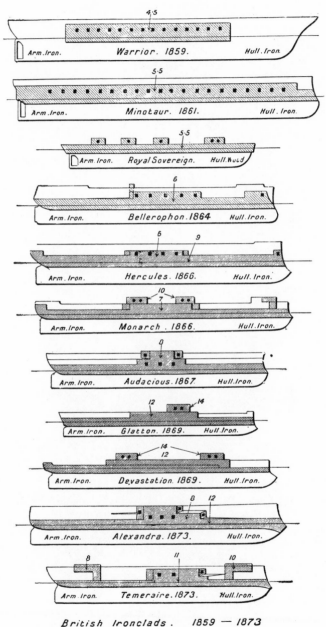

4·5
Arm. Iron.   Warrior. 1859.   Hull. Iron.

5·5
Arm. Iron.   Minotaur. 1861.   Hull. Iron.

5·5
Arm. Iron.   Royal Sovereign.   Hull. Wood.

6
Arm. Iron.   Bellerophon. 1864   Hull. Iron.

6   9
Arm. Iron.   Hercules. 1866.   Hull. Iron.

10
7
Arm. Iron.   Monarch. 1866.   Hull. Iron.

Arm. Iron.   Audacious. 1867   Hull. Iron.

12   14
Arm. Iron.   Glatton. 1869.   Hull. Iron.

14
12
Arm. Iron.   Devastation. 1869.   Hull. Iron.

8   12
Arm. Iron.   Alexandra. 1873.   Hull. Iron.

8   11   10
Arm. Iron.   Temeraire. 1873.   Hull. Iron.

British Ironclads.   1859 — 1873
Figures give the thickness of armour in inches.
(By kind permission, from Mr. H. W. Wilson's 'Ironclads in Action.')

[To face p. 24.

Phipps Coles, who had been mainly responsible for the cutting down and conversion of the *Royal Sovereign* in 1862–64, was still a living and very active advocate of the turret principle; and Mr. E. J. Reed, who was Chief Constructor from 1863 to 1870, while disagreeing with Captain Coles on most points of detail, realised that the plan of giving the maximum protection and the maximum arc of fire to an armoured ship's heaviest guns was one which deserved the most favourable consideration. Moreover, the battle of Hampton Roads, in March, 1862, and numerous other actions during the Civil War in America, demonstrated that, for work of certain kinds, the monitor, or turret-ship, was a most useful and formidable craft.

Other ideas, also, were abroad as to the best methods of compromising the claims of the various new factors which, as time went on, seemed to demand inclusion in the ideal fighting ship, yet which, it was amply evident, could not all receive equal consideration. Very heavy guns were called for by some; very thick armour was considered indispensable by others; and while one party asked for a complete water-line belt, another party urged the naval architects to devote even more attention to the protection of the armament than to the protection of the life of the ship. Yet other conflicting and almost irreconcilable claims were put forward on behalf of high speed, of great coal-capacity, of large sail-power, of lofty freeboard, of seaworthiness and steadiness of gun-platform, and of small size, shallow draught, and comparative invisibility to an enemy's gunners.

For nearly twenty years these and other problems troubled the minds of naval architects all the world over. In Great Britain they led to the construction of numerous armoured ships which are catalogued below. Some of them were not sea-going; others, though sea-going, were scarcely fit, even in their best days, for the line-of-battle; but they are all included, for the reason that each one may be deemed to have contributed something, if only a little, either to the development of that type of heavy fighting ship which was generally acknowledged to be the best at the end of the nineteenth century, or to the establishment of certain doctrines which began to be accepted about the years 1870–74, and which led later to the subdivision of all new vertically-armoured warships into three definite groups, viz., battleships, armoured cruisers, and coast-defence ironclads.

CLASS 3.—EXPERIMENTAL AND TRANSITIONAL IRONCLADS.

Name.	Type.[4]	Date of Launch.	Displacement in Tons.	H.P.I.	Speed.	Thickest Armour.	Heaviest Gun.		No. of Guns.	Complement.
					Kts.	In.	Ton.	In.		
Scorpion [1] . . .	R. T. 2.	1863	2,750	1,450	10·5	5·0	12·	9	4	150
Wivern [1] . . .	R. T. 2.	1863	2,750	1,450	10·0	5·0	12	9	4	150
Prince Albert . .	M. T. 4.	1864	3,880	2,130	11·6	4·5	12	9	4	200
Viper [2]	Br.	1866	1,230	700	9·5	4·5	6¼	7	2	80
Vixen [2]	Br.	1866	1,230	740	8·8	4·5	6¼	7	2	80
Waterwitch [3] . .	Br.	1866	1,280	780	9·2	4·5	6¼	7	2	80
Monarch . . .	R. T. 2.	1868	8,320	7,840	14·9	10·0	2	12	7	525
Captain . . .	R. T. 2.	1869	6,950	900 N.	14·0	13·0	25	12	6	500
Hotspur [2] . . .	R. T. 1.	1870	4,010	3,060	12·6	11·0	25	12	4	240
Glatton [2] . . .	M. T. 1.	1871	4,910	2,870	12·1	18·0	25	12	2	191
Cyclops [2] . . .	M. T. 2.	1871	3,480	1,660	11·0	10·0	18	10	4	175
Gorgon [2] . . .	M. T. 2.	1871	3,480	1,670	11·1	10.0	18	10	4	175
Hecate [2] . . .	M. T. 2.	1871	3,480	1,750	10.9	10·0	18	10	4	175
Hydra [2] . . .	M. T. 2.	1871	3,480	1,470	11·2	10·0	18	10	4	175
Devastation [2] . .	M. T. 2.	1871	9,330	6,650	13·8	14·0	35	12	4	420
Thunderer [2] . .	M. T. 2.	1872	9,330	6,270	13·4	14·0	38	12·5	4	420
Rupert [2] . . .	R. T. 1.	1872	5,440	4,630	13·5	14.0	18	10	4	232
Neptune [1] . . .	R. T. 2.	1874	9,310	8,000	14·2	13·0	38	12·5	6	465
Dreadnought [2] .	M. T. 2.	1875	10,820	8,210	14·2	14·0	38	12·5	4	440
Shannon . . .	Pt. Bl. Cr.	1875	5,310	3,370	12·3	9·0	18	10 [5]	9	454
Nelson [2] . . .	Pt. Bl. Cr.	1876	7,630	6,640	14.4	9·0	18	10 [5]	12	560
Northampton [2] .	Pt. Bl. Cr.	1876	7,630	6,070	13·2	9.0	18	10 [5]	12	560
Téméraire [2] . .	Bar. 2, C.-B.	1876	8,540	7,520	14·5	11·0	25	12	8	535
Inflexible [2] . .	R. T. 2.	1876	11,880	8,010	13·8	24·0	80	16 [5]	4	470
Agamemnon [2] . .	R. T. 2.	1879	8,510	6,360	13·2	18·0	38	12·5 [5]	6	405
Ajax [2]	R. T. 2.	1880	8,510	6,440	13·2	18·0	38	12·5 [5]	4	405

[1] Originally built for abroad ; purchased by the Admiralty.

[2] Twin screws.

[3] Hydraulic gunboat, designed by V.-Adm. George Elliot (4). Ruthven's propelling system.

[4] In this column, R. means rigged ; T. 1, turret-ship with one turret ; T. 2, turret-ship with two turrets ; Br., having guns behind a breastwork ; M., mastless ; Pt. Bl. Cr., partially belted cruiser ; Bar. 2, C.-B., ship with two barbettes and a central battery.

[5] These ships had armoured protective decks, intended to deflect upwards projectiles entering in the neighbourhood of the water-line.

NOTE.—All heavy guns in the above were muzzle-loaders. All the above vessels had iron hulls. Very similar to the *Cyclops* and her sisters were the *Cerberus*, built in 1868 for Victoria, and the *Magdala* and *Abyssinia*, built in 1870 for India.

The most interesting and significant ships in the above list were the *Monarch*, the *Captain*, the *Devastation* (with her two kindred ships, *Thunderer* and *Dreadnought*), the *Shannon*, the *Téméraire*, and the *Inflexible* (with her smaller cousins, *Agamemnon* and *Ajax*). It has been already pointed out that in the ten or twelve years after 1865 the central-battery rigged ironclad (class 2 above) met upon the whole with most favour at the Admiralty as the best type of heavy fighting-ship. The vessels in class 3 may be regarded as experiments in the direction of finding a yet better type.

The *Monarch*, designed under the direction of Mr. E. J. Reed, embodied an attempt to combine the advantages of a high-freeboard masted ship with those of a turret vessel. In addition to her four heaviest guns in the two turrets, she carried somewhat lighter weapons under her raised poop and forecastle; and in that respect she differed from previous British turret ships, each of which had carried the whole of her heavy armament in the turrets. It was

a gain, of course, to be able thus to carry six or seven guns instead
of only four. On the other hand, the raised poop and forecastle
masked part of the fire from the turrets, and so limited the usefulness of the powerful and well-protected guns there. This defect
constituted the *Monarch's* great drawback. Her freeboard of 14 ft.
made her a useful ship at sea.

The *Captain*, designed by Captain Cowper Phipps Coles,
R.N.,C.B., assisted by Messrs. Laird, of Birkenhead, was the production of an amateur. Coles was strongly opposed to the high freeboard, which formed one of the leading features of the *Monarch*. He
desired a low freeboard turret-ship, in order that she might present as
small a target as possible to the enemy. Curiously enough, however, he reverted to masts and sails, and rigged his vessel heavily.
Even with her intended freeboard of 8 ft. 6 in., she would have been
unsafe in a heavy sea unless very carefully handled; but unfortunately, owing to errors on the part of her designer, her actual freeboard was but 6 ft. 8 in. After having made two cruises in the
Channel, and having, by her behaviour, caused some of her bitterest
opponents to modify their opinion of her, she sailed again with the
Channel Fleet under Admiral Sir Alexander Milne, K.C.B.; and, on
the night of September 6th, 1870, during a south-westerly gale, she
capsized in a fierce squall, and went to the bottom, carrying with
her the whole of those on board except eighteen persons. The
number of souls who perished was 475, among them being her commander, Captain Hugh Talbot Burgoyne, V.C., and her misguided
designer, Captain Coles.[1] This terrible catastrophe condemned for
ever the low freeboard rigged turret-ship.

The *Devastation*, and her successors, the very similar *Thunderer*
and *Dreadnought* (all of which were closely allied to the smaller
non-seagoing ironclads, *Glatton*, *Cyclops*, *Gorgon*, *Hecate*, and
Hydra), forestalled rather than profited by the dreadful lesson taught
by the fate of the *Captain*, for the *Devastation* was laid down ten
months before the disaster. The type was designed by Mr. E. J.
Reed, C.B. In it masts and sails were frankly and completely
abandoned, the result being the creation of some most successful
and safe low freeboard turret-ships. But in one respect the new
vessels were inferior to the *Monarch*. Though they possessed all-
round fire, they mounted only four heavy guns apiece, and had no
secondary armament whatsoever.

[1] Proc. of C. M. : Parl. Paper 1871, 42.

The *Shannon*, with her larger but similar successors, the *Nelson* and the *Northampton*, is interesting for more than one reason; although the type was not a very successful one. The *Shannon* was not a battleship, but she was intended to combine some of the features of the battleship with those of the cruiser, and she was specially designed for fighting bows on. Abaft her foremast, therefore, she had a respectably thick armoured bulkhead with recessed ports. Forward of this, there was no vertical armour; but there was an under-water steel protective deck, curving downwards towards the ram, and shielding the ship's vitals. Abaft the bulkhead, as far as the stern, ran a water-line belt of vertical armour, the lower edge of which touched the lower edge of the protective deck; but, except the forward bulkhead, there was no protection for the men at the guns, so that the vessel, if regarded broadside on, might be called a partially belted cruiser, while, if regarded bows on, she resembled a central-battery battleship with an unarmoured bow. The protective deck, as employed in the *Shannon*, was built into nearly all subsequent British ironclads, and into all large cruisers, whether armoured or not.

The *Téméraire* marked a great advance, and embodied more than one valuable new feature, though she was without the protective deck, and had merely thin horizontal above-water plating to keep out light plunging fire. Near each end of the ship, above the upper deck, rose an armoured barbette, or open non-revolving turret; and in each of these was a heavy gun, which fired over the edge of the barbette and had a very wide command. The guns in this case were so arranged as to disappear behind the protection after their discharge, and to be revolved, and again brought up to the firing position by hydraulic power. Between these two barbettes, with its guns on a lower level, was an armoured central-battery, mounting six heavy pieces; and lower down, along the entire length of the ship, was a water-line belt of thick vertical armour. In this type, the biggest guns of all were in two barbettes on the upper deck, above the keel-line of the ship; and a strong secondary armament was in an armoured box-battery between them. The design, due to Mr. Nathaniel Barnaby, had in it the germ of ideas which a few years later, entered into the normal and accepted battleship types of Great Britain, the United States, Germany, Italy, and Russia, and to some extent of France also.

The *Inflexible* and her kindred were set-backs. Each of them had two very heavily armoured turrets, placed close together diagonally across the upper deck ; and in each turret each had two very heavy guns. Under and around the turrets, from the deck to below the water-line, was a thickly armoured rectangular citadel, forming the central third of the ship, but elsewhere there was neither vertical armour nor, in the case of the *Inflexible*, heavy gun of any sort. The only.armoured protection to the long ends of the ships were steel 3-in. decks, and it was generally supposed that if one of the unarmoured ends of any of these vessels were much injured by shot or otherwise in the neighbourhood of the water-line, the result would be fatal. It was an extreme instance of taking care of the gun at the expense of the ship.

At about the time when these last vessels were in process of construction several significant and revolutionary facts forced themselves before the attention of the naval architect :—

a. Not only the automobile torpedo, but also the fast torpedo-boat, had brought forward factors which could not be neglected. Provision must be made for defence against them, and also for their due utilisation.

b. The development of the power of the heavy gun had rendered the old iron armour almost useless. If, as in the case of the *Agamemnon*,[1] it were piled on in some places to a thickness of 18 inches, it would, it was true, defeat all save the very largest guns, but, at the same time, it could be carried only on a very small proportion of the total exposed surface. An armour giving equal or more resistance with less thickness and weight must be sought for.

c. Steel had become available as a building material, and was about to supersede iron entirely for that purpose.

d. The slowness of fire of heavy muzzle-loading guns, even when worked hydraulically, and their other disadvantages, taken in conjunction with the general adoption of breechloaders by foreign nations, had long since called for a change in the armament of British warships.

e. The invention of slow-burning powders for heavy guns, destined to give high velocities to their projectiles, demanded the use of a much longer barrel than could be given to any ship's muzzle-loader ; which had necessarily to be sponged and loaded from the forward end, and to be run in-board for that purpose. Therefore, unless high velocities as well as quickness of fire were to be dispensed with, long breechloading guns must be mounted. Long guns, which did

---

[1] Some of the *Inflexible's* armour was compound.

not require to be run in, could easily be fought from positions whence even much shorter and vastly inferior guns, if muzzle-loaders, could not be fought at all.

f. The appearance of the quick-firing gun, and of machine-guns, indicated that it was time to devote attention to the secondary and subsidiary as well as to the primary armaments of new ships. The ideal fighting craft could no longer afford to mount two, four, or six very heavy guns, and little or nothing else. She must be able to meet quick-firing gun with quick-firing gun, and machine-gun with machine-gun, or risk finding herself at the mercy of an opponent perhaps far smaller than herself. If heavy armour was necessary to keep out heavy projectiles, light armour was equally necessary to keep out light ones.

g. Marine engines and boilers had been immensely improved ; and the importance of speed was becoming clearer daily, from the point of view not only of tactics but also of strategy. It was obviously not sufficient that Great Britain's fastest armoured ship should have a paper speed of only 14·9 knots, and an actual continuous steaming speed of at least two knots less. Great radius of action, meaning great bunker capacity, was another desideratum, if fast vessels were to maintain their speed over long distances, and so derive full advantage from it.

h. Finally, apart from many other considerations, masts and yards had ceased to be useful in heavy fighting ships. They would be sources of danger in action, especially when exposed to the effect of quick-firing guns ; and besides involving weight to be carried, they involved weight to be carried in the most inconvenient position. They also afforded great resistance to the course of a vessel steaming against a wind. Ships of the *Devastation* type had proved that they could dispense with them. At the same time, if only for signalling and look-out purposes, masts of some sort were desirable ; and if machine-guns could be mounted in their tops, perhaps so much the better.

The result was the construction in England of a certain number of heavy fighting ships of what may be called tentative types. The time had come when the nature of most of the problems needing solution was recognised, and when it was known what desirable features presented themselves for inclusion in that all-round com-promise which, unfortunately, even the finest and largest battleship stands for. The upshot of the work done in this tentative period was (*a*) the realisation of the fact that many ironclads of earlier dates had ceased to be useful save for coast-defence or guardship purposes, although they had been built originally for sea-service, and (b) the appearance of the fast armoured cruiser as a vessel distinct from the battleship, yet capable, perhaps, of doing some of her work.

CLASS 4.—TENTATIVE TYPES OF IRONCLADS.

Name.	Date of Launch.	Type.[8]	Displacement in Tons.	H.P.I.	Speed.	Thickest Armour.	Heaviest Gun.	No. of Guns.			Complement.
								Heavy.	Secondary.	Subsidiary.[9]	
					Kts.	In.	Tons In.				
Conqueror . .	1881	{ M. T. 1. / Br. B. }	6,200	6,000	15·5	12·0	45 12	2	4	6	335
Colossus[1] . .	1882	M. T. 2.	9,420	5,500	15·5	18·0	45 12	4	5	14	396
Collingwood . .	1882	{ M. Bar. 2. / C. B. }	9,500	9,500	16·4	18·0	45 12	4	6	20	460
Impérieuse[2] . .	1883	R. Bar. 4.	8,400	10,000	17·0	10·0	22 9·2	4	10	13	527
Rodney[3] . . .	1884	{ M. Bar. 2. / C. B. }	10,300	11,500	16·7	18·0	67 13·5	4	6	22	510
Hero	1885	{ M. T. 1, / Br. B. }	6,200	6,000	15·5	12·0	45 12	2	4	12	335
Benbow . . .	1885	{ M. Bar. 2. / C. B. }	10,600	11,500	17.5	18·0	111 16·25	2	10	26	525
Camperdown[4] .	1885	{ M. Bar. 2. / C. B. }	10,600	11,500	17·2	18·0	67 13·5	4	6	22	515
Orlando[5] . . .	1886	Pt. Bl. Cr.	5,600	8,500	17·1	16·0	22 9	2	10	10	497
Sans Pareil[6] .	1887	{ M. T. 1. / Br. B. }	10,740	14,000	17·5	18·0	111 16·25	3	12	24	630
Trafalgar[7] . .	1887	{ M. T. 2. / C. B. }	11,940	12,000	17·0	20·0	67 13·5	4	6	19	520

[1] Similar to the *Colossus* was the *Edinburgh* (1882). [2] Similar to the *Impérieuse* was the *Warspite* (1884). [3] Similar to the *Rodney* was the *Howe* (1885). [4] Similar to the *Camperdown* was the *Anson* (1886). [5] Similar to the *Orlando* were the *Australia, Narcissus,* and *Undaunted* (1886), and *Aurora, Galatea, Immortalité* (1887). [6] Similar to the *Sans Pareil* was the *Victoria* (1887). [7] Similar to the *Trafalgar* was the *Nile* (1888).

[8] In this column, M., mastless; T. 1, T. 2, turret-ship with one or two turrets; Br. B., broadside battery; Bar. 2, ship with two barbettes; C. B., central battery; R., rigged; Pt. Bl. Cr., partially belted cruiser.

[9] Exclusive of machine and boat guns.

NOTE.—All the above had twin-screws and were fitted with tubes for the discharge of Whitehead torpedoes. All, also, carried breech-loading guns exclusively, and had compound vertical armour, and steel protective decks. All had steel hulls.

The above vessels, especially so far as the battleships among them are concerned, represent the efforts of the designers not only to protect the vitals of the ship and the primary armament as well as possible, but also to provide a respectable secondary armament, and to mount it in the best part of the ship. The *Conqueror* and *Sans Pareil* show a tendency in one direction. In them, as in the *Shannon*, of Class 3, the plans were based chiefly upon the assumption that the vessels would do their main fighting bows on to the foe. Both the heavy armour, therefore, and the heavy armament were put forward; the protection of the aftermost compartments was left to the armoured deck; and the stern fire was relatively weak. The *Hero* was to all intents and purposes a replica of the *Conqueror*, except that she carried her secondary armament, of 6-inch guns, on her upper instead of on her main deck. The type soon fell into disfavour.

The *Colossus* embodied a development of the *Inflexible* and *Agamemnon* types of Class 3, the diagonal arrangement of turrets being retained, but an effort also being made to provide in a satisfactory manner for a fairly powerful secondary battery. The attempt was not very successful ; and no further experiments were made along those lines. The type is one which died out quickly.

The *Collingwood*, the earliest of the " Admiral " type of battleships, was similar in general arrangement to the *Rodney, Benbow*, and *Camperdown*, which followed her, and, to some extent also, to the *Trafalgar*. She may be regarded as a development of the *Téméraire* type, in Class 3, the *Téméraire* herself being a kind of compromise between the central-battery ships of Class 2 and the sea-going monitors of Mr. E. J. Reed's design, such as the *Devastation*. It was no longer assumed by the constructors that the ship would be called upon to do her hardest fighting bows on to the enemy. On the contrary, it was sought to give the ship, so far as it could be managed, equal offensive strength in all directions. With this aim in view, the primary armament was equally divided, and placed half at one end and half at the other end of the ship in barbettes or turrets, where it could fire both parallel with and at right angles to the keel-line of the vessel ; and the secondary armament, half on each broadside, in a battery occupying the middle space on deck between the barbettes or turrets, was so arranged that all the guns on each side had a wide arc of fire, while the end guns —those at each corner of the central battery—could also fire in a direction nearly parallel with the keel-line.

This type of battleship found favour at once. The earliest exponents of it had too little water-line protection. For example, the *Collingwood*, though 325 feet long, had only 150 feet of that length protected with vertical armour. Again, the earliest exponents of the type had no armour whatsoever to cover the men at the guns in the central battery. Improvements were presently made in the direction of lengthening the armoured belt ; armouring the central battery ; dividing off the guns in the central battery by means of screens, or by placing them singly in armoured casemates ; sponsoning out the broadside guns, so as to give them a still wider radius of fire ; giving the ships higher freeboard, and raising the height above water of the primary armament ; and, in cases where turrets were not used, covering the breech-ends of the barbette guns with armoured hoods which revolved with them. The outcome of these and other improvements was the standard type of British battleship, which held its position almost unchallenged during the last twelve years of the nineteenth century, although, of course, it still continued to be improved in detail year after year.

Of the two types of armoured cruisers in Class 4, the earlier, the *Impérieuse* type, though it proved itself useful, developed no further. The later, the *Orlando* type, had an arrangement of its primary and secondary armaments similar to that which formed the peculiar feature of the *Collingwood* and her successors. For some years after the building of the *Orlando* and her consorts, the construction of armoured cruisers was neglected in England; but when it was resumed, in 1897, the standard type selected bore a strong resemblance, so far as disposition of armament was concerned, both to the *Collingwood* and to the *Orlando*.

It now remains to complete the list of British ironclads up to the end of 1900 by giving tables of the battleships and armoured cruisers of what I have ventured to call the standard types :—

CLASS 5.—STANDARD BATTLESHIP TYPES.

Name.	Date of Launch.	Displacement in Tons.	H.P.I.	Speed.	Thickest Armour.	Heaviest Gun.	No. of Guns.			Complement.
							Heavy.	Secondary.	Subsidiary.	
				Knots.	In.	Ton. In.				
Hood [1]	1891	14,150	13,000	17·5	18·0 [11]	67 13·5	4	10	22	634
Royal Sovereign [2]	1891	14,150	13,000	17·0	18·0 [12]	67 13·5	4	10	22	712
Centurion [3] . .	1892	10,500	13,000	18·5	12·0 [13]	29 10	4	10	20	620
Renown [4] . . .	1895	12,350	12,000	18·0	10·0 [14]	29 10	4	10	24	674
Magnificent [5] .	1894	14,900	12,000	17·5	14·0 [14]	46 12	4	12	28	757
Canopus [6] . . .	1897	12,950	13,500	18·25	12·0 [14]	46 12	4	12	16	750
Formidable [7] . .	1898	15,000	15,000	18·0	12·0 [15]	50 12	4	12	22	750
London [8] . . .	1899	15,000	15,000	18·0	12·0 [15]	50 12	4	12	22	750
Russell [9] . . .	bldg. 1900	14,000	18,000	19·0	12·0 [15]	50 12	4	12	16	750
Queen [10] . . .	pro. 1900	15,000	15,000	18·0	12·0 [15]	50 12	4			

[1] Laid down under the Naval Defence Act, 1889 ; a turret-ship. Otherwise practically the same as the ships of the *Royal Sovereign* type.

[2] Laid down under the Naval Defence Act, 1889 ; a barbette ship. Similar to the *Royal Sovereign* were the *Empress of India* (1891), and *Ramillies, Repulse, Resolution, Revenge*, and *Royal Oak* (1892).

[3] Estimates of 1890–91 ; a barbette ship. Similar to the *Centurion* was the *Barfleur* (1892).

[4] Estimates of 1892–93 ; a barbette ship.

[5] Estimates of 1893–94, and 1894–95 ; a barbette ship. Similar to the *Magnificent* were the *Majestic, Hannibal, Jupiter, Prince George*, and *Victorious* (1895), and the *Cæsar, Illustrious*, and *Mars* (1896).

[6] Estimates of 1896–97 ; a barbette ship. Similar to the *Canopus* were the *Albion, Goliath*, and *Ocean* (1898), and the *Vengeance* and *Glory* (1899).

[7] Estimates of 1897–98 ; a barbette ship. Similar to the *Formidable* were the *Irresistible* (1898) and the *Implacable* (1899).

[8] Estimates of 1898–99 ; a barbette ship. Similar to the *London* were the *Bulwark* and *Venerable* (1899).

[9] Supplementary Estimates of 1898, and Estimates of 1899–1900 ; a barbette ship. Similar to the *Russell* were the *Duncan, Cornwallis, Exmouth, Albemarle* and *Montagu*, all still building at the end of 1900.

[10] Estimates of 1900–1901 ; a barbette ship. Similar to the *Queen* was the *Prince of Wales*. Neither had been laid down at the end of 1900.

[11] Compound, and steel armour.

[12] Compound, and steel armour, the latter being nickel-steel in the case of the *Ramillies, Repulse, Revenge*, and *Royal Oak*.

[13] Compound, and nickel-steel armour.   [14] Harveyed steel armour.   [15] Krupp steel armour.

The modifications in the disposition of the armour on the citadel in these successive types will best be understood after an examination of the accompanying plans. It will be noticed that although throughout the heaviest armour continued to be concentrated about the vitals of the ship, a tendency gradually sprang up to armour the forward end of the ship as well, even although only comparatively thin plates could be carried there. An increasing amount of protection, also, was given to the secondary armament.

The *Formidable, London,* and *Queen* types in the above list were practically identical. Together they constituted a homogeneous group of eight first-class battleships, which may be regarded as the

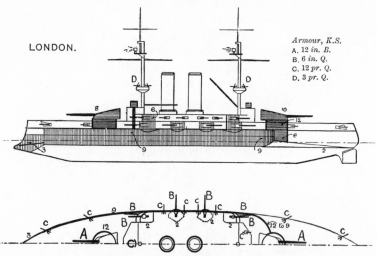

LONDON.

Armour, K.S.
A. 12 in. B.
B. 6 in. Q.
C. 12 pr. Q.
D. 3 pr. Q.

H.M. BATTLESHIPS "LONDON," "BULWARK," AND "VENERABLE," 1898–99.
(*From ' The Naval Pocket Book,'* 1901.)

best heavy fighting vessels that British naval architects and shipbuilders of the nineteenth century were capable of producing. Some additional description of them should, therefore, be given here. The following details are chiefly from my ' Naval Pocket Book ':—[1]

Hull, steel. Hooded barbettes, 2. Funnels, fore and aft, 2. Military masts with 1 top on each, 2.
Length, 400 ft. Beam, 75 ft. Mean draught, 26 ft. 9 in.
Displacement, 15,000 tons. H.P.I. 15,000. Extreme speed, 18 knots.
Coal capacity : from 900 to 2200 tons, giving a radius of action of from 3000 to 7000 miles at 10 knots.

---

[1] Edition for 1901, by L. G. Carr Laughton.

Engines: Two sets of 3-cylinder triple-expansion. Boilers, for the most part Belleville water-tube, 20 in number, with economisers, and with a heating-surface of 37,000 square feet. The *Queen* was to have Yarrow boilers.

Armour: Krupp steel partial belt, 216 ft. long, 15 ft. deep, and 9 in. thick. Cross bulkheads 9 to 12 in. Barbettes, 12, 10, and 6 in. Barbette-hoods, 10, 8, and 3 in. Protective deck, 2 to 3 in. Main deck, 1 in. From fore-end of citadel to point of ram, a 2 in. belt, 15 ft. deep. Fore conning-tower, 14 in., with 8-in. communication tube. After conning-tower, 3 in., with 3-in. tube.

Armament; 4–12 in. 50-ton wire-bound breechloaders: 12 6-in. 45 calibre quick-firers in armoured casemates; 16 12-pr. quickfirers; 2 12-pr. boat or field guns; 6 3-pr. quickfirers; 8·45-in. Maxim automatic machine-guns. The heavy guns capable of being loaded in any position. Torpedo ejectors (18 in.) 4; 3 being submerged, and 1 above water at the stern. Search-lights, 6. Boats, 18, 4 being steam-boats, and 3 being fitted to discharge 14-in. torpedoes.

The ships were divided into about 150 water-tight compartments, and had upwards of 200 water-tight doors. Apart from the main (propelling) engines, there were about 100 others, for driving pumps, fans, dynamos, steering-gear, capstans, hoisting apparatus, etc., etc. The cost of a completed ship of the type, when ready for sea, was about £1,250,000.

ESSEX.

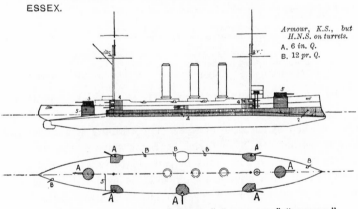

Armour, K.S., *but*
H.N.S. *on turrets.*
A. *6 in. Q.*
B. *12 pr. Q.*

H.M. ARMOURED CRUISERS "KENT," "ESSEX," "MONMOUTH," "BEDFORD,"
"CORNWALL," "SUFFOLK," ETC.

("County" Class of 1899–1901.)

(*From* '*The Naval Pocket Book,*' 1901.)

After the building of the two ships of the *Impérieuse* type in 1883–84, and of the seven of the *Orlando* type in 1886–87 (*see* Class 4), the construction of armoured cruisers by Great Britain was completely suspended for ten years. The numerous and fine cruisers which were built had no vertical armour whatsoever, except, in some cases, over their principal guns, and, in most cases, on their conning-towers; and they relied for the maintenance of their buoyancy in action upon steel protective decks, and upon the subdivision of their hulls into very numerous water-tight compartments. By 1897, however, certain foreign powers had embarked so decisively upon a policy of building fast armoured cruisers that the Admiralty could no longer hold back. Accordingly, in the Supplementary Estimates for 1897–98, and in the regular Estimates for 1898–99, 1899–1900, and 1900–1901 respectively, provision was made for the construction of twenty vessels of this class, as follows:—

CLASS 6.—STANDARD ARMOURED CRUISER TYPES.

—	Date of Launch.	Displace-ment in Tons.	H.P.I.	Speed.	Thickest Armour.	Heaviest Gun.	No. of Guns.			Comple-ment.
							Heavy.	Secon-dary.	Sub-sidiary.	
				Knots.	In.	Ton. In.				
Sutlej [1] . . .	1899	12,000	21,000	21·0	6·0 [4]	26 9·2	2	12	15	700
Kent [2]	1900	9,800	22,000	23·0	5·0 [5]	7¼ 6	—	14	13	
Good Hope [3] . .	bldg. 1900	14,100	30,000	23·0	6·0 [6]	26 9·2	2	16	17	900

[1] To this class belong also (Supplementary Estimates, 1897–98) the *Cressy* (1899), *Aboukir* and *Hogue* (1900) and (Estimates, 1898–99) *Bacchante* and *Euryalus* (building 1900): six ships in all.
[2] To this class belong also (Supplementary Estimates, 1898) the *Essex* (building 1900), (Estimates, 1899–1900), the *Monmouth* and *Bedford* (building 1900); and (Estimates, 1900–1901) the *Cornwall*, *Suffolk*, *Berwick*, *Cumberland*, *Donegal*, and *Lancaster*: ten ships in all.
[3] To this class belong also (Supplementary Estimates, 1898) the *Leviathan* (building 1900), and (Estimates, 1898–99) the *Drake* and *King Alfred* (ex *Africa*), (building 1900): four ships in all.
[4] Krupp steel and nickel steel.   [5] Krupp steel and Harveyed nickel steel.   [6] Krupp steel.

The 9·2-inch guns of the above were of the Vickers pattern on special mountings on the central-pivot system, with endless dredger hoists worked by electric motors. The training was done alternatively by hand or by electricity. Some ships of the *Kent* type had four of their 6-inch guns in pairs in turrets fore and aft, so arranged that each gun of a pair could be used independently, or that both could be trained together and fired as one piece. Later ships of the *Kent* type were to carry one 7·5-inch gun instead of each of these two pairs.

The *Sutlej* type, 440 feet long, had 230 feet of that length belted with 6-inch armour, and the forward end, to the ram, covered with 2-inch plates. The *Kent* (or "County") type, also 440 feet long, but of less beam, had a 4-inch midship belt, and 2-inch plating at the bow. The *Good Hope* type had a 6-inch midship belt, and 2-inch plating at the bow, and was 500 feet long between perpendiculars. Further particulars may be gathered from the accompanying plans.

It would be quite hopeless to attempt to analyse the very numerous designs of unarmoured cruisers which found favour at various times between the beginning of 1857 and the end of 1900.

All that can be done here is to give a few particulars of some of the more noteworthy types. These will be found over-leaf.

The gunboats built previous to 1890 had wood, composite, or iron hulls. Of sea-going gunboats, the *Bramble* type (1886–87; composite; 715 tons; 13 knots; 1 screw; 6 4-inch B.); the *Pheasant* type (1888; composite; 755 tons; 13·2 knots; 1 screw; 6 4-inch B.); and the *Lapwing* type (1889; composite; 805 tons; 13 knots; 1 screw; 6 4-inch B.), may be cited as specimens which showed a distinct advance upon the types of the period of the Crimean War. In 1897–98, the *Dwarf* class (steel, sheathed; 710 tons; 13·5 knots; 2 screws; 2 4-inch Q.) was built. Of iron coast-defence gunboats,

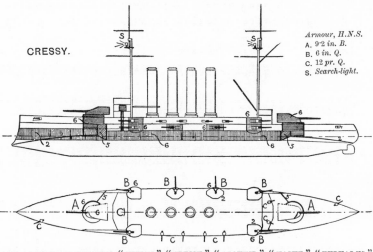

CRESSY.

Armour, H.N.S.
A. *9·2 in. B.*
B. *6 in. Q.*
C. *12 pr. Q.*
S. *Search-light.*

H.M. ARMOURED CRUISERS "SUTLEJ," "CRESSY," "ABOUKIR," "HOGUE," "EURYALUS," AND "BACCHANTE," 1899–1901.

(*From ' The Naval Pocket Book,' 1901.*)

each mounting from one to three comparatively heavy muzzle-loaders, and having twin screws but very low speed, many were built between 1870 and 1882. Their displacement was in the neighbourhood of 260 tons; and they were chiefly designed for bows-on fighting. In the last decade of the century several very shallow draught gunboats were constructed for use in the rivers of Africa and China. Some of these were fitted with a single stern-wheel, others, with twin screws working in raised tunnels. The draught of a craft displacing upwards of 100 tons was kept as low as 20 inches by the ingenuity displayed by the designers, a leader of

TYPICAL UNARMOURED CRUISING SHIPS, 1857–1900.

Class	Hull. W. = Wood. I. = Iron. C. = Composite. S. = Steel. s. = Sheathed.	Name. pp., partially protected. p., protective deck.	Date of Launch.	Displacement in Tons.	H.P.I.	Speed. Knots.	Length. Ft.	Length. In.	Beam. Ft.	Beam. In.	Heaviest Gun. M. = muzzle-loader. B. = breech-loader. Q. = quick-firer.	No. of Guns (including machine-guns).	Complement.
Old, Tentative, and Transitional Cruisers.	W.	*Mersey*	1858	5,645	[1,000 N.]	13·2	300	2½	52	0	95 cwt. 68 pr. M.	40	560
	W.	*Newcastle*	1860	4,020	[600 N.]	10·5	250	0	52	0	95 cwt. 68 pr. M.	51	
	W.	*Wolverene*	1863	2,431	[400 N.]	11·2	225	0	40	9	110 pr. B.	21	275
	W.	*Juno*	1867	2,240	1,380	10·8	200	0	40	4	6½ ton 7 in. M.	6	200
	W.	*Briton*	1869	2,150	2,150	13·1	220	0	36	0	6½ ton 7 in. M.	10	200
	W.	*Diamond*	1874	1,970	2,140	12·5	220	0	37	0	64 cwt. 64 pr. M.	12	160
	W.	*Blanche*	1867	1,760	1,950	13·6	212	0	36	0	6½ ton 7 in. M.	4	110
	W.	*Rinaldo*	1860	1,365	[200 N.]	..	185	1	33	2	58 cwt. 32 pr. M.	17	170
	I. s.	*Shah*	1873	6,250	7,480	16·0	334	0	52	0	12 ton 9 in. M.	26	600
	I. s.	*Inconstant*	1868	5,780	4,200	15·0	333	0	50	1	12 ton 9 in. M.	16	600
	I. s.	*Raleigh*	1873	5,200	4,200	14·0	298	0	49	0	90 cwt. 68 pr. M.	24	560
	I. s.	*Euryalus*	1877	4,140	5,110	14·7	280	0	45	6	90 cwt. 68 pr. M.	16	417
	I. s.	*Rover*	1874	3,460	4,960	14·5	280	0	43	6	6½ ton 7 in. M.	14	375
	I. s.	*Active*	1869	3,080	4,130	15·0	270	0	42	0	6½ ton 7 in. M.	8	350
	C.	*Emerald*	1876	2,120	2,175	13·2	220	0	40	0	64 cwt. 64 pr. M.	12	232
	C.	*Caroline*	1882	1,420	1,400	13·1	200	0	38	0	90 cwt. 7 in. M.	14	154
	C.	*Acorn*	1884	970	1,200	12·0	167	0	32	0	90 cwt. 7 in. M.	8	138
	C.	*Condor*	1876	780	770	10·9	157	0	29	6	90 cwt. 7 in. M.	3	110
	I. & S. s.	*Calliope*, pp.	1884	2,770	4,000	14·6	235	0	44	6	5 ton 6 in. B.	16[1]	291
	I. & S. s.	*Comus*, pp.	1878	2,380	2,000	12·7	225	0	44	6	90 cwt. 7 in. M.	14[1]	265
	S.	*Iris*[2]	1877	3,730	6,000	17·0	300	0	46	0	64 cwt. 64 pr. M.	10[1]	280
	S.	*Dryad*[2]	1893	1,070	3,500	18·5	250	0	30	6	2 ton 4·7 in. Q.	6[1]	115
	S.	*Alarm*[2]	1892	810	3,500	19·2	230	0	27	0	2 ton 4·7 in. Q.	6[1]	85
	S.	*Sharpshooter*[2]	1888	735	3,500	19·0	230	0	27	0	2 ton 4·7 in. Q.	6[1]	91
	S.	*Arethusa*,[2] pp.	1882	4,300	5,000	17·0	300	0	46	0	5 ton 6 in. B.	18[1]	297
	S.	*Archer*,[2] pp.	1886	1,770	3,500	16·5	225	0	36	0	5 ton 6 in. B.	14[1]	172
	S.	*Scout*,[2] pp.	1885	1,580	3,200	16·7	220	0	34	0	40 cwt. 5 in. B.	12 *	156
Standard Types at end of Century. Modern Sloops.	S. s.	*Beagle*[2]	1889	1,170	2,000	13·5	195	0	28	0	2 ton 5 in. B.	8	138
	S.	*Phœnix*[2]	1895	1,050	1,400	13·0	185	0	32	6	1 ton 4 in. Q.	10	105
	S. s.	*Condor*[2]	1898	980	1,400	13·2	180	0	33	0	1 ton 4 in. Q.	10	130
	S. s.	*Espiègle*[2]	1900	1,070	1,400	13·2	185	0	33	0	1 ton 4 in. Q.	10	135
3rd Class	S.	*Barham*,[2] p.	1889	1,830	4,700	19·0	280	0	35	0	2 ton 4·7 in. Q.	10[1]	160
	S.	*Pelorus*,[2] p.	1896	2,135	7,000	20·0	300	0	36	6	1 ton 4 in. Q.	16[1]	225
	S.	*Philomel*,[2] p.	1890	2,575	4,000	16·5	265	0	41	0	2 ton 4·7 in. Q.	16[1]	190
	S.	*Medea*,[2] p.	1888	2,800	9,000	19·0	265	0	41	0	5 ton 6 in. B.	16[1]	216
2nd Class	S.	*Latona*,[2] p.	1890	3,400	9,000	20·0	300	0	43	0	6 ton 6 in. Q.	17[1]	273
	S. s.	*Sirius*,[2] p.	1890	3,600	9,000	19·7	300	0	43	8	6 ton 6 in. Q.	17[1]	273
	S.	*Mersey*,[2] p.	1885	4,050	6,000	17·3	300	0	46	0	15 ton 8 in. B.	15[1]	325
	S. s.	*Bonaventure*,[2] p.	1892	4,360	9,000	19·5	320	0	49	6	6 ton 6 in. Q.	19[1]	318
	S. s.	*Eclipse*,[2] p.	1894	5,600	9,600	19·5	350	0	53	6	6 ton 6 in. Q.	25[1] *	437
	S. s.	*Hermes*,[2] p.	1898	5,600	10,000	20·0	350	0	54	0	7 ton 6 in. Q.	26 *	437
	S.	*Arrogant*,[2 3] p.	1896	5,750	10,000	19·0	320	0	57	6	7 ton 6 in. Q.	21 *	450
	S.	*Challenger*,[2] p.	bldg. 1900	5,880	12,000	21·0	355	0	56	0	7½ ton 6 in. Q.	25 *	475
1st Class	S.	*Edgar*,[2 4] p.	1890	7,350	12,000	20·0	360	0	60	0	22 ton 9·2 in. B.	29[1] *	544
	S. s.	*Royal Arthur*,[2 4] p.	1891	7,700	12,000	19·5	360	0	60	8	22 ton 9·2 in. B.	30[1] *	520
	S.	*Blake*,[2 4] p.	1889	9,000	20,000	21·0	375	0	65	0	22 ton 9·2 in. B.	28[1] *	590
	S. s.	*Diadem*,[2 4] p.	1896	11,000	16,500	20·5	435	0	69	0	7 ton 6 in. Q.	32[1] *	677
	S. s.	*Terrible*,[2 4] p.	1895	14,200	25,000	22·0	500	0	71	0	25 ton 9·2 in. B.	42 *	894

1 Carried torpedo-tubes (* submerged) for Whiteheads. Some earlier ships also had tubes fitted years after their completion.

3 These ships, designed as rams, had 40 ft. of their bows protected with 2-in. vertical armour, and were fitted with double rudders, the foremost being between the screws.

whom in this branch, as in other special branches of naval architecture, was Mr. A. F. Yarrow.

The most important of the special branches in question was called into existence, about the year 1877, by the demand for small fast craft suitable for the most advantageous utilisation of the Whitehead torpedo, which, at that date, was forcing its way into general notice as a weapon with immense possibilities before it. Two or three years earlier fast craft had been constructed for using with a towing-torpedo, a type which speedily became obsolete. In 1877, after the great improvements effected in the Whitehead in 1876, Messrs. Thornycroft built the *Lightning* (later known as No. 1), and Mr. Yarrow almost simultaneously produced two somewhat bigger and faster boats, subsequently known as Nos. 17 and 18, for the Admiralty. Large orders for similar vessels were quickly issued; and within the following twelve months numerous torpedo-boats were constructed for the British Government, though certain foreign powers lost no time in acquiring even more; so that for many years, as regards her torpedo-flotilla, Great Britain was inferior to some of her rivals. Particulars of a few typical British boats, arranged so as to direct notice to the developments in size, and particularly in speed, are appended. Smaller (2nd class) boats, intended for carrying on board ship, and capable of being hoisted in and out, were also built, and were eventually supplied to all battleships and large cruisers.

1st Class Torpedo-Boats.	Date of Launch.	Length.		Beam.		Draught.		Displacement.	H.P.I.	Speed.	Complement.
		Ft.	In.	Ft.	In.	Ft.	In.	Tons.		Knots.	
No. 1 . . .	1877	84	6	10	9	5	0	27	460	19·0	12
Nos. 17, 18 .	1877	86	0	11	0	4	6	33	450	21·0	15
Nos. 21, 22 .	1885	113	0	12	6	5	8	63	730	20·0	15
No. 79 . .	1886	125	0	13	0	5	6	75	1,000	22·4	15
No. 80 . .	1887	135	0	14	0	6	0	105	1,540	23·0	21
No. 93 . .	1893	140	0	15	6	5	5	130	2,200[1]	23·5	18
Nos. 98–101 .	{ bldg. 1900 }	155	0	17	0	8	5	150	2,800	25·0	20

[1] Twin-screws. The others had but one screw.

NOTE.—The number of torpedo-ejecting tubes carried by the above varied from one to five. The later boats carried a few 3-pr. quickfiring guns.

By the end of 1895, Great Britain possessed no fewer than 82 craft of the above and similar types, exclusive of boats less than 100 feet long. On the other hand, France had 195; Germany had 158; Italy had 121; Japan had 124; and Russia had 94 of corresponding classes. About three years before that date Britain's striking weakness in this respect had, however, been somewhat tardily recognised by the Admiralty ; and measures had been adopted with a view to providing compensation. These measures involved the creation of yet another class of special vessels.

Ever since the introduction of the torpedo-boat, the experts had sought for a craft wherewith to meet and checkmate it. In 1885 they had evolved the torpedo gunboat, familiarly known in the Navy as the torpedo-boat catcher, the first of the type being the *Rattlesnake*, the precursor of the vessels of the *Sharpshooter*, *Alarm*, and *Dryad* classes in the list of Typical Cruising Ships on p. 38. But the " catchers," small cruisers in effect, had proved too big, too visible, and, above all, too slow for their intended mission, which was to overhaul the torpedo-boat, and sink her by gun-fire, or by running her down. In the annual naval manœuvres of 1888–93 they failed over and over again to protect the fleets to which they were attached. It became evident that something else must be devised ; and accordingly, in 1893, the first of the torpedo-boat destroyers were ordered.

The " catcher " had been too large on the one hand, and not large enough on the other, to attain and maintain really high speed. Moreover, she had been an expensive craft, and, while useless as a snapper up of torpedo-boats, had been equally useless as a torpedo-vessel, owing to her visibility and lack of speed. It was determined that the new craft should be a " catcher " and a torpedo-boat in one, a vessel able to overhaul and reduce a hostile torpedo-boat by means of gun-fire or running down, and also able to act as a first-class torpedo-boat of the most effective sort. Mr. Yarrow's pioneer destroyer, the *Havock*, launched in the autumn of 1893 in response to the requirements of the Admiralty, was from the beginning so obvious a success that other craft of the kind were promptly ordered from various firms ; and a considerable flotilla of these boats was created by Great Britain almost before any other power secured so much as a single specimen. In the table on p. 41 will be found an epitome of the rapid development of the torpedo-boat destroyer in the few years which elapsed between its original evolution and the end of the nineteenth century.

A few miscellaneous craft of special nature remain for notice. In 1878 the importunate advocacy of the ram by Admiral of the Fleet Sir George Rose Sartorius, then eighty-eight years of age, induced the Admiralty to lay down the *Polyphemus*, a steel twin-screw vessel designed solely for ramming and for discharging torpedoes. She was of 2640 tons' displacement, and had a speed of 17·8 knots. Owing to alterations made in her plans while she was building, she was not launched until 1881, and was not ready for sea until several years later. A most expensive craft, and of doubtful value, she remained the sole representative of her class.

Destroyer's Name.	Date of Launch.	Length.	Beam.	Draught.	Displacement.	H.P.I.	Speed.	Complement.
		Feet.	Feet.	Feet.	Tons.		Knots.	
Havock . . .	1893	180	18·5	7·5	240	3,000	26·7	43
Lynx	1894	194	19·2	5·6	290	4,400	27·3	50
Handy	1895	200	19·0	7·8	275	4,000	27·8	50
Foam	1896	210	19·5	7·2	310	5,400	30·0	60
Wolf	1897	210	21·7	5·3	360	6,000	31·2	58
Express . . .	1897	227	22·0	9·0	430	9,250	33·0	60
Viper	1899	210	21·0	8·2	325	10,000	36·58	68

NOTE.—Of the above, the *Havock* was built by Yarrow; the *Lynx* and *Wolf* were built by Lairds; the *Handy* and *Express* were built by the Fairfield Co.; the *Foam* was built by Thornycroft; and the *Viper* was built by Hawthorn, Leslie and Co. The *Havock* and *Viper* had Yarrow; the *Lynx, Wolf* and *Express* had Normand; and the *Handy* and *Foam* had Thornycroft water-tube boilers. All were built of steel; all had twin-screws, except the *Viper*, which was driven by Parson's steam turbines (four shafts with two propellers on each); the usual gun armament was 1 12-pr., and 5 6-pr. quickfirers; and most of the boats carried two training ejection tubes for 18-in. Whitehead torpedoes.

The addition to the Navy of large numbers of torpedo-boats rendered it desirable that a large vessel should be provided to act as a kind of nursing-mother, storeship, and repairing shop for such craft while at sea. In 1878, the iron steamship *Hecla*, of 6400 tons' displacement, was purchased by the Admiralty for this purpose, and adapted as a torpedo depôt ship; and in 1889 a second sea-going depôt ship, the *Vulcan*, a fast steel twin-screw vessel, of 6620 tons' displacement, was added to the service. The latter was built expressly for the objects in view, and was also a mining and electric cable depôt, a floating workshop, forge, and foundry, and a repository for six second-class torpedo-boats, which she carried on her deck, and could hoist in and out by means of specially fitted hydraulic cranes. In addition, she was an efficient, though lightly armed, cruiser, with protective deck. Despatch vessels, tugs, storeships, troopships, yachts, surveying vessels, and harbour craft served throughout the period as complements of the fighting navy, but were far too numerous for mention here.

A word may be added as to the royal yachts. In 1857 the principal yacht was the second *Victoria and Albert* (ex *Windsor Castle*), particulars of which have been given in Vol. VI, p. 199. A most useful and comfortable craft, she retained her position until the end of 1900, although a third *Victoria and Albert*, a twin-screw steel ship of 4700 tons' displacement and 17 knots' speed, had been laid down in 1897 and launched in 1899. This fine vessel was nearing completion at the end of the century. At that date, the other royal yachts were the wooden paddle vessels *Osborne*, of 1850 tons' displacement and 14 knots' speed, built in 1870; *Alberta*, of 370 tons' displacement and 13 knots' speed, built in 1863; and the little tender *Elfin*, of 93 tons' displacement and 11 knots' speed, dating from as far back as 1849.

During the Russian scare of 1885, numerous fast and large merchant vessels were taken over and employed temporarily as naval cruisers,[1] one, the *Oregon*, being actually commissioned by officers and men of the Navy. Many years earlier, viz., in December, 1876, the Admiralty had opened a register for ships complying with certain stipulated conditions, and therefore suitable for employment in time f war. In 1885 the number of vessels on this list was 155, of 12 knots' speed and upwards. In the estimates for 1887–88, provision was made for the payment of small subsidies, by way of retaining fees, to the owners of a few of the most serviceable of these craft; and at the same time it was arranged that the subsidised owners should hold other ships at the disposal of the Admiralty without further retaining fee. At the end of 1900 the number of large fast vessels thus secured as " Royal Naval Reserved Merchant Cruisers," or as additional cruisers for instant use in case of need, was fifty, the contributing companies being the Cunard, the Peninsular and Oriental, the White Star, the Canadian Pacific, the Orient, the Royal Mail, and the Pacific. For each of the subventioned vessels a suitable light armament was stored at the British port to which she belonged.

The end of the Crimean War marks the end also of what may be called the stagnation period in the history of naval gunnery. In the previous half century the use of shells had become more general than before, and the shell itself had been improved, though it was still employed chiefly in mortars; and attention had begun to be directed to the problem of the diminution of windage, with a view to obtaining greater accuracy and velocity by utilising as much as possible of the elastic force of the explosion, and allowing as little of it as possible to pass the projectile and escape without doing its due share of the work. In certain small arms the problem had been

Admiralty Return of Aug. 5, 1885.

dealt with long before by the adoption of the device of rifling the interior of the barrel, and giving to the grooves of the rifling a slight but constant or even an increasing twist, which was found to increase accuracy by imparting a corresponding axial twist to the bullet in its flight. In the old muzzle-loading days, the bullet of a rifle was hammered, or violently forced down upon the powder; but very little experiment showed that it would be vain to attempt to do with an iron projectile, weighing perhaps 68 lbs., what could be done easily with a leaden bullet weighing a few grains. Whitworth and others, therefore, devised an elongated bolt or projectile which, instead of being forced into the bore of a heavy gun by the exertion of main strength, was of size and shape to permit of its being pushed home with comparatively little exertion, but which, nevertheless, acquired a twisting motion in its outward flight by reason of some peculiar correspondence between a cross section of the projectile and a cross section of the bore of the gun, the bore itself being twisted. Whitworth's section was hexagonal; the section chosen by Lancaster was slightly oval. Yet still, as the projectile would not fit with more than approximate accuracy, there was much windage; and at length it became obvious that if windage was to be reduced to the lowest practicable point, the gun must be loaded not at the muzzle but at the breech.[1]

In 1858 the first great step was taken. In that year the Committee on Rifled Cannon recommended the introduction of the rifled breechloading Armstrong gun into the naval service. In the earliest days of the new guns there was no improved velocity,[2] but there was immensely improved accuracy. Comparing, for example, the velocities and energies of the 32-pr. smooth bore and of the 40-pr. R.B.L. gun which took its place, Sir Andrew Noble puts the muzzle velocity[3] of the old weapon at 1600, and that of the newer at only 1200 foot-seconds, and the muzzle energy[4] at 570 and 400 foot-tons respectively; but he adds that, using the method of least squares to determine the relative accuracy of the rifled and of the smooth bore gun of approximately the same weight, he found that,

[1] Author, in 'Social England,' vi., 496.
[2] For a discussion of this question, *see* Noble, 'Rise and Progress of Rifled Naval Artillery'; Inst. of Nav. Arch., July, 1899.
[3] Muzzle velocity means the rate in feet per second at which the projectile moves on quitting the gun's muzzle.
[4] Muzzle energy means the power developed at the gun's muzzle, as measured by the weight in tons which that power would raise to the height of one foot.

at a range of 1000 yards, half the shot from a rifled gun fell in a rectangle about 23 yards long by 1 yard wide, while, in the case of the smooth bore, the corresponding rectangle was about 145 yards long by 10 yards wide. The velocity was afterwards improved, first by using various obturators and " driving bands," the effect of which was to enable the pressure of the gases of explosion to squeeze the basic, or part of the cylindral, periphery of the projectile into the grooves of the rifling, and so prevent those gases from escaping before the expulsion of the projectile; later by the gradual adoption of more suitable powders, which, being of slower combustion, set up growing rather than sudden pressures, and so reduced the violence of the strains; and, last of all, by the adoption of much longer guns, so as to allow of the slower burning powders perfecting their combustion while the projectile was still within the muzzle and fully subject to the pressure.

But these were the improvements of years. Armstrong's first breechloader was a tube, cut into near its rear end so as to admit of the dropping in of a breech block, which then filled the aperture and closed the bore. A hollow screw, working in the tube or bore from the rear, pressed the block home, and held it fast. The gun was loaded through the hollow screw, the block being displaced for the purpose; and for that reason it soon became known as the Armstrong screw gun. The following are particulars [1] of various types of this weapon which were used in the Navy from about the year 1860 onwards :—

R.B.L. (Screw) Guns.		Bore.		Weight of Full Charge.				
Nature.	Weight.	Length.	Diam.	Powder.	Projectile.	Projectile. Diam.	Muzzle Energy.	Muzzle Velocity.
	Cwts.	Ins.	Ins.	Lbs. Oz.	Lbs. Oz.	Ins.	Foot-tons.	Foot-seconds.
9-pr. . . .	6	52·5	3·2	1 2	8 8	3·0	66	1055
12-pr. . . .	8	61·3	3·2	1 8	11 4	3·0	118	1239
20-pr., L.S. . .	16	84·0	3·94	2 8	21 13	3·75	193	1130
40-pr., patt. G. .	35	106·3	4·96	5 0	40 2	4·75	388	1180
7-in., heavy .	82	99·5	7·2	11 0	109 0	7·0	915	1100

All these guns were rifled on the polygroove system, with a uniform twist which varied from one turn in 38 calibres in the 9-pr., 12-pr. and 20-pr., to one in 37 in the 7-in., and one in 36·5 in the 40-pr. The powders used were R.L.G. (rifled large-grain black) or P. (prism black). The 20-pr. L.S. (land-service) was used in two rather lighter forms for ship and boat service.

[1] ' Text Book of Gunnery,' 1887 ; Cat. of Mus. of Artillery, Woolwich.

This system, though embodying great improvements, proved unsatisfactory, owing, among other reasons, to the tendency of the breech-block to jump out of its place upon the firing of the gun, and to the general weakness of the breech.[1] With its introduction came the general adoption of iron or steel carriages for naval guns. The new carriages survived the new breech-loaders, which, after they had undergone but little trial in action, and before the system could be applied to weapons of larger calibre than 7 in., were abandoned, mainly on account of their danger. The 7-in. guns, and most of the 40-prs. were quickly got rid of; but some of the lighter guns remained in certain ships for twenty years or longer.

It is a strange thing that, although at the time when the R.B.L. gun was thus discredited the necessity for a breech-loader of some sort was generally recognised by experts, the British Navy reverted to the muzzle-loading system. It was about the year 1865 when the Admiralty realised that it must seek perfection in a new path. Abroad, several excellent breech-loading systems were coming into prominence; yet Great Britain went back deliberately to the muzzle-loader, and, having taken it up again, clung to it devotedly for almost twenty years, in spite of the fact that, in the interim, nearly every other naval power had armed itself with breech-loaders.

The new British muzzle-loader, however, of 7-in. calibre and upwards, was not like the old gun of Crimean war days. In one respect, indeed, it resembled the R.B.L., in that it was a built-up gun, made on the Armstrong, the Fraser, or the modified Fraser system; but it was a far larger weapon than had been employed ever before. In each case wrought-iron coils were shrunk over a steel tube with a solid end which was supported in the rear by a cascable screwed up against it through the breech. The constructions varied chiefly in the number, arrangement, and cost of the portions shrunk round the inner tube, in the diameter of the cascable, and in the thickness of the inner tube in which were cut the grooves of the rifling. All except the 16-in. 80 ton gun, were rifled on the Woolwich system of wide grooves having rounded sides; and the grooves were fitted, more or less loosely, by projecting gun-metal studs on the circumference of the projectiles, there being, of course, as many rows of studs as there were grooves. The principal heavy naval guns of this nature (M.L.) were:—

---

[1] These were not the only defects. On one occasion, in the *Thistle*, in China, a 20-pr. Armstrong breech-loader blew off the whole of the chase when firing empty common shell at target practice.

M.L. Guns.	—	Bore.	Weight of Full Charge.		—	—	—
Nature and "Mark."	Weight.	Length.	Powder.	Projec-tile.	Muzzle Velocity.	Muzzle Energy.	Penetration.
	Tons.	Ius.	lbs.	lbs.	Foot-seconds.	Foot-tons.	Ins. of wrought iron at muzzle.
7-in. M.IV. . .	7	126	30	112	1561	1895	9·5
8-in. M.III. . .	9	118	35	175	1384	2323	9·6
9-in. M.V. . .	12	125	50	253	1440	3643	11·3
10-in. M.II. . .	18	145·5	70	406	1379	5356	12·9
11-in. M.II. . .	25	145	85	543	1360	7015	14·3
12-in. M.II. . .	25	145	85	608	1292	7046	13·5
12-in. M.II. . .	35	162	140	707	1390	9469	15·9
12·5-in. M.II. .	38	198	210	809	1575	13930	18·4
16-in. M.I. . .	80	288	450	1684	1590	29530	24·7

The 7-in. gun had a rifling of uniform twist of 1 in 35 calibres. The others had an accelerating twist varying, in the case of the 10-in. gun, from 1 in 100 to 1 in 40 calibres. The powders giving the above velocities were, for the guns of 12-in. and less, Pebble; for the 12·5-in., Prism black; and for the 16-in., Prism brown. The 16-in. gun was rifled on the polygroove plain section system. For further particulars of these guns, *see* Owen, 'Modern Artillery,' 1873; 'Text Book of Gunnery, 1887,' etc.

The M.L. gun held its place in the Navy from the middle sixties until about 1881, and, during that period, was supreme. But, as early as 1877, discoveries which had the effect of increasing the initial velocities of rifled projectiles from about 1600 to 2100 foot-seconds, and the energies by nearly 75 per cent., had rendered inevitable another reconstruction of guns and their mountings. The *Thunderer* gun accident in January, 1879, tended, also, to shake faith in the muzzle-loader. At the same time, as Sir Andrew Noble points out, from the increase in the length of guns demanded by the slow-burning powders and high energies then introduced, it became necessary to return to the breech-loader. But apart from the mechanical and dynamic considerations which prompted the step, there were, so it appears to me, far more important tactical reasons; one being the impossibility of serving a broadside muzzle-loader in a ship in a hot action without exposing the crew unduly to the small projectiles of the enemy; and another being the fact, well ascertained even when Great Britain foolishly reverted to muzzle-loaders, that, weight for weight, a breech-loader is a much more rapid-firing weapon than a muzzle-loader, no matter how good or how smartly worked.

In the early eighties the new breech-loaders began to be mounted in new battle-ships and cruisers; but only very slowly did they displace the old weapons. In 1885 I went to sea with the Particular Service Squadron, under Sir Geoffrey Thomas Phipps Hornby.

There was at that time some fear of trouble with Russia, and the squadron, one of the best that could then be sent to sea by Great Britain, sailed not knowing whether it might not be in action ere it sighted England again. None of the battleships in it, however—and there were thirteen—carried so much as a single breech-loader of more than 6-in. calibre; while every one of the big ships in the navy of Russia was armed entirely with breech-loaders. In 1894 I was again afloat with the fleets which manœuvred that summer under Vice-Admiral Robert O'Brien FitzRoy, and Rear-Admiral Edward Hobart Seymour. Of twelve battleships then engaged, two still had muzzle-loaders as part of their armament; and on the last day of the century, fully eighteen or twenty years after muzzle-loaders had been finally condemned even by Great Britain, there remained on the active list of the Navy several large vessels armed in the old discredited way. Progress, therefore, was terribly slow; and it should ever be a subject of congratulation that, during the many years when the transition was in process of accomplishment, the British Navy never had to measure itself with one of the great navies, which, ere Britain had begun to move in the matter, had completed their rearmament.

The Woolwich-Armstrong breech-loading guns thus tardily introduced were of the following chief types :—

B. L. Guns.		Bore.		Weight of Full Charge.*				
Nature and "Mark."	Weight.	Length.		Powder.	Projectile.	Muzzle velocity.	Muzzle Energy.	Penetration.
	Tons.	Calibres.	Feet.	Lbs.	Lbs.	Foot-seconds.	Foot-tons.	Ins. of wrought iron at muzzle.
12-pr. 3-in .	·35	28	7·69	4	12·5	1710	254	—
4-in. 13 cwt.	·65	14·81	—	3·25	·25	1180	241	—
4-in. M.VI. .	1·3	27	10	12	25	1900	625	7·3
5-in. M.V. .	2	25	11·59	15·5	50	1770	1124	9·0
6-in. M.VI. .	5	26	14·4	48	100	1960	2665	13·3
8-in. M.III. .	13	25·6	18·8	104	210	1953	5554	16·5
8-in. M.VI. .	14	29·6	21·2	118	210	2150	6730	22·8
9·2-in. M.VII.	22	31·5	25·9	166	380	2035	10,910	24·4
10-in. M.II. .	29	32	28·5	252	500	2040	14,430	23·0
12-in. M.V. .	45	25·25	25·71	259	714	1910	18,060	22·5
13·5-in. 67-ton	67	30	36·1	630	1250	2000	34,675	30·0
16·25-in. 111-ton . .	110·5	30	43·66	960	1800	2087	54,390	36·18

* Armour-piercing shell. With common shell less powder was used.

The larger guns, including the 8-in., were built to burn Prism brown powder; the others, Pebble, or Rifle large grain The number of grooves in the rifling varied. In the 8-in. M.VI., it was 32; in the 6-in. M.VI., 24. The rifling system, except in the 16·25-in., was polygroove, with hook section. In every case there was an increasing twist. *See also* 'Text Book of Gunnery.'

The next improvements in heavy guns were indirectly the outcome of the practical supersession of gunpowder by cordite, ballistite,
and similar propellents. These give much greater energy, with
no greater chamber pressure, and, producing no smoke, possess
manifest advantages; although probably they may yet be vastly
bettered.

The new developments were in two directions, namely, in the
direction of increased power without relative increase of weight of
gun, and in the direction of accelerated rate of fire. An example of
development in the first of these directions was the 12-in. 46-ton
wire gun, which formed the chief armament of the battleships laid
down in 1894–97. This gun, with a length of 37·1 feet, or 35·43
calibres, was built to throw an armour-piercing shell of 850 lbs.,
and, with a full charge of 167·5 lbs. of cordite, gave a muzzle
velocity of 2400 foot-seconds, and a muzzle energy of 33,940 foot-
tons. It had a muzzle penetration of 36·8 inches of wrought iron ;
and, though it weighed but 46 tons, was practically as powerful a
weapon as the 13·5-in. 67-ton gun which it took the place of. A
somewhat heavier and more powerful 12-in. wire gun was introduced
for the battleships laid down in and after 1898. It weighed about
50 tons. The developments in the direction of accelerated rate of
fire must be dealt with at somewhat greater length.

Towards the end of the year 1881, the British government invited
designs for a gun which should fulfil the following among other
requirements. The weight of the gun and its mounting should not
exceed half a ton ; the projectile should weigh six pounds, and
should have a muzzle velocity of not less than 1800 foot-seconds ;
the projectile and powder charge should be made up in one cartridge ;
the gun should need a crew of not more than three men ; and the
weapon should be capable of discharging at least twelve aimed shots
per minute. In reply to this invitation, and to a somewhat similar
one for a three-pounder from the French government, the Hotchkiss
and the Nordenfelt companies, as well as other firms, drew up plans
and specifications for what afterwards became known as quick-firing
or rapid-firing guns. Weapons of this description were presently
adopted as part of the armament of every warship. As soon as it
became clear that they were destined to be successful, the Elswick
company constructed larger weapons, of 4·7-in. and 6-in. calibre,
also on quick-firing principles, and submitted them to the Admiralty.
In the case of the larger guns the projectile and the powder charge

were not made up into one cartridge ; but in most other respects the characteristics of the 6-pr. Q.F. were reproduced. The new guns speedily gained favour, and within a very few years displaced all others in the secondary batteries of warships. The general effect of the innovation, supplemented by the adoption of greatly improved mountings, was to multiply sixfold a battery's rate of fire. At a trial in 1887 on board the *Handy*, at Portsmouth, a 4·7-in. gun on centre pivot recoil mounting, the whole weighing 4 tons 12 cwt., fired ten rounds in 47·5 seconds. The gunboat *Mastiff* was subsequently ordered to fire ten rounds as rapidly as possible from her service 5-in. B.L. gun. These rounds took six minutes sixteen seconds to discharge ; so that the new gun fired ten times while the old one fired twice. The new gun afterwards fired fifteen rounds in one minute.[1]

It would be tedious, and, in a work like the present, unnecessary, to describe in detail the various types or " Marks " of British quick-firing guns, and of the mountings which have been devised for them. It will suffice to give the appended general particulars of some leading varieties of these guns [2] :—

Q.F. Guns.	Calibre.	Weight.	Length over all.	Length of Bore.	Powder Charge with Com. Shell.	Weight of Projectile.	Muzzle Velocity.	Muzzle Energy.	Penetration in Ins. of wrought iron at muzzle.
	In.	Tons.	Feet.	Calibres.	Lbs.	Lbs.	Foot-seconds.	Foot-tons.	
6-in. wire, M.II.	6	7	20·08	40	13·25	100	2200	3356	15·9
6-in. wire (Vickers) ·	6	7·4	..	45	13·25	100	2784	5373	22·7
4·7-in. . .	4·72	2·07	·15·3	40	5·6	45	2188	1494	11·9
4-in. . . .	4	1·05	..	40	3·87	25	2456	1046	11·2
3-in. 12-pr. .	3	·6	9	40	1·62	12·5	2200	423	8·1
3-in. Field 12-pr. ·	3	·4	7·3	28	·84	12·5	1584	218	5·0
Hotchkiss 6-pr.	2·24	·4	8·1	40	·49	6	1820	138	3·7
Nordenfelt 6-pr.	2·24	·3	8·7	42·3	·49	6	1820	138	3·7
Hotchkiss 3-pr.	1·85	·25	6·72	40	·4	3·3	1875	80	3·1
Nordenfelt 3-pr.	1·85	·2	..	45·4	·4	3·3	1875	80	3·1

The weights of the charges above are for cordite.
There are different " Marks " of most of the above guns.
A 7·5 in. gun was also introduced.

---

[1] Author in *U. S. Magazine*, Feb., 1891; Noble, ' Rifled Nav. Art.,' 1899; ' Mod. Nav. Art.,' 1891.

[2] ' Naval Pocket Book,' 1899.

In the meantime there were equally important improvements in the small-arms which were used in the Navy. At the close of the Crimean War, the service rifles were on the Delvigne-Minié principle, and of the 1851 pattern. These had a calibre of 0·702 in., and were muzzle-loaders. In 1856 and 1858, new patterns were adopted for different branches of the Navy; and the calibre was reduced to 0·577 in. Then, about the year 1861, came the Enfield small-bore rifle of the experimental pattern, with a calibre of 0·453 in.; but still the muzzle-loader only was employed. The first breech-loader used in the Navy was the Snider; and in 1864 a number of muzzle-loaders were converted on Snider's principle from 0·577-in. muzzle-loaders, the calibre remaining as before. A new Snider naval rifle of 0·577 in. calibre was also issued. Many years afterwards followed the Martini-Henry rifle, with a calibre of 0·45 in., to be superseded in the last decade of the century by the Lee-Metford, and the closely related Lee-Enfield, of only 0·303 in. calibre. These last were adopted nearly simultaneously with the general substitution of cordite for black powder in all arms, small as well as large. The following are some particulars of the Martini-Henry and the Lee-Metford :—

RIFLE.	Calibre.	Length of Arm.	Weight with Bayonet.		Bullet.	Powder.	Initial Velocity.
	In.	Ins.	Lbs.	Oz.	Grs.	Grs.	Foot-seconds.
Martini-Henry, M.IV. .	·45	49	10	9	480	85 [1]	1800 (?)
Lee-Metford, M.II. . .	·303	49·5	10	4	216	30 [2]	2200

[1] Black powder.   [2] Cordite.

The Franco-Prussian War of 1870–71 brought the mitrailleuse into celebrity. The weapon seems to have accomplished little in that campaign; but its use directed attention to the far more serviceable Gatling gun, another variety of small-arm battery, or "machine-gun," the object of which was to pour out a rapid and continuous hail of comparatively small bullets. Gatling guns had been shown at the Paris exhibition of 1867 by their inventor, R. J. Gatling of Indianapolis, and had attracted much notice. They were of 1 in. and 0·58 in. calibre, with six barrels revolving round a central axis. By turning a crank, cartridges, supplied by feed boxes, could be discharged at a great rate. Yet other types of machine-guns, and especially the Nordenfelt, the Gardner, and subsequently the Maxim single-barrelled automatic, won their way to favour, all being used in the Navy during the last years of the nineteenth century, although the Maxim was then rapidly displacing the others. The leading particulars [1] of them are set forth below :—

MACHINE GUNS. Nature and Calibre.	Weight.	Length.		Projectile.	Powder.	Rate of fire per Min.
	Lbs.	Ft.	In.			
Nordenfelt,						
1-in. 4 barrelled . .	447	4	9	7¼ oz.	625 grs.	360
1-in. 2 barrelled . .	180	4	7¾	7¼ oz.	625 grs.	180
·45-in. 5 barrelled .	143	3	6¼	480 grs.	85 grs.	660
Gardner,						
·45-in. 1 barrelled .	76	3	11	480 grs.	85 grs.	200
·45-in. 2 barrelled .	218	3	11	480 grs.	85 grs.	400
·45-in. 5 barrelled .	290	4	5½	480 grs.	85 grs.	650
Gatling,						
·65-in. 10 barrelled	817	5	6¼	1422 grs.	270 grs.	—
·45-in. 10 barrelled	444	4	11⅓	480 grs.	85 grs.	400
Maxim Automatic,						
1·46-in.	364	4	5	7000 grs.	1233 grs.	300
·45-in.	63	3	7½	480 grs.	85 grs.	600
·303-in.	..		..	216 grs.	30 grs.[1]	600

[1] Cordite, taking Lee-Metford ammunition.

In spite of the introduction of the torpedo, and of the fact that all large ships of war built towards the end of the nineteenth century were designed to serve as rams, the gun maintained its ancient position as the first and principal weapon of the Navy. While, however, the unshaken position of the gun was frankly recognised by all the most respectable authorities on naval tactics, the importance of good gunnery was, in practice, still strangely and culpably neglected throughout the British fleet :—so much so, indeed, that, according to the prize-firing returns for 1900, the mean percentage of hits scored by all the ships in commission in that and the previous year was no more than the following :—

GUNS.	Percentage of Hits.		Increase or Decrease.
	1899.	1900.	
B.L. 16·25-in., and 13·5-in.	33·33	28·2	− 5·13
12-in. wire B.L.	33·68	35·07	+ 1·39
10-in. wire B.L.	34·00	46·91	+ 12·91
9·2-in. and 8-in. B.L.	34·72	28·37	− 6·35
6-in. quick-firers.	28·29	36·95	+ 8·66
4·7-in. quick-firers	33·57	30·02	− 3·55

[1] For further details, *see* Clowes, ' Nav. Pocket Book,' 1900.

Looking to the easy conditions under which prize-firing was carried out, and bearing in mind that the speed of the firing ship was always relatively low, that the range was never great, and that the target, instead of being an enemy's vessel, which could retaliate and confuse the gunners, was only a floating screen of spars and canvas, these results were certainly indifferent. But in the year 1900, one ship, the first-class cruiser *Terrible*, Captain Percy Scott,[1] distinguished herself by making no less a percentage than 76·92 of hits, and so showed how very far short of attainable efficiency was the gunnery of other vessels. Her efficiency was due not only to the ingenious devices which were invented or employed[2] by Captain Scott, but also to the personal attention which he and his officers devoted to the training of their men. The consequences were that almost immediately the Admiralty turned its attention to Captain Scott's inventions, with a view to their general adoption, and that the *Terrible's* brilliant example engendered a healthy emulation which promised to lead to a very notable heightening of the standard of gunnery in every ship in commission.

The subject of engines and boilers is one into which it is not possible here to enter very deeply. Those specially interested in it will find it dealt with in a manner worthy of its importance in various technical works, to some of which the note[3] below will refer them.

Suffice it to say, as regards engines, that, at the beginning of the period under review, nearly all British men-of-war were fitted either with trunk or with return connecting-rod engines ; that, in the early " sixties," compound engines were experimented with, notably in the case of the *Constance* (built in 1846, and converted to a screw-ship in 1862), but were not then sufficiently understood to be worked successfully ; and that the earliest efficient application of compound engines to a British war-ship was made in the case of the small

[1] For some account of Capt. Scott's improvements in mountings for heavy guns for service on shore, see next chapter.

[2] Including the Barr and Stroud Range-finder.

[3] Sennett, "The Marine Steam Engine" (1888) ; Seaton, "A Manual of Marine Engineering" (1893) ; Yeo, "Steam, and the Marine Steam Engine" (1894) ; Williams, "The Steam Navy of England" (1895) ; S. W. Barnaby, "Marine Propellers" (1885) ; Bertin, "Machines Marines" (1899) ; Busley (tr. by Cole), "The Marine Steam Engine" ; Oldknow, "The Mechanism of Men of War" (1896) ; "Notes on Steam Engineering" (Annapolis, 1901) ; Tompkins, "Text Book of Marine Engineering" ; Bourne, "Catechism of the Steam Engine" ; Murray, "Marine Engines and Steam Vessels" (1886), etc. ; and works on Boilers, for which see note on p. 55.

wooden ironclad *Pallas*, of 1865. These were two-cylinder engines, by Messrs. Humphrys, with surface condensers. Not, however, until several years later were compound engines generally adopted by the Navy, for the next ironclad to be provided with them was the *Alexandra*, of 1875. At first such engines were horizontal, in order that the cylinders and machinery might be kept low in the hold, and enjoy the protection of the water; but it was all along recognised that the vertical was the proper position, and in the *Dreadnought* and the *Shannon*, both launched, like the *Alexandra*, in 1875, vertical engines were employed. To Captain Robert Anthony Edward Scott,[1] better known for his inventions in connection with gun-mountings, belongs, I believe, the credit of suggesting the use of a curved steel deck and armoured coamings over a ship's engine-room as protection for the upper parts of vertical engines, and of thus enabling such engines to be fitted in cruisers as well as in vertically-armoured vessels. Triple-expansion engines were first given in the Navy to the torpedo gun-vessel *Rattlesnake*, of 1886, and then to the battleships *Victoria*, *Sans Pareil*, and *Nile* (1887–88). Soon afterwards they became the ordinary service engines throughout the British Navy, subject, however, to various modifications. To the *Blake* and *Blenheim*, first-class cruisers of 1889–90, four sets of triple expansion inverted cylinder engines were given. Two sets remained, however, the more usual number until the close of the century.

Twin screws were fitted in numerous small craft in the later "sixties"; and in 1868 they were also given to the ironclad *Penelope*, the first of her class to have them. Not, however, until about ten years afterwards did the Admiralty make up its mind that they were necessary to all large men-of-war. It may be noted that the earlier twin screws rotated outwards, and the later ones inwards.

The earlier single screws, as applied to large vessels with full sail-power, were so fitted that they could be disconnected from the machinery, and either left to revolve with but little friction while the vessel was under canvas, or, in other cases, raised entirely out of the water, a well, generally from the upper deck, being made above them for that purpose. Yet other screws fitted to sailing vessels had feathering blades, which, when the screw shaft was not rotating, could be unlocked, and left to trail in such a manner as to offer a minimum of resistance to the water.

[1] Captain of Nov. 22, 1866; retd. Oct. 20, 1870; retd. r.-adm. Mar. 27, 1885.

Besides their main engines, all the large ships of the close of the century had numerous others, often in duplicate, for various purposes. Thus, for example, the *Vulcan* had 98 separate engines, with, in all, 194 cylinders ; the *Powerful* and *Terrible* had each 85 auxiliary engines; and the battleships of the *Royal Sovereign* class (1891–92) had each 86.

During the whole period the machine-driven screw-propeller, single or twin, advanced in favour; and, ere the beginning of the last quarter of the century, it had entirely ousted the paddle-wheel as a warship motor, although the paddle-wheel was still retained in certain tugs, surveying-vessels and harbour-craft which were not intended for fighting purposes or general service. More than once, however, experimental craft with other forms of motor were tried by the Admiralty. The armoured gun-vessel *Waterwitch*, of 1866, designed by Rear-Admiral George Elliot (4) and the Controller's Department, was driven hydraulically, but was a complete failure. The second-class 66-ton torpedo-boat, No. 98, built by Messrs. Thornycroft in 1883, was also driven hydraulically, and proved a disappointment to her projectors. Some years later, however, the success of a vessel called the *Turbinia*, the motor of which was the invention of the Hon. C. A. Parsons, drew the attention of the Admiralty to the merits of the compound steam turbine as a substitute, in certain kinds of craft, for the ordinarily driven screw. The *Turbinia* created an immense impression on the occasion of the Diamond Jubilee Review of 1897, when she appeared among the British and foreign men-of-war assembled at Spithead, and astonished all observers by her speed. The result was the fitting of somewhat similar turbines to the torpedo-boat destroyer *Viper*, which was built in 1899, and which attained the extraordinary speed of 36·58 knots, or upwards of 42 statute miles, an hour, at her trials on July 13th, 1900. She had 4 shafts, with 2 propellers on each, and Yarrow water-tube boilers ; and, on the occasion in question, with 200 lbs. of steam pressure, her propellers made 1180 revolutions a minute. Another destroyer of much the same type, the *Cobra*, built in 1900 at Elswick, for sale, if successful, to the Admiralty, did almost equally well at her first trials in June of that year ; and, although the new system of propulsion was not without some defects and drawbacks, it then became evident that it had established itself firmly as a means whereby speeds not otherwise attainable might be secured for craft of certain classes.

Triple screws, though fitted in the warships of more than one foreign power, and in several of the larger and faster of foreign merchant steamers, failed to recommend themselves to British naval constructors.

The marine boilers[1] of the period were first of the square box type, and, later, of short cylindrical or ellipsoidal shape, having, as a rule, furnaces below and in front, and fire-tubes above and behind. In all these boilers the tubes conducted the heat through the water. Other boilers of the same class had furnaces at both ends. To produce more rapid combustion in the furnaces, and quicker evolution of steam in the boilers, what was known as "forced draught" was at length employed. The stoke-holds were closed, and by means of fans, air was pumped into the stoke-hold ends of the furnaces, the air-pressure in the stoke-holds being thus increased, and additional oxygen, in proportion, being fed to the fires. The use of forced draught, however, was found to be very trying to the tubes, and especially to the tube-plates at their ends; and it was to protect the tube-plates and the ends of the fire-tubes that a strengthening device, commonly called "the Admiralty ferrule," was adopted. This enabled forced draught to be used with less damage to the boilers. Another method of feeding additional oxygen to the fires was by Mr. W. A. Martin's system of "induced draught." In this system, the air was drawn through the furnaces and tubes by means of fans placed at the bottoms of the funnels. The results aimed at were in both cases the same.

But, in practice, forced or induced draught was so seldom used in men-of-war, except at their trials; it added so little, comparatively, to their speed ; and it was, in spite of everything, so destructive to the boilers, that the wisdom of providing apparatus for it was never conclusively demonstrated. It might be important, it was recognised, to enable a ship to add a knot or two to her speed at a critical moment; but if the effort was to be accompanied by a risk of a subsequent total breakdown, possibly in presence of an enemy, it was urged, and with some justice, that the temporary extra speed might be too dearly purchased.

These and other considerations led to experiments with boilers of new types, which promised to permit of the use of higher

[1] Traill, "Boilers, Marine and Land" (1890); R. Wilson, "A Treatise on Steam Boilers" (revised by J. J. Flather, 1893); "Interim Report of the Admiralty Boiler Committee" (1901); "The Naval Annual"; and books dealing with marine engines, for which see note on p. 52.

pressures, and to facilitate a more rapid raising of steam, than the old boilers. The new types were many, but those of them which obtained any degree of success had all one feature in common. Instead of having tubes which conducted the heat through the water, they had tubes which conducted the water[1] through the heat. Of these water-tube boilers, the chief varieties which, experimentally or otherwise, were fitted in ships of the British Navy were, the Belleville, the Yarrow, the Thornycroft, the Normand, the Reed, the White, the Blechynden, the du Temple, the Babcock and Wilcox, the Mumford, and the Niclausse, though at least half a dozen other kinds were in use elsewhere.

It was recognised from the beginning that these water-tube boilers were especially suitable for destroyers, and other light fast craft, which, in all probability, would not be required to remain under steam for long periods at a time, and which, therefore, would enjoy frequent opportunities for overhauling, cleaning, and repairing their generators. When, however, upon the laying down of the gigantic first-class protected cruisers, *Powerful* and *Terrible*, which were launched in 1895, Mr. Albert John Durston, Engineer-in-Chief of the Navy, determined to fit them with batteries of Belleville boilers, fears were very widely expressed as to the unwisdom of the scheme. He persisted, however, in giving Belleville boilers not only to these vessels, but also to other large cruisers, both protected and armoured, and to all the battleships which were laid down in and after 1897. Mr. Durston won a K.C.B. in 1897 on the strength of his bold departure ; but opposition to his principles continued to grow, and by the end of the century it had become clear that the Belleville was not, upon the whole, the best of the water-tube boilers for use in big ships, while many grounds had arisen for the conviction that, although water-tube boilers possessed some striking advantages, they were in some respects unsuited for heavy war vessels from which prolonged steaming and very varying speeds would, in the nature of things, be demanded.[2] It must be remembered, however, that at the end of the nineteenth century all the naval powers were freely fitting water-tube boilers of one type or another to their warships, both small and large.

[1] A water-tube boiler, the invention of Rear-Adm. the Hon. A. L. P. Cochrane, was fitted experimentally to several vessels soon after 1870, but was presently discarded.

[2] The risk of breakdown may be estimated to some extent from the fact that in each of the armoured cruisers of the *King Alfred* class there were 5348 tubes in the 43 Belleville boilers, and 5328 tubes in the economisers.

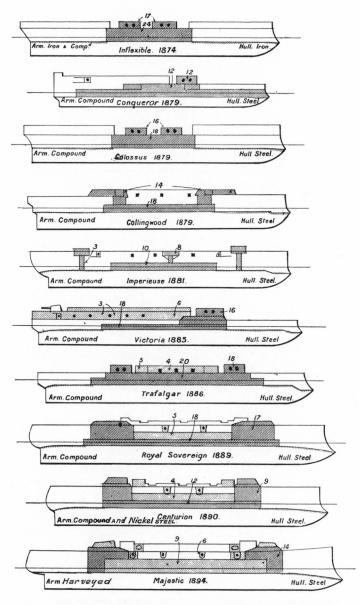

British Ironclads. 1874.–1894.
Figures give thickness of Armour in inches.

(*By kind permission, from Mr. H. W. Wilson's 'Ironclads in Action.'*)

[*To face p. 56.*

The development of armour has already been touched upon incidentally in the sketch which has been given of the history of battleship building. Until about 1875 all British vertical armour for ships of war was of wrought iron. Compound armour, or, in other words, iron armour with its face steeled, was introduced for the turrets of the *Inflexible*, which was launched in 1876. Thenceforward compound armour was generally used for about thirteen years. To some of the ships of the *Royal Sovereign* class (1891–92) nickel-steel armour was applied as protection for the central battery, nickel-steel being steel with a small toughening admixture of nickel; but the thicker belt and barbette armour continued to be compound. In the *Renown*, launched in 1895, Harvey steel was employed for the heavy armour. This is steel the surface of which, to a slight depth, has been rendered intensely hard by a process of supercarbonisation. The effect of the hardened surface was to distribute the blow of the projectile over a comparatively large extent of the softer steel beneath. In the battleships which were laid down in the last two years of the nineteenth century, Harvey steel gave place to Krupp steel, a steel surface hardened and highly tempered by a process analogous to Harvey's, but of better quality than the steel or nickel-steel which had previously been treated in England. Speaking roughly, the relative resisting powers of the various armours were as follows: 1-inch Krupp steel = 1·25-inch Harveyed nickel-steel = 1·5-inch Harvey steel = 2-inch compound armour = 2·5-inch mild steel = 3-inch wrought-iron armour. Therefore the thickest wrought-iron armour of the *Inflexible* (24 inches) may be considered as, upon the whole, inferior to the 9-inch Krupp steel belt of the ships of the *London* class, the thickest armour of which (12 inches) represents something like 36 inches of wrought-iron,—an armour which, on account of its weight, could never have been employed afloat, except over very small areas indeed.

During the period which witnessed such vast improvements in armour, there was, strange to say, no commensurate improvement in the projectiles [1] designed to attack it. Guns improved, and gunnery improved; but, after the introduction of face-hardened armour, projectiles made but little progress. Indeed, the armour-piercing shells (shells with small bursting-charges and hardened points), and common-shells (shells with large bursting charges and thinner walls)

---

[1] Generally made of chrome steel after about 1886, by the Holtzer and other processes, or of nickel-steel. American projectiles made more progress than European ones.

used in 1900 were very little different from those used in 1890, except in one feature, which, however, was extraneous to the shell itself. About the year 1894, the device of capping projectiles with a small mass of soft steel was invented by Mr. Isaac G. Johnson, in America, and, it is said, almost simultaneously in Russia. The capped projectile, when striking at right angles, was found to have a penetrating force 10, 15, or even 20 per cent. greater than that of the uncapped one. Several theories were advanced to account for this, but what seems to be the true one may be thus stated :—

"The function of the cap is to prepare the plate so that the projectile strikes it at the most advantageous moment. When the mass, consisting of the cap and projectile, strikes the plate, the hard surface of the latter is 'dished' elastically, and absorbs a considerable proportion of the energy of impact. This energy does not, however, react on the projectile, the velocity of which is barely checked, its progress through the soft cap being comparatively easy. The projectile, therefore, reaches the plate with nearly all its original inertia, and finds the hard surface of the latter already 'dished' to its elastic limit. The resistance then becomes purely local, and the hole gradually enlarges as the projectile moves on." [1]

The invention was quickly adopted by the United States, Russia, and France, but at the end of the century it had not fully commended itself to the British Admiralty, although official experiments had been made with it in England. In fact, with regard to nearly all new inventions bearing upon naval warfare, Great Britain showed herself intensely conservative.

Upon the whole it may be said that no invention of the latter part of the nineteenth century exercised a greater influence upon the principles of naval warfare than that of the automobile torpedo.

As has been shown in previous volumes, torpedoes or "infernal machines," of one kind or another, were employed by or against the Royal Navy from the middle of the seventeenth century onwards. Prince Rupert's semi-piratical attempt to blow up the *Leopard* [2] involved the use of a device of this sort; the "machine" [3] of 1694 was of similar character; the Americans endeavoured to explode mines or torpedoes under British vessels in both their wars with the parent country; the "catamaran" [4] of 1804 was a towing torpedo under another name; and the Russians did some little damage with their stationary torpedoes [5] or mines in 1855.

---

[1] *See* papers by Lieut. Cleland Davis, U.S.N., and Prof. P. R. Alger, U.S.N., in Proceedings of the U.S. Naval Inst.,' Vol. xxvii., No. 3. *See also* 'The Naval Annual,' 1901.

[2] Vol. ii., p. 127.   [4] Vol. v., p. 69.

[3] Vol. ii., p. 467 n.   [5] Vol. vi., p. 483.

The forms of torpedo principally used in the British service after the Russian war were five in number, viz., stationary torpedoes or submarine mines, to be exploded by the concussion of a passing vessel, or by electricity or mechanical means at a desired moment; spar torpedoes, or explosive charges carried at the end of a spar at a boat's bows; towing torpedoes, of which class the best known example was the short-lived and unsatisfactory Harvey; automobile torpedoes, such as the Whitehead; and controllable torpedoes, such as the Brennan. In the earlier days the charge was gunpowder; in the later ones, guncotton or some other " high explosive."

The first and most successful of all automobile torpedoes was the Whitehead, so called from the name of its inventor, to whom belongs the great credit of utilising hydrostatic pressure to regulate the depth of the weapon's immersion in the water. It seems to have been in 1864 that Mr. Whitehead's attention was originally directed to the subject, it having been then suggested to him by Captain Luppis, of the Austrian Navy, to build a surface-floating vessel which, without the aid of a crew on board, could be propelled against an enemy. Whitehead used as his motive power compressed air, which he stored in a strong steel receptacle, and which, on being released, drove an engine and worked a screw. He passed four years in study and labour, spent about £40,000 in experiments, and then produced his invention. It was still very imperfect, although of wonderful ingenuity; but after its adoption by the British Navy it was continuously improved until it became a most efficient and trustworthy weapon of considerable range and great speed. Full accounts of its history and development may be found in the works mentioned in the note below.[1]

At the end of the century two sizes of these torpedoes were used in the British service, the 14-inch, and the so-called 18-inch. The real diameter of the latter was $17 \cdot 71$ inches, or 45 centimetres. Torpedoes for the Navy were at that time made not only at Fiume, where Mr. Whitehead's parent works were, but also at the Royal Gun Factory, Woolwich [2] (R. G. F. type), at the Portland Harbour Torpedo Works (Mr. Whitehead's), and by Messrs. Greenwood and

---

[1] Clowes, "The Naval Pocket Book" (1896 and annually); "The Naval Annual" (1886 and annually); Sleeman, "Torpedoes and Torpedo Warfare" (2nd Ed. 1889); Armstrong, "Torpedoes and Torpedo Vessels" (1896); Publications of the Torpedo Station, Newport, Rhode Island (1874, etc.); "The Torpedo Manual"; Jane, "The Torpedo in Peace and War."

[2] They had previously been made at the Royal Laboratory (type R. L.).

Batley, of Leeds. All were then, however, manufactured according to the R. G. F. specifications, it having been decided to discontinue the use of other designs. Among the improvements of the last few years of the century was the fitting to the torpedo of the Obry gyroscope steering apparatus, for the automatic correction of any tendency on the part of the weapon to deflect from the original line of fire.

Particulars of a few of the numerous types of automobile torpedoes which were produced at different times for the Navy are appended.

The ranges given in the table are those to which the torpedo would travel with fairly sustained speed ; but some of the perfected long 18-inch weapons, fitted with the gyroscope, would travel accurately, although at a very much diminished velocity, up to about 2000 yards. The explosive charge in all of them consisted of

Type and " Mark."	Date.	Length.	Weight.	Speed up to 600 yards.	Range.	Explosive Charge.
		ft. in.	lbs.	Kts.	Yds.	lbs.
14-in. R.L., Mk. 1** . .	1876–80	14 6	525	19·5	600	32
14-in. R.L., and Leeds, Mk. IV* . . . . }	1885	14 11¾	670	23·5	600	60
14-in. R.L., and Leeds, Mk. VIII . . . . }	1893	14 11¾	705	26	600	65
14-in. R.G.F., Mk. IX .	1897	14 11¾	725	27	600	79
18-in., Mk. I . . .	1891	16 7½	1,140	29	800	199
18-in., Mk. II . . .	1895	16 7½	1,130	29	800	185
18-in. R.G.F., Mk. IV .	1897	16 7½	1,217	30	800	171
18-in. Short (for boats) .	1895	12 4	875	28	600	85·5

guncotton. The air-chamber, of finest Whitworth compressed steel, from ·275 to ·365-inch thick, contained air compressed by means of special pumps fitted on board the discharging ships, the pressure in some of the later " marks " of torpedo running as high as 1350 lbs. per square inch.

These torpedoes could be discharged in several ways, *e.g.*, from ejector tubes, by means of the initial impulse of compressed air, or of the explosion of a small charge of gunpowder ; or from dropping-gear—a clip-like device by means of which the torpedo was lowered overboard into the water, and there started and released without extraneous impulse. The ejector-tubes fitted to torpedo-boats and destroyers were, for the most part, training tubes mounted on deck. The tubes fitted in larger craft were chiefly either similar tubes, which were trained through above-water ports; or submerged tubes,

which were fixed in position, and which had to be aimed by means
of the vessel's helm. Towards the end of the century the tendency
lay in the direction of fitting only submerged tubes to large ships, as
it was recognised that a hostile projectile striking the detonator or
air-chamber of a torpedo in an above-water tube would probably
explode it with disastrous results.

It was sought to afford protection to ships against torpedoes by
fitting them with moveable nets, or crinolines, which could be
boomed out to a considerable distance from the hulls. Nets of this
nature were supplied to the *Thunderer* as early as 1877. They were
subsequently much improved, and after 1898 were made so substantial as to be almost impregnable to the assaults of the various
cutters, nippers, and other devices with which the noses of Whiteheads were at length provided.

Controllable torpedoes, such as the Brennan,[1] the principle of
which was purchased by the British Government in 1882, were
never part of the armament of the Navy, but were employed by the
War Department for purposes of coast defence. The Brennan was
a torpedo driven and directed by means of wires, the home ends of
which were on drums in the operating station on shore, and the
outward ends of which were on much smaller drums inside the body
of the weapon. The very rapid winding-in of the shore ends of
the wires worked the propellers of the torpedo ; and a very ingenious
device enabled the weapon to be steered with great accuracy. Such
a torpedo could not be outmanœuvred, and it possessed many other
advantages ; but it was not suitable for use by ships, which would
have been liable to have their screws fouled, or to foul the screws
of their consorts, by the wires, and which would have been obliged
to carry special engines of considerable size wherewith to drive the
drums at the necessary speed.

Akin to the torpedo is the submarine boat. Until the autumn of
1900 the British Admiralty appeared to pay but little attention to
the assiduity with which certain foreign powers had been experi-
menting with submarines during the previous twelve or fifteen years.
It then suddenly ordered the construction of five craft of the kind
by Messrs. Vickers, Sons and Maxim, of Barrow. The type chosen
was that of the American Holland boat; and the dimensions were
to be : length, 63 feet 4 inches ; beam, 11 feet 9 inches ; submerged
displacement, 120 tons. Propulsion was to be by means of an Otto

Invented in 1877 by Mr. Louis Brennan, of Melbourne.

gasolene engine for surface steaming, and by means of an electric motor of the waterproof pattern for work when submerged. The speed aimed at was 7 knots.

It was explained on behalf of the Admiralty that the ordering of these boats did not necessarily imply that the authorities had any faith in their usefulness for the purposes of war. The boats were required chiefly for experimental purposes. There were indications, however, that, even before the year 1900, the progress of invention had rendered it needless further to experiment with submarine boats which demanded the employment of officers and men in them, and which inevitably exposed their crews to extraordinary risks. Just as, by the Marconi system, it had been found possible to telegraph without wires, so, by the systems of Orling and Armstrong, Fiske, Govan, and others, it had been found possible to transmit to a distance, without the intervention of wires or other artificial connections, electrical impulses whereby automobile torpedoes or larger vessels could be started, stopped, steered, and otherwise controlled. It seemed, therefore, at the end of the century, as if the future, so far as submarine warfare was concerned, lay rather with some weapon like a wireless Brennan [1] than with the wholly self-contained and self-dependent submarine boat and its crew.

Concerning the progress of *matériel* in other directions there is room to say little here. The internal illumination of ships was revolutionised during the period under review, the old-fashioned lantern, with its dim candle, giving place first to the scarcely brighter and far more cumbrous oil-lamp, and finally to the electric light. Electric night sights, for guns, were also introduced; and, indeed, electricity on ship-board became of ever increasing importance as the century drew to its end, until at last it was employed, in preference to steam or hydraulics, as a power for the general service of many ships of war, and was applied, for example, to the loading, training, and elevating of heavy guns, as well as to the firing of them; to steering gear; to the working of ammunition hoists, capstans, and cranes; and to the transmission of orders within the vessel, by means not only of telephones, but also of speed, course, and other indicators. It was also used in search-lights; [2] in the working of mast-head and other signals, and of

[1] For convenience of reference, all torpedoes or other vessels thus controlled by electrical impulses without wires may be styled "actinauts."—Author in *New Liberal Review*, June, 1901. See also Author's paper read to the I.N.A., Mar. 21, 1902.

[2] The searchlight was fitted in the *Alexandra* in 1876.

ventilating machinery; and in a hundred other ways far too numerous to specify. Apparatus for wireless telegraphy on the Marconi system was fitted in several British ships in the year 1900.

Masts and sails died out very slowly; and, even at the end of the nineteenth century, when they had all but disappeared from the ships of the Navy, their revival, especially in sea-going training vessels, was strenuously advocated by a certain number of naval officers who had been accustomed to them in their youth, and who retained exaggerated ideas of their value, if only as a means of giving physical exercise to seamen, and developing self-reliance, smartness and resourcefulness. By that date, however, the training squadron itself, which until two or three years before had consisted exclusively of masted cruisers, was composed solely of modern vessels without a single sail among them; and almost the only sailing-craft that lingered in commission were a few old brigs attached as tenders to the stationary training-ships for boys at Portland, Portsmouth, and Devonport, the *Cruiser*, training sloop for ordinary seamen in the Mediterranean, and some semi-obsolete ironclads and cruisers of little or no fighting value, which, though they had masts and sails, seldom moved except under steam.

In the larger craft, the military mast, and, in smaller vessels, the mere pole for signalling purposes, had taken the place of the old mast with yards and sails. The military mast began to come into vogue in the early 'seventies with the advent of the low-freeboard sea-going turret ships of the *Devastation* type; and, upon the general adoption eight or ten years later of machine and small quick-firing guns, the mast was generally provided with one or more capacious fighting tops in which such weapons could be mounted so as to command an enemy's upper deck in action, and in which searchlights could be placed. The military mast was of steel, and hollow; and the top could be reached either by shrouds or by footholds let into the mast, while, in some cases, there was also a ladder or stairway within the mast. It served not only to support the top, and to furnish lofty look-out posts, but also to carry light cross-jack yards and topmasts, whence signals could be advantageously displayed. To the topmasts semaphore arms and flashing lamps were also frequently fitted, and so arranged as to be worked by men under shelter below.

Conning-towers were provided in all large war-ships of the last quarter of the century. In these, which were heavily armoured, fittings, electrical and otherwise, were placed, by means of which a commanding officer could control the general management of his vessel without quitting the position. But the conning-tower had the necessary disadvantage of occupying a known and exposed post, upon which an enemy would naturally endeavour to concentrate his fire ; and it was recognised that the protection afforded, even by very thick armour, would scarcely save an officer within the tower from disabling if not fatal shock in case the tower should be struck fairly by a heavy projectile ; while the effects of the impact would certainly involve the putting out of action of the various fittings and the delicate machinery within the tower. While, therefore, conning-towers continued to be built into all large ships of war, many officers held the opinion that their own efficiency in action would be best assured by taking up a position in some other part of the vessel. To meet their views, alternative fighting stations were almost always provided elsewhere, and furnished with facilities for transmitting orders throughout the ship.

The introduction, in 1857, of the International Commercial Code of flag-signals led to gradual improvement in the flag-signalling system in use in the Royal Navy. The Commercial Code is used by British men-of-war for communicating with merchant-vessels or foreign war-ships. This Code originally employed eighteen flags ; to which eight have since been added. The Naval Code requires as many as forty-five different flags and pennants.

Great improvements in naval night-signalling[1] began to be made in the early sixties, indirectly in consequence of suggestions put forward by Mr. Charles Babbage, and directly in consequence of the energetic advocacy of Lieutenant Philip Howard Colomb, R.N., who induced Rear-Admiral Sidney Colpoys Dacres to adopt his new system of night-signalling in the Channel Squadron towards the end of 1863, although Rear-Admiral Hastings Reginald Yelverton temporarily restored the old system in 1866. What the old systems

---

[1] Charles Babbage, in 1851, invented a numerical system of flashing signals to lighthouses and ships by night. *See* his book, " The Exposition of 1851." *See also* his letter in the *Times* of June 16, 1855, and the *Mechanics' Magazine*, 1854, and Aug. 1861. This last brought the subject to Colomb's notice, as shown in a letter of Aug. 22, 1861, from him to C. Babbage, cited in a letter of Henry P. Babbage to the *Times* of Oct. 25, 1899. Colomb's patent was sealed on Oct. 31, 1862. He adopted the Morse system ; Babbage preferred the simpler numerical system ; otherwise the inventions were much the same. See also *Journal of the R.U.S. Inst.*, 1863, pp. 285, 386.

were may be gathered from a paper contributed by Colomb to the *Journal of the Royal United Service Institution :*—

" Our naval night-signals," he said, " are now more inefficient than they were in the middle of the last [eighteenth] century. They are indeed so bad that a flag-officer recently in command assured me that he dared not make more than six out of the one hundred and three signals in the night-signal book, so much less were the chances of error with no signals at all than with the naval night-signal system. Simultaneously with the numbering of the flags, the plan adopted to get over the night-signalling difficulty was this :—One light meant one: two lights two; three lights three; four lights four ; then five was represented by false fires in any number; one gun meant ten'; two guns twenty ; three guns thirty. Each night-signal set down was then numbered as the day-signals, from one upwards. The signal twenty-one was made by two guns for twenty, and one light. The signal seventeen, by one gun for ten, false fires in any number for five, and two lights for two, making seventeen in all. This was the system in use sixty-four years ago, and I am quite satisfied that our present arrangements are not so good. It is found in practice that not more than fifteen forms of light can be used. They are all made with not more than four lights at a time. If, therefore, fifteen signals were all that could be required for night communication at sea, we might suppose that the want was fulfilled ; and neither I nor anyone else would have much to say against it. Seeing, however, that 14,000 signals are the requirements of a fleet in the daytime, it would be rather a strain upon our imagination to suppose we could contentedly drop 13,985 of them the moment darkness came on ; so that it has all along been the struggle to extend the number of our signals by night to some quantity less disproportionate than 15 to 14,000."

Lieutenant Colomb's energy was rewarded by his promotion to the rank of Commander on December 12th, 1863.

The wreck of the gun-vessel *Griffon*, in October, 1866, after collision with the *Pandora*, consequent upon the defective condition of the night-signalling system, once more directed attention to Colomb's plan of conveying night messages by means of flashing-signals based upon the Morse Code of longs and shorts ; and early in 1867 his plan was officially adopted throughout the service.

In the latter half of the nineteenth century the uniform of British naval officers underwent numerous modifications. At the end of the Russian war[1] changes were made in the distinction marks on the epaulettes ; Mates were given two shoulder-straps, or " scales " ; Midshipmen were provided with dirks instead of swords; the special engineer button was abolished ; the cap-badge was established ; and mohair instead of gold lace became the material for the cap-band. Further alterations were made in 1860,[2] 1861,[3] and 1863.[4] The curl on the sleeve of officers of the executive branch dates from 1860 ; and in 1863,[5] owing to changes which had

---

[1] Circ. of Ap. 11, 1856.   [2] Circ. of July 3, 1860.   [3] Mem. of Sept. 5, 1861.
[4] Circ. of June 5, 1863, and a subsequent codification of the regulations.
[5] Mem. of Mar. 25, 1863.

been made in the relative rank of officers, Captains were given four, Commanders three, and Lieutenants two stripes, and Sub-Lieutenants one stripe of distinction lace on the sleeve. The distinctive coloured stripes between the stripes of distinction lace on the sleeves of non-military officers also date from 1863, when scarlet was assigned to Surgeons, white to accountant officers, and purple velvet to Engineers. Blue velvet was subsequently assigned to the navigating branch, but it was abolished in 1867,[1] and afterwards given to Naval Instructors. Narrow gold lace stripes were given to Sub-Lieutenants, and chief warrant officers; and crimson and gold sashes, superseded in 1874 by aiguillettes, were ordered to be worn by naval aides-de-camp to the Sovereign. In 1867, moreover, the distinguishing marks for gunnery instructors and seamen-gunners were introduced. Beards and moustaches, if worn together and kept close trimmed, were first allowed in 1869.[2]

In 1877[3] Lieutenants of eight years' standing and upwards in that rank, and some other officers, were granted an additional narrow stripe between the two broader ones; and Honorary Physicians and Surgeons to the Sovereign were given a black and gold sash. In 1879[4] a ship-jacket was introduced, and buttons were ordered to be worn upon the sleeves below the stripes. In 1885 tunics and helmets, with puggarees for hot climates, were authorised. In 1888 torpedo-men were granted distinguishing badges. In 1889 the monkey-jacket was substituted for the blue tunic. The entire regulations were amended in 1891,[5] when shoulder-straps indicative of rank were directed to be worn on great-coats, on white undress, and on white jackets; and in December, 1900, among other alterations, the collars and cuffs of flag-officers' full dress coats were directed to be decorated with gold oak-leaf embroidery.

Seamen's uniform, very similar to that which was worn until the end of the century, was established in 1857.[6] The tarpaulin hat and blue jacket which formed part of this were, however, abolished in 1891. Further instructions, involving other modifications, were issued in 1893,[7] and February, 1897. The conferring of good-conduct badges, first established under an Order in Council of

[1] Mem. of July 2, 1867.   [2] Circ. of June 24, 1869.
[3] The regulations had been re-codified on Oct. 16, 1875: see Circ. of Oct. 30, 1877.
[4] Regs. of May 7, 1879.   [5] Circ. of Oct. 10, 1891.
[6] Circ. of Jan. 30, 1857.   [7] Jan. 11, 1893.

January 15th, 1849, was the subject of revised regulations which were promulgated in 1857,[1] and which were subsequently amended from time to time. After 1892 patterns of naval uniform were exhibited at the Admiralty, and an illustrated manual on the subject was issued, with the object of ensuring that thenceforward there should be as little divergence as possible from the established types.

The healthiness of the Navy improved astonishingly in the period under review. The improvement was due to numerous causes, such, for example, as the general substitution of iron or steel ships for wooden ones, and the consequent disappearance of bilge-water and its noxious exhalations; the better education and finer moral character of the continuous-service seaman; the fact that the crews of the ships of the last half of the nineteenth century were composed of picked individuals, trained and hardened from boyhood, and not, as had been the case previously, of men drawn from none knew whence, and often old or constitutionally broken; the general advances in sanitation; the use of antiseptics, and the progress of medicine and surgery; the practice of employing distilled water for drinking purposes; and the closer attention paid to the men's comfort on board ship. The passing of the Contagious Diseases Act in 1866 was another most beneficent factor, until the unwise agitation of a few well-meaning but fanatical enthusiasts induced the legislature, not many years later, to stultify its previous policy by resolving that the Act should no longer be enforced. But for that unfortunate retrogressive step the health of the Navy, in 1900, would have been even better than it was.

In that year, as shown by the Report which was issued in January, 1902, the death-rate in the service was but 7·27 per 1000, or about 3 per cent. less than the general death-rate in the healthiest town in the United Kingdom—and that in spite of the fact that the list included 74 deaths from wounds received in South Africa and China, and 17 suicides. The bluejacket, however, was by no means specially exempt from slight illnesses, for during the year there were no fewer than 84,550 cases under medical treatment, or, in other words, 882·29 men out of every 1000 experienced some kind of sickness or accident in the course of the twelve months. It must be admitted, on the other hand, that the seaman of the end of the century was encouraged to appeal to the surgeon upon the smallest excuse, and that every attempt was made by the medical staff to

[1] Circ. of May 20, 1857.

induce him rather to spend a day or two in the sick-bay than to
risk serious results by neglecting himself even for an hour. It is
mentioned incidentally in the Report that, during the fighting round
Tientsin, the Americans, Germans, Italians, and Russians had
neither medical officers nor hospitals, and that their sick and
wounded were tended by the British—a pleasant testimony to the
efficiency of the organisation of the medical department of the
Navy. It is also mentioned incidentally that the Boers painted the
red cross of Geneva on all sorts of vehicles; that at Belmont they
fired on the British from under the cover of " ambulance " wagons;
and that at Magersfontein they used " ambulance " wagons to
convey rifles and ammunition across exposed positions.[1]

The period of the war with Russia marks, in a rough and general
way, the line of demarcation between the old Navy of wood and
sails, and the new Navy of iron and steam-power; but it also marks
the opening of an era of progress and advancement more rapid as
well as more striking than had ever been witnessed previously.
When once the Navy began to change, it changed with almost
bewildering speed, and continued to change with steadily increasing
quickness. So much, indeed, was this the case, that it may be
said with little or no fear of exaggeration that the best ship existing
in 1867 would have been more than a match for the entire British
fleet existing in 1857, and, again, that the best ship existing in
1877 would have been almost, if not quite, equal to fighting and
beating the entire fleet of only ten years earlier. By 1890, the
ships of 1877 had become well-nigh obsolete; and by 1900 the
best ships, even of 1890, were hardly worthy of a place in the
crack fleets of the country. Nay, as a matter of fact, of the eight
battleships which belonged to the Channel squadron at the end
of 1900, the oldest had been less than eight years off the stocks;
and of the ten battleships which at the same date were attached
to the sea-going Mediterranean fleet, not one had been launched
nine years. As with the battleships, so with the cruisers. By the
end of 1900 the best cruisers of 1890 had been told off to the less
important stations; and, in the meantime, the fleets everywhere
had been reinforced with craft, such as destroyers, of types which
in 1890 had been utterly unknown.

To keep pace with these continuous changes it was early
recognised that fresh provision must be made for the technical

---

[1] Evidence of Dept.-Insp.-Genl. James Porter, R.N.

and scientific training of officers and men. Up to 1854, Naval Cadets, upon nomination, went at once, as a rule, to sea-going and regularly commissioned ships, where they had to pick up their professional education as best they could from the Naval Instructors and other officers who were their shipmates. In 1854 an improvement was made by the commissioning at Portsmouth of an old wooden ship of the line, the *Illustrious*, Captain Robert Harris, as a stationary training ship, or school, for Naval Cadets. A similar school was opened in the *Implacable*, at Devonport, in 1855; but one school was soon found to be enough for the purpose, and the Devonport establishment was closed. New regulations for the entry and training of Naval Cadets were issued in 1857[1]; and on January 1st, 1859, the *Britannia*, 120,[2] was commissioned at Portsmouth by the same Captain Robert Harris to take the place of the less suitable *Illustrious*. She was removed to Portland in 1862, and to more appropriate moorings at Dartmouth on September 30th, 1863; and although the original *Britannia* was later condemned, a new *Britannia*, previously known as the *Prince of Wales*,[3] took her place in July, 1869, and retained it until the end of the nineteenth century, at which time, however, preparations were in progress for the removal of the whole establishment to quarters on shore hard by. In 1870, the *Trafalgar*, 60, screw, was commissioned as a sea-going training-ship for cadets; and the *Bristol*, 31, *Aurora*, 28, and other vessels were subsequently used for the same purpose until the establishment of the regular Training Squadron in 1885.

Something has been written already[4] concerning the origin of the naval gunnery schools at Portsmouth and Devonport. At Portsmouth the establishment was housed afloat for many years in the *Excellent* (ex *Boyne*, built in 1810), and subsequently in another *Excellent* (ex *Queen Charlotte*, built also in 1810). In 1891, however, when barracks, practice-batteries, etc., had been erected on Whale Island, a piece of made land in Portsmouth Harbour, the establishment was transferred to the shore and housed in the commodious new buildings, although the officers and men attached to the school continued to be nominally borne afloat. The *Excellent*, which had been the *Queen Charlotte*, was in that year condemned; and the conventional headquarters of the school were lodged in a

---

[1] Admlty. Circ. No. 588, of Feb. 23, 1857.   [2] Blt. in 1820.
[3] A 131-gun ship of 6201 tons, built in 1860.   [4] *See* Vol. VI. p. 203.

508-ton gunboat, the *Handy* (built in 1883), which thereupon took over the name *Excellent*, and retained it until the end of the period under review. Numerous tenders were attached to her for gunnery training afloat; and on shore at Whale Island such parts of the gunnery course, including field exercises and theoretical instruction, as could be carried out as well or better on dry land were attended to.

The Devonport gunnery school was established in 1856 on board the *Cambridge* (built in 1815), and was eventually transferred to another *Cambridge* (ex *Windsor Castle*, built in 1858), in which it remained afloat for the rest of the century. A gunnery school on shore was subsequently established at Sheerness, the staff and other officers and men attached to it being borne in the *Wildfire*, flagship at the Nore.

In the meantime, the increasing importance of electricity and submarine mining, and the introduction of the torpedo, necessitated the establishment of torpedo schools, the *Vernon*[1] being told off for the purpose at Portsmouth in 1876,[2] and the *Defiance*[3] at Devonport in 1884. After the usefulness of destroyers had become evident, and when sufficient numbers of such craft became available, sea-going instructional flotillas of them were formed in 1895, with headquarters at Portsmouth, Devonport, and in the Medway respectively; and large numbers both of stokers and of seamen were systematically passed through them for purposes of practical training. It may be added that a signal school was established at Portsmouth in 1888; and a school of telegraphy at Devonport in 1899; and that homing-pigeon lofts were opened at Portsmouth in 1896, and at Devonport in 1897. Several years earlier, while afloat during the Naval Manœuvres, the author, from a ship thirty or forty miles from the Irish coast, sent by pigeon a message which duly reached and was published, with an explanatory note, by the *Times*. The bird used on that occasion belonged to Kingstown, and its services were lent to the writer by its owner, a naval officer.

Of the training establishments for boys for the Navy, the one at Devonport, known as the *Lion*,[4] and previously known as the

[1] The *Vernon* in 1900 was the ex-*Donegal*, 100, built in 1858.

[2] The *Vernon* had previously, from 1873, been a kind of torpedo tender to the *Excellent*. The (T) prefixed to the names of Torpedo-Lieutenants first appeared in the Navy List of November, 1878.

[3] The *Defiance* was an old 91-gun ship of 1861.

[4] The *Lion*, built in 1847.

Implacable [1] (the two ships being ultimately combined), dates from 1860; the one at Portland (formerly in Southampton Water), known as the *Boscawen*,[2] from 1861; and the one at Portsmouth, known as the *St. Vincent*,[3] from 1862. Other boys' training-ships were added from time to time, sailing brigs being attached to most of them for instructional purposes. The education of the boys was continued, at one time in the flying squadrons which were temporarily organised, and afterwards in the regularly constituted Training Squadron, which, only in the last year of the century, was modernised and made to consist exclusively of mastless ships.[4]

The education of engineer officers for the Navy was furthered by the establishment of a school for engineer students in the *Marlborough*, and by the opening of Keyham College in 1880; the advanced training of officers, and especially of executive officers, in theoretical subjects, by the opening of the Royal Naval College at Greenwich in 1873 [5]; and the development of the science of naval architecture, by the establishment of a Royal School of Naval Architecture [6] at Kensington in 1863, and by the re-organisation of the Royal Corps of Naval Constructors in 1883.[7] The training of the reserves was, perhaps rather inadequately, provided for by the stationing at various points round the coast of antiquated vessels as drill ships for the Royal Naval Reserve; for all these craft mounted guns which were obsolete and useless, and only in the last few years of the century were comparatively modern ships substituted for a few of the old ones, and better guns supplied here and there for exercise purposes. The sea-training of the Coast Guard was carried on in the Coast Guard District Ships. These, like the Drill Ships of Reserve, were often most unsuitable craft until 1870, when the ironclad *Repulse* was sent as guard-ship to Queensferry. Efficient fighting vessels gradually thenceforward found their way to the various ports, not only as coast guard-ships, but also as port guard-ships. These last, originally the flagships of the Port Admirals, were, in 1857 and for many years

---

[1] In 1900, ex-*Duguay Trouin*, taken 1805; the last surviving prize of the long French wars.

[2] The *Boscawen*, built in 1841.   [3] The *St. Vincent*, built in 1815.

[4] The Training Squadron became the Cruiser Squadron in 1901.

[5] The first President was R.-Adm. Sir Astley Cooper Key. *See* Admlty. Min. of Jan. 17, 1873.

[6] The Admiralty section of this was transferred to the R. N. Coll. at Greenwich in 1873.

[7] Parl. Paper, No. 277 of 1883.

afterwards, old sailing ships of the line, with no fighting value save perhaps as floating batteries. In course of time, however, the salutary practice arose of employing as port guard-ships fighting craft ready to go to sea at a few hours' notice. It then became the custom to fly the Port Admiral's flag, not in the guard-ship, but in some yacht or other non-fighting vessel. Thus, in 1900, the flagships at the principal ports were : at the Nore, the yacht *Wildfire*, with the battleship *Sans Pareil* as guard-ship; at Portsmouth, Nelson's *Victory*, with the battleships *Trafalgar* and *Inflexible* as guard-ships; and at Plymouth, the yacht *Vivid*, with the battleships *Nile* and *Devastation* as guard-ships.

The higher naval education was furthered somewhat, especially towards the end of the nineteenth century, by the influence of the Royal United Service Institution. The establishment of this was first advocated in 1829. The actual establishment dates from June 25th, 1831, when it was formed as " The Naval and Military Library and Museum," and was lodged in Vanbrugh House, Whitehall Yard, a small building furnished for the purpose by the Government. In 1833 a larger house, the old office of the Board of Works in Inner Scotland Yard, was also provided at the national expense, and the two buildings were connected. A lecture theatre was added in 1849–50. In the meantime the name had been changed to the one which the Institution now bears. The *Journal*, in which the proceedings of the Institution and other matters of naval and military interest are recorded, has been published periodically since 1857 ; in which year also the Government began to recognise the usefulness of the Institution by making an annual contribution to its funds. In 1860 a royal charter of incorporation was granted ; from 1874 onwards a gold medal was offered yearly for the best naval or military essay read before the members ; and in 1890 Queen Victoria granted to the Institution the use of its present quarters, the Banqueting House, Whitehall, to which additions were made at the south end. These were completed and opened by H.R.H. the Prince of Wales on February 20th, 1895.

The Institution includes a very valuable museum, a large theatre, a council room, a library, two reading rooms, and a topographical room. Lectures on naval and military subjects are delivered periodically in the theatre, and are subsequently discussed. Ordinary membership is confined to officers, active or retired, of the two services, and to officials of the naval and military departments, the entrance fee being £1, and the annual subscription a like sum.[1] The Institution deserves the support of all naval officers.

To attempt to give even a mere bald catalogue of the minor legislative and administrative changes which influenced the Navy during the second half of the nineteenth century is here impossible. A few departures of special interest which may be noted are: the establishment in 1866 of savings' banks for the Navy and Royal Marines (29 & 30 Vict. c. 43); the introduction in 1860 of uniform watch-bills, quarter-bills, and station-bills; the passing of the Naval Discipline Act of 1861, and of the New Naval Discipline Act of 1866; the issue in 1871[2] of a circular restricting the infliction of corporal punishment in peace time; the practical abolition of flogging in 1879; the withdrawal, in 1874, of flag-officers' privileges in connection with the filling of death vacancies, and with the making of haul-down promotions[3]; and the adoption, in 1875, of a special form of service, compiled by the Archbishop of Canterbury, for use at the launching of H. M. ships.[4]

On March 21st, 1862, the Royal Marine Artillery, with its headquarters at Eastney, was formed into a separate division; and in 1869 the Woolwich division of the Royal Marines was abolished. Unhappily it has been impossible in these volumes to do full justice to the splendid services of this magnificent corps, which during the reign of Queen Victoria amply maintained its old glorious reputation. When, for example, on December 14th, 1864, the screw line-of-battle ship *Bombay* was destroyed by fire off Montevideo, 34 of the 97 officers and men who perished were Marines, every sentry dying at his post. The record of the corps, indeed, has been equally fine in peace and in war. All its more conspicuous war services will, of course, be found chronicled in this book, but not, it may be feared, with as much detail as they deserve.

A valuable innovation, due, however, not to official but to private initiative, was the publication for the first time in January, 1878, of Lean's 'Royal Navy List,' a quarterly, giving the dates of all commissions, and a record of the war services of every officer of the Royal Navy and Royal Marines, retired as well as active. This indispensable work of reference continued to be edited until the end of the century by its founder, Lieut.-Colonel Francis Lean, R.M.

[1] Information kindly supplied by Lieut.-Colonel R. Holden, secretary.
[2] Dec. 18, 1871.   [3] Circ. of Nov. 10, 1874.
[4] First used on Jan. 19, 1875, at the launch of the tug *Perseverance*, at Devonport.

Several orders and distinctions which were first created during the period under review have been, or may be, conferred upon naval officers, and should, therefore, be mentioned here. Of these are the Most Exalted Order of the Star of India, established in 1861, the ribbon of which is of light blue with a white stripe near each edge; the Most Eminent Order of the Indian Empire, instituted in 1878, and enlarged in 1887, the ribbon of which is of " imperial " blue; the Distinguished Service Order, instituted in 1886, the ribbon of which is of red, with blue edges; and the Royal Victorian Order, instituted in 1896, the ribbon of which is of dark blue with a narrow edging of three stripes, red, white, and red. Open to all ranks is the Albert Medal, instituted in 1866 for gallantry in saving or attempting to save life at sea, and enlarged in 1877 so as to be available for rewarding similar acts performed ashore. The Royal Humane Society's medals for saving or attempting to save life at sea, and the same Society's Stanhope Gold Medal, granted for the greatest act of gallantry of each year, may be worn by naval officers and men, if specially authorised, upon the right breast, as also may be the medals awarded by the Royal National Lifeboat Institution, the Shipwrecked Fishermen and Mariners' Royal Benevolent Society, the honorary silver medal of Lloyd's, the Board of Trade medal, and the medal of the Liverpool Shipwreck and Humane Society.

In connection with this subject it may be added that the naval and Marine winners of the gold medal of the Royal United Service Institution, with their rank at the time, were as follows :—

1875, Commander Gerard Henry Uctred Noel; 1877, Commander Philip Howard Colomb; 1879, Captain the Hon. Edmund Robert Fremantle; 1881, Captain Lindesay Brine; 1883, Captain Charles Johnstone; 1885, Lieutenant Frederick Charles Doveton Sturdee; 1888, Captain (R.M.) John Frederick Daniell; 1889, Captain Henry Forster Cleveland; 1891, Captain Robert William Craigie; 1893, Commander Frederick Charles Doveton Sturdee; 1895, Commander Joseph Honner; 1897, Commander George Alexander Ballard; and 1899, (again) Commander George Alexander Ballard.

A few words on the subject of naval clubs may find a fit place here.

Clubs of naval officers existed in London in the seventeenth century; and, about the year 1675, one of them was in the habit of meeting at the Vulture Tavern in Cornhill on Tuesdays, and of dining there, assembling at 1 P.M., and separating at 5 P.M. Not many years afterwards a naval club existed at a tavern or coffee-house at Portsmouth. The oldest institution of the kind, however,

that survived at the end of the nineteenth century was the Royal
Navy Club of 1765, which, since January, 1889, had been united
with an organisation, the Navy Club, only a few years its junior.

The Royal Navy Club of 1765 was founded on February 4th,
1765, at a meeting which was held at the house of Captain (later
Sir) Basil Keith, R.N., among the other officers present being
Captain (afterwards Admiral Sir) Richard Onslow, and Captain
(afterwards Admiral Sir) Hyde Parker (2). The proceedings of
that day were confirmed, and rules were drawn up, at a meeting
at the St. Alban's Tavern on February 11th, when the club was
formally named " The Navy Society." In the beginning it seems
to have dined on Tuesdays during the season between November
and April, first, for a short time, at the St. Alban's Tavern, then at
the Castle Tavern, Henrietta Street, and then at the Shakespeare's
Head. At that time twelve dinners a year were held. Subsequently
the number was thirteen. In 1806 it removed to the Crown and
Anchor; in 1826, to the Piazza Coffee House, in Covent Garden ;
and in 1850, to the Thatched House Tavern, St. James's Street.
In 1829 the title of the society became " The Royal Naval Club of
1765." Among the distinguished officers who at various times
belonged to it were Kempenfelt, St. Vincent, Duncan, Hyde
Parker (1), Howe, Bridport, Collingwood, Exmouth, de Saumarez,
Nelson, Sidney Smith, Troubridge, and King William IV.

The Navy Club, founded in 1785, was also a dining club, but
with a limited membership. It met while Parliament was sitting.
Its first house was the Star and Garter, in the City, where it dined
on alternate Wednesdays. In 1800 it migrated to the Thatched
House Tavern in St. James's Street, and dined first at 4 P.M., then
at 5, and, after 1810, at 6 P.M. In 1825 the hour was 7 P.M. from
Lady Day to the end of the season, the meeting days being then,
or soon afterwards, Thursdays. In 1858 the dinner-hour became
7.30 P.M., and in 1861 the club removed to Willis's Rooms (late
Almack's). Among its members have been Keppel, Barrington,
Hotham, Cornwallis, Gardner, Keith, Gambier, Nelson, Warren,
Stopford, Hardy, Blackwood, Codrington, Hoste, and Broke. As
has been mentioned already, it amalgamated with the older society
in 1889.[1] After the closing of Willis's Rooms the club held its
dinners at various places.

---

[1] For much of the above I am indebted to Fleet-Paymaster Edward Madgewick
Roe, the Secretary of the Royal Navy Club of 1765 and 1785.

Attempts to found other exclusively naval clubs in London have not been on the whole successful; but naval, as well as military, officers are admitted to the United Service[1] (founded 1815), the Junior United Service (1827), the Army and Navy[2] (1838), the Naval and Military (1862), the Junior Army and Navy (1869), etc. At Portsmouth, however, an exclusively naval club, carried on after the fashion of the large clubs in London, has existed for many years; and there are clubs of the same kind at naval stations abroad.

England has been described as Mother of Parliaments. With almost equal fitness she may be called a Mother of Navies. Already in these volumes many examples have been given of services rendered by her officers to the rising or struggling navies of other powers, and especially to those of Russia, Portugal, and the South American republics. In the latter half of the nineteenth century she was frequently appealed to to furnish instructors and leaders to nations desirous either of creating fleets or of improving such fleets as they already possessed; and, with or without permission of the Admiralty, numerous British officers, whose names deserve to be remembered, went abroad at various times, and devoted themselves to the development of foreign navies.

Turkey, for example, secured the assistance of Captain Adolphus Slade,[3] who served her for about sixteen years, ending with 1866, and was known in the East as Muchaver Pasha. Captain the Hon. Augustus Charles Hobart[4] (later Hobart-Hampton), served her for many years from 1868 onwards, and as Pasha commanded her fleet during her war with Russia in 1877–78. Navigating-Lieutenant Henry Felix Woods[5] also entered her service about 1868, and was created a Pasha in 1883; and Commander Charles William Manthorpe[6] assumed the Ottoman uniform about the year 1877.

Egypt benefited by the services of Captain Henry Frederick M'Killop[7]; Commander George Morice,[8] who joined the Khedive in 1871, and was made a Ferik in 1886; and Lieutenant Arthur Charles Middlemass, who was lent to the Egyptian coastguard in 1884.

China obtained at various times the professional assistance of

---

[1] Known as " The Senior."   [2] Known as "The Rag."
[3] Born 1804; Capt. R.N. 1849; died v.-adm. on retd. list, 1877.
[4] Born 1822; Capt. R.N. 1863; died 1886.
[5] Nav.-Lieut. 1867; retd. 1874.   [6] Com. 1866; capt. on retd. list, 1873.
[7] Capt. R.N. 1862; retd. 1870.   [8] Com. 1869; capt. on retd. list, 1884.

Captains Richard Edward Tracey, Percy Putt Luxmoore, and William Metcalfe Lang, as well as of Commander Lawrence Ching, and of several Lieutenants and other officers. Both China and Japan also sent some of their own young officers to serve, by permission, in the British Navy, as did Germany, Chili, Denmark, Sweden, Norway, Greece, and other nationalities.

The Japanese Navy, which, in the last thirty years of the century, grew in efficiency as well as in size until it ranked with the navies of the great continental European powers, was, in its infancy, developed and trained entirely by British officers; among whom should be mentioned Commander Archibald Lucius Douglas, Lieutenant (retd. commander) Charles William Jones (who died Director of the Japanese Naval College in 1877), Navigating-Lieutenant Charles William Baillie, Lieutenant Albert George Sidney Hawes, R.M., Chief-Engineer Frederick William Sutton (2), and Engineer Thomas Skinner Gissing, all of whom served Japan during the decade 1870–1880, and Captain John Ingles, who was naval adviser to the Japanese government from 1887 to 1893.

In addition, many British officers served in the various Indian marines, all of which were amalgamated in 1877; and others had a share in the development, if not in the establishment, of the Colonial Navies which sprang into existence in the last half of the nineteenth century in New South Wales, Victoria, South Australia, and Queensland.[1] Some of these were able to contribute to the general service of the Empire during the troubles in North China in 1900.

Great Britain never derived, nor endeavoured to derive, compensating advantages from abroad. Instead of following the example of the other great powers, and appointing a naval attaché to her diplomatic representative in each country possessed of a navy of any importance, she made it a practice to appoint one attaché, who had to divide his attentions over the whole of Europe, and one other, accredited to the United States. Only occasionally and

---

[1] There were in existence in 1900 the following among other Colonial naval forces: the New South Wales Naval Defence Force; the New South Wales Naval Artillery Volunteers; the South Australia Naval Defence Force; the Queensland Naval Defence Force; the Victorian Naval Defence Force; the Victorian Naval Brigade (a militia); the Natal Naval Volunteers; and some naval or semi-naval organisations in Canada, Western Australia, New Zealand, and Tasmania, chiefly established under the Colonial Defence Act of 1865, though, in most cases, not until many years after it. In New South Wales and New Zealand naval volunteers were formed under local acts. To these may be added the Royal Indian Marine alluded to above.

temporarily did she depart from this custom, the result being that, in spite of the goodwill and energy of her representatives, she has always been very indifferently served, at least in Europe. Among the officers who did duty for her as naval attachés at different times were, in Europe, Captains Edward George Hore (who made Paris his official headquarters for eleven years prior to his death in 1871), James Graham Goodenough, Edward Henry Howard (1874–77), Henry Frederick Nicholson, Hubert Henry Grenfell, and Ernest Rice, and, at Washington, Rear-Admirals Edward Augustus Inglefield, and William Gore Jones, and Captain the Hon. William John Ward. The Naval Intelligence Department at the Admiralty, under the Director of Naval Intelligence, was formed in January, 1887. Its establishment should have been followed at once by the appointment of many more attachés; for there can be no doubt that capable and active attachés, especially if they be good linguists and professional enthusiasts, may be most valuable collectors of useful information, and that countries like France, Russia, Germany, Italy, and Japan are each worthy of having a representative sent to them by any navy which desires to keep abreast of all modern progress. At the end of the century, nevertheless, there were still only three officers so employed.

In the days of non-continuous service the British bluejacket was never properly appreciated by his country, except, indeed, during the great wars. Over and over again, when his services became urgently necessary, Great Britain was reminded by costly experience of his inestimable value, and of the difficulty of obtaining him keen, sound, and already trained for effective work in her fleets. Over and over again, when the peril had passed away, she thanklessly set him adrift in the world, and left him to shift for himself until she should again have need of men. It is true that Greenwich Hospital was open to him in the event of his disablement by wounds, disease, or old age, provided always that he could first qualify for admission to it; but, if he were still fit for service, his country was so short-sighted as to neglect him almost entirely, not only after he had been paid off, but also when he happened to be ashore for a few days' leave. Indeed, it seemed to be accepted that the country had little or no interest in him except when he was actually doing duty.

Wiser views began to prevail in the middle of the nineteenth century; and nothing, perhaps, is better illustrative of the change

which has come over the bluejackets in regard as well to the
estimation in which he is held as to the estimation in which he
holds himself, than the history of the rise and progress of the Sailors'
Home at Portsmouth, and of similar institutions there and elsewhere.

In 1850 or 1851, just before the introduction of continuous
service, and when men were still being paid off with pockets full of
money, to be the prey of sharks and harpies, far, perhaps, from
home and friends, it occurred to three officers, Sir Edward Parry,
Captain Robert Fitzgerald Gambier, and Captain William Hutcheon
Hall, to found a home where bluejackets might find shelter from
the perils and snares of the Portsmouth streets. Many excellent
people laughed at the scheme; but Queen Victoria and the Prince
Consort at once gave their support and subscriptions to it, and in
1852 the Home was established and opened, with twenty-four
cabins, containing thirty beds. Fresh accommodation was quickly
discovered to be necessary. On the first Christmas night of the
Home's existence, in spite of the fact that it had already been twice
enlarged, more than half of the 250 men who slept in it had to
lie on the bare floors. There could no longer be any doubt as to
its utility. Supported chiefly by outside contributions, it continued
to do steadily-increasing good work until 1864, when five-and-
twenty petty officers and seamen who had enjoyed its hospitality
set the example of contributing to its funds. From that time the
Home began to become a club rather than a mere refuge, and soon
seamen by the hundred subscribed to it. In 1869 a canteen for the
sale of malt liquors was opened; in 1870 an additional hundred
cabins were fitted up; and it became a common practice among
bluejackets and Marines to allot their half-pay to the manager for
safe-keeping, and to entrust him with their little valuables. In 1871
a large recreation room was added, a room which soon became a
favourite meeting-place for the members of naval friendly societies,
and for parties of various kinds. In time—and, strangely enough,
at the instigation of a distinguished teetotaler—the canteen was
authorised to supply not only beer, but also all the liquors which are
ordinarily provided at taverns, care being, of course, taken to supply
them of good quality. The experiment, though bold, was in every
way successful, and immensely increased the popularity and usefulness of this admirable institution, which was obliged to add
largely to its sleeping accommodation in 1887, and again in 1897.

At the end of the century upwards of 100,000 men per annum lodged under its roof. Its influence in developing among bluejackets self-respect, *esprit de corps*, providence, and general culture has been most beneficial. Conversely, the ever-growing intelligence and good character of the men has enabled the managers of the Home gradually to broaden its scope and its rules without imperilling its orderliness and efficiency.[1]

Miss Agnes E. Weston's Royal Sailors' Rests at Devonport (established in 1873) and Portsmouth, have done equally good work, but are conducted on somewhat narrower lines. The long devotion of this excellent lady, and her assistant, Miss Wintz, to the interests of bluejackets and other seamen, has had a powerful influence in the promotion of the cause of temperance, besides being most beneficial in other directions.

Another sign of the times was the establishment of the Royal Naval Fund. The Royal Naval Exhibition held at Chelsea in 1891 resulted in a profit of about £48,000. It was decided by the Committee to hand over this sum to trustees, who were instructed to devote the resultant income to the relief of widows, orphans, and other dependent relatives of seamen and Royal Marines dying in the service of the Crown. The Fund began work on January 1st, 1893, between which date and the end of the century it distributed £10,523, by way of relief, to 1,305 persons. The capital on December 31st, 1900, was £50,532.

Until well on in the second half of the nineteenth century the lay public seems to have taken but little practical interest in the Royal Navy. It read with natural avidity the numerous exciting accounts of maritime discovery, and the few nautical novels, such as Smollett's 'Roderick Random,' and John Moore's 'The Post-Captain,' which appeared during the eighteenth century; and, in the earlier part of the nineteenth, it eagerly perused the stirring records of polar exploration, and the nautical novels of writers like Michael Scott,[2] James Fenimore Cooper,[3] Frederick Marryat,[4] James Hannay,[5] and Frederic Chamier[6]; but, upon the whole, it

[1] Forty-ninth Annual Report of the Royal Portsmouth Sailors' Home, 1900.

[2] Mich. Scott (1789–1835), author of 'Tom Cringle's Log,' and 'The Cruise of the Midge.'

[3] Born 1789; d. 1851. From 1805 to 1811, Cooper was in the U.S. Navy.

[4] Born 1792; Com. R.N. 1815; Capt. 1825; d. 1847.

[5] Born 1827; d. 1873. From 1840 to 1845, Hannay served in the Navy.

[6] Born 1796; Com. R.N. 1826; retd. capt. 1856; d. 1870.

was content to accept the Navy as the traditional and invincible defender of the island empire, never questioning, nor even allowing itself to dream about, the fleet's permanent ability to do whatsoever work might be demanded of it. The truth is that the lay public generally regarded the Navy, nautical terminology, and naval men as mysteries which it could not hope to understand, and which certainly could not be benefited by the attentions or solicitude of landsmen. John Clerk, of Eldin, indeed, in the last quarter of the eighteenth century, offered a civilian's counsel to naval tacticians ; but he stood almost alone in his generation, and, for many years after his death, British laymen scarcely raised their voices or used their pens to make either criticisms or suggestions concerning the conduct of naval affairs.

The last half of the nineteenth century witnessed a notable change in the popular attitude. Laymen were no longer satisfied to be told that all was well with the fleet, whereon, as they knew, so much depended. They began to take a practical interest in the Navy, and to see and enquire for themselves. The meagreness of the results attained by the Navy during the Russian war aroused them from their apathy ; Mr. Hans Busk's volume on ' The Navies of the World ' [1] rendered them uneasy as to the maritime position of their country ; the naval display at the Exhibition of 1862 stimulated their curiosity with regard to the growing influence of scientific progress upon naval warfare. Then, in 1864, the Admiralty furthered the popular movement by transferring to South Kensington Museum, and throwing open to all, the collection of naval models which, since the first quarter of the century, had been gradually accumulated at Somerset House. Ten years afterwards the collection was moved to a still more suitable resting-place at Greenwich Hospital. Not without its effect, too, was the establishment, in 1860, by Dr. William Howard Russell, of the *Army and Navy Gazette*, a service periodical which, especially in the early years of its existence, was singularly able and outspoken, and which pertinaciously exposed many naval abuses and procured the granting of many naval reforms.

Fifteen or sixteen years later, when Lord Charles Beresford, then a Commander, was member for Waterford, that active officer, in order to induce some of his brother legislators to examine into naval affairs, began a practice of occasionally inviting them to accompany

[1] London, 1859.

him on a visit to Portsmouth Dockyard; and he resumed this practice, with excellent results, whenever he subsequently held a seat in Parliament.

Still, however, popular interest was not thoroughly awakened; nor was it until 1884 that the British public was induced to begin to take that intelligent and steadily growing interest in its fleet which, in the remaining sixteen years of the century, obliged successive governments, often against their will, to enlarge and improve the Navy, until it became more efficient than it had ever been before in time of peace.

The work was begun by means of the publication, in the *Pall Mall Gazette*, of the remarkable series of articles[1] entitled "The Truth About the Navy"; it was followed up, in 1885, by the exaction from the Admiralty of permission for the leading newspapers to depute correspondents to accompany the home fleets during their annual manœuvres, which date from that year. In 1888–89 the City of London, influenced not only by naval officers such as Sir Geoffrey T. P. Hornby and Lord Charles Beresford, but also by civilians, put forward demands for a stronger fleet, and had its way. In the interval the Jubilee naval review at Spithead, in 1887, had exhibited to the people the weakness as well as the strength of the Navy; and the lessons of the display had been interpreted to them by the numerous writers who, in the years immediately preceding it, had found means to make a special study of the subject, and to gain a hearing through the columns of the press. In 1888 had been made the first suggestions for a scheme which, a few years later,[2] resulted in the formation of the Navy League—an organisation, mainly civilian in its constitution, pledged to do its utmost to secure naval efficiency and a fleet entirely adequate to the needs of the Empire. All this prepared the way for the holding at Chelsea in 1891 of the extraordinarily successful and immensely instructive Royal Naval Exhibition, under the patronage of Her Majesty Queen Victoria, the presidency of H.R.H. the Prince of Wales, Honorary Admiral of the Fleet, the executive direction of Admiral Sir William Montagu Dowell, K.C.B., and the honorary secretaryship of Captain Alfred Jephson,[3] who was rewarded for the efficacy of his work with a knighthood. The Exhibition, which was open to the public on 151 days, was

---

[1] Attributed to Mr. W. T. Stead.   [2] In 1894.
[3] Com. R.N. 1873; retd. as capt. 1889.

visited by 2,351,683 people,[1] and was, undoubtedly, of the highest educational value.

In the same year the present writer had the pleasure of making public[2] a suggestion which led, in 1893, to the foundation of the Navy Records Society—a society for the printing of documents and papers connected with naval history, biography, and archæology, much of the success of which has been due to the devotion of its secretary and editor, Professor John Knox Laughton.[3] And in 1893, when, after the heavy expenditure which had been authorised by the Naval Defence Act of 1889, it appeared that the effort to raise the Navy to an adequate point of strength was to be allowed to flag, popular opinion so quickly and markedly responded to a demand[4] for additional ships and men, that the government at once increased the ordinary estimates to an amount about £3,000,000 in excess of what they had ever before been in peace time, and never afterwards, until the end of the century, suffered them to fall below the level to which they then attained. Popular and civilian interest in the Navy, thus gradually aroused, remains an important factor in the policy of the Admiralty until to-day.

The Jubilee naval review, which has been already alluded to, was held on July 23rd, 1887. The total number of vessels in line, apart from yachts, troopships, tugs, etc., was 109, of which twenty-six were ironclads. The senior officer afloat on that occasion was Admiral Sir George Ommanney Willes, Commander-in-Chief at Portsmouth, who flew his flag in the battleship *Inflexible*.

A yet more impressive review was held at Spithead on August 6th, 1889, when His Majesty William II., German Emperor,[5] visited Spithead with a detachment of his own fleet in order to be present. The number of British men-of-war in line on that day was again 109, but of them no fewer than thirty-five were ironclads. The officer then in command was Admiral Sir John Edmund Commerell, V.C., Commander-in-Chief at Portsmouth. H.R.H. Prince George of Wales,[6] as a Lieutenant, was in com-

[1] Official Report to H.R.H. the Prince of Wales, May 13, 1892.

[2] *A. and N. Gazette*, July 4, 1891, and subseq. corr. in the *Times*.

[3] Born 1830; Nav. Inst. R.N. 1853; prof. of mod. hist. at King's Coll., Lond.

[4] Made in a series of articles on "The Needs of the Navy," by the author (anonymously), in the *Daily Graphic*.

[5] Hon. Adm. of the Fleet, Aug. 2, 1889.

[6] Entered R.N. June 5, 1877; Mids. Jan. 8, 1880; Sub-Lieut. June 3, 1884; Lieut. Oct. 8, 1885; Com. Aug. 24, 1891; Capt. Jan. 2, 1893; R. Adm. Jan. 1, 1901. Served actively at sea in each rank.

mand then, and during the subsequent manœuvres, of torpedo-boat No. 79.

Very much more impressive still was the last great review of the reign, on June 26th, 1897, to commemorate the sixtieth anniversary of Her Majesty Queen Victoria's accession. Numerous foreign men-of-war were present in honour of the event, and the number of British ships in line that day was as many as 164. There were somewhat fewer ironclads than in 1889; but, on the other hand, whereas the fleet of 1889 contained numerous obsolete craft such as could scarcely have been employed actively in war time, the fleet of 1897 was composed, with very few exceptions, of modern vessels in the highest state of efficiency. At the end of the day H.R.H. the Prince of Wales, Honorary Admiral of the Fleet,[1] genially desired Admiral Sir Nowell Salmon, V.C., Commander-in-Chief, to order the main-brace to be spliced. About 35,000 officers and men manned the British men-of-war present at that final and most magnificent of the naval reviews of the century; and American, German, Russian, Spanish, French, Austrian, Swedish, Norwegian, Japanese, and Siamese men-of-war attended to witness it, and to do honour to the aged sovereign of Great Britain.

[1] July 18, 1887.

THE EGYPTIAN MEDAL. 1882.

(Similar medals, with altered dates, were granted for later campaigns.)
Silver : ribbon of blue and white stripes.

(85)

APPENDIX TO CHAPTER XLVI.,

AND INTRODUCTORY NOTE TO CHAPTER XLVII.

IN continuation of the lists given in Vol. VI. pp. 223–226, the following roll of the naval officers who held the principal commands at home and abroad from the beginning of 1857 until the end of the reign of Queen Victoria will be found useful for purposes of reference in connection with the history of the period:—

PORTSMOUTH.

Sir George Francis Seymour, K.C.B., Vice-Adm. (Adm. May 14, 1857).

Mar. 1, 1859. William Bowles, C.B., Adm.

Mar. 1, 1860. Henry William Bruce, V.-Adm. (K.C.B. 1861).

Mar. 1, 1863. Sir Michael Seymour (2), G.C.B., V.-Adm. (Adm. Mar. 5, 1864).

Mar. 1, 1866. Sir Thomas Sabine Pasley, Bart., V.-Adm. (Adm. Nov. 20, 1866).

Feb. 25, 1869. Sir James Hope, G.C.B., V.-Adm. (Adm. Jan. 21, 1870).

Mar. 1, 1872. Sir George Rodney Mundy, K.C.B., Adm.

Mar. 1, 1875. Sir George Elliot (4), K.C.B., Adm.

Mar. 1, 1878. Edward Gennys Fanshawe, C.B., Adm.

Nov. 27, 1879. Alfred Phillipps Ryder, Adm.

Nov. 28, 1882. Sir Geoffrey Thomas Phipps Hornby, K.C.B., Adm.

Nov. 28, 1885. Sir George Ommanney Willes, K.C.B., Adm.

June 20, 1888. Sir John Edmund Commerell, V.C., G.C.B., Adm.

June 22, 1891. Richard James, 4th Earl of Clanwilliam, K.C.B., K.C.M.G., Adm.

June 22, 1894. Sir Nowell Salmon, V.C., K.C.B., Adm.

Aug. 3, 1897. Sir Michael Culme-Seymour, Bart., G.C.B., Adm.

Oct. 3, 1900. Sir Charles Frederick Hotham, K.C.B., Adm.

DEVONPORT.

Sir William Parker (2), Bart., G.C.B., Adm.

May 4, 1857. Sir Barrington Reynolds, K.C.B., V.-Adm. (Adm. Nov. 1, 1860).

June 8, 1860. Sir Arthur Fanshawe, K.C.B., V.-Adm.

Oct. 11, 1860. Sir Houston Stewart, K.C.B., V.-Adm. (Adm. Nov. 10, 1862).

Oct. 27, 1863. Sir Charles Howe Fremantle, K.C.B., V.-Adm. (Adm. Feb. 9, 1864).

Oct. 26, 1866. Sir William Fanshawe Martin, Bart., K.C.B., Adm.

Nov. 1, 1869. Sir Henry John Codrington, G.C.B., Adm.

Nov. 1, 1872. Hon. Sir Henry Keppel, G.C.B., Adm.

Nov. 1, 1875. Sir Thomas Matthew Charles Symonds, K.C.B., Adm.

Nov. 1, 1878. Arthur Farquhar (2), Adm.

Jan. 9, 1880. Hon. Sir Charles Gilbert John Brydone Elliot, K.C.B.. Adm.

Dec. 1, 1881. Sir William Houston Stewart, K.C.B., Adm.

Dec. 1, 1884. Sir Augustus Phillimore, K.C.B., Adm.

May 25, 1887. Rt. Hon. Lord John Hay (3), G.C.B.. Adm.

Dec. 15, 1888. Sir William Montagu Dowell, K.C.B., Adm.

Aug. 4, 1890. H.R.H. the Duke of Edinburgh, K.G., Adm.

June 2, 1893. Sir Algernon McLennan Lyons, K.C.B.. Adm.

June 10, 1896. Hon. Sir Edmund Robert Fremantle, K.C.B., C.M.G., Adm.

1899. Sir Henry Fairfax, K.C.B., Adm.

Mar. 28, 1900. Lord Charles Thomas Montagu Douglas Scott, K.C.B., Adm.

THE NORE.

Hon. William Gordon (2), V.-Adm.

July 1, 1857. Edward Harvey, V.-Adm. (Adm. June 9, 1860).

June 28, 1860. Sir William James Hope Johnstone, K.C.B., V.-Adm.

June 25, 1863. Sir George Robert Lambert, G.C.B., V.-Adm. (Adm. Dec. 15, 1863).

Mar. 1, 1864. Sir Charles Talbot, K.C.B., V.-Adm.

Apr. 5, 1866. Sir Baldwin Wake Walker, Bart., K.C.B., V.-Adm.

Apr. 5, 1869. Richard Laird Warren, V.-Adm. (Adm. Apr. 1, 1870).

July 1, 1870. Hon. Charles Gilbert John Brydone Elliot, C.B., V.-Adm.

Feb. 11, 1873. Hon. George Fowler Hastings, C.B., V.-Adm.

Feb. 14, 1876. Henry Chads, V.-Adm.

Sept. 17, 1877. Sir William King Hall, K.C.B., V.-Adm.

Aug. 4, 1879. Sir Reginald John James George Macdonald, K.C.B., K.C.S.I., V.-Adm.

July 21, 1882. Edward Bridges Rice, C.B., V.-Adm.

Oct. 30, 1884. John Corbett, C.B., V.-Adm. (Adm. Apr. 7, 1885).

July 1, 1885. H.S.H. Ernest L. V. C. A. J. E., Prince of Leiningen, G.C.B., V.-Adm.

July 1, 1887. Charles Ludovic Darley Waddilove, V.-Adm.

July 2, 1888. Thomas Bridgeman Lethbridge, V.-Adm.

Aug. 4, 1890. Charles Thomas Curme, V.-Adm.

Feb. 27, 1892. Sir Algernon Charles Fieschi Heneage. K.C.B., V.-Adm.

Dec. 10, 1894. Richard Wells, V.-Adm.

June 10, 1896. Sir Henry Frederick Nicholson, K.C.B., V.-Adm. (Adm. Sept. 16, 1897).

Dec. 10, 1897. Sir Charles Frederick Hotham, K.C.B., V.-Adm.

July 13, 1899. Sir Nathaniel Bowden-Smith, K.C.B., V.-Adm.

THE MEDITERRANEAN.

Edmund, Lord Lyons, Bart.. G.C.B.. R.-Adm. (V.-Adm. Mar. 19, 1857).

Feb. 22, 1858. Arthur Fanshawe, C.B.. V.-Adm.

Apr. 19, 1860. Sir William Fanshawe Martin, K.C.B., V.-Adm.

Apr. 20, 1863. Robert Smart, K.H., V.-Adm.

Apr. 28, 1866. Rt. Hon. Lord Clarence Edward Paget, C.B., V.-Adm.

Apr. 28, 1869. Sir Alexander Milne, K.C.B., V.-Adm. (Adm. Apr. 1, 1870).

Oct. 25, 1870. Sir Hastings Reginald Yelverton, K.C.B., V.-Adm.

Jan. 13, 1874. Hon. Sir James Robert Drummond, K.C.B., V.-Adm.

Jan. 15, 1877. Geoffrey Thomas Phipps Hornby, V.-Adm. (Adm. June 15, 1879).

Feb. 5, 1880. Sir Frederick Beauchamp Paget Seymour, G.C.B., V.-Adm. (Adm. May 6, 1882: Lord Alcester, 1882).

Feb. 7, 1883. Rt. Hon. Lord John Hay (3), K.C.B., V.-Adm. (Adm. July 8, 1884).

Feb. 5, 1886. H.R.H. the Duke of Edinburgh, K.G., V.-Adm. (Adm. Oct. 18, 1887).

Mar. 11, 1889. Sir Anthony Hiley Hoskins, K.C.B., V.-Adm. (Adm. June 20, 1891).

Aug. 20, 1891. Sir George Tryon, K.C.B. (drowned June 22, 1893).

June 29, 1893. Sir Michael Culme-Seymour, Bart., Adm.

Nov. 10, 1896. Sir John Ommanney Hopkins, K.C.B., Adm.

July 1, 1899. Sir John Arbuthnot Fisher, K.C.B., V.-Adm.

NORTH AMERICA AND WEST INDIES.

Sir Houston Stewart, G.C.B., V.-Adm.

Jan. 13, 1860. Sir Alexander Milne, K.C.B., R.-Adm.

Jan. 7, 1864. Sir James Hope, K.C.B., V.-Adm.

Jan. 10, 1867. Sir George Rodney Mundy, K.C.B., V.-Adm. (Adm. May 26, 1869).

June 30, 1869. George Greville Wellesley, C.B., V.-Adm.

Sept. 13, 1870. Edward Gennys Fanshawe, C.B., V.-Adm.

Sept. 9, 1873. George Greville Wellesley, C.B., V.-Adm.

Dec. 22, 1875. Sir Astley Cooper Key, K.C.B., V.-Adm.

Apr. 1, 1878. Sir Edward Augustus Inglefield, Kt., C.B., V.-Adm.

Nov. 27, 1879. Sir Francis Leopold M'Clintock, Kt., V.-Adm.

Nov. 7, 1882. Sir John Edmund Commerell, K.C.B., V.C., V.-Adm.

Aug. 25, 1885. Richard James, 4th Earl of Clanwilliam, K.C.B., K.C.M.G., V.-Adm.

Sept. 4, 1886. Algernon McLennon Lyons, V.-Adm.

Dec. 15, 1888. George Willes Watson, K.C.B., V.-Adm. (K.C.B. 1891).

Dec. 15, 1891. John Ommanney Hopkins, V.-Adm. (K.C.B. 1892).

Apr. 17, 1895. James Elphinstone Erskine, V.-Adm.

Sept. 15, 1897. Sir John Arbuthnot Fisher, K.C.B., V.-Adm.

May 1, 1899. Sir Frederick George Denham Bedford, K.C.B. V.-Adm.

THE PACIFIC.

Henry William Bruce, R. Adm.

July 8, 1857. Robert Lambert Baynes, C.B., R.-Adm.

May 5, 1860. Sir Thomas Maitland, Kt., C.B., R.-Ad.

Oct. 31, 1862. John Kingcome, R.-Adm.

May 10, 1864. Hon. Joseph Denman, R.-Adm.

Nov. 21, 1866. Hon. George Fowler Hastings, C.B., R.-Adm.

Nov. 1, 1869. Arthur Farquhar, R.-Adm.

July 9, 1872. Charles Farrel Hillyar, C.B., R.-Adm.

June 6, 1873. Hon. Arthur Auckland Leopold Pedro Cochrane, C.B.

Apr. 15, 1876. George Hancock, R.-Adm. (*d. Sept.* 20).

Aug. 6, 1876. Algernon Frederick Rous de Horsey, R.-Adm.

July 21, 1879. Frederick Henry Stirling, R.-Adm.

Dec. 10, 1881. Algernon McLennan Lyons, R.-Adm.

Sept. 13, 1884. John Kennedy Erskine Baird, R.-Adm.

July 4, 1885. Sir Michael Culme-Seymour, Bart., R.-Adm.

Sept. 20, 1887. Algernon Charles Fieschi Heneage, R.-Adm.

Feb. 4, 1890. Charles Frederick Hotham, C.B., R.Adm.

May 4, 1893. Henry Frederick Stephenson, C.B., R.Adm.

June 19, 1896. Henry St. Leger Bury Palliser, R.-Adm.

June 22, 1899. Lewis Anthony Beaumont, R.-Adm.

Oct. 15, 1900. Andrew Kennedy Bickford, C.M.G., R.-Adm.

EAST INDIES AND CHINA.

Sir Michael Seymour (2), K.C.B., R.-Adm.

Jan. 25, 1859. James Hope, C.B., R.-Adm.

Feb. 8, 1862. Augustus Leopold Kuper, C.B., R.-Adm.

Feb. 15, 1864. George St. Vincent Duckworth King, C.B., R.-Adm.

(*On Jan.* 17, 1865, *the stations were separated.*)

CHINA.

Jan. 17, 1865. George St. Vincent Duckworth King, C.B., R.-Adm.

Jan. 18, 1867. Hon. Sir Henry Keppel, K.C.B., V.-Adm.

July 17, 1869. Sir Henry Kellett, K.C.B., V.-Adm.

Aug. 30, 1871. Charles Frederick Alexander Shadwell, C.B., V.-Adm.

Aug. 31, 1874. Alfred Phillipps Ryder, V.-Adm.

Aug. 31, 1877. Charles Farrel Hillyar, C.B., V.-Adm.

Sept. 26, 1878. Robert Coote, C.B., V.-Adm.

Jan. 3, 1881. Sir George Ommanney Willes, K.C.B., V.-Adm.

Jan. 3, 1884. Sir William Montagu Dowell, K.C.B., V.-Adm.

Sept. 1, 1885. Sir Richard Vesey Hamilton, K.C.B., V.-Adm.

Dec. 17, 1887. Sir Nowell Salmon, K.C.B., V.C., V.-Adm.

Nov. 29, 1890. Sir Frederick William Richards, K.C.B., V.-Adm.

Feb. 16, 1892. Hon. Sir Edmund Robert Fremantle, K.C.B., C.M.G., V.-Adm.

May 28, 1895. Sir Alexander Buller, K.C.B., V.-Adm.

Feb. 19, 1898. Sir Edward Hobart Seymour, K.C.B., V.-Adm.

EAST INDIES.

Jan. 17, 1865. Frederick Byng Montresor, Commod.

Sept. 26, 1865. Charles Farrel Hillyar, Commod.

July 29, 1867. Sir Leopold George Heath, K.C.B., Commod.

Sept. 6, 1870. James Horsford Cockburn, R.-Adm. (*died Feb.* 2, 1872).

Feb. 14, 1872. Arthur Cumming, C.B., R.-Adm.

Mar. 4, 1875. Reginald John James George Macdonald, R.-Adm.

Apr. 2, 1877. John Corbett, C.B., R.-Adm.

Aug. 4, 1879. William Gore Jones, C.B., R.-Adm.

Apr. 11, 1882. Sir William Nathan Wrighte Hewett, K.C.B., K.C.S.I., V.C., R.-Adm.

May 18, 1885. Sir Frederick William Richards, K.C.B., R.-Adm.

Feb. 25, 1888. Hon. Sir Edmund Robert Fremantle, K.C.B., C.M.G., R.-Adm.

Feb. 26, 1891. Frederick Charles Bryan Robinson, R.-Adm.

Jan. 26, 1892. William Robert Kennedy, R.-Adm.

Mar. 16, 1895. Edmund Charles Drummond, R.-Adm.

Jan. 15, 1898. Archibald Lucius Douglas, R.-Adm.

June 5, 1899. Day Hort Bosanquet, R.-Adm.

CHANNEL SQUADRON.

(*Established as such in* 1858, *but even later occasionally called a Particular Service Squadron.*)

July 13, 1858. Sir Charles Howe Fremantle, K.C.B., R.Adm.

June 2, 1859. John Elphinstone Erskine, R.-Adm.

Jan. 29, 1861. Robert Smart, K.H., R.-Adm.

Apr. 24, 1863. Sydney Colpoys Dacres, R.-Adm.

June , 1866. Hastings Reginald Yelverton, R.-Adm.

May 1, 1867. Frederick Warden, C.B., R.-Adm.

Dec. 12, 1868. Sir Thomas Matthew Charles Symonds, K.C.B., V.-Adm.

July 18, 1870. Sir Hastings Reginald Yelverton, K.C.B., V.-Adm.

Oct. 25, 1870. George Greville Wellesley, C.B., V.-Adm.

Sept. 2, 1871. Geoffrey Thomas Phipps Hornby, R.-Adm., (V.-Adm. Jan. 1, 1875).

Oct. 1, 1874. Frederick Beauchamp Paget Seymour, C.B., R.-Adm. (V.-Adm. Dec. 31, 1876).

Nov. 10, 1877. Rt. Hon. Lord John Hay (3), C.B., R.-Adm. (V.-Adm. Dec. 31, 1877).

Dec. 10, 1879. Arthur William Acland Hood, C.B., R.-Adm. (V.-Adm. July 23, 1880).

Apr. 17, 1882. Sir William Montagu Dowell, K.C.B., V.-Adm.

Dec. 3, 1883. H.R.H. the Duke of Edinburgh, K.G., V.-Adm.

Dec. , 1884. Algernon Frederick Rous de Horsey, V.-Adm.

May , 1885. Charles Fellowes, C.B., V.-Adm. (*died in com.*).

Mar. 18, 1886. Sir William Nathan Wrighte Hewett, K.C.B., K.C.S.I., V.C., V.-Adm.

Apr. 17, 1888. John Kennedy Erskine Baird, V.-Adm.

May 3, 1890. Sir Michael Culme-Seymour, Bart., V.-Adm.

May 10, 1892. Henry Fairfax, C.B., V.-Adm.

May 27, 1895. Lord Walter Talbot Kerr, V.-Adm.

June 7, 1897. Sir Henry Frederick Stephenson, K.C.B., V.-Adm.

Dec. 20, 1898. Sir Harry Holdsworth Rawson, K.C.B., V.-Adm.

AUSTRALIA.

(*Established as a separate station,* 1859.)

Mar. 26, 1859. William Loring, C.B., Commod.

Mar. 10, 1860. Frederick Beauchamp Paget Seymour, Commod.

July 21, 1862. William Farquharson Burnett, C.B., Commod. (lost in the *Orpheus*, Feb. 7, 1863).

Apr. 20, 1863. Sir William Saltonstall Wiseman, Bart., C.B., Commod.

May 23, 1866. Rochfort Maguire, Commod. (*died in com.*).

May 28, 1867. Rowley Lambert, C.B., Commod.

Apr. 8, 1870. Frederick Henry Stirling, Commod.

May 22, 1873. James Graham Goodenough, C.B., C.M.G., Commod. (*died in com.*).

Sept. 7, 1875. Anthony Hiley Hoskins, C.B., Commod.

Sept. 12, 1878. John Crawford Wilson, Commod.

Jan. 21, 1882. James Elphinstone Erskine, Commod.

Nov. 12, 1884. George Tryon, C.B., R.-Adm.*

Feb. 1, 1887. Henry Fairfax, C.B., R.-Adm.

Sept. 10, 1889. Lord Charles Thomas Montagu Douglas Scott, C.B., R.-Adm.

---

* *From that time the officer was a Com.-in-Chief.*

Sept. 12, 1892. Nathaniel Bowden-Smith, R.-Adm.

Nov. 1, 1894. Cyprian Arthur George Bridge, R.-Adm.

Nov. 1, 1897. Hugo Lewis Pearson, R.-Adm.

Oct. 1, 1900. Lewis Anthony Beaumont, R.-Adm.

CAPE OF GOOD HOPE AND WEST COAST OF AFRICA.

Apr. 1, 1857. Hon. Sir Frederick William Grey, K.C.B., R.-Adm.

Feb. 10, 1860. Hon. Sir Henry Keppel, K.C.B., R.-Adm.

Feb. 6, 1861. Sir Baldwin Wake Walker, Bart., K.C.B., R.-Adm.

(*In 1864–65 the Cape was attached to the East Indies command, but in the latter year it again became independent under a Commodore, there being, however, another independent Commodore on the West Coast. The old command was restored in 1867.*)

Sept. 9, 1867. William Montagu Dowell, C.B., Commod.

Feb. 16, 1861. Sir John Edmund Commerell, K.C.B., V.C., Commod.

Oct. 2, 1873. Sir William Nathan Wrighte Hewett, K.C.B., V.C., Commod.

Oct. 16, 1876. Francis William Sullivan, C.B., C.M.G., Commod.

Mar. 17, 1879. Sir Frederick William Richards, K.C.B., Commod.

Apr. 11, 1882. Nowell Salmon, C.B., V.C., R.-Adm.*

Mar. 6, 1885. Sir Walter James Hunt-Grubbe, K.C.B., R.-Adm.

Mar. 29, 1888. Richard Wells, R.-Adm.

Sept. 1, 1890. Henry Frederick Nicholson, C.B., R.-Adm.

Aug. 10, 1892. Frederick George Denham Bedford, C.B., R.-Adm.

May 4, 1895. Harry Holdsworth Rawson, C.B., R.-Adm.

Apr. 27, 1898. Sir Robert Hastings Harris, K.C.M.G., R.-Adm.

* *From that time the officer was a Com.-in-Chief.*

ADMIRAL SIR HENRY CHADS, K.C.B.

ADMIRAL SIR EDWARD GENNYS FANSHAWE, G.C.B.

ADMIRAL SIR JOHN KENNEDY ERSKINE BAIRD, K.C.B.

CHAPTER XLVII.

MILITARY HISTORY OF THE ROYAL NAVY, 1857–1900.

THE SECOND CHINA WAR—Case of the *Arrow*—Seizure of the Canton Forts—Bombardment of Canton—Capture of French Folly—Capture of other forts—The *Sampson* near Hongkong—Destruction of junks—Loss of the *Raleigh*—Despatch of troops to China—The action in Escape Creek—Affair in the Sawshee Channel—Action in Fatshan Creek — Chinese pirates— French co-operation— Naval reinforcements diverted to India—Blockade of the Canton River—Affair of the *Banterer's* gig— Bombardment and capture of Canton—Capture of Commissioner Yeh—Bombardment and capture of the Taku forts—Occupation of Tientsin—A treaty signed— Withdrawal of the Allies—New difficulties and outrages—Capture of Namtao— Expedition up the Yang-tse-kiang—The Nankin batteries engaged—Affairs with junks—Arrival of Rear-Admiral Hope—The Allies repulsed in the Peiho—Josiah Tatnall—Loss of three vessels—New reinforcements—Disembarkation at Pehtang —The Peiho forts taken—The Treaty of Pekin—Minor operations—The Persian War—The *Pearl* and Vivanco's Navy—THE INDIAN MUTINY—The *Shannon's* Brigade—Battle of Kudjwa—Relief of Lucknow—Fighting near Cawnpur— Action at Kallee-Nuddee—Retaking of Lucknow—Death of Sir William Peel— The *Pearl's* Brigade—Action at Amorha—Numerous engagements—Relief of Bansee—Rebels repulsed at Amorha—Action at Doomureahgunge—Final operations—The Atlantic cables—Wise in the Scarcies River, 1858–59—Troubles at Jeddah, 1858—Walker the Filibuster—Affairs in Mexico, 1859–61—Visit of H.R.H. the Prince of Wales to Canada—THE TI-PING REBELLION—British neutrality professed—Repulse of Ti-pings at Shanghai, 1860—Activity of Dew— Hope's demands—Action at Kao-Kiau—Capture of Kah-ding, 1862—Death of Protêt—Massacre at Cho-lin—Dew at Ningpo—Montgomerie at Soong-kong— Sherard Osborn's flotilla—Dew at Shou-sing—Arrival of Rear-Admiral Kuper— Second capture of Kah-ding—Chinese piracy—THE NEW ZEALAND WAR, 1860–64 Storming of Omata—Policy of Sir George Grey—Attack on Rangariri—British repulse at the Gate Pah—Concluding operations—The Niger expeditions, 1861— Burning of Porto Novo—The Gambia expedition, 1861—Capture of Saba—Operations against Quiah—Fishery disputes—The slave trade—Minor operations, 1862–63 —DIFFICULTIES IN JAPAN—Outrage near Kanagawa—Bombardment of Kagosima, 1863—Effect of Kuper's action—Conduct of Choshiu—The Strait of Simonoseki forced, 1864—Capture of the batteries—Subsequent events in Japan—Niger expeditions, 1864–65–66—Richards at Akatoo—Operations against slavers—The *Dove* in Formosa—Chinese pirates—Morant off Pyramid Point—Successes of St. John—The *Bulldog* at Cape Haytien—The Jamaica rebellion—The *Highflyer* at El Kateef—The Fenians in Canada, 1865–67—The Cretan disturbances, 1865–67 —Chinese piracy—Minor affairs—Spithead review of 1867—The Abyssinian expedition, 1868—Capture of Magdala—Domvile and Chinese pirates—Outrages at Yangchow and in Formosa—Gallantry of Gurdon—Punishment of the Coochi

pirates—Rewa shelled—Minor operations in 1868—Affairs at Bahrein—Jones near
Swatow—The East African slave trade—The Niger expedition of 1869—Pirates in
the Gulf of Tonquin—Honour to Peabody—The Bermuda Dock—Seymour in the
Congo—Robinson at Selangor, 1871—The cruise of the *Rosario*—The *Basilisk*
in the Pacific—The *Nassau* at Carang-Carang—Slavers and pirates, 1871–73—
The San Juan difficulty—Bombardment of Omoa, 1873—Woollcombe in the
Larut River—The *Virginius* affair—Yelverton and the Intransigente squadron,
1873 — THE ASHANTEE WAR — Bombardment of Elmina — Bombardment of
Aquidah—Disaster off Chamah—Destruction of Chamah—Capture of Essaman—
Affair at Ampenee—Bootry shelled—Relief of Abrakrampa—Arrival of Hewett—
Advance to Prahsu—Bradshaw at the mouth of the Prah—Battle of Amoaful—
Action at Becquah and Ordah-su—Capture of Coomassie—Honours and pro-
motions—Inspection by the Queen—Foot off Madagascar—Sulivan at Mombasa—
Affair at Tangata—Work of the *Thetis* and the *Flying Fish*—Cruise of the
Sandfly—Cruise of the *Pearl*—Death of Goodenough—TROUBLES IN THE MALAY
PENINSULA—The *Avon* on the Perak coast—Demonstration against Selangor—
The *Charybdis* and *Avon* in the Lingie River—Expedition to the Indau River—
Intervention in Sunjei Ujong—Flight of the Bandar—Murder of Mr. Birch—
Stirling in Sunjei Ujong—The Perak Field Force—The Larut Field Force—Affair
at Kotah Lamah—Close of the Malay campaign—Hewett in the Congo, 1875—
Troubles at Oman and Muscat—Ward at Barawa—Cruise of the *Dido*, 1871–76—
British interference at Samoa—Captain Stevens—Murray at Apia—Hewett in the
Niger—Bombardment of Sabogrega—Difficulties with Dahomey—Submission of
Gelelé—Purvis in the Niger—Destruction of Emblana—Keppel in the Congo—
The *Rocket* and the case of the *George Wright*—Action of the *Shah* and the
Amethyst with the *Huascar*—Activity against slavers—The *Vulture* at El Katif—
The Russo-Turkish War—Hornby in the Mediterranean—Passage of the Dar-
danelles—Commerell at Gallipoli—The Channel Squadron in the Mediterranean—
The *Swiftsure's* pinnace fired upon—The *Thunderer* gun explosion—The occupa-
tion of Cyprus—Activity of H.R.H. the Duke of Edinburgh—TROUBLES IN SOUTH
AFRICA, 1877–79—Action at Quintana—The *Active's* Brigade—The *Tenedos's*
Brigade—Action on the Inyezane River—Promptitude of Bradshaw—The *Boa-
dicea's* Brigade—Battle of Ginginhlovo—End of the Zulu War—Caffin at Tanna—
—Continued activity of the *London's* boats—The Sitka Indians—Outrages in the
Pacific—The *Boxer's* commission—Burr in the Scarcies and the Niger—The
Kestrel and the *Encounter* on the Malay coast—Loss of the *Eurydice* and the
Atalanta—The Dulcigno Demonstration—The *Wild Swan* in Conducia Bay—
The Boer Rebellion—Laing's Nek—Majuba Hill—Loss of the *Doterel*—Diffi-
culties in Egypt—BOMBARDMENT OF ALEXANDRIA—Occupation of the City—The
armoured train—Arrival of the Channel Squadron—The Marine battalions—
Hewett at Suez—Affair at Mallaha Junction—The change of Base—Seizure of the
Canal—Fairfax at Port Said—FitzRoy at Ismailia and Nefiche—Hastings at
Chalouf—Tel el Mahuta—Kassassin—The Marines at Tel el Kebir—Collapse of
Arabi's rebellion—Johnstone at Tamatave—Brooke in the Niger—WAR WITH THE
MAHDI—Occupation of Suakin—Battle of El Teb—Battle of Tamai—Usefulness
of the Marines—The Gordon Relief Expedition—Abu Klea—Abu Kru—Metem-
meh—Beresford at Wad Habeshi—Gallantry of Benbow—The river column—
Abandonment of the expedition—The second Suakin expedition—Action at Tofrik
—Affairs near Tamai—Defence of Suakin—Fatal mistake in the river Min—
Operations at Zeila and on the Gold Coast—THE CONQUEST OF BURMAH—
Surrender of Mandalay—Expedition to Bhamo—Repression of dacoity—The
Greek Blockade—Hand in the Niger—The East African Slave-trade—Death of
Brownrigg—Heroism of Lieutenant Fegen—The *Ranger* at Suweik—The *Zephyr*
in Darvel Bay—The Yonnie Expedition—Affairs at Suakin—Action at Gemaizeh

THE first China War, 1839–42, had not taught the lessons which it was designed to teach; and within a few years of its conclusion new difficulties began to arise between the British and the local authorities in various parts of the huge invertebrate empire. For a time these were arranged as they arose, without resort to war; but they were arranged, unfortunately, in a manner which too often allowed the Chinese to remain in the belief that they had won diplomatic triumphs. The result was that both locally and at the capitals, the governing classes became steadily more and more inattentive to British remonstrances concerning acts of aggression, until, in 1856, the affair of the *Arrow*, and the vigorous action of Rear-Admiral Sir Michael Seymour (2), Commander-in-Chief in the East Indies, brought about the second China War, which lasted, with intermissions, for nearly four years.

The causes of the fresh outbreak of hostilities [1] are set forth in a dispatch which was sent by Seymour to the Admiralty on November 14th, 1856; and they may be thus summarised.

On October 8th, 1856, the lorcha *Arrow*, with a colonial register from the governor of Hong Kong, was boarded, while at anchor at Canton, by a Chinese officer and a party of soldiers, who, notwithstanding the protest of the English master, seized twelve of the crew, bound them, carried them off, and hauled down the British flag. Mr. Parkes, her Majesty's consul, brought the matter before the Imperial High Commissioner, Yeh, and demanded the return of the twelve men by the officer who had abducted them, together with

[1] Perhaps the best account of the origin and early part of the Second Chinese War is in G. C. Cooke's 'China,' which has been freely made use of.

an apology, and an assurance that the flag should be respected in the future. Ultimately the men were sent back, but not in the public manner required; nor was any apology or assurance offered. On October 11th, the matter was reported to Seymour by Sir John Bowring, British Plenipotentiary in China, who suggested that an Imperial junk should be seized by way of reprisals. The making of the seizure was entrusted to Commodore the Hon. Charles Gilbert John Brydone Elliot, C.B., of the *Sibylle*, 40, senior officer in the Canton river, who was reinforced for the purpose with the *Barracouta*, 6, paddle, Commander Thomas Dyke Acland Fortescue,[1] and the *Coromandel*, steam tender. A junk was duly captured, but, as it proved to be private property, it had to be presently released. Seymour then[2] sent the *Encounter*, 14, screw, Captain George William Douglas O'Callaghan, and *Samson*, 6, paddle, Captain George Sumner Hand, to join the Commodore, hoping that the display of force in the river would bring the High Commissioner to reason. It soon, however, became clear that that official was bent upon resistance.

In the meantime, Mr. Parkes proceeded to consult with Seymour and Bowring at Hong Kong, where it was decided to seize the defences of Canton, it being evident that any more moderate measures would, as usual, be interpreted by the Chinese as symptoms of weakness. Seymour accordingly moved his flagship, the *Calcutta*, 84, Captain William King Hall, C.B., as high above the Bogue Forts as her draft would permit; and, on the morning of October 23rd, proceeded towards Canton in the *Coromandel*, accompanied by the *Samson* and *Barracouta*, with detachments of Royal Marines, and boats' crews, from the *Calcutta*, *Winchester*, 50, Captain Thomas Wilson, and *Bittern*,[3] 12, and with the Commodore and the boats of the *Sibylle*. On approaching Blenheim reach, the *Samson* and part of the force diverged up the Macao passage to keep that channel open, and to capture Blenheim fort, while the Rear-Admiral, with the *Coromandel* and *Barracouta*, went on, and anchored above the four Barrier Forts, about five miles below the city. The boats, being sent in, took possession of the works, two of which fired ere they were taken, and consequently suffered a slight loss. In the forts "were about 150 guns, from one foot bore[4] to four pounders."

---

[1] Posted, Sept. 7th, 1857.   [2] Oct. 18th.
[3] She had been condemned, and had been for some time awaiting sale.
[4] This was a brass gun.   Journal of Capt. J. S. Hand.

The *Barracouta* was ordered to follow the *Samson*; and the Commander-in-Chief, having dismantled and burnt the forts, continued his route to Canton, off which he arrived at 2 P.M., and where he learnt that boats from the *Samson* and *Barracouta* had quietly occupied the Blenheim Fort, and also the Macao Fort, a strong island position mounting 86 guns.

Mr. Parkes formally announced Seymour's arrival to the High Commissioner, and explained not only what had been done, but also that further measures of like nature would be adopted unless reparation should be forthcoming. The High Commissioner chose to remain obdurate.

On the morning of October 24th, Sir Michael landed additional Marines to aid detachments which were already ashore in Canton from the *Sibylle* and *Encounter* for the protection of the factory; and he himself went in the *Coromandel* to join the *Barracouta* off Macao Fort. Upon a preconcerted signal, the Bird's Nest Fort, mounting 35 guns, and a small fort, which being opposite the city, might have annoyed the factory, were seized without resistance. The Shameen Forts, at the head of the Macao passage, were subsequently treated in the same way; and all the guns and ammunition in them were rendered unserviceable or were destroyed.

Detecting no signs whatsoever of submission on the part of the Chinese, but rather a more intractable disposition than ever, Seymour landed the rest of his Marines and a body of small-arm men to secure the factory, and stationed boats to guard against the approach of fire rafts, and attacks by water. This necessary work was superintended by Captain William King Hall, and the Marines on shore were placed under Captain Penrose Charles Penrose, R.M., of the *Winchester*, while Captain Cowper, R.E., who had been sent for the purpose from Hong Kong, advised as to the strengthening of the weak points of the position. For the protection of American interests, officers, seamen, and marines were landed at the same time from the U.S. corvette *Portsmouth*, Commander Andrew H. Foote, U.S.N.

On October 25th possession was taken of Dutch Folly, a 50-gun fort on a small island opposite Canton; and it was garrisoned by 140 officers and men under Commander William Rae Rolland, of the *Calcutta*. All the defences of the city were then in British hands; and the Commander-in-Chief desired Mr. Parkes to write to the High Commissioner that operations would cease when his Excellency should be prepared satisfactorily to settle the points in dispute.

His Excellency did not reply as Seymour had anticipated. At 12.30 P.M., a body of Chinese troops, part of a much larger force in its rear, attacked the position at the factory, in spite of Mr. Parkes's warning; but Penrose, with his Marines, drove back the enemy, killing and wounding about 14 of them. On the 26th, it being Sunday, the men were allowed to rest.

Early on the morning of the 27th, Seymour caused a new letter to be written to the High Commissioner, informing him that, since satisfaction had not been offered for the *Arrow* outrage, operations would be continued. At Bowring's suggestion an additional demand was made to the effect that all foreign representatives should be allowed the same free access to the city, and to the authorities at Canton, as was enjoyed under treaty at the other four ports, and denied at Canton only.

No reply being vouchsafed, fire was opened at 1 P.M. on the High Commissioner's compound from the 10-in. pivot gun of the *Encounter*, and kept up at intervals of from five to ten minutes until sunset. At the same time, the *Barracouta*, from a position which she had taken up at the head of Sulphur Creek, shelled some troops who were on the hills behind Gough's Fort. The High Commissioner retaliated by publicly offering a reward of 30 dollars for the head of every Englishman. A few gunners of the Royal Artillery, who had joined under Captain Guy Rotton, R.A., were that day stationed in the Dutch Folly, where two 32-prs. from the *Encounter* had been mounted.

On the 28th, these guns opened with the object of clearing a passage to the city wall. In the course of the day, Captain the Hon. Keith Stewart (2), of the *Nankin*, 50, joined the Rear-Admiral, with 140 of his men, and a couple of field-pieces; and 65 officers and men from the U.S. corvette *Levant* reinforced the American guard ashore. During the following night, the enemy apparently mounted guns on the city wall; and, anxious to give them no further opportunity for improving their defences, Seymour reopened fire early on the 29th. In the course of the morning, Commander William Thornton Bate, late of the *Bittern*, and acting Master Charles George Johnston, at some personal risk, ascertained that the breach was practicable; and a body of Marines and small-arm men, about 300 in number, was told off for the assault, under the command of Commodore Elliot.

The Rear-Admiral accompanied the advance from the boats, which landed the force, and two field-pieces at 2 P.M. The seamen were led by the Commodore, Captain the Hon. Keith Stewart (2), and Commanders Bate and Rolland ;[1] the Marines by Captains Penrose, and Robert Boyle, R.M. ; and the gun-detachment by Lieutenants James Henry Bushnell and James Stevenson Twysden ; Bate gallantly showing the way, and carrying an ensign to the summit of the breach, the wall on each side of which was quickly occupied. Penrose moved to the gate next on the right, and, having signalled his presence there, opened it to a further detachment which was instantly landed under Captain William King Hall, Commander Fortescue, and Flag-Lieutenant George Campbell Fowler.[2] The gate was then blown to pieces,[3] and the archway above it partially destroyed. In the meantime the guns had been placed in the breach, and had opened on some Chinese who began a desultory fire from their gingals, by which three people were killed, and eleven (two mortally) wounded. The latter were sent to Dutch Folly, where they were attended to by Surgeon Charles Abercromby Anderson, M.D., and Assistant-Surgeon George Bruce Newton. The Rear-Admiral, with the Commodore and Mr. Parkes, visited the house of the High Commissioner, and, at sunset, re-embarked with all his force, his object being, as he said in his dispatch, to demonstrate his power to enter the city. It is right, however, to add, that in the squadron the retirement was attributed to the impossibility of making a lodgment.[4] At all events, its moral effect was bad ; and it is scarcely astonishing that, in the night, the enemy filled up the breach with sandbags and timber. On the 30th and two following mornings it was cleared again by fire from the ships.

Seymour once more wrote to the High Commissioner, sending him indeed two letters, neither of which produced a satisfactory reply. In the interval, in order to protect the factory from the dangers of incendiary fires, the houses between it and the city were pulled down ; and copies of the Rear-Admiral's letters, with a *précis* of the whole affair by Mr. Parkes, were distributed among the people through the medium of the native boatmen, who, in spite of what was going on, continued to furnish supplies to the ships. On the

[1] Posted, Aug. 10th, 1857.   [2] Com., Aug. 10th, 1857.   [3] By Capt. Rotton, R.A.
[4] Hand: Journal. See also Officer's letter in *Naut. Mag.*, 1857, p. 153.

31st, Captain Thomas Wilson joined, with 90 officers and men from his ship, the *Winchester*.

On November 3rd, the *Encounter*, *Samson*, and Dutch Folly began a slow fire on the government buildings in the Tartar city, and on Gough's Fort, and continued it till 5 P.M. Seymour also addressed yet another letter to the High Commissioner. At night an attempt was made to blow up the English clubhouse, in which were some seamen and Marines; and, in consequence, no native boats were thereafter allowed to approach the sea-wall of the factory.

On the 4th, fire was resumed for four hours, and on the 5th, one of the *Samson's* 68-prs. in Dutch Folly threw shells into a distant fort on a hill behind the city. That day information was received to the effect that an attack was intended upon the ships and the factory, and that twenty-three war junks were at anchor below Dutch Folly, protected by French Folly Fort, which mounted 26 guns.

Commodore Elliot was ordered to take the *Barracouta*, *Coromandel*, and ships' boats, and disperse or capture the junks; and, Commander Bate having buoyed the narrow channel, the force proceeded at daylight on the 6th, and Fortescue presently anchored the *Barracouta* 800 yards above French Folly, and within 200 yards of the nearest of the hostile vessels, which were all ready for action. The *Barracouta*, in order to prevent the Chinese from training their guns on her, fired her bow pivot gun as she approached, and so provoked the enemy, who, from more than 150 pieces, retaliated ere she could bring her broadside to bear. In about five-and-thirty minutes, however, her grape and canister, and the approaching boats, under Captain Thomas Wilson, drove the people from their vessels; and the sloop was then able to give her undivided attention to French Folly, which, being soon silenced, was taken possession of by a landing-party under Captain King Hall. Its guns and ammunition were destroyed. Two 32-prs. in Dutch Folly rendered material help during the engagement. The junks, being aground, or sunk, were burnt, with the exception of the admiral's ship, which was brought off, and two more, which escaped for the time, though one of them was afterwards burnt by Captain King Hall. Seymour mentions with praise the conduct of Commander Fortescue, of his senior Lieutenant, William Kemptown Bush, and of Lieutenant Henry Hamilton Beamish, of the *Calcutta*, who, under a very heavy fire, carried out the anchor by means of which the *Barracouta*[1] was enabled to spring her broadside. The affair, very bloody to the enemy, cost the British a loss of but 1 killed and 4 wounded.

On November 7th, the *Niger*, 13, screw, Captain the Hon. Arthur Auckland Leopold Pedro Cochrane, C.B., arrived from England ; and a detachment from the frigate *Virginie* landed to protect French interests at the factory.

At 4 A.M. on the 8th, the squadron was suddenly alarmed by a bold attempt on the part of the enemy to destroy it with fire-vessels. The Chinese sailed four large junks down the river, and anchored them when they were close to the *Barracouta*, *Samson*, and *Niger* ; whereupon they instantly burst into a blaze. The *Barracouta* must infallibly have been burnt had she not slipped her cable with extra-ordinary promptitude. The junks were backed up by war-boats ; but no damage was done, except to the Chinese. To prevent any similar occurrence Seymour caused lines of junks to be drawn across the river, above and below the shipping ; nor was the precaution needless. On the 12th, one of the junks of the upper line was burnt by means of a stinkpot ; and on the 13th, two small fire-boats which had been sent from the shore, exploded alongside the *Niger*. Thenceforward no native boats whatsoever were allowed within the lines of junks.

In the meantime, at the advice of Sir John Bowring, the Rear-Admiral threatened the High Commissioner with the destruction of the Bogue forts ; but, failing, as before, to coerce him into submission, he left Commodore Elliot, with the *Samson* and *Niger*, to protect the factory, and on the afternoon of the 11th proceeded in the *Encounter* below the Bogue, where he found the *Calcutta*, in which he rehoisted his flag, *Nankin*, 50, *Barracouta*, *Hornet*, 17, screw, Commander Charles Codrington Forsyth, just arrived from Hong Kong, and *Coromandel*. On the 12th, the mandarin in charge was summoned to deliver up the forts, pending the Emperor of China's decision concerning the conduct of the Viceroy and High Commissioner ; and the *Calcutta* and *Nankin* were placed in positions favourable for action. As the demand was refused, the ships opened fire at 10.45 A.M. against the two Wantung Islands forts from the Bremer Channel side ; and, after a considerable but ill-directed

[1] Her hull was pierced by 28 large shot, besides smaller ones. *Naut. Mag.*, 1857, p. 154.

resistance for about an hour,[1] sent ashore parties which took possession of them. In the *Nankin* a boy was killed, and 4 men were wounded ; but fortunately there were no other casualties. The forts were fully manned, and mounted upwards of 200 guns ; and they were stronger than when taken in 1841. On the 13th, the Anunghoy forts, on the opposite side of the Bogue, were attacked and taken in a similar manner. They mounted 210 guns, but were captured without loss to the British. On the 14th, the Commander-in-Chief returned to the *Niger* off Canton. Concluding his report of these events, Seymour wrote : —

"The command of the river being now in our hands, I have no operation in immediate contemplation beyond the security and maintenance of our position ; and it will remain with H.M. Government to determine whether the present opportunity shall be made available to enforce to their full extent the treaty stipulations which the Canton government has hitherto been allowed to evade with impunity. . . . The original cause of dispute, though comparatively trifling, has now, from the injurious policy pursued by the Imperial High Commissioner, assumed so very grave an aspect as to threaten the existence of amicable relations as regards Canton. Though I shall continue to take steps, in conjunction with H.M. Plenipotentiary, in the hope of being able to bring matters to a successful termination, I shall be most anxious to receive the instructions of H.M. Government on this important question." [2]

The *Encounter* was stationed close off the factory as a guard ; and the *Samson* was sent below the Barrier forts to join the *Comus*, 14, Commander Robert Jenkins, which was subsequently moved to below the Bogue to protect trade, and was relieved by the *Hornet*. On December 2nd, the *Samson* was ordered to the neighbourhood of Hong Kong, where petty piracy had become very troublesome. While, however, Seymour allowed the Chinese a short respite, the foolish conduct of the mandarins, and the intractableness of Yeh, provoked a conflict with the United States' ships in the river.

On December 6th, at the back of Stonecutters' Island, near Hong Kong, the *Samson*, after an exciting chase of a couple of hours, drove ashore several junks and destroyed five, besides liberating two market boats with passengers on board. These petty pirates flew the flag of the Ti-ping rebels ; and it was consequently somewhat difficult for Captain Hand to make certain of their true status until he caught them, as it were, red-handed.[3] In the Canton

---

[1] The majority of the logs make the time to have been nearer two hours.

[2] Seymour to Adlty., Nov. 14th.

[3] Hand to Seymour, Dec. 6th, 1856. Hand took two more piratical boats on Dec. 29th, off Tongboo, he having been sent in the interim to Amoy.

river little was done by the British during the winter months, beyond what was rendered necessary by the provocative action of the Chinese. On December 6th, it became advisable to capture French Folly Fort, which had been reoccupied ; and the work was easily accomplished by the *Encounter* and *Barracouta*, and landing parties from the squadron. On January 4th, 1857, an attack on Macao Fort, which was garrisoned by Marines of the squadron, was repulsed with no greater difficulty ; and, later in the course of the same month, an attempt by war junks on the ships in the Macao channel was frustrated by the action of the *Hornet, Comus, Encounter, Niger,* and *Coromandel.* In returning to Canton with stores for the squadron, the *Samson* had an experience which brought much adverse criticism upon her gallant Captain, who, as will be seen, did not in the least deserve it. On the morning of January 17th, 1857, while passing above the second bar, she fell in with a large fleet of mandarin junks,[1] which opened a heavy fire on her, and mortally wounded her pilot. Hand returned the fire as he approached, and, when abreast of the enemy, gave the order to stop the engines, with the object, no doubt, of doing as much damage as possible ere he went on. But although the Chinese shot had hulled the steamer in a dozen places, and wounded three people, Commodore Elliot, who happened to be taking passage, directed the *Samson* to proceed. Hand admits in his journal that he believes that he did no harm to the enemy, but chivalrously says nothing about the Commodore's order. I have the fact, however, from an officer who heard the order given.

The harrying tactics of the Chinese, who seldom left the squadron alone for many hours together, annoying it almost every night with rockets, fire rafts, and all sorts of devilments, led Rear-Admiral Seymour to doubt the possibility of keeping the river communication open with the small force at his disposal ; and, learning from India that no troops could be spared thence, he was disposed partially to withdraw from his position. The *Niger* left her station off the factory and anchored abreast of Macao Fort ; the *Encounter* did likewise ; and Dutch Folly was evacuated, and instantly reoccupied and burnt by the enemy. But it was finally determined to hold Macao Fort, and to keep at least the lower reaches of the river open. The mandarin junks which had attacked the *Samson*

---

[1] Fast armed craft, otherwise called "snake boats." Cf. ancient "esnecca," Vol. I., 101.

on January 17th, and which generally lay in Escape Creek, had a brush with the *Hornet* in February, and lost one of their number, a vessel mounting sixteen guns, some of which were British Board of Ordnance 32-prs.; but they remained very troublesome, and, as they were about 120 in number, the *Hornet* and *Samson* were for a time stationed off the mouth of the creek to observe them. In March, in Sandy Bay, the *Hornet* destroyed 17 large lorchas and junks. On April 6th, the two vessels, with the tenders, *Hongkong* and *Sir Charles Forbes*, stood in to Deep Bay, as far as the depth of water would permit, in search of some junks, and, finding several, sent their boats, and those of the *Sibylle* and *Nankin*, up a creek, where 11 junks and 2 lorchas were taken and destroyed. Numerous other craft were taken or burnt up and down the coast during the six or seven weeks following; and in the course of that period the British force in the river was reinforced; but the *Raleigh*, 50, Commodore the Hon. Henry Keppel, C.B., one of the vessels which should have joined the flag, struck on an obstruction between Hong Kong and Macao on April 14th, and had to be beached between the Koko and Typa Islands, where she ultimately became a total loss. Keppel shifted his broad pennant to the *Alligator* (hospital ship), and managed to save all his stores, guns, etc. At about the same time there arrived the good news that, although there was nothing like unanimity in England on the Chinese question, and although Seymour and Bowring were held to have acted imprudently, 5000 troops were to be sent out, and strong measures were to be adopted for the settlement of all difficulties, seeing that the action of those on the spot had put the credit of the country at stake, and that it must be supported.

Towards the end of May, therefore, active operations were resumed, the first blows being dealt at the troublesome mandarin fleet in Escape Creek, an eastward branch of the Canton River,[1] by a flotilla under the orders of Commodore Elliot.

On May 25th, Elliot went on board the tender *Hongkong*, and, followed by the gunboats *Bustard*, Lieutenant Tathwell Benjamin Collinson, *Staunch*,[2] Lieutenant Leveson Wildman, and *Starling*, Lieutenant Arthur Julian Villiers, and the tender *Sir Charles Forbes*, in the order named, towing boats manned from the *Sibylle*, *Raleigh*, *Tribune*, *Hornet*, *Inflexible*, and *Fury*, steamed into the creek, and

---

[1] See Map, Vol. VI., p. 286.

[2] The *Staunch* seems to have subsequently fallen astern.

soon sighted 41 junks, which were moored across the stream, and
which opened a spirited fire from their guns – in each case a 24- or
32-pr. forward, and four or six 9-prs. The attacking craft then
formed in line in as wide order as possible, and replied warmly, the
Chinese sticking to their guns wonderfully well, but finally cutting
their cables, hoisting their sails, getting out their sweeps, and fleeing
further up. The steamers pursued until they grounded ; and then
their people abandoned them temporarily, and, jumping into the
boats, pulled hard after the enemy. One by one, several of the
junks were overhauled. In most cases the Chinese, when a boat
got alongside, fired a last broadside of grape and langridge at her,
leapt overboard on the other side, and swam for shore. Thus sixteen
craft were disposed of in the main channel, by boats led by Captain
Harry Edmund Edgell, of the *Tribune*, 31, screw. Ten more took
refuge up a minor creek on the left, and were chased by a division
of boats under Commander Charles Codrington Forsyth ; whereupon
their crews set them on fire and abandoned them. One vessel,

ADMIRAL SIR WILLIAM GRAHAM, K.C.B.

which made for a creek on the right, was abandoned so hastily
that her people had no time to fire her ; and she was taken and
towed out. The other junks got away by dint of hard pulling.
The heat was terrible, and, although there were only two casualties
from the enemy's shot, some damage was done by sunstroke.

   In addition to some of the officers named above, the following
were mentioned by the Commodore with approval, in consequence
of their share in that day's work : Commander John Corbett ;[1]
Lieutenants Arthur Metivier Brock,[2] and Edward Frederic Dent ;[2]
acting-Mates Ralph Abercrombie Brown,[3] and Thomas Keith
Hudson ;[4] and Second-Master John Molloy.

   On the following day, the outlets into the main stream of all
the creeks communicating with Escape Creek were guarded : the

---

[1] Posted, Aug. 10th, 1857.   [3] Actg. Lieut., May 25th, 1857.
[2] Coms., Aug. 10th, 1857.   [4] Actg. Lieut., Aug. 10th, 1857.

Sawshee channel by the *Tribune*, Captain Harry Edmund Edgell ; the Second Bar Creek by the *Inflexible*, Commander John Corbett ; and Escape Creek itself by the *Hornet*, Commander Charles Codrington Forsyth, the idea being to scour the inland waters, and oblige all junks in them either to fight or to flee towards the guarded passages. At daybreak on the 27th, the Commodore and the boats, towed for ten or twelve miles by the steamers, proceeded up the Sawshee channel. About ten miles above where the steamers had been left, the city of Touan-Kouan was sighted, and the mastheads of many war junks were observed over the land. The boats, although threatened by a small battery, pulled on with such speed as to take the enemy completely by surprise. Both battery and junks were abandoned almost as soon as the boats opened fire on them ; and orders were at once given to destroy all the vessels except one, the finest and heaviest armed war junk Elliot had ever seen in China. Owing, however, to the opposition of the enemy, who plied their gingals from among the houses on the banks of the narrow creek, all the junks had to be burnt. Even this could not be accomplished until landings had been effected to clear the neighbourhood. The force then withdrew. Elliot, in his letter to Seymour, says nothing about the number of people wounded ; but it was much more considerable than on the 25th.[1] He mentions, however, with approval Captain Edgell ; Commanders Forsyth,[2] Corbett,[2] and Edward Winterton Turnour [2] (late of the *Raleigh*) ; Lieutenants Edward Nares, and William Lowley Staniforth ; [3] acting-Mate Thomas Keith Hudson ; Chaplain and Naval Instructor the Rev. Samuel Beal, who was very useful as Chinese interpreter, and Lieutenant George Lascelles Blake, R.M.[4]

During all this time the Chinese force, consisting of the large fleet of war junks which had attacked Macao Fort on January 4th, and which had afterwards tried to block the Macao channel, lay in Fatshan Creek. The Commander-in-Chief had been for some days at Hong Kong, when, leaving Captain William King Hall there in the *Calcutta*, he embarked on May 29th in the paddle tender *Coromandel*, Lieutenant Sholto Douglas, and, accompanied by

---

[1] No one was killed ; but 31 people were wounded, including Lieuts. Francis Martin Norman (*Tribune*), and Henry Edmund Bacon (*Inflexible*); Mids. Arthur Edward Dupuis, and Edward Pilkington (*Inflexible*); and Asst.-Surg. Miles Monk Magrath (*Inflexible*).

[2] Posted, Aug. 10th, 1857.　　　　　　　　　　[3] Com., Aug. 10th, 1857.

[4] Elliot to Seymour, May 29th.

several gunboats, and by the boats of the flagship, under Commander William Rae Rolland,[1] entered the Canton River and proceeded as far as the second bar. His immediate object was to deal with the junks in Fatshan Creek, as those in Escape Creek had been already dealt with by Commodore Elliot. Some way up the creek, and nearly south of Canton, is Hyacinth Island, a flat expanse which very much narrows the channels. On the south side of the creek is a high hill, upon which the Chinese had built a 19-gun fort; opposite to it was a 6-gun battery; in the channel, moored so as to command the passage, were seventy junks; and

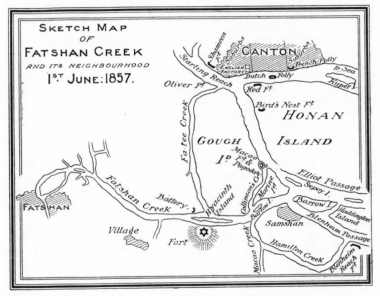

the whole position was so strong as to be deemed impregnable by those who held it. Seymour caused his force to make rendezvous on May 31st, a short distance below the obstruction; and before dawn on June 1st he led to the attack in the *Coromandel*, with the *Haughty* following, each vessel having on board a detachment of seamen, under Commodore Elliot, and Marines, under Captain Robert Boyle, R.M., and towing boats manned and armed. This force constituted the first division, the mission of which was to capture the 19-gun fort and its outworks. Commodore the Hon. Henry Keppel, in the *Hongkong*, Lieutenant James Graham Goodenough, with the second, third, and fourth divisions, was ordered;

[1] Posted, Aug. 10th, 1857.

upon seeing the assaulting party mounting the hill, to advance up the channel on the other side of Hyacinth Island, and attack the junks.[1]

Sir Michael Seymour, in his dispatch, gives the following account of what occurred :—

" The flight of several signal rockets showed that the Chinese were fully alive to our proceedings. When within about 1000 yards of the fort, the *Coromandel* grounded on a barrier of sunken junks filled with stones; and the enemy opened fire. The leading party of seamen and Marines were immediately put in the boats, and sent ahead; and, under a very heavy fire of round and grape, in which the junk fleet joined, the fort was almost immediately in our possession, Commodore Elliot setting the good example of being one of the first in it. The landing was partially covered by the fire of the *Haughty*. One or two of the guns in the fort were immediately turned on the war junks. Happily this important service was effected without loss.

" The position was a remarkably strong one, and, defended by a body of resolute troops, might have bid defiance to any attack. The *Haughty*, having landed her party, went on, with Commodore Elliot and the boats of the first division, to co-operate with Commodore Keppel. I ordered a portion of the Royal Marines, under Lieutenant and Adjutant Burton,[2] to remain as a garrison in the fort, and sent Captain Boyle,[3] with the remainder, about 150 in number, to the scene of operations by land, to cut off the enemy retreating from the junks, and to prevent the advancing boats being annoyed by gingals or matchlocks from a large village adjoining—a favourite tactic with the Chinese. One half of this force was ultimately sent back to the fort, and the remainder rejoined the squadron up the creek.

" As soon as Commodore the Hon. H. Keppel perceived the men of the first division ascending the heights, he advanced up the channel on the east side of Hyacinth Island, with the gun and other boats of the second, third, and fourth divisions, in the order stated in the programme. With the exception of the *Haughty* and *Plover*, the gunboats soon grounded, but, agreeably with my instructions, the boats were pushed ahead. The junks, which were admirably moored in position to enfilade the whole of the attacking force, soon opened a very heavy fire, keeping it up with great spirit, until our boats were close alongside, when the crews commenced to abandon their vessels, and to effect

---

[1] Vessels employed in the action in Fatshan Creek :—

Coromandel, padd. tender	R.-Adm. Sir Michael Seymour (2), K.C.B.
	Lieut. Sholto Douglas (Com., Ap. 28th, 1858).
Hongkong, padd. tender .	Commod. Hon. Henry Keppel, C.B.
	Lieut. James Graham Goodenough (Com., Feb. 26th, 1858).
Haughty, scr. g.-b. . . .	Commod. Hon. Chas. Gilb. Jno. Brydone Elliot, C.B.
	Lieut. Richard Vesey Hamilton (Com., Aug. 10th, 1857).
Plover, scr. g.-b. . . .	Lieut. Keith Stewart (3).
Opossum, scr. g.-b. . .	Lieut. Colin Andrew Campbell (Com., Feb. 26th, 1858).
Bustard, scr. g.-b. . .	Lieut. Tathwell Benj. Collinson.
Forester, scr. g.-b. . .	Lieut. Arthur John Innes.
Starling, scr. g.-b. . .	Lieut. Arthur Julian Villiers.
Staunch, scr. g.-b. . .	Lieut. Leveson Wildman.

and boats from the *Calcutta*, *Nankin*, *Raleigh*, *Tribune*, *Highflyer*, *Inflexible*, *Niger*, *Sibylle*, *Hornet*, *Fury*, *Elk*, *Acorn*, and *Cruiser*.

[2] Lieut. Cuthbert Ward Burton, R.M.

[3] Capt. Robert Boyle, R.M.

their escape across the paddy fields. The blowing up of one or two junks hastened this movement. In about twenty minutes we had possession of fifty junks.

"Leaving the third and fourth divisions to secure the prizes, Commodore Keppel then proceeded about three miles further up the creek, where more mastheads were visible; and found twenty junks moored across the stream in a very strong position, which opened such a well-directed and destructive fire that he was obliged to retire, and wait for reinforcements. The launch of the *Calcutta* was sunk by a round shot; the Commodore's galley had three round shot through her; and several other boats were much injured. On additional boats coming up, the Commodore shifted to the *Calcutta's* black barge,[1] and again advanced; and, after a severe action, the enemy gave way. They were pursued as far as Fatshan, a distance of seven miles, and seventeen of them captured and burnt. In consequence of my orders not to molest this large and important city, the three junks which passed through the creek on which it is built effected their escape.

"The result of this expedition was the capture of between seventy and eighty heavily-armed junks, mounting, on an average, from ten to fourteen guns (many of them long 32-pounders), nearly all of European manufacture. As no object would have been gained by removing the prizes, I caused them, with a few exceptions, to be burnt; and the flames and numerous heavy explosions must have been seen and heard far and wide.

"This engagement opens a new era in Chinese naval warfare. Great judgment was shown in selecting the position for the fleet; and the Chinese, particularly the last division attacked by Commodore Keppel, defended their ships with skill, courage, and effect.

"I enclose a list of casualties, which, I regret to say, is large, amounting to 3 officers, and 10 seamen and Marines, killed, and 4 officers, and 40 seamen and Marines wounded;[2] but it is to me a matter of surprise that, under the circumstances of the case, the loss was not greater."

Declaring that all did their duty, the Commander-in-Chief recommended the Admiralty, in the bestowal of marks of its approval, to have regard to the seniority and services of those engaged. He mentioned by name only the two Commodores,[3] and Master George Raymond, of the *Encounter*,[4] who had volunteered his services as pilot, and taken the *Hongkong* up Fatshan Creek—"a service of danger." Nor did Keppel, in his letter, dated from "the *Raleigh's* tender, *Sir Charles Forbes*," on July 2nd, single out individuals for special praise, beyond saying that Captain the Hon. Arthur Auckland Leopold Pedro Cochrane led the final seven miles' chase; but in a letter to his sister, the Hon. Mrs. H. F. Stephenson, the Commodore

---

[1] In this he returned to the *Hongkong*, where he shifted into the (late) *Raleigh's* cutter.

[2] The officers killed were Master's-Assistant E. C. Bryan (*Highflyer*), Mids. H. Barker (*Tribune*), and Major Kearney. The officers wounded were Capt. Hon. A. A. L. P. Cochrane; Lieut. John Stanley Graham; and Mids. Edward Pilkington, and Henry Nelson Hippisley. Master's-Assistant B. Staunch, who was slightly hurt, is not included.

[3] Keppel, in consequence, was made a K.C.B., and Elliot a C.B. on Sept. 12th, 1857.

[4] Then lying off Macao.

gives some characteristic details. After describing the grounding of the *Hongkong,* Keppel goes on :—

" Took with me Prince Victor of Hohenlohe,[1] having previously been commanded by her Majesty, through Sir Charles Phipps, to take every care of him, and left Victor Montagu,[2] my proper gig's Mid., on board; but the lifting tide soon put him in the midst. The first division of the Chinese were attacked simultaneously by about 1900 men. I had not more than a quarter of that number to attack the second division, which was three miles higher up the river. . . . Boarding nets were dropped on our boats, but not until our men were alongside ; and it enabled them all the quicker to sever the cables connecting the junks. *Raleigh's* boats well up, and did not require cheering on. The Chinese fired occasional shots to ascertain exact distance, but did not open their heaviest fire until we were within 600 yards. Nearly the first fellow cut in two by a round shot was an amateur, Major Kearney[3]. . . . We cheered, and were trying to get to the front when a shot struck our boat, killing the bow man. Another was cut in two. Prince Victor leant forward to bind up the man's arm with his neck-cloth. While he was so doing, a shot passed through both sides of the boat, wounding two more of the crew : in short, the boat was sunk under us. . . .

" The tide rising, boats disabled, our oars shot away, it was necessary to re-form. I was collared, and drawn from the water by young Michael Seymour,[4] a Mate of his uncle's flagship, the *Calcutta.* We were all picked up except the dead bow man. . . As we retired, I shook my fist at the junks, promising I would pay them off. We went to the *Hongkong,* and re-formed. I hailed Lieutenant Graham[5] to get his boat ready, as I would hoist the broad pennant for next attack in his boat. I had no sooner spoken than he was down, the same shot killing and wounding four others. Graham was one mass of blood ; but it was from a Marine who stood next to him, part of whose skull was forced three inches into another man's shoulder. When we reached the *Hongkong,* the whole of the Chinese fire appeared to be centered on her. She was hulled twelve times in a few minutes. Her deck was covered with the wounded who had been brought on board from different boats. From the paddle-box we saw that the noise of guns was bringing up strong reinforcements. The account of our having been obliged to retire had reached them. They were pulling up like mad. The *Hongkong* had floated, but grounded again. A bit of blue bunting[6] was prepared to represent a broad pennant, and I called out, 'Let's try the row-boats once more, boys,' and went over the side into our cutter (*Raleigh's*), in which were Turnour,[7] and the faithful coxswain, Spurrier.[8] At this moment there arose from the boats, as if every man took it up at the same instant, one of those British cheers so full of meaning that I knew at once it was all up with John Chinaman. They might sink twenty boats, but there were thirty others which would go ahead all the faster. It was indeed an exciting sight. A move among the junks ! They were breaking ground and moving off, the outermost first. This the Chinese performed in good order, without slacking fire. Then commenced an exciting chase for seven miles. As our shot told they ran

---

[1] H.S.H. Prince Victor F. F. E. A. C. F., of Hohenlohe-Langenberg, Count Gleichen, died a retired vice-admiral in 1891. He was a nephew of Queen Victoria.

[2] Hon. Victor Alexander Montagu, retd. as a Capt., 1877.

[3] D.A.Q.G. of China Exped. Force.

[4] Later Adm. Sir Michael Culme-Seymour, G.C.B.

[5] Lieut. James Stanley Graham, of the *Calcutta.* Died a Capt., Feb. 3rd, 1873.

[6] Keppel was then Commod. of the Blue, or third class.

[7] Edward Winterton Turnour, late Com. of the *Raleigh.*

[8] Wounded.

mostly on to the mud banks, and their crews forsook them. Young Cochrane [1] in his
light gig got the start of me. . . . Seventeen junks were overtaken and captured.
Three only escaped. . . ." [2]

These operations had a great moral effect upon the Chinese, and
would, perhaps, have inclined them to listen to reason and to concede
Seymour's demands, had it been found possible to follow them up
promptly and with vigour. Unhappily, as will be seen, the sky was
just then black for England, and she could not for the time concentrate her attention on the Chinese question, having to wrestle elsewhere for the very life of her Eastern Empire.

It may be mentioned here that, at the beginning of June, the
Samson, being away on detached duty, learnt of the presence of
some piratical junks in Mirs Bay, off which place Captain Hand
accordingly presented himself early in the morning of June 8th.
Getting out three of his boats, under Lieutenant George Henry
Wale,[3] he sent them to cut off a craft which was seen standing into
Double Haven, and himself went round in the frigate to Crooked
Harbour, where he came upon a pirate mounting nine guns, and
having 70 men, all of whom leapt overboard and made for the shore,
only to be massacred there by the villagers. Wale, after some
resistance had been offered, took two lorchas and a junk, mounting
in all 22 guns, which were convoyed to Hong Kong, where owners
were found, and salvage money paid for them. They had apparently
been captured by the other vessel.[4] Commander John Corbett, in
the *Inflexible*, took a pirate at about the same time. It may be mentioned, too, that on June 18th, the most southern of the defences of
the Canton River, near the Bogue, and known as Chuenpee, was occupied by the British without resistance, and found to have been not only
abandoned, but also partly dismantled. It was entrusted to the command of Captain Edgell, of the *Tribune*. On July 6th, the *Samson*
towed the *Alligator*, bearing Keppel's pennant, to Hong Kong.[5]

France, like Great Britain, had with China treaties which were
not observed, and her squadron in Chinese waters would have made
common cause with Seymour's at once, had it been a little stronger
than it was. The French government, however, unwilling to let

---

[1] The Captain of the *Niger*, who was wounded. He was then 33, but his father,
Adm. Lord Dundonald, was alive.

[2] Keppel, iii., 2. The letter was printed in the *Times*.

[3] Com. Feb. 26th, 1858.   [4] Hand to Seymour, June 9th.

[5] Keppel soon afterwards went home, Sir Charles Wood disapproving of his hoisting
a broad pennant, in view of the loss of the *Raleigh*.

slip so good an occasion for settling long-standing difficulties, decided to strengthen its forces, so as to enable it to act with effect, and to send out Baron Gros with instructions to co-operate with Lord Elgin,[1] who was being despatched from England with special powers to treat concerning all pending questions. Rear-Admiral Rigault de Genouilly, who went out in the *Némésis*, 50, arrived in Chinese waters on July 8th, 1857, and, on the 15th of the same month, superseded Rear-Admiral Guérin. Thenceforward he was reinforced from time to time. Baron Gros did not reach China until October.[2]

In the meantime, large reinforcements, naval as well as military, had been sent out from England; and the *Shannon*, 51, screw, Captain William Peel, C.B., had conveyed Lord Elgin to the scene of action. But Elgin, on reaching Singapore, had learnt of the outbreak of the Mutiny in India, and, not underrating its character, had wisely taken upon himself to divert thither the troops intended for China. On July 14th, still graver news reached Seymour, who was then preparing for a trip with Lord Elgin to the gulf of Pechili; and he thereupon sent to Calcutta the *Shannon*, with 300 Marines who had arrived in China in the *Sanspareil*, 70, screw, Captain Astley Cooper Key, C.B., together with the *Pearl*, 21, screw, Captain Edward Southwell Sotheby. The two ships sailed on July 15th, and, as will be shown later, were able to render most valuable services. The *Sanspareil* herself also proceeded in August to Calcutta with artillery and stores,[3] but did not, as the other ships did, land a brigade for service with the troops in the interior of India. A party from her garrisoned Fort William for a time, but she returned to the Canton River on December 17th, in time for the operations then pending. Lord Elgin, seeing that, until the major danger should be crushed, little could be done in China, retired to Calcutta, to await a better opportunity, and left Seymour to blockade the Canton River. The blockade was declared as from August 7th, and, in the opinion of naval officers on the spot, was established not so much to annoy the Chinese as to prevent foreign vessels from going up to load, and so getting the trade into their hands at a time when the British and French were unable to enjoy a share of it.[4]

Lord Elgin returned to Hong Kong at the end of September, but

---

[1] James Bruce, 8th Earl of Elgin and Kincardine, Kt.   [2] Chevalier, 297.
[3] She was towed 745 miles of the way by the *Samson*, which expended 245 tons of coal on the run. Hand's Journal.   [4] Hand's Journal.

for some time afterwards nothing could be done, owing to the slowness with which the French squadron was reinforced, and to the absence of troops. Although, however, the 5000 men originally intended for China had, as has been shown, been diverted from their destination to meet the pressing need in India, 1500 men under General Charles T. van Straubenzee, chiefly Royal Marines, Royal Artillery, the 59th Regiment, and the 38th Madras native infantry, were placed at Seymour's disposal.

On December 10th, the French squadron anchored at the Bogue ; and Rear-Admiral Rigault de Genouilly issued a proclamation to the effect that from the 12th he should associate himself with his British colleague in the blockade of the river. On the 13th he took his force up to Whampoa; and on the day following, Seymour, transferring his flag to the *Coromandel*, also proceeded to the front with the British gunboats.

A bloody and lamentable affair occurred on December 14th. Lieutenant Bedford Clapperton Tryvellion Pim, commanding the gunboat *Banterer*, took his second gig, with fourteen people in her besides himself, up a winding creek opposite High Island to a point near the town of Sai-lau, where, leaving two men in charge, he landed with the rest of his party, and entered the place. His object, according to the correspondent of the *Illustrated London News*, who accompanied him, was partly recreation and partly information. On his return, he found that a number of Chinamen were assailing the two boat-keepers with brickbats. He charged the mob, and so got the whole of his people to the boat; but no sooner were they on board than a sharp fire was opened upon them with gingals, and later with a small gun. Pim, who displayed extraordinary personal courage, conducted the retreat along the narrow creek, standing in the stern-sheets, and using his revolver with great effect; but the fire was so hot, and victory seemed so hopeless, that one by one the people who were in a condition to do so waded ashore, and bolted in the direction of the *Nankin*, whose hull was visible over the paddy fields. Pim stuck to the boat until every other living person had deserted her, and then, using his last cartridge to shoot the Chinese leader, also leapt to land and took to his heels. Of fifteen people in the boat, five were killed outright, one died afterwards, and five more, including Pim, who was hit in six places, were wounded. On the 15th, the *Nankin*, by way of reprisals, shelled Sai-lau, and landed 250 men, who, after a determined resistance, entered the place, part of which they burnt, not, however, without suffering a loss of four wounded. Pim's [1] expedition was a most foolhardy one, and, seeing that little or no good could possibly have been derived from it, should never have been undertaken.[2] A court of inquiry, nevertheless, found that he was justified in all he had done. His gallantry gained him his promotion on April 19th, 1858.

On December 15th, the Marines, and a French detachment intended for the attack on Canton, were landed without opposition on the island of Honan, where they found excellent quarters; and in the course of the next few days the lighter vessels of the combined fleet were all stationed in readiness for the projected attack [3] upon Canton.

A final demand for satisfaction and concession had been sent to Commissioner Yeh on December 12th, and ten days had been assigned to him wherein to reply. In the interim, a battery for mortars was erected on Dutch Folly rock, and a conference of the allied chiefs was held on board the *Audacieuse*, the headquarters of Baron Gros.

Captain Chevalier explains very lucidly the situation, and the difficulties which confronted the allied Admirals.

[1] Capt. Ap. 16th, 1868; retd. rear-adm. July 5th, 1885; died, 1886.
[2] *Ill. Lond. News*, Feb. 27th, 1858. Cooke, 286.
[3] The stations of the larger vessels of the allied fleets during the bombardment were, beginning at the eastward end of the line:—

Ships.	Guns.	Commanders.	Stations.
Fr. *Primauguet*, scr.	8	Com. Vrignaud	Outside east end of Kuper Island.
Fr. *Durance*, scr.	4	Lieut. Thoyon	
Br. *Furious*, pad..	16	Capt. Sherard Osborn, C.B.	
Fr. *Dragonne*, scr. g.-v.	4	Lieut. Barry	Off French Folly.
Br. *Surprise*, scr. g.-v.	4	Com. Saml. Gurney Cresswell	Off S.E. corner of wall.
Fr. *Marceau*, scr. disp. v.	4	Com. Lefer de La Motte	Outside the island (with gunboats).
Br. *Nimrod*, scr. g.-v.	6	Com. Roderick Dew	
Fr. *Avalanche*, scr. g.-v.	4	Lieut. Lafond	
Br. *Niger*, scr.	13	Capt. Hon. A. A. L. P. Cochrane	
Br. *Hornet*, scr.	17	Com. Wm. Montagu Dowell	Off Yeh's Yamen.
Br. *Cruiser*, scr.	17	Com. Chas. Fellowes	
Br. *Bittern*, sailg.	12	Lieut. Jas. Graham Goodenough	Outside Dutch Folly.
Fr. *Mitraille*, scr. g.-v.	4	Lieut. Béranger	Inside Dutch Folly.
Fr. *Fusée*, scr. g.-v.	4	Lieut. Gabrielli de Carpégua	
Br. *Actæon*, surv.	—	Capt. Wm. Thornton Bate	Off the Factories (with gunboats).
Fr. *Phlégéton*, scr.	8	Com. Lévêque	
Br. *Hesper*, scr. store-s.	—	Mast. Jas. Stephen Hill	Off N.W. of Honan Island.
Br. *Acorn*, sailg.	12	Com. Arth. Wm. Acland Hood	

"The task to be performed with the feeble means at their disposal was," he says, "to strike a blow worthy of the strength of France and England, and, at the same time, of such a nature as to destroy Commissioner Yeh's illusions on the subject of the possibility of resisting the allies. It was one thing to make a way into Canton by main force, and altogether another thing to maintain oneself, with a few thousand men, in a city of a million inhabitants. Nor was there any doubt that, if order should cease to reign there, part of the Chinese population would give itself up to pillage, and would commit acts of brigandage which would strike at the honour of the two nations. In order to avoid such misfortunes, the Admirals and the General, after careful study, made the following dispositions. The gunboats and the lighter vessels, going in as close as their draught of water would permit, were to bombard the south face of the massive walls which surrounded Canton, so that the resulting breach would prevent the Chinese

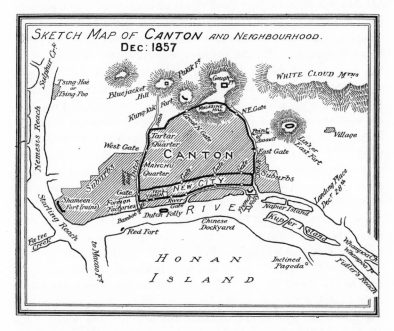

troops from communicating by way of the walls with the eastern portion. The expeditional corps, landed on that same side of the city, was to make its way along the walls, its aim being the capture of the positions which command Canton on the north. Supposing the double operation to succeed, the allies would hold Canton under the guns of the forts on the north, and under those of the squadron, which would still be ready to open on the south side; and it would then be seen whether the Imperial Commissioner would accept, without further delay, the terms offered to him."

Active hostilities were not resumed until daybreak on December 28th, when, it having become clear that the Chinese authorities would not give way an inch unless forced to do so, a general bombardment of the city was opened by the ships of the combined fleets, thirty-two in number, while the troops from Honan Island,

and a French naval brigade, were conveyed to the place of disembarkation, a point about two miles below French Folly.

After the army and the French had landed, the British Naval
Brigade, of 1500 men, commanded by Commodore Elliot, and formed
in three divisions under Captains the Hon. Keith Stewart (2) (*Nankin*),
Astley Cooper Key (*Sanspareil*), and Sir Robert John Le Mesurier
M'Clure (*Esk*),[1] also disembarked, and advanced to some rising
ground to the eastward of the city.   Lin Fort, a work on the same
side, was quickly seized by the French and the 59th; but the naval
advance was checked; and the Brigade ultimately took up a position
for the night in some buildings about 800 yards to the right of
Gough's Fort, which annoyed it with a desultory fire during the
hours of darkness.   On the morning of the 29th the Brigade joined
the rest of the force for the storm, and moved up behind a hillock,
about 800 yards from the east gate, where the men had breakfast.
At about that time, while examining the ditch and wall, and pointing
out to Seymour a good place for scaling, Captain William Thornton
Bate, of the *Actæon*, a most valuable officer, and a noted surveyor,
was shot dead with a gingal ball.[2]   At 8.30, the scaling ladders were
sent to the front, under Commander John Fane Charles Hamilton[3]
(*Elk*); and at 8.45 the general advance was sounded, the point
chosen for escalade being one which was sheltered by an angle of
the wall from the fire of Gough's Fort.   The French assaulted at a
point 500 yards distant, and were the first up, but only by a minute
or two.   Commander Charles Fellowes,[3] of the *Cruiser*, is generally
credited with having topped the wall before any other officer or
man of the Naval Brigade.   In an hour after the assault, the whole
of the heights were in possession of the allies.   The Navy opened
the north-east gate to the Marines and artillery, and some of the
Samson's and *Calcutta's* dragged up two or three field-pieces where

[1] With the First Division were Capt. Geo. Sumner Hand (*Samson*), and Coms. Jno.
Fane Chas. Hamilton (*Elk*), and Geo. Aug. Cooke Brooker (*Inflexible*), and parties
from the *Nankin, Sibylle, Samson, Racehorse,* and *Inflexible:* with the Second Division
were Coms. Arth. Wm. Acland Hood (*Acorn*), and Julian Foulston Slight (*Sanspareil*),
and parties from the *Calcutta, Sanspareil,* and *Acorn,* and from Macao Fort: with the
Third Division were Capts. Sherard Osborn, C.B., and Hon. A. A. L. P. Cochrane, C.B.,
and Coms. Wm. Montagu Dowell (*Hornet*), and Chas. Fellowes (*Cruiser*), and parties
from the *Highflyer, Esk, Niger, Furious, Hornet,* and *Cruiser.*   Genl. Order of
Dec. 26th.

[2] Mids. Henry Thompson, of the *Sanspareil*, was mortally wounded by a rocket at
about the same time.

[3] Posted, Feb. 26th, 1858.

the wall had been scaled, the guns being subsequently sent towards
the heights under Lieutenant Henry Hamilton Beamish.[1]   In the
course of a movement in the direction of Magazine Hill, where the
enemy made a stand, some further casualties, which, however, were
not very numerous,[2] took place, and Lieutenant Viscount Gilford[3]
was badly wounded.

After the city had been occupied, and Gough's Fort had been
evacuated by the Chinese, resistance ceased, though there was some
sniping till nightfall.   On the 30th, flags of truce appeared in various
places, and a message arrived from the Tartar general to the effect
that he was willing to discuss matters.   As, however, he did not
appear upon the expiration of the time assigned to him, a party
went the round of the ramparts of the old city, and spiked, or
knocked the trunnions off, all the guns there.   About 400 were

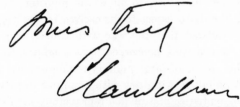

THE RT. HON. RICHARD JAMES, EARL OF CLANWILLIAM, G.C.B., K.C.M.G.,
ADMIRAL OF THE FLEET.

thus dealt with; but most of them were already honeycombed,
and almost useless.

The Chinese authorities were still obdurate.   Every proposal
made to the Imperial Commissioner was put aside by him; and
although Canton was at the mercy of the allies, it was, or presently
would be, still more at the mercy of the bands of robbers who were
gathering round it from the country, unless, indeed, the Tartar
troops, who were also assembling in the neighbourhood, should
succeed, as no doubt Yeh hoped they would, in forcing the allies to
quit both the city and the river.   A further step, therefore, had to
be taken, and, on January 5th, 1858, at daybreak, three detachments,

---

[1] Com., Feb. 26th, 1858.

[2] In the whole operations, the Naval Brigade had 7 killed or mortally wounded, and
32 wounded.   The officers killed were Capt. Wm. Thornton Bate, and Mids. Henry
Thompson : those wounded were Com. Chas. Fellowes, and Lieuts. Visct. Gilford, and
William Ormonde Butler.   The Marine Battalion lost 4 killed and 32 wounded, among
the latter being Lieut.-Col. Thos. Holloway, R.M.A., and Lieut. Wm. Fredk. Portlock
Scott Dadson.

[3] Later Adm. of the Fleet the Earl of Clanwilliam : Com. Feb. 26th, 1858.

in pursuance of a pre-arranged plan, entered the city.   One laid
hands on, and carried off, the Tartar general, Muh ; another, British,
kidnapped the governor of the city, Peh-Kwei ; and the third, also
British, abducted, and ultimately carried on board the *Inflexible*,
Yeh himself.   Captain Cooper Key, indeed, took the Commissioner
with his own hands.   The general and the governor were afterwards
sent back to carry out their duties and maintain order, under the
supervision of an international commission.   This arrangement
worked well, and it was found possible to raise the blockade of the
Canton river on February 10th.

  But China remained defiant.   After having waited in vain for
plenipotentiaries from Peking, Lord Elgin and Baron Gros determined
to go northward, hoping that a naval demonstration in the vicinity
of the capital of the empire would tend to accelerate the course of
events.   In order, moreover, to allow the ministers of the United
States and of Russia to associate themselves in the negotiations, it
was formally declared that the war with China, so far as Great
Britain and France were concerned, was confined to the city of
Canton.   The arrival of large military reinforcements in the river
enabled the Admirals to withdraw with a number of their ships.[1]

  The plenipotentiaries first invited representatives of the Emperor
of China to meet them at Shanghai, whither they proceeded ; but,
no one appearing there, they went on to the mouth of the Peiho,
where Lord Elgin anchored on April 14th, 1858.   A commissioner
named Tan was sent down to the town of Taku to negotiate, or
rather, no doubt, to procrastinate.   Soon, however, it became apparent that the enemy had no serious intention of treating on such
lines as would be agreeable to the allies.   Seymour and Rigault de
Genouilly reached the mouth of the river in April ; but part of the
naval force was slow in making the rendezvous, owing to bad
weather, the lateness of the monsoon, and the small steam power of
some of the gunboats ; and the Admirals were only just ready to act
when, on May 19th, recognising the uselessness of further delay, the
plenipotentiaries placed the matter in the hands of their fighting
colleagues.

  The British screw gun-vessels, *Nimrod*, 6, and *Cormorant*, 4,
with the French gunboats *Dragonne*, *Fusée*, *Avalanche*, and
Mitraille, had already lain for several days within the bar, and
within easy shot of the forts, though a little below them.   On the

[1] Chevalier, 305.

evening of the 19th these craft were joined by the small gun-boats *Slaney*, bearing during the attack the flags of both Admirals, *Firm*, *Opossum*, *Leven*, *Staunch*, and *Bustard*; the *Slaney*, *Firm*, *Staunch*, and *Bustard* having British, and the *Leven* and *Opossum* French landing parties on board.

"The Chinese," says Seymour, "have used every exertion to strengthen the forts at the entrance of the Peiho. Earthworks, sandbag batteries, and parapets for the heavy gingals, have been erected on both sides for a distance of nearly a mile in length, upon which eighty-seven guns in position were visible; and the whole shore had been piled [1] to oppose a landing. As the channel is only about 200 yards wide, and runs within 400 yards of the shore, these defences presented a formidable appearance. Two strong mud batteries, mounting respectively thirty-three and sixteen guns, had been also con-structed about 1000 yards up the river, in a position to command our advance. In the rear several intrenched camps were visible, defended by flanking bastions." [2]

At 8 A.M. on May 20th, Captain William King Hall and the French Flag-Captain Reynaud delivered to Commissioner Tan a summons to deliver up the forts within two hours. By 10 o'clock no reply had arrived; and a signal was hoisted for the attack to be made in the prescribed order, Commander Thomas Saumarez (2) [3] leading in the *Cormorant*, and being followed by the *Mitraille*, *Fusée*, *Avalanche*, *Dragonne*, *Nimrod*, and *Slaney*, successively, and by the five small gunboats. The vessels were directed not to fire until specifically ordered to do so; and, while the *Slaney*, 2, Lieutenant Anthony Hiley Hoskins,[4] bearing the flags of both Admirals, placed herself where she could be of most service, and could best direct operations, the other craft, having on board, or towing, landing parties, British and French, which numbered in all 1178 officers and men, were told off as follows:—

| ATTACKING THE NORTH FORTS. | | | ATTACKING THE SOUTH FORTS. | | |
| LEFT BANK. | | | RIGHT BANK. | | |
Ships.	Commanders.	Commanding Landing Party.	Ships.	Commanders.	Commanding Landing Party.
Br. *Cormorant*, 4	Com. Thomas Saumarez (2)	Capt. Sir F. W. E. Nicolson (*Pique*).	Fr. *Avalanche*, 4	Com. Lafond	Capt. W. K. Hall (*Calcutta*).
Fr. *Mitraille*, 4	Com. Béranger	Capt. Sherard Osborn, C.B. (*Furious*).	Fr. *Dragonne*, 4	Com. Barry	Com. Chas. T. Leckie (*Fury*).
„ *Fusée*, 4 .	Com. Gabrielli de Carpégua	Com. S. G. Cress-well (*Surprise*).	Br. *Nimrod*, 6	Com. ——	Com. Jas. G. Goodenough.
Br. *Staunch*, 2	Lieut. Leveson Wildman	Major Robt. Boyle, R.M.	„ *Opossum*, 2	Lieut. ——	Lieut. E. G. M'Callum, R.M.
„ *Bustard*, 2	Lieut. Fred'k. Wm. Hallowes		„ *Leven*, 2 .	Lieut. Jos. S. Hudson	
		Capt. —— Lévêque (*Phlégéton*).	„ *Firm*, 2 .	Lieut. ——	Capt. Reynaud (*Némésis*).

[1] *I.e.*, lined with piles driven into the mud.   [2] See plan, p. 126.

[3] Posted, July 27th, 1858.   [4] Com., Feb. 26th, 1858.

The *Cormorant* led off at full speed; and the Chinese opened fire almost immediately. Although Saumarez was somewhat checked by warps which the enemy had thrown across the river, and which he broke, his French consorts did not keep pace with him, and, in consequence, suffered more than he did. The signal to engage was quickly made from the *Slaney*; and, ere the vessels had anchored in their assigned positions, the effect of the return fire was very apparent, the shells bursting well in the embrasures, and dispersing men, guns, and carriages. The smaller vessels passed beyond the forts, and landed their parties on both banks on the flanks of the Chinese positions, while the larger craft, opposite the forts, occupied their direct attention. On the south side, the first fort was entirely dismantled and abandoned, and the second one partially so; and on the north side, the *Cormorant* and her French consorts completely crushed opposition. At the end of an hour and a quarter, the Chinese fire almost ceased. The landing then took place, the Admirals themselves joining Captain Hall's party; and the enemy ran. Fifty yards of mud, two feet deep, had, however, to be floundered through ere the works could be reached. In a few minutes they were covered with flags, for half the French officers had tricolors in their pockets. Soon afterwards, the French sustained severe losses by the accidental explosion of a magazine. During the operations the enemy sent down numerous junks full of flaming straw; but the *Bustard* drove off the people who were trying to guide them by means of ropes from the shore; and the craft burnt themselves out innocuously.

After the action, Nicolson and Lévêque moved up against two other forts on the north side, the 33- and 16-gun forts described by Seymour; and, supported by the fire of the *Bustard*, *Staunch*, and *Opossum*, took them with but slight loss, and also destroyed some entrenched camps in their vicinity. Everything was over by 2 P.M. When the necessary arrangements had been made at the mouth of the river, the force advanced to the town of Taku, which was occupied by Captain King Hall, Flag-Lieutenant Michael Culme-Seymour, and a party. Eighteen field-pieces were found there; and opposite the place was a boom of junks filled with combustibles, which was burnt on the 21st. The British loss in the fighting of the 20th was only 4 killed, including the Carpenter of the *Fury*, and 16 wounded, including Second-Master

Charles Prickett,[1] of the *Opossum*. The French, however, had 67 killed and wounded.[2]

On May 23rd, Seymour, in the *Coromandel*, with two other British gunboats, and Rigault de Genouilly in the *Avalanche*, with the *Fusée*, moved slowly up the river, towing a number of manned boats, and burning all the stacks of straw and small timber which might have been used for loading incendiary vessels. Such junks as were met with were ordered out of the river ; and those which did not promptly obey the order were destroyed, so that the enemy should not be left with vessels out of which he could improvise fireships. A few shells also were fired at bodies of troops ; but otherwise no hostile acts were committed by the allies, who arrived on May 26th at Tientsin, where there was no resistance.[3]

The Court of Pekin was at last seriously impressed, and sent down to the Admirals a note announcing that a high official, armed with full powers, would instantly appear to treat. Lord Elgin and Baron Gros reached Tientsin in the *Slaney* on May 30th, and were followed, at an interval of twenty-four hours, by the ministers of the United States and of Russia. In the meantime, reinforcements had been sent to the mouth of the Peiho ; and 1000 British troops, together with 500 French, were forwarded to Tientsin, which they garrisoned. There was no further dallying ; and peace was signed on June 27th.

The treaty of Tientsin contained no fewer than 56 articles, its most important provisions stipulating for : the confirmation of the treaty of Nankin ; the appointment of a British minister to Pekin ; his right of access to the Secretary of State at Pekin on a footing of equality ; toleration of Christianity ; the opening to travellers of all parts of China ; the opening, as ports, of Chinkiang, and three other ports on the Yang-tse-kiang, besides Niuchang, Tungchow, Taiwan, Swatow, and Kiungchow ; a revised tariff ; the visiting by British ships of war of any port in the Empire ; the concerting of measures for the repression of piracy ; and the arrangement of an indemnity.

---

[1] Master, Sept. 17th, 1858.

[2] Seymour's disp. in *Gazette* of July 27th : Chevalier, 306 : Corr. of *Ill. Lond. News*, and *Times*.

[3] There was, nevertheless, some friction ere the negotiations were completed. Seymour was hooted while walking in the town, and on the following day Capt. Roderick Dew and Com. Saumarez were pelted with stones ; whereupon the Com.-in-Chief ordered the Marines into the place. The Chinese endeavoured to keep them out by shutting the gates ; but Capt. Sherard Osborn and Com. Saumarez scaled the walls with their boats' crews, and admitted the Marines, who marched through the town. Hand's Journal : L. Oliphant's 'Earl of Elgin's Mission.'

It looked as if all difficulties were settled, and as if all possible causes of future difficulty were removed. The forts on the river were destroyed and evacuated; and presently the allies withdrew from the Gulf of Pechili. But appearances were deceptive. The authority of Pekin did not suffice to coerce immediately the mandarins in all other parts of the Empire; and in many districts there was at the time open rebellion. Canton was besieged, and repeatedly assaulted; on July 3rd men from the *Sanspareil* had to be landed to reinforce the army of occupation; and on July 19th, a cutter belonging to the *Amethyst*, 26, Captain Sidney Grenfell, manned by eight seamen and a Marine, under Master Richard Cossantine Dyer, while in chase of a junk in the Canton river, was attacked by a mandarin row-galley, with seventeen men armed with gingals, rockets, and stinkpots, and defended by iron plates in the vessel's bow. Dyer made an excellent fight of it for half an hour, and killed 13 of his assailants, while no one in his boat was hurt. The British made every effort to disseminate the fact and terms of the treaty among the natives; but it was extremely dangerous to do so; and an outrage perpetrated on a party from the *Starling*, 2, Lieutenant Arthur Julian Villiers, and *Nankin*, involving the killing of one seaman, and the wounding of two more at Namtao, near Hong Kong, obliged Commodore the Hon. Keith Stewart (2), of the *Nankin*, 50, and General van Straubenzee to adopt severe punitive measures, and to occupy the town on August 11th. In this affair, in addition to the troops, the *Samson*, and five gunboats with a brigade from the *Sanspareil, Cormorant*, and *Adventure*, were engaged. Among those who distinguished themselves in the action were Captain Julian Foulston Slight[1] (*Sanspareil*), Commander Thomas Saumarez (2) (*Cormorant*), and acting-Commander Edward Madden[2] (*Sanspareil*), the last of whom was severely wounded. Two brass guns, each weighing about 30 cwt., were brought off, and the place was pillaged and partially burnt.[3]

Lord Elgin went on a diplomatic mission to Japan; and, on his return, started from Hong Kong on November 8th upon an expedition up the Yang-tse-kiang as far as Hankow, a city seven hundred miles from the sea. Nankin and its neighbourhood was in the hands of the Ti-ping rebels. The Ti-pings were perfectly prepared to be friendly; but, on November 20th, misunderstanding

---

[1] Posted, Ap. 28th, 1858. [2] Com. Aug. 11th, 1858.
[3] Hand's Journal: *Ill. Lond. News*, Oct. 16th.

the objects of the gunboat *Lee*, 2, Lieutenant William Henry Jones, which had been sent ahead of the squadron to communicate if possible, their batteries opened fire on her; whereupon the other vessels of the escort, the *Retribution*, 28, paddle, Captain Charles Barker, *Furious*, 16, paddle, Captain Sherard Osborn, *Cruiser*, 17, screw, Commander John Bythesea, and *Dove*, 2, Lieutenant Charles James Bullock, attacked them, causing considerable loss.[1]   There were one or two other collisions with the Ti-pings during this expedition, notably on the following day, when the ships returned and re-engaged the Nankin forts, and on November 26th at Nganking; and, although it is now known that the rebels were acting under misapprehension, they were reported not only as having fired upon the British flag, but also as having violated a flag of truce,[2] which it is clear they did not know to be one.   These affairs, and the somewhat similar trouble with the *Hermes* in 1853, were largely responsible for the attitude taken later by Great Britain with regard to a movement which was one of the most extraordinary of the century, and which, if assisted instead of discouraged, might perhaps have effected the regeneration of China, and saved the powers of Europe from much subsequent perplexity.

In the interim various ships under the orders of the Commander-in-Chief had been active in repressing the piracy which had begun to flourish anew during the prolonged hostilities.

On August 4th, 1858, the gunboat *Staunch*, Lieutenant Leveson Wildman,[3] while on passage from Shanghai to Hong Kong, chased three pirate junks off Taon Pung, and endeavoured to lash herself alongside the largest of them, but was driven off by a shower of stinkpots, and lost a gallant seaman, Edward George, who had leapt on board the enemy in order to secure her to the *Staunch*. Wildman had only two 24-pr. howitzers on board; and they were quickly dismounted, owing to being fired rapidly; but he remounted them, renewed the engagement, boarded and captured another of the junks, and, leaving her in charge of Second-Master George Morice, chased the third in his gig, and took her also.   The big junk got away.

On August 22nd, 1858, Commander Samuel Gurney Cresswell,[4]

---

[1] In the *Retribution* Mids. Geo. Anthony Wyrley Birch lost an arm, and a blue-jacket a leg.   There were no other casualties.

[2] Wade's Report. 'Ti-ping Tien-Kwoh,' I. 220.   *North China Herald* (acc. by an officer of the squadron). L. Oliphant.

[3] Com., Oct. 15th, 1858.   [4] Posted, Sept. 17th, 1858.

with his screw gunboat the *Surprise*, 4, her boats, and the boats of the *Cambrian*, 40, attacked a number of heavily-armed piratical junks under Lingting Island, near Hong Kong. The enemy opened fire at 1600 yards as the *Surprise* approached; but she did not return it until within 1000 yards; when she steadily poured in shot and shell, and gradually closed under a storm of round shot and rockets, canister and grape. In the meantime, the *Cambrian's* boom boats, under Lieutenant John Whitmarsh Webb,[1] went in-shore of the gunboat, and took the enemy in flank. The action began at 8 A.M. By 8.35 the pirates' fire had slackened; and, at about 9, two of their largest lorchas blew up. Firing then ceased; whereupon Cresswell pushed in with his own boats, joined the boats of the *Cambrian*, and landed near the junks, just after the crews of the latter had deserted their vessels and fled to the hills. Advancing to the top of a ridge, the British discovered some more piratical craft in a snug creek on the other side of it, and, from their commanding position, killed a number of the people with their rifles, and drove off the rest. The sun was so hot that Cresswell, determining to spare his men as much as possible, returned to the gunboat, which, with the boats in tow, he took round to the creek. Having fired a few shells, he sent in the boats. No serious resistance was offered, though there was a little sniping from the neighbouring hills; and the work of burning such junks as could not be moved, and of bringing out the remainder, was accomplished without difficulty. Of twenty-six piratical craft at the island, nineteen were destroyed, and seven were carried to Hong Kong.

A third operation of a similar kind was conducted by Captain Nicholas Vansittart, C.B., of the *Magicienne*, 16, paddle, who, with the *Inflexible*, 6, paddle, Commander George Augustus Cooke Brooker, *Plover*, 2, screw, Lieutenant Robert James Wynniatt, and *Algerine*, 2, Lieutenant William Arthur, between August 26th and September 3rd, 1858, destroyed Coulan, an old piratical headquarters, together with a 14-gun stockade, 26 armed junks, and 74 row-boats, mounting 236 guns; and killed 372 pirates.[2]

In April, 1859, Rear-Admiral Sir Michael Seymour (2) returned to England, upon the expiration of his term of service, and his supersession by Rear-Admiral James Hope, C.B.; and on May 20th he was rewarded for his work in China with a G.C.B. Hope was soon confronted with difficulties, most of which arose out of the

[1] Com., Nov. 5th, 1858.　　　[2] Seymour's disps. *Gazette*, Nov. 2, 1858.

fact that the Chinese placed one construction upon the terms of
the treaty of Tientsin, while the British and French placed another.
Lord Elgin had also returned to England; and in his stead, as
Plenipotentiary and Envoy Extraordinary, his brother, the Hon.
Frederick W. A. Bruce, had been sent out to proceed to Pekin, with
the new French envoy, M. de Bourboulon, who arrived in the
corvette *Duchayla,* accompanied by the dispatch vessel *Norzagaran.*

SIR JAMES HOPE, G.C.B., ADMIRAL OF THE FLEET.

*(By permission of Mr. T. McLean, from the engraving by T. Davey, after the painting
by Sydney Hodges, at Greenwich.)*

Hope, with a squadron,[1] and the French vessels, arrived off the
island of Sha-lui-tien, in the gulf of Pechili, on June 17th, 1859;
and, on the following day, proceeded to the mouth of the Peiho
in order, as he explains, to intimate to the local authorities the
intended appearance of the ministers, and to reconnoitre " the

[1] *Chesapeake,* 51, screw (flag), *Magicienne,* 16, padd., *Highflyer,* 21, screw, *Cruiser,* 17,
screw, *Fury,* 6, padd., *Assistance,* screw store-ship, *Hesper,* screw store-ship, and the
gun-vessels and gunboats named later in the text.

existing state of the defences of the river." These last seemed to consist principally of the reconstruction, in earth, and in an improved form, of the works destroyed in 1858, with additional ditches and abattis. There were, moreover, stronger and better booms across the channel. Few guns were seen; but numerous embrasures were masked with matting, obviously in order to conceal what was behind them.[1]

The officer who was sent on shore to communicate was met by a guard, and assured that there were no officials nearer than Tientsin. He was prevented from landing; but, on telling the people that the Commander-in-Chief desired that the obstructions in the river should be removed to enable the envoys to go up to Tientsin, he was promised that the necessary work of clearing should be begun within the next forty-eight hours. On June 19th, the whole squadron was moved to the anchorage off the mouth of the river; and the smaller craft were sent inside the bar. On the 20th, Hope again examined the channel; and, finding that nothing had been done towards carrying out the promise of the 18th, he addressed a letter to the Taotai at Tientsin, repeating the announcement of the arrival of the envoys, and the request for free passage. To this letter an evasive answer was returned on the 22nd.

In the meantime, Bruce and de Bourboulon had formally desired Hope to take the matter into his own hands, and to adopt such measures as he might deem expedient for opening the way up. Hope, in consequence, informed the Taotai that, if the obstructions were not removed, he should remove them, using force if needful. This communication received no answer; and on June 24th, the whole of the rest of the squadron was taken inside the bar; and intimation was sent in to the effect that unless a satisfactory answer were received by 8 P.M., the Rear-Admiral would feel at liberty to take his own course.

There were three booms or obstructions. The first, or lowest, was of iron piles; the second was of heavy spars of wood, apparently moored head and stern, and cross-lashed with cables; the third consisted of large timber baulks, well cross-lashed together, tied with irons, and forming a mass about 120 feet wide and 3 feet deep. It was made in two overlapping pieces, as indicated in the plan; and the opening between these might have just admitted the

---

[1] It was generally believed that the new defences were the work of Russian engineers.

passage of a gunboat, though the strength of the current would have rendered it difficult and even dangerous for such a craft to attempt to get through.

That night three boats, under Captain George Ommanney Willes, of the *Chesapeake*, passing through or circumventing the first boom, pulled up to the second, and cut one, and blew away with powder two, of the cables forming part of it. The boats he had with him were one from the *Chesapeake*, under Lieutenant John Crawford Wilson, one from the *Magicienne*, under acting-Mate Frederick

ADMIRAL SIR GEORGE OMMANNEY WILLES, G.C.B.

Wilbraham Egerton, and one from the *Cruiser*, under Boatswain W. Hartland. Before the return of the party, Willes examined the third or inner boom ; and, in consequence of his report on it, the Rear-Admiral concluded that he would not be able to pass the works and attack them from above, but must attack them, if at all, from the front, and, upon silencing them, endeavour to carry them by storm. By morning, the Chinese had repaired the damage done overnight to the second boom. Hope determined to try to carry out both plans, and to employ the following craft :—

SHIPS (all screw).	GUNS.	COMMANDERS.
Opossum, g.-b. . . .	2	(Capt. Geo. O. Willes.) / Lieut. Chas. Jno. Balfour.
Starling, g.-b.. . . .	2	Lieut. Arth. Julian Villiers.
Janus, g.-b.	2	Lieut. Herbert Price Knevitt.
Plover, g.-b.	2	(R.-Adm. James Hope, C.B.) / Lieut. Wm Hector Rason.
Cormorant, g.-v.	4	Com. Armine Wodehouse.
Lee, g.-b.	2	Lieut. Wm. Hy. Jones.
Kestrel, g.-b.	2	Lieut. Geo. Dacres Bevan.
Banterer, g.-b . . .	2	Lieut. John Jenkins.
Forester, g.-b.. . .	2	Lieut. Arthur Jno. Innes.
Haughty, g.-b. . . .	2	Lieut. Geo. Doherty Broad.
Nimrod, slp.	6	Lieut. Robt. Jas. Wynniatt (actg.-Com.).

The above nine gunboats varied from about 235 to about 270 tons (B.M.) and seem to have carried each one 68-pr. of 95 cwt., and one 32-pr. of 56 cwt., besides, in some cases at least, two howitzers. Their proper complements were about forty, all told, but extra officers and men were in most of them. The remaining two vessels (*Cormorant* and *Nimrod*) were considerably more powerful.

The morning of June 25th was occupied in putting these vessels into position. The *Starling, Janus, Plover, Cormorant, Lee, Kestrel,* and *Banterer* were stationed on a line parallel with the works on the south side, or right bank, of the river; and the *Nimrod* was put in rear of that line, with her guns bearing on the more distant north fort. The *Opossum* was stationed in advance, close up to the boom of piles; and the *Forester* and *Haughty* were in reserve in rear of the line, the former having orders to move up to the *Plover's* post, should that vessel advance to the support of the *Opossum*.

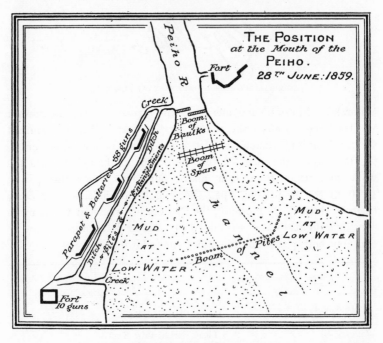

The vessels on the right were under the direction of Captain Charles Frederick Alexander Shadwell of the *Highflyer*, and those on the left, under Captain Nicholas Vansittart, of the *Magicienne*. The strength of the tide, and the narrowness of the channel (about 200 yards) had rendered it a matter of extreme difficulty to take up the positions above described; and the *Banterer* and *Starling*, the vessels on the extreme right and left of the line, both took the ground, the former in a good position, but the latter in one which, unfortunately, prevented her from taking much share in the action.

At 2 P.M. the *Opossum* was ordered to open a passage through the first barrier. She made fast a hawser to one of the iron piles, and, by 2.30, had pulled it out; whereupon, supported by the *Plover*, and closely followed by the *Lee* and *Haughty*, she moved up to the second boom. As she reached it, the forts opened a simultaneous fire from between thirty and forty guns, ranging from 32-prs. to 8-in. pieces. Hope at once ordered the ships to engage.

It was a hot day, with a clear blue sky; and the Chinese had the range to a nicety. The *Plover* posted herself close to the barrier, with the *Opossum*, *Lee*, and *Haughty*, in succession, astern of her. By 3 P.M., the four craft inside the outer barrier had suffered severely, and were rapidly becoming disabled. The *Plover* had lost her gallant young commander, Rason, who was cut in two by a round shot, and whose place was temporarily taken by George Amelius Douglas, Hope's Flag-Lieutenant. In her also fell Captain T. M‘Kenna, of the 1st Royals, who was attached to the Major-General commanding the forces in China; and among her wounded were the Rear-Admiral

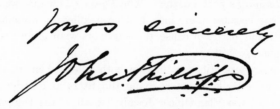

STAFF-CAPT. JOHN PHILLIPS, R.N.

himself, and Second-Master John Phillips (acting). The four vessels were, consequently, dropped down[1] into fresh positions below the first barrier, where, having received fresh men, they renewed the action. The *Plover* was so badly mauled that Hope shifted his flag from her to the *Cormorant*; and at 4.20, finding himself too weak for the work, he was obliged to summon Captain Shadwell, and to entrust him with the more immediate command of the squadron.

It should be mentioned here that the French dispatch vessel *Norzagaray* was not armed in such a manner as to enable her to share in the attack; and that the *Duchayla* drew too much water for the purpose. Although, therefore, the French were as much concerned as the British in asserting the right of free passage for their representative to Tientsin, they bore no part in this naval attack; at which, indeed, they were represented only by Commander

---

[1] The *Plover* dropped down because her cables were cut by shot; and she drifted unmanageable until she grappled the *Cormorant*, and so brought herself up.

Tricault, of the *Duchayla*, who attached himself to the Commander-in-Chief, and remained with him until the landing.   The Americans and Russians, less intimately concerned, were not represented at all ; and, in fact, were professedly neutral.

At 5.40 the *Kestrel* sank in her position; and the *Lee* had to be put upon the mud to save her from the like fate.   At about that time, or a little before,[1] there occurred an incident which has ever since most happily affected the relations between the two great English-speaking nations.

The *Cormorant*, flying the Rear-Admiral's flag, lay with her port broadside facing, and engaging, the works on the right bank. Lashed on her starboard side was the almost disabled *Plover*, in such a manner that the latter's bow gun cleared the *Cormorant's* bows by a yard or so, and could be fired across them at the forts. The *Banterer* was aground on the *Plover's* starboard bow ; the *Haughty* lay across the *Cormorant's* stern ; and the *Lee* was aground on the *Haughty's* port quarter.   The *Plover's* bow gun was almost silent, partly because many men had been killed or wounded while serving it, and partly because the survivors were almost worn out with fatigue.

The firing was still very hot on both sides, when up the river came a double-banked cutter, flying the Stars and Stripes in the stern.   In her was Flag-Officer Josiah Tatnall, of the United States' navy, senior American officer in Chinese waters, who had pulled up from his flag-ship below the bar, in spite of the storm of shot.   He had fought against the British in the war of 1812.   His coxswain took him alongside the *Plover's* starboard gangway ; and, even as the bow-man was getting out his boat-hook, the coxswain was hit by a Chinese projectile.   Tatnall boarded the *Plover*, crossed her bloody deck, and went to visit Hope, who was lying wounded in the *Cormorant's* cabin.   He expressed his sympathy ; said that he trusted he might be of some use in removing and tending the numerous wounded ;   and remained for a short time with the British Com-mander-in-Chief.   While he was in the *Cormorant's* cabin, his boat lay under the *Plover's* shelter ; and her men watched the *Plover's* weary bluejackets working intermittently at the bow gun.   At length, one of the Americans, and then others, climbed shyly on deck, and began to help, saying little or nothing, but gradually relieving the

---

[1] It may have been as early as 4.40 P.M.   Accounts of those present vary as to the exact time.

proper gun's crew, until the gun was wholly manned by Tatnall's men.   They had fired it at least once when Tatnall reappeared.

" Hulloa there ! " he cried, somewhat sharply, as he crossed the *Plover's* deck to the gangway; " don't you know that we are neutrals ? "

" Beg pardon, sir," said one of the Americans, drawing off shamefacedly with his mates to the boat, " they were very short-handed at the bow-gun; and so we thought we'd lend them a hand for fellowship's sake."

By 6.30 the fire from the north forts had ceased altogether; and by 7, that from the south ones was also silent, save that a single gun in the outer, another in the centre bastion, and a third in the detached fort on the south continued to ply the ships with shot.

A landing force, chiefly made up of about 350 Marines and a few bluejackets, was brought from the vessels below the bar.   There is strong evidence that Tatnall's steam boat, the *Toey-whan*, was allowed to assist in towing part of it up the river, though, no doubt, the nominal mission of the little craft was to fetch wounded from the gunboats below the barrier.

At 7.20 P.M. a landing was effected opposite the outer bastion of the south fort, the spot being selected because it seemed to have suffered most, and because an attack there could be best supported by the guns of the squadron.   The force consisted of a detachment of Sappers and Miners, under Major Fisher, R.E., a brigade of Marines, under Lieutenant-Colonel Thomas Lemon, a division of seamen under Captain Vansittart, assisted by Commanders John Edmund Commerell, V.C., and William Andrew James Heath, and a small body of French seamen under Commander Tricault; the whole being under the orders of Captain Shadwell.

The party was met by a heavy fire from guns, gingals, and rifles, and, in addition, had terrible obstacles to contend with in the shape of stakes planted in the shallows and mud, and two, if not three, ditches.   In the advance, Shadwell, Vansittart, and Lemon, with many others, were disabled, and the command devolved upon Commerell.   About 150 officers and men struggled as far as the second ditch, and about 50 even got close under the wall of the fort; but, although those positions might have been held for a time, further advance, or a storm, was impossible without reinforcements.   Such was Commerell's unwilling conclusion after he had consulted with Fisher, Tricault, and Captain Richard Parke, R.M.; and he reported it to Shadwell, who ordered a retirement. This was effected in the darkness with the utmost deliberation and coolness, the force proceeding to the boats in detachments, and bringing off its wounded. It was accomplished by 1.30 A.M. on June 26th, the last to leave the shore being Commerell and Heath.

The *Kestrel*, *Starling*, and *Banterer* were raised or floated. The *Lee* became a total loss. After the action the *Plover* grounded within range of the forts, and, being necessarily abandoned, was also lost. The *Cormorant* went to her assistance, and grounded. She got off again on the night of the 27th, but piled up once more while endeavouring to move down, and on the 28th was swept by such a heavy fire that she presently sank.

This lamentable affair, therefore, cost the Navy three vessels. The expenditure of human life was even more serious. No fewer than 25 officers and men were killed; 39 others were badly wounded; and 54 more received slighter injuries, during the preliminary attack; and the subsequent landing, and attempted capture of the south forts added to the total 64 officers and men killed; 162 badly wounded; and 90 slightly wounded. The whole British casualties, therefore, amounted to the appalling number of 89 killed, and 345 wounded—a much heavier loss than that suffered by the entire British fleet at the famous battle of Cape St. Vincent, in 1797. In addition, the French had 4 killed, and 10 wounded.

Among the officers killed were: Lieuts. William Hector Rason (comdg. *Plover*), Alfred Graves (*Assistance*), and Charles Henry Clutterbuck (*Chesapeake*); Lieuts. (R.M.) Hamilton Wolrige, and Henry Langton Tollemache Inglis; Capt. T. M'Kenna (1st Royals); and Mids. T. H. Herbert (*Chesapeake*). Among the officers severely wounded were: Rear-Admiral James Hope, C.B.; Capts. Charles Frederick Alexander Shadwell, C.B. (*Highflyer*), and Nicholas Vansittart,[1] C.B. (*Magicienne*); actg.-Lieut. Claude Edward Buckle (*Magicienne*); Master Augustus John Burniston (*Banterer*); actg.-Mate Nathaniel Bowden Smith (*Chesapeake*); Midshipmen Armand Temple Powlett (*Fury*), and G. Armytage (*Cruiser*); Gunner W. Ryan (*Plover*); Lieut.-Col. Thomas Lemon, R.M.; Capt. William Godfrey Rayson Masters, R.M.; Lieut. John Chesterton Crawford, R.M.A.; Lieut. G. Longley, R.E.; and the Rev. H. Huleatt, Chaplain to the Forces.
Rear-Admiral Hope, in his dispatch, mentioned with commendation Capts. C. F. A. Shadwell, N. Vansittart, and George Ommanney Willes; Commanders John Edmund Commerell, William Andrew James Heath, and Armine Wodehouse; Lieuts. John Jenkins, Robert James Wynniatt, Arthur John Innes, George Dacres Bevan, William Henry Jones, Charles John Balfour, George Doherty Broad, Herbert Price Knevitt, George Parsons (2), and John Crawford Wilson; Master William Donaldson Strong; Mates Claude Edward Buckle,

---

[1] Capt. Vansittart succumbed to his injuries.

George Spotswood Peard, Frederick Edward Gould, and Visct. Kilcoursie;
Mids. G. Armytage and Charles Lister Oxley; Paymaster and Secretary James
William Murray Ashby; Asst.-Paymaster John St. John Wagstaffe; Second-
Master Oscar Samson; Staff-Surg. Walter Dickson (2) M.D.; Surg. John
Little, M.B.; Asst.-Surg. William James Baird, M.D.; Lieut.-Col. Thomas
Lemon, R.M., Capts. (R.M.) Richard Parke, W. G. R. Masters, and Ponsonby
May Carew Croker; Lieuts. (R.M.) Langham Rokeby, John Frederick
Hawkey, Harry Lewis Evans, and John Straghan; Sergt.-Maj. Woon, R.M.,
Q. M. Sergt. Halling, R.M.; Major Fisher, R.E., and Lieuts. (R.E.) J. M.
Maitland and G. Longley.[1]

As this hotly contested action resulted in a defeat, those who
participated in it were never directly rewarded by the issue of medals
or clasps, the granting of honours, or promotion; yet it must be
admitted that, as, indeed, the exceedingly heavy loss indicates,
officers and men behaved in a manner which added distinctly to
the glories of the Navy, and which could have been scarcely more
creditable had victory rewarded their efforts. The attack failed,
firstly, because the narrowness of the channel, and the artificial
obstructions crippled the usefulness of the ships, and, secondly,
because the assault, a frontal one, was made over most difficult
ground against works which were supposed, but wrongly supposed,
to have been silenced; and was attempted with insufficient force. It
must also be admitted that, as usual, the British were very ignorant
of the exact strength and dispositions of the enemy.

" After the retirement," writes a distinguished officer who was
present, " the *Coromandel* received as many wounded as she could
stow; and the rest were sent down by boats towed by the U.S.
steamer *Toey-whan*, obligingly placed at our disposal by Flag-Officer
Tatnall, in, as he put it, ' the cause of humanity.' This is when the
expression, ' Blood is thicker than water,' was used by him to my
chief, Sir James Hope. It was on the day after the action."

As the officer from whom I quote this was the Rear-Admiral's
Secretary, there can be no doubt that Tatnall used the expression on
the occasion referred to; but there is some evidence that he also
used it on the day of the action; and also that his men used it
when on board the *Plover.* I think, therefore, that, in all probability,
it was an habitual expression with Tatnall at the time, and that it
was imitated by his people.

Tatnall, it may be added, took the unfortunate side in the struggle

---

[1] Hope's disp. of July 5th. The above account is the result also of conversation and
correspondence with numerous officers who were present. See, too, Chevalier, 328; and
corr. in *Times.*

which soon afterwards so nearly rent his country permanently in twain; and, in consequence of his action, he was obliged to withdraw to Halifax, Nova Scotia, where he lived in something approaching poverty. His attitude to the British in China in 1859 was not, I am pleased to say, forgotten by those whom he had befriended. As soon as his misfortunes were known in the Navy, a number of officers who had served in China, and of others who remembered what had occurred there, subscribed a sum of money which, happily, saved the last days of Commodore Josiah Tatnall from absolute penury.[1] His name can never be forgotten in the British service.

On July 3rd the British squadron repassed the Peiho bar, and proceeded to Shanghai, to allow the wounded opportunity to recover on shore, and to begin preparations for an attack on a more adequate scale, and so for repairing British prestige in China. Operations could not be resumed for twelve months. Both France and Great Britain decided to send out considerable bodies of troops from home, as well as large naval reinforcements; flat-bottomed boats, rafts, and stages for landing the armies had to be constructed; and not until June 25th, 1860, did the expedition begin to concentrate in Talienwan Bay, near Port Arthur, a spot which had been fixed upon for the purpose in consequence of representations made by Commander John Bythesea, of the *Cruiser*, who, in the interval, had thoroughly surveyed the Gulf of Pechili.[2] The forces ultimately assembled included about 12,600 British and Indian troops, under Lieutenant-General Sir Hope Grant, and nearly 8000 French under General Cousin de Montauban. Rear-Admiral James Hope[3] still commanded the British fleet on the station. Montauban left France with the title of "Commandant en Chef des Forces de Terre et de Mer"; but the French government, preferring to imitate the arrangements of its ally, and to keep separate the naval and military commands, sent out after him Vice-Admiral Charner, who reached Shanghai on April 19th. Although, in the circumstances, such procedure was perhaps hardly necessary, war had been formally declared against China on April 8th, that power having previously refused reparation for its action in the Peiho in the summer of 1859.

[1] Letter to W.L.C. from the late Adm. Sir G. O. Willes.
[2] Other surveys, which were most useful as preparation for the operations of August, were made by Com. John Ward (2), of the *Actæon*. Hope to Admlty., Aug. 27th, 1860.
[3] With temp. rank as Vice-Adm.

One of the most troublesome questions to be settled by the admirals and generals was where best to disembark the army. It was necessary to find a spot or spots where the water should be deep enough to allow the transports to approach within reasonable distance of the shore, and spots, moreover, where the coast should be less muddy, and more healthy, than the major part of the coast-line of the Gulf of Pechili. It was at length arranged that the French army should land at a point to the south of the mouth of the Peiho, and should then proceed to attack the defences on the right bank of that river; and that the British should disembark at Pehtang, about nine miles to the northward of the river's mouth, and should devote their attention to the defences on the left, or north bank : but the French soon found that they could not carry out their part of the agreement without some risk, and without exposing their troops to the probability of being cut off from communication with their fleet. The result was that both armies were ultimately taken to Pehtang. As had been the case at the time of the invasion of the Crimea, the French squadron was overcrowded with troops, while the British war-ships, the army being in hired transports, were fit for anything that might befall, and were free and unencumbered. Captain Chevalier expresses his strong sense of the advantages of this method, which, it may be hoped will be always followed when the British Navy and Army co-operate on any expedition of the kind.

The main part of the work done on this occasion was done by the allied armies ; and may, therefore, be passed over briefly here.

Pehtang stands at the mouth of the small river of the same name, and on the south bank of it. To the south of the town is a con-siderable extent of hard ground ; and from Pehtang, south-westward to Sin-ho, about five miles distant, ran a raised causeway, flanked on each side by a ditch. From Sin-ho south-eastward to Tong-ku, a distance of little more than two miles, ran a somewhat similar causeway ; and from Tong-ku, when taken, the Peiho forts on the north side of the river could be approached and attacked from the rear.

The transports stood in towards the mouth of the Pehtang on August 1st, 1860. Some gunboats had previously entered the river, and passed beyond two forts which overlooked the estuary, it being , intended that if these forts should assume a hostile attitude, they should be shelled from above, a point from which no Chinese river forts of that day were capable of withstanding attack by water. The forts were found to have been abandoned; but one at least of them had been ingeniously mined in such a manner that any incautious entry by the troops would have caused an explosion. The disembarkation began at once at a point below the tract of hard ground about half a mile south of the town; and the British, although by far the more numerous, completed the operation forty hours before the French,[1] chiefly in consequence of the foresight which had provided plenty of small craft capable of crossing the bar, on which, even at high tide, there were only ten feet of water. A battalion of Royal Marines under Lieutenant-Colonel John Hawkins Gascoigne, and a battalion of French seamen joined the army, which, on August 12th, marched to, and occupied Sin-ho, driving back a considerable body of the enemy, and taking two entrenched positions; and, on the 14th, attacked and captured Tong-ku,[2] the Chinese then retiring into the northern forts, or across the river. On the right of the main force, during its advance, moved a smaller body under Brigadier-General Sir Robert Cornelius Napier.[3] Grant advised Hope of his intention to attack the Taku northern forts on August 21st; and, in order to co-operate, Hope and Charner, on the previous day, sent the French and British gunboats, and the rocket-boats of the fleet into the Peiho.

When, at about daybreak on the 21st, the troops began to attack the inner fort on the north side, the vessels were prevented by the want of sufficient water from at once reaching the positions assigned to them; and, indeed, the gunboat *Dove,* Lieutenant Charles James Bullock, temporarily bearing the flag of Rear-Admiral Lewis Tobias Jones, who was in immediate command of the operations in the river, grounded in six and a half feet; and Jones had to transfer his flag to the *Clown,* Lieutenant William Frederick Lee. By six o'clock, however, the gunboats were able to open; at 6.15 a shell blew up a magazine in the inner north fort; and at 6.25 there was a similar explosion in the outer one. The Chinese fought well; but at about 9 A.M. the inner north fort was stormed; and although there was firing until near 11, the enemy then prudently relinquished further efforts, and, having lost terribly, hoisted white flags on all the works that remained in his hands.

In the afternoon, the outer north fort was taken possession of; and in the evening, the south fort, which had been evacuated, was

[1] Chevalier, 343. [2] A party from the *Chesapeake* being present. [3] Afterwards Lord Napier of Magdala.

occupied, and the booms across the river were removed. The iron piles, however, which formed the outermost barrier, were fixed with so much firmness that a passage could not be opened through them until noon on the 22nd. The gunboats then passed through, and anchored off Tong-ku. In this affair the ships employed[1] had no casualties; but the Marines who were with the army had 1 killed, and 29 wounded. On the 23rd, the *Coromandel*, bearing the flag of Vice-Admiral James Hope, together with a number of British gunboats, and subsequently of French ones, passed up to Tientsin, which, being destitute of troops and pacifically inclined, was occupied.

Lieut.-Colonel Gascoigne, in describing the work done by his battalion of Royal Marines, reported with approval the conduct of Lieut.-Colonel Joseph Oates Travers, Captains Jermyn Charles Symonds, John Charles Downie Morrison, and John Basset Prynne; Lieutenant T. Herbert Alexander Brenan; Surgeon John Little, M.B.; Assistant-Surgeon Doyle Money Shaw; Sergeants Teacle, Knapp, and H. Trent; Corporal Kelly; and Privates Bray and Bowerman.[2]

On August 31st a mandarin of high rank reached Tientsin; and Lord Elgin and Baron Gros entered into negotiations with him; but on September 7th he was nowhere to be found. It therefore became necessary for the allied armies to advance upon Pekin. The Chinese attempted to cause further delay; and two battles had to be fought ere they were finally induced to submit. Not until Pekin had been taken, and the palace burnt, did the enemy agree to the terms demanded; and the Treaty of Pekin was concluded only on October 24th. During the advance up the river, the boats of the fleet[3] rendered immense assistance in transporting the siege train, and stores for the army. The treaty provided for the opening of Tientsin to commerce; the occupation of that town, and of the Peiho Forts pending the payment of a certain proportion of an indemnity; an apology from the Emperor; the cession of Kowloon to Great Britain; and the ratification of the previous treaty of

---

[1] Vessels employed in the Peiho, August 20th, and onwards: *Coromandel*, pad., temp. flag of V.-Ad. Hope, C.B.; *Dove*, scr., temp. flag of R.-Adm. Lewis Tobias Jones, C.B.; and (under Capt. Jas. Johnstone M'Cleverty, C.B.), *Havock*, scr., *Staunch*, scr., *Opossum*, scr., *Forester*, scr., and *Algerine*, scr.; with (under Capt. Lord John Hay (3), C.B.), *Clown*, scr., *Drake*, scr., *Woodcock*, scr., and *Janus*, scr.; besides rocket-boats contributed apparently by the *Chesapeake*, *Cambrian*, *Centaur*, *Encounter*, *Impérieuse*, *Magicienne*, *Odin*, *Pearl*, *Urgent*, etc. Hope's disp. is very meagre.

[2] Gascoigne to Hope, Aug. 24th.

[3] Especially those of the *Chesapeake*, *Cambrian*, *Impérieuse*, *Scout*, and *Simoon*.

Tientsin.   In 1860, as at a later date, the Chinese distinguished themselves by their bad faith ; and their barbarous treatment of Messrs. Parkes, Loch, de Normann, Bowlby, and other Europeans who fell into their hands, rendered them totally undeserving of the merciful light in which their long course of misconduct was viewed when the time came for the exaction of penalties.   The evacuation of Pekin was concluded on November 9th.

In recognition of their services, Rear-Admiral Hope was at once made a K.C.B.,[1] and a few officers were promoted, while a few others received honours at a somewhat later period.[2]   The work done was not, however, very lavishly rewarded.   A monument to those of Hope's flagship, the *Chesapeake*, who perished during the commission, 1857–61, has been erected on Clarence Esplanade, Southsea.

While the China War was in progress, some of the small craft on the station were busily occupied in dealing with the pirates, who, taking advantage of the situation, were particularly active up and down the coasts.   Lieutenant Henry Knox Leet, first commanding the *Firm*, and afterwards the *Slaney*, and Lieutenant Joseph Samuel Hudson, commanding the *Leven*, were among the officers who distinguished themselves in this branch of duty ; but many others might also be named.   On the east coast of Africa, where the slave trade then flourished exceedingly, the *Lynx*, 4, screw, Lieutenant Henry Berkeley, was one of the most active cruisers.   In the course of 1859 she also landed a small brigade to co-operate with a force from the East India Company's steamer *Assaye* in an attack upon some rebellious subjects of the Sultan of Zanzibar and in the destruction of a small fort.   In 1860, the *Torch*, 5, screw, Commander Frederick Harrison Smith, began on the west coast a useful commission, in the course of which she captured seven slavers ; and some exploits of other vessels on that station will demand notice later.   But the repression of piracy and slavery was by no means the only kind of minor service rendered by the Navy.   In 1860, for example, Captain Thomas Miller, of the *Clio*, 22, screw, was instrumental in saving the city of Panama from capture by a mob, and in protecting some French subjects from infuriated negro

---

[1] Nov. 9th, 1860.

[2] *E.g.*, Rear-Adm. Lewis Tobias Jones, a K.C.B. June 28th, 1861; Col. Jno. Hawkins Gascoigne, and Lt.-Col. Joseph Oates Travers, C.B.'s, Feb. 28th, 1861; Capt. Geo. Ommanney Willes, a C.B., July 16th, 1861.

rioters; and a party of seamen and Marines from the *Satellite*, 21, screw, Captain James Charles Prevost, under Lieutenant Thomas Sherlock Gooch, was marched many miles up country in British Columbia in order to overawe certain miners who were causing anxiety to the Government.

During the Persian War of 1856–57, a few officers of the Royal Navy were employed in those vessels of the East India Company which were engaged along the Persian coast, especially at the capture of Reshire fort on December 7th, and the occupation of the island of Karak, and of part of Bushire, on December 10th, 1856; but the Navy itself did not share in the operations, which were under the maritime direction of Sir Henry John Leeke, Kt.,[1] and Commodore Ethersey, of the H. E. I. Co.'s navy. In the years 1857–61, however, the repression of piracy in the Persian Gulf provided plenty of occupation for several of her Majesty's cruisers, among which may be mentioned the *Ariel*, 9, screw, Commander Charles Bromley, and the *Lyra*, 9, screw, Commander Radulphus Bryce Oldfield. In the same years, in the West Indies, the *Styx*, 6, paddle, Commander Charles Vesey, rendered excellent service against the slavers in Cuban waters.

Early in 1857, Peru was in the throes of one of its too frequent revolutions. A politician named Vivanco, who was said to possess the sympathies of the richer classes, and especially of the ladies, was engaged in an attempt to depose the President, General Ramon Castilla, who was supported by the army, and by the mass of the people. Vivanco's chief power lay in the fact—an important one in a country having so large a sea-board as Peru—that he had with him the greater part of the small Peruvian navy. On March 24th, Vice-Admiral Henry William Bruce, Commander-in-Chief on the Pacific station, being then in the *Monarch*, 84, at Callao, received intelligence to the effect that two of Vivanco's war-steamers, the *Loa* and the *Tumbes*,[2] had stopped the British mail-steamer *New Grenada*, while on her way to Panama, and, having boarded her, had taken from her 32,000 dollars, besides sundry goods, which, though shipped in the names of merchants at Valparaiso, had in reality been sent by Castilla to supply his troops in the northern

---

[1] A Capt., R.N., of 1826, who had become a rear-adm. on reserved half-pay in 1854, and who died in 1870.

[2] Gunboats, built in England for Peru. The *Loa* had four long 32-prs., the *Tumbes* two, and a smaller brass gun.

part of the republic. Bruce at once despatched the *Pearl*, 21, screw, Captain Edward Southwell Sotheby, in search of the delinquents; and she sailed at noon on the 25th. Early on the 28th, Captain Sotheby found the rebel craft off Lambeyaque, and, going to quarters, steamed alongside them, and sent to the *Loa*, the senior officer's ship, a boat under Lieutenant Nicholas Edward Brook Turnour, to demand the stolen money and goods, and the officers and men who had taken them. In default, the surrender of both craft was required within five minutes. As the money had been distributed, it could not be returned. The two Peruvian captains, therefore, wisely surrendered. The people who had not been implicated personally in the outrage were allowed the option of going ashore or of being carried to Callao; Lieutenant Seymour Walter Delmé Radcliffe was given charge of the *Loa*, and Lieutenant Henry Duncan Grant, of the *Tumbes*; and, with one prize on each quarter, the *Pearl* steamed back to Callao, arriving there on March 31st. One of the craft was quickly given back to her temporary owners; the other was detained for some time as security that similar depredations should not be committed again.[1]

It has been shown how, after their arrival at Hong Kong, in the summer of 1857, the *Sanspareil, Shannon*, and *Pearl* were hastily despatched to Calcutta by Rear-Admiral Sir Michael Seymour (2), K.C.B., in order that they might assist in quelling the Mutiny in India.

The *Sanspareil*, 70, screw, Captain Astley Cooper Key, C.B., landed a brigade in August to garrison Fort William, Calcutta; but, after two or three months, returned, as has been seen, to Chinese waters, without having taken any active part in the suppression of the rebellion. The two other ships, however, sent their officers and men up country, and were able to render the most valuable assistance to the troops.

The *Shannon*, 51, screw, had been launched at Portsmouth in November, 1855, and, though other vessels exactly like her were launched in the years immediately following, she was for a time the largest steam frigate afloat. Her tonnage (B.M.) was 2667, or about one-fourth more than that of the *Victory*; and her nominal complement was 560 officers and men, though, on her arrival in India, she had more than that number on board.

The frigate had been commissioned at Portsmouth on Septem-

---

[1] Williams: 'Cruise of the *Pearl*,' 15.

ber 13th, 1856, by Captain William Peel, C.B., V.C., who has been
already mentioned many times in these pages. On August 6th, 1857,
she arrived in the mouth of the Ganges, and Peel at once offered the
services of himself and his people to proceed to the front, and co-
operate with the army. On the 14th, the Captain, several officers,
and about 390 seamen and Marines, embarked in a flat, and were
towed up the Hoogly to join the Lucknow relief force; and on
the 18th they were followed by another party of 5 officers and 120
men,[1] the frigate then being left with 140 people in her, under the
command of Master George A. Waters. The officers with the
Brigade were:—

Captain William Peel, C.B.; [2] Lieutenants James William Vaughan,[3] Thomas James
Young,[4] William Charles Fahie Wilson,[5] Edward Hay,[5] Henry Rushworth Wratislaw,[5]
and Nowell Salmon; [6] Brevet-Lieutenant Colonel Henry H. Maxwell (attached);
Captain Thomas Carstairs Grey, R.M.; Second Lieutenant William Stirling, R.M.;
Mates Henry P. Garvey,[7] and Edward Hope Verney; [8] Midshipmen or Naval Cadets
Edmund John Church, William Henry Richards, Martin Abbot Daniel,[7] John Lewis
Way, Edward St. John Daniel, Lord Walter Talbot Kerr, Lord Arthur Pelham Clinton,
Edward S. Watson, and H. A. Lascelles; Chaplain Edward Lawson Bowman; Assist.-
Surgeon James Flanagan [9] (actg.); Assist.-Paymaster William Thomas Comerford; [10]
Assist.-Clerk James Edward Stanton; Assist.-Engineers John W. Bone, Frederick
William Brown, and Henry A. Henri; Gunner Robert Thompson; and Carpenter
Henry Brice. Lieut. Lind af Hazeby, Swedish navy, was also attached to the Brigade:
and Captain Oliver John Jones, R.N. (half-pay), joined it as a volunteer.

As the Brigade took with it both guns and howitzers, as the
towing vessels were of but small power and shallow draught, and
as the current was strong, progress was slow; and Peel did not
reach Allahabad, near the junction of the Jumna with the Ganges,
until the second half of October. By the 20th the strength of the
brigade assembled there was 516 of all ranks. Of these about 240,
under Lieutenants Wilson, Wratislaw, and af Hazeby, were left in
garrison at Allahabad. On October 23rd 100 more, under Lieutenants Vaughan and Salmon, with four siege-train 24-prs., went
to Cawnpur, and thence joined the army before Lucknow; and on
the 27th and 28th the rest of the brigade, with four 24-prs. and
two 8-in. howitzers, followed, and was presently amalgamated with

---

[1] Some of these were recruited from merchant vessels at Calcutta.
[2] K.C.B., and died 1858.
[3] Com., Jan. 30th, 1858; C.B., June 29th, 1858.
[4] Com., March 22nd, 1858; V.C., Feb. 1st, 1859.
[5] Com., March 22nd, 1858.
[6] Com., March 22nd, 1858; V.C., Dec. 24th, 1858.
[7] Killed in action.   [8] Actg.-Lieut., March 22nd, 1858.
[9] Surg., Aug. 3rd, 1859.   [10] Paym., March 22nd, 1858.

a small force which, under Lieutenant-Colonel Powell, of the 53rd regiment, was marching in the same direction. Late on October 31st the column camped near Fatehpur, and, on the following day, marched twenty-four miles and defeated 4000 of the enemy at Kudjwa, capturing two guns. Powell fell, and Peel took command, and completed the rout of the mutineers, ultimately securing a third gun. The British lost 95 in killed and wounded, among the latter being Lieutenants Hay, R.N., and Stirling, R.M.; but the rebels lost 300 in killed alone. Peel then pressed on for Cawnpur. Writing to Sir Michael Seymour (2) on November 6th, from a camp between Cawnpur and Lucknow, he said :—

"Since that battle was fought, with the exception of one day's rest for the footsore men who had marched seventy-two miles in three days, besides fighting a severe engagement, we have made daily marches. . . . At Cawnpur I was obliged to leave Lieutenant Hay with fifty men to serve as artillerymen for that important position. . . . I am much gratified with the conduct of all the Brigade ; and there is no departure whatever from the ordinary rules and customs of the service."

Peel and Vaughan rejoined one another on November 12th before Lucknow, which had been relieved by Havelock and Outram, who, however, were so weak in force that they had been soon afterwards themselves besieged with the original defenders. On the 14th, when the Brigade's guns were in action, one of them burst, killing Francis Cassidey, captain of the main-top, and wounding several other men. On November 16th, during the successful attack on Secunderabagh, Midshipman Martin Abbot Daniel was killed by a round-shot, and Lieutenant Salmon was severely wounded. Salmon, however, won the Victoria Cross for that day climbing up a tree touching the angle of the Shah Nujjif, to reply to the fire of the enemy, for which dangerous service Peel had called for volunteers. Boatswain's Mate John Harrison displayed similar gallantry, and was similarly rewarded.[1] The total loss of the Brigade on that occasion was 4 killed and 13 wounded. Fighting went on almost continuously until the 25th, when the relief was fully accomplished and the town evacuated.[2] It was quickly occupied by the rebels, strongly fortified and heavily garrisoned.

Sir Colin Campbell, accompanied by the Naval Brigade, repaired to Cawnpur. On November 28th, on the way thither, a party of 36

---

[1] On the same day Com. Thos. Jas. Young, and Wm. Hall, capt. of foretop, gained the Victoria Cross for gallant handling of a 24-pr. *Gazette*, Dec. 24th, 1858, and Feb. 1st, 1859.

[2] Campbell to Gov.-Genl., Nov. 18th and 25th, 1857.

bluejackets, with two 24-prs., under Lieutenant Hay, Mate Garvey, and Naval Cadet Lascelles, who was then acting as A.-d.-C. to Captain Peel, was engaged, in company with the 88th regiment, and did distinguished service.   It was at about that time that Captain Oliver John Jones joined as a volunteer.

In the fighting near Cawnpur, between December 6th and December 9th, the Brigade had a share; and on January 2nd, 1858, it behaved with great gallantry at the action at Kallee-Nuddee. Lieutenant Vaughan was attacked while repairing a bridge across the river, which he then promptly crossed with three guns.   On the further side he held in check a body of cavalry, and, himself aiming and firing one of his guns, made such good practice at the rebel gun which had originally annoyed him, that in five shots he dismounted the piece, destroyed its carriage, and blew up its ammunition waggon. Towards the end of the day Captains Peel and Jones, with three men

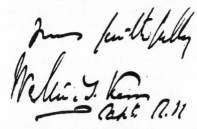

ADMIRAL THE RT. HON. LORD WALTER TALBOT KERR, K.C.B.
(Signature as Captain.)

of the 53rd regiment, while passing through a captured battery, were unexpectedly attacked by five sepoys who had lain in ambush.   All the assailants were killed, the last falling to Jones's revolver.

During the subsequent marching, the Brigade excited the admiration of the army by the manner in which it moved its guns.   If a weapon drawn by bullocks stuck in heavy ground, the seamen never failed to extricate it, manning both wheels and drag-ropes, and, if necessary, getting an elephant to push behind.   The cheerfulness, too, of the Brigade was much remarked on; and, doubt-less, it contributed to the keeping up of the spirits of all engaged throughout a terribly trying time.

In the fighting previous to the final capture of Lucknow in March, 1858, Peel and his men took a very active part, being present on the 3rd at the action at the Dilkoosha.   On the 9th, while looking out for a suitable spot on which to post some guns for breaching the

Martinière, the leader of the Brigade was severely wounded in the thigh by a musket-ball. His six 8-in. guns and two 24-prs. were chiefly employed in battering the Begum's palace; and it was while riding to them with a message on March 12th that Mr. Garvey was killed by a shell from one of the rebel coehorns. Captain Jones, on the same day, most devotedly exposed himself on the parapet of a battery in order to direct the fire of the guns behind it. On the 13th, when the guns had been placed in a somewhat more advanced battery, a coloured Canadian seaman named Edward Robinson betrayed extraordinary coolness in extinguishing a fire which had caught hold of some sandbags forming the face of the work. Under a storm of bullets from loopholes not forty yards away from him, he leapt out, and either quenched or tore away the burning canvas, being, however, severely wounded. He was awarded the Victoria Cross.

On the 14th, the Brigade, and especially a detachment under Commander Vaughan, Lieutenant Hay, Mate Verney, and Midshipman Lord Walter Kerr, took part in the blowing open of a gate leading to one of the courts of the Kaisarbagh; on the 16th the guns were advanced to the Residency; on the 22nd the rebels evacuated the town; and on March 29th the Brigade handed over the six 8-in. guns which it had brought up from the *Shannon*, and which were put into park in the small Imaumbarah, with the word " Shannon " deeply cut into each carriage.

The naval contingent from the *Shannon* saw no more fighting in India. The gallant Peel, slowly recovering from his wound, was to have been carried down from Lucknow in one of the King of Oude's carriages which had been specially prepared for him by the *Shannon's* Carpenter. When he saw the gorgeous equipage, he declared that he preferred to travel in a doolie, like an ordinary bluejacket. Unfortunately, the doolie selected for him must have been an infected one; for, soon afterwards, he was attacked with small-pox, to which, being already weakened by his wound, he succumbed at Cawnpur on April 27th, aged only thirty-four. He was, perhaps, the most brilliant naval officer of his day.[1]

Sir Edward Lugard, with whose division the Brigade served in the advance to Lucknow, and during the operations there, bore the following high testimony to the behaviour of Peel and his men :—

[1] A monument to Peel and the officers and men of the *Shannon's* Brigade stands on Clarence Esplanade, Southsea.

" The men were daily—I may say hourly—under my sight; and I considered their conduct in every respect an example to the troops. During the whole period I was associated with the *Shannon's* Brigade, I never once saw an irregularity among the men. They were sober, quiet, and respectful; and I often remarked to my staff the high state of discipline Sir W. Peel got them into. From the cessation of active operations until I was detached to Azimghur, I commanded all the troops in the city; and all measures for the repression of plundering were carried out through me, and, of course, every irregularity committed was reported to me. During that period not one irregularity was reported to me. Indeed, in the whole course of my life I never saw so well conducted a body of men. . . . Many a time I expressed to Peel the high opinion I had of his men, and my admiration of their cheerfulness and happy contented looks, under all circumstances of fatigue and difficulty." [1]

The Brigade returned slowly to Calcutta, and on August 12th and the following days, rejoined the ship, which, on September 15th, sailed for England.[2]

On her way from China to Calcutta, the *Pearl* called at Singapore, and there picked up two companies of the 90th Regiment, which, on July 10th, 1857, had been wrecked in the Strait of Banca in the iron trooper *Transit*. Proceeding, the *Pearl* disembarked those troops at Calcutta on August 12th. Captain Sotheby, like Captain Peel, offered his services to the Government, and, on September 12th, he embarked some of the officers and part of the crew of his corvette in the paddle-steamer *Chunar*. This detachment, of 158 men, with one 12-pr. howitzer, one 24-pr. howitzer, and 24-pr. rockets, reached Dinapur on October 7th. There it was found that no carriage suitable for the 24-pr. howitzer could be procured. The weapon was therefore left to be sent back to the ship. In lieu of it a 12-pr. howitzer and two 12-pr. mountain guns were supplied, and with them Sotheby landed at Buxar on October 10th, and took up his quarters in the fort. On the 23rd the detachment was summoned to Chupra, and the whole of it was in quarter there by the afternoon of the 26th. Thence it moved successively to Sewan and Myrwa. By that time another detachment, under Lieutenant Radcliffe, had joined from Calcutta, bringing up the force of the *Pearl's* Brigade to about 250 in all. A few had been raised from among volunteers from the merchant vessels at Calcutta; but the vast majority were seamen and Marines belonging to the corvette. The officers of the Brigade were :—

Captain Edward Southwell Sotheby; Lieutenants Nicholas Edward Brook Turnour, Seymour Walter Delmé Radcliffe, Henry Duncan Grant, and

---

[1] Lugard to Vaughan.
[2] Disps. of Peel and Vaughan; Journal of Lieut. É. H. Verney.

Hawkesworth Fawkes; Mates Alexander Wighton Ingles, and Thomas Moore Maquay; Midshipmen Lord Charles Thomas Montagu Douglas Scott, Hon. Victor Alexander Montagu, Henry Frederick Stephenson, Charles Edward Foot, and Herbert Holden Edwards; Lieutenant (R.M.) Frederick George Pym; Second-Master (actg.) John Fowler; Chaplain and Naval Instructor, Rev. Edward Adams Williams, M.A.; Assistant-Surgeon William James Shone; Assistant-Engineer John George Shearman; Master's-Assistant T. R. Merewether; Clerk Thomas Henry Lovelace Bowling; Gunner Parkin; Boatswain Charles Band; [1] and Carpenter John Burton.

The Brigade was attached to the Sarun Field Force, of which, on November 27th, Colonel Rowcroft took command at Myrwa. It first came into action with the mutineers on December 26th at Sohunpore, where an entrenched position was taken, and the enemy was dispersed. No one belonging to the Brigade was hurt.

By February 8th, 1858, the force arrived at Burhul, whence it moved up the Gogra in 150 boats, escorted by the small steamer *Jumna*, reaching Ghopalpur on the 10th; and on the 17th the strong fort of Chanderpur was captured by Captain Sotheby with 130 of the Brigade, 35 Sikhs, and 60 Gurkhas, acting in concert with the *Jumna*, which was under the orders of Second-Master John Fowler. Two guns were captured. The casualties on the side of the attack were insignificant, only about four people being wounded. On the evening of February 19th, Nourainie Ghat was reached. That night a fort on the Oudh side of the river was seized; and, on the afternoon of the following day, an attack was made upon a body of rebels at Phoolpur. After a gallant and well-sustained action, the enemy was driven from the field, with a loss of three guns. Two days afterwards, the Brigade recrossed the river by a bridge of boats which it had constructed. There had been some friction with the native allies; and it was deemed advisable to keep a British force to guard the rear of the advance, large numbers of rebels being reported in the vicinity of Fyzabad.

The Brigade marched to Amorha on March 2nd. Colonel Rowcroft was there informed that the fort of Belwa, seven miles further on, was occupied by the mutineers. In the afternoon, 168 men of the Brigade, with four guns, some 24-pr. rockets, 35 Sikhs, and a regiment of Gurkhas, moved to Belwa, and, being there joined by the Bengal Yeomanry Cavalry, 250 strong, opened fired on the fort at 5 P.M. The place, however, proved stronger than had been anticipated; and, when darkness came on, the whole force withdrew

[1] So says the Medal Roll at the Admiralty. Williams gives the Boatswain's name as Cooley.

to the Yeomanry camp, and, on the day following, returned to
Amorha. That night and the succeeding day the rebels received
very large reinforcements, chiefly from Fyzabad, but also from
Nawabgunge, Gondah, and elsewhere. The retirement from before
Belwa had been interpreted as a British defeat; the Sarun Field
Force, including the sick, was not then more than 1500 strong; and
the mutineers, having collected many thousands of men and fourteen
guns, were eager and confident. The little camp was, therefore,
rendered as defensible as possible by means of an enclosing line of
rifle-pits, and the clearing away of all jungle and houses which could
shelter an advance.

On the morning of March 5th, it was reported that the rebels
were about to attack. The force thereupon moved out, and took up
a position about half a mile to the west of the village of Amorha,
with the Naval Brigade and four guns under Captain Sotheby in the
centre, astride of the road, a Gurkha regiment and the small detachment of Sikhs on the left, and another Gurkha regiment on the right.
On each flank was a squadron of the Bengal Yeomanry Cavalry.
The enemy was in such force as to overlap the British force by at
least a mile in each direction; and he came on in excellent order in
rear of a cloud of skirmishers. The naval guns, under Lieutenant
Turnour, opened, and were replied to by ten pieces. After an
artillery duel which lasted for some time, Colonel Rowcroft threw
out his skirmishers, and began a steady forward movement, which
never ceased until the mutineers were driven from the field; for the
cavalry, supported by the Gurkhas, cleared the foe from the flanks
of the advance. As soon as it was evident that the enemy had been
checked, Rowcroft reinforced his Royal Marines, who were in the
skirmishing line, with a detachment of seamen, and pressed the foe
all along his front. One of the first guns abandoned by the rebels
was turned upon them, and worked by Lieutenant Grant, Assistant-
Engineer Shearman, Midshipman Lord Charles Scott, and a seaman
named Jesse Ward; and, as there was no port-fire wherewith to fire
it, a rifle was discharged into the vent, and the retreating foe was
plied with his own grape. A brilliant cavalry charge threw the left
wing of the mutineers into confusion; and soon the entire body fled,
leaving behind it eight unspiked guns. The enemy was pursued for
six miles, and, making a brief stand at one point, killed Second-
Master John Fowler (actg.) and one Gurkha. Heat and fatigue at
length put a stop to the action, which had lasted from 8.30 A.M. to

12.30 P.M.   The rebels had attacked with about 14,000 men and ten guns, and had been completely defeated, with a loss of about 500, by 1261 men, with but four guns.   The Naval Brigade had 1 officer killed and about 15 people wounded.

After the battle, in order to indicate to the enemy that the forces of the Government were confident of being able to take care of themselves, the line of rifle-pits was filled up, and the camp at Amorha was pitched in the open plain.   A small fort, however, was built to contain the sick, and the spare ammunition and baggage.   There were many alarms until the end of April; and, during that period, the force was joined by the left wing of Her Majesty's 13th Light Infantry, while one of the Gurkha regiments was withdrawn from it and sent to Goruckpur.   On April 17th, a detachment went out and defeated a body of marauding rebels near the village of Tilga, capturing a gun; and, on April 25th, another body was met near Jamoulee.   Owing to the intense heat, this affair was an unsatisfactory one, for the rebels would not stand and could not be followed far.   On the next day, the force moved to Kuptangunge.   The enemy was then all round it.   With a view to freeing it somewhat, an attack was made on April 29th on the fort of Nuggur by a detachment which included 96 officers and men, two guns, and a rocket tube from the Naval Brigade.   The place was taken with but very trifling loss; and in the evening the detachment returned to camp. For some time afterwards the Brigade remained at Bustee, where it went into huts on June 13th.   From Bustee, several small expeditions were made against detached bodies of the enemy.   One of these expeditions, on May 31st, turned a party of mutineers out of a position near Amorha; and on June 18th, another party of more formidable strength, was defeated at Hurreah, but withdrew in good order.

On August 29th, a section of the Brigade, 50 strong, under Lieutenant Fawkes, with two guns, took part in an engagement near Lumptee, and did good and steady service; and on the same day, another section, under Lieutenant Turnour, also with two guns, assisted in repelling an attack on an outpost at Hurreah, and, following the enemy, routed him on September 1st at Debreah.   On the evening of September 6th, Commander Grant,[1] with 73 seamen and Marines, two 12-pr. howitzers, a 24-pr. rocket-tube, and a detachment of the 13th Regiment, left Amorha, with a view to

[1] He and other officers had by that time been promoted. *Vide infra*, p. 149.

relieving a small garrison of Sikhs in the friendly town of Bansee.
At Gondah, Grant was joined by Captain Mulcaster, who arrived
with a squadron of cavalry, and took command.   Bansee was
reached on the 8th, after a splendid march of 50 miles in 39 hours,
the men being often up to their knees in mud, and sometimes up to
their waists in water.   Bansee was relieved only just in time, for
the gallant Sikhs holding it had but three percussion caps per man
remaining.   From Bansee, the expedition, which had been reinforced
on the 10th by Brigadier Fischer, marched on the 12th, reaching
Doomureahgunge on the 13th, and driving back a body of the rebels.
The howitzers, under Lieutenant Ingles, were most excellently
handled.   On the 14th, an effort was made to catch a body of
mutineers at Intwa ; but the roads were so bad that the attempt
had to be abandoned ; and on the 17th, the expedition returned to
Bustee.   Another naval force, under Lieutenant Ingles, formed part
of an expedition which left Bustee on September 27th for Bansee,
and which, having crossed the Raptee, got up with, and dispersed,
some mutineers at Mowee on September 30th, after most exhausting
marches.

On October 1st, the outpost at Amorha, which included 50 of
the *Pearl's* people, with two howitzers, under Lieutenant Fawkes,
was attacked by about 1200 mutineers, with two guns.   The enemy
was repulsed, after Lieutenant Maquay, who directed the howitzers,
and four seamen, Lee, Williams, Rayfield, and Simmonds, had
especially distinguished themselves.

On October 23rd, yet another expedition had to be despatched
towards Bansee.   On October 26th, when an insufficient British
force was foiled in an attack on the jungle fort of Jugdespore,
twenty-five miles north-west of Bustee, it was reported that the
Brigade lost its guns in the retreat.   There was no foundation for
the story, which, however, gave rise to some amusing correspondence
in the Indian papers.

In the middle of November, all the outlying parties were recalled,
and the whole force left Bustee on the 24th for the northern jungle
on the Nepal frontier, only a field hospital and guard remaining.   A
siege train had, in the meantime, arrived at Bustee, and had been
handed over to the *Pearl's* people.   On the 25th, Bhanpur was
reached, and a Madras battery joined; and on the 25th, the force
moved on to Doomureahgunge, where the rebels were very bloodily
defeated, and a halt was made for some days, during which a bridge

L 2

of boats was thrown across the Raptee, in face of a considerable army under Balla Rao, a near kinsman of Nana Sahib. On the evening of December 2nd, Brigadier Rowcroft learnt that another native force, under Nazim Mahomed Hossein, was six or eight miles up the river, intending to cross and join Balla Rao. On the 3rd, therefore, a detachment, which included 2 guns and 50 men of the Naval Brigade, under Captain Sotheby, went out to the attack, and found the rebels at Bururiah in a strong position. The enemy stood with unusual steadiness, until his flank was threatened; whereupon he retired and scattered, carrying off his guns. The detachment then returned to camp; and on December 5th, the Naval Brigade crossed the Raptee, the rest of the force soon following.

The movement was part of a concerted plan to encircle the shattered armies of the Begum, Lord Clyde being to the westward, Sir Hope Grant to the southward, and Brigadier Rowcroft drawing round from the eastward, while to the northward were the jungles of Nepal. A guard was left at the bridge at Doomureahgunge; and the remainder of the force marched to Intwa and camped there. The siege train, consisting of two 18-prs., one 8-in. howitzer, two 8-in. mortars, and two 5·5-in. mortars, arrived on the 18th and gave the Naval Brigade as much artillery as it could possibly manage. The mortars were entrusted to Lieutenant Pym, R.M. On the 20th, the force advanced from Intwa to Biskohur, in Oudh, and, on the 22nd, to Goolereah Ghat, five miles from Toolseepur, where the remnants of the enemy were collected in great force. On the 23rd, in concert with the army of Sir Hope Grant, the force crossed the Boora Raptee, and attacked. Near the centre were the four naval guns and two 24-pr. rocket tubes, under Commander Turnour, Lieutenant Maquay, and Midshipman Foot. The rest of the Naval Brigade, and the siege train, under Captain Sotheby, was as close up as the nature of the ground would admit. In about an hour and a half, the rebels were completely routed, though they carried off most of their guns, and although the pursuit was somewhat ineffective, owing to lack of enough cavalry to undertake it properly. The mutineers numbered about 12,000; the attacking force, which had but 4 killed and about a dozen wounded, only 2500.

This was the last affair in which the *Pearl's* Brigade took part, and, indeed, the last general action of the Mutiny. The seamen and Marines hoped to enjoy a quiet Christmas at Toolseepur, but were ordered on almost immediately with Brigadier Rowcroft. After a useless pursuit, nearly as far as the Nepal frontier, the force returned. On the last day of the year, the Brigade lay at Puch-purwah ; and on January 1st, 1859, it was ordered back to the ship at Calcutta. Brigadier Rowcroft, on taking leave of it on the 2nd, said : " The successes we have gained are mainly due to your courage and gallantry. I have also observed the excellent discipline and conduct of your Brigade, which reflects great credit on Captain Sotheby, and the officers, as well as on yourselves. I therefore regret to lose your services ; but I am glad that, upon your departure, you are homeward bound, which you all so much desire."

On the 3rd, the Brigade departed, and, having embarked on the 17th in the steamer *Benares*, reached Calcutta on February 2nd. A ' Gazette Extraordinary,' published at Allahabad on January 17th, when the Brigade passed through that city, expressed the high satis-faction of the Government of India with the great services of the *Pearl's* officers and men. The ship left Calcutta on February 13th, called at Madras, whence she sailed again on the 26th, and reached Spithead on June 6th, after having circumnavigated the globe, and been absent from home for three years and a week. She was paid off on June 16th, 1859 ; and a "paying-off" dinner on the evening of that day revived an old custom which had long been nearly extinct in the service, and brought officers and men all together for the last time.[1]

The principal honours and promotions granted in respect of the services of the *Pearl's* Brigade were as follows :—

Captain E. S. Sotheby, to be C.B., June 29th, 1858.
To be Commanders : Lieut. N. E. B. Turnour, May 21st ; Lieut. S. W. D. Rad-cliffe, and Lieut. H. D. Grant, June 18th, 1858.
To be (actg.) Lieutenants : Mate A. W. Ingles, May 21st ; Mate T. M. Maquay, June 18th, 1858.

As in South Africa, forty years later, so in India during the Mutiny, the landed guns of the Navy, and the indefatigable and resourceful manner in which they were moved and worked in diffi-cult country, went far towards saving a very precarious situation. Yet it should not be forgotten that the Navy does not exist for such work as had to be done by it on those occasions ; and that it would scarcely have been called upon to do it had the British Empire been

---

[1] Williams, ' Cruise of the *Pearl.*' Disp. of Sotheby, Macgregor, and Rowcroft ; Ind. *Gazettes* of Mar. 9th, 23rd ; April 27th ; May 11th ; June 22nd ; July 6th, 13th ; Aug. 13th ; Oct. 12th, 19th ; Nov. 23rd, 26th, 1858 ; and Jan. 11th, 1859.

properly prepared to bear its immense responsibilities. It was only because the military administration failed at the pinch that the Navy had to step in and adapt itself to duties which did not belong to it, and which, for the moment at least, diminished its efficiency for services more peculiarly its own.

The Navy was intimately concerned in the laying of the first submarine telegraph cable across the Atlantic. An unsuccessful attempt was made in August, 1857, after the intended route, between Ireland and Newfoundland, had been surveyed by the *Cyclops*, 6, paddle, Lieutenant Joseph Dayman.[1] About half the cable was put into the U.S. screw frigate, *Niagara*, 40, Captain Hudson, U.S.N., and half into the screw battleship *Agamemnon*, 91, Master Cornelius Thomas Augustus Noddall; the programme being that the *Niagara* should lay the section between Valentia and mid-Atlantic, where a splice should be made, and that the *Agamemnon* should complete the laying to Newfoundland.

The two cable ships quitted Valentia on August 7th, accompanied by the *Leopard*, 18, paddle, Captain James Francis Ballard Wainwright, the *Cyclops*, and the U.S. paddle-vessel *Susquehanna*, 15. When 335 miles of the cable had been payed out, it parted.

In July, 1858, a more fortunate essay was made. It had been determined that the cable ships should proceed to a rendezvous in mid-Atlantic, there make the splice, and then steam away from one another in opposite directions. Again the *Agamemnon* and the *Niagara* were employed, the former, however, being commanded by Captain George William Preedy, with, as navigators, Master Henry Augustus Moriarty, and Second-Master Samuel Libby.[2] The splice was effected on July 29th, and the *Agamemnon* then made for Kingstown Bay, Valentia, escorted by the *Valorous*, 16, paddle, Captain William Cornwallis Aldham, while the *Niagara* made for Trinity Bay, Newfoundland, escorted by the *Gorgon*, 6, paddle, Commander Joseph Dayman. At the western terminus there waited the *Porcupine*, 3, paddle, Captain Henry Charles Otter, and, at the eastern one, the gunboat *Shamrock*, Master William Barnerd Calver; and, with the assistance of these, both shore ends were safely landed on August 6th. Unhappily, this cable worked only for a short time. It then became useless, and telegraphic communication beneath the Atlantic was not again effected until 1866.

Towards the end of December, 1857, Commodore Charles Wise,

[1] Com., Jan. 1st, 1858.   [2] Mast., Sept. 3rd, 1858.

of the *Vesuvius*, 6, paddle, senior officer on the west coast of Africa, was instructed by the Admiralty to proceed up the Great Scarcies river, about thirty miles to the northward of Sierra Leone, and to punish the Sooso tribe, which had gone to war with the Timmanees, allies of the British, burning several British factories, and even threatening Sierra Leone.

With his own vessel, and the *Pluto*, 4, paddle, Lieutenant William Swinburn, *Spitfire*, 5, paddle, Lieutenant James Carter Campbell, and *Ardent*, 5, paddle, Commander John Halliday Cave, and a party from the *Teazer*, 2, screw, Lieutenant William Henry Whyte, the Commodore anchored off the mouth of the river on January 21st, 1858. The Soosos refused to evacuate the town of Kambia, which they had occupied, and which belonged to the Timmanees; and, in consequence, on January 31st, a force consisting of eight paddle-box boats carrying 24- and 12-prs., a rocket cutter, a colonial gunboat having on board the governor and staff, and a detachment of about 250 seamen and Marines, proceeded up the river, and anchored off Kambia on February 1st. The town was strongly stockaded, and defended by an inner mud wall and flanking towers, while the plain between the place and the river's bank was studded with rifle-pits. Within a quarter of an hour, however, the town was set on fire by means of rockets; and a bombardment with shell killed, it was said, 200 of the enemy. Kambia being in ashes, the force descended the stream, destroying in succession Robelli, Makanka, Robaiyan, and Rokon, besides other villages. Although the people were exposed to a brisk fire from each place, the casualties among them were only 2 officers and 8 men wounded. Thanks to a liberal use of quinine, there was no fever in the force, which rejoined the ships on February 4th.

For this service Lieutenants Swinburn, Whyte, and Campbell were promoted, and three Mates were made Lieutenants.

The force had not landed to occupy the site of any of the destroyed towns; and the enemy, attributing the omission to weakness, presently became more aggressive than before; whereupon, in March, 1859, a fresh expedition, again under Commodore Wise, went up the river in 52 boats. The landing force consisted chiefly of Marines, and the 1st West India Regiment. The stockade was stormed; the Soosos were driven out with heavy loss; and the Timmanees were put in possession of the town. The casualties were trivial; and, as before, there was happily no fever.

At about the same time the vessels on the station were both active and successful in the repression of slavery. An armed slaver of considerable size and force was captured by the *Vesuvius's* cutter, under Mate Robert Henry More Molyneux,[1] assisted by the *Pluto's* gig.

In the course of June, 1858, a dispute arose at Jeddah, the port of Mecca, concerning the ownership of a vessel which belonged to Indian subjects of her Majesty. In consequence of this dispute, rioting took place; and on the evening of June 15th, the British vice-consul, the French consul, and several other Christian residents in the town were massacred. Several more only escaped massacre owing to the intervention of local officials, or to the opportune despatch to the shore of an armed boat from the *Cyclops*, 6, paddle, Captain William John Samuel Pullen, which was lying off the town.

Pullen took the fugitives to Suez, and, having received orders, returned to Jeddah, where he arrived on July 23rd. He demanded satisfaction within thirty-six hours, and, getting no reply by the morning of the 25th, began a bombardment. At 11 A.M. an unsatisfactory answer from the local pasha was sent off to him ; whereupon he resumed firing, and continued, with intermissions, until the evening of the 26th. On the 27th Turkish troops appeared in a transport, and were landed. Their commander seized the murderers, but professed that he had no power to execute them, although they had been found guilty by the native court. Pullen insisted upon their execution ; and, on the morning of August 5th reopened the bombardment in order to enforce his determination. More troops, and an officer of superior rank, arriving from Egypt, eleven of the murderers were executed in sight of the town and shipping on the morning of the 6th, and four more were sent to Constantinople.[2] The business was a natural result of the lamentable weakness of Turkish authority in Arabia ; but, as proper satisfaction was given by the Sultan, the matter proceeded no further.[3]

William Walker, the famous filibuster, who had been a thorn

---

[1] Actg.-Lieut. in consequence, June 28th, 1859.

[2] Cons. Green to For. Off.   Lord Malmesbury in Ho. of Lords, July 19th, 1858.

[3] The *Roebuck*, 6, screw, Lieutenant (actg.-Commander) Edwin Charles Symons, was also employed at Jeddah, during this year, in connection with the attacks on the local Christians, and subsequently at the Andaman Islands, on the occasion of a mutinous outbreak there.

in the side of the Central American governments since 1853, had
been driven out of Nicaragua in 1857 by the concerted action of
the other states, and, making an effort to return in 1858, had
been shipwrecked, and obliged to accept the hospitality of a British
man-of-war.   He, or his partisans, made yet another abortive
attempt in 1859; and in 1860, after having written a curious
history of his adventurous career, he set out from Mobile on what
proved to be his last expedition.   Previous to his departure, Great
Britain had joined the United States in declaring that any further
action by Walker against Nicaragua would be forcibly resisted.
Until a few years before, Ruatan, the principal of the Bay Islands,
had been under British guardianship; but, under the Clayton-
Bulwer Treaty, it had been ceded to Honduras; and the filibuster
imagined that he might take advantage of this circumstance to
make the island his base of operations against the republic of
which he had been, for a short time, president.   He therefore

SIR NOWELL SALMON, G.C.B., ADMIRAL OF THE FLEET.

proceeded thither with a number of his old followers.   Unfortunately for him, the British flag was still flying over Ruatan, the
cession not having been actually carried out, owing to certain
financial disputes between Great Britain and Honduras not having
been settled.

While Walker was standing on and off, waiting for the British
flag to be hauled down, the *Icarus*, 11, Commander Nowell
Salmon, V.C., arrived at Ruatan from Belize, having on board
the Superintendent of Belize, who, with Salmon, was to complete
the 'cession of the islands.   Seeing what was the state of affairs,
and unwilling to do anything which might enable Walker to seize
Ruatan ere Honduras could take possession of it, the British
officials went to Jamaica for further orders.   Upon returning,
Salmon found Walker still in the neighbourhood, and learnt that
he had endeavoured to utilise for his purposes the adjoining island
of Bonacea.   Chafing at being able to accomplish nothing in the
islands, Walker and his people sailed over to Truxillo on the

mainland, and captured it.   Salmon followed him, and was informed that the filibuster had " annexed " the town, and made it a free port.   The inhabitants, who had been maltreated, had taken to the forest.

With some little difficulty Salmon put himself in communication with the expelled Honduran governor, and discovered that the customs' receipts of the place had been mortgaged to the British government in payment of a debt.   He therefore wrote to Walker, telling him that in the circumstances his acts could not be recognised, and that he must evacuate the town within twenty-four hours, and take shipping, which should be provided, for New Orleans.   After some correspondence, in the course of which Walker magniloquently declared that he had come to introduce the code of Alfred into benighted lands, the filibuster agreed to the terms, and undertook to embark on the following morning. This was on August 20th.   Pressed, however, by Honduran forces, he evacuated the town over night, and retreated down the coast, with but seventy men.   On his way, he looted some mahogany-cutting settlements ; and, upon hearing of this, the Honduran government applied to Salmon for assistance.   Salmon satisfied himself that there was precedent for giving it ; and, taking in tow a barque with General Alvarez and 200 troops, went in chase down the coast.   Off the Rio Negro, it was ascertained that Walker and his companions were making themselves at home on the mahogany-cutting station of an Englishman, near Lemas. Salmon proceeded up the river with his boats manned and armed ; and, when within sight of the station, landed with General Alvarez, and walked to the building which Walker had made his headquarters.   To a demand for an unconditional surrender, and a threat that the guns in the boats would open fire on him if he refused, the filibuster asked for certain terms, which Salmon declined, alleging that, as Walker had already broken faith, he would not be allowed another opportunity for doing so.   Walker then inquired whether he was surrendering to the Queen of England. The reply was that the surrender was to the Commander of the *Icarus* ; whereupon Walker fell his men in, and ordered them to lay down their arms.   Both men and arms were taken on board the sloop and carried to Truxillo, where all but Walker, and Rudler, his chief of staff, were transferred to the *Gladiator*, 6, paddle, Commander Henry Dennis Hickley, and conveyed to New Orleans.

Walker declined to plead American nationality, and claimed to be president of the Nicaraguan Republic. Salmon, therefore, could not persuade the Honduran authorities to release the two leaders ; nor, acting with and on behalf of them as he did, did he feel justified in taking up the position that the filibusters ought not to be punished. However, he appointed a Mr. Squire to watch the case on behalf of the United States government. Walker was tried by court-martial on September 11th, and condemned to be shot on the following morning. Ere he died, he admitted the justice of his sentence.[1]

Walker's allusion to King Alfred indicates that he regarded himself as an enlightened law-giver. This singular man also regarded himself as a disinterested liberator ; for, after his surrender, he sent for Salmon, and asked : " Would you have treated Garibaldi like this ? " But Salmon, who seems to have had but little sympathy with liberators, even of Garibaldi's type, replied to the effect that, if it fell to his lot to be able to do so, he might possibly not hesitate. The " last of the filibusters " was little more than thirty-six at the time of his death.

Between 1821 and 1868 the form of government in Mexico was changed ten times ; upwards of fifty persons became in succession rulers of the country as presidents, dictators, or emperors ; and there are said to have been no fewer than three hundred *pronunciamientos*. It is hardly astonishing, therefore, that during that period Mexico got into occasional difficulties with foreign powers.

In 1857, what is known as the " Struggle of Reform " broke out. Ignacio Comonfort, who had been made provisional president of the republic by Alvarez, in 1855, had assumed a dictatorship, with the support of the clergy and the conservatives. Benito Pablo Juarez, the chief justice, and leader of the advanced liberals, or "Puros," headed the opposition. In 1858 Comonfort was deposed by Zuloaga, who resigned in favour of the conservative General Miramon, but was presently restored by him. Juarez claimed that, the president having been unconstitutionally displaced, the chief justice, as vice president, thereupon became legal president of the republic, and, accordingly, he ignored Zuloaga and Miramon, and himself acted as president. Civil war resulted. An able, honest, and patriotic statesman, Juarez had the misfortune, throughout his active career,

---

[1] J. J. Roche: 'Story of the Filibusters,' 173–177; Disp. of Salmon; Letter of Salmon to author, Oct. 12th, 1900 ; *A. and N. Gazette*, Oct. 6th, 1860.

to be regarded with suspicion and intolerance by most of the Europeans with whom his energetic behaviour brought him into contact; and certainly his methods were sometimes extremely high-handed. As early as the autumn of 1859, the *Amethyst*, 26, Captain Sidney Grenfell, which was then serving a commission during which she circumnavigated the globe, found occasion to interfere with the proceedings of his supporters at Mazatlan, and at San Blas, both on the Pacific coast. Trade was taken possession of; Mazatlan was blockaded; an American brig, which had been seized, and which lay under the batteries there, was pluckily cut out one October night by three of the frigate's boats, under Master Richard Cossantine Dyer; and Royal Marines, under Lieutenant Alfred Henry Pascoe, R.M., were disembarked at San Blas.

At length the Puros were triumphant, and Juarez was duly elected by congress to be president of the republic of Mexico. He readily agreed with Great Britain and France as to the payment of indemnities to persons of those nationalities who, residing in Mexico during the civil commotions, had suffered in consequence; and a convention to that effect was signed on March 16th, 1861. But the country, exhausted by the long strife, was in grave financial difficulties; and on July 17th, following, congress was induced to pass a law, in virtue of which the payment of all public debts, including the indemnities, was to be postponed for two years. The representatives of Great Britain and France endeavoured, in vain, to procure the repeal of this measure, and then broke off relations with the Mexican government. Spain, which also had claims, took parallel action, and, on October 31st, 1861, the three powers signed a convention providing for their co-operation with a view to obtaining satisfaction.

France dispatched a large naval and military force; Spain sent 6000 troops; Great Britain contributed only a battalion of Marines, and a few vessels which happened to be on the station, including the *Challenger*,[1] 22, screw, Captain John James Kennedy, C.B., the *Desperate*, 7, screw, Commander John Francis Ross, and the *Barracouta*, 6, paddle, Commander George John Malcolm. The British participated in the occupation of Vera Cruz in January, 1862, but on the following April 9th, wisely decided, in concert with Spain, to press matters no further, and to withdraw from Mexican territory. France, which had larger views than her allies, was left

---

[1] Bearing the broad pennant of Commodore Hugh Dunlop, from Jamaica.

to prosecute alone an undertaking which became disastrous both to herself and Mexico, and to France's *protégé*, the Austrian Archduke, Ferdinand Maximilian Josef, who was made emperor in 1863.

In 1860, accompanied by a large suite, H.R.H. the Prince of Wales paid a visit to Canada and the United States. The screw battleship *Hero*, 91, Captain George Henry Seymour, C.B., was selected as the vessel in which he was to cross the Atlantic; and he embarked in her at Plymouth, and sailed on July 12th, escorted by the screw frigate *Ariadne*, 26, Captain Edward Westby Vansittart, and the screw sloop *Flying-Fish*, 6, Commander Charles Webley Hope. The outward voyage was made without incident. Returning, the Prince embarked at Portland, Maine, on October 29th, and, encountering head winds and bad weather nearly all the way home, did not reach Plymouth until November 16th, by which day the *Hero* had only about one week's ship's provisions left, and even the royal party was living on salt and preserved meat. The ships had plenty of coal, but, with the relatively low-powered engines of those days, had been unable to make head against the continuous gales. "Our cousins in the United States," as Lord Palmerston said, "received the eldest son of our gracious Sovereign, not as if he were a stranger belonging to another land, but as if he had been born in their own country." Of the loyalty of the reception in Canada there is no need to speak.

The history of the events which led up to Great Britain's active interference with the Ti-ping rebellion in China must be told at some little length. It affords an interesting study, and, I think, supplies examples rather of what to avoid than of what to emulate in dealing with great reform movements in Oriental lands.

After the collision with the Ti-ping rebels at Nankin, and elsewhere on the Yang-tse-kiang, in 1858, Great Britain, which had always recognised the Ti-pings as belligerents,[1] re-adopted a professed policy, so far as they were concerned, of non-intervention. The rebels were, however, from time to time reminded that they must neither interfere with British trade nor imperil British interests. Thus, for example, a proclamation by the Hon. F. W. A. Bruce, dated Shanghai, May 26th, 1860, pointed out that, Shanghai being a port open to foreign trade, commerce would receive a severe blow, were the place to be attacked and to become the scene of civil war; and went on to declare that, without taking any part in the contest,

---

[1] Bowring's Ordinance of 1855.

or expressing any opinion as to the rights of the parties to it, the British might justifiably protect the city, and assist the Chinese authorities in preserving tranquillity within it.[1] Mr. Bruce did not, unfortunately, wait for the rebels actually to attack Shanghai ere he began to make a distinction between them and the Imperial party, such as, apparently, he had no right to make so long as the Ti-pings were officially recognised as belligerents ; for, a few months after his proclamation above alluded to, he refused to allow the consuls to hold any communication with certain insurgent authorities at Soo-chow, and ordered them to take no notice of a dispatch which had been received from one of the insurgent leaders. This attitude was inconsistent, and, as events proved, dangerous. Neutrality, such as Mr. Bruce professed, should not have allowed him to take more notice of Imperial than of Ti-ping dispatches ; nor could he complain if, so long as he declined to notice communications from the Ti-pings, the Ti-pings paid little attention to communications from him. It was the anomalous and contradictory situation created by Mr. Bruce which, I believe, was originally responsible for the many bloody collisions which followed between the British forces and the rebels, who, it is notorious, were particularly anxious to gain European countenance, and most unwilling deliberately to provoke European hostility.

On August 18th, 1860, the rebel leader sent to the foreign ministers a notification of his intention to come to Shanghai,[2] and of his determination to respect foreign churches and property, upon yellow flags being hoisted over them. This was the dispatch which Mr. Bruce ordered his subordinates to take no notice of. Instead of acknowledging it, and directly stating in reply that the rebels must on no account approach, he issued a " notification," based ostensibly on " reports " which had reached him, to the effect that, armed

---

[1] Yet, writing to Lord John Russell from Shanghai on June 10th, 1860, Mr. Bruce had said : " I am inclined to doubt the policy of attempting to restore, by force of arms, the power of the Imperial government in cities and provinces occupied, or rather overrun, by the insurgents." And, after deprecating intervention, went on, " . . . the Chinese, deprived of popular insurrection—their rude but efficacious remedy against local oppressors—would, with justice, throw on the foreigner the odium of excesses which his presence alone would render possible. . . . No course could be so well calculated to lower our national reputation as to lend our material support to a government, the corruption of whose authorities is only checked by its weakness." *See also* Sykes' 'Taeping Rebellion,' 18.

[2] In response, he afterwards explained, to an invitation from the French. The Chung-wang to the Consuls, Aug. 21st.

forces being understood to be in the neighbourhood, he thereby made known that the city of Shanghai, and the foreign settlement, were militarily occupied by the British and French, and that any armed force approaching would be treated as hostile. He sent a copy of this, not to the chief who had addressed him, but to a place out of the line of the march of the Ti-pings ; and, in consequence, it was not delivered. Had he communicated with the Chung-wang,[1] who had written to him, what followed might have been avoided.

On August 18th, 1860, the Ti-ping army, or rather, part of it, arrived before Shanghai, and drove in the Tartar outposts, subsequently advancing to the walls. They were met with shot, shell, and musketry from the European garrison of the settlement, and especially from Royal Marines, and Indian troops, Lieutenant John William Waller O'Grady, R.M., being particularly active, and Captain Frederick Edward Budd, R.M., keeping up a very hot fire from another position. It is said that, during the whole time, the rebels did not reply.[2] At any rate, about 300 of them fell, while there was not a single casualty on the part of the Europeans. When the Ti-pings had retired, parties were sent out to burn down such houses in the suburbs as might afford cover to the rebels. On Sunday, August 19th, the French burnt more houses, and, in the afternoon, the gunboats *Kestrel*, Lieutenant Henry Huxham, and *Hongkong*, together with Lieutenant O'Grady's Marines, re-opened fire on any rebels who could be seen. It is said that again the Ti-pings did not return a shot. It is certain, however, that, on the 20th they advanced in greater strength than before, determined, perhaps, to endeavour to avenge their comrades slaughtered, as they conceived it, in bad faith. Once more they were driven back ; and during the following night, the *Pioneer*, 6, screw, Commander Hugh Arthur Reilly, added to their discomfiture by steaming up the river and dropping shells into their camp.

When, after the conclusion of peace with China, it became desirable that a British expedition should proceed up the Yang-tse-kiang to provide for the opening of the treaty ports there, it was necessary to make some preliminary agreement with the Ti-pings, who commanded many of the important points on the river. Sir James Hope, therefore, communicated with the Ti-ping authorities

[1] Ti-ping general-in-chief.

[2] Corr. of *Nonconformist*, Nov. 14th, 1860; *Overland Register*, Sept. 10th, 1860 ; 'Ti-ping Tien-Kwoh,' i., 275, etc.; *Times of India*, Oct. 24th, 1860.

at Nankin, and once more pledged British neutrality. He was instructed by Lord Elgin[1] to say that the British did not appear as enemies, nor with the intention of taking part in the civil war. Mr. Parkes, who accompanied the Vice-Admiral on the subsequent expedition up the river, was instructed by Lord Elgin[2] to the same effect. But, when Hope, in the *Coromandel*, reached Nankin, he directed[3] Commander Elphinstone d'Oyley d'Auvergne Aplin, of the *Centaur*, 6, paddle, to tell the Ti-ping authorities that the British and French governments had ordered that any attempt to enter Shanghai or Woosung would be repelled by force, and that therefore the Ti-pings would do well not to go within two days' march of those cities. If such orders had then been given, they were secret ones; but the Foreign Office approved[4] of Hope's measures, and also of his having assured the Ti-pings that, if they obeyed him in this matter he would exert his influence to prevent any hostile expedition from leaving those places in order to attack Ti-ping troops. While expressing his approval, Lord John Russell added : " You will understand, however, that Her Majesty's government do not wish force to be used against the rebels in any case, except for the actual protection of the lives and property of British subjects."

The upshot was that the Ti-pings ultimately promised not to attack Shanghai or Woosung that year (1861) ; and requested that, on the other hand, the Imperial troops might not be allowed into those places. Mr. Parkes accepted and reported this request as a condition. It was also arranged that if the Ti-pings should attack other treaty ports and not molest British subjects in their persons and property, commanders of British vessels, in accordance with instructions to be given them, would not interfere in the hostilities, except for the purpose of protecting their countrymen, if necessary.

The Ti-pings adhered to their undertaking relative to the year 1861, and refrained from advancing within 100 li, or about 30 miles, of Shanghai or Woosung. They might easily have taken both places had they wished, and had they had only the Imperial forces to contend with, for, during that year, they were extraordinarily successful, and made themselves masters of nearly the whole of the two rich provinces of Chekiang and Kiangsu.

That friction, nevertheless, occurred almost immediately was but natural, looking to the forward policy which Sir James Hope thought

---

[1] *See* Parl. Corr. on Opening of Yang-tse-kiang.   [2] Jan 19th, 1861.
[3] Hope to Aplin, Mar. 28th, 1861.   [4] Russell to Bruce, July 24th, 1861.

fit to adopt throughout. Mr. Bruce, writing to Lord John Russell
on January 3rd, 1861, said that he had directed the British consul at
Ningpo not to undertake the defence of that city, and, should it be
attacked, to confine his efforts to a mediation, " which may save
the place from being the scene of pillage and massacre " ; and, in
a letter to Hope, Bruce declared that he did not consider himself
authorized to protect Ningpo. In his instructions to Mr. Sinclair,
the local consul, he wrote : " Your language should be that we take
no part in this civil contest, but that we claim exemption from
injury and annoyance at the hands of both parties." All this was
approved by Lord John Russell in a dispatch of March 28th, 1861.
Yet, on May 8th, Sir James Hope, at Nagasaki, ordered Captain
Roderick Dew, of the *Encounter*, 14, screw, to put himself into communication with the rebel leaders, and to require them to desist
from all hostile proceedings against the town of Ningpo. At the
same time, Dew was directed to communicate also with the Imperial
authorities at Ningpo,

" for the purpose of ascertaining what their means of resistance are, and the probabilities
of their proving successful; and, should you find them amenable to advice, you will
point out to them such measures as circumstance may render expedient, and you will
place every obstruction in the way of the capture of the town by the rebels."

This was not neutrality. Lord John Russell was being hurried
on by Hope, but hurried on unwillingly ; for, commenting on the
" every obstruction " policy of the Vice-Admiral, Lord John, writing
to Bruce, said :—

" I have caused the Admiralty to be informed, in reply, that I am of opinion that
Vice-Admiral Hope's measures should be approved. . . . You will understand, however, that Her Majesty's government do not wish force to be used against the rebels in
any case, except for the actual protection of the lives and property of British subjects."

Captain Dew, in pursuance of instructions, proceeded on May 24th
in the gunboat *Flamer*, Lieutenant Henry Maynard Bingham, to
convey Hope's ultimatum to the rebels in the vicinity of Ningpo.
They were not to approach within two days' march of Ningpo upon
penalty of coming into hostile contact with British forces. Dew,
being unable to reach the rebel positions in the gunboat, put his
little party into pulling boats. Upon reaching a town which was
occupied by the Ti-pings, he noticed a discharge of gingals from the
walls, though whether directed against him is doubtful ; and he
withdrew, after having left Hope's communication in a cleft bamboo
stuck into the ground before the place. If there was any firing at

the party, it was probably the work of some ignorant underling or the result of mistake; for when, on June 11th, with the *Encounter* and *Flamer*, Dew took another copy of the ultimatum to Chapoo, which had been occupied by the Ti-pings, and landed with it under a flag of truce, he was not fired at; and the local commandant went out and received the letter in person. The document, dated "*Encounter*, June 11th," says nothing about any hostile act having been committed on May 24th; and therefore it may be assumed that whatever occurred on that day was officially regarded as not calling for an apology.

The Ti-pings, be it remembered, were under no undertaking not to occupy Ningpo. The British, however, were under an undertaking to be neutral. Yet almost while Lord John Russell, writing on August 8th[1] to Mr. Bruce, said that the desire of the government was to remain neutral as before, and to "abstain from all interference in the civil war," Captain Dew was assisting the Imperialists with plans for the defence of Ningpo, and fitting twelve heavy guns with carriages to mount on the walls. It is not astonishing that Mr. Bruce thought that

"Captain Dew had gone farther than he was strictly warranted in doing in his desire to save the city of Ningpo."[2]

In June, moreover, Captain Dew appeared in the *Flamer* off the Ti-ping town of Loochee, some distance up the Wong-poo river, and demanded the restitution of some boats and silk which had been detained for non-payment of duty at a time when duty was being paid as a matter of course at the same station by many European traders. It could not be contended that the Ti-ping occupation had injured the silk trade, duty or no duty; for Mr. Bruce himself, in a dispatch to Lord John Russell said that the export from June, 1860, to June, 1861, had been 85,000 bales; and that was, with one exception, the largest annual export ever then known.

By November, the only places in the Chekiang and Kiangsu provinces south of the Yang-tse-kiang not held by the Ti-pings were the treaty ports of Shanghai, Chinkiang, and Ningpo. Those places were strongholds of the Imperialists; and the rebels were bound by all the principles of strategy either to complete their conquest of the provinces, or criminally to leave their cause in a

---

[1] Blue Book on China, p. 46.　　　　[2] Blue Book on China, pp. 50, 64.

position of great danger and peril.   In spite, therefore, of Sir
James Hope's communications, they approached Ningpo ; whereupon
the British and American Consuls, with Lieutenant Henry Huxham,
commanding H.M.S. *Kestrel*, and a French naval officer, proceeded
on November 28th to the Ti-ping headquarters, and verbally
informed the leaders

" That the undersigned take no part in this civil contest, but that they claim exemption from injury and annoyance at the hands of both parties."

Hwang, the Ti-ping general, agreed with the principle thus
laid down, assured the Consuls of his desire to keep well with
foreigners, and promised to behead any of his followers who should
offer them annoyance.   On December 2nd the Consuls visited
another Ti-ping general, Fang, who was advancing from a different
direction.   They endeavoured to dissuade him from capturing the
place, chiefly on the ground of the difficulty of keeping order
afterwards.   Fang replied that he could not allow Ningpo to remain
in the hands of the Imperialists ; but, at the wish of the Consuls,
he consented to postpone the attack for a week.   At the expiration
of that period, the Ti-pings, on December 9th, 1861, took Ningpo,
after it had offered a feeble resistance for about an hour, the
Imperialists then fleeing.   Hope, in his account of the affair,
admits that—

" everything had been done to assist the Imperialists in the defence of the town, except
the use of force in their favour; and their Lordships will not fail to observe how
utterly useless such measures proved, in consequence of the cowardice and imbecility
of the mandarins. . . . The behaviour of the rebels has been good hitherto; and they
profess a strong desire to remain on good terms with foreigners."

The British Consul, writing to Lord John Russell, also said :—

" Up to the present time there has been no slaughter, or massacre, or fires within
the walls. . . . With the exception of a few men killed, and a certain amount of
destruction of property, the rebels have, so far, conducted themselves with wonderful
moderation."

A few days afterwards, Sir James Hope proceeded to Nankin
in order, if possible, to obtain from the Ti-ping leaders a renewal
of their promise not to attack Shanghai for one year—that is, during
the course of 1862.   This they declined to give, partly because
they considered that the British had not strictly interpreted their
own promise to prevent the Imperialists from using Shanghai as
a base for aggressive purposes ; partly because Shanghai had

become an Imperial arsenal and rallying place; and partly because they could not further forego their rights as recognised belligerents.

Upon that Sir James Hope, through Lieutenant Henry Maynard Bingham, of the *Renard*, on December 27th, 1861, put forward demands which, I think, can have been formulated only with an intention of finding a *casus belli*. He alleged that certain British subjects, by robberies committed in territories held by the Ti-pings, had suffered a loss amounting to 7563 taels, 1 mace, and 7 candareens, 4800 dollars, 20 bales of silk, and 2 muskets. The cash value of all this in British currency may have been as much as £3500. He further demanded that junks carrying British colours should be regarded as British vessels, no matter whether British or foreign built, and should be allowed to pass free on the river from examination or other molestation. He went on to declare that the Ti-ping promise that troops should not approach within 100 li of Shanghai and Woosung had not been faithfully observed; and he ended by requiring that no Ti-ping troops should go within 100 li of Kiukiang and Hankow, and that Silver Island, the residence of the British Consul at Chinkiang-foo, should not be molested. The general tenor of the reply[1] of the Ti-ping leaders was to the effect that compliance with the demands, some of which were new and of a distinctly unfriendly nature, would fetter the Ti-ping cause, and could not, therefore, be granted. It was objected that no proofs had been advanced as to the alleged losses by British subjects, or that such losses had been caused by the Ti-pings; and that, if the losses had taken place, the British ought to have complained at once to the local officers, instead of waiting many months before complaining at all. It was also pointed out that, if the British flag were permitted to cover non-British vessels, the Ti-pings might see themselves deprived of nearly the whole of their customs revenue.

Bingham, by Hope's direction, at once answered with a threat to use force. It would occupy much more space than can be afforded here were I to follow out the arguments by which Sir James persuaded himself that it was his duty to prevent the Ti-pings from occupying Shanghai; but I cannot blind myself to the conclusion that, had not Hope desired hostilities, hostilities could very easily and honourably have been avoided. It was a case, and a case not

[1] Jan. 1st, 1862.

altogether creditable, of the "prancing pro-consul" leading his
countrymen into devious and dangerous paths ere they realised
whither they were bound, or had time to inquire whether or not
good reasons summoned them. There is a proverb that adversity
makes us acquainted with strange bed-fellows. A forward policy
did as much for Hope. Not many months earlier, Commander
Nowell Salmon, in Central America, had seized the filibuster
William Walker, and handed him over for execution to the
authorities of Honduras. Sir James Hope now associated himself
with William Townsend Ward, who had been one of Walker s
lieutenants, and who, still a filibuster, happened to be, in 1862,
engaged on behalf of the Chinese Imperialists.

On February 21st, 1862, Hope began operations against the
rebels by landing a naval brigade of 350 men and a 6-pr. rocket-tube,
which, with about 600 disciplined Chinese under Ward, and 160
French seamen under the French Rear-Admiral Protêt, drove the
small and ill-armed Ti-ping garrison from the village of Kaokiau,
killing more than 100 of them, and suffering a loss of only 1 French
seaman killed. A similarly one-sided engagement took place on
February 28th at Seadong; and on March 1st, having been
reinforced from Shanghai, the allies attacked the fortified village
of Hsiautang, near Minghong, about twenty miles from Shanghai.
About 100 rebels were killed and 300 taken prisoners, the assailants
not losing a man. On April 4th a stockaded camp at Wongkadzu,
twelve miles from Shanghai, was shelled till the rebels quitted it.
They were pursued, and about 600 of them were killed, while the
allies, who had been again reinforced, had but 1 killed and
2 wounded. On April 5th 300 rebels were killed at the capture of
Lukakong, the assailants once more having no casualties. They
had, however, been repulsed on the previous day, and Hope himself
had been slightly wounded. On April 17th, Chepoo, a village seven
miles up a creek running into the Woosung river, twelve miles
above Shanghai, was bombarded and rushed, the allies having
but 1 killed and 2 wounded, but the Ti-pings suffering a loss
estimated at 900. On May 1st, after four days' operations, the city
of Kahding was taken, the European allies capturing 1000
prisoners and killing "some hundreds," while their Chinese
colleague, General Lee, cut off the retreat of many others and
"destroyed 2500 of the enemy." [1] These operations cost the

[1] Staveley's disp. of May 3rd.

allies not more than five or six people wounded. On May 12th the walled city of Tsingpoo was escaladed. About 2500 Ti-pings were killed, and the whole of the rest of the garrison was taken prisoners. The allies here had but 2 killed and 10 wounded, though they also lost an artillery officer from exposure and over-exertion. The village of Najoor was taken on May 17th. This capture cost the life of the French Rear-Admiral Protêt and the wounding of 15 other British and French; but the Ti-pings had 500 killed. On May 20th the small town of Cholin, twenty-six miles S.S.W. of Shanghai and two miles from the sea, was bombarded and stormed. Here a most disgraceful and indiscriminate massacre took place, even women and children not being spared.[1] About 3000 Chinese perished. The allies had 1 killed and 4 wounded. Up to that time Sir James Hope and General Staveley, in the neighbourhood of Shanghai, had met only ill-armed Ti-pings. Upon receipt of intelligence that the Chung-wang, with a large and probably a more formidably-equipped army, had taken the field, and invested Kahding, and was threatening Tsingpoo, they returned to the treaty port. A half-hearted attempt to relieve Kahding was abandoned, owing to the immense numbers of rebels near it; but the only loss suffered by the British ere they retreated was 1 killed and 4 wounded. The Naval Brigade employed in these various affairs was drawn mainly from the *Impérieuse*, 51, screw (flag), Captain George Ommanney Willes, C.B.; *Pearl*, 21, screw, Captain John Borlase, C.B., who generally commanded; and *Vulcan*, 6, screw trooper, Commander Augustus Chetham Strode.

All this was done professedly in the interests of European commerce. It would hardly have been done had the merchants been first consulted. Messrs. Jardine, Matheson and Co., in their circular of February 27th, complained, not of what had been done by the Ti-pings, but of what was about to be done by the allies. They wrote:—

"The policy the allied commanders are adopting will, it is feared, lead to disastrous consequences. . . . Our interests call for a strict neutrality; but, so far from this course being pursued, our last advices report a combined expedition of English and French marines and sailors, in conjunction with a force of Imperialists, commanded in person by their respective admirals, against a body of some 6000 rebels which, of course, they defeated with great slaughter."

[1] *Overland Trade Report*, June 10th. See also *North China Herald*. The French, announcing that they were avenging Protêt, were the worst offenders.

Nor, after he had begun hostilities, was Sir James Hope consistent. He grounded his action on the possibility that the advancing Ti-pings might destroy supplies. After describing his operations, he said :—

"All these camps, which contained large quantities of rice collected from the surrounding country, were burnt, and the grain destroyed."

Moreover, only a few days before the attack on Wongkadzu, the *Flamer* destroyed a flotilla of 300 Ti-ping boats "deeply laden with rice and live stock."

In the meantime Ningpo had been taken by the rebels. Mr. Consul Harvey reported that it was held with "wonderful moderation." On April 22nd, during certain rejoicings there, some shots were fired wildly in the direction of the foreign settlement, and, it was alleged, killed two or three Chinese. The true facts were never established; but when Commander Robert George Craigie, of the *Ringdove*, 4, screw, wrote to the local authorities on the subject, he received a civil reply and a promise that the offenders, when discovered, should be severely punished. On April 29th Captain Roderick Dew, in the *Encounter*, arrived off Ningpo from Shanghai. On the 27th he wrote to the local authorities, expressing his satisfaction at the replies and promises, and added that, in consequence of their nature—

"we shall not insist on the demolition of the battery at the point, but we still do that you remove the guns. . . . We again inform you that it is the earnest wish of our chiefs to remain neutral, and on good terms with you at Ningpo. . . ." [1]

But on the very day after he had written so condonatory an epistle, he addressed the local authorities with a demand for the pulling down of the battery alluded to, and for the removal of all guns opposite the foreign settlement. After professing his unwillingness to be obliged to resort to force, and his desire to be neutral as between the rebels and the Imperialists, he threatened to destroy the battery and capture Ningpo if his demands were not complied with within twenty-four hours. The rebel leaders protested that the battery was designed, not to injure foreigners but to defend the city, and that the guns had the same object; whereupon Captain Dew, who acted, no doubt in accordance with the private instructions of Sir James Hope, made further demands in a letter of May 2nd. The rebels, on the 3rd, referred to the explanations

[1] These extracts are from the 'Further Papers' issued in August.

which had been already tendered and accepted as satisfactory, and, while once more pointing out that the offending guns were absolutely necessary for the defence of the position against the Imperialists, went so far as to offer to block up the embrasures of certain pieces.

Thus matters rested for a day or two. On the 5th Consul Harvey heard from the ex-governor of Ningpo that he was about to attack the city with a strong force, and that the support of the British and French admirals was solicited. Harvey communicated this to Captain Dew, who, going down the river, saw the ex-governor and the leader of the Imperial fleet which was to take part in the attack. A forward policy, as we have seen, had made Hope and Protêt the abettors of a filibuster. The same vicious system now made Dew the accomplice of a pirate ; for the leader of the Imperial fleet was none other than Apak, a notorious freebooter, whom, like other criminals and scoundrels, the Chinese government did not hesitate to take into favour and to employ in its hour of need. Reporting on the 7th to Hope, Dew wrote :—

" I told them that, in consequence of the rebels refusing certain demands we had made, I should have no objection to their passing up, but that they were not to open fire until well clear of our men-of-war."

In consequence of Dew's permission, Apak and his junks passed up ; and on May 9th Consul Harvey reported to Mr. Bruce that the Chinese fleet was " lying in front of our settlements," making preparations for an assault on Ningpo. Dew, on April 18th, had written to the Ti-ping chiefs that he would " not even allow the foreign settlement to harbour the Imperialists," provided that a battery (which on the 27th he had said might remain) were pulled down. He knew that the place could not be defended without the battery ; and he knew that, if the Imperialists were allowed to place themselves opposite the foreign settlement, that settlement might be said to " harbour the Imperialists," since the Ti-pings could not then defend themselves at all without endangering the settlement, besides endangering the European men-of-war which were lying beyond it.

Early on May 10th the Imperialists, who had previously informed Captain Dew and Consul Harvey " in a private manner " [1] of their intention, began to attack Ningpo, advancing from the

[1] Harvey to Bruce, May 9th.

direction of the foreign settlement, and then manœuvring round and round the British and French vessels, and firing when in such positions as prevented the Ti-pings from replying without imperilling the Europeans. Dew never enforced his stipulation that the Imperialists should keep clear of his men-of-war; and, in his dispatch,[1] he was so disingenuous as to say nothing of the methods whereby, at length, the Ti-pings were unwillingly induced to fire in a direction of the settlement and ships. He does not say, as is perfectly true, that for some time the Ti-pings did not reply at all; and that, when they did at length fire in self-defence, they began by firing muskets only, deeming that they had less control over the projectiles from their heavy guns. What he does say in his letter to Hope is:—

" You are aware, Sir, that the rebel chiefs had been informed that if they again fired either on our ships or in the direction of the settlement, we should deem it a *casus belli.* This morning at 10 A.M., the *Kestrel,* and French vessels *Etoile* and *Confucius* were fired on by the point battery. I cleared for action in this ship, when a volley of musketry was fired on us from the bastion abreast. The undermentioned vessels, viz., *Encounter, Ringdove,*[2] *Kestrel,*[3] and *Hardy,*[4] with the *Etoile* and *Confucius,* French gunboats, now opened fire with shell on the walls and batteries, which was replied to with much spirit from guns and small-arms. . . ."

It must be admitted that, on the 8th, in an ultimatum to the Ti-pings, he had written:—

" We now inform you that we maintain a perfect neutrality; but if you fire the guns or muskets from the battery or walls opposite the settlement on the advancing Imperialists (thereby endangering the lives of our men and people in the foreign settlement), we shall then feel it our duty to return the fire and bombard the city."

It was equivalent to saying: " We are neutral, provided that you do not defend yourselves."

At 2 P.M., after a continuous bombardment, the city was stormed; and at 5, when all opposition had ceased, the ex-governor and his troops landed, and received charge of the city from Captain Dew, who re-embarked his brigade. The rebels, on evacuating the place, left behind them 100 killed. The British loss was 3 killed and 23 wounded.

The rebels had at least behaved with moderation during their occupation of Ningpo. According to the correspondence of the *China Mail* of May 22nd, the pirates who supplanted them

---

[1] To Hope, May 10th.
[2] Com. Robert George Craigie.
[3] Lieut. Henry Huxham.
[4] Lieut. Archibald George Bogle.

committed the most revolting atrocities on the 10th, 11th, and 12th. The *Hongkong Daily Press* began its comments on the affair by saying: "There never was a falser, more unprovoked, or more unjustifiable act than the taking of Ningpo by the allies from the Taipings." The *Overland Trade Report* said: "So much mystery and double-dealing has been practised by the allies to wrest this port from the Taipings, and so little regard for veracity pervades the official dispatches regarding their doings, that the truth is most difficult to arrive at, and has certainly never yet been published. . . . The mode of ɩaccomplishing this design reflects indelible disgrace on British prestige. . . ."

It has been mentioned that, upon learning that the Chung-wang had collected a huge army for the recovery of his posts near Shanghai, Sir James Hope and General Staveley withdrew to that city. The only place of importance which they continued to hold beyond its immediate precincts was Soongkong, which they garrisoned in conjunction with some of Ward's disciplined Chinese. The rebels made a determined effort at daylight on May 30th, 1862, to carry Soongkong by storm, but were bloodily repulsed, mainly by the instrumentality of a detachment from the *Centaur*, 6, paddle, Commander John Eglinton Montgomerie. On June 2nd, however, the Ti-pings won a small success outside the town, driving a body of Imperialists from a stockade, and capturing a gig belonging to the *Centaur*, and a number of Chinese gunboats in a neighbouring creek. By means of a sortie, the gig and some of the gunboats were retaken by the British and Ward's Chinese; and it is noteworthy that, in spite of what had happened at Ningpo and elsewhere, the gig's crew, and other Europeans who were taken in the gunboats, were not harmed during the time when they remained in Ti-ping hands. Other Europeans, including one Forrester, a filibuster friend of Ward, were liberated after the recapture of Tsingpoo by the Ti-pings on June 10th, although European advisers of the Chung-wang advocated the wisdom of retaining the prisoners as hostages.

Sir James Hope raised the siege of Soongkong by despatching thither reinforcements under Captain John Borlase, C.B.; whereupon the Chung-wang, with the bulk of his army, withdrew to Nankin.

At about that time the Imperial government at Pekin was warned from London that Great Britain would "not go on protecting Shanghai for ever,[1] and was encouraged to procure foreign ships and foreign officers for the purpose. Captain Sherard Osborn, C.B., R.N., was induced to engage himself as admiral; and the British government, suspending the Foreign Enlistment Act, passed an Order in Council[2] on August 30th, which authorised the fitting out and manning of vessels of war for the service of the Emperor of China. Vessels were accordingly fitted out in England;[3] and they proceeded to China; but the entire arrangement, entered into by Prince Kung in an unofficial capacity, was disavowed by the Emperor and his advisers when the flotilla reached what was to have been the scene of its operations. The Imperialists were willing even then to take over the flotilla, provided it should be placed under the control of the provincial authorities; but to such a course Captain Osborn refused to agree; and ultimately he returned to England, the vessels also returning, or being sold. During the brief stay of the flotilla in Chinese waters, some of the officers and men belonging to it behaved in such a fashion that there was a general sense of relief among the European

---

[1] *See* China Blue Book, 1863, pp. 13, 67; and Lay, ' Our Interests in China.'

[2] *Gazette*, Sept. 2nd, 1862.

[3] The vessels which went out from England to join this extraordinary force (others were procured, and armed and manned in China), and the officers of the Royal Navy who found employment in them, were as set forth below. Other officers were taken from the Indian Navy and from the mercantile marine:—

Keangsoo (flag), wooden, paddle, 1000 tons, 300 H.P. nom. (built at Southampton, 1862–63, for the Chinese service):

    Com. Charles Stuart Forbes (capt.); Sub-Lieut. Francis Charles Vincent (lieut.);

    Surg. John Elliott (surg.-in-chief).

Kwangtung, iron, paddle, 522 tons, 150 H.P. nom. (built by Messrs. Laird, 1862–63, for the Chinese service):

    Lieut. William Allen Young, R.N.R. (com.); Lieut. Charles Edward Burlton (lieut.)

Tientsin, iron, screw, 445 tons, 80 H.P. nom. (built by Messrs. Laird, 1862, for the Chinese service):

    ex-Com. Beville Granville Wyndham Nicolas (capt.).

Pekin (ex-H.M.S. *Mohawk*), screw sloop:

    Capt. Hugh Talbot Burgoyne, V.C. (capt.); Lieut. Henry Mortlock Ommanney (lieut.); Asst.-Surg. Frederick Piercy (surg.).

Amoy (ex-H.M.S. *Jasper*), screw gun-vessel:

    Lieut. Arthur Salwey (com.); Sec.-Master Alfred Frederick Pearce (sub-lieut.)

China (ex-H.M.S. *Africa*), screw sloop:

    Lieut. Noel Osborn (com.); Lieut. George Morice (lieut.); Asst.-Surg. Henry Fegan (surg.).

Thule, purchased screw schooner; tender to *Keangsoo*.

Ballarat, purchased steam store-ship:

    Master Stephen J. W. Moriarty (com.).

residents upon its departure. The disappearance of the "Vampires," as they were called, probably saved some of them from having to meet charges of piracy; for they had no commission whatsoever.

In the meantime, Captain Dew,[1] of the *Encounter*, being left a nearly free hand in the vicinity of Ningpo, associated himself with Ward, a Franco-Chinese force, and the Imperialists, and, aided by the British gunboat *Hardy*, and the French gunboat *Confucius*, conducted with varying fortunes a bloody campaign in the district comprising Tsekie, Yuyaou, Fungwha, and Shousing.

Shousing is more than a hundred miles from Ningpo—quite outside the radius, that is to say, of any operations ever contemplated by Hope and Bruce, when they determined to keep clear a certain region round the treaty ports; so that when, early in 1863, after the Imperialists, with their Anglo-Chinese and Franco-Chinese allies, had been badly defeated before that town, and Dew went to the spot with a 68-pr., in charge of Lieutenant Edward Charles Tinling, the Captain of the *Encounter* was at length checked by his superiors. The fact that Tinling, a young officer who had been promoted for his gallantry at Ningpo, was mortally wounded in the course of another vain attempt to storm the city, called attention to the loose and semi-piratical manner in which the war was being conducted; and Rear-Admiral Augustus Leopold Kuper, C.B.,[2] who, at the end of the previous October, had relieved Sir James Hope as Commander-in-Chief, was, perhaps, less tolerant of such excesses than his capable but too truculent predecessor had been. There was at once an outcry, in England as well as in China, in Parliament as well as in the street; and, by direction of the Admiralty, Captain Dew was at length informed officially that he had exceeded his instructions. It was high time. Not only in China had Great Britain been venturing upon paths which, with more honour, might have been avoided. The same newspapers which chronicled the doings of Dew, and the fitting out of the Anglo-Chinese flotilla under Captain Sherard Osborn, recorded the operations of the Confederate cruisers, which would have never harried the Federal trade at sea had Lord Palmerston, Lord John Russell, and Mr. Gladstone been thoroughly scrupulous in their interpretation of the word "neutrality."

The Navy was concerned in yet one more operation against the Ti-pings ere Sir James Hope handed over his command to Rear-

[1] C.B., Aug. 26th, 1862.   [2] Apptd. Feb. 8th, 1862.

Admiral Kuper.   In October, 1862, the Imperialists informed
General Staveley that if he would recapture Kahding for them,
they would place a garrison in it.   The town was accordingly bombarded for two hours on October 24th, and then taken by storm
by a force made up of the disciplined Chinese, who, since Ward's
death, were commanded by an American named Burgevine; some
French troops, some more Chinese, under Lieutenant Kingsley, R.A.,
and Lieutenant Crane, R.A., and a Naval Brigade, composed of
570 officers and men from the *Impérieuse, Euryalus, Pearl, Vulcan,
Starling,* and *Havock,* under Captain John Borlase, C.B.   The
brigade lost 11 men wounded, one mortally.   General Staveley, in
his dispatch, mentioned with approval the names of Commander
Augustus Chetham Strode, of the *Vulcan,* and Lieutenant John
Frederick George Grant, of the same ship; and among others who
were employed on the occasion were Lieutenants Arthur Hart
Gurney Richardson, Edward Hobart Seymour (who will be heard
of again in connection with operations in China), Henry Holford

E. H. Seymour

VICE-ADMIRAL SIR EDWARD HOBART SEYMOUR, G.C.B.

Washington, Duncan George Davidson, Horace William Rochfort,
John Hamilton Colt, James Edward Hunter, Robert Peel Dennistoun, John Gabriel Yarwood Holbrook, Herbert Price Knevitt,
George Henry Barnard, and George Poole; together with Captains
John Yate Holland, R.M., and Ebenezer Tristram Thomas Jones,
R.M., and Lieutenant William Stewart, R.M.A.   The rebels are
said to have had 1500 killed and wounded, while the Imperialists
and allies had but 34 casualties in all.   The place was at once
handed over to Burgevine, who stained his success by ordering
many of the 700 prisoners who fell into his hands to be blown
from guns.   It may be mentioned here that Burgevine was soon
afterwards deposed from his command by his Chinese superiors, in
consequence not of this but of other offences, and his place given
to Captain Holland, R.M., aforesaid.   In his hands the disciplined
Chinese force did not prosper; and, upon his resignation, it was
taken charge of by Major Charles George Gordon, R.E., who,
engaged in a less questionable cause, perished heroically at
Khartoum in 1885.

From the time of Rear-Admiral Kuper's assumption of the

command in Chinese waters, the active and systematic employment of the Navy on behalf of the corrupt and unworthy
government at Pekin, and against rebels who, according to their
lights, were struggling for reformation, came to an end.

During the operations against the Ti-pings, the hunting down
of Chinese pirates continued, among the officers most active and
successful in the work being Commander John Moresby, of the
Snake, 4, screw, who captured or destroyed fourteen craft belonging
to these freebooters. The *Pearl*, 21, screw, Captain John Borlase, C.B., was conspicuous in the same kind of service, especially
in May and June, 1861. The *Cockchafer*, 2, screw, Lieutenant
Henry Lowe Holder, also distinguished herself. The scene of
operations was, for the most part, off the coast of the province of
Kwangtung.

A renewal of the disputes over land-titles produced another native
outbreak in the North Island of New Zealand early in 1860, the
scene of hostilities being the neighbourhood of Taranaki, and the
native leader being William King, the chief of the local tribe. A
force, including two companies of the 65th Regiment, was sent to
the spot, whither also the *Niger*, 13, screw, Captain Peter Cracroft,
proceeded. A landing was effected at Waitara, on March 5th, no
resistance being offered; and, on the following day, the ship was
about to proceed to New Plymouth, when signals were made to
her to the effect that the enemy, during the darkness, had built a
stockade, which threatened to cut off the communication of the
troops with their land base. King, however, eventually abandoned
this stockade without fighting. On the 17th he was discovered to
have erected another pah, which he resolutely defended,' until a
bombardment obliged him to quit it also. In the meantime, the
Niger had gone to Auckland for supplies, leaving only a few of her
people to assist the troops. On the 26th William King murdered
three men and two boys, and boasted that he would drive the
Europeans into the sea. On the 28th, therefore, by which day the
Niger had returned, the naval detachment on shore accompanied
the troops into the country to bring into town some settlers who
lived in exposed and outlying places; and Cracroft, at the desire of
Governor Gore Browne, landed further officers and men to hold
the town during the absence of the expedition. He disembarked in
person, with sixty seamen and Marines.

The rescuing force had not advanced more than four miles when

it found itself warmly engaged with a strongly-posted body of the
enemy. Word was sent back for reinforcements, and Cracroft went
at once to the front with his men and a 24-pr. rocket-tube. King
occupied a pah at Omata on the summit of a hill, and had severely
handled the British force ere Cracroft's arrival; and of the small
naval contingent, the leader, Lieutenant William Hans Blake, had
been dangerously wounded, and a Marine killed. Cracroft determined to storm the pah, and, addressing his men, pointed to the
rebel flag, and promised £10 to the man who should haul it down.

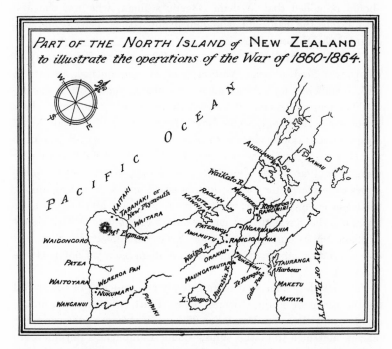

He then moved to within 800 yards, and opened fire from his rocket-
tube, which, however, made no impression. It was then nearly
dark, and Colonel Murray, who led the military force, announced
his intention of retreating to the town, whither he had been ordered
to return by sunset, and advised Cracroft to do the same. "I
purpose to take that pah first," said the Captain. The visible withdrawal of the troops from the front of the position probably had the
effect of rendering the enemy more careless than he might otherwise
have been to what was going on on his flank. The result was that
Cracroft managed to get close up to an outlying body of natives

before his presence was detected.   Within 60 yards of the enemy he gave the word to double.   With a volley and a cheer the men were instantly in the midst of the rebels, who, after a brave resistance, took refuge in the pah behind them, or escaped.   The seamen and Marines rushed onwards, met tomahawk with bayonet, and soon annihilated all resistance.   Cracroft, who had not force enough to hold the position with, returned leisurely with his wounded, who were not numerous, and was not molested.   On the following day, the enemy retired to the southward, having lost very heavily.[1]   It should be added that William Odgers, seaman, who was the first man inside the pah, and who pulled' down the enemy's flag, was awarded the Victoria Cross.[2]

Hostilities continued.   On June 23rd a reconnoitring party of troops was fired at near Waitara; and, in consequence, an attack, with insufficient force,[3] was made on a strong rebel pah in the immediate neighbourhood on June 26th, in the early morning.   Part of the 40th Regiment, some Royal Engineers, and a small Naval Brigade under Commodore Frederick Beauchamp Paget Seymour, of the *Pelorus,* 21, screw, were engaged.   After a hot fight, lasting for more than four hours, the British were obliged by overwhelming forces to retreat, after having lost 29 killed and 33 wounded, among the latter being Seymour, eight seamen, and one Marine.   Besides Seymour, the naval officers engaged were Lieutenant Albert Henry William Battiscombe, Midshipmen Ernest Bannister Wadlow, and —— Garnett, and Lieutenant John William Henry Chafyn Grove Morris, R.M.A.[4]

The war was somewhat more actively prosecuted after the arrival on the scene of Major-General T. S. Pratt, who won an initial success, and then, on December 29th, with troops, guns, and 138 officers and men from the ships,[5] under Commodore Seymour, entrenched himself at Kairau, opposite the strong position of Matarikoriko, which, during the two following days, he obliged the enemy to evacuate.   He fought the action entirely with cannon, rifle, and spade, and, not unduly exposing his men, had but 3 killed and 21 wounded.   After this success, Pratt adopted the practice of reducing the successive positions of his opponents by means of regular

[1] Corr. of *A. and N. Gazette,* July 14th, 1860; Fox, ' War in New Zealand,' 30.
[2] *Gazette,* Aug. 2nd, 1860.
[3] Three hundred and forty-seven in all.   The natives were thrice as numerous.
[4] *Taranaki Herald,* June 30th, 1860.   Desps.
[5] Chiefly from the *Cordelia* and *Niger*; and from colonial steamer *Victoria.*

approaches. These tactics broke up the rebel combinations. A chief named William Thompson, whose tribe, the Waikato, had joined the Taranaki natives, finally proposed a suspension of hostilities, and on May 21st, 1861, a truce was arranged.

Governor Gore Browne had mismanaged matters; and he would, almost immediately, have provoked a new outbreak had not the home Government, realising that the position of the colony was becoming serious, recalled him by means of a dispatch which, while otherwise complimentary, informed him that he was superseded by Sir George Grey, who, as has been seen, had already been appointed governor in 1845, and who had since governed the Cape.

Grey seems to have used his best endeavours to pacify the natives. He even offered to submit the still unsettled land questions to arbitration by two Europeans and four Maoris, three to be appointed by him and three by the natives. This was refused. Grey then determined to abandon the disputed territory at Waitara, but to insist upon the restitution of the district of Tataraimaka, which had been seized by the rebels and held by them since 1861, in spite of the fact that there was no doubt whatsoever of the validity of the purchase of it in 1848 or 1849. Unfortunately, as it turned out, he sent a force to occupy Tataraimaka, without simultaneously proclaiming his intention of giving up Waitara. The resident natives made no opposition, but sent to William Thompson, of Waikato, for orders. He and the other leaders of the King party decided for war; and the Maoris at once began operations by falling upon a small escort party on May 4th, 1863, and murdering two officers and eight rank and file of Imperial troops. Grey then committed a worse mistake. He announced hurriedly that Waitara was to be abandoned, thereby encouraging his enemies, and sapping the attachment of his friends among the natives by unwittingly suggesting that he was influenced by fear and the consciousness of weakness. A few weeks earlier, Mr. John Eldon Gorst,[1] civil commissioner in the Waikato country, who had established a newspaper there to combat the teachings of Kingism, had had his press and material violently seized by the partizans of the King paper, *Hokioi*; and the timber ready for the erection of a court-house and barracks in lower Waikato had been forcibly taken and thrown into the river, while Mr. Gorst had been expelled soon afterwards.[2]

Aware, after what they had done, that they were committed to a

---

[1] Sol.-Genl., 1885–86; Und.-Sec. for India, 1886–91, etc.   [2] Fox, 43–60.

serious struggle, the natives determined to invade Auckland; and Grey, getting early intelligence of their intention, decided to forestall matters by advancing into the Maori country. The senior military officer, Lieut.-General D. A. Cameron, C.B., who was at New Plymouth, endeavouring to punish the perpetrators of the massacre, was therefore recalled to Auckland, leaving behind him only enough troops to garrison New Plymouth; and the available British forces were soon afterwards concentrated along the Waikato river and the Maungatawhiri creek, the boundary between the settled districts and the unsold Maori lands. The boundary was crossed on July 12th; on July 17th a small British detachment was defeated between Queen's Redoubt and Drury; and on the same day a body of rebels was driven back and scattered near Koheroa; but then there ensued a long and almost inexplicable period of comparative inaction, so far as the army was concerned.

In the meantime, however, the Navy made itself useful. On June 4th, 1863, the *Eclipse*, 4, screw, Commander Richard Charles Mayne, co-operated in an attack which was made by the garrison of New Plymouth on a rebel position near the mouth of the Katikara; and on the night of August 1st, a detachment from the *Harrier*, 17, screw, Commander Francis William Sullivan, took part in a reconnaissance of Paparoa and Haurake. On August 3rd, Commander Sullivan, in the lightly-armoured colonial steamer *Avon*, also reconnoitred the Waikato river above Kohe-Hohe, and, for about half an hour, engaged a body of the enemy near Merimeri. On September 7th, the *Harrier's* boats, under Sullivan's direction, were employed to convey a force which was intended to support an unfortunate and costly raid made in the direction of Cameron Town.

While the army, under Lieut.-General Cameron, was getting ready for offensive operations, Commodore Sir William Saltonstall Wiseman, Bart., of the *Curaçoa*, 23, screw, who, in April, had been appointed senior officer on the Australian station, concentrated as large a proportion as possible of his available strength in New Zealand waters, and himself left Sydney, with troops on board, and one or two vessels in company, on September 22nd, arriving at Auckland on October 2nd. The *Curaçoa* herself at once landed 232 officers and men, who were sent up country to the support of the troops; and she remained as guardship at Auckland under Lieutenant Duke Doughton Yonge, with but three other officers and 90 men in her. She was kept ready for action in case of a sudden descent of the Maoris on the town. The other ships which then, or soon afterwards, co-operated with the senior officer in New Zealand waters were the—

Miranda, 15, screw . . .	Captain Robert Jenkins
Esk, 21, screw	Captain John Fane Charles Hamilton
Harrier, 17, screw . . .	Commander Francis William Sullivan [1]
Eclipse, 4, screw	Commander Richard Charles Mayne [2]
Falcon, 17, screw . . .	Commander George Henry Parkin

Besides the *Pioneer, Avon, Sandfly, Corio*, and other colonial vessels.

Late in October, General Cameron and Commodore Wiseman, in the colonial steamer *Pioneer*, made two reconnaissances up the Waikato, pushing, on the 31st, as far as Rangariri. On that occasion they passed the strong Maori position at Merimeri, and, having discovered a good landing-place about six miles above it, it was arranged with the Commodore to embark a force from Queen's Redoubt. This force, in the colonial steamers *Pioneer* and *Avon*, with four lightly-plated gunboats [3] in tow, got under way at 2.30 on the morning of November 1st, and reached the landing-place at about 6 A.M. The troops disembarked unopposed, and began to construct a breastwork, pending the arrival of further forces. In the afternoon, however, the natives at Merimeri, seeing that their position had been turned, abandoned their works, and made off in canoes up the Maramarua and Whangamarino creeks. Cameron at once proceeded to Merimeri, and occupied it with a force which included 250 seamen under Commander Mayne. The place was afterwards fortified.

Between November 16th and November 25th, an expedition, under Captain Jenkins and Colonel G. J. Carey, was engaged to the northward, and up the Firth of Thames, to the eastward of the country occupied by the enemy. It was made in the *Miranda, Esk, Sandfly*, and *Corio*. Although it took possession of some positions, and so accomplished part of its purpose, it did not come into actual collision with the enemy, and was therefore unable to deal any serious blow. The *Miranda* remained for a time in the Firth of

---

[1] Capt. Nov. 9th, 1863. He was succeeded by Com. Edward Hay.

[2] After Mayne's disablement, Lieut. Henry Joshua Coddington acted until the arrival of Com. Edmund Robert Fremantle.

[3] These gunboats, named *Flirt, Midge, Chub* and *Ant*, were originally cargo boats, and were thinly armed by Capt. Jenkins at Auckland, and then transported by him overland, *viâ* Manakau, to the Waikato.

Thames.[1]   During the absence of the expedition an important success was won on the Waikato.

After the abandonment of Merimeri, a strong force of rebels entrenched themselves at Rangariri, a village about twelve miles higher up the river.   There, on November 20th, General Cameron, with troops, the four plated gunboats, and a Naval Brigade from the *Curaçoa, Miranda, Harrier*, and *Eclipse,* under Commodore Wiseman, numbering about 400 men, attacked them.   He had in all about 1200 men, while the Maoris were but about 400; but the latter had the advantage of a strong position, though it was one from which there was no easy way of retreat, and one, too, which required a much larger force to hold it properly.   The two divisions did not arrive simultaneously before the works.   One, coming by land, threatened the front, while the other, brought in the steamers, was to have threatened the rear; but part of the latter was delayed by the strength of the current.   For an hour and a half the position was bombarded, and then, at 4.30 P.M., an assault was ordered.   The Maoris soon concentrated themselves in a very formidable redoubt in the centre of their lines, and bloodily repulsed four separate attempts to carry it—one by the 65th Regiment, one by a party of Royal Artillerymen, and two by 90 men of the Naval Brigade, gallantly led by Commander Mayne and Commander Henry Bourchier Phillimore.   It was then nearly dark.   An attempt on the part of some of the brave defenders to get away across Lake Waikarei, and a swamp on their right flank, was partially prevented by the 40th Regiment, and a detachment of the Marines, who, having by that time arrived by water, had moved round to the rear; but it was supposed that two of the most important leaders, King Matutaere, and William Thompson, escaped ere the way was blocked.   The rest were trapped, and, although they kept up a desultory fire during the night, they surrendered unconditionally on the morning of November 21st.   Those who thus gave themselves up numbered 183 men and 2 women.   The others had fallen or had escaped.   It had been a magnificent defence; and the success was a very costly one; for, on the British side, 36 were killed and 98 wounded, many mortally.[2]   The naval casualties were 5 killed, including Midshipman

---

[1] Wiseman to Admlty., Nov. 30th.

[2] The British tactics at Rangiriri were adversely criticised at the time.   The enemy was driven, without much trouble or loss, into the central redoubt, where he might have been either approached by sapping, or starved into surrender, if he had not previously succumbed to bombardment.   Instead, he was stormed, at great expendi-

Thomas A. Watkins (*Curaçoa*), and 10 wounded, including Commander Mayne [1] (*Eclipse*), and Lieutenants Edward Downes Panter Downes [2] (*Miranda*), Henry M'Clintock Alexander [2] (*Curaçoa*), and Charles Frederick Hotham (*Curaçoa*). After the surrender, William Thompson, with a small party, approached the place with a white flag, but, having parleyed, withdrew again, not being able to make up his mind to submit.[3]

In addition to the naval officers already named, the following were mentioned in the dispatches : Captain Francis William Sullivan ; Lieutenants Charles Hill, and William Fletcher Boughey ; Acting-Lieutenant Robert Frederick Hammick,[4] commanding the small gunboats ; Sub-Lieutenant Frederic John Easther, commanding the *Avon* ; Midshipmen Sydney Augustus Rowan Hamilton, Frank Elrington Hudson, and Cecil George Foljambe ; Assistant Surgeons Adam Brunton Messer,[5] M.D., and Duncan Hilston, M.D. ; and ordinary seaman William Fox (*Curaçoa*).

The prisoners were temporarily confined on board the *Curaçoa*, at Auckland.

For some days after the action, the flotilla was laboriously employed in bringing up supplies to Merimeri, Rangiriri, and Taupiri, to which last the General advanced on December 3rd. On the same day, Commodore Wiseman and Captain Sullivan, having lightened the *Pioneer* by removing the armoured turrets from her, pushed on in her to Kupa Kupa Island, about four miles ahead of the troops. Immense natural difficulties were encountered, but no enemy was seen.

There is no doubt that the Maoris were, for the moment, greatly disheartened ; for, on December 8th, without further resistance, General Cameron was allowed to occupy Ngaruawahia, at the junction of the Hurutiu and Waipa rivers, which together form the Waikato. Ngaruawahia was an important political centre, as it had been the headquarters of Kingism, the burial place of King Potatau, and the capital of his successor Matutaere. If Sir George Grey had seen his way to go thither to negotiate, as, at one time, he intended, terms might then have been arranged. Instead, he wrote to the

---

ture of life. Fox thinks that he might have been reduced, with little or no loss, in a few hours, as he could not escape.

[1] Capt., Feb. 12th, 1864.   [2] Coms., Feb. 12th, 1864.
[3] Wiseman's disp. of Nov. 30th ; Cameron's disp. of Nov. 24th ; Fox, 80.
[4] Lieut., Feb. 12th, 1864.   [5] Surg., Feb. 12th, 1864.

natives that he would receive a deputation from them at Auckland. It is, however, not certain that William Thompson, the leading spirit, then really desired peace; for no reply to the Governor's letter was ever received. Cameron remained for some time at Ngarua-wahia to collect supplies, but, at the end of January, moved up the Waipa, and arrived before Pikopiko and Paterangi, two posts which were very strongly fortified. While this movement was in progress, Lieutenant William Edward Mitchell, of the *Esk*, who was in command of the *Avon*, was fatally wounded by a chance shot from Maoris in ambush on the river bank. He was only two-and-twenty years of age. Acting-Lieutenant Frederic John Easther, of the *Harrier*, succeeded him in command of the *Avon*.

Before the *Miranda* quitted the Firth of Thames, all the posts between that estuary and Queen's Redoubt, on the Waikato, were taken possession of, and held by detachments of the 12th and 70th Regiments, the Waikato militia, or the Auckland Naval Volunteers, which had been brought round with the expedition commanded by Captain Jenkins. On January 20th, 1864, with troops under Colonel Carey, of the 18th Royal Irish, Jenkins weighed, and proceeded down the coast to Tauranga, leaving the *Esk* in the Thames. The *Miranda*, which was accompanied by the *Corio*, encountered no resistance on the shores of the Bay of Plenty; and, when the troops had established themselves at Te Papa, the natives at first supplied them with provisions, though afterwards they became less willing to assist them.

At that time, the *Curaçoa* was at Auckland, while most of her people, under the Commodore, were serving at the front; the *Harrier* was in the Thames or at Manakau, also with most of her people at the front; and the *Eclipse* was in the Waikato, with a detachment, under Lieutenant William Fletcher Boughey, co-operating with the troops. Sir Duncan Cameron lay for some weeks in the neighbour-hood of the native strongholds of Pikopiko and Paterangi; but on the night of February 20th, he turned those positions by making a sudden flank march to Awamutu. The formidable works on the Waikato were instantly evacuated by the Maoris, who concentrated at Rangioawhia, where, on the 22nd, they were defeated, with con-siderable loss in killed and prisoners. The majority of the rebels in what are now Waikato, Raglan, and Waipa counties then retired to Maungatautari, a stronghold on the Hurutiu. During these opera-tions the Navy appears to have suffered no loss; and in the few

succeeding movements which terminated what has been called the
Waikato campaign, the Navy had practically no share.

In April, Sir Duncan Cameron had his headquarters at Pukerimu,
on the Hurutiu, a place only about forty miles as the crow would fly,
from Tauranga, on the east coast. Most of the Tauranga people
had been engaged in the actions in Waikato ; and on April 1st, the
Miranda, lying in the Bay, had been obliged to disperse a number of
them who had come down to the coast in a threatening manner.
Lieut.-Colonel Greer, 68th Regiment, had by that time succeeded
Colonel Carey in command at Te Papa ; and, believing his position
to be precarious, he asked Sir Duncan Cameron for reinforcements.
Cameron not only sent them, but also went himself to Tauranga, and
procured the assistance of some of the squadron in conveying thither
a part of the troops. The landing of these was completed on April
26th. The force then ashore numbered 1695 of all ranks, and included
429 officers and men from the *Curaçoa, Miranda, Esk, Eclipse,* and
Falcon. In the Bay were the *Miranda, Esk,* and *Falcon,* together
with the colonial steamers *Sandfly, Alexander,* and *Tauranga.* The
troops consisted mainly of the 43rd, 68th, and 70th Regiments, some
Royal Engineers, and some Royal Artillery ; and the guns landed
were: one 110-pr. Armstrong, two 40-pr. Armstrongs, two 6-pr.
Armstrongs, two 24-pr. field howitzers, two 8-in. mortars, and six
coehorn mortars. A body of Maoris, said not to have exceeded 300
in number, and alleged by themselves not to have exceeded 150, had
constructed a formidable work about three miles from Te Papa, on a
neck of land which on each side fell off into a swamp. It is known
in history as the Gate Pah. On the highest point of the neck was
an oblong palisaded redoubt ; and from the redoubt to the swamps
were lines of rifle-pits. The rear of the position was accessible,
though with difficulty ; and across it Colonel Greer, with the 68th
Regiment, succeeded in posting himself on the night of April 28th,[1]
while a feigned attack was being made on the enemy's front ; and he
stationed himself in such a manner as to cut off the supply of water
to the work, and also, theoretically, to be able to intercept the retreat
of the garrison. It is clear that the rebels, deprived of their water,
and having no guns, might have been easily reduced without any
resort on the part of Cameron to the costly and disastrous tactics
which he chose to pursue.

---

[1] On that day the *Falcon* had shelled the enemy out of a position at Maketu, and
driven them along the beach to Otamarakau.

The guns were planted in four positions at distances varying from 800 to 100 yards from the pah ; and soon after 6.30 A.M. on April 29th, after the Maoris had fired a volley at the British skirmishers, the guns opened simultaneously. Sir Duncan Cameron reported that the practice was excellent, but other eye-witnesses have declared that it was extremely wild. The rebels lay low in their schanzes, and made but little reply. At about noon, a 6-pr. gun was taken across the swamp on the enemy's left, and hauled on to the high ground, whence it enfiladed the rifle-pits on that side and presently caused their abandonment. The latter part of the bombardment having been directed chiefly against the left angle of the main work, the fence and palisades in that neighbourhood were destroyed, and a breach was effected by 4 P.M., when Cameron ordered an assault. For that purpose, 150 seamen and Marines, under Commander Edward Hay of the *Harrier*, and an equal number of the 43rd Regiment, under Lieut.-Colonel Booth, had been told off. In addition, 170 men of the 70th Regiment had been directed to extend, keep down the enemy's fire until the last possible moment, and then follow the assaulting column into the breach ; while the rest of the seamen and Marines, and of the 43rd, were to bring up the rear as a reserve.

The assaulting column, favoured by the folds of the ground, gained the breach with but little loss, and entered the works, the 68th, from the rear of the position, closing up at the same moment and driving back the Maoris, who were already attempting to bolt. Inside the pah the rebels fought with desperation, both Hay and Booth being mortally wounded soon after they had got through the breach. But the place would have been carried had not a panic, which Cameron professed himself unable to explain, seized the assaulting column, or, rather, as would appear, the part of it belonging to the 43rd. The men turned round, communicated the contagion to their fellows, and rushed out pell-mell, shrieking, " There's thousands of them " ; and in an instant they were flying madly back. Captain John Fane Charles Hamilton, of the *Esk*, with the reserve of the Naval Brigade, pushed up, but was shot dead on the top of the parapet. Nothing could be done to stop the disgraceful retreat ; and the rebels, boldly showing themselves and firing into the backs of the fugitives, did terrible execution.

The force was at length rallied ; but Cameron cared not to renew the assault. Instead, he ordered a line of entrenchments to be thrown up within a hundred yards of the pah, intending to conduct further operations on the following morning.

The night of the 29th was extremely dark. For a time the rebels, as was their custom in such circumstances, howled and shouted. Suddenly the noises ceased, and the sound of firing was heard from the rear. The Maoris, with very little loss, had escaped through the lines of the 68th ; and a British officer who crept into the pah at about midnight found it completely evacuated, save by a few British wounded, who had not been maltreated. Cameron, in his dispatch, says that the loss of the natives must have been very heavy, yet admits that only about 20 Maori killed and 6 wounded were found about the position. Natives afterwards estimated their total loss at no more than between thirty and forty.[1]

"Allowing," says the correspondent of the *Times*, "that the best way of taking a Maori pah is to storm it in front, everything was done that skill and diligence could do to this end." The premise can hardly be admitted, seeing that Cameron had means of knowing that the pah was waterless, and therefore could not be held by the enemy for many hours ; nor, even admitting the premise, can the conclusion be granted. One of the rules of war is that, when a force of given strength has to be employed, a homogeneous force is better than a mixed one, unless it be necessary to utilise more than one arm, as, for example, cavalry and infantry. Another rule is to employ for any given service the force best suited by tradition and training for the work in hand. Cameron had with him nearly 300 officers and men of the 43rd, and more than double that number of the 68th ; yet, instead of taking what he appears to have deemed the necessary detachment of men for the assault from one of those corps, he took 150 from the 43rd, and added to them, not 150 from the 68th, but 150 from the Naval Brigade, a force which, looking to all the circumstances, ought, I venture to think, to have formed the reserve, and to have been given no other post. No doubt, the Navy craved to be allowed to share the dangers of the storm ; but to say that is far from saying that the General was wise in permitting it to do so. It should be added here that at Te Ranga, on June 21st following, the 43rd amply redeemed its laurels.

The lamentable affair of the Gate Pah cost the British no fewer than 27 killed and 66 wounded. Of this tale, the casualties of the Navy were 3 officers and 8 men killed or mortally injured, and

[1] Col. Parl. Papers, 1864, E. 3, p. 60.

3 officers and 19 men wounded. The officers who lost their lives were Captain John Fane Charles Hamilton[1] (*Esk*), Commander Edward Hay[2] (*Harrier*), and Lieutenant Charles Hill[3] (*Curaçoa*) ; and the officers wounded were George Graham Duff (*Esk*), Lieutenant Robert Frederick Hammick (*Miranda*), and Sub-Lieutenant Philip Reginald Hastings Parker (*Falcon*).[4]

The Naval Brigade behaved admirably, and retired only when nearly all its leading officers had been shot down. The Commodore and Captain Jenkins had most marvellous escapes. After Commander Hay had been mortally hit, a seaman named Samuel Mitchell went to his assistance, and, although ordered by his officer to leave him and consult his own safety, carried Hay out of the pah. The act of devotion gained the brave fellow the Victoria Cross.[5]

In recognition of the gallantry displayed by the Navy in New Zealand, and especially in the affair of the Gate Pah, the Admiralty made the following promotions :—

To be Captain: Com. Henry Bourchier Phillimore (July 14th, 1864).

To be Commanders : Lieut. George Graham Duff (Ap. 29th, 1864) ; Lieut. Charles Frederick Hotham (upon completing sea-time, Ap. 19th, 1865) ; Lieut. John Thomlinson Swann (July 14th, 1864).

To be Lieutenants : Sub-Lieut. Philip Reginald Hastings Parker (Ap. 29th, 1864) Actg.-Lieut. Archer John William Musgrave (on passing required examination, to date Ap. 29th, 1864) ; Sub-Lieut. Paul Storr (July 14th, 1864) ; Sub-Lieut. John Hope (July 14th, 1864).

In addition, the names of Lieuts. Robert Sidney Hunt, and Robert Frederick Hammick, and Lieut. (R.M.A.) Robert Ballard Gardner, were ordered to be favourably noted.

In the latter part of this unfortunate war, which dragged on for a considerable period, and which owed its prolongation not only to the bravery of the enemy, but also to the supineness and divided counsels of the British, the Navy had comparatively little share ; nor was it called upon to do anything of importance in connection with the repression of the brief New Zealand rebellion of 1869. Among the vessels which were more particularly concerned, especially in the earlier part of the period, were the *Eclipse*, 4, Commander

[1] Aged 42 ; a Capt. of 1858.

[2] Aged 28 ; a Com. of 1858. A memorial to those of the *Harrier's* people who fell in New Zealand was erected in 1865 in Kingston Church, Portsmouth.

[3] A survivor of the wreck of the *Orpheus*.

[4] *Gazette*, July 15th, 1864 ; Corr. of *Times* ; Fox, 112.

[5] *Gazette*, July 20th, 1864.

Edmund Robert Fremantle; *Brisk*, 16, Captain Charles Webley Hope; and *Esk*, 21, Captain John Proctor Luce.

Several effective blows were struck at the West African slave trade in 1861, especially in the Niger, and in the Gambia.

The chief, or petty king, of Porto Novo, in the Niger river, a creature of the King of Dahomey, having been troublesome for some time, Commander Henry Rushworth Wratislaw, of the *Ranger*, 5, screw gun-vessel, put seventeen seamen and Marines, and a gunner on board the paddle tender *Brune*, Lieutenant John Edward Stokes, and escorted that craft up to Badagry on February 24th, whence she proceeded alone to Porto Novo. Consul Foote, who accompanied the little expedition, sent ashore a message to the effect that, if his demands were not previously complied with, the *Brune* would open fire on the town at 11 A.M. on the 25th; and then the vessel, dropping three miles down the creek, anchored for the night. On the following day, though no reply had been vouchsafed, the British waited until 1.20 P.M., when they opened fire, which was returned. During the action a number of friendly Lagos men, who desired to take refuge on board the tender, were mistaken for enemies, and unfortunately fired upon. After some hours' bombardment, the *Brune* returned to Badagry to await results. The king presently sent down to the Badagry chiefs, asking them to intercede for them; whereupon the Consul consented to await the arrival of an envoy at Lagos, and to give the king three weeks wherein to comply with his requirements.

The king was so ill-advised as to allow himself to be influenced by the king of Dahomey to refuse satisfaction, and to boom the river. A further expedition was therefore necessary. The Consul called on Commodore William Edmonstone, of the *Arrogant*, 47, screw, for assistance; and, in consequence, an expedition, consisting of the *Brune*, *Fidelity*,[1] Lieutenant Robert Barclay Cay, and boats of the squadron on the station, the Commodore accompanying it, moved up from Lagos to Badagry Creek on April 23rd, 1861. On the 26th it proceeded to Porto Novo, and, on approaching the town, opened fire with rockets, grape, canister, and shell, the enemy making a brisk return. In an hour the place was ablaze; but the natives, driven from the buildings, concealed themselves in the thick grass at the edge of the stream, whence they were not dislodged until a party under Commander Henry James Raby, V.C.,

[1] A hired Liverpool vessel.

of the *Alecto,* 5, paddle, had landed and expelled them. It was computed that about 500 of the enemy fell. The British loss was but 1 killed, and 4 or 5 wounded. As soon as possible, the slave barracoons at Porto Novo were destroyed; and the expedition, which had in no way suffered from fever, returned to Lagos on April 28th. The results were excellent, the king conceding all demands.[1]

At the time of the first attack on Porto Novo, the Commodore and part of his command had been occupied to the northward. The King of Baddiboo, on the Gambia, had robbed some British merchants, and, upon being called upon to pay a fine of bullocks, had offered to fight the British. He had been so unwise as to annoy his French neighbours at the same time; and an international expedition had accordingly been organised against him.

The British portion of the force consisted of the *Arrogant,* 47, screw, Commodore William Edmonstone, the *Falcon,* 17, screw, Commander Algernon Charles Fieschi Heneage, and the *Torch,* 5, screw, Commander Frederick Harrison Smith, or detachments from them, together with the 1st and 2nd West India Regiments, the Gold Coast Artillery, and the Bathurst Rifles. The *Forte,* 51, flagship of Rear-Admiral the Hon. Sir Henry Keppel, Captain Edward Winterton Turnour, also proceeded as far as the mouth of the river; but, finding that the services of his ship did not appear to be indispensable,[2] Keppel sailed again at once in order generously to leave the Commodore to acquire the whole of whatever credit might result from the coming operations.

A Naval Brigade under the Commodore in person, with Lieutenant Walter James Hunt-Grubbe as second in command, was formed; and a landing was effected, under cover of the guns of the *Torch,* in Swarricunda Creek, the banks of which were lined with rifle-pits and held by the enemy. When the natives had been dispersed, the Brigade began a march of several hours' duration in the direction of the strongly stockaded and well-garrisoned town of Saba. On February 21st, the place was vigorously bombarded, rockets as well as shells being employed; and, as soon as the defence showed signs of having been shaken, the position was attacked in flank by the Naval Brigade, which, gallantly led by the Commodore, successfully rushed it, and inflicted very heavy loss upon the enemy, but itself lost 6 killed and about 15 wounded.

[1] Foote's Rep.   [2] Keppel, III., 71, 72.

In December of the same year, part of the West Coast command was employed in retributive operations against the petty King of Quiah, Massongha being captured and destroyed on the 10th, and some stockades at Madonika being taken on the 19th of that month.

In 1861 there were frequent and troublesome disputes between the Scots and French fishermen in the home seas, the latter at one time assuming a very offensive attitude. The *Lizard*, 1, paddle, Lieutenant Edward Eyre Maunsell, tender to the flagship at Sheerness, did good work by capturing twenty-four French luggers which, with numerous others, had contravened the fishing regulations, or wilfully annoyed the north countrymen; and the lesson had a most beneficial effect, and was not forgotten for years.

The minor operations of the Navy in 1862 were neither numerous nor, except in China, very interesting. During her commission, which had begun in 1860, the *Ariel*, 9, screw, Commanders John Richard Alexander and William Cox Chapman, was particularly successful against slavers on the east coast of Africa, capturing no fewer than eighteen in 1862–4. On the west coast, one of the most energetic cruisers was the *Zebra*, 17, Commander Anthony Hiley Hoskins, which commissioned in the spring of 1862. Among her numerous prizes was the large slaver *Maraquita*, commanded by the famous American skipper, Bowen. On the same station the *Flying Fish*, 6, screw, Commander Warren Hastings Anderson, was also active and successful, especially just prior to her recall in the summer of 1862. A disturbance at Cape Coast Castle in October, arising out of the mutinous attitude of the Gold Coast Artillery, was put down with the assistance of the *Brisk*, 16, screw, Captain John Proctor Luce, and the *Zebra*. In other seas, it fell to the lot of the squadron under Rear-Admiral Richard Laird Warren, on the south-east coast of America, to carry out a few mild reprisals against Brazil in consequence of a brief and unimportant misunderstanding with that empire, and to that of the *Harrier*, 17, screw, Commander Sir Malcolm MacGregor, Bart., to chastise some troublesome natives of the Fiji Islands.

The minor naval events of 1863 were still more few and unimportant. In consequence of the difficulties with Ashantee, some officers and men from the West Coast of Africa squadron were employed for a time at Cape Coast Castle; and, as in many other years, a small naval expedition ascended the Congo. In the Mediterranean, during the revolutionary troubles in Greece, Captain

Charles Farrel Hillyar, of the *Queen*, 74, screw, had occasion more than once to land Marines, especially in July, when a force under Lieutenant James Woodward Scott, R.M., undertook the protection of the British Legation at Athens.

It is very difficult to understand the nature of the events which led to American and European interference in the affairs of Japan, without first glancing briefly at the ancient political condition of the island empire.

The old constitution of the land was a despotism, feudal, military, and hierarchical, under a Mikado. About the twelfth century of the Christian era there arose a "Mayor of the Palace" in the person of an officer known eventually as the Tycoon, or, more properly, as the Shogun—an officer who assumed the political and military management of the country, the Mikado retaining, as years passed, little more than the religious headship. The office of Shogun descended through three families and many vicissitudes ; and its powers were gradually modified by the upgrowth of a very large class of Samurai, or retainers of great nobles—men of birth and education, but hereditary fighters—or, in peace time, hereditary idlers. The highest class of these, as head retainers of the Daimios, came to occupy with regard to their nominal masters much the same kind of relationship as was held by the Shogun to the Mikado ; for both Mikado and Daimios, brought up apart from the people and surrounded with every indulgence, had temporarily lost the fire and energy of their ancestors. This condition of affairs was a fruitful source of discontent and intrigue.

The position of the Shoguns was a curious one. They steadily increased their power and importance in the state, yet, though actual rulers of the empire, professed a most abject deference to the person of the Mikado, and, moreover, were social inferiors of many of the Daimios. Indeed, a Shogun, unless by birth so entitled, was not allowed even to look upon the face of the Mikado ; while, at the same time, such was his authority that he was able to compel the Daimios to spend every alternate year at his capital, Jeddo, and to override their views. The Daimios had a right of appeal to the Mikado, but seldom exercised it.

In the nineteenth century the Daimios had begun to chafe under this state of things ; and those of them who came in contact with the Mikado, as periodical protectors of his person and palace, resenting the nonentity of their master, set on foot an agitation in favour of a return to a more natural system, with the Mikado as ruler, and the Shogun as commander-in-chief, and no more. When, in 1853, Commodore M. C. Perry first appeared in Japan with an American squadron, and demanded a treaty, threatening hostilities in the event of a refusal, matters were ripening for a change. The Shogun and his advisers, called Bakufu by the Japanese, were thrown into consternation, and having no precedent to guide them— a lack which is as puzzling to the Oriental mind as it is to the British Admiralty—were unable to act with decision. The opinions of the Daimios were asked, and ideas were welcomed from any one who was capable of giving them. The Americans, made aware of the perplexities of the situation and of the tumults which took place near Jeddo in consequence, withdrew, to return in the following year; and in the meantime the Shogun died, and was succeeded by his son, Jyesada, thirteenth of the Tokugawa dynasty.

In 1854 Perry returned; and hot debates ensued at Jeddo. Prince Mito, a powerful noble, objected to the opening up of the country; but the officials of the Shogun, better educated, pointed out the impossibility of excluding foreigners at that time, when Japan was unprepared for war, and urged that, while complying for the moment, the country might learn the drill and tactics of the strangers, purchase foreign ships and guns, and, when ready for action, unite and drive the interlopers into the sea, and perhaps even embark on a career of foreign conquest. The result was the signing of the convention with the United States in 1858, and the subsequent conclusion of similar engagements with other powers, Yokohama at the same time being opened for trade.

The Mikado and his counsellors at Kioto disapproved of the action of the Shogun, and unanimously declined to sanction the treaties. This course injured the prestige of the Shogun in the eyes of the people; and the Shogun, realising his weakness, selected a Regent to support him. The action of the Mikado encouraged the prevalent anti-foreign feeling. Of the idle and warlike Samurai, there were 30,000 in the country, and attacks on foreigners became inevitable.

In the autumn of 1858 the Shogun died, it is supposed by poison. Prince Mito nominated for the succession his own kinsman, Hitosubashi; but one Jyemochi, of the Kishiu family, obtained the office, whereupon a powerful clique of Daimios, headed by Mito, privately banded themselves together against the new Shogun, and memorialised the Mikado to expel the barbarians at once. The Regent, on his part, suspecting that Jyesada had met his death by foul play, ordered several of the Daimios to retire to their estates, and directed Prince Satsuma and others to confine themselves to their palaces in Jeddo. This policy led to fighting, the Regent having the best of it, but carrying things with so high a hand as to increase the exasperation of the growing anti-foreign party, and to bring about numerous murders of foreigners and their servants. In 1860 the Regent was assassinated by the followers of Mito, greatly to the loss of the party of the Shogun, which in consequence was obliged to temporise, and to isolate the foreigners as much as possible. The Shogun, indeed, who in 1858 had been strong enough to punish even nobles for opposing intercourse with the outer world, dared not in 1860 set the laws in motion against the murderers of Americans and Europeans. The Shogun tried to improve his position by inducing his friends to bring about a marriage between himself and the sister of the Mikado; and the marriage took place in 1861; but it did not mend matters. Prince Mito instigated an attack on the British Legation at Jeddo in the same year; and, as he had in his possession a secret document from the Mikado, commanding him to endeavour to reconcile the differences at Jeddo, and to induce the Shogun to exterminate the barbarians, he had authority for his action. The Shogun was then obliged to admit his inability to protect strangers. He made all kinds of efforts, which were not then understood, to persuade the Legations to remove from Jeddo to Yokohama, where they could be more easily defended. The people who had attacked the British Legation were, it is true, executed; but the government was so afraid of popular feeling that it had to announce that the culprits were punished, not for assaulting foreigners, but for highway robbery.

The strength of popular feeling showed itself again in January, 1862, when, although Mito, the great anti-foreigner, had died in the previous September, Ando Tsushima, one of the Shogun's council, and a protector of foreigners, was nearly murdered in the street, and upon his recovery was made to retire into private life, thanks to the influence of the Mikado's party. Up to that time, however, no Daimio had openly declared himself against the Shogun, although many retainers of Daimios had voluntarily outlawed themselves in order to gain freedom of action against the foreigners.

In the spring of 1862 a new force appeared upon the scene, in the person of Shimadzu Sabura, uncle of the then Prince of Satsuma. While on his way to obtain an amnesty for the political prisoners who had been sentenced by the Regent in 1860, he was met by a large body of the outlaws, or Ronins, who begged him to memorialise the Mikado to go forth in person against the barbarians, to abolish the Shogunate, and to punish the Shogun's council. Shimadzu Sabura presented the petitions, and soon afterwards an amnesty was granted to the political prisoners. Choshiu, Prince of Nagato, was in Kioto at about the same time; and to him and Shimadzu Sabura was entrusted the somewhat difficult task of keeping the Ronins quiet. Thus the great clans of Satsuma and Choshiu became for a time associated in a combination against the Jeddo government, and in an opposition which had the Mikado at its back.

Another attack on the British Legation occurred in June, 1862. The Shogun's council was too feeble to take active measures against the culprits, and, in face of the attitude of the surrounders of the Mikado, was unable either to satisfy the foreign representatives or to appease the enmity of its political opponents. In June, 1862, the Mikado ordered the Shogun to expel the foreigners, and to appear at Kioto to consult with the Court, leaving proper persons at Jeddo to carry out his functions there. The chief of the persons so left was the same Hitosubashi who had been Mito's nominee for the Shogunate. There could have been no more conclusive evidence of the decadence of the once great authority of the Shogun. In September, 1862, Shimadzu Sabura was greatly incensed at the scant courtesy shown to him by the ministers of the Shogun, and, it is probable, was only too ready to countenance the outrage[1] which led, in 1863, to hostilities between Great Britain and Japan.

The *Euryalus*, flagship of Vice-Admiral Kuper, arrived at Yokohama on the day of the outrage, the nature of which will be explained later. Upon representations being made, the Shogun's council expressed its regret, but frankly admitted its inability to force so powerful a Daimio as Satsuma to surrender the guilty parties. In the meantime Shimadzu Sabura had received the thanks of the Mikado for his services, and Prince Tosa had arrived at Kioto and joined Satsuma and Choshiu in the policy of opposition to foreigners. This seems to have stimulated the Mikado's advisers

[1] The outrage was committed on Sept. 14th, 1862.

to order the Shogun, who had not yet left Jeddo, to take command of the clans in the spring of 1863, when he was due at Kioto, and drive the foreigners into the sea. The unfortunate Shogun, continuing to temporise, agreed to obey the commands of the Mikado, and, at the same time, while keeping peace with the foreigners, tried, by making their position intolerable, to induce them to leave the country. The foreign representatives, on the other hand, were daily becoming more and more convinced that the Shogun had little real power, and no authority to sign treaties.

Strengthened by the arrival of numerous Daimios, the Mikado called a meeting at Kioto on April 8th, 1863, a fortnight before the appearance of the Shogun, and, ordering the expulsion of foreigners from Japan, directed that his will should be conveyed to the Samurai. Strangers were, in consequence, liable from that moment to be murdered, and were deprived of all protection and all redress, save what might be obtained by the exercise of force.

The Legations were, one by one, driven from Jeddo; and the cordon round Yokohama, where they took refuge, was gradually narrowed in preparation for their final expulsion. A large force of European ships was kept close at hand; seamen and marines were landed to protect the settlement; and, off each of the other ports in which there were Europeans, a man-of-war lay with banked fires, ready, at an instant's notice, to embark the fugitives. The old custom, in virtue of which the Daimios had spent every alternate year in Jeddo, and had always left their wives and families there, had been abrogated at the end of 1862; so that a wholesome restraint upon the conduct of the malcontent princes, and a formidable instrument of power in the hands of the Shogun, had disappeared.

On June 5th, 1863, at the instigation of Shimadzu Sabura, the 25th of the same month was fixed as the day on which the complete expulsion of the foreigners was to be effected; and it then became necessary for the Shogun to make up his mind whether he would carry out the behests of the Mikado, or would join hands with the foreigners, bolster up his own power, and try to overthrow his opponents. In his perplexity, he asked for permission to return to Jeddo. It was refused, and his rival, Prince Mito, was sent thither instead of him.

Since April the Shogun's council had tried to procrastinate in its replies to the demands for satisfaction on account of the outrage of the previous September. It had at last promised to pay the indemnity on June 18th; but as soon as Prince Mito reached Jeddo, a refusal to pay was announced. On June 24th, moreover, a decree was promulgated by the Shogun, who was stated to have received "orders" to that effect from the Mikado, "to close the open ports and remove the subjects of the treaty powers." The indemnity was, however, handed over when the Council learnt that the settlement of the business had been placed in the hands of Vice-Admiral Kuper. A little later the Council secretly approached the treaty powers with a request for assistance in overthrowing the Mikado and his party. This was refused; but while the answer of the foreigners was still unknown, the Council, through Hitosubashi, reported that the orders of the Mikado could not be carried out.

The apparent lack of patriotism displayed by the Shogun's party proportionably increased the fanaticism of the Kioto faction, the result being that on June 25th Choshiu opened fire on some French, American, and Dutch vessels at Simonoseki. At this crisis the Shogun behaved very well. He might have made capital by joining the popular movement, and encouraging a general massacre of foreigners; and, as he was at Kioto, he might have pleaded duress. His council, too, at Jeddo, though playing a double game, succeeded in causing the defence of Yokohama to be handed over to the foreign executive authorities. Choshiu, for his part, received the approval of the Mikado; and although, on July 20th, the French Rear-Admiral Jaurès, with a couple of ships, bombarded the Simonoseki batteries, and, landing, spiked some of their guns, the United States corvette *Wyoming*, which tried single-handed to punish Choshiu in the same manner, ran aground under the forts, and did not get off until she had been rather roughly handled.[1]

I may now revert to the outrage of September, 1862, and describe the hostilities which resulted from it.

The cause of the quarrel is sufficiently explained in a letter addressed on August 1st, 1863, by Lieut.-Colonel Edward St. John Neale, Her Majesty's *Chargé d'Affaires* in Japan, to the Prince of Satsuma. The important part of this communication is as follows:

"YOUR HIGHNESS,—It is well known to you that a barbarous murder of an unarmed and unoffending British subject and merchant was perpetrated on the 14th of the month of September last . . . upon the Tokaido, near Kanagawa, by persons attending the procession, and surrounding the norimon of, Shimadzu Sabbura, who, I

---

[1] *See* Griffis, in *N. Amer. Review*, 1875; Adams, 'History of Japan'; Hübner's 'Prom. autour du Monde'; For. Off. Corr.; and Farret, 'Opérats. de Guerre Marit.'

am informed, is the father[1] of your Highness. It is equally known to you that a murderous assault was made at the same time by the same retinue upon a lady and two other gentlemen, British subjects, by whom he was accompanied, the two gentlemen having been severely and seriously wounded, and the lady escaping by a miracle. The names of the British subjects here referred to are as follows:—Mr. Charles Lenox Richardson, murdered; Mrs. Borradaile; Mr. William Clarke, severely wounded; Mr. William Marshal, severely wounded. . . . Ten months have now elapsed since the perpetration of this unprovoked outrage . . . but I have had occasion to report to my Government that, removed in your distant domain from the direct influence of the supreme Government, and shielded also by certain privileges and immunities . . . you had utterly disregarded all orders or decrees of the Japanese Government calling upon you to afford justice by sending the real criminals to Yeddo. . . . In the meantime, I have received the explicit instructions of my own Government how to act in this matter. . . . When British subjects are the victims of those acts, Japan, as a nation, must, through its Government, pay a penalty, and disavow the deeds of its subjects, to whatever rank they may belong. . . . I demanded from the Tycoon's Government an apology and the payment of a considerable penalty. . . . Both these demands have been acceded to. But the British Government has also decided that those circumstances constitute no reason why the real delinquents and actual murderers should be shielded by your Highness, or by any means escape the condign punishment which they merit. . . . I am instructed to demand of your Highness as follows:—First. The immediate trial and execution, in the presence of one or more of Her Majesty's naval officers, of the chief perpetrators of the murder of Mr. Richardson, and of the murderous assault upon the lady and gentlemen who accompanied him. Secondly. The payment of £25,000 sterling, to be distributed to the relations of the murdered man, and to those who escaped with their lives the swords of the assassins on that occasion. These demands are required by Her Majesty's Government to be acceded to by your Highness immediately upon their being made known to you. And upon your refusing, neglecting, or evading to do so, the Admiral commanding the British forces in these seas will adopt such coercive measures, increasing in their severity, as he may deem expedient to obtain the required satisfaction. . . ."

On August 13th the Minister of the Prince of Satsuma replied with a temporising and otherwise unsatisfactory letter; and on the 14th Lieut.-Colonel Neale, by dispatch, requested Vice-Admiral[2] Augustus Leopold Kuper, C.B., Commander-in-Chief on the East Indies and China station, to enter upon such measures of coercion as he might deem expedient.

The Vice-Admiral's available force consisted of H.M.S.[3]—

Ships.	Guns.	Tons.	Nom. H.P.	Compt.	Commanders.
Euryalus (flag)	35	2371	400	515	{ Capt. John James Stephen Josling. { Com. Edward Wilmot.
Pearl . .	21	1469	400	275	Capt. John Borlase, C.B.
Coquette .	4	677	200	90	Com. John Hobhouse Inglis Alexander.
Argus . .	6	981	300	175	Com. Lewis James Moore.
Perseus .	17	955	200	175	Com. Augustus John Kingston.
Racehorse .	4	695	200	90	Com. Charles Richard Fox Boxer.
Havock .	2	235	60	40	Lieut. George Poole.

[1] Apparently he was uncle. [2] Temporary rank only.

[3] The *Euryalus*, a wooden screw frigate, originally of 51 guns, was built at

From the Vice-Admiral's dispatch of August 17th to Lieut.-Colonel Neale, and from that of August 22nd to the Secretary of the Admiralty, is compiled the succeeding account of what occurred :—

On the forenoon of the 14th inst., Kuper quitted the *Euryalus* and proceeded in the *Havock* in order to satisfy himself as to the position of three steamers, the property of the Prince of Satsuma, which were lying in a bay to the northward of Kagosima. These steamers were the *England*, screw, 1150 tons, purchased for 125,000 dollars ; the *Sir George Grey*, screw, 492 tons, purchased for 85,000 dollars ; and the *Contest*, screw, 350 tons, purchased for 95,000 dollars. He found deep water in the bay, there being generally fifty fathoms within a hundred yards of the shore. A strong breeze from the eastward had sprung up, and, the rapid falling of the barometer indicating the probable approach of a typhoon or heavy gale, the top-gallant masts were sent on deck.

Kuper received the dispatch of the 14th inst. on the evening of that day ; and the *Pearl, Coquette, Argus, Racehorse,* and *Havock* were sent at daylight on the 15th to seize the three steamers already referred to. Captain Borlase, the senior officer, was directed to avoid as much as possible all unnecessary bloodshed or active hostility.

"The steamers were accordingly taken possession of without opposition, and brought down to our anchorage during the forenoon of the 15th, lashed alongside the *Coquette, Argus,* and *Racehorse,* which vessels anchored in the same bay as before. . . . The weather still looked threatening. At noon, during a squall, accompanied by much rain, the whole of the batteries [1] on the Kagosima side suddenly opened fire upon the *Euryalus,*[2] the only ship within range; but although many shot and shell passed over and close around her, no damage was done beyond cutting away a few ropes. Finding that the springs on the cable would not keep the ship's broadside on, and as it was impossible, with the comparatively small force at my command, to engage the batteries under way, and, at the same time, to retain possession of the steamers, I signalled to the *Coquette, Argus* and *Racehorse* to burn their prizes, and then to the whole squadron

---

Chatham in 1853. The *Pearl,* a wooden screw corvette, was launched at Woolwich in 1854. The *Coquette,* a wooden screw gun-vessel, was built in 1855. The *Argus,* a wooden paddle-wheel sloop, was built at Portsmouth in 1849. The *Perseus* was a wooden screw sloop, built at Pembroke in 1861. The *Racehorse* was a wooden screw gun-vessel built in 1860. The *Havock,* of the "*Albacore* class," was one of 116 similar wooden screw gun-vessels built at the time of the Russian War.

[1] About 88 guns and mortars were in position, including at least three 10-in. and two 8-in. guns. and forty 32- and 24-prs.

[2] The *Euryalus* was taken entirely by surprise. The late Sir Alfred Jephson told me that she hastily weighed, while her band played, "Oh dear, what can the matter be ? "

to weigh and form the line of battle according to seniority,[1] the *Havock* being directed
to secure the destruction of the three steamers. Previous to this, the *Perseus,* having
slipped her cable, was directed to fire on the north battery until the signal was made
to form line of battle, which service was executed by Commander A. J. Kingston with
great promptness.

"Although the weather was now very dirty, with every indication of a typhoon, I
considered it advisable not to postpone, until another day, the return of the fire of the
Japanese, to punish the Prince of Satsuma for the outrage, and to vindicate the honour
of the flag; and, everything being now ready, I proceeded towards the batteries,
opening fire upon the northernmost one with considerable effect; and passed, at slow
speed, along the whole line within point-blank range. Owing, probably, to the un-

favourable state of the weather, the ships astern did not maintain their positions in as
close order as I could have wished, and the *Euryalus* was consequently exposed to a
very heavy and well-directed fire from several of the batteries at the same time, and
suffered somewhat severely. About this time, also, and whilst in the thickest of the
action, I deeply regret to state that I was deprived, at the same moment, of the
assistance of Captain Josling[2] and Commander Wilmot,[3] both of whom were killed by
the same shot, whilst standing by me on the bridge of the *Euryalus,* directing the fire

---

[1] This order is observed in the tabulated list given on p. 196.

[2] Captain John James Stephen Josling's commissions bore date: Lieutenant,
July 25th, 1847; Commander, Nov. 2nd, 1854; and Captain, Jan. 31st, 1861.

[3] Commander Edward Wilmot's commissions bore date: Lieutenant, Sept. 26th,
1853; Commander, Dec. 24th, 1861. He had served in the Black Sea, in the *Royal
Albert,* during the Russian War.

of the quarters and setting an example of coolness and gallantry which was emulated throughout the entire ship.

"In consequence of the dense smoke, and occasional heavy showers, it was difficult to ascertain the extent of the damage done to the earthwork batteries, but by the time the *Euryalus* got abreast of the last, or southernmost battery, I could observe the town to be on fire in several places; and, the weather having now assumed a most threatening appearance, I considered it advisable to discontinue the engagement, and to seek a secure anchorage for Her Majesty's ships. The *Racehorse*, owing to a momentary stoppage of her engines, unfortunately took the ground opposite the northern battery : but by the prompt energy of the commanders of the *Coquette*, *Argus*, and *Havock*, which vessels were despatched to her assistance, she was got off without damage. The steady fire kept up by Commander C. R. F. Boxer prevented the *Racehorse* receiving any serious injury from the battery, which had already been much disabled by the fire of the other ships. The *Havock* was then ordered to set fire to five large junks belonging to the Prince of Satsuma, which Lieutenant George Poole accomplished in a most satisfactory manner; and these, as well as a very extensive arsenal and foundry for the manufacture of guns, shot, and shell, together with large storehouses adjoining, were also completely destroyed.

"During the whole of the succeeding night it blew almost a hurricane, but all the vessels of the squadron rode it out without accident, with the exception of the *Perseus*, which vessel dragged her anchors off the bank into 60 fathoms water, and was compelled to slip her cable during the following afternoon, when the gale had somewhat moderated. The gale subsided gradually during the 16th, and, as I had observed the Japanese at work, apparently erecting batteries on the hill above the anchorage, enveloped in trees and bushes, which might have inflicted much damage upon the small vessels lying within pistol-shot of the shore, I became anxious for their safety, and determined to move the squadron out of the anchorage we had occupied upon the night of our arrival in the gulf, for the purpose of repairing damages, fishing spars, and refitting previous to proceeding to sea. The squadron accordingly weighed at three P.M. of the 16th, and, passing in line between the batteries of Kagosima and Sakurasima, steamed through the channel and anchored to the southward of the island, taking advantage of the occasion to shell the batteries on the Sakura side, which had not been previously engaged, and also the palace of the prince in Kagosima. A feeble fire only was returned from the batteries which had not been closely engaged in the first attack, and this, happily, without effect upon Her Majesty's ships. . . . With much regret I have to add that the returns received from the various ships present a list of casualties unusually great, being no less than 13[1] killed and 50 wounded, the half of which occurred in my flagship alone. . . . I left the gulf of Kagosima, in company with the squadron, on the afternoon of the 17th inst., on my return to Yokohama."

This engagement did much to discredit a type of gun which was then new to the Navy. An officer who was present in the *Euryalus* wrote to me :—

"We had on our main-deck 32-pr. 56 cwt. muzzle-loaders; and they, of course, gave no trouble. On our quarter-deck we had four 40-pr. Armstrongs, and we got two or three from the port side over to the spare ports on the starboard side to make a larger battery. These all worked well. But in the forecastle we had a 7-in. B. L. 110-pr. Armstrong. Whether the men in the heat of the action became hurried I cannot say; but certain it is that the breech piece of this gun blew out with

---

[1] In addition to the two officers already named, Gunner Thomas Finn, of the *Coquette*, was killed.

tremendous effect, the concussion knocking down the whole gun's crew, and apparently paralysing the men, until Webster, captain of the forecastle and of the gun, roused them by shouting: 'Well; is there ere a b—— of you will go and get the spare vent piece?'"

It is of first-rate importance that men should have confidence in the safety of their weapons. Naturally the type of gun in question never again commanded much confidence.

During the engagement, a 10-in. shell from the batteries exploded near the muzzle of one of the guns on the main deck of the *Euryalus*, killing seven men, and wounding Lieutenant Alfred Jephson, and five others. The remaining officers wounded were Assistant-Paymaster George Washington Jones, and Gunner W. Sale (*Euryalus*); Carpenter M. Armstrong (*Pearl*); Lieutenant D'Arcy Anthony Denny, and Gunner W. Harris (*Coquette*); and Lieutenant Francis Joseph Pitt, Master Robert Gilpin, and Midshipman John Robert Aylen (*Perseus*).[1]

The promotions consequent upon this engagement were:—

> To be Captains: Coms. John Hobhouse Inglis Alexander (Aug. 16), and Lewis James Moore (Nov. 9).
> To be Commanders: Lieuts. James Edward Hunter, and Arthur George Robertson Roe (Aug. 16), and James Augustus Poland, and George Poole (Nov. 9).
> To be Surgeon: Asst. Surg. Charles Richard Godfrey (Nov. 9).

Because of the typhoon, and the rolling of the ships, many of the shot intended for the batteries fell in the wood and paper town, and set it on fire. For this, Vice-Admiral Kuper was strongly blamed in the House of Commons; and was as warmly defended by a brother flag-officer, who, in the heat of argument, used the word "damn," and, upon being called to order, created much amusement by apologising for having uttered language which, he said, "so seldom fell from the lips of sailors." Master William Hennessey Parker, of the flagship, steered his vessel with great judgment, taking her at times within 400 yards of the batteries; yet Kuper continually spurred him with: "Go in closer, Parker; go in closer!" Owing to the heavy sea in which the action was fought, the decks were afloat.

It should be mentioned that, previous to the action at Kagosima, the Shogun had quitted Kioto, with the expressed intention of returning to Jeddo overland. He had, however, embarked in a

---

[1] *Gazette,* Oct. 30, 1863; *Japan Comm. News,* Aug. 26; corr. of *Times*; For. Off. corr.

steamer at Osaka, and so had reached Jeddo on July 31st.   No
doubt he feared for his safety.

The effect of Kuper's action was immense, especially on the
powerful Satsuma following. That great clan learnt, and never
again forgot, that Japan was not the strongest power in the world,
and that there were other nations which, though far away, were,
even in Japan, to be feared as being both stronger and more
civilised. Satsuma's people subsequently took the lead in general
progress, and in introducing European machinery and inventions to
their compatriots.

Yet, although the conversion of the anti-foreign party had begun,
the Shogun did not regain his prestige. In the autumn of 1863, a
European-built steamer, carrying Japanese colours, and bearing
envoys from him, was fired upon by Choshiu. Choshiu, however, soon
went too far. Early in October, 1863, he formed a plan to carry off
the Mikado from his palace, one of the gates of which was in charge
of the Nagato clan. The plot was discovered in time; Satsuma's
people were summoned in haste; and Aidzu, the Shogun's Resident
at Kioto, with some small Daimios, rallied to the Mikado's person,
the upshot being that Choshiu, and many of his confederates, had to
withdraw in disgrace. This conspiracy had its influence upon the
Mikado's advisers; and although the Emperor declared that he was
still determined to expel the foreigners, he added that he should
delay taking the field. News of this announcement reaching Jeddo,
and, it being there interpreted with prudence, the Shogun's council,
on November 12th, withdrew the decree of June 24th, relative to the
closing of the ports, and the removal of foreigners; and Satsuma's
envoys gave the satisfaction and indemnity which had been demanded
by Great Britain. From that time the scheme for expelling " the
barbarians " fell to pieces. The Shogun, with others, received marks
of the Mikado's favour, and, at the same time, promised to confine
his functions to those of a military vassal, and to endeavour, by
improving the military resources of the country, to enable Japan
to hold her own against other powers. The authorities thenceforth
frankly recognised the superiority of foreign ships and arms; and a
decree on the subject was issued by the Mikado, and sent to all the
Daimios. A copy of this decree fell into the hands of the British
Minister in April, 1864; and the Shogun's council was then taxed
with cherishing a deliberate intention of expelling foreigners when
the time for doing so should have arrived. The council answered

blandly that the necessary preparations would take a long time to make, if the foreigners should continue to keep at hand a large coercive force. This led to a permanent occupation of Yokohama by the British and French.

Choshiu, the restless, though in disgrace, was not idle. In February, 1864, he sank a steamer which had been lent to Prince Satsuma by the Shogun; and in July, 1864, accompanied by an armed body of Ronins and adventurers, he ascended the river from

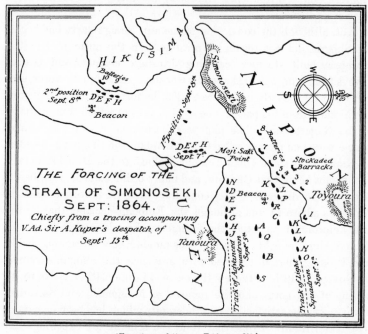

(*For reference letters, see Table on p.* 203.)

Osaka, and appeared before Kioto. The Mikado refused to listen to those who advised him to deal leniently with the truculent prince; and heavy fighting resulted, the Shogun's people, under Hitosubashi, and Satsuma's men, assisting in the defence of the palace, and in the defeat of the assailants, but not until there had been great slaughter, and until thousands of houses, sixty Shinto shrines, and one hundred and fifteen Buddhist temples, had been destroyed. After the repulse, the Mikado ordered the Shogun to march an army into the rebel vassal's territory at the south-western extremity of Nipon, and in the island of Choshiu, and to bring to his senses

"Matz daira Daizen no Daibu, Jiusi no Choshiu," Prince of Nagato.

Here was a good opportunity for punishing Choshiu for having fired upon European vessels, to aid a government which showed some signs of entertaining wiser and more liberal sentiments than before, and to open the Inland Sea to trade. The Shogun gave a secret assent to the suggestion that the ships of the powers should assist ; and Sir Rutherford Alcock, then British Envoy Extraordinary in Japan, gladly seized so favourable an occasion for dealing a blow at the chief of the anti-foreign party, who, moreover, for the previous twelve months, had interrupted the trade at Nagasaki.

The associated powers were Great Britain, France, Holland, and America. The Americans had no suitable vessel available on the spot ; but anxious to take part, they put an officer, some men, and a gun from the U.S. corvette *Jamestown*, on board a chartered steamer, the *Takiang*, and added her to the combined forces, which, when assembled, comprised the following ships :—

ALLIED SQUADRONS AT THE FORCING OF THE STRAIT OF SIMONOSEKI,
SEPTEMBER, 1864.

NATION.	Ref. to Plan.	SHIPS.	Tons B. M.	Guns.	COMMANDERS.
Br.	A	*Euryalus*, scr. frig.	2,371	35	V.-Ad. Sir Augustus Leopold Kuper, K.C.B.
					Capt. Jno. Hobhouse Inglis Alexander.
Fr.	B	*Sémiramis*, scr. frig..	..	35	R.-Ad. C. Jaurès.
					Capt. Du Quilis.
Br.	C	*Conqueror*,[1] scr. batt.-ship . . .	2,845	78	Capt. Wm. Garnham Luard.
Br.	D	*Tartar*, scr. corv.	1,296	20	Capt. Jno. Montagu Hayes.
Fr.	E	*Dupleix*, scr. corv.	..	10	Capt. Franclieu.
Dut.	F	*Metalen Kruis*, scr.	..	16	Capt. J. F. De Man.
Br.	G	*Barrosa*, scr .corv.	1,700	21	Capt. Wm. Montagu Dowell.
Dut.	H	*Djambi*, scr.	..	16	Capt. van Rees.
Br.	J	*Leopard*, padd. frig..	1,406	18	Capt. Chas. Tayler Leckie.
Br.	K	*Perseus*, scr. sloop	955	17	Com. Aug. Jno. Kingston.
Dut.	L	*Medusa*, scr.	..	18	Capt. de Casembroot.
Fr.	M	*Tancrède*, scr. disp. v.	..	4	Lieut. Pallu.
Br.	N	*Coquette*, scr. g. v.	677	4	Com. Arth. Geo. Robertson Roe.
Br.	O	*Bouncer*, scr. g. b.	..	..	Lieut. Hy. Lowe Holder.
Br.	P	*Argus*, padd. sloop	281	6	Com. Jno. Moresby.
Dut.	Q	*Amsterdam*, padd.	..	8	Com. Müller.
Am.	R	*Takiang*, chartd. str.	..	1	Lieut. Pearson, U.S.N.
Br.	S	*Pembrokeshire*, collier	..	..	

Advanced Squadron. applies to C, D, E, F, G, H, J rows. *Light Squadron.* applies to K, L, M, N, O, P, Q, R, S rows.

[1] Having on board a battalion of Royal Marines.

Sir Augustus Kuper quitted Yokohama on August 29th, and sailed again from the rendezvous, off Himesima Island, in the Inland Sea, on September 4th, anchoring in the afternoon out of range of the batteries in the Strait of Simonoseki. The defences then existing there are shown in the accompanying plan. The nature of the guns in the various forts is specified in the table on p. 206.

Kuper, with the French Rear-Admiral Jaurès, reconnoitred the position of the various works which were held by the Prince of Nagato ; and it was arranged that the attack should be made on September 5th, as soon as the tide should serve.

At 2 P.M. on the 5th, therefore, the ships took up their assigned positions, and, immediately they had reached them, the action was opened by the flagship *Euryalus*, the Japanese replying smartly and with spirit. The positions of the ships, as described in Kuper's dispatch of September 15th, were as follows :—

" The advanced squadron, under the command of Captain J. M. Hayes, consisting of the *Tartar, Dupleix, Metalen Kruis, Barrosa, Djambi*, and *Leopard*, moved into the bay off the village of Toyoura, as shown on the plan, within easy range of batteries 3 to 8 [1] inclusive, while the *Euryalus* and *Sémiramis* opened fire upon the same works. The light squadron, under Commander Kingston, consisting of the *Perseus, Medusa, Tancrède, Coquette*, and *Bouncer*, were directed to take the batteries in flank. The *Argus* and *Amsterdam* being at first kept in reserve to render assistance to any ship that might be disabled or grounded, were afterwards ordered to close and engage ; and the *Conqueror*, having the battalion of Marines on board, was, in consequence of the difficult navigation, directed to approach only sufficiently near to admit of her Armstrong guns bearing on the nearest batteries. During this operation, the *Conqueror* grounded twice on a knoll of sand, but came off again without assistance, and without sustaining any damage. The *Takiang* also fired several shots from her one Parrot gun, doing good service. The *Coquette*, towards the close of the engagement, was withdrawn from her position with the flanking squadron, and sent to assist the foremost of the advanced corvette squadron, a service which Commander A. G. R. Roe performed with great promptness."

By about 4.30 P.M. the fire from batteries 4 and 5 evidently slackened ; and soon afterwards it ceased. By 5.30 batteries 6, 7, and 8 were also silenced. It was, however, then too late in the day to admit of landing-parties being disembarked. Nevertheless, the *Perseus* and the *Medusa* being very close to battery 5, and it being too dark to signal for instructions, Commander Kingston, with Lieutenant Francis Joseph Pitt, and a party from the *Perseus*, followed by Captain de Casembroot, and Lieutenant De Hart, of the *Medusa*, gallantly pulled ashore, spiked most of the guns in that battery, and returned to their ships without casualties. A curious and significant feature of this first day's action was the receipt of a request from Buzen, on the side of the strait opposite to Simonoseki, that the people there should be permitted to fire blank cartridges at the squadron during the attack, and yet not be molested. They desired to keep in the good graces of both parties, with a diplomatic view to the future.

At daylight on September 6th, battery 8 re-opened fire upon the advanced squadron, doing some damage to the *Tartar* and *Dupleix* ;

---

[1] The dispatch says " 3 to 9 " an obvious error.

but, on a return being made by the squadron, it was silenced, only
a few straggling shots being afterwards fired from it. Kuper
continues :—

"The arrangement for the disembarkation having been completed, the allied forces,
composed of the small-arm companies of the *Euryalus* and *Conqueror*, under the command of Captain J. H. I. Alexander, of the *Euryalus*, the battalion of Marines, and
Marines of the squadron, under that of Lieut.-Colonel William Grigor Suther, R.M.,
and detachments of 350 French, and 200 Dutch seamen and marines, the former under
the command of Captain Du Quilis and Lieutenant Layrle, chef d'état major, and the
latter under that of Lieutenant Binkis, were distributed in the boats of the squadron
and towed to the opposite shore by the *Argus, Perseus, Coquette, Tancrède, Amsterdam,
Medusa,* and *Takiang,* the *Bouncer* assisting to cover the landing, which was effected
without accident, under the able superintendence of Captain W. G. Luard, of the *Conqueror,* assisted by Commander Edward Thomas Nott of that ship; and the force proceeded, under my personal direction, to assault and take possession of the principal
batteries; which was accomplished with only trifling opposition. All the guns having
been dismounted and spiked, carriages and platforms burnt, and magazines blown up,
and deeming it inexpedient, from the very rugged and almost impenetrable nature of the
country, to retain possession of any post on shore during the night, I directed the whole
force to re-embark at 4 P.M.

"The French and Dutch detachments were already in their boats, when the naval
brigade stationed at battery No. 5 was suddenly attacked by a strong body of Japanese
assembled in the valley in the rear of the battery. Colonel Suther's battalion of Marines
coming up at this moment, a joint attack was instantly organised, and the enemy
driven back upon a strongly-placed stockaded barrack, from which they were dislodged after making a brief but sharp resistance, leaving seven small guns in our
possession."

On this occasion, Captain Alexander, while leading his men, was
badly wounded in the foot, and numerous other casualties took place.
The force re-embarked without further incident. The *Perseus,*
while assisting in the landing operations in the morning, was driven
on shore by a strong eddy of the current, and remained fast until
midnight on the 7th, when, having been lightened, she was towed
off undamaged by the good management of Commander Moresby.
An extraordinary incident of the second day's work was the arrival
of envoys from Choshiu, with a request for a cessation of hostilities
for forty-eight hours, it being alleged that the Japanese troops were
tired and hungry, but would be prepared to renew the engagement
at the expiration of the period. The episode recalls the easy-going
behaviour of the Belgian and Dutch troops, who, during the four
days' fighting in Brussels in 1830, desisted each day for dinner, as
by common consent, and even allowed each other time for a brief
siesta afterwards.

The batteries from 1 to 8 inclusive being in possession of the
Allies, working parties were landed early on September 7th, and

began to embark the captured guns. In the afternoon, the *Tartar, Metalen Kruis, Djambi,* and *Dupleix* moved round to the westward of Moji Saki Point, preparatory to an attack on batteries 9 and 10.

On September 8th, accompanied by Jaurès, Kuper shifted his flag to the *Coquette,* and, with the four ships above mentioned, proceeded to open fire on batteries 9 and 10. The fire was not returned; and soon afterwards parties were landed from the squadron to destroy the works and embark the guns, the whole operation being completed by the evening of September 10th. Sixty-two pieces in all were brought away.[1]

On the 8th, while the work on shore was still in progress, an envoy from Choshiu went on board the British flagship under a flag of truce, and produced letters and documents which induced Kuper and Jaurès to allow a two days' truce, at the expiration of which a Japanese officer of high rank brought humble and satisfactory submissions from Choshiu, his promise to erect no more batteries, and his consent to open the strait.[2]

In the course of the operations, the allies had 12 people killed, and 60 wounded. The British loss was, *Euryalus,* 5 killed, 18 wounded; *Tartar,* 8 wounded; *Conqueror,* 2 killed, 4 wounded;

[1] ORDNANCE CAPTURED AT SIMONOSEKI, SEPT., 1864.

BATTERY.	GUNS.	HOWITZERS.	MORTARS.	FIELD PIECES.
No. 1 . . .	1—9-pr.	1—32-pr.		2—12-prs.
No. 2 . . .	1—9-pr.			
No. 3 . . .	Removed by the Japanese.			
Stockaded } Barracks }	..	1—12-pr.	1 coehorn	{ 2—6-prs. 3 swivels.
No. 4 . . .	4—30-prs.			
No. 5 . . .	{ 1—8-ton 6—24-prs.			
No. 6 . . .	{ 2—11-in. 3—78-prs. }	..	..	3—12-prs.
No. 7 . . .	..	..	{ 1—8-in. 1—13-in.	
No. 8 . . .	{ 1—8-in. 3—24-prs. 7—30-prs. }	2—5-in.		
Nos. 9 and 10 .	{ 6—30-prs. 1—24-pr. 2—9-prs. }	1—5-in.	..	{ 4—6-prs. 2—3-prs.
Total . .	38	5	3	16

[2] Disps. and letters of Kuper, Alexander, Hayes, and Suther; Journals of Capt. Payne and Chf. Paym. R. R. A. Richards; Corr. of *Times,* and of *A. and N. Gazette.*

Barrosa, 1 wounded; *Leopard*, 2 wounded; *Perseus*, 2 wounded; *Bouncer*, 1 wounded; and the battalion of Royal Marines, 1 killed, and 12 wounded: total, 8 killed, 48 wounded. No officers were killed, but the following were wounded: Captain John Hobhouse Inglis Alexander, Lieutenant Frederick Edwards, and Midshipman C. W. Atkinson (*Euryalus*); Lieutenant William Arthur de Vesci Brownlow, and Midshipman Edward John Wingfield (*Tartar*); and Lieutenant-Colonel Charles William Adair, R.M., Captain Nevinson William de Courcy, R.M., and Lieutenant James Weir Inglis, R.M., of the Marine battalion.

The promotions consequent upon the action were:—

To be Captains: Commanders John Moresby and Augustus John Kingston (Nov. 21st).

To be Commanders: Lieutenants Henry Lowe Holder, William Henry Cuming, William Arthur de Vesci Brownlow, Richard Hastings Harington, and Richard Edward Tracey (Nov. 21st).

To be Master: Second-Master James Greenwood Liddell (Nov. 18th).

To be Surgeon: Assistant-Surgeon Richard Lovell Bluett Head (Nov. 18th).

ADMIRAL SIR WILLIAM MONTAGU DOWELL, G.C.B.

Most of the British casualties occurred on September 6th, when the Naval Brigade and Marines were engaged on shore. It was then that Captain Alexander was wounded, the command of the Brigade devolving on Lieutenant Harington. In the course of that afternoon's fighting some gallant deeds were done, and no fewer than three Victoria Crosses were gained; one by Midshipman Duncan Gordon Boyes of the *Euryalus*, "who carried a colour with the leading company, kept it with headlong gallantry in advance of all, in face of the thickest fire, his colour-sergeants having fallen, one mortally and the other dangerously wounded, and was only detained from proceeding further yet by the orders of his superior officer. The colour he carried was six times pierced by musket balls."[1] The others were gained by Thomas Pride, captain of the afterguard, who, until he fell disabled, had supported Boyes; and by William Seeley, seaman, who daringly ascertained the position of the enemy,

---

[1] Alexander to Kuper, Sept. 10th.

and afterwards, though wounded, continued in the front of the advance.[1]

In addition to most of the officers who have been already named, the following were mentioned in the dispatches :—

"Lieutenants Robert Peel Dennistoun (flag), Cottrell Burnaby Powell, and Alfred Jephson; Masters George Williams, John Charles Solfleet, and John Emanuel Chapple; Paymaster Hemsley Hardy Shanks (Secretary); Surgeons David Lloyd Morgan, and Christopher Knox Ord, M.D.; Assistant-Surgeons Samuel M'Bean, Edward Alfred Birch, and John Thomson Comerford; Midshipmen Henry Hart Dyke, and Edward Plantagenet Hume; Clerk Robert N. Haly; Lieut.-Colonel Penrose Charles Penrose, R.M.; Captain Ambrose Wolrige, R.M.; Lieutenant John Christopher Hore, R.M.; Lieutenant William Henry Townsend Morris Dodgin, R.M.A.; and a Prussian officer, Herr von Blanc, who was attached to the *Tartar.*"

After much further negotiation, some internal outbreaks, and a demonstration by the fleets of the powers at Osaka, the Mikado ratified the treaties at the end of 1865. In 1866 the Shogun, or Tycoon, Jyemochi, died, and was succeeded by Hitosubashi, under the name of Keiki. At about the same time Choshiu, who had previously repulsed the Shogun's forces, became reconciled both with the Mikado and with Satsuma. In 1867 the Mikado also died, and the crown devolved upon Mutsu Hito, then a boy of fifteen, who later distinguished himself as a most successful and enlightened ruler. There was thenceforward no serious difficulty with foreigners. An attack in May, 1867, on two British subjects who were travelling between Osaka and Jeddo was promptly punished; and the murder of two men of H.M.S. *Icarus*, at Nagasaki, was as quickly inquired into, the perpetrators being executed. In November of the same year, the dual government was terminated by Keiki's surrender of the remains of his power to the Mikado.

It is not necessary to follow further the evolution of the modern régime in Japan. It was not accomplished without much violence; and in 1868 seamen and Marines had again to be landed on Japanese soil, this time at Kobe. They had, however, little or no fighting to do; and, soon afterwards, the conservative chiefs formally admitted that the long efforts to close the country were a mistake, and prayed that relations of amity with foreigners might be encouraged. In March, 1868, the European and American ministers were invited for the first time to visit the Mikado at Kioto. Isolated outrages continued for some time; and even on the occasion of this visit to the Mikado, the British minister narrowly escaped assassination;

[1] *Gazette,* April 21st, 1865.

but proper punishment was instantly meted out to the offenders ; and it was generally admitted that these crimes were the work of individual fanatics, and were in no sense instigated by the government.

Japan, under the Emperor Mutsu Hito, began, very soon afterwards, to astonish her friends by the rapidity with which it assimilated European methods and civilisation ; and, ere the end of the nineteenth century, she won her way to recognition as one of the great powers of the world.

In 1864, and again in 1865 and in 1866, various expeditions proceeded up the Niger to maintain British prestige, and to keep the turbulent chiefs in order. For this work the *Investigator*,[1] 2, paddle, drawing as she did only about 4 feet 4 inches of water, proved most useful. She was employed almost constantly during those three years, either up the river, or in the Lagos lagoons, where, in March, 1865, she participated in the action at Ikorudu. Among the officers who successively commanded her on these services were Lieutenant Charles George Frederick Knowles, Lieutenant John George Graham M'Hardy, Lieutenant George Truman Morrell, and Lieutenant John William Jones. In the Congo, in 1865, the boats of the *Archer*, 13, screw, Captain Francis Marten, were engaged against the river pirates.

Early in 1865, while the *Dart*, 5, screw, Commander Frederick William Richards, lay at Akatoo, on the West Coast of Africa, a rumour arose to the effect that the natives were about to plunder the British factories. One factory, indeed, had been actually looted, and a schooner had been stripped and set adrift. Richards therefore landed some men from his gun-vessel, and, also a small detachment from the *Lee*, 5, screw, Lieutenant Oliver Thomas Lang. Several boats were capsized in the surf, and two people drowned ; and, in a subsequent collision with the natives, one seaman was wounded.

Of the captures of slavers made in the same year, no case was more gallant and creditable than one in which the pinnace and cutter of the *Wasp*, 13, screw, Captain William Bowden, were concerned. On May 12th, the boats in question, containing 24 seamen and two Midshipmen, under Lieutenants Charles Compton Rising, and Charles Barstow Theobald, found an Arab

[1] Built at Deptford in 1861.

dhow, with 283 slaves and a crew of 76 Arabs on board, about nine miles off Zanzibar, and captured her, after the enemy had made a desperate resistance, and had killed the pinnace's coxswain, John New, and wounded 11 people, including Rising,[1] Theobald,[2] and Midshipman William Wilson.[3] The *Wasp* made several more captures, resistance, however, not being offered in most cases. Another vessel which, at about the same time and on the same station, greatly harassed the slave-trade, was the *Lyra,* 7, Commander Robert Augustus Parr. At her paying off, in April, 1868, after a fifty-two months' commission, she had eleven dhows to her credit.

In June, 1865, while surveying off the south cape of Formosà, a boat party from the screw gunboat *Dove,* Master George Stanley, was set upon by cannibal natives, and had one man wounded. The vessel, upon the return of the party, opened fire with effect upon the assailants, who crowded the beach. The scene of the outrage is now known as Attack Bay.

In consequence of the long-continued outrages committed by certain of the inhabitants of the New Hebrides, Commodore Sir William Saltonstall Wiseman, Bart., in the *Çuraçoa,* 23, screw, bombarded Tanna and Erromanga in 1865. At Tanna one British seaman was killed by a native. On the native side the damage done was confined chiefly to property.

On December 12th, boats' crews from the *Salamis,* paddle despatch-vessel, Commander Francis Grant Suttie, and *Janus,* gunboat, Lieutenant Cecil Frederick William Johnson, had a brush with some Chinese pirates at Tia Nia, on the west coast of the island of Tonqua. Acting on information received from the mandarins, Commander Suttie landed with 45 officers and men, and, approaching three junks and five snake-boats which lay in a creek, was fired upon from several directions by a force of about 200 people, who presently fled to the hills. Lieutenant Johnson, with only six men, followed the main body of these, and fought them gallantly until he was recalled. About a dozen of the enemy were killed and wounded, and all their craft were destroyed. On the British side there were no casualties.

Among the numerous engagements which took place during these years between H.M. ships and Chinese pirates, few were more

---

[1] Com., Nov. 26, 1865.   Pension of £100 for wounds, Aug. 9, 1866.
[2] Com., Nov. 16, 1865.   [3] *Gazette,* July 21, 1865.

noteworthy than one fought by the gunboat *Grasshopper*, Lieutenant George Digby Morant, in November, 1865. The vessel, on several other occasions, rendered useful service of the same sort, and, at her paying off, she was able to claim prize-money in respect of 20 pirate vessels, and 483 men. Morant, while lying in Chimmo Bay, near Amoy, learnt that three pirate lorchas, which were then at Port Matheson, had lately captured five cargo junks. Arriving off Pyramid Point at about 8 A.M. on November 23rd. Morant found the three pirates under sail, and their prizes at anchor inside of them. He gave chase, and, at 8.45, fired a gun to bring them to. They replied at once, and formed line of battle at the shoal end of the bay, tacking backwards and forwards. Having little more water under him than he drew, Morant was obliged to engage them at 1200 yards. At 11 A.M, one of his 68-pr. shells blew up the magazine of the largest pirate, a Macao lorcha, and set fire to the hull. The other two tried to make off through a rocky channel. The *Grasshopper* steamed round outside, and drove them back, and, upon the tide rising, was able to close within 800 yards. At 12.45 the people of one of the lorchas began to jump overboard ; whereupon Morant ordered his Gunner, Mr. H. Gardner, to take the cutter and capture her. This was done. The third lorcha kept up the engagement until 1.15, when she struck, her crew leaving her. Morant, in the gig, went and took possession of her. The gunboat had no casualties, and was hulled only twice. Upon seeing the *Grasshopper* approach, the pirates had deliberately beheaded 34 of the prisoners whom they had on board, and disembowelled two boys, sons of the masters of two of the prizes. Lieutenant Morant, who was promoted[1] for this affair, was fortunately able to capture 23 of the scoundrels who had jumped overboard. The largest of the lorchas mounted two long 16-prs. and six 6-prs. Each of the others had five guns, and among them the three had about 150 men on board.[2]

In the previous month, the *Opossum*, 2, Lieutenant Henry Craven St. John, tender to the *Princess Charlotte*, had been sent in search of some pirates who were reported to be lying in Mirs Bay. She had there found two pirate junks, which she burnt, and their prize, which she restored to her owners, from whom St. John received news which induced him to proceed at once to Tooniang Island, where he discovered three more piratical craft in a creek.

___

[1] Com., Feb. 6th, 1866.   [2] Morant to King.

Having landed a force to take them in rear, he attacked in the
gunboat from seaward, the result of his excellent dispositions being
that he captured all three without suffering any loss. This exploit
was, for the moment, the last of a series of operations, during
which, in about a year, St. John had captured 35 pirate vessels,
mounting, in the aggregate, 140 guns.

One of the most brilliant bits of hard fighting done by the Navy
in the second half of the nineteenth century stands to the credit of
the paddle-sloop *Bulldog*, 6, of 1124 tons, and 500 nominal horse-
power. She was on the North America and West Indies station
in 1865, when Sylvestre Salnave was endeavouring to wrest the
presidency of the Haytian Republic from Fabre Geffrard.   On
October 22nd, off Acul, and in sight of the sloop, a Salnavist
steamer, the *Valorogue*, fired into a British Jamaica packet.
Captain Charles Wake, of the *Bulldog*, having approached, and
inquired into the matter, informed the commander of the *Valorogue*
that, unless he ceased firing, his ship should be sunk under him.
The rebel officer thereupon desisted, and took his vessel into Cape
Haytien.   As soon as he heard what had happened, Salnave ordered
the arrest by force of a number of fugitives who had sought refuge
in the British Consulate there.

On the morning of the 23rd, Wake,[1] who was accompanied by
three Geffrardist war-steamers, appeared off the mouth of the
harbour. The Consul had informed him in the interval that the
refugees had been not only seized but also shot, that the Consulate
had been wrecked, and that the flag had been insulted in other
ways. Wake demanded satisfaction, and, getting only a refusal,
began to shell Fort Cirolet at 8.45 A.M. The work replied five
minutes later. Pushing further in, and engaging all the batteries,
Wake presently caught sight of the *Valorogue*, which, perhaps
rather unwisely, he endeavoured to ram at full speed. Unfortunately, he was in waters which were strange to him ; and his
navigating officer, Acting-Master Edwin Behenna, was a young
man fresh to the station. The result was that the sloop ran on a
reef within short musket-shot of the enemy's vessel, and within
point-blank range of a masked shore battery, which instantly opened
on her. Nevertheless, the *Bulldog* sank the *Valorogue* at 9.45 ; and
at 10.10 A.M. the largest schooner of the Salnavist fleet was also

---

[1] The two Lieutenants of the *Bulldog* were John Lewis Way, and Frank
Rougemont.

sunk. In addition, the sloop blew up the Salnavist powder-magazine, set fire to the town, and dispersed with grape and canister the riflemen who had assembled on the shore. At 11.30, Wake sent a message to the United States' war-steamer *De Soto*, requesting her captain, Lieutenant-Commander Howell, to tow him off. Some steps in this direction seem to have been taken, but in vain, by the Americans, who, at noon, through Lieutenant Sumner, kindly offered to receive and tend the sloop's wounded. This Wake thought proper to decline at the moment. During the whole time, and, indeed, until dark, the engagement continued. When the firing had ceased, the gallant British Captain, who had no intention of allowing his ship to fall into the hands of the blacks, and who had little ammunition left, set fire to and abandoned her, transferring himself, his people, his wounded, and his killed (with the exception of a few who were sent to the friendly *De Soto*), to the Geffrardist steamer *Vingt-deux Décembre*. The sloop, still fast aground, finally blew up.

Of her complement of 175 officers and men, the *Bulldog* had 3 killed, and 10 wounded. A court-martial, which was held at Devonport, considered that Wake and Behenna were to blame for having run the sloop on to the reef, and that she had been abandoned and destroyed prematurely; and it severely reprimanded Wake, and reprimanded Behenna. Captain Wake called the attention of the Admiralty to his sentence, which, according to public opinion, was a somewhat harsh one, and was informed that their lordships " did not consider that any imputation was cast on his honour or his courage.[1] This gallant officer, as will be seen on reference to the Flag-Officers' List, died in 1890. It is pleasant to be able to add that he was soon again employed afloat.[2]

On November 9th, following, the offending forts at Cape Haytien were bombarded, and silenced one after the other, by the *Galatea*, 26, scr., Captain Rochfort Maguire, and *Lily*, 4, scr. Commander Algernon Charles Fieschi Heneage. The firing lasted from 9 A.M. until 6 P.M. The *Galatea* had no casualties; but the *Lily* had

---

[1] Disps.: Wake's account in *Army and Navy Gazette*, Dec. 2nd, 1865; letter of officer of the *De Soto*. Mins. of C.M., Jan. 15th, 1866.

[2] *Punch* ended some verses on the affair and its sequel with:

> " Then here's three cheers for Captain Wake; and, while we sail the sea,
> May British Bulldogs always find Captains as stout as he,
> That's all for biting when they bite, and none for bark and brag,
> And thinks less about court-martials than the honour of the flag."

several people hurt. As the forts were reduced they were occupied by the Geffrardists.

In opening the Legislative Session of 1865, Governor E. J. Eyre, of Jamaica, made the following reference to the part played by the Navy in repressing the very serious disturbances which had then recently taken place in the island :—

"To the senior naval officer, Captain de Horsey, of H.M.S. *Wolverene*, we owe it that we were enabled to carry out with promptitude and efficiency the arrangements necessary to control and suppress the rebellion. The *Wolverene* and her gallant Captain were kept almost unceasingly at work, day and night, in all weathers, and off a lee coast; but all was done with hearty good will, zeal, and cheerfulness. . . . Lieutenant Brand, of H.M.S. *Onyx*, is entitled to the highest praise for the unceasing and valuable services rendered by the little gunboat under his command."

Captain de Horsey was the Admiral Algernon Frederick Rous de Horsey, the dates of whose commissions, etc., will be found in the Flag Officers' List. Lieutenant Herbert Charles Alexander Brand, commanding the *Onyx*, one of the smallest of the gunboats which had been built for the purposes of the war with Russia, became a victim of a hot and foolish agitation in England, the result of which was that, with Brigadier-General Nelson, he was arraigned at the Old Bailey on a charge of wilful murder. The prisoners were happily acquitted; and, after further honourable service, Brand retired in 1883 with the rank of Commander. He died in 1901.

In 1865 the piratical depredations of the Arabs on the west coast of the Persian Gulf, and especially of those of El Kateef, became so troublesome that, towards the close of the year, the screw corvette *Highflyer*, 21, Captain Thomas Malcolm Sabine Pasley, was sent thither to exact satisfaction. Failing to obtain it, Pasley, in January, 1866, destroyed two forts, and burnt some dhows belonging to the marauders. Misapprehending the nature and strength of a fort near El Kateef, he subsequently sent his boats ashore there, and landed a party which, in an attempt to rush the work, succeeded in getting inside the outer wall only, and was at length obliged to retreat thence with a loss of 3 killed and 8 wounded,[1] one of the latter also dying on the following day. After the repulse, the *Highflyer* sent in her boats, and shelled the fort at long range, but apparently did it little damage.[2]

[1] Among the wounded was Lieut. John Fellowes : see Disps.
[2] *Bombay Gazette.*

During the Fenian disturbances in Canada, in 1865–67, a number of Her Majesty's ships and vessels were employed, under the direction of Captain de Horsey, on the river St. Lawrence, and lakes Ontario, Erie, and Huron. Their services were not, for the most part, of a very exciting character, being mainly of a preventive nature; but, in respect of them, a medal and clasp were granted in 1899 to officers and men who were in the following vessels on the occasion:—

> *Aurora*, 35, screw, Captain Algernon Frederick Rous de Horsey; *Pylades*, 21, Captain Arthur William Acland Hood; *Niger*, 13, screw, Captain James Minchin Bruce; *Rosario*, 11, screw, Commander Louis Hutton Versturme; the gunboats *Heron*, Lieutenant Henry Frederick Stephenson; *Britomart*, Lieutenant Arthur Hildebrand Alington; and *Cherub*, Lieutenant Spencer Robert Huntley; and the armoured hired gunboats *Canada*, Lieutenant Thomas Hooper; *Royal*, Lieutenant John Henry Vidal; *Hercules*, Lieutenant Archibald Lucius Douglas; *St. Andrew*, Lieutenant Seymour Spencer Smith; *Michigan*, Lieutenant Frederick William Burgoyne Heron Maxwell Heron; and *Rescue*,[1] Lieutenant Henry James Fairlie.

The Cretan revolt, which began in 1866, caused so little anxiety to the British authorities in the Mediterranean that it is not mentioned in the autobiography and journals of Vice-Admiral Lord Clarence Edward Paget, who was Commander-in-Chief there at the time. Nevertheless, precautions were taken for the protection of British interests; and for some months in 1866–67, the gunboat *Wizard*, Lieutenant Patrick James Murray, was stationed off the coast for that purpose.

Lieutenant Henry Craven St. John, who was reappointed to command the gunboat *Opossum*, 2, at the beginning of 1866, signalised his fresh term of command, and earned his promotion, by the zeal which he again displayed in the repression of Chinese piracy. In February, he left Hongkong on a cruise, and, hearing of the presence of a number of pirates near Pakshui, on the west coast beyond Macao, he at once went in search of them. He discovered fifteen vessels at the head of a small creek, mounting among them 43 guns, and protected by a battery mounting three others. He had but about thirty men on board; yet he silenced the battery, and drove the pirates from their vessels, which he seized, and many of which he destroyed, handing over the rest to the Imperial Chinese authorities. His loss was 5 people

---

[1] Twin-screw, of 248 tons, and 100 H.P.

wounded. Two days later, he recaptured a junk which had been stolen from her owners and used for piratical purposes by her skipper. Not long afterwards, he made another prize. After his promotion, which was dated April 12th following, he made a further attack on Pakshui, where he captured nine snake-boats, and again destroyed a battery. He was then superseded by Lieutenant Karl Heinrick Augustus Mainwaring. In June, 1866, the *Osprey*, 4, Commander William Menzies, with the *Opossum*, left Hongkong in search of some more pirate junks, which, to the number of twenty-two, were found in Sama creek. Among them they mounted upwards of 200 guns. The *Osprey* approached within 1200, and the *Opossum* within 700 yards, and, after a two hours' cannonade, landed parties, which took the junks in rear, and compelled their abandonment. The vessels were all burnt, and the village of Sama, which had sheltered them, was destroyed. The only person killed on the side of the attack was a Chinese mandarin, who had accompanied it in order to identify the freebooters.[1]

In the course of the year 1867 several of her Majesty's ships were actively employed on the coast of Ireland in connection with the repression of the Fenian disturbances there. The Navy took part, however, in no fighting deserving of the name.

Early in the same year, the British consul at Cartagena, Colombia, having complained that his letters were opened and detained by the local authorities, Commodore Sir Francis Leopold M'Clintock, in charge at Jamaica, despatched to the spot the *Doris*, 24, screw, Captain Charles Vesey. Vesey made certain demands which the governor of the town declared that he had not power to grant; whereupon, on February 26th, the Colombian Government steamer *Colombiano* was seized by an armed party in three boats from the frigate. This measure induced the governor to adopt new views as to his powers, and, matters having been settled satisfactorily, the steamer was released on March 1st.

On June 26th, the gunboats *Bouncer*, Lieutenant Karl Heinrick Augustus Mainwaring, and *Havock*, Lieutenant Yelverton O'Keefe, with a mandarin accompanying them from Kowloon Bay, found two piratical Chinese vessels at anchor in Starling Inlet, and, getting out their boats, took and destroyed both, and released their prize, a trading junk. Such pirates as escaped were followed to the shore, but in vain. On the 28th, fifty miles further up the coast,

[1] *A. and N. Gazette*, Sept. 22, 1866.

the same gunboats attacked, captured, and destroyed a considerable flotilla of piratical craft, preserving, however, one prize which, on the 29th, was towed by the *Havock* into Hong Kong. In the course of 1867, when the treaty port of Cheefoo, in north China, was threatened by a large horde of rebels, a British force was landed there for its defence. The senior officer on the spot at the time was Commander Frederick William Hallowes, of the paddle-sloop *Argus*, 6.

On July 17th, 1867, Her Majesty Queen Victoria reviewed a large fleet at Spithead. Admiral Sir Thomas Sabine Pasley was in command, with his flag in the *Victoria*, screw wooden three-decker. The port column on this interesting occasion consisted exclusively of vessels of the old and doomed types. The starboard column, under Rear-Admiral Frederick Warden, who had his flag in the *Minotaur*, consisted exclusively of ironclads, and included not only iron-hulled armoured battleships, like the *Bellerophon*, but also wooden-hulled ones, like the *Lord Clyde*, together with coast-defence turret-ships, such as the *Royal Sovereign* and the *Prince Albert*, and armoured gun-vessels, such as the *Vixen* and the hydraulic-driven *Waterwitch*. No non-steamers were present in the lines. Accompanying the Queen were the Sultan of Turkey and the Viceroy of Egypt. Lieutenant William Robert Kennedy acted as Flag-Lieutenant to the Board of Admiralty at the review, and was promoted, on the following day, to be Commander. In August, 1869, when their Lordships went for a cruise in the *Agincourt* with the Channel Squadron, which was then commanded by Vice-Admiral Sir Thomas Matthew Charles Symonds, in the *Minotaur*, Captain James Graham Goodenough, Lieutenant the Hon. Edward Stanley Dawson was appointed Flag-Lieutenant to the Board. The Admiralty flag was hauled down on September 30th, and Mr. Dawson received his promotion on the following November 11th.

Numerous acts of piracy and murder by the natives of the Nicobar Islands led to the despatch thither from the Straits Settlements on July 19th, 1867, of the *Wasp*, 13, screw, Captain Norman Bernard Bedingfeld, and the *Satellite*, 17, screw, Captain Joseph Edge, the latter having native troops on board. Some villages and war-canoes were burnt, and one or two prisoners were released; but, disturbances having in the meantime broken out at Penang, the ships had to return thither in the middle of August. The *Wasp* had been originally commissioned in November, 1863, for the suppression of the slave-trade on the east coast of Africa. One of her exploits there in the year 1865 has been already recorded.

The Navy had but a modest, though an altogether creditable share in the Abyssinian Expedition of 1868. The naval arrangements in the Indian seas were in the hands of Captain Leopold George Heath, C.B., who flew a broad pennant, as Commodore of the First Class, in the *Octavia*, 35, screw, Captain Colin Andrew Campbell. To the *Octavia* was attached, as Director of the Transport Service, Captain George Tryon, who had on his staff Paymasters Thomas Henry Lovelace Bowling, and Thomas Nelson Firth, and Assistant-Paymaster Thomas Edmund Goodwin. These officers did most of their work at the base at Zoulla, in Annesley Bay, one of the hottest places on earth, and were fully employed, seeing that no fewer than 291 transports, besides tugs, lighters, and native craft, were engaged in the operations.[1]

More interesting experiences fell to the Naval Brigade which, with rockets and Sniders, was landed at Zoulla on January 25th, under Commander Thomas Hounsom Butler Fellowes,[2] of the *Dryad*, 4, screw, and which accompanied the army to Magdala. The ships which chiefly contributed were the *Octavia*, the *Dryad*, Commander Fellowes, and the *Satellite*, 17, screw, Captain Joseph Edye ; though medals for the campaign were also granted to the *Star*, 4, screw, Commander Richard Bradshaw ; *Argus*, 6, paddle, Commander Frederick William Hallowes ; *Daphne*, 4, screw, Commander George Lydiard Sulivan ; *Nymphe*, 4, screw, Commander Thomas Barnardiston ; *Spiteful*, 6, paddle, Commander Benjamin Langlois Lefroy ; and *Vigilant*, 4, screw, Commander Ralph Abercrombie Otho Brown ; these ships being engaged on various services in connection with the campaign.

The Brigade marched on February 29th, reached Senafé on March 5th, and, advancing again on the 7th, arrived at Antalo on March 16th. It consisted of but 100 European officers and men, with 2 farriers, 13 grasscutters, 3 water-carriers, 6 sick-bearers, 1 hospital-sweeper (Indian natives), and 88 battery mules, 54 baggage and provision mules, or their equivalent in camels, 11 officers' horses, and 3 bullocks for carrying water. At Antalo it was attached to the 2nd brigade, 1st division. At Lat, on March

---

[1] Fitzgerald, " Life of Tryon," 99.

[2] In his absence the *Dryad* was temporarily commanded by Lieut. George Woronzow Allen.

23rd, it joined the first division under Major-General Sir Charles
Staveley, and thence continued on the 25th towards Magdala.   On
joining Lieutenant-General Sir Robert Napier, the commander-in-
chief, at Santara, on March 30th, the force was drilled, and fired
rockets, under his Excellency's inspection.   It was then attached to
the 1st Brigade under Brigadier-General Schneider, which moved
forward on the 31st.   On April 10th it rendered valuable service
during the action in the Arrogie Pass, where it led the attack up
the King's Road.   On April 13th it threw rockets into Magdala, and
took part in the assault on the place.   Two or three days later it
again used its rockets to disperse Galla plunderers.   In the
distribution of the loot, the Brigade received as its trophy " a
valuable and handsome shield, with gold filigree and lion's skin,
and a solid silver cross."   At the review on Dalanta Plain, on
April 20th, the Brigade was placed on the right of all the troops,
excepting the cavalry.   The return march was begun on the 22nd.
In the meantime another Brigade, under Captain Colin Andrew
Campbell,[1] had been landed for the defence of Senafé, but was not
required there, and was re-embarked.

Throughout the operations the men behaved admirably, and
marched very well indeed, although, in many cases, their boots gave
out.   Commander Fellowes, who was himself mentioned in the
despatch of Sir Robert Napier, specially brought to the notice of
the Admiralty (in his despatch dated Marrawah, May 2nd) the
names of the following officers and men of his little command : *viz.*
Lieutenant Charles Searle Cardale (*Satellite*), Assistant-Surgeon
Henry Nanton Murray Sedgwick (*Octavia*), Chief-Gunner's Mate
Charles Henry Jones, Gunner's Mate Robert Smith, Boatswain's
Mates Thomas Vaughan, and John Graham, coxswain of the barge
Benjamin Starkes, and second captain of the foretop Charles
Austin.   There were no casualties.[2]   For their services Commodore
Heath received a K.C.B., and Captains Edye, Tryon, and Fellowes
each a C.B.[3]   In addition, Commanders Fellowes and Barnardiston
were posted ; Lieutenants John Fiot Lee Pearse Maclear, Edmund
Lyons Green, and Charles Searle Cardale were made Commanders ;

---

[1] In his absence Com. William Henry Maxwell commanded the *Octavia*.

[2] *Gazette,* June 16th, 1868.   Fellowes to Admlty., May 2nd (in *A. and N. Gazette,*
June 27th, 1868).   Hozier, " Brit. Exped. to Abyssinia " (1869).   Heath to Admlty.,
June 10th, 1868.   The last makes favourable mention of a number of officers.

[3] All dated Aug. 15th, 1868.   Capt. Edye died on Sept. 13th, 1868, at Hong Kong.

acting Sub-Lieutenant George Lambart Atkinson was made acting Lieutenant; Navigating-Lieutenants Daniel John May, and Thomas Pounds were made Staff-Commanders; Surgeon James Nicholas Dick was made Staff-Surgeon; Assistant-Paymaster William Edwin Boxer was made Paymaster; and Engineer William Henry Grose was made Chief-Engineer.[1]

This year is remarkable for the unusual number of cases of piracy and outrage which, in various quarters of the world, necessitated the active employment of ships of the Navy.

Lieutenant Compton Edward Domvile, of the *Algerine*, 1, screw, who had already done useful service against Chinese pirates, continued to be very active in the summer. On May 26th, 1868, the gun-vessel left Hong Kong in search of a piratical junk or snake-boat, which had committed piracy just outside the harbour. She found a junk of about 100 tons in an inlet of Mirs Bay, and, acting upon information received, took her, burnt her, and drove her people away, then proceeding to Stanley for further directions. Early on the 31st she again started, calling at Macao, and thence going to Namoa. On her way back, when between that place and St. John's, on June 3rd, she fell in with a squadron of thirteen heavily-armed pirates. Domvile hailed them, and demanded their papers, whereupon they fired into him. The mandarin with him assured him that they were pirates, and the fire was promptly returned. In a few minutes the action became general. The gun-vessel rolled badly, but made fairly good practice. She cut off and boarded one junk, which was endeavouring to run in-shore, and then she chased the others, which were going off in a body to the westward. She got up with them at about dusk, having first engaged them at a little after 3 P.M. A fresh and close action followed, and lasted for an hour and a half. Owing to the darkness and the shoaling water the pursuit had then to be abandoned; but the already captured junk, which made off to seaward, was retaken two hours after dark, and towed into Hong Kong on June 9th. Whether the Chinese were really pirates is more than doubtful; for, on trial, the prize was judged to be a trader, and was released. Domvile, indeed, though with the best intentions, acted too hastily. Otherwise the affair was most creditable; for while on the Chinese side about 800 men and 130 guns seem to have been engaged, the *Algerine* had on board but one large and two small pieces, and about

[1] All dated Aug. 14th, 1868.

20 people ; among whom there were, strange to say, no casualties.[1] On July 15th the *Algerine* captured three other alleged piratical junks in a bay in Tychan Island. Domvile was promoted on September 2nd following. British officials, both consular and naval, were at that time rather too ready to employ force in China. In 1869 the Foreign Office strongly censured Consul Sinclair, of Foochow, for having unnecessarily induced Lieutenant Leicester Chantrey Keppel, of the *Janus*, 1, to intervene on behalf of a certain missionary.

At Yangchow, on August 22nd, 1868, the unpopularity of the British missionaries led to a serious outrage, which only by great good fortune did not terminate in the whole household of the Rev. Mr. Taylor being burnt. Happily, the entire British party escaped to Chinkiang. Consul Walter Medhurst, and the *Rinaldo*, 7, screw, Commander William Kemptown Bush, proceeded as soon as possible from Shanghai to Chinkiang, whence, with an escort of 80 officers and men from the sloop, the Consul went to Yangchow on September 8th, and made certain demands. Some of these the local authorities professed themselves powerless to grant, whereupon the Consul and his party moved up to Nankin ; but, Commander Bush falling ill, the *Rinaldo* was withdrawn ; and the Governor-General, seeing the Consul deprived of his supports, assumed an intractable attitude. Medhurst had to return to Shanghai, and refer the matter to Pekin. The affair was most injurious to British prestige, and Commander Bush was much blamed for withdrawing his sloop instead of leaving her at Nankin and himself going to Shanghai in one of the regular steamers.[2] After some negotiations, Sir Rutherfold Alcock was obliged to place the matter of the attack on the missionaries in the hands of Vice-Admiral the Hon. Sir Henry Keppel, who, accordingly, sent up the *Rodney*, 78, screw (flag[3]), Captain Algernon Charles Fieschi Heneage, *Rinaldo*, 7, and *Slaney*, 1, screw, Lieutenant William Francis Leoline Elwyn, to Nankin, where the *Icarus*, 3, screw, Commander Lord Charles Thomas Montagu Douglas Scott, and the *Zebra*, 7, screw, Commander Henry Anthony Trollope, subsequently joined them. The squadron seized the Chinese gunboat *Tien Chi*, on November 8th,

---

[1] *China Mail* ; Admiralty Corr. in *A. and N. Gazette*, May 22nd, 1869.

[2] *Shanghai News Letter. Friend of China.* Shanghai Corr. of *Times* in letter of Oct. 13th, 1868.

[3] But Keppel was temporarily elsewhere, in the *Salamis*.

as a material guarantee; and a strong landing party, under Captain Heneage, was then despatched, in November, to Yangchow, where it remained until the whole of the British demands had been conceded.[1]

There were other outrages, arising chiefly out of the local opposition to missionaries, and the attempt of the Chinese to monopolise the camphor trade, in the island of Formosa. Claims for redress were evaded, and at length Consul Gibson requested Lieutenant Thornhaugh Philip Gurdon, commanding the *Algerine,* 1, screw, to occupy the Amping and Zelandia forts, which constituted the key to the capital, Taiwan. At Amping, forty-one guns were already in position. To prevent the mounting of more, Gurdon, on November 25th, 1868, opened fire with his pivot-gun at 2000 yards; but, finding that he could not stop the construction of earthworks, he very pluckily landed at night in his gig and cutter, accompanied by two officers and twenty-three men. The gig was swamped, but he disembarked in safety through the surf, two miles below the town. Advancing carefully, as it was moonlight, he took shelter under some rising ground, 800 yards from the works, until 2 A.M., when he made a rush, and carried the place almost instantly, killing several Chinamen, and driving off the rest. At daylight he also took possession of Zelandia, and, when attacked there by a force from Taiwan, repulsed it with heavy slaughter. This brilliant action led to the submission of the local authorities, the punishment of those who had committed the outrages, and the breaking down of the camphor monopoly. On the other hand, Consul Gibson, Lieutenant Gurdon, and Sir Henry Keppel were severely attacked, besides being blamed by the Admiralty, for having had recourse to such active measures, although, in fact, fruitless negotiations had been going on for five months ere any blow was struck.[2] Gurdon was, however, promoted on June 1st, 1869.

On February 2nd and 3rd of the following year, the *Algerine,* then commanded by Lieutenant Henry Rowland Ellison Grey, destroyed twelve piratical snake-boats off Tonqua, subsequently releasing four valuable prize junks.[3]

The town of Choochi, on the river Han, above Swatow, was

---

[1] Keppel, "A Sailor's Life," iii. 221.

[2] Keppel, "A Sailor's Life," iii. 223.   *A. and N. Gazette,* Feb. 13th and Mar. 13th, 1869.

[3] *Hongkong Daily Press,* Feb. 10th, 1869.

long the headquarters of a band of pirates, who interfered with the transport of merchandise from the interior to the coast, and even plundered vessels in sight of Swatow itself. In 1868 some of these people foolishly fired upon and robbed a boat which, in charge of a British subject, was bringing down stores for the *Bustard*, 2, screw, Lieutenant Cecil Frederick William Johnson. Johnson demanded the punishment of the offenders, but the local mandarin declared that Choochi was fortified, and far too strong for him to meddle with; whereupon, on June 29th, the *Bustard* steamed up the river, and anchored a mile and a quarter from the pirate stronghold. The co-operation of some mandarins, with 300 Chinese troops, had been obtained. The town having been summoned, and having refused to surrender, Johnson landed, and led the troops to the attack of the place, which was stoutly held and mounted two guns. The Chinese soldiers did well until they became entangled among spikes and other obstructions under a heavy fire inside the outer stockade. Johnson was then obliged to retire, as he had with him too few Europeans to attempt a storm, and the enemy could concentrate 600 men at any given point. Returning to the gunboat, he began a bombardment which he kept up until dark. In the night he landed sixteen of his men with a 24-pdr. howitzer, which, posted within 600 yards of the works, opened fire at dawn on the 30th. When, after some hours, the inner fortifications were breached, the Chinese troops were again induced to advance. Johnson led them gallantly, but they were once more repulsed. On the two following days the bombardment was continued. At length, the town being on fire in several places, Johnson, with twenty-four of his own small ship's company, succeeded in taking it. After levelling the works and burning the stockades, he handed it over to the Chinese authorities.[1] Johnson was recommended for his services, but was not promoted until 1873.

Owing to Mr. Baker, a missionary, and some of his dependents having been murdered, the *Challenger*, 18, screw, Commodore Rowley Lambert, C.B., proceeded in August, 1868, to Rewa, in the Fiji Islands, and despatched her launch, and first and second cutters, under Commander Charles James Brownrigg, who shelled one or two villages as a punitive measure, and, it was believed, killed several natives. On the British side two persons only were wounded. On September 11th and 12th the *Blanche*, 6, Captain

[1] *Hongkong Daily Press*, Aug. 10th, 1868. Johnson to Keppel.

John Eglinton Montgomerie, executed similar punitive measures at Rodora Bay, in the Solomon Islands.

As in so many previous years, some of the piratical tribes on the Congo gave trouble in 1868. They were effectively punished, particularly at Maletta Creek in November. The vessels whose officers and men participated in the affair were the *Myrmidon*, 4, screw, Commander Henry Boys Johnstone, *Pandora*, 5, screw, Commander John Burgess, and *Plover*, 3, twin screw, Commander James Augustus Poland.

Towards the end of the year a schooner under the British flag was captured by pirates near Malluda Bay, and three of her people were killed. Upon hearing of the outrage the Governor of Labûan went in pursuit in the *Dwarf*, 2, screw, Lieutenant Charles Francis Walker. The pirates made a stand on the island of Ubean, and, refusing to deliver up their leader, were punished by a landing party, which burnt their village, and brought about their submission. Governor John Pope Hennessy left the question of compensation to be settled by an official of the Sultan of Sulu.

Piracy in the Arabian Gulf received a check at the hands of Commander Benjamin Langlois Lefroy, of the *Spiteful*, 6, paddle, who, during a month's cruise in the early part of 1868, captured and destroyed six vessels, and rescued 200 slaves. Two of the slavers taken were armed with 6-pr. carronades. On one occasion determined resistance was offered; and on another the fugitive crew of a captured dhow returned, and made a bold but vain effort to regain the prize, which had to be blown up.

In the late summer of 1868, as soon as she could be spared from service with the Abyssinian Expedition, the *Vigilant*, 4, screw, Commander Ralph Abercrombie Otho Brown, was sent, with three vessels [1] of the Bombay Marine, to deal with the troublesome chief, Mahomet ben Kuleef, of Bahrein, in the Persian Gulf, and with his neighbours and allies, who had greatly oppressed Indian traders. Mahomet ben Kuleef's fort, war-vessels, and guns were destroyed after a two days' bombardment; reparation was made; fines were imposed; and certain chiefs were deposed and outlawed. The Bombay vessels subsequently proceeded to Muscat, which was found to have been captured by rebels on the day previous to their arrival; and assistance was rendered to the Sultan. [2]

[1] *Sir Hugh Rose, Sinde,* and *Clyde.*
[2] *Times of India,* Oct. 2, 1868; *A. and N. Gazette,* Nov. 7, 1868.

At Bahrein matters did not remain quiet for long ; and towards the end of 1869 it became necessary again to take action there. The matter was entrusted to Commander George Amelius Douglas, of the *Daphne*, 4, screw, who, accompanied by the *Nymphe*, 4, screw, Commander Edward Spencer Meara, and two vessels of the Bombay Marine, proceeded to the spot, and, in October and November, blockaded the island of Bahrein, took the fort of Menameh, and seized or obtained the surrender of several truculent chiefs, who were presently carried to Bombay as prisoners. It may be added that, previous to this expedition, both the *Nymphe* and the *Daphne* had been unusually successful while slave-cruising. During the commissions which they were then serving they captured between them about sixty slave vessels of one kind or another. The *Star*, 4, screw, Commander Walter Sidney de Kantzow, was also conspicuously successful.

Another craft which, on the same station, did good service against slavers in the years 1868 and 1869 was the *Dryad*, 4, screw-sloop, Commander Philip Howard Colomb, who subsequently wrote an interesting account of his work, and published it under the title of ' Slave-Catching in the Indian Ocean.'

Early in January, 1869, when Vice-Admiral the Hon. Sir Henry Keppel happened to be with the British Consul at Canton, information reached him from Captain Oliver John Jones, Commodore at Hong Kong, concerning an outrage which had just been committed by the Chinese in the vicinity of Swatow. The crew of the *Cock-chafer*, 2, screw, while exercising in the boats up the River Han, under the commander of the gunboat, Lieutenant Howard Kerr, had been attacked by the inhabitants of some neighbouring semi-piratical villages, and, having been landed, had found itself opposed by about 600 people, and ultimately obliged to retire, with a loss of 11 wounded. Keppel communicated with the Chinese authorities, who undertook to co-operate in punishing the assailants ; and he ordered the Commodore to proceed to the spot with the *Rinaldo*, 7, screw, Commander Frederick Charles Bryan Robinson, *Perseus*, 15, screw, Commander Charles Edward Stevens, *Icarus*, 3, screw, Commander Lord Charles Thomas Montagu Douglas Scott, *Leven*, 2, screw, Lieutenant Orford Somerville Cameron, *Bouncer*, 2, screw, Lieutenant Rodney Maclaine Lloyd, and a detachment of seamen and Marines from Keppel's flagship, the *Rodney*, which was making good defects at Hong Kong. Keppel did not intend Jones to act before his senior's arrival, and, having proceeded to Hong Kong, sailed thence on January 30th, 1869, in the *Salamis*, 2, paddle, Commander Henry Matthew Miller.

The impetuous Commodore, however, probably fearing to be superseded in the command of the expedition, did not wait for the arrival either of his chief, or of the whole of the Chinese forces, but, having landed a sufficient detachment, advanced on January 28th along the banks of Outingpoi Creek, burnt two or three villages, killed or wounded 88 natives, re-embarked, and returned to his ships. The British loss was only five wounded, including Lieutenants Herbert Frederick Gye (*Rodney*), Philip Bennet Aitkens (*Rinaldo*), and Rodney Maclaine Lloyd (*Bouncer*).[1]

The slave trade persisted on the east coast of Africa many years after it had become practically extinct elsewhere; and, indeed, slavers continued to be captured there, though with diminishing frequency, until the end of the nineteenth century. In 1869 the traffic was extremely active, as may be judged from the fact that between January 4th and April 9th of that year, the *Nymphe*, 4, screw, Commander Edward Spencer Meara, took no fewer than sixteen slave-dhows on the station. On April 11th, when the sloop was at Zanzibar, her two cutters were ordered away, at the request of the Sultan, to stop another dhow, which was putting to sea. She was made prize of, but in the struggle, and by subsequent fire from the shore, a seaman was killed, and two officers were wounded.[2] On May 21st, while on her way to Aden, the *Nymphe* took two more large slavers, making nineteen in less than five months. Other vessels were almost equally successful at about the same period.

An expedition, consisting of the *Lynx*, 4, twin screw, Commander James Wylie East, and the *Pioneer*, 2, paddle, Lieutenant William Wiseman,[3] left Lagos, on July 21st, 1869, in order to proceed as far as possible up the Niger in support of British trade and influence. The bar of the river was crossed on July 23rd, but only very slow progress could be made, owing to the sandbanks· and natural obstacles. After a point upwards of 400 miles from the

[1] Keppel, "A Sailor's Life," iii. 233 (untrustworthy especially as regards names). *A. and N. Gazette*, Feb. 20th, March 6th, March 13th, and March 27th, 1869. *Saturday Review*, May 29th, 1869.

[2] Sub-Lieut. Norman Leith Hay Clark, who commanded, and Sub-Lieut. Thomas Tarleton Hodgson (severely). Both were presently promoted.

[3] Afterwards Capt. Sir Wm. Wiseman, 9th Bart., died Nov. 1, 1893.

sea had been reached, the vessels, which had become very sickly, returned; but the difficulties of navigation prevented them from recrossing the bar until September 13th. On the arrival of the *Lynx* at Ascension, every one of her people except four had to be sent to hospital. The expedition was purely a peaceful one, yet it narrowly escaped being of the most costly nature.

In June, 1869, the *Bouncer*, 2, Lieutenant Rodney Maclaine Lloyd, tender to the *Princess Charlotte*, receiving-ship at Hong Kong, proceeded, in company with two Chinese gunboats, on a cruise in search of pirates. On the night of June 12th, off Gowtow Island, in the Gulf of Tonquin, the *Bouncer* took five large junks, after her landing-party had had a sharp engagement with some of the freebooters on shore, who, swimming off at length, turned the guns of one of the junks upon the others as they were attacked. A Marine, James Murphy, had previously distinguished himself by swimming in the darkness to reconnoitre the enemy's position. By the 26th the *Bouncer* had captured twelve piratical craft, and her consorts nine more. Some of the prizes were excellently armed. Lloyd was specially thanked by the Hong Kong Government, and promoted on his return to England.

Upon the death in England of the American philanthropist, George Peabody, who had contributed half a million sterling to the relief of the poor of London, it was decided by the British Government, at the suggestion of H.M. the Queen, to send the body of England's dead benefactor across the Atlantic in a man-of-war, in order to let it be seen how greatly his generosity was appreciated by the nation. It was at first intended to employ the large iron cruiser *Inconstant*, but the new turret battleship *Monarch*, Captain John Edmund Commerell, C.B., V.C., was ultimately selected as being more worthy of the occasion. Mr. Peabody's coffin was, accordingly, placed in the specially fitted stern cabin of the ironclad at Portsmouth on December 11th, 1869, under a salute of twenty minute guns; and the ship then went to Spithead, where, however, she was delayed for several days by heavy weather; and she did not sail for Boston until December 21st. She was escorted by the U.S. corvette *Plymouth*.[1]

In the same year, when an iron government floating-dock,[2] then the largest in the world, was towed across the Atlantic to Hamilton,

[1] *A. and N. Gazette*, Dec. 11th, 18th, and 25th, 1869.
[2] Length over all, 381 ft.; width at entrance, 84 ft.; lifting power, 11,000 tons.

Bermuda, one of the vessels which convoyed her was the twin-screw gun-vessel *Lapwing,* 3, Commander Philip Ruffle Sharpe.   Towards the end of the year, having seen the dock to its destination, the *Lapwing* was usefully employed off Nassau in watching and intercepting blockade runners bound for Cuba.   She captured four of these craft ; and she also disarmed and embarked 296 filibusters whom one of them had landed on Nurse Key.

On January 28th, 1870, when the twin-screw gun-vessel *Growler,* 4, Commander Edward Hobart Seymour, was lying in the mouth of the Congo, she was boarded by some men belonging to the British schooner *Loango,* who reported that their vessel had been attacked by pirates on the previous afternoon.   The *Growler* weighed at once, and steamed up to the scene of the outrage.   At 1 P.M., having sighted the schooner, she manned and armed three boats, which pursued the freebooters, who abandoned their prize. Thirteen canoes and a prisoner were captured ere the boats returned. It was discovered that the *Loango* had been pillaged, and that her master and a boy were missing.   Seymour suspected a chief named M'pinge Nebacca to be implicated, and decided to surprise him in his town.   On the 29th, three boats were again manned and armed. First a visit was paid to a village belonging to the chief's brother, and some plunder was there recovered.   The expedition then pushed on, and landed two miles from the town, towards which the force advanced under a dropping fire from the retreating natives.   In the place the missing master, badly wounded, was discovered by Sub-Lieutenant Henry Bingham Chesshyre Wynyard ; and much gunpowder, which had been looted from the schooner, was found and blown up.   The town was burnt before the force retired.   Still anxious to find the missing boy, Seymour sent his cutter, with the wounded master, back to the *Growler,* and, with his gig and whaler, moved up two miles further to Nebuila.   He landed in a narrow creek, exposed to a desultory fire, which wounded Navigating Sub-Lieutenant William Stephen Robert Gow, and, after the village had been burnt, struck down Seymour himself. When the party had withdrawn, word was sent that, in exchange for a certain quantity of cloth, the missing boy would be released. Seymour, however, replied that, unless the boy were released unconditionally, all the villages in that direction would be burnt, whereupon the youngster was at length sent down to the ship. Seymour's wound, a serious one in the right leg, obliged him to

invalid some weeks later.[1]   Only a few months earlier the recall of
the cruisers from the West African coast had been foolishly urged
upon the Admiralty.

In consequence of the piratical depredations of certain Malays,
and, of the resistance offered by them and their friends to the
colonial officers sent to secure the culprits, Colonel Anson, Administrator of the Straits Settlements, desired Commander George
Robinson (2), of the *Rinaldo*, 7, screw, to take under his orders the
colonial steamer *Pluto*, and to proceed with her to Selangor.   The
two vessels anchored off the mouth of the Selangor river early on
July 3rd, 1871 ; and the sloop's boats, being manned and armed,
were sent with a field-piece party to the *Pluto*.   The party from the
Rinaldo consisted of ninety-five officers and men under Commander
Robinson, Lieutenant Grosvenor Stopford, and Acting-Lieutenant
Eustace Downman Maude.[2]   At 7.30 A.M., the *Pluto* got under
way to proceed with the boats, but at 9 A.M. grounded, and did not
arrive off Selangor until 2 P.M.   Parties were detached to search the
houses, shipping, and river banks.   Lieutenant Maude's party, in
a cutter which was armed with a rocket-tube, landed, and, upon
returning to the beach, was fired at, one man at once falling
mortally wounded.   The party, pursued by a hot fusillade, made
the best of its way to the *Pluto*, which then returned the fire.   In
the scuffle and the retreat, seven members of the party were
injured.   The Malays, however, seem to have suffered much more
heavily.

Commander Robinson ordered the *Pluto* to weigh, her position
and that of the boats being unduly exposed.   Later in the day he
sent her to Penang with the wounded, and with a request for troops
and a surgeon.[3]   On the 4th, the *Rinaldo* steamed into the river
alone.   At 6.15 A.M. the forts near the southern side of the entrance
opened on her at about 400 yards, the northern forts soon afterwards
joining in with such good effect that in less than five minutes the
sloop had three men wounded, and her hull and rigging much cut.
She replied, and, steaming on, took the batteries from the rear,
quickly knocking them to pieces and dismounting their guns.   At
6.40 A.M. Robinson anchored off the town, and laid out an anchor

---

[1] *A. and N. Gazette*, July 23, 1870.   [2] Wounded.

[3] The *Rinaldo* was without any medical officer, her Surgeon being ill, and her
Assistant-Surgeon having been appointed by the C.-in-Chief to the Naval Hospital at
Hong Kong.   *A. and N. Gazette*, Sept. 16, 1871.

astern so as to keep his battery bearing on the forts. By 8 A.M. he had driven the enemy from all his works. Occasional guns were fired during the day to prevent the Malays from remanning their pieces. At 4.30 P.M., after having been aground for several hours, the *Rinaldo* weighed, and steamed leisurely down again, ceasing fire at 5.30, and re-anchoring in the road at 6. The *Pluto* returned on the 5th with a detachment of Royal Artillery, and another of the 19th Madras Native Infantry. On the 6th, these troops were landed, but there was no further resistance,[1] and the place was quietly occupied.

On September 20th, 1871, Bishop J. C. Patteson, of Melanesia, was murdered by a native of Nukapu Island, one of the Swallow group of the Santa Cruz archipelago in the Pacific. At about that time, largely, it must be admitted, in consequence of the iniquities of the labour traffic, the natives were exceedingly hostile to white men, and had recently committed numerous outrages. Not too soon, therefore, did the *Rosario*, 3, screw, Lieutenant Albert Hastings Markham (acting Commander),[2] undertake a cruise among the islands where the worst troubles had arisen. In the middle of November, 1871, she reached Havannah Harbour, in Vate, one of the New Hebrides, and thence sent her boats to Montague Island[3] hard by to enquire into the murder of some people belonging to the schooner *Fanny*. The natives declined to give up the murderers, and, attacking the party, were punished by the destruction of their village. On the 15th the *Rosario* steamed round, and made a harmless but effective demonstration with her guns. On November 23rd, the sloop anchored off Cherry Island, in connection with an outrage on the people of the ship *Marion Rennie*[4]; but, although the natives seemed friendly, no satisfaction could be got out of them. Probably they were innocent. On the 29th, the sloop reached Nukapu. Markham's object was to acquire information concerning the murder of the Bishop. He sent in a boat, which was fired at with arrows. It was recalled, but, being sent in again, was again fired at, whereupon the *Rosario* opened with her two 40-pr. Armstrongs and her 7-inch muzzle-loader.

[1] Robinson to Anson, July 6; Robinson to Admiralty. Col. Papers, c. 466: 1872.

[2] Com. Henry Joseph Challis, of the *Rosario*, had been appointed acting Captain of the *Blanche* on Oct. 12, 1871, and his place had been taken by Lieut. Markham, who retained it until Feb. 10, when Challis, superseded in the *Blanche*, relieved him.

[3] Otherwise Nguna.

[4] See *Fiji Times*, Feb. 1, 1871.

At high-water a party landed and destroyed the village and canoes. Two of the sloop's crew were wounded in this affair, one mortally; and about five-and-twenty natives are said to have been killed.[1]

Nitendi, or Santa Cruz, where Goodenough fell in 1875, and Espiritu Santo, the largest of the New Hebrides, were also visited. At Cape Lisburn, the south-west point of the latter, the natives were interrogated, on December 16th, as to the murder of the crew of the New Zealand craft, *Wild Duck*. They admitted having killed the men, and were believed to have also eaten them. Markham would have let them off very mercifully with a fine of twenty-five pigs, but, as only four of these were paid, he burnt the village and destroyed the canoes. Pentecost and Aurora Islands were next touched at. At Aurora, where the natives at first seemed friendly, Paymaster Shuldham Samuel Crawford Hill, who had confidingly sat down to rest on the beach, was treacherously clubbed and badly hurt on December 27th; and there also the villages and canoes were wrecked in retaliation. The sloop returned to Sydney on February 8th, 1872.[2]

The fact that the offending natives were treated with a consideration which they did not merit is proved by Markham's offer to allow the Nitendi people to compound by the payment of a few pigs for the murders which they admitted having been guilty of. Nevertheless, the proceedings of the *Rosario* gave great offence to certain pseudo-philanthropists in England. Questions on the subject were even put in the House of Commons, where eventually Mr. Goschen quieted clamour by laying the despatches on the table.

On the other hand, the Pacific natives were sometimes frightfully ill-treated. A letter written from the *Basilisk*, 5, paddle, Captain John Moresby, and dated from Cardwell, Queensland, February 5th, 1872, contains the following :—

"This morning at about 11 o'clock, just after we had passed the entrance to the bay, there was the report of a sail, and the Captain, wishing to send letters, stood for her. She was soon made out to be a schooner of about 80 tons. When we got close to her we saw a lot of Polynesians in her. We immediately sent the first Lieutenant and the gig to board her; but, as they seemed inclined to show fight, we sent the cutter, armed, to assist. When they got on board they found twelve blacks all right, one dying, and three dead of starvation, the ship stinking like a pest house, so that all

---

[1] Markham himself seems to doubt whether any were killed. 'Cruise of the *Rosario*,' 150–156.

[2] *Sydney Empire*, Feb. 9, 1872: *A. and N. Gazette*, Ap. 6 and 20, 1872. Markham, 'Cruise of the *Rosario*.'

our men were as sick as possible. It appears she was a kidnapping schooner from
Samoa, and, running short of provisions, besides being waterlogged, the white men,
supposed to be Portuguese, deserted her four days ago, and left nothing for the poor
blacks (seventeen) but a bucket of water, and not a scrap of provisions, so that they
had eaten one of their own number. They were the most frightful looking wretches I
ever saw, being so fearfully attenuated, and quite naked. The very bones were
sticking through their skin ; and, as for the dead men, they were quite putrid and blue,
so that, when they hoisted them out of the hold, a hand or a foot would be left
behind. . . ."

This schooner was the *Peri*. Subsequent inquiry showed that
she was from Rewa, Fiji, not from Samoa, and that she had sailed,
with 50 Polynesians and three white men on board, on December
27th, 1871. It was suspected that the natives had really risen and
murdered their kidnappers ; but the truth seems never to have been
fully ascertained.[1]

During the same cruise, the *Basilisk* sent an expedition, under
Lieutenant Francis Hayter, which severely punished some Australian
aborigines who had murdered part of the crew of the brig *Maria*,
wrecked on the Great Barrier Reef.[2] Navigating-Midshipman
Hubert Heath Sabben, who had charge of a schooner, tender to
the *Basilisk*, went in a boat with a small party early in 1872 in
search of survivors of the brig's people. He was attacked by a
large body of natives, and being shamefully deserted by his crew,
and left ashore with only a single supporter, a gallant bluejacket
named Springay, he was in serious peril. The two Englishmen,
however, drove off the enemy, no fewer than sixteen of whom were
killed or wounded by the steady fire from their Snider rifles.[3]

In May, 1872, while the *Nassau*, 4, screw surveying vessel,
Commander William Chimmo, was engaged in the performance of
her duties in the Sulu Sea, she had occasion to land a boat's crew
on the north-east end of Sulu Island, where it was desired to take
bearings. The party was attacked on May 11th by forty or fifty
Illanoon pirates, and had to retreat fighting, several people, including Navigating-Lieutenant Francis John Gray,[4] being wounded.
Attempts were made to secure satisfaction, it being at first supposed
that the natives had mistaken the British for Spaniards ; but, as
the enemy, during prolonged negotiations, displayed a truculent
attitude, the *Nassau* eventually shelled and destroyed their village,

---

[1] Many examples of the barbarity of the kidnappers are given by Markham.
[2] *A. and N. Gazette*, June 15, 1872.   [3] *A. and N. Gazette*, July 20, 1872.
[4] Transferred on Apr. 1, 1873, to the Lieutenants' list with seniority of Mar. 2,
1866, in recognition of this service.

Carang-Carang.[1] During the operations about 190 of the pirates were believed to have been killed.

A very creditable capture of a slave-dhow was made in the same year by the boats of the *Vulture*, 3, twin-screw, Commander Robert Barclay Cay, off Ras-el-Had, in the Persian Gulf. The affair, which gained promotion for Sub-Lieutenant Frank Hannam Henderson, revealed in their most repulsive forms some of the horrors of the middle passage.   Of 169 slaves on board, no fewer than 36 were found to be down with small-pox. Forty-four wretches, who, before the capture, had been recognised by the crew and slave-merchants to be infected, had been flung overboard alive ; and when it had been seen that this procedure did not check the spread of the plague, the owners had run to the other extreme, and had forced sick and sound to huddle together until the vessel became so foul that the captors could hardly endure to board her.[2]

The *Bittern*, 3, twin-screw, Commander the Hon. Archibald St. Clair, rendered some useful services on the West Coast of Africa.   In January, 1872, she undertook active operations against the piratical natives of Corisco and Elobey Islands, after the loss of the mail steamer, *McGregor Laird*, and succeeded in capturing Coomba, the chief of Corisco.   She was subsequently engaged in the mouth of the Congo in protecting the Banana Creek factories from native attack.

For many years the ownership of the San Juan, or Haro Islands, an archipelago lying between Vancouver Island and the mainland, had been disputed by Great Britain and the United States.   In July, 1859, when the group was in the joint occupation of the two powers,[3] General Harney, commanding in Washington Territory, largely reinforced the American garrison in San Juan, and made an unqualified declaration of United States sovereignty.   The Governor of British Columbia remonstrated, but General Harney persisted, and, indeed, persisted in a most provocative manner.   Happily the government of the United States assumed a more friendly attitude, and despatched to the scene of the dispute General Winfield Scott, with whom it was amicably arranged that the American reinforcement should be withdrawn, and that both powers should maintain only a very small number of troops in the islands, pending the ultimate settlement of their ownership.   In consequence of the

---

[1] *Straits Times.*   [2] *Times of India* ; *A. and N. Gazette*, Oct. 26, 1872.
Under a provisional arrangement come to in 1855.

temporary friction, a small British squadron had been ordered to the scene. This thereupon dispersed, leaving behind it, however, a few Royal Marines to serve as garrison under the agreement. Thenceforward, for many years, Marines were stationed in the islands. After General Harney's recall, in 1860, the joint occupation was managed with good feeling on both sides. At length, by arbitration of the German Emperor, on October 21st, 1872, the dispute was settled in favour of the United States; and the British Marines, then commanded by Captain William Addis Delacombe, evacuated the islands on November 22nd following.

Among the vessels most active in their operations against the slave-trade on the east coast of Africa and in the Red Sea at about the time when Sir Bartle Frere, as envoy to Zanzibar and Muscat, was specially exerting himself against it, were the *Columbine*, 3, screw, commanded in 1871–3 by Commanders John Collier Tucker, and Edward William Hereford; the *Daphne*, 5, screw, Commander Richard Sacheverell Bateman; and the *Thetis*, 13, screw, Captain Thomas Le Hunte Ward. The *Columbine* took numerous dhows, especially in 1871; the *Daphne*, which also made many prizes, had the misfortune to lose one of her officers, Sub-Lieutenant Marcus M'Causland, in a treacherous affair with natives at Kiunga, near Barawa, on the Somali coast, in the autumn of 1873; and the *Thetis*, though then only passing through the station on her way to China, captured ten dhows in May, 1873. Most of them, however, seem not to have been slavers, for they were not condemned. After the murder at Kiunga, Sub-Lieutenant Percy Hockin,[1] who was boat-cruising in company with the dhow from which M'Causland had landed, took his men ashore with great determination, and forcibly obliged the murderers to give up the body. He afterwards proceeded to the southward, until he fell in with some boats of the *Briton*, 10, screw, under Lieutenant Arthur Stephens Phillpotts, with whom he returned, and partially destroyed Kiunga.[2]

In 1872–73, disputes relative to the then partly-built interoceanic railway led to the overthrow of President Medina, of Honduras, and to the installation in his place of Señor Arias. A movement was thereupon begun in Honduras and Guatemala for the reinstatement of Medina, who lay imprisoned at Comayagua; and the troops assembled for the purpose from both states were placed under the

---

[1] Promoted to be Lieutenant, Sept. 23, 1873.
[2] *A. and N. Gazette*, Nav. 22, 1873.

orders of General Palacios, who had been Guatemalan minister in London. As the railway was being built largely with British capital and under British supervision, British interests suffered considerably from the disturbances, and from the consequent insecurity. Puerto Cortez, the Atlantic terminus of the line, lies near the Honduran town of Omoa; and at Omoa is the ancient Spanish casemated fort of San Fernando, which was occupied by a certain General Streber, on behalf of Arias; the old governor, General Alvarez, being superseded, but remaining as commandant of the port. In view of this situation, the *Niobe*, Commander Sir Lambton Loraine, Bart.,[1] was despatched from Jamaica to Omoa in June, 1873, with instructions to protect British interests and to enforce treaty obligations. On her way, she called at Truxillo, where Loraine was informed of certain acts of oppression which had been committed in the Bay Islands against neutral persons who were under treaty protection. At Puerto Cortez Streber was found to have made military exactions from the railway

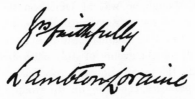

REAR-ADM. SIR LAMBTON LORAINE, BART.

company, and to have tried to force the company's labourers to join him. He was duly cautioned; and the *Niobe* then proceeded to Belize,[2] to gain further intelligence from the Lieutenant-Governor, and from Mr. Debrot, British vice-consul at Omoa, who had taken refuge in British Honduras, to escape from the outrages and tyranny of Streber. That general had also obliged the Spanish and Portuguese consuls to flee with their families; and the people had taken up their residence on the Zapotillo Cays, dependencies of British Honduras; whither Streber had had the audacity, on July 4th, to send an expedition which captured and handcuffed the fugitives, and carried them off, after threatening the inhabitants. They were

[1] A few months earlier, Sir Lambton had exhibited a salutary display of determination at Puerto Plata, San Domingo, where three refugees had been kidnapped from the British Consulate. The governor himself was forced to remove the shackles from the feet of his prisoners, and then to deliver them up on board the *Niobe*. The San Domingan troops were also obliged to replace the ensign above the consulate, and to salute it with twenty-one guns. *A. and N. Gaz.*, May 17, 1873.

[2] Arriving on July 12th.

fortunately retaken on their way to Omoa by a steamer belonging to Palacios.

When Sir Lambton Loraine returned to Omoa, he learnt that, in his absence, Palacios had secured military possession of the railway works at Puerto Cortez, and, by occupying San Pedro, had wholly cut off Streber from connection with Arias and the interior. Streber was communicated with, and was induced to promise that, upon proof being given that British territory had been violated, he would give satisfaction, and that, in the meantime, he would abstain from further raids in that direction. The discussion about the Zapotillo affair occupied nearly a fortnight; and, during much of that period, the *Niobe*, as she had yellow fever on board, usually kept under sail in the offing, or visited Puerto Cortez. Thus, her Commander could not continuously observe what was going on in Omoa; nor did he learn immediately after the occurrence that on July 29th some of Streber's soldiers had rifled a building belonging to Mr. Debrot. Indeed, though he was at Omoa on the 30th and 31st, he heard no news of the outrage until his return on August 15th from a cruise to the Bay Islands. He was then met with sworn evidence, not only of the events of July 29th, but also of further outrages, including the tearing down of the British flag, the robbing of Mr. Debrot's premises, the firing on the troops of Palacios under a flag of truce, and the sacking of Omoa in celebration of this treachery, foreign property suffering to the extent of £20,000, and four British subjects being imprisoned, after one of them had been flogged.

Having satisfied himself as to the facts, Sir Lambton Loraine took on board the acting British vice-consul, Mr. Bain, and, on August 18th, anchored in a suitable position opposite the fort of San Fernando. Early on the following morning Streber was supplied with a précis of the evidence, and desired to give his explanations, to deliver up the prisoners, and to state what reparation he purposed to offer. Four hours were allowed him for a reply. In the interim General Alvarez visited the *Niobe*, informed himself as to what terms would be accepted, expressed his sense of their fairness, and obtained an additional three hours' delay. At the end of that time, it being 2 P.M., Alvarez returned with a verbal refusal of satisfaction from Streber, whose folly he denounced, and who, at the moment, paraded his troops on the ramparts, and fired shots of defiance, though not towards the *Niobe*. Loraine sent ashore a letter stating

what course he intended to pursue, and, at 2.30, Alvarez remaining
on board, opened a bombardment of the fort with his 7-in. and
40-pr. guns. The troops promptly disappeared from the ramparts,
and returned the fire only with badly aimed musketry. The *Niobe*
pounded the 20-foot walls for three hours and three quarters, and
then withdrew until 1 A.M. on August 20th, when she closed again,
and fired at long intervals until 4 A.M. At 9 A.M. a white flag was
shown, and Streber's secretary went off to the ship with a verbal
request for a 72 hours' truce. This was refused, and a renewed
bombardment promised for 2.30 P.M. unless a satisfactory written
communication should be received in the interval. Nevertheless,
some further delay was accorded; and it was not until 1 P.M. on
the 21st that Streber at last yielded, promising surrender of the
prisoners, restitution of stolen goods, and compensation for damage
done. He subsequently signed a formal declaration to the same
effect; but he so badly carried out parts of his undertaking that, on
September 10th, a detachment had to be landed from the *Niobe* to
secure and seal up the plundered houses, and to nail a British flag
over the vice-consulate. The vessel sailed on September 13th for
Jamaica. She had suffered neither loss nor damage.[1]

Sir Lambton Loraine's proceedings in this matter were so
warmly approved by the British at Belize, and so well supported
by Commodore Algernon Frederick Rous de Horsey and Vice-
Admiral George Greville Wellesley, Commander-in-Chief, that Mr.
Gladstone's government, perhaps unwillingly, realised their necessity,
and stood by the action of the Commander, who, very soon afterwards, had a further opportunity of showing his readiness to assume
serious responsibilities.

Some piratical Chinese freebooters in the Larut River, on the
Perak coast, gave much trouble in 1873, especially in connection
with an attack which they made upon the British steamer, *Fair
Malacca*. At length it was decided to take the severest measures
against them; and, on September 19th, by arrangement, the
Thalia, 6, screw, Captain Henry Bedford Woollcombe, met the
Midge, 4, twin-screw, Commander John Frederick George Grant,
which already had had peculiar experience both of the local waterways and of the habits of the pirates throughout the Straits of
Malacca. Indeed, on September 16th, while two of her boats were
searching a creek, they had been set upon by row-boats, supported

[1] Disps. Priv. accounts of eye-witnesses. *A. & N. Gazette,* Oct. 18, Oct. 25, 1873.

by fire from a 7-gun stockade. After a hot action, in which the
British had employed both small-arms and rockets, the Chinese had
been driven off with heavy loss, but not until Sub-Lieutenants
William Rooke Cresswell, and Abraham Hamilton Lindesay had
been badly wounded.

At the mouth of the river the two commanders consulted ; and,
on the morning of September 20th, towed by the *Midge*, and by
the yacht of the friendly Rajah Muntri, the ships' boats went up
the stream. At about 11 A.M., being near the fort, the stockade,
and the three heavy war junks which belonged to the pirates,
the boats cast off, led by the *Thalia's* galley under Woollᴉ-
combe in person, and covered by the fire of the *Midge*, while,
soon afterwards, the Rajah's yacht, brought up by Grant, steamed
close to the fort, and there anchored. The enemy fired briskly ;
but, apparently the attack was delayed owing to the yacht drifting
ashore under the Chinese guns. She was, however, got off, thanks
largely to the energy of Gunner Alexander Ellis, of the *Thalia*, who
gallantly laid out an anchor for the purpose ; and, soon after 2 P.M.,
the attack was most daringly delivered. The Chinese fought
stubbornly, and, being about 4000 in number, while only 150
seamen formed the assaulting party, were a formidable enemy.
But at length they were driven from all their positions, and the
fort, the stockade, and the three junks were taken possession of,
and destroyed, all the guns being spiked. The boats then proceeded
further up the river in company with the yacht, burnt a fourth
junk, captured a fifth, and destroyed a second stockade ; whereupon
the pirate chiefs surrendered unconditionally with the whole of their
forces. They had lost about 200 men in the fighting.[1] The British
had two people (one mortally) wounded.

In the same year there occurred an affair which has provided the
international lawyers with some famous precedents, and which is
also interesting as an illustration of the kind of good work which is
often done for humanity at large by the British Navy.

The *Virginius*, an American steamer secretly engaged in the
cause of the rebellion in Cuba, after causing some anxiety and
trouble to the British authorities at Jamaica, who suspected her
true character, but could obtain no proof of it, sailed from Kingston
on October 23rd, 1873, ostensibly bound for Port Limon, in Costa

[1] *Penang Gazette*, Oct. 4, 1873. Disps., especially Woollcombe's of Oct. 4. Col.
Papers, c. 1111, 1874. *A. & N. Gaz.*, Aug. 19, 1876.

Rica, for which place she had been advertised to sail with passengers, having been cleared in due form by the United States Consul. She carried 155 people, of whom 103 were passengers, while the remaining 52 included the crew and certain poor persons who had been engaged to work their passage to Port Limon. Among the 155 were 32 British subjects, and 14 citizens of the United States. The rest were principally Cubans ; and four of them were chiefs of the Cuban rebellion, and were named Varona, Cespedes, Del Sol, and Ryan. The steamer was commanded by Captain Fry, formerly of the United States Navy.

Soon after leaving Jamaica the *Virginius* began to leak, and directed her course to Haiti, ostensibly for repairs, but really to embark arms and ammunition. This done she left her anchorage on October 30th, and steered for the coast of Cuba, to the dismay of the British passengers and all who, like them, had paid their passage money to Costa Rica.

On the afternoon of October 31st the *Virginius* was sighted eighteen or twenty miles off the coast of Cuba by the Spanish man-of-war *Tornado*, whose commander, suspecting her intentions, gave chase, and, though without any international right to do so, captured her that same night on the high seas while running towards Jamaica. It is said that the arms embarked at Haiti had been thrown overboard during the chase.

On the following day, November 1st, the *Tornado* arrived with her prize at Santiago de Cuba. All on board the *Virginius* were at once declared by the Spanish authority, and in defiance of public law, to be pirates. Their property was taken from them. The crew, brought into harbour ironed and corded, was then conveyed on board Spanish gunboats to await trial by a naval court-martial. The passengers were thrown into prison to await trial by a military one.

Brigadier-General Don Juan Nepomuceno Burriel y Lynch was at that time departmental governor of the district of which Santiago is the capital. This officer found himself in the fortunate position— so far as concerned the immediate purposes which he cherished—of being cut off for a time from his superior authority at Havana, as well as from Spain and all Europe, by the fortuitous interruptions of telegraphic communication between Santiago and the western end of the island.

It may be added that General Jovellar, then Captain-General of

Cuba, and Señor Castelar, head of the republican government in Spain, both stated afterwards that they had received no information of the proceedings at Santiago until it was too late to interfere. General Burriel, on his own part, had mendaciously affirmed to his interlocutors, all through, that he was acting under the orders of superior authority.

General Burriel's first step was to stop the sending of telegrams to Jamaica (that line being open) on the part of the United States Consul at Santiago, to whose protests against the *Virginius's* capture and the impending trials by courts-martial he had responded insultingly. On November 4th the four captured insurgent chiefs were shot. This news reached Jamaica on November 5th. The fate of the Cuban chiefs inspired there no particular regret, and, had the justly exasperated Spanish authorities gone no further, their illegalities of procedure might have been condoned by the British. When, however, the following day brought to Jamaica further telegrams from Santiago to the effect that thirty-seven of the *Virginius's* crew—half of them British subjects and mostly innocent cooks, stewards, servants, and firemen—were about to be condemned to death, the community received a shock. Sir John Peter Grant, Governor of Jamaica, and Commodore Algernon Rous de Horsey, commanding the West Indies division, at once telegraphed strong protests against these summary and bloodthirsty proceedings, and H.M.S. *Niobe*, Commander Sir Lambton Loraine, Bart., was ordered by the Commodore to sail the same night (November 6th) for Santiago de Cuba to stop them.

The protests just mentioned, together with the prospect of a man-of-war's interference, had no other effect than to cause General Burriel to hurry on his summary courts and to execute their sentences with all rapidity. The naval court-martial sat through the night of the 6th, and on the morning of the 7th the aforesaid thirty-seven captives—among them Captain Fry, with eight other Americans and nineteen innocent British subjects—were sent from the Spanish men-of-war to the gaol under sentence of death. Their consuls had been denied access to these friendless persons, and, on protesting, had received contemptuous replies. The Spanish priests, however, had free access to them, and seized the opportunity to assail the faith of all who did not belong to their own communion. At about 4 P.M. the thirty-seven were marched from the gaol, bound with cords and followed by the exultant shouts of the crowd, to the common slaughter-house of the town ; and there, ranged in line against the wall surrounding this place, all on their knees and facing the wall, they were shot. So clumsily was the execution performed that, although four soldiers were detailed to each victim and ordered to pour their fire into his back at close quarters, seven minutes of struggling and butchery were counted by a spectator before the last man was completely despatched. The bodies were carted off in loads and shot into a trench hard by.

On the following morning, November 8th, at 7 A.M., and while the *Niobe* was nearing her goal, twelve of the more prominent Cuban prisoners were shot in like manner. At 9.30 A.M. the *Niobe* arrived and cast anchor. Not many minutes afterwards, her Commander, accompanied by Mr. Theodore Brooks, British acting Vice-Consul, presented himself at Government House and called for a cessation of the executions. He was passionately answered by Burriel that the prisoners were in the power of Spain, and that any more of them sentenced to death would infallibly be shot. Written arguments impeaching the legality of his proceedings were next addressed to the Governor by the Commander. Burriel only found fault with his interference, and would give no guarantee. All, indeed, that could be obtained from him was permission for Sir Lambton Loraine and the acting Vice-Consul to visit the prison, with liberty there to see and question in open court such of the accused as were of their own nationality. The British Commander, therefore, authorised his Consulate to give out that the shedding of more innocent blood would be the signal for him to sink the Spanish man-of-war lying nearest to the *Niobe*.

Nothing was heard of executions thereafter ; and Burriel, for the first time, consented to refer to his Captain-General. But for this check on his vindictive intentions, it is probable that of the remaining prisoners fifty-seven would have been shot, and forty-five (being mere youths and boys) sent to penal servitude for life. All instead were freed. The citizens of Santiago, ultra patriots all, had been looking forward eagerly to their Governor prolonging the executions through several days. " No hay carne fresca esta mañana ? " (Is there no fresh meat this morning ?) they would say. In the written language of the commander of the *Tornado*, their " enthusiasm was turned into frenzy." Meanwhile, the British Commander, attended by the acting Vice-Consul and two Spanish magistrates, examined, in the hall of justice in the gaol, the prisoners claiming to be British.

In course of time, the circumstances became known in Europe and America, and on November 15th (a week after the last executions) a telegram reached Santiago de Cuba to announce that the British Government had notified Spain that her government and all concerned would be held responsible for any further executions of British subjects. This was the *coup de grâce*, and it was followed next day by the necessary telegraphic orders from Spain, extended so as to apply to the prisoners of all nationalities.

Up to that time no foreign power but Britain had been represented in Santiago harbour; and the foreign consulates were without instructions. Of Spanish men-of-war there had been six present; but two were detached on November 13th to escort the *Virginius* to Havana. The town itself and the fortifications of the harbour were amply garrisoned. Even when, at length, ships of war from the United States and from France appeared on the scene (November 26th–December 2nd), it was left to the *Niobe*, on an occasion when the Spanish Governor, Morales, acting in Burriel's place, clandestinely removed the prisoners in the night (December 3rd) and shipped them off in a gun-vessel outside the harbour, to pursue that vessel as far as Havana, and there procure orders from the Captain-General of Cuba for her immediate return, with the prisoners, to Santiago.

The first result of diplomatic negotiations was that, on demand of the United States, the *Virginius* was surrendered to the American flag. This took place at Bahia Honda on December 15th. Next, the surviving prisoners, 102 in all, were delivered up to the U.S. corvette *Juniata* at Santiago on the 18th, the *Niobe* being present. There, for the last time, a refined cruelty was practised by the Spanish officials on the captives, in informing them they were being taken out of prison to be shot. The *Virginius* herself speedily came to an end. She sank off the American coast while being towed from Bahia Honda towards New York. The released captives were in due time dispersed by the United States' authorities to their own homes. In the sequel the British Government demanded from Spain a national recognition of the wrong done to Great Britain, and compensation to the families of the British subjects executed. The United States demanded further the trial of General Burriel, but that was not conceded; and after a time the man was appointed to an important governorship in the Peninsula. He died in January, 1878.

For his services in this affair, Sir Lambton Loraine received the thanks of the British and French Governments, the freedom of the city of New York, and other well-deserved recognition, but, probably because he was only a Commander, not the honour of a C.B.

Early in 1873, King Amadeus, after a brief and anxious experience of its discomforts, resigned the crown of Spain, and, quitting the country, left it a prey to various factions. Of these the strongest for the moment was the republican party, which, under Señores Salmeron and Castelar, assumed power at Madrid; but in the north the Carlists were active, and in more than one town on the Mediterranean littoral a separate cantonal government of communist type was proclaimed.

One of the places to take this course was the important naval port of Cartagena, in Murcia, where the Intransigentes seized a considerable part of the Spanish fleet, including the four ironclads, *Numancia, Vitoria, Tetuan,* and *Mendez Nuñez,* together with several unarmoured craft. On July 20th, President Salmeron proclaimed these vessels to be pirates, and his foreign minister duly brought the fact to the notice of the diplomatic corps in Madrid.

In the meantime, in consequence of the action of the British consul at Valencia, the British and German senior naval officers on that part of the coast had entered into an agreement each to afford protection to the subjects and interests of the other as well as of his own nationality. The senior German officer was Captain Werner, of the ironclad *Friedrich Carl.* He at once quitted Valencia for Alicante, where the Intransigentes were believed to be about to cause trouble. The British force on the coast was small, but information as to the state of affairs at Cartagena and elsewhere was promptly despatched to Malta, whence, in pursuance of orders from the Admiralty, the ironclad *Swiftsure,* Captain Thomas Le Hunte Ward, departed westward on July 25th, followed, on the 26th, by the ironclads *Lord Warden,* Captain Thomas Brandreth, bearing the flag of Vice-Admiral Sir Hastings Reginald Yelverton, K.C.B., *Invincible,* Captain John Clark Soady, and *Pallas,* Captain Charles John Rowley. The *Helicon,* dispatch vessel, Lieutenant Frank Rougemont, was left behind to await the arrival of the English mail, viâ Italy, and then to press after the other ships with all speed.

Werner's prompt appearance before Alicante checkmated the

R 2

designs of the Cartagena Intransigentes there. He discovered the *Vitoria*, which, with the revolutionary leader Galvez Arce on board, had sent in a demand for the instant payment of a war contribution of $80,000, and which, upon the refusal of the local authorities to comply, had already bombarded the place, but had wisely desisted upon learning of the *Friedrich Carl's* approach. The pirate had committed this outrage under the red flag, but she hoisted, and saluted with, the Spanish flag when Werner was sighted. She then steamed to sea, and as soon as she was out of gunshot rehoisted the red flag. On July 22nd, as Werner was about to return to Cartagena, Salmeron's proclamation of the 20th was brought on board to him by the German consul. He reached Cartagena on the 23rd at 1 A.M., and found the *Vitoria* already anchored there. As day broke there came in the dispatch-vessel *Vigilante*, which hoisted the new unauthorised flag, and, moreover, had been seen on the previous day in company with the *Vitoria*. She paid no heed to Werner's orders, enforced with an unshotted gun, to bring to ; and, as soon as the German captain had been assured by his consul that the newcomer was one of the Intransigente ships, he decided to take possession of her. He instantly seized her, capturing with her the insurgent leader Galvez Arce; and she was placed securely in a berth between the *Friedrich Carl* and the British gun-boat *Pigeon*, 2, Lieutenant John Archibald Harvey Trotter, which had arrived that morning, and which happened to be the craft with whose commander Werner had made the compact at Valencia a few days earlier. The Cartagenans were furious, and threatened reprisals.

With the co-operation of a British Captain, who soon afterwards reached the spot, Werner arranged with the Intransigentes that no ship should quit Cartagena until July 28th, by which date he hoped to receive instructions from his government. Galvez Arce and his friends promised to take care of the lives of all German and British subjects on shore, and when, in addition, they formally admitted that the *Vigilante*, having been taken under unrecognised colours, was good prize, Werner released his prisoners.

In the interim the whole Spanish coast, from Barcelona to Cadiz, was carefully watched by British and German vessels ; and a large international squadron began to assemble in Spanish waters.

Early on August 1st, the *Friedrich Carl* appeared off Malaga, which was threatened with bombardment by the Intransigentes. A few hours later, the *Swiftsure*, which, as has been shown, had left

Malta on July 25th, also arrived there.   Malaga, like Cartagena, had declared itself independent of the central government at Madrid ; but this fact did not prevent the Cartagenans from desiring to levy a contribution from the town, money being very scarce in Murcia. At Malaga lay the French frigate *Jeanne d'Arc.*

Werner and Ward put to sea together, and found in the offing the Intransigente ironclad *Vitoria,* and frigate *Almansa,* flying no flags, and declining to hoist any, until a shot from the *Friedrich Carl* across the *Almansa's* bows brought the Spanish flag to the peak, and a flag of truce to the truck.   Werner then ordered the insurgent General Contreras to quit the *Almansa* and go on board the *Friedrich Carl.*   The rebel chief did so, and was made prisoner ; the *Almansa* was taken possession of by the Germans, and simultaneously the *Swiftsure's* people seized the *Vitoria.*   The two captains were about to conduct their prizes back to Cartagena, and there to liberate them, when they were fallen in with by Vice-Admiral Yelverton, who directed that the vessels should be retained, and that Contreras should be kept as a hostage, but that the crews might be released upon certain conditions.   Werner and Ward, accordingly, took the ships to Cartagena, and on August 3rd anchored them in Escombrera Bay.   Yelverton, who was overtaken by the *Helicon* shortly before he reached Gibraltar, anchored there on August 2nd.

At Cartagena the people belonging to the prizes were put ashore. Malaga was delighted at Werner's conduct, and the British Captains were loud in their praises of his behaviour.   Unfortunately he was disavowed by his political superiors in Berlin, and, on August 14th, was superseded, though he was immediately employed elsewhere. Berlin made a mistake, and a few months later Werner's successor found himself obliged to deliver an ultimatum to the Cartagenan insurgents, and to claim payment of an indemnity of $15,000 under threat of bombardment.   Had Werner's action been supported throughout, German interests would have been respected by the Intransigentes from August 1st onwards.

The *Vitoria* and *Almansa* remained in Escombrera Bay in charge of Yelverton, who proceeded in person to the scene.   He was anxious to hand them over to the Madrid government, which, however, seemed at the time to be almost impotent, and which was then able to send to sea only a wooden frigate and three old paddle-vessels.   Occasional shots from the insurgent batteries fell near the British ships and boats, but Yelverton diplomatically assumed that these were fired unintentionally in his direction. While he waited at Cartagena with the ironclads *Lord Warden*, *Triumph*, Captain John Dobree M'Crea, and *Swiftsure*, the *Helicon*, and the gun-vessel *Torch*, 5, Commander Hugh M'Neile Dyer, he kept the *Pallas*, and the *Rapid*, 11, Commander the Hon. Alexander Montagu, at Barcelona; the *Hart*,[1] 4, Commander Thomas Harvey Royse, at Valentia; the *Pheasant*,[1] 2, Lieutenant George Woronzow Allen, at Malaga; the *Invincible* at Cadiz; and the rest of his immediately available force[2] at Gibraltar.

Towards the end of August, as the Spanish Admiral Lobo seemed to be less able than ever to meet the Intransigentes with any reasonable prospect of beating them, Yelverton made up his mind to remove the prizes to an anchorage where their custody would be less troublesome to him. On August 31st he caused all the merchantmen in harbour to be towed out of the way, ordered all his ships to get up steam and to be prepared to slip, and warned the Consul and British subjects ashore to be ready to go off to the squadron in case of need; and, on September 1st, in spite of the threats of the insurgents, he brought out the *Vitoria* and *Almansa*, under their own steam, and with British crews on board. The prizes and their escort passed the three ironclads, *Numancia*, *Mendez Nuñez* and *Tetuan*, and the forts, all of which had their guns loaded and run out; but nothing happened. Had a shot been fired, the three ironclads were to have been taken or sunk by the *Lord Warden*, *Triumph* and *Swiftsure*, and the forts were to have been afterwards silenced.

The *Vitoria* and *Almansa*, which were in a disgustingly filthy condition when captured, were convoyed by the *Swiftsure* and *Triumph* to Gibraltar, where they arrived on August 3rd. They were eventually handed over to Admiral Lobo, who was waiting there for them, and who, on October 11th following, employed them in a long-range indecisive engagement, which he fought off Cartagena. As for the rest of Yelverton's squadron, after the bringing out of the prizes it returned to its anchorage in Escombrera Bay, where it was not molested.[3] After the action of October 11th,

---

[1] Later summoned to Cartagena.

[2] Including the detached squadron under Rear-Adm. Fredk. Archibald Campbell.

[3] Disps., Brit. and German; Tesdorpf, 'Gesch. der k. d. Marine'; *A. and N. Gazette*, Aug. 16, Aug. 30, Sept. 6, Sept. 13, 1873.

Yelverton sent Lieutenant Tynte Ford Hammill to Cartagena, and Commander Royse to Admiral Lobo with offers of surgical assistance. Lobo professed to have no killed or wounded. The Intransigentes appeared to need no help. In the middle of the month, Sir Hastings was happily instrumental in preventing the insurgent ships from Cartagena from bombarding Valencia. A blockade of the port was afterwards established.

On March 5th, 1867, a convention had been concluded between Great Britain and the Netherlands, in virtue of which a transfer of territory had taken place in that part of West Africa known as the Gold Coast. Great Britain handed over to Holland Apollonia, Dixcove, Secondee, Commenda, and the protectorate of Denkira, East and West Wassaw, and native Apollonia, while she received part of Accra, Cormantine, Moree, and Apam.

The negroes were not pleased with the transaction. The king of Apollonia, and other chiefs, protested; and the people of Commenda, refusing to accept the arrangement, attacked a boat's crew from a Dutch man-of-war, killed some seamen, captured others, and were punished by having their town bombarded. At Dixcove there was another conflict; nor were affairs much more satisfactory in the new British protectorate.

It seemed, however, that the country might soon settle down if the whole coast were subjected to a uniform system of customs duties, and if only one European flag flew there; and as the Dutch were not enthusiastically in love with their possessions, it was found easy to begin negotiations with them for the cession to Great Britain of all their remaining Gold Coast territory.

The attitude of the coast tribes for generations had been greatly influenced by that of the King of Ashantee,[1] a considerable tract of country forming the Gold Coast hinterland. In 1868 a new king, Coffee Calcallee, young, warlike, and ambitious, mounted the Ashantee throne, and embarked at once upon an anti-European policy. He committed several outrages to the westward, in the neighbourhood of the River Volta; and a relative of his, Prince Atjempon, stirred up some of the Fantees and Denkiras to assist him in an attack upon the Dutch forts at Elmina.

---

[1] General authorities for the history of the causes and events of the Ashantee War: Winwood Reade, 'The Ashantee Campaign' (1874); Stanley, 'Coomassie and Magdala' (1874); Hay, 'Ashanti and the Gold Coast' (1873); H. Brackenbury, 'Narrative of the Ashanti War' (1874); Boyle, etc.

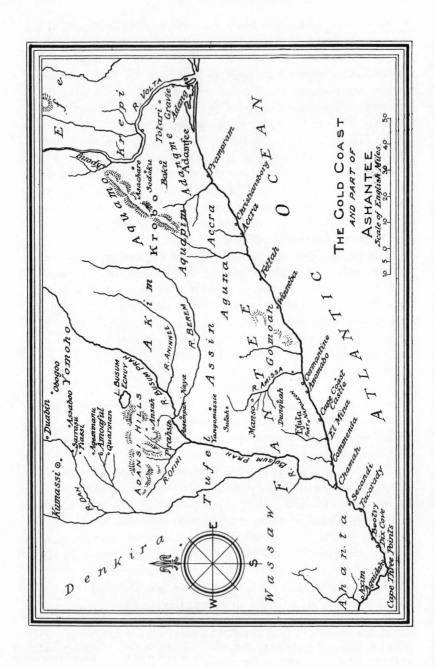

THE GOLD COAST
AND PART OF
ASHANTEE.

Scale of English Miles.

Mr. Salmon, British Administrator of Cape Coast Castle, interfered to prevent tribes under British protection from going to war
with Great Britain's allies, and checked the formation of a Fantee
Confederation, which had been projected by speculative traders and
ambitious natives.

On the other hand, the attack on Elmina rendered Sir Arthur
Kennedy, Governor of the British West African settlements, unwilling to contemplate the proposed transfer of Elmina to Britain
so long as there was danger of Ashantee complications arising out
of the transaction.   The position of Holland was that Ashantee
had no claim whatsoever upon Elmina.   Coffee Calcallee, however,
maintained that from time immemorial the Elmina forts had paid
regular tribute to his predecessors, and that Elmina was practically
his.   It had brought him in, he said, £80 a year; but the Dutch
contended that the £80 was neither tribute nor rent, but merely
a present.

To induce Coffee Calcallee to adopt their view, the Hollanders
arrested his relative, Atjempon, and stopped the payment of the
£80 ; and by these and other methods they secured from Coffee
an unwilling retractation of his former statement.

This seemed to remove the objections on the part of Great
Britain to accepting the transfer of Elmina ; and when, in April,
1872, Mr. John Pope Hennessy succeeded to the governor-general-
ship, he arrived with instructions to complete the business.   The
cession was thereupon effected, mainly on the strength of British
confidence in Dutch representations.

Coffee Calcallee was displeased ; and, upon demands being made
to him for the release of some missionaries and others who had been
taken prisoners during the raids to the westward in 1869, he declined
to surrender them, save upon payment of 1800 oz. of gold.   The
result was a blockade of the trade-routes leading from the coast into
Ashantee.

If the British Government, as represented by Mr. Pope Hennessy,
had been firm and consistent in its attitude, it is possible that war
might have been avoided, in spite of the disturbances which broke
out at Elmina and elsewhere when it became known that the
transfer had been decided on.   Unfortunately, Coffee Calcallee was
by turns threatened and cajoled.   He was given to understand that
on no account would the British pay him the 1800 oz. of gold,
but it was suggested that perhaps the missionary society whose

missionaries had been captured might be disposed to spend £1000 on effecting their liberation.   Moreover, a present of gold-embroidered silks was forwarded to the King : he was told that his roads should be opened again to traders ; and he was promised a yearly gratuity double that which he had received from the Dutch.   In addition, a turbulent Ashantee, who had 'been imprisoned at Cape Coast Castle, was liberated, and his expenses up country were paid.   But the still more turbulent and dangerous native, Atjempon himself, was arrested, and then inconsequently released before the European captives had been freed ; and although the imprisoned missionaries had been sent down as far as the River Prah, and their society had supplied the £1000 for their ransom, it was foolishly determined that the money should not be handed over until the poor people were safe at Cape Coast Castle.

The indecision, weakness, delay, and haggling of the administration, coupled with the fact that Atjempon returned to Coomassie, the capital of Ashantee, on the eve of a " grand custom," or court orgie, brought matters to a crisis.   Coffee Calcallee, flattered by his subjects, spurred on by his war chiefs, annoyed by the story of Atjempon's imprisonment, and excited by what he had eaten and drunk, swore that he would conquer all lands from Coomassie to the sea, and would wash his royal stool in British blood at Cape Coast Castle.

On January 22nd, 1873, he began his invasion of territories which, though absolutely undefended, were under nominal British protection.   The chiefs of Assin, Abrah, Annamaboe, and Mankassim applied in terror for aid.   Fifty Houssa police were sent from Lagos, but only as far as Dunquah, where, even had they been ten times as numerous, they would have been useless.   Sixty thousand Ashantees, having crossed the Prah, were advancing in three armies towards the coast.   At that time Mr. Pope Hennessy was relieved by Mr. Keate.

The idea of a Fantee Confederation, for defence, was revived ; volunteers were organised ; and arms and ammunition were sent to a native contractor named Bentill, who had offered to raise 20,000 men : but the tide of invasion was almost unchecked ; and on March 1st the victorious Ashantees occupied Yancomassie, only about five-and-twenty miles from Cape Coast Castle.   The Fantee allies proved useless ; and as for the available regulars, all of them, and more, were needed for the defence of the coast settlements.

On April 11th a great but indecisive battle was fought between Dunquah and Yancomassie, and 40,000 Ashantees, under Amanquatia, received a slight check. On the 14th, there was another action, the result of which was that the Fantee allies, after committing some outrages, dispersed. It was vain to attempt any more fighting in the field at that time. Cape Coast Castle, Annamaboe, and Elmina were garrisoned as well as might be by the aid of detachments from the *Druid*, 10, Captain William Hans Blake, *Argus*, 6, paddle, Commander Percy Putt Luxmoore, *Merlin*, 4, Lieutenant Edward Fitzgerald Day, *Decoy*, 4, Lieutenant John Hext, and *Seagull*, 3, Commander Ernest Augustus Travers Stubbs. Even then Colonel Harley had barely a thousand men with whom to defend the coast settlements.

The news of the situation reached England in the middle of May; whereupon the Government, instead of sending out at once

[signature]

ADMIRAL THE HON. SIR EDMUND ROBERT FREMANTLE, G.C.B., C.M.G.

a body of troops sufficiently large to permit of the offensive being assumed, contented itself with slightly reinforcing the West India and Houssa detachments in the colony, and with despatching thither 110 Royal Marines,[1] under Lieutenant-Colonel Francis Worgan Festing, while augmenting the small squadron on the coast by adding to it the *Barracouta*, 6, paddle, Captain Edmund Robert Fremantle. This craft reached Elmina on June 7th, when Fremantle became senior naval officer.

In the meantime, the Ashantees, instead of making straight for Cape Coast Castle, had struck somewhat to their right, in the direction of Elmina, in and around which town they had many sympathisers; and Atjempon, with 3000 fighting men, had proceeded further to the westward in order to attempt to raise the Apollonia tribes against the British. Had Coffee Calcallee pushed ahead from the beginning, things must have gone badly with the defence.

---

[1] With two mountain guns and 200 rockets.

It was quickly seen that the state of affairs at Elmina was most dangerous. The suburb known as King's Town was furnishing the enemy with arms, stores, and information, and the local chiefs were disaffected. Harley ordered these last to come in and surrender their weapons. They did not obey; and it was determined to punish the Elmina rebels swiftly and severely.

On the night of June 12th, Festing occupied the land side of Elmina with Marines, West India and Houssa troops, and volunteers to the number of 300. As many officers and men from the squadron were told off to co-operate; and the twenty-one boats containing them were all ready, inside the bar of the river, by daybreak on the 13th. There were four paddle-box boats, each with a 20-pr. R.B.L. gun on a swivel mounting ; one cutter with a 7-pr. gun ; eight cutters with rocket-tubes; two pinnaces also with rocket-tubes; five whale boats ; and one jolly-boat, all posted opposite the hostile quarter of the town, above the bridge that led from the loyal quarter to the esplanade of the castle. The officers in command were Captain Fremantle, Lieutenant Hext, who was to lead, as he knew the river mouth well, and Lieutenants Lewis Fortescue Wells, William Marrack, Edmund George Bourke, and Gordon Charles Young.

A final summons was addressed to the rebels, and delay was granted for the removal of their women and children. Then, at noon on June 13th, a bombardment of their town began both from the boats and from the castle. In ten minutes Elmina was on fire in several places, and the natives, leaving it, took to the bush, whither they were pursued by Festing, Fremantle, with most of the bluejackets, also landing to assist. While the boats continued to ply their guns and rockets, Hext and Young, with a very few men, and at considerable risk, went along the windward side of the native town with torches, and completed its destruction.

Scarcely had the bluejackets and troops returned from the pursuit ere an attack was made upon the loyal part of the town by about 600 Ashantees. A brisk engagement resulted ; but the Ashantees fired badly, and, though sometimes at very close range, succeeded in hitting only about half-a-dozen of the defenders, of whom three were killed. The enemy drew off towards 6 P.M., having lost very heavily. They carried away their wounded, but left behind them some hundreds of dead, and six prisoners.

It was by that time evident that the Ashantee war was not to be concluded without a serious effort ; for the Ashantees, while not again attacking Elmina, lay around both that place and Cape Coast Castle, confined the British and their allies within a comparatively small tract beyond range of the guns of the ships and forts, and plainly awaited only what they should deem a good opportunity for sweeping the whites into the sea. Yet in England the situation was not grasped for some time; and, in the interim, little more than purely defensive measures could be undertaken by the feeble forces on the spot. In those services the Navy proved very useful, especially on August 28th, at Aquidah, ten miles from Dixcove, where the *Druid* co-operated with the Dixcove natives in taking revenge upon their Aquidah cousins, who had attacked them without provocation. The corvette shelled the offending village, and then covered the successful attack of the native allies by sending in three of her boats. During this waiting period two strong outposts were formed inland, about six miles behind the two threatened towns. Fort Abbaye, to the rear of Elmina, and Fort Napoleon, to the rear of Cape Coast Castle, served as stations from which any movement of the enemy could be observed promptly, and whence information could be sent to the shore in such a manner as to prevent undue panic there.

In August, when at length the home authorities were beginning to take a proper view of their difficulties, Commodore John Edmund Commerell, V.C., C.B., in the *Rattlesnake*, 17, Commander Noel Stephen Fox Digby, arrived on the scene; and it was decided, pending the receipt of further military forces from England, to make a reconnaissance up the river Prah, which comes down from the Ashantee country, passes through or near the district then held by the right of the Ashantee army, and falls into the sea at Chamah, midway between Commenda and Secondee. It was supposed that on an island in that river, which is navigable for about twenty-five miles inland, there was a large force of the enemy. It was an unfortunate and costly decision.

On August 13th the Commodore went to Secondee, and at 9 A.M. on the following day quitted the *Rattlesnake* with the following boats manned and armed, viz., the steam-cutter of the *Simoon*,[1] under Lieutenant Frederick Edwards, of the *Rattlesnake*, who had with him Navigating Sub-Lieutenant Peregrine William Pepperell Hutton; the gig of the *Rattlesnake*, under Sub-Lieutenant Archibald

---

[1] The *Simoon*, troopship, Capt. Mountford Stephen Lovick Peile, which had arrived, lent her steamboat for the occasion.

James Pocklington; the *Rattlesnake's* whaler, under Surgeon Charles Frederick Kennan Murray, M.D.; the colonial steam-launch, under Sub-Lieutenant Charles Henry Cross, of the *Argus*, and, towed by the latter, his own galley, in which were himself, Commander Luxmoore, and Captain William Helden,[1] civil commandant at Secondee.

Commerell landed unarmed at Chamah, and had what was deemed to be a friendly interview with the chiefs there, who, however, expressed a wish to be neutral in the quarrel, and who declined to allow two of their number to accompany the expedition. Soon afterwards the *Rattlesnake* anchored off Chamah, while the boats entered the river, the colonial launch, however, breaking down almost immediately, and being left behind, with the gig to assist her.

Supposing the Chamah people to be neutral, if not actively friendly, the Commodore ascended the stream on the Chamah side. The stream is seventy or eighty yards broad, and the banks are covered with dense brushwood. The boats had advanced about a mile and a half against a two-knot stream when, without the slightest warning, they were saluted with a most murderous fire from the Chamah bank, where an ambuscade had been prepared. The fire was returned, but the rockets could not be used, as they were in the *Simoon's* steam-cutter, which was then towing the two other boats. Commerell, Luxmoore, and Helden were severely hit at the first discharge, and a number of men were wounded. The boats were ordered into mid-stream, and, in view of the numerous casualties, were then directed to return to the *Rattlesnake*. Luxmoore behaved most pluckily. He continued to carry on, and no one save himself knew that he was wounded until he nearly fainted.

At 6 P.M. the *Rattlesnake* was reached, and the injured people were transferred to her. On the way down Surgeon Murray not only attended to them, but also steered, and directed the fire of, the whaler.

In the meantime another act of treachery had been perpetrated. It had been arranged that the fort at Chamah was to be occupied by ten policemen. A cutter, under Sub-Lieutenant William Pitt Draffen, took these men ashore from the *Rattlesnake* while the other boats were still up the river. After Draffen and the police

[1] 2nd W.I. Regt.

had landed, the cutter was swamped in the surf; and while
Midshipman Richard Henry Francis Wharton Wilson [1] and the
crew were endeavouring to right her, and to land the stores, they
were fired into by the natives on the beach. Draffen,[2] who had
remained at hand, coolly did all that was possible, by forming up
the police, and throwing them out as skirmishers, to cover the
people in the water; and he certainly saved many lives; but a
seaman, a Krooman, and two Fantee policemen were killed, and
several of the boat's crew were wounded.

As soon as he saw what was happening on the beach,
Commander Digby despatched further boats under Lieutenants
Henry Holden Wilding and John Dundas Nicholls; but, ere they
reached the shore, the natives had made off to the bush. Upon the
return of the boats from the river, the *Rattlesnake* was cleared for
action, and the town of Chamah was bombarded and burnt. It was
not, however, believed that the treacherous natives suffered heavily
from the fire either of the boats or of the corvette. During the
bombardment, the *Merlin*, 4, arrived on the scene. The Commodore
at once sent her to Secondee with Sub-Lieutenant Edward Henry
Bayly, of the *Rattlesnake*, who was ordered to take the place of the
wounded Captain Helden as civil commandant there. Commerell
subsequently himself proceeded to Secondee, whence he sent on the
Merlin to communicate with Dixcove and Axim. Although severely
wounded in the right side, he decided to endeavour to continue to
exercise the command of the squadron. Word to that effect was
carried to Cape Coast Castle by the *Simoon's* steam-cutter. On the
14th, Commander Digby, and Assistant-Paymaster William Nichols
Thomas, the Commodore's Secretary, held a palaver with such of the
Secondee chiefs as could be induced to attend; and on the 15th,
the *Argus* having arrived that morning, the *Rattlesnake* weighed,
and proceeded for Cape Coast Castle. In addition to the officers
already named, Commerell mentioned Charles Godden, coxswain,
and William Sermon, ordinary seaman, both of Lieutenant Wilding's
party, who, he said, had "evinced great pluck."

The total casualties in these two lamentable affairs amounted, on
the British side, to 4 killed and 20 wounded.[3]

During August and the first half of September great preparations
were made in England for the prosecution of the military part of

---

[1] Wounded.   [2] Slightly wounded.
[3] Wilding to Commerell, Aug. 14; Commerell to Admlty., Aug 15, 1873.

the campaign; and on September 11th, Major-General Sir Garnet Joseph Wolseley, who had been selected to conduct it, embarked with his staff for Africa. On October 2nd he landed at Cape Coast Castle; but he preceded the greater portion of the force which was to be employed under him. Nevertheless he began work without delay, and set to work at once to clear the enemy from the neighbourhood of Elmina.

Commerell, greatly to his disgust, had been obliged to relinquish active command,[1] his wound at length vanquishing his will; and Fremantle was left senior naval officer upon the coast. The first operation undertaken owed much of its success to the Navy, for, except officers, the only white people taking part in it were 22 bluejackets and 1 Marine, with a 7-pr. gun, from the *Barracouta,* 158 Royal Marine Artillery and Light Infantry, from the *Simoon;* 38 seamen and 19 Marines from the *Argus;* and 15 seamen and 10 Marines from the *Decoy.* The total force landed from the ships, including 19 Kroomen, and 17 officers, numbered 299, the officers being:—

Captain Fremantle, Lieutenant Thomas Edward Maxwell, Staff-Surgeon Francis Hamilton Moore, and Assistant-Paymaster Edmund Hickson (*Barracouta*); Captain John Frederick Crease, R.M.A., Captain William Winkworth Allnutt, R.M., Lieutenant Thomas Moore, R.M.A., Lieutenant Montague Philip Hall Gray, R.M., and Surgeon Archibald Adams, M.D. (*Simoon*); Commander Luxmoore, Lieutenants Gordon Charles Young, and John Leslie Burr, Sub-Lieutenant Edward John Sanderson, and Staff-Surgeon Leonard Lucas (*Argus*); and Lieutenant John Hext, Boatswain William Jinks, and Surgeon James William Fisher, M.D. (*Decoy*).

Some miles in rear of Elmina was an Ashantee camp at Mampon. To the westward of Elmina, and along the coast between it and Commenda, were the disaffected villages of Amquana, Akimfoo, and Ampanee; and between these villages and Mampon was the town of Essaman, which the Ashantees held. The ships[2] left Cape Coast Castle on the night of October 13th, ostensibly for the eastward, a baseless rumour having been intentionally allowed to circulate to the effect that Commander John Hawley Glover, R.N.[3] (retired), Official Administrator of Lagos, who was raising native forces for an expedition up the Volta, was in difficulties at Ada, at the mouth of that river. Instead of going eastward, the ships steamed westward; and at

[1] He left for the Cape on Aug. 22.
[2] *Barracouta* and *Decoy. Argus* was already to the westward.
[3] Born 1825; Com. 1862; retd. 1870; G.C.M.G. 1874; later Govr. of Newfoundland and of Leeward Islands; died 1885.

3 A.M. on the 14th disembarked the major part of the intended landing force at Elmina, the *Decoy* and *Argus* then proceeding, and anchoring off the coral reef in front of Akimfoo and Ampanee, while the *Barracouta's* steam-launch and the *Argus's* paddle-box boats placed themselves inside the reef. Meantime, the land forces, including the main part of the Naval Brigade, marched from Elmina, and at 7 A.M. on the 14th approached Essaman.

The enemy was on the alert, and opened fire. Though the Ashantees were completely concealed in the bush, the fire was returned; and the party pressed on, the gun and rocket-trough being quickly placed in position within 200 yards of the place. By 8.30, after some sharp fighting, the enemy retired, and Essaman was taken. It was promptly burnt. From Essaman the column marched six miles to Amquana, which was taken and set on fire. Most of the Marines were left there temporarily, and the rest of the force proceeded four miles along the shore to Akimfoo, where, at 3 P.M., it was joined by the landing-parties from the *Argus* and *Decoy*, which vessels had been engaged during the day in shelling Akimfoo and Ampanee. Both villages were found to be deserted, and were destroyed; but, upon leaving Ampanee, the party was attacked by an ambushed force of the enemy, and while the Naval Brigade was being re-embarked, a further attack was made upon it, the West India troops,[1] however, driving the Ashantees back.

This day's work went far towards securing the safety of Elmina and Cape Coast Castle, and, indeed, it caused the whole of the Ashantee army to fall back several miles; but it was not carried out without some loss. Fremantle was wounded severely; four other people from the ships were injured, and on the side of the land forces there were 21 casualties.[2]

Although nothing like a general advance could yet be attempted, owing to the non-arrival of troops from England, the Navy did not cease to be engaged almost continuously up and down the coast. On one occasion a party from the *Argus* landed at Tacorady to destroy some canoes, but had to retire with a loss of 12 wounded, including Lieutenant Gordon Charles Young, who commanded it. Brief bombardments of the unfriendly coast villages occurred frequently. On October 28th, Bootry, three miles east of Dixcove,

---

[1] Two hundred of these were with the column.
[2] Wolseley to Sec. for War; Wolseley to Col. Sec., both of Oct. 15; Fremantle in *Gazette* of Nov. 11.

was shelled by the *Argus* and *Decoy*, and was then burnt by a landing-party under Lieutenants J. Hext and G. C. Young. There were no casualties.[1]

At about the same time Sir Garnet Wolseley undertook another short inland expedition with the object of endeavouring to break up a detached Ashantee force which, he had reason to believe, was near Dûnquah, some miles on the main route between Cape Coast Castle and the interior, viâ Mansu. He sent a small military force from Cape Coast Castle to Dunquah on October 25–26th, and on the 26th another force marched out of Elmina, which was garrisoned in its absence by a party from the *Druid*, while a third force, with which were Sir Garnet and a detachment of bluejackets and Marines[2] from the squadron, moved out to Assayboo in support. At Assayboo some Houssas and native levies were picked up, and thence an advance was made to Abrakrampa, where more native troops were found, some of these being under Lieutenant George Northmore Arthur Pollard, R.N.; but in such fighting as occurred on October 27th and 28th near Dunquah the Brigade had little share. After that fighting, Lieutenant Wells, with 50 men, was left to form part of the garrison of Abrakrampa, and the rest of the landed force returned to Cape Coast Castle.[3]

On November 5th, Abrakrampa, where Major Baker C. Russell commanded, was attacked by the enemy in force, just as Lieutenant Wells, with his seamen and Marines, was about to set out on his return to Assayboo and the coast. The firing was heavy, and the little garrison, though well entrenched, was for a time hard pressed. News of its precarious situation reached Wolseley at 2 A.M. on the 6th, and he appealed at once to Fremantle for a landing force wherewith to attempt a relief. The Navy, of course, responded with cordiality, every man who could be spared being put promptly ashore, and the Brigade,[4] with Wolseley and Fremantle accom-

---

[1] Luxmoore to Fremantle, Oct. 28.

[2] Under Captain Fremantle: from the *Barracouta*, 64 men under Lieut. Lewis Fortescue Wells; from the *Simoon*, 66 men under Capt. Mountford Stephen Lovick Peile, and 101 Marines under Capt. William Winkworth Allnutt, R.M.; and from the *Bittern*, 3, twin-scr., 34 men under Com. Prescot William Stephens; besides 48 Kroomen. Owing to lack of Marine officers, Lieut. Horatio Fraser Kemble (*Bittern*), and Sub-Lieut. Francis Avenell Brookes (*Barracouta*) did duty as such. Capt. Allnutt breaking down on the march, Capt. Crease, R.M.A., took his place.

[3] *Gazette*, Nov. 25, 1873.

[4] Three hundred and twenty-five officers and men from the *Barracouta*, *Simoon*, *Beacon*, *Bittern*, and *Encounter*.

panying it, marching inland soon after 7 A.M., together with some Houssa artillery and miscellaneous troops. The march was most exhausting. At Assayboo, 100 bluejackets and Marines were left, but at Accroful a detachment of the 2nd West India Regiment was added to the expedition, which pushed on, and reached Abrakrampa at 6.30 P.M., while fighting was still in progress. It soon, however, ceased. This march, and a demonstration made on the following morning by some cowardly native levies, caused a regular panic among the Ashantees, who retired hastily, abandoning many stores, and, indeed, almost everything except, as Wolseley put it, "the actual weapons in the hands of the fighting men." In these operations no white man was wounded, though many suffered terribly from the heat. Thenceforward the enemy stood almost exclusively on the defensive, and soon recrossed the Prah, retiring on Coomassie. Its retreat was hastened by Colonel Evelyn Wood,[1] who, however, experienced a check on November 27th at Faysowah, on the road between Mansu and Prahsu; whereupon a small naval contingent,[2] which afterwards became the nucleus of the Naval Brigade in the general advance, was despatched to reinforce him at Sutah.

On November 14th, Fremantle was superseded as senior naval officer, Commodore William Nathan Wrighte Hewett, V.C., who had succeeded Commerell, arriving in the *Active*, 10, screw, Commander Robert Lowther Byng. Fremantle had done so well that Wolseley paid him the compliment of saying that, but for him, the operations leading to the retreat of the Ashantees could not have been carried out. This was, no doubt, perfectly true; but Wolseley's praise of Fremantle was constructive censure of the authorities at home, who, for nearly a year after the commencement of hostilities, had left the colonies without white troops, and who had thus obliged the Navy to undertake work for which it was never intended. When, at the end of the year 1873, troops in plenty arrived on the scene, the Naval Brigade might well have been released from further service ashore. It continued, however, to be employed, and although its unnecessary employment was economically unsound, the Brigade, by its gallant and cheerful behaviour, gained further laurels, which, perhaps, even the bitterest critics of the administration would have been sorry to see it shut out from.

---

[1] Later Gen. Sir Evelyn Wood. He had begun his career in the Navy. *See* Vol. VI. 435.   [2] Three officers and fifty men.

In December, 1873, the troopships *Himalaya*, Captain William Burley Grant, and *Tamar*, Captain Walter James Hunt-Grubbe, and the hired transport *Sarmatian*, arrived off the coast with the 42nd Highlanders, the 2nd battalion of the Rifle Brigade, and the 23rd Regiment, but were sent to sea again until all was ready for the advance. Other troops also, and Royal Marines, went out. On December 26th Wolseley left Cape Coast Castle for Prahsu; on the 27th, a new Naval Brigade landed, and marched up to Prahsu, which it reached on January 3rd; and on January 1st the troops were disembarked.

Almost at the last moment before the general advance was begun a somewhat amusing affair occurred to the westward. The Commenda natives, burning to prove their loyalty by attacking Chamah, begged the British to convey a body of them across the mouth of the Prah. The *Encounter*, 14, Captain Richard Bradshaw, and *Merlin*, 4, Lieutenant Edward FitzGerald Day, accordingly transported 635 natives to the west bank of the Prah on December 24th. A day later the valiant natives, who were like to have been annihilated by the Chamah people, were glad enough to be ferried back again. On the 26th, Bradshaw, before returning to Cape Coast Castle, bombarded and burnt a village on Alboaddi Point, where the Chamah natives had congregated. The three boats concerned in this affair were respectively commanded by Lieutenant Day (*Merlin*), and Lieutenants Edward Seymour Evans, and Alfred Churchill Loveridge (*Encounter*).[1] Ere the loyal natives were removed, they succeeded in burning Chamah, and in capturing about 50 canoes.

During the final advance, the chief difficulties which the Naval Brigade had to contend with were natural ones; and it was not until the last five or six days of the campaign that it took part in any serious fighting. It was the first European part of the expedition to cross the Prah, which it passed on January 20th. The force, which was about 500 strong, was commanded by Commodore Hewett.

On January 29th, there being a hostile force under the King of Adansi on the left flank of the British advance, Borumassie was captured, and the enemy driven out of it. A much more important battle was fought on January 31st, at and around Amoaful, on the main line of the advance. Says Hewett :—

[1] Hewett, of Dec. 26; Bradshaw, of Dec. 24 and Dec. 26.

" Without attempting to give the details of the General's plan of operations, I will endeavour to afford such particulars as will enable their Lordships to gain some idea of the position occupied by the Naval Brigade during the engagement. The first encounter took place at 8 A.M., when the village of Egginnassie, about a mile from Amoaful, was carried by a rush of the scouts under Lord Gifford. The Naval Brigade was divided into two wings, one, under Captain Walter James H. Grubbe, of her Majesty's ship *Tamar*, being attached to the left column, and the other, under Acting-Captain Percy P. Luxmoore, of her Majesty's ship *Druid*,[1] to the right. On the advance being made, the right and left columns were ordered to cut paths at right angles to the main road for a distance of 300 yards into the bush and then to form upon the flanks of the 42nd Regiment, who, in the front column, were making their way through the thick bush on either side of the road. The enemy's centre was at Amoaful, and, throwing out two columns towards us in a diagonal direction, they formed, as it were, a broad arrow with the main path, in which order they received our attack. After suffering very heavy losses, the 42nd Highlanders eventually captured the town at 1.45 P.M. I have great pleasure in acquainting their Lordships with the steady behaviour of the Naval Brigade. During a very trying time they showed the greatest coolness, and, advancing slowly under a continuous and heavy fire, steadily drove back the enemy until 3 o'clock, when they forced them to make a precipitate retreat, and the day was ours." [2]

On February 1st, the Brigade was sent on to Becquah, three miles beyond Amoaful, where a large force of Ashantees was attacked, and driven back with considerable loss.

The naval casualties during these three days were as follows :—

At Borumassie, Jan. 29th: two seamen of the *Active*, and one seaman and one Marine of the *Argus* wounded.

At Amoaful, Jan. 31st: Capt. Hunt-Grubbe (*Tamar*), Lieut. Angus MacLeod (*Barracouta*), Actg.-Lieut. Gerald Rivers Maltby, and Sub-Lieuts. Robert Leyborne Mundy, and Wyatt Rawson (*Active*), and Mids. Charles Goodhart May (*Amethyst*), wounded. Petty officers, seamen, and Marines, twenty wounded (*Active, Druid, Amethyst*, and *Argus*).

At Becquah, Feb. 1st: one seaman killed (*Active*), and three petty officers and seamen wounded (*Active*).

On February 4th, there was further fighting at Ordah-su, where the Naval Brigade had an officer [3] and four men wounded; and in the afternoon of that day the army entered Coomassie, which Sir Garnet Wolseley, on the 6th, ordered to be burnt. A few days afterwards, Commander Glover, who had advanced by way of Akim, from the Volta, joined hands with the main force. On his way, on January 16th, he had captured the town of Obogo just in time to save the lives of 40 slaves who were to have been sacrificed that day at the funeral of a local chief. On February 13th peace was concluded.

[1] Capt. Wm. Hans Blake died of dysentery on Jan. 22, 1874. Com. Luxmoore had taken his place upon his being invalided.

[2] Hewett, of Feb. 2. *See also* Hunt-Grubbe, of Feb. 18, and Luxmoore, of Feb. 7.

[3] Lieut. Adolphus Brett Crosbie, R.M.L.I. (*Active*).

Among the officers favourably mentioned in the despatches of Wolseley and Hewett, or in their enclosures, were:—

Lieutenant Ernest Neville Rolfe, Naval A.d.C. to the Commander-in-Chief, Captains Hunt-Grubbe, Richard Bradshaw (*Encounter*), Alfred John Chatfield (*Amethyst*), and George Henry Parkin (*Victor Emmanuel*); Commanders John Hawley Glover (retd.), Thomas Henry Larcom, Percy Putt Luxmoore, Herbert Franklyn Crohan, John Hext (actg.), and Robert Lowther Byng; Lieutenants Robert Beaumont Pipon, Edward FitzGerald Day, Gerard Henry Uctred Noel, George Henry Moore, Gerald Rivers Maltby, William Frederick Stanley Mann, and Angus MacLeod; Sub-Lieutenants Henry Ponsonby, Henry Horace Adamson (retd.), Wyatt Rawson, and Harry Seawell Frank Niblett; Navigating-Lieutenant Hugh Halliday Hannay; Captain (R.M.) James William Vaughan Arbuckle; Lieutenant (R.M.) Adolphus Brett Crosbie; Midshipman Charles Elsden Gladstone; Gunner Thomas Cowd; Staff-Surgeons Ahmuty Irwin, James William Fisher, John Watt Reid (2), and William James Hamilton; Surgeons Henry Fegan, Henry Thompson Cox, and Walter Reid; and Assistant-Surgeon James McCarthy.[1]

In addition to numerous promotions for services in the campaign, the following honours to naval officers were gazetted:—

To be K.C.B., Capt. John Edmund Commerell, V.C.; Capt. William Nathan Wrighte Hewett, V.C.

To be C.B., Capt. Walter James Hunt-Grubbe; Capt. Hon. Edmund Robert Fremantle; Capt. Percy Putt Luxmoore; Dept. Insp. of Hosps. Ahmuty Irwin; Staff-Surg. Henry Fegan; and Col. Sir Francis Worgan Festing, R.M.A.

To be K.C.M.G., Col. Francis Worgan Festing, C.B., R.M.A.

To be C.M.G., Capt. Hon. Edmund Robert Fremantle, C.B.

Her Majesty's ships which were concerned from first to last in the campaign, and their commanding officers (where these have not been already named), were:—

Active, Amethyst, Argus, Barracouta, Beacon (Com. Hamilton Dunlop), *Bittern, Coquette* (Lieut. Edward Downes Law, and later Lieut. William Eveleigh Darwall), *Decoy, Dromedary* (Nav.-Lieut. William Wallis Vine), *Druid, Encounter, Himalaya, Merlin, Rattlesnake, Seagull, Simoon, Tamar,* and *Victor Emmanuel.*

On April 23rd, 1874, the Queen graciously inspected the Ashantee Naval Brigade, and the Royal Marines who had been sent to Africa. The *Barracouta's* and *Simoon's* officers did not, unfortunately, arrive in time to be present; but in the grounds of the Royal Clarence Victualling Yard, Gosport, there were 61 naval officers and seamen, 11 officers and 209 men of the Royal Marine Light Infantry, and 8 officers and 104 men of the Royal Marine Artillery.

At about this time much success attended British efforts to repress the slave-trade, especially on the east coast of Africa.

[1] Glover, of Feb. 25; Hewett, of Mar. 3; Hunt-Grubbe, of Feb. 19; Hewett, of Mar. 4, 1874.

On March 13th, 1874, the *Daphne*, 5, screw, Commander Charles Edward Foot, made prize, off Madagascar, of one of the finest slave-dhows ever taken in those seas, a vessel of upwards of 200 tons' burden, with 230 slaves and forty other people on board. She had then been eight days at sea, and had already lost thirty slaves. Unfortunately, owing to the unwillingness of the acting agent of the Union Steamship Company at Mozambique to incur the responsibility of taking over, and giving a receipt for the captives, Foot, after carrying them thither, was obliged to proceed with them to Zanzibar; and on the way he encountered a cyclone, the results of which, and the insanitary nature of the surroundings, cost the loss of about forty more of the poor wretches ere the survivors could be landed.[1] The affair naturally made some stir at the time, it being at first believed that Commander Foot was to blame for the terrible mortality, or that it was in consequence of orders from the Commander-in-Chief in the East Indies that the slaves could not be landed earlier.

In April, 1874, Captain George Lydiard Sulivan, who was selected on account of his wide experience in dealing with the slave trade, was appointed to the *London*, storeship at Zanzibar. During his period of command[2] he displayed great and ceaseless activity; and no fewer than 39 dhows were captured by the boats of the ship between October, 1874, and April, 1876. He was also instrumental in quelling a dangerous native insurrection which, at the end of 1874, broke out at Mombasa, about 140 miles north of Zanzibar.

Mombasa, or Mombas, which was visited by Vasco da Gama, was for many years a station of the Portuguese, who built there a fort called Mozambique in 1594, and a citadel in 1635. The Portuguese were, however, expelled by the Imaum of Oman in 1698; and soon afterwards the town passed into the possession of the Mazara family, which placed it under British protection in 1823. The British soon abandoned it; whereupon, after much fighting, it was secured, in 1834, by Sayyid Said, of Zanzibar. The outbreak of 1874 was the work of a rebel named Abdallah, who, with about 400 fighting men, seized the Portuguese fort, provisioned it for a year, and set himself up as independent. Early in January, 1875, he

---

[1] *A. and N. Gazette*, May 16, June 6, July 18, 1874.

[2] He was superseded on Sept. 27, 1875, by Capt. Thomas Baker Martin Sulivan, who was also very active.

attacked the Sultan's people and burnt the town of Mombasa; and the Sultan, while preparing to send a force of his own to the scene of trouble, asked for British assistance.

Captain Sulivan, with 100 of his bluejackets and Marines, and accompanied by the British Consul, Captain W. F. Prideaux, of the Indian army, proceeded northward at once in the screw surveying vessel *Nassau*, 4, Lieutenant Francis John Grey. The *Rifleman*, 4, Commander Stratford Tuke, also went to the spot, and on January 19th, 1875, the vessels and their boats, after a five hours' bombardment, drove out the rebels, who lost 17 killed and 51 wounded, and occupied the fort, subsequently handing it over to the Sultan's representatives. The British suffered no casualties.

In the following November, some of the *London's* people, and five of her boats, under Lieutenant William Martin Annesley, were engaged at Tangata, where two hostile villages were taken and burnt.[1]

Another vessel which, at about the same period, and on the same station, was most useful in the repression of the slave trade was the screw corvette *Thetis*, 14, Captain Thomas Le Hunte Ward. During her commission, 1873–77, her boats were repeatedly employed, especially in river work, on the east coast of Africa; and on one occasion they came into collision with the natives of Madagascar. The *Flying Fish*, 4, Commander Herbert Franklyn Crohan, was also active and successful. The supply of steam-boats, in addition to pulling and sailing boats, for use by men-of-war was then a novelty. It greatly increased the utility of such cruisers as were provided with the new craft, and led to the capture of numerous dhows which otherwise must have escaped.[2]

On July 2nd, 1874, the sailing schooner *Sandfly*, 1, Lieutenant William Henry George Nowell, cleared Sydney Heads for a cruise

---

[1] A daring act of bravery was related by the Zanzibar correspondent of the *Western Morning News*. Richard Trigger, captain of the *London's* launch, and two blue-jackets named Quint and "Hope," were cruising in Captain Sulivan's yacht *Victoria*, off Pemba, when they saw a dhow becalmed about seven miles away. With an interpreter, they manned their dingy, and, after a two hours' pull, reached the dhow. There was some opposition; but Trigger, with his cutlass between his teeth, boarded over the bows. He and his comrades, seeing that the craft was full of slaves, knocked down and tied up the Arab master, put him into the dingy, made sail on the dhow, and, with the dingy in tow, fetched back to the *Victoria*. The dhow was eventually condemned at Zanzibar. This was in 1875. I believe that these men were Richard Harris Trigger (Boatswain, Sept. 30, 1876), Stephen Quint (Gunner, July 26, 1883), and Stephen Hopes (Gunner, Sept. 10, 1881).

[2] *Western Daily Mercury.* Zanzibar letter of July 2, 1875.

among the Pacific islands. Nothing of importance befell her until
she reached Tapoua, or Edgecumbe Island, one of the Santa Cruz
group, where the natives, at first very friendly, made a sudden and
unprovoked attack upon the vessel on September 17th. They were
then fired at and dispersed, twenty of their canoes were destroyed,
and two of their villages were burnt. On September 20th, the
schooner anchored off Nitendi, or Santa Cruz Island. Armed
canoes quickly put out, and presently a general attack was made
upon the *Sandfly*, many of the natives having previously climbed
on board. Something like a hand-to-hand fight took place ere the
assailants, who lost about thirty men, were driven off. Nowell then
lowered his boats, destroyed as many abandoned canoes as he could
lay hands on, and burnt two villages. On the 21st and 22nd the
parties sent ashore for water had to be covered by rifle-fire, and a
couple of shells were thrown into the bush. On the 23rd, the
natives were again dispersed.   These collisions were the cause of
the visit which Commodore Goodenough paid to the island nearly
a year later, and which had so fatal a result. In the course of the
cruise, the *Sandfly* also called at Api, or Tasiko Island, in the New
Hebrides, where she shelled a village by way of punishing certain
natives who, some time before, had murdered and eaten a boat's
crew belonging to a vessel named the *Zephyr*. She returned to
Port Jackson on December 10th, 1874.

On May 22nd, 1873, Captain James Graham Goodenough had
been appointed to the *Pearl*, 17, as Commodore on the Australian
station; and in the following August he arrived at Sydney. After
having taken part in the inquiries which preceded the annexation of
the Fiji Islands in October, 1874, he conveyed Sir Arthur Hamilton
Gordon,[2] as Governor, to Levuka, and then sailed for a cruise to
the New Hebrides and Santa Cruz groups. He visited Ambrym,
Mallicolo, Saint Bartholomew, Espiritu Santo, and Vanikoro. On
August 12th, 1875, accompanied by some officers and men, the
Commodore landed in Carlisle Bay, Santa Cruz Island, his intention
being to conciliate the natives, and to open friendly intercourse with
them. The people assembled on the beach, showed no signs of
hostility, and were ready to barter. They even received Goodenough in their village, and allowed him to mix freely with them.
But, as the party was re-embarking, a man discharged a poisoned
arrow, which struck the Commodore in the left side; and, before the

[1] *Sydney Empire*, Dec. 11, 1874.   [2] 1st Baron Stanmore, 1893.

British could get to their arms, several flights of arrows were fired at them, and six people were wounded,[1] Goodenough also being again hit, though slightly. On returning to the ship the Commodore resolved to punish the act of treachery by burning the village which had been the scene of the attack; and he therefore sent in four boats for the purpose; but he expressly ordered that no life should be taken. He might, with reason, have been much more severe, for,

CAPTAIN JAMES GRAHAM GOODENOUGH, C.B., C.M.G., COMMODORE.

(*From the bust by Adm. Count Gleichen.*)

[By permission of the Lords of the Admiralty.]

as has been noted, the *Sandfly* had been attacked at the same place in the previous September. Moreover, he had more than a suspicion that the wounds had been inflicted with poisoned arrows, and would prove fatal. Unhappily, they did so, in three cases out of seven. A seaman died on August 19th, Goodenough himself on the 20th, and another seaman on the 21st. The *Pearl* returned to Sydney

---

[1] Including Sub-Lieut. Henry Colley Hawker.

on the 23rd with the Commodore's body, which was publicly buried on the 24th at St. Leonard's cemetery in the presence of thousands of people, and of officers, seamen and Marines, from the *Pearl* and *Sappho*. Goodenough's grave lies near that of the eminent surveyor and Arctic navigator, Captain Owen Stanley, who died in 1850. That officer's brother, Dean Stanley, in a sermon at Westminster Abbey on November 1st, 1875, spoke of the Commodore as " one of England's best seamen, a man tender as he was brave, a man of science, full of the highest aspirations, fit for any great work—such a one as no nation can afford to lose lightly." It is a strange coincidence that Goodenough's last public act in New South Wales was to unveil at Randwick a statue of Captain James Cook (1), an officer who, besides having many characteristics in common with him, met death in almost exactly the same way—at the hands of savages who attacked without provocation.[1] Goodenough had received the C.M.G. in 1874, and the C.B. in 1875.

In November, 1873, Sir H. St. George Ord, C.B., had been succeeded as Governor of the Straits' Settlements by that distinguished administrator, General Sir Andrew Clarke, K.C.M.G. Up to that date the relations between the British authorities and the various native states of the Malay peninsula had been generally unsatisfactory. It is true that these relations had been regulated by treaties, as, for example, those of 1818 and 1826 with Perak, and those of 1818 and 1825 with Selangor; but frequent civil wars, chronic piracy, the tyranny, weakness, and self-indulgence of the local princes, and the numerous disputes between the dominant chiefs and the Chinese settlers within their territories prevented the development of the country, especially on the west coast, crippled trade, and gave perpetual cause for active British intervention. The new Governor might have found plenty of excuse for conquering and annexing the more troublesome provinces. Instead, he set about thoroughly mastering the origin and history of the disorders which prevailed among his semi-civilised neighbours, and then, while maintaining a firm and inflexible attitude with regard to piracy, embarked upon a policy of attempting to arrange all difficulties by pacific methods, and of endeavouring to induce the chiefs to accept British counsel and assistance in the management of their affairs. The work which he thus mapped out for himself was of a

[1] C. R. Markham: 'Commodore J. G. Goodenough.' Goodenough to Admiralty, Aug. 19th, 1875.

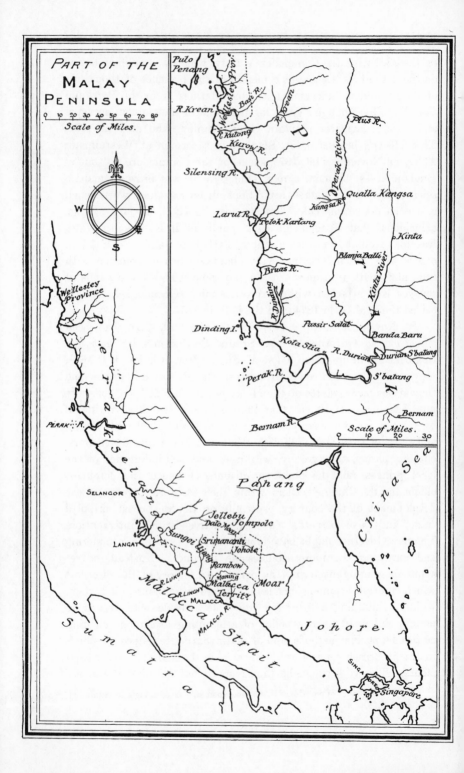

PART OF THE
MALAY
PENINSULA

0 10 20 30 40 50 60 70 80
Scale of Miles.

W E

S

Pulo Penang

R. Krean

Wellesley Prov.

Basi R.

R. Kean

Plus R.

R. Kulong

Kurow R.

Silensing R.

Perak River

Larut R.

Telok Karlang

Kangsa R.

Qualla Kangsa

Kinta

Blanja Balli

Kinta River

Bruas R.

R. Dinding

Dinding I.

Passir Salat

Banda Baru

Kota Stia

R. Durian

Durian S'batang

Wellesley
Province

Perak R.

S'batang

Perak R.

Bernam

PERAK R.

Bernam R.

Scale of Miles.
0 10 20 30

Selangor

Pahang

China Sea

SELANGOR

Jellebu

Jompole

Dato Moar

Sungei Ujong

Srimananti

Johole

LANGAT

R. LUKUT

Rambow

Manning

Malacca
Territ?

Moar

R. LINGHY

MALACCA

Malacca

MALACCA R.

Johore

Sumatra

Malacca Strait

SINGAPORE

Singapore

I. of

very laborious nature, and for a time the results were disappointing; but the outcome of Clarke's wise and far-sighted action was ultimately the addition to the British Empire of a number of protected states which, while retaining much of their independence, submitted contentedly to British methods of government, and became valuable outworks of civilisation instead of irritating centres of turbulence along its borders.

As early as January 20th, 1874, Sir Andrew concluded with Perak a treaty in virtue of which the Raja Muda was recognised as Sultan of that long distracted country, and a resident and an assistant-resident were appointed to aid him in preserving order in his state. Later in the same year residents were also appointed to Selangor and Sungei Ujong. Even that measure of success, however, was not secured until the imagination of the chiefs had been stimulated by naval demonstrations, which, owing to the fortuitous presence in that part of the station of Vice-Admiral Charles Frederick Alexander Shadwell and a considerable part of the China command, could, when desirable, be carried out upon an impressive scale.

The coast of Perak at that time swarmed with pirates; and on the night of December 11th, 1873, the *Avon*, 4, Commander John Conyngham Patterson,[1] being near the Dindings, was so fortunate as to come upon three trading craft at the moment when they were being attacked by six boats full of these cut-throats. She fired upon the scoundrels, and drove them off with loss, but did not succeed in capturing any of them at the time. Proceeding in January, however, to Silemseng, near the mouth of the Larut river, and taking with him the armed steamer *Johore*, Sub-Lieutenant Charles Skelton Nicholson, Patterson, who had satisfied himself as to the complicity of some of the local people, enforced the surrender of a number of junks, many men, and a quantity of arms, and burnt some houses.[2] This action sufficed to convince the people of Perak that the British were in earnest. To convince the other states, more imposing action was employed.

Previous to the inception of negotiations with Selangor, it was deemed necessary to induce the Sultan of that state to promise to make reparation for certain serious piratical acts which, not long

---

[1] Patterson had retired with the rank of captain Oct. 1, 1873, but remained in command pending the arrival of his successor.

[2] Patterson to Woollcombe, Dec. 13, 1873; Jan. 21, 1874.

before, had been committed by some of his subjects to the prejudice
of British residents at Malacca; and, to attain the object in view,
Vice-Admiral Shadwell himself appeared in his flagship, the *Iron
Duke*, Captain William Arthur, off the mouth of the Klang and
Langkat Rivers, where, by appointment, he met the Governor on
February 6th, 1874. There were also assembled the *Thalia*, 6,
Captain Henry Bedford Woollcombe; *Salamis*, 2, dispatch-vessel,
Lieutenant the Hon. Algernon Charles Littleton; *Rinaldo*, 7,
Commander George Parsons; *Frolic*, 4, Commander Claude Edward
Buckle; *Midge*, 4, Commander John Frederick George Grant;
Avon, 4, Commander Armand Temple Powlett; and the colonial
steamer *Pluto*. Shadwell and Clarke went up the Klang river to
Langkat on the 7th, and, on the three following days, effected a
satisfactory arrangement with the Sultan of Selangor, who agreed
upon measures for the punishment of the pirates, and assented to
the destruction of certain stockades. Captain Woollcombe remained
as senior officer, with the *Thalia*, *Rinaldo*, *Midge*, and *Avon*, and
eventually occupied two stockades near the mouth of the Jugra
river. These, after having been held for a fortnight, were burnt.[1]

   Another focus of piratical activity was the Lingie river, between
the British state of Malacca and the friendly native state of Sungei
Ujong, where stockades had been erected under the alleged authority
of the chief of Rumbow. At the beginning of May, 1874, Sir
Andrew Clarke went to the Lingie river in the *Charybdis*, 17,
Captain Thomas Edward Smith, accompanied by the *Avon*, 4,
Commander Armand Temple Powlett, and the colonial steamer
Pluto. The chief of Rumbow made excuses for not attending a
conference to which he had been invited, whereupon the Governor,
on May 4th, gave his support to the chief, or Klana, of Sungei
Ujong, who, without opposition, occupied the offending stockades at
Bukit Tiga. They had been abandoned a few hours earlier. This
action was of great commercial importance, as it reopened the
Lingie river to the trade to and from the rich tin mines in the
interior.

   In the following September the *Charybdis* and *Avon*, together
with the *Hart*, 4, Commander Thomas Harvey Royse, took part in
an expedition to the Indau river, a stream which runs into the sea
on the east coast of the peninsula, and which forms the frontier

---

[1] All corresp. relating to these events is to be found in Command Paper 1111,
of 1874.

between Johore and Pahang.   Sir Andrew Clarke's object in going
thither was to compose some differences between the rulers of those
two states.   He was very successful.

Soon afterwards serious disputes arose in Sungei Ujong between
the Klana, or ruling chief, and the Bandar, a feudatory of great
wealth and influence.   As the former had already asked for a
British resident to be sent to his court, and as the latter was
intractable in spite of Sir Andrew Clarke's repeated efforts to
persuade him to adopt reasonable courses, it was decided to support
the Klana, who had been forced to begin hostilities on November
16th, 1874.   On November 24th, accordingly, Clarke proceeded to
the mouth of the Lukut river in the *Charybdis*, with the *Hart* in
company, and a small military force including men of the 10th
Regiment and of the Royal Artillery.   On the 26th the troops
were disembarked, together with a small Naval Brigade [1] under
Lieutenant John George Jones, Acting-Lieutenant Gerard Marma-
duke Brooke, Lieutenant Robert Evans Montgomery, R.M.L.I.,
Surgeon George Gibson, Gunner Edwin Bishop, and Midshipman
Charles Brownlow Macdonald, and on the 27th began to march
inland,[2] ten Marines under Montgomery being, however, left in
charge at Lukut.   Clarke in the meantime went on in the *Hart* to
Langkat, in order to warn the Selangor authorities against affording
assistance to the insurgents.

The force which included the Naval Brigade had a most trying
two days' march ere it arrived, on November 28th, within three
miles of Campayang, the Bandar's headquarters, where a halt was
called.   A reconnaissance, however, brought on some firing, and the
advance was resumed in consequence.   As soon as the leading body,
under Brooke, showed itself, it was fired at from the stockades.   A
rocket-tube was brought up; and after about half-an-hour's action,
in the course of which Robert Chambers, captain of the main-top,
was fatally wounded, the enemy was nearly silenced.   As darkness
was falling the expedition withdrew for the night.   On the following
morning it was announced that Sir Andrew Clarke had sent up
orders that the Bandar was to be given twenty-four hours in which
to come to terms.   On the 30th, no reply having been received from
the rebel, the force again advanced, but discovered to its disgust
that the place had been evacuated by the Malays, and occupied by

---

[1] Officers 6, seamen and Marines 67: from the *Charybdis*.
[2] Smith to Shadwell, Nov. 26; Jones to Smith, Dec. 10, 1874.

a number of Chinese coolies, who were already quarrelling over the loot, and who did not desist until about fifty of them had been killed.[1] The guns found were four of iron, about 12-prs., and two of brass, about 2-prs. Yet another gun, which had been captured from the British on some previous occasion, was recovered. The place was burnt. Parties were afterwards sent out in all directions to look for the Bandar; but he could not be caught, and the Naval Brigade had to return empty-handed to the *Charybdis*, which was reached on January 10th, 1875. The chief surrendered later.

Towards the middle of 1875 Governor Sir Andrew Clarke was succeeded by Sir W. F. D. Jervois. The affairs of the peninsula had settled down, and the general outlook was exceedingly encouraging when, on November 2nd, 1875, Mr. J. W. W. Birch, the resident in Perak, was murdered near Passir Sala, together with several of his attendants. Jervois at first mistook the outrage for one of a personal and isolated character, and ordered to the spot 100 troops from Singapore, 60 from Penang, and armed police from various quarters. He also went thither himself. Upon arriving in the Perak River on November 8th, he learnt that on the 7th a small party, including a naval officer and four seamen [2] with a rocket-tube, had attacked the village in which Birch had been killed, and had been defeated with loss. Jervois then came to the conclusion that the disturbance was much more serious than he had at first supposed ; and he applied for reinforcements, naval and military.

The only men-of-war on the spot were the *Thistle*, 4, Commander Francis Stirling, and the *Fly*, 4, Commander John Bruce, which went up the Perak River on the 8th with such few additional troops as by that time had been collected. From the China station were despatched the *Modeste*, 14, Captain Alexander Buller, the *Egeria*, 4, Commander Ralph Lancelot Turton, and the *Ringdove*, 3, Commander Uvedale Corbet Singleton, and, from the East India station, the *Philomel*, 3, Commander Edmund St. John Garforth. There being trouble in Sungei Ujong, a detachment from the *Thistle* was left in the Lingie and Lukut rivers when the gun-vessel herself

---

[1] Corr. of *A. and N. Gazette*, Feb. 20, 1875.

[2] Sub.-Lieut. Thomas Francis Abbott, of the *Thistle*, had been left at Banda Bahru, with four men, for instructional purposes. Stirling to Jervois, Oct. 16, 1875 ; Jervois to Carnarvon, Nov. 16, 1875. Abbott behaved admirably. Going up under fire from Banda Bahru to Passir Sala, upon hearing of the murder, he took charge of the residency, and entrenched himself on the island on which it was built. It was after this that he joined in the attack on the village. He was promd. Jan. 28, 1876.

went to the northward. The *Ringdove*, upon her arrival, steamed
up the Perak River to Durian S'batang, where she established a
base ; and a small brigade from the *Thistle* and *Fly*, under Commander Stirling,[1] pressing on with some troops, made such rapid
progress that, on November 15th, the force was able to attack the
stronghold of the chief in whose district Birch had been assassinated.
Four stockades and six guns were taken, without loss on the British
side, the houses and villages of the offending people were destroyed,
and the resident's papers and effects were recovered.[2]

The trouble in Sungei Ujong was soon quelled. The insurgent
Malays were badly defeated on December 7th by a purely military
force, and on December 22nd were again attacked and dispersed by
a detachment which included 32 officers and men from the *Thistle*
under Commander Stirling.[3] The later operations in that state
were carried out without much further help from the Navy.

In the meantime the chiefs responsible for the Perak outrage,
and for the political movements with which it was connected, had
withdrawn to the district on the upper reaches of the Perak River ;
and it was decided to attack them simultaneously from two directions,
viz., by a force, under Major-General Sir Francis Colborne, moving
up the Perak upon Blanja, and by another force under Brigadier-
General J. Ross, disembarked at Telok Kartang, near the mouth of
the Larut River, and moving overland thence eastward to Qualla
Kangsa, on the Perak, afterwards, if necessary, advancing down the
stream upon Blanja.   While the movements were in preparation,
the *Thistle* lay for a time in the Perak, near the point at which that
river is joined by its north-east affluent, the Kinta ; and the *Modeste*,
Fly, and *Egeria* blockaded the Perak littoral from the mouth of the
Bernam to that of the Krean.   The *Egeria* also sent her boats up
the Kurow River, and destroyed or carried off some guns, arms, and
ammunition which might have been useful to the enemy.[4]

---

[1] Naval Brigade employed near Passir Sala on Nov. 14–16, 1875, under Commander
Francis Stirling (*Thistle*): from *Thistle*, Lieut. Arthur Hill Ommanney Peter Lowe,
Sub-Lieut. Thomas Francis Abbott, Boatswain Joseph Tyler, and twenty-five men ;
from *Fly*, Commander John Bruce, Lieut. William Codrington Carnegie Forsyth,
Sub-Lieut. Duncan Munro Ross, Surgeon Edward Thomas Lloyd, Boatswain George
Vosper, and twenty-five men; with one 7-pr., two 12-pr. howitzers, one coehorn
mortar, and two 24-pr. rocket-tubes. Stirling to Ryder, Nov. 16, 1875.

[2] Dunlop to Jervois, Nov. 16, 1875.   The Naval Brigade here employed was
eighty-five strong.

[3] Jervois to Carnarvon, Dec. 28, 1875.

[4] Turton to Buller, Dec. 2, 1875.

To Major-General Sir F. Colborne's advance up the Perak River from Durian S'batang and Banda Bahru was attached a Naval Brigade from the *Modeste, Ringdove,* and *Thistle,* consisting of 10 officers[1] and 60 seamen. To Brig.-General Ross's advance across country from the mouth of the Larut to Qualla Kangsa was attached a Brigade from the *Philomel, Modeste,* and *Ringdove,* consisting of 7 officers[2] and 98 seamen and Marines.

Buller records that the advance from Banda Bahru was begun on December 8th, and that Blanja was entered on the 13th, without opposition. The chiefs implicated in Mr. Birch's murder were reported to have fled eastward to Kinta, the capital. The Perak Field Force left 50 soldiers and 22 naval officers and men at Blanja, and started in pursuit on the 14th. Two miles out of Blanja opposition was met with, but the enemy was easily driven off. Later in the day a Malay stockade made a brief stand, but was evacuated upon a rocket-tube being brought into action. The Brigade halted for the night seven miles from Blanja, the advance having been intensely arduous, and, on the 15th moved forward six or seven miles further to Pappan. On the 16th the Brigade got within half a mile of Kinta, and, after some interchange of shot, entered it, the enemy fleeing up the Kinta River, and abandoning nine brass guns. The fugitive chiefs escaped into Lower Siam.

Garforth records that he landed his men at the mouth of the Larut River on December 11th and 13th, with a 24-pr. rocket-tube and a 7-pr. gun. He reached Qualla Kangsa without adventure.

Brig.-General Ross lay for some days at Qualla Kangsa, and on January 4th, 1876, proceeded thence with a force, which included 32 officers and men of Garforth's Brigade, to inflict punishment upon the village of Kotah Lamah, three miles further up the Perak River on the left bank. A detachment of the troops were un-

---

[1] Naval officers employed with the Perak Field Force, Dec. 1875: from *Modeste*, Capt. Alexander Buller, senior naval officer, Straits' Division, Lieut. John Pakenham Pipon, Sub-Lieut. Walter Travers Warren, Gunner John Grant, Mids. Mansfield George Smith, Surgeon Charles Cane Godding, and Asst.-Paymaster William Codgbrooke Gillies; from *Ringdove*, Com. Uvedale Corbet Singleton, Nav. Sub-Lieut. Valentine David Hughes, and Surgeon Anthony Gorham. Buller to Admlty., Dec. 19th and 29th, 1875.

[2] Naval officers employed with the Larut Field Force, Dec. 1875, Jan. 1876: from *Philomel*, Com. Edmund St. John Garforth, Lieut. Robert Thomas Wood, Sub-Lieut. Richard Poore, and Surgeon Robert William Williams; from *Modeste*, Lieut. Henry Townley Wright, Sub-Lieut. James Pipon Montgomery, and Mids. Thomas Philip Walker. Garforth to Ryder, Dec. 13, 1875.

expectedly attacked by a concealed body of Malays, and, it was generally admitted, would have been cut to pieces, but for the extreme gallantry displayed by the seamen, who had been formed up as a guard for the Brig.-General. Lieutenant Wood, Sub-Lieutenant Poore, and seamen Henry Thompson, Henry Bonnet, and David Sloper gained special commendation for their bravery in this affair.[1] The naval casualties were two killed or mortally wounded.

Stirling's share in the operations in Sungei Ujong was of a most creditable character, and his despatches single out for special mention Navigating Sub-Lieutenant Michael Stephens Beatty, and Assistant-Paymaster Thomas Foley Harrison, the latter of whom did duty as an executive officer.[2]

These operations, and a punitive attack made on a village near Blanja by a small force which included a naval detachment under Lieutenant Henry Townley Wright, of the *Modeste*, practically brought the brief campaign to a satisfactory conclusion, though for some time afterwards much unrest prevailed on the Perak River. Ismail, the principal offending chief, surrendered at Penang on March 20th, 1876, and most of the other persons implicated also fell one by one into British hands. Garforth remained for some time in the neighbourhood of Qualla Kangsa, and, on February 4th, 1876, was slightly engaged at Enggar, but suffered no casualties.

Among the consequent rewards and promotions were the following :—

To be C.B.: Captain Alexander Buller, Mar. 25, 1876.
To be Captains: Commanders Francis Stirling, Mar. 9, and Edmund St. John Garforth, Aug. 18, 1876.
To be Commander: Lieutenant Henry Townley Wright, Mar. 9, 1876.
To be Lieutenants: Sub-Lieutenants Richard Poore, and Walter Travers Warren, Mar. 9, 1876.

In the autumn of 1875 a punitive expedition was once more sent up the river Congo. At the beginning of that year the trading schooner *Geraldine* had stranded while proceeding up the stream, and had been attacked and looted by native pirates, four of her people being killed while endeavouring to defend their ship. It having been determined to punish the marauders, the paddle-sloop *Spiteful*, 6, entered the river early in August to reconnoitre the

---

[1] Jervois to Carnarvon, Jan. 14, 1876, with enclosures: Garforth to Ryder, Jan. 6.
[2] Stirling to Buller, Dec. 21, 1875, and Jan. 7, 1876.

various creeks ; and on August 30th, the following vessels proceeded up the Congo :—

SHIPS.	GUNS.	COMMANDERS.
Active, scr. . .	10	Sir Wm. Nathan Wrighte Hewett, K.C.B., V.C., Commod. Com. Robert Lowther Byng.
Encounter, scr. .	14	Capt. Richard Bradshaw.
Spiteful, padd. .	6	Com. Mervyn Bradford Medlycott.
Merlin, scr. g.b. .	4	Lieut. Wollaston Comyns Karslake.
Foam, scr. g.b. .	4	Lieut. Henry Chapman Walker.
Ariel, scr. g.b. .	4	Lieut. Orford Churchill.
Supply, st. ship. .	2	Staff-Com. Frank Inglis.

At 6 A.M. on August 31st the boats of the *Active, Encounter,* and *Spiteful* left their ships, and were towed to the entrance of Chango creek, four miles up which 150 Marines, under Captain Bradshaw, were disembarked. The party destroyed three villages, and, though it sighted no enemy, was fired at from the dense jungle, but had no casualties. On September 2nd, the gunboats and the boats of the larger vessels bombarded several villages on the northern bank. A detachment which was landed discovered in the houses some relics of the plundered merchantman. There was again firing from the jungle, but only one man was wounded. All the villages on the north bank, as far as Melilla creek, were destroyed. On the 3rd, other villages were bombarded ; and a force which was landed, burnt yet other villages, and marched to the town of the chief Armanzanga, who had been marked out for severe punishment. In spite of dropping shots from the bush the place was taken and destroyed ; and Captain Bradshaw, on his way back to the creek, burnt additional villages. On the 4th, the *Encounter* and *Spiteful* steamed further up the river and punished the natives in Luculla creek ; and the *Merlin* and other craft proceeded to Punta da Lenha, where Commodore Hewett summoned the local chief to give up the murderers of the *Geraldine's* people within forty-eight hours.

No reply being vouchsafed, the place was attacked by a landing party on the 7th ; and, in spite of a brisk fire, it was taken and delivered to the flames. On the 8th, the boats returning down the north bank, a landing was effected under fire near Manoel Vacca's town, which was found to be deserted, and was razed to the ground. On the 10th, the smaller craft entered Sherwood creek, where two chiefs came off, and, visiting the Commodore, were assured that people who had behaved themselves would not be interfered with. On the 11th Commander Medlycott, with the *Spiteful's* boats and a detachment of bluejackets and Marines, destroyed Polo Bolo, having one man wounded. On the 12th, the Commodore, with the three gunboats, ascended the river to Emboma, seventy-three miles from the mouth, and there, on the 15th, had an interview with seven kings or chiefs, who expressed satisfaction with the work which had been done, and hoped that, since the pirates had been so severely punished, the peaceful trade in the river would increase. Sir William Hewett returned on the 17th, and a few days afterwards the ships separated.[1]

The labours of the expedition were most arduous, some of the creeks being literally overgrown with luxuriant vegetation which had to be cut away to admit of an advance, and the country generally being difficult to a degree. The entire loss by the enemy's fire, however, was only one killed (a Portuguese guide), and six wounded (including Engineer Robert Dixon, of the *Ariel*). Nor was there, at the time, much sickness. Later, however, the effects of the malarious climate showed themselves; and among those who perished from the results of the brief campaign were Navigating Lieutenant Edmond Carter Smith, and Paymaster William Alfred Brown, both of the *Encounter*. Numerous officers were mentioned as having rendered conspicuous service, the list including Captain Bradshaw, Commander Medlycott,[2] Lieutenant Karslake;[3] Lieutenant Adolphus Brett Crosbie, R.M., Lieutenant Thomas Peere Williams Nesham, Lieutenant Ernest Neville Rolfe, Fleet-Surgeon Henry Fegan, C.B., Paymaster William Alfred Brown, and Sub-Lieutenants Arthur Charles Middlemass[4] and Percy Moreton Scott.[4]

In these years there was much unrest along the shores of the Gulf of Oman and the Persian Gulf. In 1873, Commander Robert Moore Gillson, of the *Rifleman*, 4, had to land a party, under Sub-Lieutenant Harry George Grey, for the protection of the Indo-European Company's telegraph station at Gwadur, Baluchistan; and in March, 1874, the fort of Masnaah, Gulf of Oman, was attacked and reduced by a naval force under Commander Edmund St. John Garforth, of the *Philomel*, 3, who was assisted by the *Nimble*, 5, Commander Henry Compton Best, and the *Hugh Rose*,

---

[1] Hewett's disps., and *St. Helena Guardian*.   [2] Posted, Nov. 1, 1875.
[3] Com., Nov. 1, 1875.   [4] Lieuts., Nov. 1, 1875.

of the Bombay Marine, the last named having on board a party from the *Rifleman* to work her guns.   In August, 1875, intervention again became necessary in consequence of a disturbance at Muscat.

The reigning Sultan, Sayyid Turki, had occasion to visit Gwadur, which belonged to him, and, proceeding thither in the *Rifleman*, then commanded by Commander Francis Starkie Clayton, left Oman and Muscat in charge of his brother Abdul Ayuz.   When, on August 25th, the *Daphne*, 5, Commander Charles Edward Foot, happened to call at Muscat, the place was found to be in possession of the Bedouins.   The presence of the man-of-war, however, which despatched four of her boats to police the coast, prevented the commission of any outrages; and, the situation having quieted down, trade was resumed.   On October 3rd, up to which time the *Daphne* remained off the town, news arrived that a former Sultan, Salim bin Thoweynee, who had been warned by the Indian government not to enter Oman, was about to return and seize the throne. Commander Foot, in consequence, weighed and cruised to intercept him, and, after several disappointments, discovered the pretender on the 10th off the Suadi Islands.   Boats were manned and armed, and he and his two dhows were captured without resistance.   Two or three hours later he would have disembarked on the mainland, and would have been able to elude pursuit.[1]

A hostile collision between Great Britain and Egypt was within a little of taking place towards the end of 1875.   Both Egypt and Zanzibar claimed the coastline north of the river Juba.   It was occupied, however, by, and was eventually confirmed to, Zanzibar. Nevertheless an Egyptian squadron, under M'Killop Pasha,[2] had sailed down the coast, and substituted the Egyptian for the Zanzibari flag at Barawa.   Upon hearing of this Dr. John Kirk, British consul at Zanzibar, proceeded to the spot in the *Thetis*, 14, Captain Thomas Le Hunte Ward, in order to see how matters stood, and to look after the interests of the numerous Indian subjects of the Queen who resided there.   Kirk and Ward landed, but other persons from the corvette were prevented from doing so, the Egyptians threatening to fire on them.   Having returned on board the consul demanded an apology, and the concession of the right of British officers to land without interference.   Both demands were refused; and the *Thetis* had actually cleared for action and

[1] Muscat letter of Oct. 16 in *A. and N. Gaz.*, Nov. 20, 1875.

[2] Henry Fredk. M'Killop, a Capt. R.N. of 1862, who had retired in 1870.

prepared to land bluejackets and Marines ere the commandant on shore changed his mind, and hurriedly gave way.[1]

For some time afterwards the *Thetis* was very active in the suppression of the slave trade off the east coast of Africa, capturing numerous dhows in the course of 1876–77.

The *Dido*, 8, Captain William Cox Chapman, which was paid off in the summer of 1876 after having been absent from Portsmouth for more than five years, served a singularly useful commission, owing largely to the tact and good temper of the officer in command. In the autumn of 1871 she was instrumental in settling without bloodshed a dispute among the kings of New Calabar, Bonny, and Ekrika, on the Niger, and in procuring safety for British trade in that river. In 1873 she was similarly successful in effecting a peaceful solution of difficulties which had arisen in Fiji between the native government and the white settlers. She also returned to their homes in the New Hebrides and other groups a number of South Sea islanders who had been kidnapped by a notorious brig named the *Carl*. In 1874 she assisted the crew of the French man-of-war *Ermite*, which had been wrecked on Wallace Island, and was present at the formal transfer of the Fiji Islands to the British flag. On the death of Commodore Goodenough, Captain Chapman was appointed Commodore on the Australian station pending the arrival there of Captain Anthony Hiley Hoskins. A large proportion of the officers who left England with her in 1871 returned in her in 1876. The record of her commission, though unexciting, serves as a good example of the unostentatious but valuable work which is often done by British men-of-war of whose proceedings little or nothing is ever heard at home.[2] It may be added that, on the occasion of one of her visits to Fiji, the *Dido* was so unfortunate as to introduce measles among the native population, and that lamentable loss of life followed.[3]

For many years, from 1868 onwards, a series of petty civil wars raged almost without intermission in the Navigators' Islands, better known as Samoa. At first nothing occurred to excuse active British interference, but in 1876 Captain Charles Edward Stevens, of the paddle-sloop *Barracouta*, 5, who was then at Apia, considered it to be his duty to intervene. It appears that an American named Steinberger had been appointed by the King to be prime minister

---

[1] Zanzibar corr. of *Western Morning News.*
[2] *A. and N. Gazette,* June 10, 1876.   [3] Proc. of Ho. of Commons, Aug. 1, 1876.

for life, and that the King nevertheless desired to get rid of him. It was alleged that both the King and the American consul requested Stevens to take charge of Steinberger. The premier, therefore, was arrested, and conveyed on board the *Barracouta*. This procedure was bitterly resented by the other ministers and the holders of offices, nearly all of whom owed their places to Steinberger; and they retaliated by seizing the King and transporting him to an outlying island. The *Barracouta* took on board Malietoa, the exiled monarch; and Stevens, landing with fifty seamen and Marines at Apia, the capital, on March 13th, marched to the council-house, where the legislature was assembled, with a view to the restoration of his majesty. The natives resisted; the Marines were ordered to disarm them; a fight ensued; and two Marines and one seaman were killed, and five Marines and three seamen wounded. Only three natives fell in the struggle. Stevens withdrew to the ship with his wounded, and then landed again with guns, and erected breastworks which he held for a fortnight. During that time he was not re-attacked; and finally he went back to the *Barracouta* on March 27th with three chiefs as hostages. Upon being relieved by the *Sapphire*, 14, Captain Elibank Harley Murray, the *Barracouta* transferred the native prisoners to her, and, with Steinberger on board, proceeded to Auckland by way of the Fiji Islands.[1] This was the earliest of a number of interventions which would have been justifiable only if the home government had been consistently determined that British influence should be always paramount in Samoa. Seeing, however, that no steady policy was ever formed with regard to the islands, and that at length, in 1899, the group, with the assent of Great Britain, was divided between the United States and Germany, it is, perhaps, to be regretted that on several subsequent occasions, as in 1876, British life was sacrificed in support of causes which were in no adequate sense of imperial interest.

Stevens's interference was, there is no doubt, particularly unwise. He was a truculent and imperious officer, and, a little later, was tried, and dismissed the service, for tyrannical conduct.[2] The action of the Samoans could not, however, be overlooked. The *Pearl* visited the islands to make enquiries; and eventually a claim for 6000 dollars, on account of the loss of life among the *Barracouta's*

[1] London newspapers of May 25, 1876; Stevens's disp. of Mar. 20; *A. and N. Gazette* of May 13 and 27, 1876.   [2] C. M. of Ap. 11, 1877.

people, was lodged by the British Government. In the spring of 1878, the *Sapphire*, still commanded by Captain Murray, was sent to Apia to enforce the demand. As the natives declined to pay, preparations to bombard the town were made on March 18th. Happily the Samoans gave way at the very last moment, and so saved further effusion of blood.

In June, 1876, some native chiefs on the banks of the lower reaches of the river Niger took it into their heads to interfere with the navigation of the stream, and especially to endeavour to obstruct the outward passage of a British merchant steamer, the *Sultan of Sokoto*. As there had been previous outrages and unrest Commodore Sir William Nathan Wrighte Hewett, V.C., K.C.B., transferred his broad pennant from the *Active*, as being too large a ship for the work, to the *Sultan of Sokoto*, and directed the composite gun-boats, *Cygnet*, 4, Lieutenant Robert Frederick Hammick, and *Ariel*, 4, Lieutenant Orford Churchill, to send their spare stores and their upper spars on board the corvette. On July 29th, the two gunboats, being thus lightened, crossed the Nun bar and anchored in Akassa creek; and, on the following day, in company with the *Sultan of Sokoto*, which had taken on board four guns and thirty Marines from the *Active*, they moved up to a point half a mile above the village of Akado, where a party was landed, and three small guns were taken possession of without resistance.

On the 31st the ships weighed, and, after stopping at various places to communicate with the natives, anchored off Sabogrega at 5 P.M. The *Active's* steam launch was sent in to palaver with the people, who, however, made signs to Lieutenant Ernest Neville Rolfe, who was in charge, to keep off, and then opened fire. Sir William Hewett at once signalled to the gunboats to bombard the town, which was of considerable size and strongly defended with rifle-pits and stockades formed of trunks of trees. The natives replied in a spirited manner both with heavy guns and with small arms. At dark the shelling was discontinued, and preparations were made to assault the place on the following day.

At 5.30 A.M. on August 1st, accordingly, the bombardment was re-commenced, and a landing-party of bluejackets and Marines was assembled round the *Cygnet* in boats under the command of Commander James Andrew Thomas Bruce (*Active*). The rocket-party was under Lieutenant Thomas Peere Williams Nesham ; the

Royal Marines were under Lieutenant Adolphus Brett Crosbie, R.M.L.I.; the boats of the *Cygnet* were under Sub-Lieutenant Francis John Oldfield Thomas; and the boats of the *Ariel* were under Sub-Lieutenant Frederick Rigaud Gransmore. When everything was ready the boats dashed in under a galling musketry fire, dislodged the enemy, burnt the lower town, flung the heavy guns into the river, and blew up a quantity of powder. The force then re-embarked, and pulled up stream a quarter of a mile to the upper town. Commander Bruce's gig, and the *Cygnet's* cutter, being in advance, did not wait for the main body, but landed at once, whereupon their people were set upon by an overwhelming force of the enemy, and somewhat roughly treated ere the other boats got up. The upper town was then destroyed, and the force, returning on board, moved up to Agberi, which, in the course of the afternoon, was burnt without much resistance. That day's work cost the squadron the loss of one Marine killed, and of five officers[1] and nine men wounded.

On August 2nd, 3rd, and 4th, the force proceeded steadily up the river, and on the 5th it reached Onitcha, about 170 miles above the Nun bar. Commodore Hewett there, on the 6th, had a satisfactory interview with the king, after which he returned, stopping, however, to burn Akado, at the point where the channel had been obstructed in June. The expedition re-anchored in Akassa creek on the 10th, and, on the 11th, recrossed the bar, after having accomplished its objects in a most satisfactory manner.[2]

In order to carry out this Niger Expedition, Sir William Hewett was temporarily called away from troublesome business which occupied him elsewhere, and which, indeed, was his chief preoccupation during nearly the whole of the year 1876. Quite early in that year, Gelelé, King of Dahomey, who had succeeded his father Gezo in 1858, and who ever since had been intractable and anti-British, committed certain outrages on the persons of British subjects at Whydah. Hewett proceeded to the spot in February, and, having held an enquiry, sentenced the King to pay a heavy

---

[1] Lieut. T. P. W. Nesham; Sub-Lieuts. F. J. O. Thomas, and John Casement (*Mallard*); Rev. Fras. Chas. Lang, Chaplain; and Paym. Hy. Cecil Wm. Gibson, Secretary. Nesham, Thomas, and Casement were promoted on Oct. 3, 1876. Sub-Lieuts. Harry Campbell Reynolds and Tom Bowden Triggs, both of the *Active*, were also promoted on Oct. 13.

[2] Hewett's disps.; Madeira telegram of Sept. 5; Corr. of *Times*, Sept. 14.

fine, and threatened that, unless the fine were paid within three months, the coast would be blockaded from June 1st onwards.[1] When the terms of this warning were conveyed to the Admiralty, their Lordships, for some not very obvious reason, directed that no blockade should be established until after June 30th,[2] and so, it would appear, unwittingly encouraged Gelelé in his contumacy ; for he showed no signs of any intention to hand over the 500 puncheons of palm oil demanded.

On and from July 1st, accordingly, a blockade was declared between 1° 30″ and 2° 35″ East, the *Spiteful*, 5, paddle, Commander Armand Temple Powlett, being stationed at Whydah, and the gunboat *Ariel*, Lieutenant Orford Churchill, being stationed at Little Popo to enforce it, and to protect British interests.[3] Vessels already in the blockaded ports were, however, allowed thirty days wherein to load and depart. Gelelé retaliated by seizing some French subjects ; and, as he held them practically as hostages, considerations for their safety thenceforth fettered Hewett to a very inconvenient extent. And so the affair dragged on. In the course of it, Captain Charles Pringle, of the *Sirius*, 12, one of the vessels engaged, succumbed to coast fever, and was ultimately succeeded by Captain George Lydiard Sulivan, who, towards the end of the blockade, was senior officer on the coast. Hewett, too, whose period of command expired in due course, was succeeded as Commodore by Captain Francis William Sullivan, C.B., who flew his broad pennant in the *Tourmaline*, 12, but who took little direct share in the dreary and unhealthy work. The most arduous part of the duty fell to the *Sirius*, *Seagull*, 3, Commander Frederick William Burgoyne Maxwell Heron, *Cygnet*, 4, Lieutenant Robert Frederick Hammick, *Contest*, 4, Lieutenant George Woronzow Allen, *Mallard*, 4, Lieutenant Alfred Wilmot Warry, *Avon*, 4, Commander Leicester Chantrey Keppel, *Pioneer*, 6, paddle, Lieutenant Edwin Hotham, *Spiteful*, *Ariel*, and *Supply*, 2, storeship, Staff-Commander Frank Inglis.

The whole conduct of the latter part of the blockade was left to Captain George Lydiard Sulivan, with the result that on May 4th, 1877, Gelelé found it expedient to open negotiations with him at Whydah. On May 10th a preliminary instalment of 200 puncheons of oil was handed over; and two days later the blockade was

[1] Hewett's letter to Brit. traders, dated off Lagos, Mar. 4, 1876.
[2] *Gazette*, May. 23, 1876.   [3] *A. & N. Gaz.* July 20, 1876.

formally raised.[1] Sulivan received the approval of the government for the arrangements into which he entered.

Scarcely had affairs been settled with Dahomey ere, in consequence of the refusal of some of the Niger natives to release prisoners whom they had taken from the *Sultan of Sokoto*, it became necessary to undertake a fresh expedition into the lower reaches of that pestilential river. Accordingly, Captain John Child Purvis (2), of the *Danae*, 12, shifted his pennant to the *Pioneer*, 6, Lieutenant Edwin Hotham, and in her, with the *Avon*, 4, Commander Leicester Chantrey Keppel, and *Boxer*, 4, Commander Arthur Hildebrand Alington, in company, proceeded up the stream on August 15th, 1877. There had been previously transferred to the *Pioneer* from the *Danae* 6 officers, 42 seamen, and 17 Marines. Two British consular officers were also with the expedition. On the 17th the flotilla brought to off Emblana, and, after an unsatisfactory interview had been held with the head men, the people were ordered out of the village, which was promptly subjected to a fire of shell, case, and rockets. A landing party, under Lieutenant John Salwey Halifax, supported by another under Lieutenant Edward Henry Arden, then burnt the place, and a number of canoes. Off Osomari, on the evening of the 18th, the *Avon* piled up on a sandbank, delaying the advance for some hours. On the following day, Onitcha was reached, and on the 21st the local chief gave assurances of friendliness. The vessels next dropped down to Oko, on the other side of the river. The chief of that place, though contumacious and defiant, escaped punishment. On the 26th, when Emblana was repassed, the natives opened fire, whereupon a party landed, chastised them severely, and burnt more of their huts. A village on Stirling Island was subsequently destroyed, with but slight opposition. In these affairs the only loss suffered by the expedition was three men slightly wounded. The ships quitted the river on August 28th.[2]

At about the same period there was trouble of a similar character in the river Congo. On December 27th, 1876, when the *Avon*, 4, Commander Leicester Chantrey Keppel, lay at Loanda, the British steamer *Ethiopia* arrived there, having on board the master and crew of the American schooner *Joseph Nickerson*. These people, who had been picked up at Banana Creek, reported that their

---

[1] *Times* corr. in *A. & N. Gaz.*, June 23, 1877.

[2] Desps., and corr. in *A. & N. Gaz.* of Oct. 6 and 13, 1877.

vessel had run on shore at Shark's Point, while endeavouring to enter the Congo, and had been plundered by natives, who had fought a serious skirmish with some Dutch settlers who endeavoured to interfere. The *Avon* thereupon proceeded to the mouth of the river, and Keppel held a palaver on December 30th with the chiefs at Shark's Point, and demanded that the stolen goods should be returned. There being no sign of compliance, he landed six officers, forty men, and four guides on January 2nd, 1877, and burnt two villages. The party was fired at as it returned. The *Avon* consequently proceeded higher up, burnt three more villages, and fired rockets into others. The effect was excellent, for quantities of the stolen goods were subsequently given up by the people. The *Avon* suffered no loss, and Keppel's action received the full approval of the government.[1]

On another occasion, at about the same time, did it fall to a British ship to avenge an outrage on the crew of an American vessel. In 1873 a steamer, the *George Wright*, while on her voyage to Alaska, had been lost in Queen Charlotte Sound, off the coast of British Columbia. About fifteen of her people had escaped to land, and had been brutally robbed, and then murdered by the Indians. Early in 1877 some of the belongings of these poor people were reported to be in possession of a tribe in Deane's Inlet, on the mainland. The gun-vessel *Rocket*, 4, Lieutenant Charles Reynold Harris, with an interpreter and a sergeant of police, sailed for the spot on March 14th from Vancouver, and soon discovered that men who had been implicated in the massacre were still in the neighbourhood. Harris seized some chiefs as hostages, and demanded that the culprits should be given up; but, this being in vain, he was ultimately obliged to shell and burn the village, ere he could secure compliance. Two of the culprits were thus taken.[2]

In the course of a revolutionary movement which occurred in Peru in 1877, some adherents of the insurgent leader, Nicolas de Pierola, persuaded the officers of the Peruvian turret-ship *Huascar*,[3]

[1] *A. & N. Gaz.*, Ap. 7, and June 23, 1877.

[2] Corr. of *Western Daily Mercury*, May, 1877.

[3] The *Huascar*, an iron single-turreted monitor of 1130 tons displacement, was built by Laird Brothers, of Birkenhead, in 1865, and fitted by them with simple jet condenser engines indicating 1200 horse-power, and working a single, four-bladed, non-raising screw. The dimensions were: length, 196 ft.; beam, 35 ft. 6 in.; depth of hold, 21 ft.; freeboard, 4 ft. 6 in.; draught, 15 ft. forward, 16 ft. aft. The hull was

to rebel against the central government. With the connivance of the officers, a number of the insurgents seized the vessel in the harbour of Callao, and, under cover of the darkness, put to sea, making for the southward. At Cobija, then a port of Bolivia, the *Huascar* took Pierola himself on board, and then returned to the northward with a view to effect a landing. Soon after the seizure of the turret-ship, Rear-Admiral Algernon Frederick Rous de Horsey, British Commander-in-Chief in the Pacific, arrived at Callao in his flagship, the *Shah*;[1] and, being informed of what had occurred, and learning also that the *Huascar* had committed outrages against British subjects and British property, he made formal complaint

---

divided into five watertight compartments by four traverse $\frac{3}{8}$-in. iron bulkheads with watertight doors. There was also a collision bulkhead forward; and on each side of the fire-room there was a longitudinal $\frac{3}{8}$-in. iron bulkhead extending to the traverse bulkheads forward and aft, and leaving a space 3 ft. wide between it and the ship's side. The bottom was double. The turret, on Captain Coles's plan, was supported on rollers, and revolved by hand gearing. Its exterior diameter was 22 ft. The turret armour was $5\frac{1}{2}$ in. thick, backed by 13 in. of teak set on end, and by a $\frac{1}{2}$-in. iron inner skin, except around the two oval ports, where the armour was increased by 2-in. plates, and the backing proportionately reduced. The turret roof was of 2-in. plates, and slightly convex, and was provided with two bullet-proof sighting hoods. The side-armour, extending 3 ft. 6 in. below the load water-line, had a thickness of $4\frac{1}{2}$ in. abreast of the turret-chamber and the fire and engine-rooms, and diminished to $2\frac{1}{2}$ in. at the bow and stern. It was backed by 10 in. of teak, and a $\frac{1}{2}$-in. inner iron skin. The bow was strengthened and shaped for ramming. The deck was protected by 2-in. plates. Forward was a small top-gallant forecastle, 6 ft. high. Aft was an open poop. Abaft the turret was an hexagonal conning-tower 7 ft. 6 in. high and 8 ft. wide, by 5 ft. 2 in. long, carrying 3-in. armour in vertical slabs, backed by balks of teak 8 in. thick, placed on end. The summit of it supported a bridge. Abaft the conning-tower was an unarmoured funnel; and around this was the fire-room hatch, with a high wooden coaming, and no bomb-proof grating. Abaft the funnel was an iron mainmast with wire rigging set up to the rails without channels. The foremast was a tripod of iron tubes, and the rig was that of a brig with movable bowsprit. The coal capacity was 300 tons; the turning period, through 180°, was 2 minutes 0·3 seconds; and the maximum speed was 11 knots. Her armament consisted of two 10-in. $12\frac{1}{2}$-ton 300-pr. Armstrong R.M.L. mounted in the turret, and commanding 138° of the horizon, *i.e.*, from 10° on either side of the bow line to 32° on either side of the stern line; and two 40-pr. Armstrong R.M.L., placed one on each side of the quarter-deck.

[1] The *Shah*, an iron, wood and copper sheathed unarmoured frigate of 6250 tons displacement and 7480 indicated horse-power, was built at Portsmouth in 1873, and engined by Messrs. Ravenhill. At her official trials in April, 1876, her mean speed was 16·4 knots. Her armament at the time of the action consisted of two 9-in. 12-ton R.M.L., sixteen 7-in. $6\frac{1}{2}$-ton R.M.L., and eight 64-pr. R.M.L., with Gatlings in the tops, and with three above-water torpedo ejectors. The complement was 602 officers and men. She was ship-rigged, with a single screw, and two funnels; and her dimensions were: length, 334 ft. 7 in.; beam, 52 ft.; mean draught, 26 ft. $5\frac{1}{2}$ in. In 1892 the *Shah* was towed to Bermuda to serve as a hulk there. She was commanded at the time of this action by Captain Frederick George Denham Bedford.

to the Peruvian Government, which, in reply, disclaimed responsibility, declared the *Huascar* to be a pirate, and offered a reward
for her capture. The Rear-Admiral determined, therefore, to
proceed against the rebel vessel with his flagship and the corvette
Amethyst.[1]

The following brief account of the resultant proceedings is taken
from ' The War Ships and Navies of the World,' a valuable work
by Chief-Engineer King, U.S.N. :—

"Having put to sea for the purpose, the Rear-Admiral sighted the *Huascar* off the
town of Ilo on the afternoon of May 29th, and summoned her to surrender. This
summons the commanding officer refused to entertain. The *Shah* then fired, first a
blank cartridge, and then a shotted charge, but, the *Huascar* still refusing to surrender,
a steady and well-sustained fire from both the *Shah* and *Amethyst* was directed against
her. The fight was partly in chase and partly circular, the distance between the
combatants being, for the greater part of the time, from 1500 to 2500 yards. The time
employed in the engagement was about three hours, the fight being terminated by
darkness coming on and the *Huascar* running close in shore where the *Shah* could not
follow, consequent upon her greater draught. Of the projectiles thrown from the
English ships, it is reported that some seventy or eighty struck the ironclad, principally
about the upper decks, bridge, masts, and boats. One projectile from a heavy gun
pierced the side on the port quarter 2 feet above the water, where the armour was
$2\frac{1}{2}$ or 3 in. thick, and brought up against the opposite side, killing one man and
wounding another. Two other projectiles dented in the side armour to the extent of
3 inches. The turret was struck once by a projectile from the heavy guns of the *Shah*.
It was a direct blow, but penetrated 3 inches only. The hull showed that several
64-pr. shot had struck it, only leaving marks. When at close quarters—which the
Huascar sought for the purpose of ramming—the Gatling gun in the *Shah's* fore-top
drove the men from the quarter-deck guns of the former. On one of these occasions
a Whitehead torpedo was launched at the ironclad, but, as she altered her course at
about the same instant, the torpedo failed to strike its mark."

Neither British ship suffered any loss; neither, in fact, was
struck about the hull. The action began at 3.6 P.M. and terminated
at 5.45 P.M. The *Shah's* firing was telling and well-sustained, but
the turret-ship, being a small and low target, and frequently end on,
was a difficult object to hit, and the atmospheric conditions were
not, it is reported, altogether favourable for good practice. The
Shah's guns also were more than once ordered to cease firing, when,
owing to the *Huascar* placing herself close under the town of Ilo,
there was risk of injuring the buildings and property on shore. The
Amethyst's fire was conducted with great precision; but, for the
business in hand, her guns were, of course, useless. The *Shah's*

---

[1] The *Amethyst*, a single-screw unarmoured wooden corvette, of 1970 tons displacement and 2140 indicated horse-power, carried fourteen 64-pr. R.M.L. guns, and
had a complement of 226 officers and men. She was commanded on the occasion by
Captain Alfred John Chatfield.

movements were impeded by the narrowness of the waters in which she was operating; by her great length; and by the danger of stopping in view of the possibility of being rammed. The *Huascar* lost one killed and three wounded. A boat expedition, despatched in the course of the following night under Lieutenant Charles Lindsay to attack the rebel ship, failed to find her, owing to darkness and fog.[1] Lieutenant Thomas Francis Abbott, Sub-Lieutenants Hugh Talbot, and Scott William Alfred Hamilton Gray, Navigating Sub-Lieutenant Henry William Steele, Surgeons Marcus Allen, and Thomas Martyn Sibbald, and Assistant Engineer William Walter White volunteered for this service.

Two British officers who subsequently inspected the *Huascar* were of opinion that seventy or eighty projectiles,[2] as mentioned by Mr. King, had struck her. Numbers of pieces of shell were sticking in the woodwork. One 9-inch common shell had struck the hull on the starboard side, about 2 feet from the water-line and 50 feet from the stern, in the foremost wardroom cabin. It had burst in the backing, the head splintering in all directions, and the base continuing its course until brought up against the inner skin on the opposite side. Don Manuel Carrasco, in his official report, stated that the explosion of this shell killed one seaman and wounded an officer and two men.

"The plating at the spot where it struck was about $3\frac{1}{2}$ in. thick. Two 64-pr. shells left indentations on the plating. One heavy shot, evidently a ricochet, hit the upper edge on the starboard side, scoring it to a depth of 3 in. after going through the bulwark. Another hit the plating 2 ft. from the water-line at an angle, making a dent 2 in. in depth and 18 in. in length. On the port side there was a shot similar to the ricochet. The hull showed that several 64-prs. had struck it, only leaving a mark. One shot struck the poop on the port quarter, and went out on the starboard side, splintering an iron beam. The funnel-casing and funnel had been hit about twelve times by shot and pierced by the Gatling gun. The turret had only been struck once—by a 7-in. projectile hitting direct and penetrating 3 inches."

---

[1] *A. & N. Gazette*, July 14, and July 21, 1877. Desps. (laid on table of House of Commons July 27, 1877).

[2] The small effect produced by the *Shah's* 9-in. and 7-in. projectiles is very remarkable, seeing that theoretically their penetration of wrought iron, striking direct, should have been—

	At 1000 yds. in.	At 2000 yds. in.
9 in. .	9·6	8·4
7 in. .	6·5	5·6

The projectile of the 9-in. gun weighed 253 lb., and the powder-charge 50 lb. The projectile of the 7-in. gun weighed 112 lb., and the powder-charge 30 lb. The muzzle velocities should have been 1440 and 1525 foot-seconds respectively.

This account does not agree strictly with that given by Mr. King; but, no very important facts being at stake, it is not deemed necessary or worth while to endeavour to harmonise or explain the apparent differences.

The *Huascar* was afterwards surrendered to the Peruvian Government.

On the east coast of Africa, in 1877, the vessels there employed for the repression of the slave trade found plenty to do, the boats of the *London*, Captain Thomas Baker Martin Sulivan, continuing their activity and capturing numerous dhows. On one occasion Lieutenant William Rooke Cresswell, when about to board one of these craft, had a narrow escape of his life. The slavers intended to allow him to board, and then to shoot him; but the officer was saved by the interpreter, who, catching sight of a half-hidden Arab, with his gun cocked and levelled, gave warning of the danger. Among other officers of the *London* whose names figure in the despatches of the time were Lieutenant Lloyd William Mathews, and Sub-Lieutenant Robert Maitland King. The *Lynx*, 4, Commander Francis Metcalfe Ommanney, which received permission to search vessels bearing the Portuguese flag, was another active cruiser on the station. The *Vulture*, 3, Commander Henry Holford Washington, also made herself useful on the same coast, and continued to do so, first under that officer, and then under Commander John Eliot Pringle, during great part of her commission, 1876–80. In the Persian Gulf, in 1878, Pringle's boats were engaged in an action of some importance.

The *Vulture* proceeded to Bahrein in October of that year in order to exact certain fines from the head men of the island for the infraction of a treaty which had been concluded in 1861. On arriving, she learnt that all communication with El Kateef, on the mainland, was suspended, and that that town was beleaguered by about 3000 Bedouins. Pringle, in consequence, went on to El Kateef, and communicated with the governor, who informed him of the presence of a considerable piratical fleet of dhows near Ras Tinnorah. The *Vulture* steamed thither, and on October 10th found the dhows close in shore in shoal water. Although it was blowing half a gale, Pringle manned and armed his boats, and led them to the attack. Six of the largest dhows made sail and stood out to engage, while the others, and many people on shore, opened a brisk fire. The British, however, pushed in, drove the Arabs from their vessels, and harassed their retreat with shrapnel and rockets.   It was ascertained that the enemy lost no fewer than 34 killed and 85 wounded, while the attacking party escaped scot free.   Twenty dhows were taken possession of, and, each in charge of a bluejacket, were navigated to El Kateef.   The capture of the flotilla relieved the governor, who had long suffered from the depredations of the marauders and of their allies on shore.[1]

In 1875 Bosnia and Herzegovina revolted from Turkey.   At that time the Ottoman Empire was bankrupt, misrule was general throughout the country, and Russian influence was all powerful at Constantinople.   On May 30th, 1876, a palace conspiracy cost the Sultan Abdul Aziz his throne.   His feeble, if not imbecile successor, Murad V., made way in three months for Abdul Hamid II., and, while these changes were going on, the Bosnian revolt extended to Bulgaria; and Servia and Montenegro also took up arms against the Porte.   It was then, with a view to signifying to the revolted provinces and to their Russian instigators that she would not suffer Constantinople to become a prize to any of the Sultan's enemies, and with a view also to the protection of her own interests as a great eastern and Mahometan power, that Great Britain found it necessary to make a naval demonstration by dispatching her Mediterranean Fleet to Besika Bay, near the entrance to the Dardanelles.   It assembled there in June, and the greater part of it remained there, or in the immediate neighbourhood, for many months.   There was then but one British flag-officer permanently employed afloat in the Mediterranean, but, as soon as the demonstration had been decided upon, Rear-Admiral Edward Bridges Rice, Superintendent of Malta Dockyard, shifted his flag from the guardship *Hibernia* to the armoured battleship *Triumph,* Captain George Henry Parkin, and joined the Commander-in-Chief, Vice-Admiral the Hon. Sir James Robert Drummond, K.C.B., who flew his flag in the armoured battleship *Hercules,* Captain Nathaniel Bowden-Smith.   Rear-Admiral William Garnham Luard was also sent out as a temporary Superintendent to Malta.   The British Naval force in the Mediterranean in November, 1876, comprised ten ironclads, inclusive of the small and inefficient *Pallas,* corvette, and *Research,* sloop, among the number being the *Sultan,* then commanded by H.R.H. Captain the Duke of Edinburgh, K.G.   It also comprised about a dozen unarmoured vessels, the only really valuable one of which, however,

[1] *A. & N. Gaz.,* Jan. 11, 1879.

was the iron screw frigate *Raleigh*. Had the Mediterranean fleet of that year been obliged to undertake a campaign, it would have found itself even worse off for efficient cruisers and scouts than the same fleet was when Nelson most complained of its shortcomings in that direction. Happily Drummond was not called upon to adopt active measures.

In the early spring of 1877 Drummond was succeeded in command by Vice-Admiral Geoffrey Thomas Phipps Hornby, an officer

SIR GEOFFREY THOMAS PHIPPS HORNBY, G.C.B., A.D.C., ADMIRAL OF THE FLEET.
(*From a photo by Russell.*)

who, although he had not seen a shot fired in anger since 1840, had, at the age of fifty-two, established for himself a reputation scarcely second to that of any British naval officer then living. It is not astonishing. He was a great student of professional history; he had a wonderfully clear head, and a scientific mind; he was a natural diplomatist, and an unrivalled tactician; and, to a singular independence and uprightness of character, he added a mastery of technical detail, and a familiarity with contemporary thought and progress that were unusual in those days among officers of his standing. He might have derived no small additional advantage from the fact that he was a kinsman and close friend of the Earl of Derby, the Foreign Secretary with whom it became his duty to co-operate, so that his qualifications for the post were, upon the whole, greater probably than were possessed by any other man of the moment. Unfortunately, Lord Derby was one of the weakest Foreign Secretaries of his age.

Hornby hoisted his flag and went out in the battleship *Alexandra*, Captain Robert O'Brien FitzRoy, reaching Malta on March 17th. In July he took the fleet to Besika Bay, Russia having by that time declared war against Turkey, and crossed the Danube. Thenceforward, until December, Besika Bay remained the headquarters and usual anchorage of the fleet, which, in the interval, thanks to the energy and administrative ability of the Commander-in-Chief, was brought up to a very high degree of efficiency. As the Russians continued to advance, Rear-Admiral Sir Edmund Commerell, V.C., was sent out in the *Agincourt*, Captain Richard Wells, as second in command.

On December 27th, the fleet weighed from Besika Bay, and proceeded to Vourla Bay, at the entrance to the Gulf of Smyrna, a place which Hornby had selected as a more suitable winter station ; and, it then seeming improbable that the Russians could penetrate much further southward until the spring, the Admiral quitted the fleet and went to Malta on January 4th. In consequence of a telegram which reached him there on the night of the 11th, he returned to Vourla Bay in the *Sultan*, Captain the Duke of Edinburgh, leaving in the hands of the dockyard authorities his own flagship the *Alexandra,* the *Achilles,* the *Devastation,* and the *Raleigh*, with orders to rejoin him as soon as possible. At that time, and indeed for many months previous, he was most anxious to be supplied with troops from England to enable him, if necessary, to occupy the lines of Bulair,[1] above Gallipoli, and so to secure his own communications, and threaten those of the Russians, in case he should be required to undertake hostile action within the Dardanelles. As these troops were never sent to him, it is perhaps fortunate that, after all, he was not called upon to fight. He was also an importunate advocate for a more determined policy than found favour at Whitehall.

---

[1] Across the narrow neck of the peninsula of Gallipoli,—a position easily defensible by troops supported by ships.

On January 18th, 1878, Mr. (afterwards Sir) Austen Henry Layard, British Ambassador to the Porte, telegraphed to the Vice-Admiral at Vourla :—

"Russians advancing upon Adrianople, which they will probably occupy immediately. . . . Austria and England have remonstrated at St. Petersburg. Panic amongst ministers here."

On the 20th came a further telegram :—

"Consul at Dardanelles reports that he thinks a further series of torpedoes have been laid at the entrance of the Straits between Castles Koum-Kali and Sed-ul-Bahr, and also at the northern extremity of the narrows between Forts Nagara and Bovali. The mid-channel at bottom of the places not believed to be obstructed. . . . About sixty heavy rifled guns are mounted now in the four principal forts in the narrows. The 50-ton Krupp gun at Sultanieh Fort may be called ready for service."

This was followed by :—

"*Admiralty, London, 6.40 p.m., Jan. 23, to Admiral, Vourla, 11.55 a.m., Jan. 24. Secret.*
"Sail immediately for Dardanelles, and proceed with the fleet now with you to Constantinople. Abstain from taking any part in contest between Russia and Turkey, but waterway of Straits is to be kept open ; and, in the event of tumult at Constantinople, protect life and property of British subjects. . . ."

Thereupon Hornby, on the 24th, telegraphed to the Ambassador :—

"Have received orders to proceed to Constantinople with the fleet, and to keep Dardanelles open. I sail at 5 P.M. to-day. Request firman may be sent for the fleet to pass Tchernak, but orders do not permit me to wait for firman."

And to his wife he wrote :—

. . . "With a determined enemy in possession of the Gallipoli peninsula, this '(the keeping open of the Dardanelles)' is not possible for ships to guarantee. I fear from the vacillation our orders denote that we are not well commanded,[1] and I do not anticipate much credit will accrue to the country. . . ."

When the fleet sailed, no one but the Commander-in-Chief, who led the starboard line in the dispatch-vessel *Salamis*, Commander Frederick Wilbraham Egerton, knew whither nor on what mission it was bound, though everyone guessed. By 8 A.M. on the 25th the fleet was off Besika. No fresh orders met it there, and it passed on. Close to the mouth of the Dardanelles, Hornby transferred his flag to the *Sultan*, and began to make such preparations for action as were possible without betraying a hostile purpose. The *Salamis* was sent in to Tchernak [2] with the message :—

[1] *I.e.*, not well directed from London.
[2] On the Asiatic shore at the mouth of the narrowest part of the Dardanelles. See chart in Vol. V., p. 223.

" We came as friends, but I was bound to go on. If you fired at me I should be obliged to fire at you; and then we should only be playing the Russian game, which would be very disagreeable to me."

The commandant at Tchernak had the firman granting permission to pass, and handed it to Egerton, who was on the point of taking it off to the flagship, when a telegraph clerk ran after him with a message as follows :—

"*Admiralty, London, Jan. 24, 7.39 p.m., to Admiral, Tchernak, Jan. 25, 3.30 p.m.*
"Annul former orders. Anchor at Besika Bay and wait further orders. Report arrival there."

This sudden reversal of policy was most annoying to the Commander-in-Chief, who feared not only that it would be prejudicial to British material interests, but also that it would be most injurious to British prestige throughout the East. He anticipated that it would encourage Russia, and would drive the Sultan into the hands of the Czar. The truth seems to be that the British Cabinet had been apprised in the interim of certain terms upon which Russia was willing to make peace, and regarded those terms as admissible. However this may have been, a different view presently recommended itself to the Ministry, for, on February 9th Hornby, then in Besika Bay, received orders to proceed, if possible that afternoon, for Constantinople to protect the life and property of British subjects. He was informed that the Ambassador had been directed to obtain the necessary firman, to induce the Porte to send pacific orders to the forts, and to communicate the results to the Vice-Admiral. Again, therefore, he proceeded for Tchernak, weighing at 6 P.M.; but at Tchernak there was neither firman nor message from Mr. Layard, and, to make matters worse, the Pasha in command protested against the fleet entering the strait. After anchoring for some hours, Hornby returned to Besika Bay, and curtly telegraphed home to ask whether he was to go on and force a passage, or to wait for permission to pass. On the 10th he heard from the Ambassador that permission had been asked for and had been refused, and next that the Russians had threatened to occupy Constantinople in case the ships should pass the Dardanelles.

On February 12th more definite and satisfactory instructions arrived from London. The Vice-Admiral was to proceed into the Sea of Marmora without waiting for a firman, and if he were fired upon and his ships were struck, was to return the fire, but not to wait to demolish the forts.[1] I take the following description of those works from Mrs. Fred Egerton's biography [2] of her father :—

" There were then only four formidable forts in the Dardanelles. The lowest of these was Fort Namasghia,[3] in which were sixteen Krupp breechloading rifled guns, supposed to be about 26 centimetres,[4] also one Krupp and two Armstrong 7-inch muzzle-loading guns. Nearly opposite is the Sultanieh Fort,[5] in which the monster 50-ton Krupp gun had been mounted to command the approaches to the Narrows. This was, however, the only formidable piece of ordnance in the fort. A mile above is the Medjidieh Fort, probably the strongest of all, having been reconstructed by a German officer, Blum. It had thirteen 6-inch breech-loading Krupp guns, seven of which enfiladed the channel. The fort of Nagara,[6] two and a half miles further on, completed the defences, as the other forts were supplied only with obsolete guns, or the modern ones intended for them had not been mounted." [7]

No mines were feared ; for, although a number had been laid down, Hornby believed that recent gales, aiding the always strong current, had washed all of them into the Ægean Sea. Woods Pasha, who had to do with the laying and recovery of them, has since informed me that Hornby was mistaken.

The *Raleigh*, 22, Captain Charles Trelawny Jago, was detached to Dedegatch to embark fugitives ; the *Salamis* was sent forward to communicate once more with the Pasha commanding at Tchernak ; and with the following six battleships, cleared for action and with their upper spars sent down, the Vice-Admiral, who had weighed at daylight, entered the mouth of the Dardanelles, a snowy gale blowing from the eastward :—

Battle-Ships.	Heavy Guns.	Commanders.	Orders.
Alexandra . .	12	V.-Adm. G. T. P. Hornby. Capt. Robt. O'Brien FitzRoy. Com. Atwell Peregrine Macleod Lake.	To destroy the 50-ton gun.
Agincourt . .	17	R.-Adm. Sir J. E. Commerell, K.C.B., V.C. Capt. Richard Wells. Com. Thomas Sturges Jackson.	To silence Namasghia.
Achilles . . .	16	Capt. Sir Wm. Nathan Wrighte Hewett, K.C.B., V.C. Com Wm. Hargraves Mitchell Molyneux.	To silence Namasghia.
Swiftsure . .	14	Capt. Nowell Salmon, C.B., V.C. Com. Hilary Gustavus Andoe.	To attack Medjidieh Fort.
Téméraire . .	8	Capt. Michael Culme-Seymour. Com. Albert Baldwin Jenkings.	To attack Medjidieh Fort.
Sultan . . .	12	Capt. H.R.H. the Duke of Edinburgh, K.G. Com. Richd. Fredk. Britten.	To destroy the 50-ton gun.

Note.—The *Hotspur*, 3, Capt. St. George Caulfield d'Arcy-Irvine, and *Ruby*, corvette, Capt. Robt. Hy. More Molyneux, which had quitted Besika Bay with the fleet, had been detached to assist the *Raleigh*, she having run ashore near Rabbit Island. Numerous other vessels were in the Mediterranean, but not then upon the spot.

---

[1] At the same time the Channel Squadron was ordered to Gibraltar, and, a day or two later, to Malta.

[2] ' Admiral of the Fleet Sir G. T. Phipps Hornby ': London, 1896.

[3] Below Kilid Bahr.   [4] *I.e.* of about 10.5-in. calibre.   [5] Near Tchernak.

[6] The ancient Abydos.   [7] See the chart in Vol. V., p. 223.

As Egerton landed at Tchernak he noted that the tompion had not been taken out of the big gun. That was reassuring. The Pasha, however, appears to have handed to Egerton a written protest, although he qualified it by saying, as he dismissed that officer, " Return to the Admiral, and tell him that from motives of humanity I refrain from firing."

The flagship grounded on the edge of a shoal just below the narrowest part of the strait. Retaining the *Sultan* to assist the *Alexandra*, Hornby sent on the other four ships to Gallipoli. As soon as the *Alexandra* had been got off, she proceeded to Nagara Point, where she anchored for the night. On the 14th the Commander-in-Chief learnt that the Russians were within twelve miles of the Bulair lines. He therefore left the *Agincourt* and *Swiftsure* off Gallipoli, ordered forward the *Salamis* to communicate with Mr. Layard, and, with the *Alexandra*, *Achilles*, *Sultan*, and *Téméraire*, steamed leisurely across the Sea of

[signature]

SIR GEOFFREY THOMAS PHIPPS HORNBY, G.C.B., ADMIRAL OF THE FLEET.

Marmora, and appeared off Constantinople on the morning of February 15th. He anchored near Prince's Islands, within sight of the Russian and Turkish tents that faced each other close to San Stefano.

Hornby's opinion always was that, had the Turks tried to obstruct his passage, he could have silenced their batteries, and, with relatively small damage to himself, have reached Constantinople. Had the *Alexandra*, however, or any one of the ships grounded under fire, it might have been impossible to save her. He knew nothing of the mines. He believed, nevertheless, that if either the Turks or the Russians had determined seriously to hold the northern bank of the Dardanelles against the fleet, they could, with but little special preparation, have accomplished their purpose, or at least have prevented the passage of the Narrows by any vessels not armoured. His ships, he asserted, could have dealt with the existing guns, which were near the water level, but they could not have dealt with the guns which might have been quickly mounted on the cliffs above; and guns so mounted might have entirely prevented the upward passage of colliers, storeships and transports, and so have deprived the fleet off Constantinople of all resources. It was for this reason that he ardently desired that he should be placed in a position to occupy the lines of Bulair and the peninsula of Gallipoli when ordered to pass the Dardanelles ; and, as he was never placed in that position, it must be admitted that his situation in the Sea of Marmora was a most precarious one, his communications not being in any way secured. Fortunately, the Russians believed that the ships were crowded with troops. Fortunately, too, they remembered that their own long line of land communications northward to the Danube was a difficult one to protect, and that they had pushed southward with more hardihood than the rules of sound strategy warranted. Austria lay on the flank of the Russian advance, and was excessively irritated. And thus, although the Grand Duke had threatened to occupy Constantinople if Hornby should enter the Sea of Marmora, the very appearance of Hornby deterred him from risking so extreme a measure. Constantinople was saved.

The anchorage of the body of the fleet was presently removed to Touzla Bay, an inlet on the mainland, a little to the southward of Prince's Islands, Commerell, however, with the *Agincourt* and *Swiftsure*, remaining off Gallipoli to hearten the Turks there, and having orders to blow up the Dardanelles' forts rather than permit them to be occupied by the Russians, and to prevent any Russian force from embarking and crossing to the Asiatic shore. Having received news on March 4th that preliminaries of peace had been concluded on the previous day, Hornby, on the 9th, took his ships to pleasanter quarters off Ismid. Before Easter Lord Derby resigned, and the home government, adopting a firmer policy, authorised the naval chiefs, if necessary, to take the Turkish troops at Bulair into British pay, and to land officers and men for the defence of the lines. On the other hand, the Turkish Ministry became rather less anti-Russian and rather more anti-British than it had been ; so that the prospects of peace did not immediately improve. In May, Lord Beaconsfield tellingly reminded both the late belligerents that he was prepared to interfere, with or without the Turkish alliance, if necessary ; and his summoning of 10,000 Indian troops to Malta produced a powerful impression. At about the same time, the battleship *Devastation*, Captain Walter James Hunt-Grubbe, C.B., Commander Charles John Balfour, took the place of the *Sultan* in the Sea of Marmora, the boilers of the latter ship being worn out.[1]　Captain Algernon Charles Fieschi Heneage also superseded Captain Hewett in command of the *Achilles*.　On June 18th, the squadron returned to the anchorage off Prince's Islands, the neighbourhood of Touzla Bay being reputed unhealthy in summer.

In the meanwhile, in order to strengthen the hands of the British representatives at the Congress which had been called at Berlin to arrange final terms of peace, the Channel Squadron,[2] under Vice-Admiral Lord John Hay (3), C.B., in the *Minotaur*, Captain Harry Holdsworth Rawson, had been dispatched to the Mediterranean, anchored in Suda Bay, and placed under Vice-Admiral Hornby's orders.　At the end of June, Hay was sent to Larnaca, in Cyprus, where presently the battleship *Invincible* and the cruiser *Raleigh* (both of the Mediterranean fleet) joined him. On July 8th the conditional cession of Cyprus to Great Britain was announced in Parliament, and, on the same day, Lord John Hay was directed to take possession of it.　This and the decisions of the Congress marked the end of the period of extreme tension in the vicinity of the Dardanelles, although, on July 14th, the *Swiftsure's* steam-pinnace was fired upon by the Russians near Xeros, and two British officers were taken prisoners.　General Todleben, the Russian commander-in-chief, offered, however, satisfactory explanations and regretful apologies.

On August 6th Hornby was deservedly rewarded with a K.C.B. "How wonderfully complete," wrote Lord Charles Beresford, "your organisation must have been, as, if even a Midshipman had lost his temper, he might have run the country into war."　The San Stefano lines were evacuated by the Russians on September 23rd, and, in accordance with an agreement which had been arrived at, the fleet moved to Artaki on the 28th.　There it remained until January 1st, 1879, when it sailed for Ismid.

On January 2nd, while the battleship *Thunderer*, Captain Alfred John Chatfield, which had relieved the *Devastation* about two months earlier, was practising at quarters in the Gulf of Ismid, one of the 12-in. 38-ton Woolwich muzzle-loaders, supposed to be charged with 85 lb.[3] of powder and a common shell, burst in

---

[1] The *Sultan* turned over her officers and crew to the *Black Prince*, of the Channel Squadron, at Malta on May 9.

[2] The place of the Channel Squadron in home waters was taken by the Reserve Squadron, under Rear-Adm. Henry Boys.

[3] The full charge was 110 lb.; and a charge of that weight, with an empty Palliser shell, had, as was imagined, been fired a few minutes earlier.

her fore-turret. The muzzle, from about two feet in front of the trunnions, was blown off, and terrible destruction was done. Two officers, Lieutenant Augustus Heyliger Coker, R.N., and Lieutenant Edward Daniel, R.M.A., with nine men, were killed, and thirty-five persons were injured. Only one of those who were in the turret survived. The accident seems to have been due either to double loading or to a shifting forward of the projectile after it had been hydraulically rammed home in the depressed muzzle. The committee which reported upon the subject adopted the former theory.[1] Lord Charles Beresford, writing to the *Times*, said : " that any of the Woolwich pattern guns could burst, except under conditions unfair to the gun, I do not believe." There was evidence, however, that flaws in the material might, in certain circumstances, cause an explosive burst, for on no other hypothesis can the bursting of a 9-in. 12-ton Woolwich gun in the turret ship *Wivern* in 1867 be explained. On that occasion, although about thirteen persons were inside the turret, and the breech of the gun, weighing about a ton, was blown off, there were happily no casualties. While the great balance of probability indicates that the *Thunderer's* gun had been doubly loaded by mistake, owing to a previous miss-fire during the discharge of an electric broadside not having been noticed, it cannot be said that the truth of this theory was ever demonstrated beyond all doubt.

Not until March 19th, when the Russians were withdrawing from Adrianople, did Sir Geoffrey Hornby repass the Dardanelles.

For many months Europe had been upon the verge of a general war. No individual, perhaps, did more to avert that catastrophe than the Vice-Admiral ; yet certainly no Englishman was more determined than he to champion what he conceived to be British interests, and to fight for them if necessary. His fine performance affords a good example of the old truth that obvious readiness to strike more often saves than provokes a quarrel. How he would have fared, had he had to strike, is another question. His squadron, it is true, was small. On the other hand, he had under him, in Sir Edmund Commerell, Sir W. N. W. Hewett, Captain Nowell Salmon, Captain Culme-Seymour, and many others, officers who, in their day, were among the very best in the Navy, and who,

---

[1] Report issued Mar. 1, 1879. The correctness of the conclusion was to a great extent confirmed by experiments which were made with the sister gun at Woolwich in the following December and January.

almost without exception, believed in Hornby as, so more than one of them has told me, they believed in no other Commander-in-Chief of their time.

During the time of tension, Russia made numerous purchases, especially in America, of vessels suitable for service as privateers. Most of these were carefully watched by British cruisers. From the same period dates the formation of the Russian " Volunteer Fleet " —a flotilla consisting for the most part of large and fast craft which are chiefly used at ordinary times as transports and storeships,·but which carry formidable armaments in their holds, and can mount them promptly in case of need.

It is not necessary to say much concerning the occupation of Cyprus. The ships concerned in it were the—

SHIPS.	GUNS.	COMMANDERS.	REMARKS.
Minotaur, b.s.	17	V.-Adm. Lord John Hay (3), C.B. Capt. Harry Holdsworth Rawson. Com. John Fellowes.	Flagsh'p, Channel Squad.
Black Prince b s.	28	Capt. H.R.H. Duke of Edinburgh, K.G. Com. Rich. Fredk. Britten.	Channel Squad.
Monarch, b.s. . . ·. . .	7	Capt. Algernon McLennan Lyons. Com. Alan Brodrick Thomas.	Channel Squad.
Invincible, b.s.	14	Capt. Lindesay Brine Com. Wm. Fredk. Stanley Mann.	Medit. Fleet.
Pallas, armd. corv. . . .	8	Capt. Hy. Hamilton Beamish, C.B.	Medit. Fleet.
Raleigh, cr.	22	Capt. Chas. Trelawny Jago. Com. Day Hort Bosanquet. ¡	Medit. Fleet.
Foxhound, g.b.	4	Lieut. Wm. Hy. Geo. Nowell.	Detained on way home from China.

These reached the neighbourhood of the island on July 7th, 1878, and, after the *Raleigh* had been sent in to take soundings, the squadron anchored in Larnaca Bay on the 8th. On the 10th the British dispatch-vessel *Salamis,* 2, Commander Frederick Wilbraham Egerton, arrived from Constantinople with the Pasha who had been empowered to transfer the island to British rule; and on the night of the 11th the flagship landed 53 Marines, under Captain Henry Holdsworth Kelly, R.M.A., to take possession of the capital, Nicosia. Other detachments of Royal Marines, and a force of bluejackets, under Lieutenant Jasper Edmund Thomson Nicolls, were subsequently disembarked. The honour of having first hoisted the British flag in the island appears to be due to Lieutenant Horatio Fraser Kemble, first of the *Minotaur*.[1] Lord John Hay assumed the governorship of the place pending the arrival of Sir Garnet Wolseley, who had been appointed to the post, and who quickly assumed it.

[1] *A. & N. Gaz.*, July 20, and Aug. 3, 1878.

Troops were soon sent to the island to relieve the bluejackets and Marines on shore. An open beach was the only landing-place for them, but the Navy improvised facilities. That the labour involved in doing so was very arduous may be gathered from the fact that the working hours for the ships' companies were from 3.15 A.M. to 9.30 P.M., with an interval of only one hour for rest, and that many of the men were up to their necks in water while

H.R.H. ALFRED ERNEST ALBERT, DUKE OF SAXE-COBURG AND GOTHA, DUKE OF EDINBURGH, K.G., K.T., G.C.B., K.P., G.C.S.I., G.C.M.G., G.C.I.E., G.C.V.O., A.D.C.,
ADMIRAL OF THE FLEET.

(*From a photo by Downey.*)

engaged in pier-building. Captain the Duke of Edinburgh personally superintended the landing of the whole of the men and stores. The following extract from a letter sent to the *Scotsman* by a non-commissioned officer of the 71st Highlanders gives an interesting glimpse of the energetic manner in which his Royal Highness threw himself into his work, and affords room for regret that this was one of the very few occasions when the lamented Prince was able actively to exert himself in a service which he loved ardently to the day of his death, twenty-two years later :—

"The order was given for the regiment to disembark at 4 A.M. on the 24th, and so good were the arrangements (which were under the entire control of H.R.H. the Duke of Edinburgh) that at 4.20 A.M. there was not a 71st man left in the ship. We were taken on shore in large horse-boats, tugged by steam launches. As we came alongside the pier the first man I saw was the Duke of Edinburgh, who was helping the men out of the boats. As each of us carried our valise in one hand, and our rifle in the other, and as there was a swell on the water, you will understand that a man jumping out is apt, if he does not jump at the proper time, to find himself between the pier and the boat, with a very good chance of being drowned or crushed the next time the boat comes up. To prevent this, the Duke, and others with him, caught each man by the arm as he jumped out; and so well was this attended to that not a single man, or rifle, or valise fell into the water. I can assure you that it will be a long time before we forget the cheery word and smile his Royal Highness had for each of us as he helped us on to the pier. Early as it was, the sun was blazing hot, and though we had our helmets on, he had only his navy cap, with a white cover on it. After we were all out of the boats, and when I was going to fall in with the regiment, I saw him amongst the baggage, directing and encouraging, all his anxiety being to get us out of the sun."

What is remembered in South Africa as the Transkei, or "Old Colony" war, but which was, in fact, a number of small simultaneous campaigns against rebellious Galekas, Gaikas, Griquas, and other turbulent native tribes in 1877–78, was carried out mainly by the land forces; but the screw corvette *Active*, 10, Commodore Francis William Sullivan, C.B.,[1] bore a certain share in the operations. Her boats having been unable to effect a landing through the surf at Bowker's Bay in presence of a large body of Galekas, she turned her guns on the natives, and, it was said at the time, impressed them so powerfully that, if only their responsible leaders had been on the spot at the time, peace might have been then and there concluded. A little later, on January 14th, 1878, she landed a Naval Brigade of 196 officers, seamen, and Marines at East London, under Commander Henry Townley Wright. This took part in the action at Quintana on February 7th, and rendered most useful service, Lieutenant William des Vœux Hamilton doing valuable work in command of the rocket party.[2] On July 3rd following the Commodore and his officers[3] received an address and vote of thanks from the House of Assembly of Cape Colony. These disturbances

---

[1] C. M. G. May 24, 1878.   [2] Norbury: 'The Naval Brigade in S. Africa.'

[3] The officers landed, besides those already mentioned, were Lieut. Robt. Wm. Craigie; Lieut. (R.M.) Townley Ward Dowding; Sub-Lieuts. Arth. Hy. Loring, Reg. Purves Cochran, and Lionel Aubrey Wallis Barnes-Lawrence; Staff-Surg. Hy. Fredk. Norbury; Gunner Hy. Bays; and Clerk Ralph Balsom Marwood.

led incidentally to the annexation of Walfisch Bay, which was formally taken possession of on March 12th, 1878, by Staff-Commander Richard Cossantine Dyer, of the storeship *Industry*, 2. They also, no doubt, had some effect in encouraging the Zulus to become restless, and actively to prosecute their ancient feuds with their white neighbours.[1]

Before the actual outbreak of the Zulu war, the *Active* again landed a Brigade. The detachment disembarked at Durban on November 19th, 1878, and proceeded to the neighbourhood of the Zululand boundary line, there to garrison Fort Pearson and other posts on the Lower Tugela with a view to preventing incursions into Natal.

The Zulu question as it then stood may be thus summarised.

Cetewayo, the king, had had a dispute of long standing with the South African Republic concerning some land between the Buffalo and the Pongola which had been occupied as Transvaal territory. After the annexation of the Transvaal by Great Britain, Cetewayo had built military kraals on that territory, and had given its inhabitants notice to quit. Attempts had been made to arrange the difficulty, with the result that a commission had been appointed, and had reported in June, 1878; but the final award had been left for the consideration of Sir Bartle Frere, High Commissioner for South Africa.

Frere proceeded to Natal in September, 1878, and, in dealing with the situation, took account not only of the boundary question, but also of the general relations of Cetewayo with his neighbours. After making a careful survey of those relations,[2] which was very unsatisfactory, he decided that the award on the boundary question should be made known to Cetewayo simultaneously with certain demands, the concession of which was regarded as necessary for the welfare as well of the Zulus as of the inhabitants of Natal and the Transvaal. The award, which was favourable to the Zulu claims, and the demands, were delivered to Cetewayo's representatives on December 11th, 1878; and twenty days were allowed the king for compliance with the most pressing requirements of the ultimatum. When those twenty days had expired without any sign of submission

---

[1] The Transvaal had been annexed to Great Britain on Apr. 12, 1877, by Sir Theophilus Shepstone, who continued to administer it until Mar., 1879. Great Britain, however, inherited the Boer feuds both with Cetewayo, of Zululand, and with Sikukuni, chief of the Bapidi tribe of the Bechuanas.

[2] Frere's Mem. of Jan., 1879.

on the part of the Zulus, Sir Bartle Frere transferred the further conduct of the affair to Lieutenant-General Lord Chelmsford.

For some months before the delivery of the ultimatum preparations for a struggle had been made by both the parties concerned. The Imperial authorities had landed troops and munitions of war at Durban, had called out the mounted volunteers of Natal, had formed three regiments of Natal natives, and had massed all their forces on the Zululand border, in three columns. The first of these, at the mouth of the Tugela, was under Colonel Pearson, and included the Naval Brigade from the *Active*. The second, or main column, under Colonel Glyn, had its headquarters at Helpmakaar; the third, under Colonel Evelyn Wood, V.C., had Utrecht as its base, and lay in territory the ownership of which was in dispute.

Colonel Wood crossed the Blood River into Zululand on January 6th, 1879, and, on the 17th, moved towards the sources of the White Umfolosi, and thence to Kambula, where he entrenched himself. Colonel Glyn crossed the Buffalo at Rorke's Drift on January 11th, gained a facile and delusive success over the Zulus at Usirayo's stronghold on the 12th, and then moved tediously towards Isandhlwana, a mountain at the base of which he encamped on the 20th. On the 22nd, Lord Chelmsford and Colonel Glyn moved out of camp to reinforce Major Dartnell, who had proceeded with a patrol in the direction of Matyana's stronghold; and, during their absence, the rest of the column, under Colonels Pulleine and Durnford, about 1100 strong, was surprised, overwhelmed, and practically annihilated.[1] The little commissariat and hospital post at Rorke's Drift, ten miles to the rear, was afterwards attacked by the victorious Zulus, but was heroically defended by Lieutenants Chard, R.E., and Bromhead (24th Regiment), until the enemy was beaten off, leaving 350 dead behind him. Lord Chelmsford did not learn what had befallen his camp until comparatively late in the day. On the 23rd, after having passed an anxious night in the devastated camp, he moved back to Rorke's Drift.

Colonel Wood, from his post at Kambula, harried the enemy very successfully, though not without some reverses. Colonel Pearson crossed the Tugela River near its mouth on January 22nd,

---

[1] The only representative of the Navy present at Isandhlwana was William Aynsley, a signalman belonging to the *Active*. He was seen, "his back against a waggon-wheel, keeping the Zulus at bay with his cutlass; but a Zulu crept up behind him, and stabbed him through the spokes." Hallam Parr: 'Sketch of the Kaffir and Zulu Wars.' Lieut. A. B. Milne, R.N., was at the time with Lord Chelmsford.

and on the same day was attacked by, and defeated, a Zulu force at the Inyezane River. He then resumed his march, and next day reached Ekowe.[1] He had intended to move upon Cetewayo's kraal at Ulundi, but, upon hearing of the disaster at Isandhlwana, he decided to hold Ekowe fort, sending, however, his mounted troops back to the border. He retained about 1,300 men, inclusive of the Naval Brigade, and plenty of ammunition; and he held his position until his relief on April 3rd. He was never attacked.

After Isandhlwana and Rorke's Drift, Lord Chelmsford evacuated Zululand, and awaited reinforcements. At the beginning of April he advanced to relieve Ekowe, and, on the 2nd, defeated the enemy at Ginginhlovo, six miles south of the Inyezane River. Pearson, freed on the 3rd, returned to the Tugela. From that time forward no considerable action was fought until July 4th, just after the arrival in South Africa of Sir Garnet Wolseley to take over the supreme command. On that day Lord Chelmsford signally defeated the Zulus at Ulundi, and virtually ended the war; and on August 28th Cetewayo was captured in the Ingome Forest by Major Richard Marter, of the King's Dragoon Guards. The Zulu King was sent to Port Durnford, where, embarking in the transport *Natal*, under the charge of Lieutenant Crawford Caffin, he was escorted to Cape Town by the gunboat *Forester*, 4, Lieutenant Sidney Glenton Smith.

The general course of the war having been thus briefly summarised, the share taken in it by the Royal Navy may be followed in somewhat greater detail.

It has been mentioned that the *Active* disembarked a detachment at Durban on November 19th, 1878, and that Commodore Francis William Sullivan[2] sent it to the neighbouring Zululand boundary line. This detachment garrisoned Fort Pearson, on the Natal side of the mouth of the Tugela, and established and worked a pontoon, by which eventually Pearson's column crossed into Zululand. The naval force consisted of 174 blue-jackets, 42 Marines, about 14 West African Kroomen, two 12-prs., one 10-barrelled Gatling gun, and two rocket tubes, under Commander Henry John Fletcher Campbell (acting Captain); Lieutenants Robert William Craigie, and

---

[1] Or Etshowe.

[2] Rear-Adm. Dec. 31, 1878. Soon afterwards Commod. Fredk. Wm. Richards arrived in the *Boadicea*, Sullivan, however, remaining on the station for some little time, and surrendering the command only on Mar. 24.

William des Vœux Hamilton; Sub-Lieutenant Thomas Guthrie Fraser; Navigating Sub-Lieutenant John George Heugh; Staff-Surgeon Henry Frederick Norbury; Surgeon William Thompson; Lieutenant (R.M.) Townley Ward Dowding; Midshipman Lewis Cadwallader Coker[1]; and Boatswain John Cotter. Lieutenant Archibald Berkeley Milne, who was also landed from the *Active*, was attached as naval aide-de-camp to Lord Chelmsford's staff.

On December 20th, 1878, the *Tenedos*, 12, Captain Edward Stanley Adeane, arrived at Durban; and on January 1st, 1879, she also landed a Naval Brigade of 3 officers and 58 men, under Lieutenant Anthony Kingscote, who took them to the Zulu side of the mouth of the Tugela, and there built and garrisoned Fort Tenedos.

When Colonel Pearson advanced into Zululand, he was accompanied by the *Active's* Brigade, of the behaviour of which at the action of the Inyezane River on January 22nd, Commander Campbell wrote[2]:—

"All were remarkably steady under fire. Those employed on the ridge were exposed to a cross fire for nearly two hours, after which they responded to my call for the final assault with alacrity, and led the rush till success was secured. I particularly recommend Lieutenant Hamilton, whose company was in front during the action. Sub-Lieutenant Fraser also did good service in command of the reserve, being under fire the whole time. Boatswain Cotter was most successful with the rockets I placed in his charge. Lieutenant Craigie . . . rendered valuable services as acting-adjutant. . . . I beg to recommend to your notice E. White, P. O. First Class, who continued to fight after having been struck by a ball; E. Futcher, P. O. First Class, who took a leading part in the movements; Thomas Harding, ordinary, who was the first unmounted man in enemy's position."

The Brigade had seven men wounded.

In the meantime the disaster of Isandhlwana had struck Natal with panic, and had caused the Colony to fear an immediate Zulu invasion. When the *Boadicea*, 16, Commodore Frederick William Richards, which had gone from England to relieve the *Active*, reached the Cape, small-pox had broken out in her, so that it was impossible for her to land a Brigade as promptly as she would otherwise have landed one. There was also small-pox in the *Flora*, guardship at Simon's Bay, so that people could not be drawn from her. Chelmsford's column was shattered; Pearson's was shut up; Wood's was fighting in the enemy's country; the cry was for steady fighting men. It was unexpectedly answered from the sea.

---

[1] Died in Ekowe.   [2] Report to R.-Ad. Sullivan.

The screw iron frigate *Shah*, 26, Captain Richard Bradshaw, on her way home from the Pacific, called at St. Helena, the Governor of which island, having heard of Isandhlwana, allowed him to take on board all the available troops, 200 in number. With them Bradshaw sailed for Simon's Bay on February 12th, arriving on February 23rd. He acted on his own responsibility, and was rewarded with the full approval of the Admiralty and the country. From Simon's Bay he was ordered up to Durban, where, on March 7th, he disembarked 16 officers and 378 men, under Commander John William Brackenbury, thus at once doubling the strength of the naval detachments in, and on the borders of, Natal. On March 18th the *Boadicea* also was able to land a Brigade of 10 officers and 218 men, under Commander Francis Romilly. These two detachments, together with the one from the *Tenedos*, joined the force which presently proceeded to the relief of Ekowe, where the *Active's* contingent remained shut up with Pearson. They had a conspicuous share, consequently, in the battle of Ginginhlovo on April 2nd, 1879, when Brackenbury was in command of the united Brigades, Commodore Richards, however, being present.[1] The Navy held the corners of the British square, and its guns rendered excellent service. The naval casualties that day were one officer (Staff-Surgeon William Digby Longfield) and 6 men wounded.

On April 4th, the day after the relief of Ekowe, Acting-Captain Campbell, of the *Active*, was placed by the Commodore in command of the entire Brigade, then numbering upwards of 800 officers and men ; and he retained that position until the *Active's* and *Shah's* contingents re-embarked on July 21st ; but, up to the time of the general forward movement in June, Commander Brackenbury commanded that part of the Brigade which remained with the advanced force on the Inyezane River. The *Tenedos's* contingent had by that time been withdrawn, having re-embarked on May 8th. Says Commodore Richards :—

"During the occupation of Fort Chelmsford, several reconnaissances were made for the examination of the different drifts for the passage of the Emlalazi River; in which Commanders Brackenbury and Romilly, and Sub-Lieutenants (James) Startin, and (Arthur Hale) Smith-Dorrien took part. These reconnaissances were made under fire. The division encamped on the Emlalazi plain on the coast, at the position known as Port Durnford; and, on the arrival of the *Forester* with the surf-boats, and of store-ships, for the purpose of opening communications with the shore at that place, the

---

[1] Richards's disps. of Apr. 11, and Sept. 13, 1879. The Royal Marines were commanded in the battle by Capt. Joseph Philips, R.M.L.I.

services of the Brigade were immediately put in requisition for this operation; and so well was the work done that in three weeks' time over 2000 tons of commissariat and ordnance stores had been landed on the open beach, to the entire relief of the land transport."

The last naval contingent to re-embark was that from the *Boadicea*, which returned to its ship on July 31st. The only other vessel which had any of her people serving ashore during the war was the *Flora*, which sent two officers to the front on April 20th; but it may be mentioned that two members of the Royal Naval Artillery Volunteers went up country at their own expense, and joined the *Active's* Brigade, and that some others attached themselves to other commands. A Royal Marine battalion sent out from England was so unfortunate as to land in Africa too late to participate in the final actions of the campaign. It was also a matter of great disappointment to both the Royal Navy and the Royal Marines that they were not represented at the battle of Ulundi, save by Lieutenant A. B. Milne, who still served as Lord Chelmsford's aide-de-camp, and who was wounded; but they had the satisfaction, previous to their re-embarkation, of being inspected by Sir Garnet Wolseley, who, in his General Order, declared :—

" The conduct of the men has been admirable, and their bearing in action in every way worthy of the service to which they belong, while they have worked hard and cheerfully in their laborious duties, which constitute so important a part of all military operations."

The *Forester*, 4, Lieutenant Sidney Glenton Smith, made herself indispensable in surveying the coast with a view to finding suitable landing-places for troops and supplies; and she enabled Port Durnford to be utilised as a base. Her second visit to that neighbourhood was made on April 22nd. On the 24th, when the gunboat was lying off Port Durnford, and two of her boats were sounding close in shore, a large body of Zulus suddenly appeared and opened fire from the beach. The boats retired, firing as they went; and the *Forester* then shelled the coast and bush, killing a number of cattle, and probably causing other casualties.[1]

The transport service during the war was managed mainly by Captain Guy Ouchterlony Twiss, Commander Edward Henry Meggs Davis, Lieutenants Crawford Caffin, and Frederick Streatfield Pelly, Staff-Surgeon James Hamilton Martin, and Paymaster William Besley Ramsey (all borne in the *Boadicea*), and by Lieutenant Alexander Milne Gardiner, of the *Shah*. Among the numerous

[1] *Natal Mercury.*

officers whose names were mentioned in the dispatches, the
following were rewarded with honours or promotion :—

To be K.C.B.: Rear-Admiral Francis William Sullivan, Nov. 27, 1879.

To be C.B.: Captains Frederick William Richards, Richard Bradshaw, Henry
John Fletcher Campbell, and Fleet-Surgeon Henry Frederick Norbury,
Nov. 27, 1879.

To be C.M.G.: Captains Edward Stanley Adeane, and John William Brackenbury,
Dec. 19, 1879.

To be Captain: Commander Henry John Fletcher Campbell, July 3, 1879.

To be Commanders: Lieutenants Crawford Caffin, and Anthony Kingscote,
July 3, 1879, and Frederick Ralph Carr,[1] and Robert William Craigie,
Nov. 6, 1879.

To be Lieutenants: Sub-Lieutenants James Startin, and Thomas Guthrie Fraser,
and Navigating Sub-Lieutenant John George Heugh, Nov. 6, 1879.

To be Chief-Boatswain: Boatswain John Cotter, Nov. 6, 1879.

To be Major, R.M.: Captain Joseph Philips, R.M., Nov. 9, 1879.

To be Captain, R.M.: Lieutenant Townley Ward Dowding, R.M., Nov. 15, 1879.

To be Fleet-Surgeons: Staff-Surgeons Henry Frederick Norbury, and William
Digby Longfield, July 3, 1879.

In 1878 much needless importance was given, in Parliament and
elsewhere, to an incident which had occurred at Tanna, in the New
Hebrides, in September, 1877. The schooner *Beagle*, 1, Lieutenant
Crawford Caffin, had proceeded thither in order to make inquiries
with respect to the murder of a white man named W. Easterbrook ;
had demanded the murderer from the head men of the village of
Numukur; had been refused ; and, in concert with the commander
of the schooner *Renard*, 1, Lieutenant Horace John Moore Pugh,
had seized a number of hostages. As a result, one Nokwai, a
younger brother and accomplice of the actual murderer, had been
surrendered, though the chief criminal, Yuhmaga, had not been
given up. Nokwai had thereupon been sentenced to death, and on
September 25th had been hanged at the fore yard-arm of the *Beagle*.
Before dying the prisoner had admitted his guilt.[2]

In his comments to the Admiralty on the case, Commodore
Anthony Hiley Hoskins, while expressing the opinion that Caffin's
proceedings deserved general approval, had added :—

"that it would have been more satisfactory had the man executed been the actual
murderer, Yuhmaga, and had it been clearly established that Easterbrook was free from
all imputation of having given provocation. I also think that it would have been
better in any case that the execution should have taken place on shore—if possible, on
the scene of the murder : and I purpose so informing Lieut. Caffin."

Upon these facts certain well-meaning people based an agitation
which lasted for five or six months. Eventually it was decided that

---

[1] Gazetted, but subsequently cancelled.   [2] Caffin to Hoskins, Sept. 26, 1877.

Lieutenant Caffin was not deserving of censure, but that, upon the whole, it was undesirable that executions of the kind which had taken place should be carried out on board H.M. ships.[1]

The *London*, store ship at Zanzibar, to which Captain Hamilton Edward George Earle was appointed in the summer of 1878, continued to be invaluable as a centre of operations against the slave trade. Her boats were unceasingly active, and on several occasions her officers and men were under fire. A petty officer named Cornelius Duggan specially distinguished himself. In a dinghy, with one seaman, William Clark, only, he was stationed one night to watch a channel between an outlying island and Pemba, with a view to noting whether slaves were being removed from the former. In the small hours, two canoes full of people suddenly quitted the small island. Although his possible opponents[2] were at least thirty or forty in number, Duggan instantly gave chase. The Arabs opened fire, and several bullets struck the dinghy, while one passed through Duggan's clothes. The pursuit was, however, most pluckily persisted in, until one of the dinghy's oars broke; where-upon Duggan and his companion had to content themselves with emptying their revolvers after the fugitives.[3] At about the same time Sub-Lieutenant Neville Edmund Cornwall Legh behaved with great gallantry in an affair at Uzi, and also made numerous captures of slaves at Pemba.

Early in 1879 the white inhabitants of Sitka, in the United States' territory of Alaska, had reason to fear that their Indian neighbours were about to rise and massacre them, and, having in vain petitioned their own government for assistance, sent an urgent appeal for help to the senior British naval officer at Esquimalt, the result being that in February the *Osprey*, 6, Commander the Hon. Henry Holmes à'Court, was ordered to the threatened spot, where she remained until the arrival on the scene of a United States' corvette. During the *Osprey's* presence off the coast, her commander was boastingly informed by the Indians that, whenever they might choose to do so, they could make themselves masters of the little United States' revenue steamer *Oliver Wolcott* which lay there. To prevent the possibility of anything of the sort, à'Court, by permission of the American naval officer in charge of

---

[1] Procs. of Ho. of Com., Aug. 5, 1878.
[2] About half seem to have been slaves, and half Arab dealers and their men.
[3] Corr. in *A. and N. Gazette*, Dec. 14 and Dec. 28, 1878.

the feeble craft, put a body of British bluejackets and a Gatling gun
on board of her to supplement her crew; and with these the *Oliver
Wolcott* undertook an expedition to intercept some war canoes
belonging to the turbulent chiefs.[1]

In the Pacific several small punitive expeditions were undertaken
by her Majesty's ships in the course of 1879. A boat's crew
belonging to the British trader *Mystery* had been massacred by the
natives of Aoba, or Lepers' Island, in the New Hebrides, and there
had been other murders of white men in the Louisiade Archipelago
and elsewhere. The vessels employed were the *Cormorant*, 6,
Commander James Andrew Thomas Bruce, which visited, among
other places, Brooker Island, New Guinea, and Brother Island,
shelling and burning villages at each; the *Wolverene*, 17, Commodore
John Crawford Wilson; *Conflict*, 1, schooner, Lieutenant John
George Musters; and *Beagle*, 1, schooner, Lieutenant Thomas
de Hoghton, which proceeded to Aoba, Marau Sound, and the
Louisiades; and the *Danae*, 12, Captain John Child Purvis (2),
which also went to Marau Sound, in the Solomon Islands. Wilson
spared the Marau natives, understanding that they had already been
sufficiently dealt with by traders, but inflicted severe punishment
at Ferguson Island, and in the Louisiades. Purvis, being subsequently despatched to Marau Sound, where, after all, the people
had not been taught a sufficiently instructive lesson, destroyed some
villages and canoes, but suffered a loss of one killed and two
wounded.[2]

Elsewhere some useful police work was done in the same year
by the *Boxer*, 4, Commander Arthur Hildebrand Alington, first on
the west coast of Africa, where the gun-vessel was employed to
lodge a protest against the French occupation of the island of
Matacong, was engaged in the delimitation of the Liberian
boundary, and hoisted the British flag on the Scarcies River; and
subsequently off the coast of Haiti, where, in the summer, a
revolution was in progress. At Port-au-Prince, besides protecting
British interests, she embarked a number of refugees, including a
rebel leader who had sought shelter in the British consulate; and
more than once, while lying there, she was threatened with attack

[1] *A. and N. Gazette*, Mar. 22 and Apr. 12, 1879: Corr. of *Times* and *Hampshire
Telegraph.*

[2] *A. and N. Gazette*, Mar. 29, Apr. 19, May 24, Aug. 16 and 30, Sept. 6, and
Dec. 6, 1879.

from the shore.   Unhappily, owing to the insanitary condition of
the town and of the people whom she saved from it, yellow fever
attacked her officers and crew, and carried off, among others,
Lieutenant Edward Henry Arden, and Paymaster James King Bell.
The *Decoy*, 4, Lieutenant Victor Edward John Brenton von Donop,
in the earlier half of 1879, rendered useful police service in the
Coanza River, where the negroes had risen and murdered two white
people and several natives.

More serious business fell to the lot of another vessel of the
West African command, the *Pioneer*, 6, paddle, Lieutenant John
Leslie Burr.   In April, 1879, she proceeded into the Scarcies River
with a force under Governor Rowe, of Sierra Leone, in order to
re-hoist the British flag, which had been hoisted there in March by
the *Boxer* in face of some opposition, and which had afterwards
been hauled down by the natives.   The island of Kikoukeh, which
was the chief point annexed, was occupied as a set-off to Matacong,
which, a short time before, had been annexed by the French.
Lieutenant Burr had some trouble with the natives, who resented
the seizure of their territory ; but he managed the affair with
singular success.   A little later he took his ship about 700 miles up
the River Niger, carrying presents from the imperial and colonial
governments for the Emir of Nupi.   On his return he attacked and
destroyed the village of Onitsha, the inhabitants of which, not for
the first time, had murdered British traders and committed other
outrages ; and, making a short overland expedition, he burnt
another town about three miles from the river.   The effect of his
action was excellent, and earned him the thanks of the African
Company, which also presented him with a piece of plate.[1]

The African slave-trade languished, though a few captures of
dhows were made upon the east coast, especially by the *Spartan*, 12,
Captain Richard Edward Tracey, by the *Vestal*, 9, Commander
Dashwood Goldie Tandy, and by the boats of the *London*, Captain
Hamilton Edward George Earle.   In the Malay Archipelago,
however, the kidnapping piratical tribes, the Balinini and Illanuns,
were so active in seizing fishermen whom they subsequently sold
as slaves along the east coast of Borneo, that, at the desire of
Governor Treacher, of Labuan, the *Kestrel*, 4, Commander Frederick
Edwards, proceeded against them in August, 1879.   Having traced
certain outrages to the inhabitants of the Balinini village of

[1] Disps., and *A. and N. Gazette*, June 7, Dec. 6, Dec. 20, 1879.

Tarrebas, Edwards invited the local chief to pay him a visit on
board the gun-vessel. The man made excuses, and declined to
appear; whereupon, after due notice had been given, Tarrebas, and
about fifteen piratical craft, many of which had bullet-proof
bulwarks of iron-wood, were burnt.[1] Shortly afterwards, with the
Encounter, 14, Captain the Hon. Albert Denison Somerville
Denison, the *Kestrel* took part in a demonstration in the Larut
River, on the west coast of the Malay peninsula, with a view to
overawing the natives who threatened disturbances.

Early in 1880 the Royal Navy sustained a disaster somewhat
similar to the loss of the *Eurydice* in 1878.[2] The sixth-rate
Atalanta, employed on training service, sailed from Bermuda for
England on February 1st and was never heard of again. On
June 29th a reward was offered by the Admiralty for information
concerning her, but it was never claimed. There were lost in the
ship Captain Francis Stirling, the crew of 113 officers and men, and
170 ordinary seamen who were under training. A committee which
was appointed to inquire into the vessel's efficiency reported[3] to the
effect that: the *Atalanta* was sound when she left England for the
West Indies in November, 1879; she was on the whole a very stable
ship, save at large angles of keel; Captain Stirling was most able
and experienced; the other officers had been carefully chosen; and
nothing could be more satisfactory than the character of the crew.
All that is known and that bears on her fate is that storms of
exceptional violence raged at that time in the part of the Atlantic
which she would have had to cross. Just before her last cruise the
ship had been very thoroughly repaired in the dockyards. The
original estimate had been £11,000, but it had grown to £28,000.
As the *Atalanta* had been built in 1844, and as it was estimated that
a new ship of the class could be had for £36,000, it was naturally
argued at the time that she was not worth so large an expenditure.
From a comparison of her dimensions with those of the *Eurydice*—

Ship.	Length between Perpendicular.	Length for Tonnage.	Beam.	Depth.	Builder's Measurement.
	Ft. in.	Ft. in.	Ft. in.	Ft. in.	Tons.
Atalanta . . .	131 0	107 2	40 3	10 10	923
Eurydice . . .	141 3	117 10	38 4	8 9	921

[1] *Straits Times* in *A. and N. Gazette*, Nov. 8, 1879.   [2] *See* Appendix of Ships Lost.
[3] Sessional Papers, 1881. Report of *Atalanta* Committee.

it will be seen that the *Atalanta* should have had considerable advantage in point of stability.[1]

In the same year the Eastern question once more necessitated action on the part of the great Powers. It had been decided at the Berlin Conference that Turkey should hand over Dulcigno to Montenegro ; but, although the resources of diplomacy had been exhausted, the Porte still refused to carry that decision into effect. England, therefore, proposed, and France, Russia, Austria, and Italy agreed, that a combined naval demonstration should be made off the Albanian coast, there being an understanding that no troops were to be landed. It was further agreed to regard as commander-in-chief the senior flag-officer present,[2] and thus Vice-Admiral Sir Frederick Beauchamp Seymour, then in command of the British Mediterranean fleet, assumed command of the allied squadrons at Ragusa on September 20th, 1880. The ships of the Royal Navy present were the *Alexandra* and *Téméraire*, ironclads, with the *Condor*, gun-vessel, and the despatch-boat *Helicon*. The display was enough. Negotiations followed, and on November 26th Dulcigno was handed over to Montenegro. Consequent on this it was determined that the squadrons should part company after communicating their respective destinations ; and on December 5th the force dispersed.

Early in 1881 the sloop *Wild Swan*, 6, Commander Seymour Henry Pelham Dacres, was ordered to coöperate with the Portuguese authorities, who were making efforts to suppress the slave trade which had long been carried on by the Makuas of the Mozambique coast. With that object she left Zanzibar on January 22nd, and proceeded down the coast to Chuluwan, subsequently moving, in company with some Portuguese gunboats, to Conducia Bay, where she arrived on February 12th. A Portuguese landing-party, which was presently disembarked, was accompanied by Commander Dacres, Sub-Lieutenant Arthur Henry Stuart Elwes, Clerk Warwick Arthur Green, and three men from the sloop ; but the only important work done by the British was accomplished by the *Wild Swan's* guns, and by that vessel's rocket apparatus in her steam cutter.[3] The behaviour of the Portuguese on shore was not good ; and, had it not been for the support afforded by the ships, the landed force would have met with serious disaster.

[1] Brassey, 'British Fleet,' iv. 434.   [2] *Times*, Sept. 13, 1880, etc.
[3] *A. & N. Gaz.*, Feb. 26, Mar. 12 and 26, 1881; Letters of Offrs.

On December 16th, 1880, the Boers of the Transvaal, after a brief experience of British rule,[1] had re-proclaimed the South African Republic, and then, without delay, had laid siege to nearly all the British military posts in the country.

General Sir George Pomeroy Colley, who, at the time, was governor and commander-in-chief in Natal, and high commissioner for South-East Africa, began immediate preparations, though on a very inadequate scale, for the relief of the threatened towns and the suppression of rebellion, and, while collecting such military forces as were within reach, appealed for help from the Navy. The appeal reached Commodore Frederick William Richards, C.B., of the *Boadicea*, 16, a few hours after that vessel's arrival off Durban, on January 5th, 1881, and was instantly and loyally responded to. On the following day Commander Francis Romilly, of the *Boadicea*, with whom were Lieutenants Cornwallis Jasper Trower, and Reginald Purves Cochran, and Sub-Lieutenant Augustus Lennox Scott, accompanied by Surgeon Edward Elphinstone Mahon, of the *Flora*, guardship at Simon's Bay, landed with 124 petty officers and men, two Gatling machine-guns, and a couple of rocket-tubes, and proceeded to Pietermaritzburg, there to place himself under Colley's orders.[2]

The morning of January 28th, 1881, found the combined force encamped at Mount Prospect, inside a spur of the Draakensberg, opposite, and about four miles distant from, the pass of Laing's Nek, where the Boers were known to be in force and to have erected defences. At 6 A.M. camp was struck: two companies of infantry, and Lieutenant Cochran, with 40 *Boadicea's* and the two Gatlings, were left behind to hold three entrenched positions for the defence of the laager; and at 6.10 A.M., Colley, with the remaining 1211 officers and men,[3] moved forward to the attack. The *Boadicea's* 4 officers and 84 men, with their rocket-tubes, were in the centre of the column.

At 9 A.M. Colley, with whom was the Commodore, placed his guns on an undulating ridge facing the Nek, and 2200 yards from it, and ordered Romilly and his detachment to take up a station in advance. Behind knolls above and to the right, and about

[1] Consequent upon the annexation by Sir Theophilus Shepstone, who, in 1877, had been sent into the country, and who saw no other way of protecting the settlers against the natives.
[2] Parl. Papers, 1881. Vol. LXVII. contains three Blue Books on S. Afr.
[3] Besides 196 horses and 9 guns.

1700 yards off, bodies of Boers could be seen. Only on the left was the position assailable. A mealie field and the garden of a farm house enabled the Naval Brigade finally to bring its rocket-tubes within about 1500 yards from the pass, and to post a covering party in skirmishing order along a stone wall where, to the right, the line was continued by a company of the 60th Rifles. Half an hour later, when these dispositions had been completed, the guns and rocket-tubes opened upon the enemy; and, as soon as it was supposed that the bombardment had shaken the Boers, the British infantry and mounted troops charged up a grassy spur on the right of the Nek to assault the left of the hostile entrenchments. For a time success seemed possible; yet the Boers fired so well and so heavily that soon the troops were driven down again with serious loss, nearly all the mounted officers falling. The enemy not only followed up, but also appeared on the British right. The Naval Brigade sent rockets in the latter direction, and presently found itself engaged on both flanks as well as in front. But for the stone wall, it must have lost heavily. As a matter of fact, it had only two killed,[1] ere it was ordered to fall back on the guns.

After the retirement had been effected, a flag of truce was sent out, and the dead and wounded were brought in. At 4 P.M., the force returned to camp, and learnt from Lieutenant Cochran that, during its absence, a body of 400 Boers had reconnoitred the laager, but had moved away without attacking. Colley, in his despatch, expressed his indebtedness to Commodore Richards and the Brigade, and made special laudatory mention of Surgeon Mahon, Lieutenant Trower, and Sub-Lieutenant Scott.[2]

The general decided to remain at Mount Prospect until reinforcements, which were on their way in the transports *Euphrates*, *Crocodile*, and *Tamar*, could reach the front; and, in the mean-time, at his request, Commodore Richards caused an additional 50 men, with two field-guns, to disembark from the *Boadicea* and the *Dido*,[3] under Lieutenant Henry Asgill Ogle, of the latter vessel.[4] These men, however, did not join until after February 8th, when Colley fought the battle of Ingogo with the object of

---

[1] Including Gunner's Mate Henry Ransome, who was mentioned in desps.
[2] Colley to Sec. for War, Feb. 1, 1881.
[3] Captain Compton Edward Domvile.
[4] Richards to Admlty., Feb. 7, 1881.

keeping open his communications with Newcastle. In that unfortunate action the Naval Brigade had no share.

The Boers made no important advance, but concentrated most
of their energies upon the strengthening of the works in the pass
leading from Natal into the Transvaal. Dominating the western
extremity of their lines was the flat-topped hill of Majuba, which,
nevertheless, they made no attempt to hold. Colley, reinforced
during the second and third weeks of February, came to the
conclusion that Majuba was the key to the enemy's position, and,
in an evil hour, decided to occupy it with a detachment which
proved utterly inadequate to the end in view.

At 10 P.M., therefore, on February 26th, the general in person
moved from Mount Prospect with 554 officers and men only,
including 64 petty officers and men of the Navy under Commander
Romilly, Lieutenant Trower, Sub-Lieutenant Scott, and Surgeon
Mahon. Neither guns nor rocket-tubes were taken. Small though
the original detachment was, three companies which had left camp
with it were dropped at various points to guard the line of communications, so that but four companies and the little Naval
Brigade reached the front.

The top of the hill was reached by a very precipitous route;
but all the men were at their assigned stations by 4 A.M. on
Sunday, the 27th, there having been no opposition whatsoever.
A section of the Brigade, under Lieutenant Trower, remained
near that end of the mountain where the ascent had been made.
The rest of the force was placed in a hollow at the end closest
to the Boer lines; and at dawn the enemy's laagers could be
seen below. The summit was not entrenched, in spite of the
fact that its conformation was such that the people holding it
could not properly command the exterior slopes without dangerously exposing themselves; and an extraordinary degree of over-
confidence seems to have prevailed.

Soon after daylight the Boers showed some signs of activity
about the base of Majuba, and steady firing followed; but for a
time it did not look as if any serious object had occurred to the
enemy, who, on the other hand, was deemed to be throwing
away his ammunition. Sub-Lieutenant Scott, with the second
section of the Naval Brigade, was presently sent to line the edge
of the mountain top in the rear, and, a little later, part of the
58th Regiment was withdrawn from the left, where its post was

taken by portions of the first and second sections. The men lay down under good cover, seeing very little of the Boers, most of whom appeared to be out of range, and firing seldom. Trower and Scott were with them. So also was Romilly during great part of the morning; but at about 11 A.M. a dozen men were ordered to be sent from the left to the front, and Romilly went across to fetch them. In returning, the gallant Commander was shot through the body, and fell close to the general. Mahon attended to the mortally wounded officer, who presently was carried into the hollow, out of reach of gun-fire. At about that time, Scott, with six men, was stationed by Trower on a ledge about twenty feet below the summit on the right side of the mountain, near the track by which the ascent had been made.

During the whole of the morning, and more especially during the half hour or so after noon, the people on the top of Majuba had their attention held by the general firing, and failed to see that a small force of Boers was working its way stealthily up the mountain, covered by the much larger force below. Shortly before 1 P.M., the firing increased greatly. Hearing that the enemy was close at hand, Scott ventured to take his men from the ledge, and lead them to the point which appeared to be most threatened. He found the 92nd Highlanders and part of the 58th Regiment firing on the foe, who was then nearing the top, but he was at once ordered back by the general. A few moments later the Boers gained the summit, and the British began a retreat which soon became a rout. Colley, until he fell, shot through the head, and his officers, did all that lay in their power to stem the panic; but the frightened troops were not to be stayed. Many rushed at break-neck speed down the almost precipitous sides of the mountain, exposed to a terrible fire from the Boers, and, for the most part, losing their arms in the descent. Seeing how few in number were the assailants, the flight is one of the most extra-ordinary in history. It can be explained only by the completeness of the surprise, and by the men's sudden realisation of the fact that no due precautions had been taken by their own leaders.

Earlier in the day a hospital had been established behind a ridge of rocks near the centre of the plateau. The enemy crowned the rocks, and fired upon all indiscriminately,[1] shooting down a doctor while he was caring for the wounded. Perceiving how

---

[1] Mahon to Richards, Mar. 4.

things had gone, Surgeon Mahon, who but lately had quitted
Romilly in order to cross to the hospital, returned to his Commander's side, and, to save further slaughter of the wounded
and non-combatants, hoisted a white flag. All the fugitives, however, were not then clear of the top, and firing continued on the
summit. To avoid the bullets, Mahon, and Assistant Sick-Berth
Attendant Bevis, who was with him, lay down till the plateau
was clear of their flying friends, and until the enemy was within
a few paces from them. When they rose, they were not molested,
and were suffered to carry poor Romilly to the hospital from the
point where he had lain sheltered on the south-west front.

Throughout that afternoon and the following night Mahon
remained on the mountain, seeking out and attending to the
wounded, and receiving much kindly help from the enemy. He
took upon himself to send four blue-jacket prisoners to carry
Romilly back to camp ; but, soon after they had started, they
were ordered back by the enemy, the result being that the unfortunate Commander had to lie in the open during the whole of
the wet, dark, and chilly night of the 27th. At 6 A.M. on the
28th, Lieutenant Cochran came up from camp with a burial
party, and with stretchers and medical comforts. Of the fifty-
three men who were buried on the summit, ten belonged to the
Naval Brigade. But these were not the whole of the naval
casualties. The *Boadicea* lost Lieutenant Trower [1] and 10 men
killed, and Commander Romilly and 5 men mortally wounded.
The *Dido* lost 3 men killed. In addition, 10 *Boadicea's* and 3
Dido's were wounded; so that of the total naval force engaged,
33 (being practically 50 per cent.) were put out of action. [2]

Trower's body was found on the extreme ridge, and, being
taken back to camp, was buried there. Romilly [3] died on March
2nd. A Boer commandant pointed out to Cochran the bodies of
two men who had most bravely stood their ground and perished
there. They were those of George Hammond and Samuel
Witheridge, quartermasters, R.N. Mahon, who reached camp
at 5 P.M. on the 28th, with five ambulances full of wounded,
behaved throughout with magnificent devotion and gallantry, and

[1] Lieut., Apr. 28, 1876.
[2] Admlty. to Col. Off., May 2, enclosing Richards to Admlty. of Mar. 14, covering
Ogle to Richards, Mar. 3, and Scott to Ogle, Mar. 1, 1881.
[3] Com., Apr. 14, 1877.

was specially promoted.[1]   In the opinion of all those who were left on the fatal hill, he deserved the Victoria Cross.

Upon the death of General Colley, the command of the troops devolved temporarily upon General Sir Evelyn Wood; and on March 4th, Captain Compton Edward Domvile, of the *Dido*, went up from Durban to take charge of the remnant of the Naval Brigade. On the same day a detachment of 50 seamen, who had been sent out in the *Danube*[2] to fill vacancies, left for the front under Lieutenants George Morris Henderson, and Andrew Henry Farrell Duncan.   Sir Evelyn Wood went from Newcastle back to Pietermaritzburg, where he assumed for the nonce the functions of governor of Natal; but ere the new permanent governor and commander-in-chief, General Sir Frederick Sleigh Roberts, arrived on the scene, Wood had held a prolonged conference with the Boer general, Piet Joubert, and had concluded an armistice, which resulted, on March 24th, in a peace.

This is not the place in which to enter into any wide criticism either of the tactics pursued by the British leaders in the field, or of the policy directed by Mr. Gladstone's government at home. Colley paid for his negligence and his contempt for the enemy with his life: Mr. Gladstone, who was animated by motives some at least of which were doubtless excellent, but who was congenitally incapable of understanding the Boer character, patched up an unsatisfactory arrangement which, it was generally felt, could not be lasting.   In spite of what had happened at Laing's Nek, Majuba, and elsewhere, the Boers might have been brought to reason with comparative ease in March. They did not realise that fact, and they mistook British generosity and quixotism for pusillanimity. Less than twenty years later, both parties had to pay a frightful price for their misapprehensions. Yet in 1881, as in the subsequent struggle, the Navy, happily, had nothing with which to reproach itself.[3]

The *Doterel*, 6-gun sloop of 1,137 tons, while at anchor off Sandy Point, Straits of Magellan, was destroyed by an explosion on April 26th, 1881.   Commander Richard Evans, Lieutenant John Martin Stokes, three other officers, and seven men were saved, but the rest of the crew of 156 perished. The ship was a new one,

---

[1] Staff-Surgeon, July 18, 1881.   [2] Merchant steamer.
[3] Among naval officers who did good service in Natal in connection with transport work were Capt. Hilary Gustavus Andoe and Lieut. Edward Chichester.

being then on passage to the Pacific station for her maiden commission. Commander Evans reported that the explosion had been so sudden and destructive that there was no possibility of lowering boats to save life. He, with the surviving officers and men, was acquitted of all blame by the finding of the court-martial, September 3rd, 1881.[1] It was decided that the destruction of the ship had been due to an explosion of gas given off by coal in the bunkers, and that this had communicated with the fore magazine, causing that also to explode. It was never proved how the explosions had originated, but it was suggested that, as the ship had been about to complete with coal, a light may have been introduced into one of the bunkers. Another theory was that the disaster had originated with a spontaneous explosion of xerotine siccative, a material which, on November 23rd of the same year, undoubtedly brought about an explosion in the *Triumph,* off Coquimbo, and caused the loss of three lives.

The history of the most serious naval operation in which British men-of-war were engaged during the last quarter of the nineteenth century has next to be followed.

Owing to the extravagance of the Khedive, Ismail Pasha, the finances of Egypt had fallen into great disorder ; and, in November, 1875, partly in order to relieve them, and partly to strengthen the interests of Great Britain in a country which lay on the direct route to India, Lord Beaconsfield's administration, acting on the advice of Mr. Frederick Greenwood, had purchased, for £4,080,000, the shares in the Suez Canal held by Ismail. The bondholders did not greatly benefit; and in 1876, first Mr. Cave, and afterwards Messrs. Goschen and Joubert, made certain recommendations which, in September, 1878, resulted in the appointment of Mr. Rivers Wilson as Minister of Finance, and of M. de Blignières as Minister of Public Works, the object being the control by Europeans of the inordinate expenditure. The Khedive soon found their interference irksome, and he dismissed them in April, 1879 ; whereupon the Great Powers, acting in the interests of the bondholders, called upon the Sultan to depose his vassal, who was accordingly dethroned in June. Ismail retired to Naples with an immense fortune, and was succeeded by his son, Mohammed Tewfik. To liquidate the debt, and to effect various reforms, the Anglo-French, or " Dual " control was

[1] *Times*, Aug. 27 and Sept. 5, 1881.

established, with Messrs. Evelyn Baring[1] and de Blignières as controllers.

Great Britain and France, the two Powers chiefly interested in the well-being of Egypt, did not pull well together; and their jealousies encouraged the gradual formation of a popular party which had for its motto, "Egypt for the Egyptians." Owing to the growing strength and machinations of this party, and to the manner in which its propaganda appealed to the army, there were two significant mutinies in 1881. The second of these was ended only by the resignation of the ministry, and the appointment of a new one, which presently gave to Arabi Pasha, the leader of the Egyptian party, the post of under-secretary for war, and, through an "Assembly of Notables," claimed a right to regulate the budget in defiance of the control. Among the agitators there were, no doubt, men of sterling patriotism, as well as others of more selfish aims ; but, having regard to the huge indebtedness of Egypt, the Powers were bound to guard their own interests, and could not afford to allow the untried and headstrong Egyptian party to seize the reins of government. In the next ministry, Arabi took the post of minister for war; and on May 10th, upon his initiative, the chamber repudiated the authority of the Khedive, who was regarded as the creature of the Powers. Great Britain and France threatened to intervene, and Arabi was obliged to resign ; but on May 27th, he was reinstated, practically as dictator. He then set to work to strengthen and modernise the fortifications of Alexandria, where, in spite of the presence off the port of an international squadron, a rising against Europeans took place on June 11th.[2] This led to the departure from the city of most of the foreign residents ; while the Khedive became, for the time, the unwilling tool of Arabi.

But for international jealousies, matters would never have grown so serious. If clear injunctions had been given at an early stage both to the French and to the British naval commanders on the spot, the "national" movement might have been crushed without much difficulty or bloodshed ; but France was playing a double game, and, while willing enough to profit by any action which might be taken in defence of the interests of the bondholders, shrank—although she would not confess it until the last moment[3]—from being implicated

---

[1] Afterwards Lord Cromer.

[2] Among the 68 Europeans who were killed on the occasion were Engineer James Pibworth, of the *Superb*, and two men belonging to the *Helicon*.

[3] The French Squadron withdrew to Port Said just previous to the bombardment.

in what many of her people regarded as something like a tyrannical repression of the *vox populi* in Egypt. Puzzled by the hesitations of French diplomacy, the British cabinet pursued an unsteady course for some time ; and, at last, took action alone.

The British fleet lying before Alexandria in July, 1882, under the command of Admiral Sir Frederick Beauchamp Paget Seymour, G.C.B., was as given in the Table on the following page.

Some days before hostilities were decided upon, the *Invincible, Monarch*, and *Penelope* lay inside the harbour of Alexandria. The *Alexandra* drew too much water to get in with ease ; and Seymour temporarily shifted his flag from her to the *Invincible*, not only in order to be as close at hand as possible during the negotiations, but also to be able to exercise a personal supervision over the Egyptians, and to prevent them from laying down mines, of which they had a large number in readiness.

After the riotous outbreak of June 11th, Arabi's officers began systematically to strengthen the works lying along the neck of land which separates Lake Mareotis from the sea, and to mount additional guns in them. Seymour remonstrated, and demanded that the operations should be stopped. He was informed in reply that no operations of the kind mentioned were in progress ; and appeals were made to his humanity, the foreign consuls backing these up with assurances that if he should bombard the place, as he had threatened to do in case of non-compliance, neutral property would inevitably suffer. In the meantime, labour at the batteries went on night after night, and the people working there could be seen plainly from the ships. At length, when Lieutenant Henry Theophilus Smith-Dorien, of the *Invincible*, who had been ashore on leave, made a declaration to the Admiral that he had actually witnessed the mounting of two guns in Fort Silsileh, Seymour summoned a council of war on board the *Helicon*, and decided to send in a strongly worded ultimatum. The Egyptians were informed that unless the batteries of Ras el Tin, and the south side of the harbour, were " temporarily surrendered for purposes of disarmament," the fleet would attack them. To this an Egyptian officer replied that three guns in the batteries named should be dismounted ; whereupon most of the foreigners who had remained in Alexandria, seeing that fighting was inevitable, quitted the city. Seymour expressed his dissatisfaction, and, on July 10th, supplemented his ultimatum with the declaration that unless the works were given up at once, he would open fire on the 11th.

Ships, with date of launch. b. s. = battleship, g. v. = gun vessel, disp. v.=dispatch vessel	Displ. Tons.	I.H.P.	Mean Draught. ft.	Thickest Armour. in.	Guns: ALL RIFLED.													Compt.	Commanders.
					80-ton 16-in. M.	25-ton 12-in. M.	25-ton 11-in. M.	18-ton 10-in. M.	12-ton 9-in. M.	9-ton 8-in. M.	5½-ton 7-in. M.	4½-ton 7-in. M.	64-cwt. M.	64-pr. M.	40-pr. B.L.R.	20-pr. B.L.B.	Light.		
Ironclads. Inflexible, turret b. s., blt. 1876.	11,880	8,010	25·5	14 to 24	4											8	22	484	Capt. John Arbuthnot Fisher. Com. Albert Baldwin Jenkings.
Monarch, turret b. s., blt. 1868.	8,320	7,840	26	4 to 10		4			2		1						17	515	Capt. Henry Fairfax, C.B. Com. Tynte Ford Hammill.
Téméraire, cent. bat. and barbette b. s., blt. 1876.	8,540	7,520	27·2	5 to 11			4	4									31	534	Capt. Hy. Fredk. Nicholson. Com. Enst. Downman Maude.
Alexandra, cent. battery b. s. (flag), blt. 1875.	9,490	8,610	26·5	6 to 14			2	10									30	670	Adm. Sir Fredk. Beauchamp Paget Seymour, G.C.B. Capt. Charles Fredk. Hotham. Com. Alan Brodrick Thomas.
Sultan, cent. battery b. s., blt. 1870.	9,200	7,720	27·5	6 to 9				8	4							7	19	400	Capt. Walter James Hunt-Grubbe, C.B. Com. Chas. Jno. Balfour.
Invincible, cent. battery b. s. (temp. flag-ship), blt. 1869.	6,010	4,830	22·7	5 to 8					10				4			6	23	450	Capt. Robt. Hy. More Molyneux. Com. Reg. Friend Hannam Henderson.
Superb, cent. battery b. s., blt. 1875.	9,170	6,580	26·2	5 to 12				16								6	25	620	Capt. Thomas Le Hunte Ward. Com. Harry Fras. Hughes Hallett.
Penelope, cent. battery b. s., blt. 1867.	4,470	4,700	17·5	4½ to 6						8					3	2	12	223	Capt. S. John Caulfield D'Arcy-Irvine. Com. John Pakenham Pipon.
Beacon, g. v., blt. 1869.	603	510										1	2		2	2		75	Com. Geo. Weightman Hand.
Bittern, g. v., blt. 1869.	805	850	10·1									1				2	3	90	Com. Hon. Thos. Seymour Brand.
Condor, g. v., blt. 1876.	780	770	13·2									1	2				3	100	Com. Lord Chas. Wm. Delapoer Beresford.
Cygnet, g. v.	455	530	8·5										2			2		60	Lieut. Hugh Cuthbert Dudley Ryder.
Decoy, g. v.	430												2			2		50	Lieut. Arth. Herb. Boldero.
Helicon, padd. disp. v., blt. 1865.	1,000	1,290	10·5													2		80	Lieut. Wm. Llewellyn Morrison.
Total number of guns in the Fleet					4	4	6	38	16	8	1	3	12		5	39	185		
Number of Rounds fired during the Bombardment					88	117	184	752	224	231	21	114	412		152	621	§		

§ From 9-prs. and 7-prs. . . . 282
From Nordenfelts 16,233
From Gatlings 7,100
Rockets 37
Martini-Henry cartridges . . 10,160

NOTE.—The *Hecla*, torpedo-depôt ship, Captain Arthur Knyvet Wilson, was also present, and supplied ammunition during the engagement.

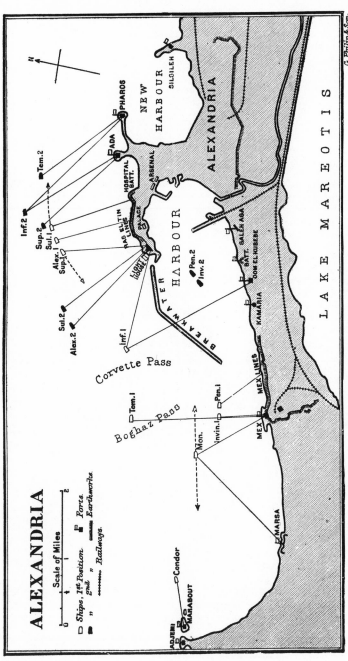

THE BOMBARDMENT OF ALEXANDRIA, 1882.

(*Reproduced, by permission, from Mr. H. W. Wilson's 'Ironclads in Action.'*)

G. Philip & Son.

[*To face p. 324.*]

This was the signal for all neutral vessels to leave the harbour. As the foreign men-of-war which were present departed, the British battleships played them out. In the meantime, the telegraph steamer *Chiltern*, which was at Alexandria, had picked up the cables to Malta and Cyprus, and, establishing an office on board, had placed the fleet in independent communication with home.

The position of the seaward defences of Alexandria will be seen on the plan. The guns actually mounted in them in July, 1882, were much inferior to those carried by the British ships, and were as follows :—

—	Rifled.					Smooth Bores.			Mortars.				Total.	
	Muzzle-loaders.				B. L.									
	10-in.	9-in.	8-in.	7-in.	40-pr.	15-in.	10-in.	6·5-in.	20-in.	13-in.	12-in.	11-in.	Rifled.	Others
Fort Silsileh .	..	1	1	..	..	..	3	..	..	1	.	..	2	4
Fort Pharos .	1	3	2	.	2	..	6	31	..	4	.	..	8	41
Fort Ada . .	1	3	1	..	..	..	14	..	..	5	..	..	5	19
Ras el Tin lines	1	3	2	2	1	4	15	11	1	6	1	2	9	40
Fort Ras el Tin	1	4	1	..	..	2	5	21	..	1	..	2	6	31
Fort Saleh Aga	..	..	..	..	..	..	4	8	..	..	.	..	..	12
Battery . .	..	..	..	..	..	..	2	2	..	..	..	..	..	4
Fort Oom el Kubebe . .}	..	..	2	.	..	..	6	10	.	1	1	..	2	18
Fort Kamaria .	..	..	..	..	.	..	2	3	..	1	..	..	..	6
Fort Mex . .	1	1	3	.	..	..	4	5	..	3	2	..	5	14
Mex lines . .	..	..	..	..	..	4	11	9	..	..	..	..	..	24
Fort Marsa. .	..	..	..	..	..	..	3	1	..	..	..	..	..	4
Fort Marabout.	..	3	2	2	..	..	9	16	..	2	..	5	7	32
Totals . .	5	18	14	4	3	10	84	117	1	24	4	9	44	249

293

The smooth-bores and mortars may almost be ruled out as non-effective, especially as the carriages and platforms of many of them were out of repair, and as the powder used with them seems to have been of defective quality, while the gunners were in-experienced. Of rifled heavy guns, as will be seen, the Egyptians had but forty-four to the British ninety-seven. Moreover, Forts Marabout and Adjemi were not engaged by the ironclads, but only by the gun vessels ; Fort Kamaria took no part what-sover in the action ; and Fort Marsa is reported to have received no shot. As for the works themselves, none were of very modern or perfect construction, and some were very old. With the exception of Fort Pharos, they were low, and of irregular trace. The parapets of the heavy rifled guns had regular embrasures, but the smooth bores fired over the parapets, and their crews were, therefore, much exposed to the British shrapnel, machine-gun, and small-arm fire. Behind the forts, or inside them, were buildings, such as shell stores and magazines, showing over the parapets, and offering good targets. The magazines, or many of them, had open ventilators and iron floors, and were rendered conspicuous by their lightning conductors. The more ancient forts were constructed of very soft limestone, and the mortar used was bad. The masonry was backed with sand, and the parapets were of sand, sloping at an angle of 30 degrees. It cannot be said that the defences were of a formidable nature; and, judging from the manner in which Seymour ordered them to be

ADMIRAL SIR CHARLES FREDERICK HOTHAM, K.C.B.

attacked, he must have despised them; for, as will be seen, he allowed his Captains some discretion as to whether they would or would not anchor within range of the batteries during the action; and he prepared to attack a number of works simultaneously, instead of concentrating the whole of his fire against the strongest fort opposed to him, and then dealing with the others in succession. This would have been the natural procedure of a Commander-in-Chief who regarded his task as a really serious and difficult one. At the same time, it is by no means clear that Sir Beauchamp had any very definite ideas as to the strength of the defences, and the resistance which they were capable of offering; for he contemplated the possibility that it might take the fleet two or three days to accomplish the object which he had in view.

Seymour's plan of action is laid down in the appended extract from a General Order, which was issued by him on July 10th :—

" In the event of my not receiving a satisfactory answer to a summons which I shall send to the Military Governor of Alexandria, calling on him to deliver up to me temporarily the works on the southern shore of the harbour, and those on the Ras el Tin peninsula, the squadron under my command will attack the forts as soon as the twenty-four hours given to neutrals to leave the place have expired ; which will be at 5 A.M. of the 11th.

" There will be two attacks :

" 1. From the inside of the harbour,[1] in which the *Invincible, Monarch,* and *Penelope* will take part.

" 2. By the *Sultan, Superb, Téméraire, Alexandra,* and *Inflexible,* from outside the breakwater.

" Action will commence by signal from me ; when the ship nearest the newly-erected earthwork near Fort Ada will fire a shell into the earthwork.

" On the batteries opening on the off-shore squadron in reply, every effort will be made by the ships to destroy the batteries on the Ras el Tin peninsula, especially the Lighthouse battery, bearing on the harbour. When this is accomplished, the *Sultan, Superb,* and *Alexandra* will move to the eastward, and attack Fort Pharos, and, if possible, the Silsileh battery.

" The *Inflexible* will move down this afternoon to the position off the Corvette Pass assigned to her yesterday, and be prepared to open fire on the guns in Mex Lines in support of the in-shore squadron when signal is made. The *Téméraire, Sultan,* and *Alexandra* will flank the works on Ras el Tin.

" The gun-vessels and gunboats will remain outside, and keep out of fire until a favourable opportunity offers itself of moving in to the attack on Mex.

" Ships must be guided in a great measure by the state of the weather whether they anchor or remain under way. If they anchor, a wire hawser should be used as a spring. The men are to have breakfast at 4.30 A.M., and are to wear their working rig.

" The in-shore squadron will be under my personal command; the off-shore ships under that of Captain Hunt-Grubbe, C.B., of the *Sultan.* The *Helicon* and *Condor* will act as repeating ships.

" Finally, the object of this attack is the destruction of the earthworks and the dismantling of the batteries, on the sea-fronts of Alexandria. It is possible that the work may not be accomplished under two or three days. Shell is to be expended with caution, notwithstanding that the *Humber,* with a fair proportion of reserve ammunition, may be expected here on the 12th. Should the *Achilles* arrive in time, she is to attack Fort Pharos, or place herself where the senior officer of the off-shore squadron may direct. . . ."

Towards evening the ships took up the positions assigned to them, the *Alexandra* 1500, the *Sultan* 1750, and the *Superb* 1950

---

[1] Sir Beauchamp meant "in-shore, near the mouth of the harbour," as is shown by his more detailed instructions.

yards from the Lighthouse Fort; the *Inflexible*, in the Corvette Pass, 3750 yards from Mex; the *Téméraire*, outside the Boghaz Pass, 3500 yards from Mex;[1] the *Penelope* and *Invincible* in-shore, 1000 yards from Mex; and the *Monarch* somewhat more to the westward, and 1300 yards from Mex. Such ships as were in company with others were at intervals of two and a half cables. All were cleared for action on the 10th, top-gallant masts being struck, and bowsprits rigged in. The small craft sent down all their yards, but the ironclads only their upper ones.

The morning broke fair and clear, with a smooth sea, and a light N.W. breeze, which, when the action began, carried the smoke in-shore, and obscured the target, making good shooting a little difficult.

At 7 A.M., by order, the *Alexandra* fired the first shot at the battery near Fort Ada; and a signal for general action was hoisted in the *Invincible*, where the Commander-in-Chief still flew his flag. It was greeted with cheers. Indeed, throughout the action there seems to have been more noise and chaff on some of the British decks than would have been desirable, or even safe, had the enemy been a more serious one. The Egyptians replied quickly and pluckily, their officers not hesitating to leap upon the parapets in order to direct and encourage the gunners; and the guns' crews sticking manfully to their work in spite of the overpowering fire. In the British ships, officers stationed in the tops, or elsewhere aloft, gave such information as the smoke would permit them to collect to the people at the guns below. The shooting on the part of the attack, though not brilliant, was, perhaps, as good as could be looked for in the circumstances; but an undue proportion of the large shells failed to burst; and the unsuitableness of ships of the *Inflexible* type for war service was shown by the fact that the concussion of her guns smashed her boats (which ought to have been hoisted out, and sent to a place of safety, though not too far away), and damaged her superstructure. In fact, no man-of-war, if she can temporarily get rid of her boats, ought to go into action with them on board. It is very important that, in the event of her sustaining serious injuries, they should be available for the saving of her crew; and, if they be kept on board, they must suffer severely, if not from the concussion of the ship's own guns, at least from the quick-firing and machine-guns of the enemy. Moreover, they become a fertile

---

[1] The *Téméraire* grounded there, but got off again during the action.

source of splinters; and they increase the risk of fire, which, even though it may not actually imperil the ship, must impair her efficiency by the production of smoke.

By 7.10 all the ships were engaged; and all the forts that could bring their guns to bear on them were replying. Of the in-shore squadron, the *Invincible* fought at anchor, using a hawser as a spring; the *Penelope*, after first fighting at anchor, steamed out to a range of about 1200 yards, and then allowed herself to drift

ADMIRAL THE RT. HON. FREDERICK BEAUCHAMP PAGET SEYMOUR, LORD
ALCESTER, G.C.B.

(*From a photo by the London Stereoscopic Co.*)

in to a range of about 700, afterwards repeating the manœuvre; and the *Monarch* steamed up and down, parallel with the Mex lines, and, at 8.30, blew up a magazine in the rear of Fort Marsa. The *Téméraire*, further out, supported the fire of the in-shore squadron; and the *Inflexible*, from outside the centre of the breakwater, divided her fire between earth and masonry works—Oom el Kubebe at 4000 yards, and Ras el Tin at 2700. The *Alexandra*, *Superb*, and *Sultan,* first under steam at from 1500 to 2000 yards, and then at anchor at about 2200 yards, engaged the works between Ras el Tin and Pharos. The firing of the fleet was for the most part very slow and deliberate. Nevertheless, by 10.30, the Mex works began to show signs of having had enough of it; and by about 12.30 the *Inflexible* and *Téméraire* moved eastward, and devoted their attention to Pharos and Ada. The *Superb,* which had previously fired chiefly at the Ras el Tin lines and Lighthouse battery, also attacked Ada, which she silenced at about 2 P.M., after having exploded the magazine. At nearly the same hour, it being seen that the gunners in the lower battery of Mex had abandoned their guns, a party of twelve volunteers,[1] under Lieutenant Barton Rose Bradford, landed through the growing swell and breaking surf, spiked six smooth-bores, and disabled two 10-inch rifled muzzle-loaders by exploding charges of gun-cotton in their muzzles. This was done without casualty, though it cost the loss of the *Bittern's* dinghy.

Oom el Kubebe had been silenced at about 1 P.M.; part of the Ras el Tin works ceased to reply an hour and a half later; the Lighthouse end of the Ras el Tin lines became quiet at nearly the same time; and the Hospital end of the same lines fired only from a single gun after about 3 P.M. Pharos held out till about 4.30; and not till after 5 did the last gun near the Hospital desist from replying. For a little longer the bombardment was continued. At 5.30, however, the signal was made to cease firing.

In the meantime the gunboats, and especially the *Condor,* had not been idle. Early in the day Lord Charles Beresford, noticing that Fort Marabout was endeavouring to annoy the in-shore squadron, stood in to the work so close that its guns could barely be depressed sufficiently to reach him, and, anchoring, warped his little craft to and fro, veering away and heaving in cable, and pouring in such fire as he could. He had been at that work for about an hour and a half, when, at 10 A.M., the Admiral ordered in the other gunboats on the same duty. They all gained positions in which they could not be touched, and, no doubt, distracted the attention of the enemy to a considerable extent. When, at length, the gunboats were recalled, the *Condor* was cheered from the flagship, which made the signal, "Well done, *Condor.*"

During the morning a 10-in. shell from a smooth-bore pierce

an unarmoured part of the *Alexandra's* side, and lodged on her main deck. Hearing a cry to that effect, Gunner Israel Harding, who was below, rushed up the ladder, and, seeing that the fuse was burning, flung some water over it, and then picked up the projectile, and immersed it bodily in the contents of a tub that stood at hand. For this act he was promoted to be Chief Gunner as from the day of the engagement, and, in the following September, was awarded the Victoria Cross.

The casualties on the side of the attack were insignificant. The *Alexandra* had 1 killed, and 3 wounded; the *Superb*, 1 killed, and 1 wounded; the *Sultan*, 2 killed, and 8 wounded; the *Inflexible*, 1 killed, and 2 wounded (one mortally) ;[1] the *Invincible*, 6 wounded ;[2]

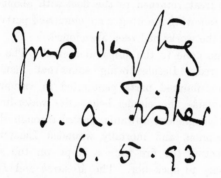

VICE-ADMIRAL SIR JOHN ARBUTHNOT FISHER, K.C.B.
(Signature when a Rear-Admiral.)

and the *Penelope*, 8 wounded ;[3] making in all, 5 killed, and 28 wounded. The Egyptian loss, never accurately ascertained, has been estimated at as high as 2000, and as low as 300. It was probably about 150 killed, and 400 wounded, out of the 2000 men who appear to have been engaged in the forts; and, doubtless, there were many further casualties among the troops who were to the rear of the works.

That night the ships repaired damages, and swept the forts and harbour with their search-lights, in order to prevent the Egyptians from working, or from using mines and torpedoes. The morning of the 12th was windy and gloomy. The dead were committed to

[1] The two fatally hit were Lieut. Francis Sydney Jackson, and Carpenter Wm. Shannon.

[2] Including Mids. Walter Lumsden.

[3] Among these was Lieut. Francis Harvey Davies.

the sea; but, although the *Achilles*, armoured battleship, Captain Edward Kelly, had arrived, little else could be done until the weather moderated. When that -happened the *Inflexible* and *Téméraire* fired a few shots into Pharos and Ada, whereupon a flag of truce was hoisted. The Admiral sent his Flag-Lieutenant, the Hon. Hedworth Lambton, in the *Bittern*, to receive the surrender of the forts; but, the governor refusing to give them up, it was announced that the bombardment would be renewed; and, at 4 P.M., a shot was fired at Pharos. Immediately another white flag was hoisted. The day was so far advanced that Sir Beauchamp decided to postpone further operations until the 13th. The *Helicon*, however, steamed into the harbour, and, though she found no one with whom to treat, returned to the fleet with about 170 refugees. When, on the following morning, a reconnoitring party landed, it was found that all the works had been abandoned.

The damage done to the ships was small. The *Inflexible* was the most injured. Besides being somewhat mauled aloft, and having her unarmoured parts penetrated in various places, she was struck outside the citadel below the water-line by a 10-in. rifle shot,[1] which glanced upwards, passed through the deck, killed Carpenter Shannon, and mortally wounded Lieutenant Jackson, who was directing the fire from a 20-pr. on the superstructure. It was necessary to dock her. The *Monarch* and *Téméraire* were untouched. The *Alexandra* had twenty-four hits from shot or shell outside her armour, and was struck, in all, about sixty times. The *Sultan* had a plate dented and started on the water-line, four boats damaged, a shot through one funnel, and another through the mainmast. The *Invincible* had several dents on her armour, and was penetrated more than once outside of it. The *Superb* was badly hit, just above the water-line and belt, by a shell, which burst and blew a hole ten feet long and four feet wide. She also had two other holes, one near her fore torpedo-port on the port side, and another on the port side abaft the battery. The *Penelope* was hulled eight times. One shot, entering the battery and striking the engine-room hatch-coaming, fell into the engine-room, but was caught on the grating. One of her guns on the port side had its muzzle chipped, but could still be fired. The armour in all cases afforded considerably better protection in action than on the proving

---

[1] A Palliser shot. In the course of its career it struck an iron bollard, base first, and impressed its maker's name on it. It also wrecked the Captain's cabin.

grounds, and it was not penetrated. As for the ships themselves, all were perfectly in condition to re-engage on the following day.[1]

It was supposed at first that the forts had suffered very severely indeed from the fire of the ships; but, especially after they had been carefully inspected by the Royal Engineers, it appeared that they had by no means been crushed, and that they were capable of being easily repaired, and quickly fought again. Some of the guns had been capsized by their own recoil, owing either to the defective nature of their mountings, or to their having been improperly handled; but only 10 out of the 44 rifled guns had been silenced by the fire of the fleet. Briefly summarised, the effect of the bombardment of the forts was as follows:—

Fort Silsileh, a regular fort, chiefly of earthwork, had been not much engaged, and had suffered little.

Fort Pharos, a masonry work with casemates, had had several of its casemates riddled and choked. Three guns and carriages were wrecked, and others were masked by fallen débris. One gun on the reverse face had been carried away, and pitched upon its muzzle into the ditch, thirty feet off. Five out of six of its heavier rifled guns were, however, capable of being still worked.

Fort Ada, an earthwork riveted with masonry, was cut about, but its parapets were not materially damaged. Three guns had been struck and put out of action; yet, but for the havoc wrought by the explosion of the magazine, the work might have gone on firing.

Ras el Tin lines, from the Hospital battery on the east, to Ras el Tin Fort, or the Lighthouse Fort, on the west, were constructed of masonry and earth. These lines and their forts had fought more stubbornly than any other part of the defences, and had been badly mauled, but no guns had been actually disabled in the lines, though some had been struck. In the Hospital Battery the fronts of the embrasures were destroyed, and the guns laid bare, but although one of the weapons bore as many as forty-nine marks of shrapnel, none had been materially damaged. In Ras el Tin Fort, three guns had been dismounted, but not disabled by the ships. One gun had turned over and crushed its gunners.

Fort Saleh Aga, a work insignificant except that it had a command of 60 feet, had a 6·5-in. smooth-bore dismounted.

Fort Oom el Kubebe, a masonry and earthwork, with good profile, and a command of 80 feet, also had a 6·5-in. smooth-bore dismounted. The heavy shells from the *Inflexible* had caused much damage to the parapet.

Fort Kamaria was untouched, and appears never to have engaged.

The Mex lines, with an extreme command of about 25 feet, had their guns firing *en barbette* over earthen parapets from 15 to 18 feet thick. One, if not two of the guns, had been dismounted by the fire of the fleet.

Fort Mex, with 22 feet of command, also had its guns *en barbette*, with unriveted earth parapets. These last were hardly injured, but the buildings in rear of them were swept away. Three guns were struck by shells, and put out of action; others bore marks of machine-gun and shrapnel bullets.

Fort Marsa was an impotent work.

Fort Marabout, attacked only by the gunboats, had no guns put out of action.

---

[1] Desps.: 'Nav. Annual,' 1886: Farret, 'Ops. de Guerre Marit.' 47: 'Journal of R.U.S.I.,' xxvii., 200: Private journals: Corr. of the *Times*, etc.

The large shells, it was found, had produced remarkably little effect against the earthworks. Many burst prematurely, and many others did not burst at all. Some even split on striking, and did not burst in spite of it. An unexploded 8-in. shell from the *Penelope* was found in an Egyptian magazine which contained 400 tons of powder. Apart from all that, the amount of ammunition expended was incommensurate with the results attained. The two ships, the *Inflexible* and *Téméraire*, which had guns that were worked hydraulically, seem to have made, upon the whole, the best shooting.

Let it be admitted that the bombardment of Alexandria was no very brilliant or dangerous exploit. The place was not a Toulon, or a Cherbourg; its defenders were, for the most part, not highly trained; five-sixths of its guns were obsolete; and the operations of the attack were not impeded, as they would have been before many another fortress, by the presence of mines, or by the moral effect of the vicinity of torpedo boats. The Egyptians had plenty of mines, no fewer than 87 of 250 or 500 lbs., and 500 of 100 lbs, being afterwards found in the magazines; but, owing to causes already noted, they were unable to lay them down. Again, the numerous mortars mounted in the works were but little employed, and were fired without skill or discretion. A 13-in. shell dropped on the deck of any ship engaged would probably have put her out of action, and might have been fatal to her; for, of the eight ironclads, only three, the *Inflexible, Alexandra*, and *Téméraire*, had any armoured decks at all, and those had comparatively weak ones. In face of well served mortars, it would certainly have been extremely risky for the ships to anchor, as some of them did.

One of the most suggestive accounts of the bombardment is to be found in the report[1] which was furnished to Washington by Lieutenant-Commander Caspar F. Goodrich, of the United States Navy, who witnessed it. The main conclusions, other than some of those already formulated, of this able and observant officer, were that :—

Command is important for forts.
Thirty feet of earth stops all projectiles.
Embrasures should be cut deep below the crest.
No non-disappearing guns should be mounted *en barbette*.
Guns should be painted the same colour as the works.
Flat-trajectory guns are not the best for attacking earthworks.
Some ships should carry howitzers.

---

[1] 'Information from Abroad,' iii.

Vertical fire is important against earthworks, and should be studied.
Disappearing guns, firing *en barbette*, are very efficient.
Projectiles not specially aimed at guns or magazines are thrown away.
Ships do not fight on even terms with forts ; yet
Forts cannot stop ships.[1]
Opposed to forts, ships gain more than they lose by anchoring.
In a heavy swell, broadside guns are not as accurate as axially mounted ones.

There is much to be said in favour of nearly all these conclusions ; and I do not know that anything has since occurred to modify the majority of them.   But it is impossible to agree that, looking to the manner in which accuracy of fire was improved in the last years of the nineteenth century, and to the means which may be adopted by a vigilant enemy for judging ranges in front of a permanent position, ships have any right to anchor before forts.   Indeed, even when under way, ships before forts are always exposed to extreme risks, if the defenders have adopted such precautions as are open to them. At Kagosima, in 1863, Captain Josling, and Commander Wilmot were killed just when the *Euryalus* was close to a target which had been laid out by the Japanese, and of which, no doubt, they knew the exact range.

If Sir Beauchamp Seymour had been only slightly mistaken in his estimate of the nature of the defences, and of the capacity of the people who manned them, he would scarcely have escaped without very serious loss.   The attack of a place such as Alexandria can be conducted prudently only by such methods as were afterwards pursued by the Japanese during their war with China in 1894.   The function of a fleet before a naval fortress of any pretensions seems to be to hold the nut while forces landed on each side of it close and crack it.

The official Egyptian account of the engagement ought not to be omitted.   It runs :—

"On Tuesday, Shaban 25th, 1299, at 12 o'clock in the morning, the English opened fire on the forts of Alexandria, and we returned the fire.   At 10 A.M. an iron-clad foundered off Fort Ada.   At noon, two vessels were sunk between Fort Pharos and Fort Adjemi.   At 1.30 a wooden man-of-war of eight guns was sunk.   At 5 P.M. a large ironclad was struck by a shell from Fort Pharos, her battery was injured, and a white flag was immediately hoisted by her as a signal to cease firing, whereupon the firing ceased on both sides, having lasted for ten hours without cessation.   Some of the walls of the forts were destroyed, but they were repaired during the night. The shot and shell discharged by the two sides amounted to about 6000; and this is the first time so large a number of missiles has been discharged in so short a period.

[1] This was often demonstrated during the operations at Rio de Janeiro, 1893-4.

"At 11 A.M. on Wednesday the English ships again opened fire, and were replied to by the forts.; but after a short time the firing ceased on both sides, and a deputation came from Admiral Seymour, and made propositions to Toulba Pasha which he would not accept. No soldiers ever stood so firmly to their posts under a heavy fire as did the Egyptian under the fire of twenty-eight ships during ten hours. At 9 A.M. on Thursday an English man-of-war was seen to put a small screw in place of the large one which she had been using; and it was then known that her screw had been carried away by a shot from the forts. On examining other ships, it was observed that eight had been severely battered on their sides, and that one had lost her funnel."

Various honours were granted for this in conjunction with the subsequent work done by the Navy in Egypt. For the bombardment of Alexandria alone the following executive promotions were made, as from the day of the action :—

To be Captains: Commanders George Weightman Hand, Charles John Balfour Lord Charles William Delapoer Beresford, Albert Baldwin Jenkings, and Alan Brodrick Thomas.

To be Commanders: Lieutenants Hugh Cuthbert Dudley Ryder, Edward Payne, Arthur Herbert Boldero, Duke Arthur Crofton, William Codrington Carnegie Forsyth, William Llewellyn Morrison, William Harvey Pigott, Henry John May, Barton Rose Bradford.

To be Lieutenants: Sub-Lieutenants Charles Eustace Anson, Herbert Willoughby Meredith, George Frederick Godfrey Purvis, George Sarsfield Walsh, William Henry du Caurroy Chads, Robert Burlton Abdy, Reginald Ambrose Cave-Brown-Cave, Norman Burgoyne Youel, Norman Godfrey Macalister.

Several other officers were noted for promotion.

For some time after the bombardment the Navy continued to take a conspicuous share in controlling the course of events, not only in and near Alexandria, but also in other parts of Lower Egypt. Seymour, however, was cruelly hampered, especially at the outset, by the impossibility of putting ashore a force strong enough to undertake operations on any but the most modest scale. The authorities at home had failed to make adequate provision for the occupation of a large city, and the management of a turbulent mixed population; and the consequences were not creditable to the foresight of the British Government, though they did no small honour to the British bluejacket and his officers.

On July 13th the *Invincible, Penelope, Monarch, Condor, Beacon,* and *Bittern* steamed into harbour, and the Admiral landed from them a detachment of 150 bluejackets and 450 Royal Marines to keep some kind of order in the place. The city was still burning, partly as the result of the bombardment, partly in consequence of incendiary fires which had been lighted by released convicts. It was supposed, moreover, to be mined on an extensive scale, so that the streets were regarded as extremely unsafe. The guns in several batteries were spiked; the Khedive's palace at Ras el Tin was garrisoned; and efforts were made to clear the streets. On the following day, when a number of additional Marines had been disembarked for police duties, the *Penelope*, with Rear-Admiral Anthony Hiley Hoskins on board, left for Port Said.[1] The Khedive was visited by Seymour and some civilian officers, and invited to go on board one of the warships; but he preferred to remain at Ras el Tin. By the evening all the most important positions in the city had been taken possession of, though the available men were, of course, far too few to hold them properly, and, indeed, too few to repress at once the looting and continued incendiarism that prevailed. Captain Fisher was in command of all the British naval forces ashore, and, with small means, accomplished wonders. On the 15th, when the senior American officer on the spot had landed a number of his marines to assist in the restoration of order, these, and the British naval police, were placed in charge of Commander Lord Charles Beresford, who rendered very sterling service. The Americans, as usual, co-operated in the most loyal and friendly fashion with the British. In consequence, apparently, of the example set by them, the senior naval officers of one or two other nationalities also offered to land men; and their offers were gratefully accepted.

In the meantime Arabi and the Egyptian forces had withdrawn without the city, and, upon the whole, neither they nor the tribes-men caused much trouble, though, on one occasion, about 150 Bedouins, bent probably upon looting, appeared close to the Gabari gate. When, however, Midshipman Eustace William Clitherow Stracey,[2] at the head of twelve bluejackets, attacked them, and killed two, the rest fled, the Egyptian army not attempting to intervene. Lieutenant Charles Eustace Anson, of the *Helicon*, was employed on another occasion to destroy the railway line above Mallaha Junction, the station at which was garrisoned without opposition; and, on the 17th, when Commander Eustace Downman Maude, of the *Téméraire*, with four bluejackets and four men of the Khedive's Guard, rode towards Kafr-dawar, and within 300 yards of Arabi's lines, he found all quiet. Had the Egyptian

---

[1] *Times* of July 14 and 15, containing telegs. from Seymour, etc. Hoskins seems to have returned, and to have gone again to Port Said on Aug. 16.

[2] Of the *Alexandra*.

general maintained an actively offensive attitude, the difficulties of the British officers in Alexandria would have been greatly increased in those early days. While he lay almost inactive, reinforcements arrived, and he lost such chances as he may have had at first.

On July 17th, the ironclads *Agincourt*,[1] Captain Elibank Harley Murray (flag of Rear-Admiral Sir Francis William Sullivan), and *Northumberland*,[1] Captain George Stanley Bosanquet, and the despatch vessel *Salamis*,[1] Commander Frederick Ross Boardman, together with the troopship *Tamar*, Captain Thomas Harvey Royse, reached the scene; and a stream of much-needed troops began to pour into Alexandria. The reliefs enabled most of the disembarked bluejackets to be recalled to their ships on the 18th, though the Marines, of course, remained ashore, and their strength there was increased. The Navy, moreover, continued to take charge of the town, Major-General Sir Archibald Alison,[2] who had been sent out, commanding the army which at length was assembling. The naval officers holding the most responsible positions in Alexandria, under the Admiral, were Captain Hotham (Chief of the Staff), Captain Edward Kelly, of the *Achilles* (Head of the Transport Service), Captain Fisher (Chief of the Naval Brigade), Commander Lord Charles Beresford (Chief of Police), and Paymaster James Edward Stanton, of the *Invincible* (Head of the Commissariat). Immense keenness and energy were displayed by all ranks and ratings. Captain Wilson, of the *Hecla*, who landed for the purpose at Mex, and then moved along the coast, destroyed about 100 guns in the seaward defences, and Lieutenant William Harvey Pigott, of the *Inflexible*, mounted the damaged lighthouse at great risk, and relighted the lamp in it, though, with the seaman who accompanied him, he found it impossible to descend unaided from the tower, and had to wait there until he could be rescued. As for the Marines, who, during the earlier part of the occupation, were under Major Joseph Philips, of the *Alexandra*, they were insatiable, working on many occasions until they were absolutely

---

[1] Detached from the Channel Squadron. The other ships detached from the Channel Squadron were the *Achilles*, which had reached Alexandria immediately after the bombardment, and the *Minotaur* (flag of Vice-Adm. Wm. Montagu Dowell, senior officer), Captain John Fellowes. Vice-Adm. Dowell became, therefore, second in command in the Mediterranean, Rear-Adm. Sullivan being third, and Rear-Adm. Hoskins fourth. The last had been specially appointed on July 7, 1882, and hoisted his flag in the *Penelope* upon his arrival.

[2] Sub-Lieut. James Erskine, of the *Helicon*, was attached to Alison as naval A.D.C.

exhausted.[1] It was during this period of the campaign that Captain Fisher, assisted by Lieutenant Richard Poore, devised and improvised an armoured train which at once became exceedingly useful for reconnoitring purposes, and which seems to have been first employed in action on July 28th.[2] In a skirmish near Ramleh, four days earlier, a couple of naval guns took part; and these, or two other naval 9-prs., were subsequently posted on the high ground eastward of the palace to defend the ridge east of the city. They were commanded first by Captain Alan Brodrick Thomas, and, after July 29th, by Commander Tynte Ford Hammill. On the 29th Captain Fisher and Lieutenant the Hon. Hedworth Lambton, with 300 Marines, 2 Nordenfelt machine-guns, and a 9-pr., accompanied Sir Archibald Alison on a railway reconnaissance from Gabari Station.[3] It was on the 29th, also, that Midshipman Dudley Rawson De Chair, of the *Alexandra*, while carrying dispatches between Ras et Tin and Ramleh, lost his way, and fell into the hands of the rebels, near Siouf.[4] He was well treated by Arabi Pasha, but liberated only upon the occupation of Cairo by the British Army. Mex forts were occupied on August 2nd by Marines from the *Inconstant*, *Superb*, and *Achilles*, under Lieut.-Colonel Frederick Gasper Le Grand.[5] A considerable force of both arms of that invaluable and historic corps had arrived, in the interim, from England, and subsequently, as will be seen, distinguished itself greatly.

While preparations were being made for grappling with the Egyptian rebellion from the Mediterranean side, the Navy also secured a foothold and a shore base on the Red Sea coast of Egypt. Rear-Admiral Sir William Nathan Wrighte Hewett, V.C., Commander-in-Chief in the East Indies, had come westward with a portion of his squadron, and, on August 2nd, learning that Suez was in danger of being burnt, he disembarked several hundred Marines, and occupied the town. No resistance was offered, the Egyptian troops fleeing at once. The vessels which contributed the landing force were the corvettes *Euryalus* (flag), Captain Alexander Plantagenet Hastings, *Ruby*, Captain Charles Edward

---

[1] *Times*, July, 18, 19, 22.

[2] On that day there were still ashore, under Capt. Fisher, 900 Marines and 850 seamen.

[3] *Times*, July 31. When, two days later, Fisher relinquished some of his shore duties, the Khedive sent for him, and complimented him on his services.

[4] *Times*, Aug. 1.   [5] *Times*, Aug. 3.

Foot, and *Eclipse*, Captain Edmund St. John Garforth, and the sloop *Dragon*, Commander Edward Grey Hulton.[1]

The armoured train had a busy day on August 4th, when it accompanied a strong reconnaissance to Mallaha Junction, and there came into contact with Arabi's outposts. Upon returning to Gabari Station, the train took on board Captain Arthur Knyvet Wilson, of the *Hecla*, and one of his 40-pr. Armstrong breech-loaders, and steamed to the Mex lines. There the gun was disembarked, and employed with extraordinary success against the Mariout earthworks, distant about 6000 yards. In the evening, Admiral Seymour and Rear-Admiral Sullivan used the train to make a further inspection of Arabi's lines to the eastward. On the day following the train, for the first time, was seriously engaged.

On the 5th it steamed out under Captain Fisher at about 4 P.M. On board were Sir Archibald Alison, Admiral Seymour, Lieut.-Colonel Henry Brasnell Tuson, R.M.A., Major Henry Harford Strong, R.M.L.I., Commander Reginald Friend Hannam Henderson, Lieutenants the Hon. Hedworth Lambton, and Richard Poore, Major Joseph Philips, R.M.L.I., and Midshipmen Edward Ernest Hardy, and E. W. C. Stracey. A train followed with 700 men of the Marine battalion. In conjunction with the railway expedition a military force[2] acted from Ramleh. Apart from that, 200 blue-jackets, and 1000 Marines, in all, with one 40-pr., and two 9-prs., were engaged, the naval contingent being drawn from the *Invincible*, *Inflexible*, *Alexandra*, *Inconstant*, *Hecla*, and *Helicon*.

Within about 800 yards of Mallaha Junction, the Marines detrained, formed up under cover of the railway embankment, and then advanced. The enemy's vedettes quickly appeared on the left front, the 40-pr. opened on them, and, when a company of Marine Infantry moved forward under Captain Leaver Henry Gascoyne Cross, R.M., the Egyptians were subjected to a brisk rifle fire. Cross was supported by another company under Captain Edward Berry Byrch, R.M. The 40-pr. quickly dislodged the enemy, whereupon a company of Marine Artillery, under Major Andrew Donald, R.M.A., occupied the Egyptian entrenchments. Donald was supported by a company of Marine Infantry under

---

[1] From Suez, on Aug. 8th, departed Lieut. Harold Charrington, of the *Euryalus*, with Capt. Gill, R.E., and Prof. Palmer, to make arrangements with the Arabs for the supply of camels. All three were murdered by the Bedouins.

[2] 60th Rifles and part of 38th and 46th Regts.

Captain Robert Walker Heathcote, R.M., who took up a position in extension of Donald's left. At 6.30 P.M., daylight failing, and the General's object having apparently been accomplished, the men began to be withdrawn; whereupon the Egyptians commenced an extremely galling fire upon the British right. The Marines instantly faced round, and retired company by company, the units supporting one another as each fell back. The operation was very well performed; and the whole day's work of the seamen and Marines elicited high praise from Sir Archibald Alison, who afterwards visited their barracks. Six prisoners were taken. The casualties of the Marines and Brigade in this affair were 1 Marine killed, 12 Marines wounded; 1 seaman killed, 4 seamen wounded.[1] The number of the enemy engaged was about 2000, with 6 guns, and 6 rocket-tubes. The armoured train continued to make reconnaissances of this kind;[2] but the value of them was considered to be doubtful, as the positions taken were never held, and no immediate objects seemed to be served.

In the meantime a number of Bedouins were seen to be employed upon some earthworks east and south of Ramleh. Accordingly, on the afternoon of August 8th, the *Superb* weighed, and, steaming down the coast, shelled them, and drove the labourers away. At night the ship's searchlights were turned upon the shore; but the chief effect of them was to confuse the British pickets. Searchlights, indeed, are of but little value except to observers posted behind or in the neighbourhood of the projectors. In the early days of their introduction, they were often employed, especially during manoeuvres, in such a way as to be a positive source of danger to their users and their users' friends.

On August 11th, the greater part of the Naval Brigade was recalled to the fleet, two 9-prs., and two Gatling machine-guns, with their crews, being, however, left with the army. General H.R.H. the Duke of Connaught, who had arrived on the 10th, caused great satisfaction by requesting' that the Royal Marines might form part of his brigade. On August 12th, when, by the way, the foreign landing-parties were all re-embarked, a party from the *Hecla* distinguished itself by destroying a quantity of

---

Adml's. and Genl's. desps.; and *Times*, Aug. 7. The First Lord, in the Queen's name, subsequently cabled thanks.

[2] *E.g.*, on Aug. 9 and Aug. 14. On the latter day, when it moved towards Mex, it was fired upon by the enemy, of whom it killed or wounded about 20.

gun-cotton while exposed, during some minutes, to a smart fire from the enemy.

General Sir Garnet Wolseley, who, with Lieut.-General Sir John Adye as chief of his staff, had been appointed to the supreme military command in Egypt, and who reached the scene of action at about this time, had decided not to use Alexandria as his base of operations against Cairo, but to advance instead from Ismailia, a port on the Suez Canal nearly midway between Port Said and Suez. The expeditionary force, however, consisting of about 17,000 troops of all arms,[1] made preliminary rendezvous at Alexandria, while Rear-Admirals Hewett and Hoskins took the necessary measures to secure the Canal and the desired base, a misleading demonstration being made simultaneously in the direction of Aboukir.

Under Hoskins's direction, Captain Fairfax, of the *Monarch*, occupied Port Said, and Captain Robert O'Brien FitzRoy, of the ironclad *Orion*, occupied Ismailia on August 20th.

At Port Said no difficulties were experienced. At 3.30 A.M. on that day a party of 216 seamen and 276 Marines,[2] with 2 Gatling machine-guns, landed in silence under Captains Fairfax, and Edward Hobart Seymour (*Iris*). The Egyptian troops in the barracks were surrounded, and seamen were posted right across the isthmus, from Lake Menzaleh to the sea. The troops surrendered immediately. Captain Seymour then seized the Canal Company's office, so as to prevent the alarm from being transmitted thence to other stations.[3]

At Ismailia there was more trouble. The landing-force consisted of 565 officers and men, drawn from the *Orion*, and the *Northumberland*, from the corvette *Carysfort*, Captain Henry Frederick Stephenson, and from the gunboat *Coquette*, Lieutenant Lenox Napier, with a 7-pr. and 2 Gatlings. The European part of the town was occupied in silence, and without fighting; but some skirmishing took place in the Arab quarter, and it was found necessary to shell certain guard-houses. In the meantime, too, a large body of the enemy collected at Nefiche station, other troops coming thither from Tel el Kebir, and preparing to attack Ismailia.

---

[1] Besides an Indian contingent of about 7000 men.

[2] From the ironclad *Monarch*, and the cruiser *Iris*, with a few from the ironclad *Northumberland*.

[3] Royle, 144.

When, however, the *Orion* and *Carysfort*, from their positions
in the Canal, opened fire at about 4000 yards, the concentration
was checked, although the Egyptian position was visible only
from the corvette's mast-head, and every gun had to be aimed
by means of bearings taken from that point of vantage. To
enable the *Orion's* guns to be given the requisite elevation, the
ironclads port boilers had been emptied and her projectiles shifted,
so as to give the ship a list to starboard. When, at length, she
burst a shell under a train which was bringing up reinforcements,
the Egyptians, who by that time had had enough of it, abandoned
Nefiche.[1] The corvette *Tourmaline*, Captain Robert Peel Dennistoun, the gun-vessel *Ready*, Commander Herbert Holden Edwards,
and the gunboat *Dee*, Lieutenant Frank Archdall Harston, were
sent promptly by Hoskins to FitzRoy's support, with a reinforcement of 340 Marines, but do not seem to have been needed. In
this affair Commander Henry Coey Kane, of the *Northumberland*,
was wounded.

During the previous night, that of the 19th, all the dredgers
and barges in the Canal, the Company's telegraph system, and the
village of Kantara, had been seized by a force of 100 officers and
men acting under direction of Commander Edwards, of the *Ready*;
so that by the afternoon of the 20th the Canal and all its machinery
were in British hands. M. de Lesseps, on behalf of the Company,
made vigorous protests, and was, to some slight extent, backed up
by his compatriots; but, in the circumstances, he could not be
listened to. Eventually he consoled himself by bringing ridiculous
charges of barbarism against Captain FitzRoy,[2] whom he compared unfavourably with Arabi Pasha.

The Canal having been secured, the gun-vessels *Beacon*, Commander William Frederick Stanley Mann, and *Falcon*, Commander
John Eliot Pringle, the dispatch-vessel *Helicon*, Lieutenant Alfred
Leigh Winsloe, and the special service vessel *Stormcock*, entered
it to undertake patrol and other duties; and on August 21st, the
waterway was temporarily closed to all vessels save those under
the orders of the British Government. The Dutch Hotel, commanding the Port Said entrance to the Canal, was purchased for
£78,000, and occupied by two companies of seamen from the
Monarch, under Commander Hammill, and Lieutenants William
Crawford Reid, and Thomas Henry Fisher, and by three com-

[1] Royle, 137.   [2] *Times*, esp. of Sept. 5 and 6.

panies of Marines drawn respectively from the *Monarch*, the *Inflexible*, and the *Alexandra*.

From the Suez end of the Canal, on August 20th, Captain Hastings, of the *Euryalus*, with seamen and Marines from the gun-vessel *Seagull*, Commander Mather Byles, and the gunboat *Mosquito*, Lieutenant the Hon. Francis Robert Sandilands, and 200 of the 72nd Highlanders, proceeded to Chalouf, where he landed,[1] and defeated 600 of the enemy, capturing a number of prisoners, a small gun, and a quantity of arms, ammunition, and stores.[2] His losses were only 2 Highlanders drowned, and 2 seamen wounded, while the Egyptians had 168 killed.

Previous to the advance of the army from the Canal westwards, the work of the Royal Navy and Royal Marines was chiefly confined to the preservation of order in the Canal, although on several occasions the *Minotaur*, lying in Aboukir Bay, bombarded the enemy's works, and although in the brisk action at Tel el Mahuta, near Ismailia, on August 24th, a creditable part was borne by a detachment of seamen and Marines, with 2 Gatlings, from the *Orion*[3] and *Carysfort*. Marines also took a leading part in the preliminary affair at Kassassin[4] on August 28th.

Preparations for a general movement from Ismailia along the Fresh Water Canal towards Cairo went on steadily, until, at the end of the first week in September a considerable British force was concentrated at Kassassin, where, on the morning of the 9th, the Egyptians attacked again. On that occasion the Marines were on the left of the British line, and, with the King's Royal Rifles, soon began to drive the enemy back. After the Egyptian artillery, which was posted on a ridge, had been shelled, Captain Roger Pine Coffin, R.M.L.I., and Lieutenant Herbert Cecil Money, R.M.L.I., led a successful charge of Marines up the slope, and captured two Krupp guns, whereupon the enemy retired within his earthworks. That day Lieutenant Charles Kennedy Purvis, of the *Penelope*, was wounded while directing the fire of a 40-pr. Armstrong, and was obliged to have a foot amputated. Towards evening the small Naval Brigade at the front was reinforced by 15 officers, 197 seamen, and 6 Gatling machine-guns from the *Téméraire*, *Orion*,

---

[1] The naval landing party was under Lieut. Ebenezer Rae, and Sub-Lieut. Wm. Oswald Story.

[2] *Times*, Sept. 1.   [3] Under Lieut. Gerald Lycidas King-Harman.

[4] On that occasion, Capt. Wm. Guise Tucker, R.M.A., mounted a captured Krupp gun on a railway truck and worked it most effectively against the enemy.

Alexandra, Monarch, Superb, and *Carysfort,* the whole being then under Captain FitzRoy, and numbering about 250 of all ranks and ratings.

For three days longer the concentration at Kassassin continued. Then, on the night of September 12th, Sir Garnet Wolseley moved forward the bulk of his army over the intervening six and a quarter miles, marching in the gloom of a moonless night; and early in the morning of the 13th he surprised Arabi's army in its positions eastward of Tel el Kebir, and, attacking it at once, defeated it with great slaughter.

The Naval Brigade on that day moved along the railway. A battalion of Royal Marine Artillery,[1] under Lieut.-Colonel Henry Brasnell Tuson, and another of Royal Marine Light Infantry, under Lieut.-Colonels Howard Sutton Jones, and Samuel James Graham, also took part in the action, the latter especially distinguishing itself. It formed the left of Major General Graham's (2nd) brigade of Lieut.-General Willis's (1st) division. After a long march, the brigade, as dawn was breaking, found itself 1200 yards from the front of the northern portion of the Tel el Kebir lines, but, having mistaken its way in the darkness, it was facing in the wrong direction. While a change of front was being effected the enemy opened fire, and ere the brigade was properly formed the fire had become heavy. Lieut.-Colonel Jones sent forward three companies into the firing line, and kept three in support, and two more in reserve, and so attacked over ground which afforded absolutely no cover. But the men moved forward with extraordinary steadiness, mounted the glacis, and reserved their fire until they were within little more than 100 yards of the ditch. The reserves, under Lieut.-Colonel Graham, then came up, and the whole force dashed into the ditch with a cheer, scrambled over the eight-foot parapet on the other side, and engaged the Egyptians at hand grips. The enemy, after a brief resistance, broke and fled, and was pursued for about four miles. The casualties in the Light Infantry battalion were; killed, Major Henry Harford Strong, Captain John Charles Wardell, one non-commissioned officer, and 10 men; wounded, Captains Roger Pine Coffin, and Leaver Henry Gascoyne Cross, Lieutenants John Hulke Plumbe, and Edwin Loftus McCausland, and 43 men. Lieutenant Wyatt Rawson, R.N., who was acting as naval A.d.C. to Sir Garnet Wolseley, was

---

[1] Employed as Sir G. Wolseley's bodyguard.

mortally wounded. He had undertaken to guide part of the force
during the night by means of the stars. "Did I not lead them
straight?" he asked the commander-in-chief, who rode back to
visit him. He was specially promoted to the rank of Commander,
but died on the 21st.[1]

The Naval Brigade was withdrawn to the ships on September 16th,
and the gallant Marines saw no more fighting, for Tel el Kebir had
been the decisive battle of the campaign. On September 19th and
20th, Vice-Admiral Dowell, who lay meanwhile in Aboukir Bay,
landed a force of Marines, under Major Arthur French, R.M.A.,
of the *Minotaur*, and occupied the forts there. On the 21st, a
blockade of the Damietta mouth of the Nile was established by
the *Iris, Beacon,* and *Decoy* ; but the operation was almost needless,
for the Damietta forts surrendered on the 23rd without opposition,
and a few days later the last sparks of Arabi's rebellion had
flickered out.

The naval honours granted in respect of this campaign were
gazetted, for the most part on August 14th, and November 17th,
1882, and included the following :—

> To Adm. Sir F. P. B. Seymour, G.C.B., a peerage, as Baron Alcester.
> To Vice-Adm. W. M. Dowell, C.B., and Rear-Adm. A. H. Hoskins, C.B. (Nov. 17),
> and to Capt. W. J. Hunt-Grubbe (Aug. 14), the K.C.B.
> To Capts. T. Le H. Ward, St. G. C. D'Arcy-Irvine, H. Fairfax,[2] H. F. Nicholson,
> C. F. Hotham, R. H. M. Molyneux, and J. A. Fisher, and Dept. Insp.-Genl.
> Doyle Money Shaw (Aug. 14), and to Capts. R. O'B. FitzRoy, Harry
> Holdsworth Rawson[3] and A. P. Hastings; Chf. Insp. of Mach. James Roffey,
> Colonels H. S. Jones, R.M.L.I., and H. B. Tuson, R.M.A., and Lieut.-Col.
> S. J. Graham, R.M.L.I. (Nov. 17), the C.B.

In addition to the promotions which had been dated July 11th
in recognition of the bombardment of Alexandria, the following,
among other advancements, were made on November 18th, 1882 :—

> To be Captains, Coms. M. Byles, H. H. Edwards, and H. C. Kane.
> To be Commanders, Lieuts. Wm. Wilson, Lenox Napier, Geo. Hy. Moore,[4] Jno.
> Edric Blaxland, Edw. Chichester,[4] Alex. Cook, Chas. Jas. Norcock, Gerald
> Chas. Langley, Hon. Fras. Robt. Sandilands, and Chas. K. Purvis.
> To be Staff Commanders, Nav.-Lieuts. Hy. Emilius Wood and Jno. Baker Palmer.
> To be Chief Engineers, Geo. Swinney, Wm. Thos. Hy. Bills, and Geo. Rigler.
> To be Staff Surgeons, Surgs. Chas. Cane Godding, Herb. Mackay Ellis, and Evelyn
> Rd. Hugh Pollard.
> To be Colonels in the Army, Lt.-Cols. H. B. Tuson and H. S. Jones, R.M.

---

[1] *Times*, and Desps.; Journ. of R.U.S. Inst., *Standard, A. & N. Gaz.*
[2] Mil. He had been made a Civ. C.B. in 1879.
[3] Rawson served as Principal Transport Officer.   [4] Transport Offrs.

Before giving any account of the operations which, in 1883 and later, were rendered necessary by the fact that, after Arabi's rebellion, Great Britain assumed responsibility for the management of the affairs of Egypt, it will be convenient to glance at some useful and interesting work which was done by the Navy on other parts of the coast of Africa.

In virtue of an obscure clause in an agreement dating from the days of Richelieu, France for many years had taken a special interest in the affairs of the island of Madagascar, the whole of which, indeed, she formally annexed in 1896. In 1883, however, when first she adopted a forward policy in her dealings with the island, and when she sent a Commissary of the Republic, M. Baudais, to advance her interests on the spot, her ambitions seemed to limit themselves to the occupation of certain points on the coast. In the spring of that year Rear-Admiral Pierre bombarded and took possession of the villages in Ampassandava Bay, the Hova fort of Amorantsanga, and the customs' house and town of Majunga ; and on May 31st he arrived off Tamatave. On the day following he made demands on the part of the French government, and declared that, unless they should be complied with by midnight on June 9th, he would adopt hostile measures.

At that time Mr. Pakenham, the British Consul at Tamatave, was dying.[1] His successor had not been appointed, and, consequently, Commander Charles Johnstone, of the sloop *Dryad*, took upon himself to assume the post of acting British Consul, in order to watch over the local interests of his countrymen. He removed the consular records on board his ship.

Two days later, Rear-Admiral Pierre issued a notice to the effect that French subjects and foreign consuls (after having hauled down their flags on shore) would be received in his vessels, and that otherwise he would not be responsible for their safety. This caused something like a panic in the town ; and on June 7th Commander Johnstone deemed it desirable to land a guard of 19 Marines for the protection of the consulate, and to put the *Dryad's* steam cutter and pinnace at the disposal of such persons as might desire to take refuge in the sloop. For this purpose the boats lay near the landing-place.

On June 9th the French consul was handed a refusal of the ultimatum ; and he embarked at once on board the French flagship

[1] He died on June 22nd.

Flore. On the 10th the town was bombarded by the *Flore* and the *Forfait,* and set fire to in various places; but the British guard, assisted by a few Europeans, succeeded in staying the progress of the most serious conflagration, which broke out in the market-place. Nevertheless, Rear-Admiral Pierre had the hardihood to declare that that particular fire had been caused by an incendiary, and that, since Johnstone had landed a guard, he must be held responsible for the outbreak.

The Hovas, acting on British advice, did not reply to the French guns, and evacuated the fort early on the 10th; but it was not until the morning of the 12th that the French put ashore any force capable of keeping order in the place. This force behaved in a tyrannical manner, and, among other outrages, arrested Mr. Shaw, an agent of the London Missionary Society, on a ridiculous charge of having harboured spies, and drugged wine which he gave to French soldiers. Meanwhile, the *Dryad's* officers and crew were forbidden to communicate with the shore, and the sloop *Dragon,* Commander Edward Alverne Bolitho, which had arrived on the 10th, was ordered into quarantine, apparently without adequate excuse. Not until July 28th did the rear-admiral permit the foreign consuls to resume the exercise of their functions; and during great part of the interval the tension between Pierre and Johnstone was extreme. Ultimately Mr. Shaw, who was released when the charges brought against him were proved to be baseless, was paid an indemnity of £1000 by the French government.[1]

The episode was a most extraordinary one, for there is very little doubt that Commander Johnstone, who was deservedly promoted[2] for his services, had to deal with a madman, Pierre's mental condition becoming obvious soon afterwards. Yet, though the French had upon the spot a large frigate-built cruiser of 3500 tons,[3] another cruiser of 2400 tons,[4] and various other vessels of force, Johnstone, with his feeble and ill-armed 1620 ton sloop,[5] reinforced by another sloop of 1130 tons, not only prevented French interference with the mails, and saved much valuable property, but also added to the glory of the flag by resolutely clearing for action in order to prove his readiness to stand up to the death for the

---

[1] *Times,* July 16, July 18, Aug. 25, Sept. 11, etc.: Parl. Paper C. 3838 (1884).

[2] Posted Nov. 21, 1883 : retd. as r.-adm. Jan. 1, 1899.

[3] *Flore.* She carried 22 5·5-in. guns, besides other weapons.

[4] *Forfait.* She carried 15 5·5-in. guns, besides other weapons.

[5] The *Dryad* seems then to have carried 9 64-prs.

rights of his countrymen, undeterred by the overwhelming odds against him. An officer less firm, spirited, and tactful might easily have met with disaster, even if the French officer opposed to him had been free from every suspicion of insanity.

An affair which, unfortunately, involved the loss of British lives took place a few months later on the other side of Africa. There having been trouble with the natives of Igah and Aboh, on the river Niger, Captain Arthur Thomas Brooke, of the *Opal*, left his corvette at the mouth of the stream, and, transferring his pennant to the paddle-vessel *Alecto*, Lieutenant Frank Archdall Harston, proceeded in her to Igah, accompanied by the twin-screw gun-vessel *Flirt*, Commander Robert Frederick Hammick, and the gunboat *Starling*, Lieutenant Francis William Sanders. The *Opal's* steam-cutter, under Sub-Lieutenant Alexander Ludovic Duff, and one of her pulling-boats were also with the expedition. Brooke met the chiefs on October 25th. The natives, however, showed hostility, and the chiefs, upon being required to disperse them, refused, whereupon the British officer withdrew to his ship.

The natives then opened fire on the vessels, which retaliated by beginning a general bombardment. Later, bluejackets under Hammick and Harston, and a body of Marines under Sanders, landed, and completely destroyed Igah.

On the day following the three ships steamed to Aboh, where a British subject had been ill-treated; and Brooke ordered the local chiefs to assemble for a palaver. The chief who was specially implicated refused to attend. A party under Lieutenants Sanders, and Leslie Creery Stuart (first of the *Opal*) was sent ashore to take charge of the Sierra Leone man whose complaint had brought the expedition to the spot, and Brooke dispatched to the recalcitrant chief a warning that, if he did not go on board the *Alecto*, the town would be shelled. The chief still refused, and, moreover, expressed his willingness to fight. On the 29th, indeed, about four or five thousand natives assembled on the shore, and attacked the various parties which had been landed. After a smart action they were driven back with heavy loss, but not until two seamen of the *Opal* had been killed, and Lieutenant Charles Henry Hodgson Moore, and Midshipman Edward Hay had been wounded, the last fatally.[1]

The course of events in Egypt may now be returned to.

As early as 1881 a religious leader, Mahommed Ahmed, who

[1] *Times*, Nov. 29, 1883; *A. & N. Gaz.* Jan. 19, 1884.

called himself the Mahdi, had attained a commanding position in the Soudan, and had revolted against the Egyptian government. In that year he had destroyed a small force which had been sent to arrest him. In 1882 he had annihilated a much larger force under Yusef Pasha. In 1883 a still larger army, under Hicks Pasha, had been almost totally cut to pieces by the rebels near El Obeid. By that time the Mahdi's [1] authority had extended greatly, and had reached the Red Sea littoral, where the prophet's lieutenant, Osman Digna, an ex-slave dealer of Suakin, raised the local Arabs and invested Sinkat and Tokar. On October 16th, and again on November 4th, 1883, he intercepted and crushed Egyptian reinforcements which were intended for the former town.

It was in consequence of Osman Digna's activity that, in November, 1883, Rear-Admiral [2] Sir William Nathan Wrighte Hewett, V.C., Commander-in-Chief on the East Indies Station, ordered the gun-vessel *Ranger*, Commander William Eveleigh Darwall, to Suakin, to support Egyptian interests. On November 26th, and December 1st, the Suakin forts were attacked by the enemy, and on December 2nd an Egyptian force which had been sent out from the town was annihilated near Tamanieb. For some little time afterwards, the safety of the place depended upon the *Ranger*, which, on December 6th, opened fire with some effect upon the Arabs. [3]

In the meantime it was decided in London and at Cairo temporarily to abandon Kordofan and the Upper Nile; and General Charles George Gordon was ordered to Khartum to give effect to that decision. Valentine Baker Pasha was simultaneously sent to Trinkitat, with 2500 fresh men, and ten British officers, to effect the relief of Sinkat and Tokar. Hewett was given full powers on the Red Sea littoral, and 300 Marines from the Mediterranean fleet were despatched to him, the corvette *Carysfort*, Captain Walter Stewart, and the torpedo-depôt ship *Hecla*, Captain Arthur Knyvet Wilson, being also ordered thence to the threatened spot. On February 4th, 1884, there was a further catastrophe. Baker's heterogeneous force, which was then moving between Trinkitat

---

[1] The activity of the Mahdi caused a certain amount of sympathetic unrest in Egypt proper. In Ap. 1883, the *Iris*, Capt. Ernest Rice, and in Feb., 1884, the *Monarch*, Capt. Fredk. Geo. Denham Bedford, and another vessel, had to land men at Port Said by way of precaution against serious disturbances.

[2] With local rank of Vice-Adm.

[3] *Times*, Nov. 16 and 24: Dec. 10 and 12, 1883.

and Tokar, was routed with terrible loss at El Teb by a numerically inferior body of the enemy.

Upon this, Hewett landed at Suakin 150 seamen and Marines from his flagship, the *Euryalus*, Captain Alexander Plantagenet Hastings, from the *Ranger*, and from the gunboat *Coquette*, Lieutenant Fritz Hauch Eden Crowe, to assist in manning the fortifications; and the British government determined to send a British force, chiefly made up of troops from Egypt and returning drafts from India, under Maj.-General Sir Gerald Graham, to relieve Tokar. Sinkat, unhappily, fell at about the same time, after a gallant defence, its garrison being killed almost to a man.[1]

General Graham, like Baker Pasha, began his march inland from Trinkitat, a coast town a few miles south of Suakin, and utilised in his advance a fort which Baker had constructed, a few bluejackets and Marines being sent ahead to hold it. At 8 A.M. on February 29th, the whole force, about 3900 strong, moved forward, and was soon upon the scene of Baker's defeat. The British marching formation was practically that of a hollow square, with the transport in the centre. Half a battery of the Naval Brigade, with 2 Gatling and 1 Gardner machine-guns, was on the left front under Flag-Lieutenant Walter Hodgson Bevan Graham, of the *Euryalus*; another half battery, with 2 Gardners and 1 Gatling, under Captain Walter Stewart, of the *Carysfort*, was on the right front; and in the rear centre was the bulk of the Brigade,[2] 115 strong, with two 9-prs., under Commander Ernest Neville Rolfe,[3] of the *Euryalus*. With the column were also about 400 Royal Marine Light Infantry and Artillery, under Colonel Henry Brasnell Tuson, R.M.A. Rear-Admiral Hewett, and Commander Crawford Caffin were with General Graham.

At about 11.20 A.M., the enemy, nearly 10,000 in number, and entrenched on rising ground near El Teb, in front of the advance, opened fire as well from musketry as from several Krupp guns, some of which were worked by Egyptian artillerymen who had been made prisoners on the occasion of Baker Pasha's disaster. The position was shelled, and the line of advance was changed in such a manner that the column had passed nearly to the rear of

---

[1] *Times*, Nov. 16, 24, etc., 1883; *A. & N. Gaz.*, Dec. 15, 1883; Feb. 9 and 16, 1884.

[2] From the *Euryalus*, *Carysfort*, *Hecla*, *Briton*, Capt. Andrew James Kennedy, *Dryad*, Com. Edward Grey Hulton, and *Sphinx*, Com. Crawford Caffin.

[3] With Lieut. William Hughes Hallett Montresor, of the *Euryalus*, as adjutant.

the entrenchments ere the final attack took place. Thus the rear of the square became ultimately the face which was nearest to the enemy. It was in the course of this movement that Lieutenant Frank Massie Royds, of the *Carysfort*, was fatally hit. He was taken back to Trinkitat at great risk by a party under Surgeon Thomas Desmond Gimlette, of the *Euryalus*, but died next day.

The tribesmen made repeated and most heroic attempts to rush the square, coming on in dense masses, but being mown down in hundreds at close quarters by machine-gun and rifle fire. At length they were driven back.

Captain Wilson, of the *Hecla*, had attached himself to the right half battery of machine-guns, in place of Lieutenant Royds, and moved out from the square to the attack of the first of the enemy's batteries. At the same moment, the Arabs made a dash upon a corner of the square where a detachment was dragging one of the Gardners. Wilson rushed to the front, endeavouring especially to protect a Marine who was hard pressed, and was at once surrounded by five or six Arabs, who engaged him in personal combat. His sword broke short off, but he continued to fight with his fists and sword-hilt, until some men of the York and Lancaster Regiment intervened with their bayonets. He received a scalp wound, but, after having it dressed, was able to remain with the advance. For this piece of gallantry he was deservedly awarded[1] the Victoria Cross.

The guns in this first battery were captured by 12.20 P.M., and, under the direction of Major William Guise Tucker, R.M.A., were turned at once upon the enemy's second position—a large brick building with loopholed walls, surrounded by rifle-pits. In the capture of this position, the Naval Brigade, headed by Lieutenant W. H. B. Graham, bore a leading part. The village of El Teb was then cleared ; and the last position was rushed at about 2 P.M., two Krupp guns, one Gatling, one brass gun, and two rocket-tubes being captured in it. Thereupon the Arabs fled, after having suffered an estimated loss of 1500 in killed alone. In the assault, both Sir William Hewett and Commander Caffin participated.[2] Besides Lieutenant Royds, three seamen were killed.[3]

In his general order after the action, Sir Gerald Graham wrote :

[1] May 21, 1884.
[2] *Times*, Mar. 3 : Desps. of Hewett, Graham, and Buller : *A. & N. Gaz.* Mar. 8, 1884.
[3] Total British loss, 34 killed, 155 wounded.

"The General Officer thanks the Naval Brigade for their cheerful endurance during the severe work of dragging the guns over difficult country, when suffering from heat and scarcity of water, and for their ready gallantry and steadiness under fire while serving the guns. The Naval Brigade contributed materially to the success of the action, and the General Officer commanding cannot too highly express his thanks for their services."

Among those who were favourably mentioned in the various despatches were Commander Ernest Neville Rolfe, Lieutenants W. H. B. Graham, W. H. H. Montresor, Walter Byrom Almack, Crawford James Markland Conybeare, and Houston Stewart (2); Surgeon T. D. Gimlette; Midshipman Edward Matson Hewett; and Gunner Richard Archibald Cathie, of the *Sphinx*. The last displayed great bravery in personal encounters with the enemy, and was specially thanked both by Rear-Admiral Hewett and by Commander Rolfe. It was in consequence of his admirable conduct on this and other occasions that he received the exceptional recognition of promotion to the rank of Lieutenant in 1887.

The inhabitants of Tokar were relieved on the 30th. The Egyptian garrison of the place had already made terms and surrendered to Osman Digna. The force began its return to Trinkitat on March 2nd, re-embarked[1] for Suakin on March 5th, and completed its disembarkation there on March 9th. The next object to be attained was the dispersal of the Arabs who were beleaguering Sinkat.

The new advance began on the evening of March 11th. At night the force lay in a zeriba about eight miles from Suakin. There information was received to the effect that Osman Digna's army was assembled in Khor Ghob, a ravine between the zeriba and the village of Tamai. At 8.30 A.M. on the 12th the force again moved forward in two echeloned squares, the left and leading one of which, composed of the second brigade, under General J. Davis, comprised the Naval Brigade, which was constituted much as before, though without any contingent from the *Carysfort*. The Naval Brigade marched just behind the front face of the square, and in front of the reserve ammunition. The left front face and left flank were filled by the York and Lancaster Regt., and the right front face and right flank by the Royal Highlanders (42nd). The rear was formed of the Royal Marines.[2] About 4 P.M., being then in touch with the enemy, General Graham, after firing a few

---

[1] Under superintendence of Capt. A. J. Kennedy, of the *Briton*.

[2] The Naval Brigade and Roy. Marines numbered 14 officers and 464 men, with 3 Gardners, and 3 Gatlings.

rounds from his guns, made a second zeriba, whence, at 8.20 A.M.
on the 13th, the advance was resumed. During the night the
sniping had been very troublesome, and the enemy close at hand.
Nevertheless, in the darkness, Commander Rolfe had stolen out,
passed the Arab lines, and secured some very valuable information.
At sunrise the guns and machine-guns had opened on the enemy,
and driven him to his main position. General Graham joined, and
led, the second brigade.

The first, or rearmost brigade, did not get in motion quite so
promptly as had been expected. There was consequently a gap of
unpremeditated breadth between the two squares. Across the line
of advance lay the Khor. A few minutes after starting, the second
brigade was halted, reformed, and moved up towards the edge of
the ravine, beyond which many Arabs could be seen. Some ugly
rushes were made by the Dervishes, but they were stopped ; and
within about 200 yards from the Khor the word was given to charge.

The Naval Brigade, with its guns, and the 42nd, dashed forward
instantly at the double, leaving the York and Lancaster, to which
no order had been given, still holding the left front and flank of the
original square. The guns were already in hot action ; the smoke
hung heavy in the breezeless air ; and, taking advantage of this, a
mass of tribesmen who had lain concealed in a small nullah running
at right angles with the Khor, crept up and rushed upon the York
and Lancasters from behind. Terrible confusion ensued, and the
brigade was broken up, although there was no actual panic. On the
contrary, the troops displayed great gallantry, and presently rallied
round their officers, forming a number of little squares, and fighting
back to back. Major George Harrie Thorn Colwell, R.M., collected
about 150 of his men, and made a most useful stand ; yet the
remnant of the square was driven about 800 yards to the left rear.

In the meantime, the Naval Brigade, which had advanced with
its guns to the verge of the Khor, found itself cut off from its
ammunition, and unable to continue the offensive. The men formed
round their useless pieces and fought desperately ; but, after they
had lost three of their officers, Lieutenants William Hughes Hallett
Montresor (*Euryalus*), Walter Byrom Almack (*Briton*), and Houston
Stewart (2) (*Dryad*), besides seven bluejackets, they disabled and
abandoned their guns, and also fell back as best they could.

With the help of the first brigade's fire, order was at length
restored. The first brigade then checked the enemy, advanced in

splendid order, and, aided by dismounted cavalry, retrieved the situation; whereupon the second brigade rallied on the Marines, and once more presented an unbroken front. As soon as fresh ammunition had been served out, it advanced again over the lost ground; and the Naval Brigade had the satisfaction of regaining possession of all its lost guns except one Gatling, which, with its limber, had been rolled into the ravine. Indeed, even this gun was eventually recovered, though the limber was found to have been burnt.

When the Khor had been cleared, the first brigade crossed it. The Arabs, by that time, had had enough of fighting, and offered but little further resistance. By noon their camp and wells were occupied. In this action at Tamai they had lost 2000 killed. The total British loss had been 109 killed and 104 wounded. In addition to the three officers and the seven men of the Naval Brigade who were killed, Lieutenant Crawford James Markland Conybeare (*Hecla*) and six seamen were wounded. On the 14th, the force returned to its first zeriba, and, on the 18th, re-entered Suakin.

Among those whose names were specially mentioned by Commander Rolfe for gallant conduct at Tamai were Midshipmen Edward Carey Tyndale-Biscoe and Edward Matson Hewett, both of the *Euryalus*. At the critical moment, when the three Lieutenants fell, these youngsters took command of the subdivision, and acted with great coolness and bravery. Lieutenant Walter Hodgson Bevan Graham was also praised. At Tamai, however, there were many heroes.[1]

Rear-Admiral Hewett put a price on Osman Digna's head, but, at the instance of the British Government, withdrew the proclamation. He also made various efforts to bring in the rebellious tribes, and to keep open the road to Berber, so as to preserve a way of retreat for the garrison at Khartum. In these, however, he was not very successful; and at the end of March he went to Massowah, whence he presently proceeded on a very interesting and useful mission to King John of Abyssinia. In view of his absence, Captain Robert Henry More Molyneux was appointed[2] Commodore in the Red Sea, with his broad pennant in the *Sphinx*. In spite of the station where he served, he was attached to the Mediterranean fleet.

---

[1] *Times*, Mar. 12, 14, 17, etc.; Royle, 'Egyptian Campaigns,' 291, etc.; Burleigh, 'Desert Warfare,' 159, etc.; Desps.; Genl. Order of Mar. 16.

[2] May 1, 1884.

Among the honours and promotions granted for this brief but bloody campaign were the following :—

> To be C.B., Capts. Hilary Gustavus Andoe[1] and Ernest Neville Rolfe (May 21, 1884).
> To be Capt., Com. E. N. Rolfe (May 20).
> To be Com., Lieuts. Henry Charles Bigge,[2] William Douglas Morrish,[3] Walter Hodgson Bevan Graham, and Crawford James Markland Conybeare (May 20).
> To be Lieut., Sub.-Lieut. Percy Douglas Melville Henderson (May 20).
> To be Staff-Com., Nav.-Lieut. Frederick Hire[4] (May 20).
> To be Insp. of Mach., Chf. Eng. George Thomas Crook[5] (May 20).
> To be Staff-Surg., Surg. Horace Edward Firmin Cross (May 20).
> To be Fleet-Surg., Staff-Surg. James Hamilton Martin (May 20).
> To be Paym., Asst. Paym. James Auten Bell (May 20).

As part of the garrison of Suakin, a battalion of Royal Marines was left, first under Lieutenant Colonel Albert Henry Ozzard, and afterwards under Lieut.-Colonel Nowell FitzUpton Way. It did long and arduous service in and about the wretched town, and, as will be seen, fought again there, and consistently maintained the ancient credit of the force. More trying, however, than any enemy were the climate and dismal surroundings, against the subtle influences of which, be it said, the *moral* of the Marines stood as firm as against the onslaughts of the Arabs. This history records only incidentally and briefly the gallant work of this splendid force, the main purpose being to chronicle the progress and services of the Royal Navy proper ; but it would be as unwelcome to the Navy as to the author to attempt wholly to dissociate the exploits of the sea-soldiers from those of the bluejackets with whom they are so commonly shipmates and comrades in arms, and who have such excellent and lasting reasons for being proud of the fellowship. Indeed, an apology is needed for the somewhat curt manner in which, owing to considerations of space, the history of the Royal Marines has necessarily been dealt with here.

As early as March, 1884, it became apparent that General Gordon's withdrawal from Khartum would be difficult, if not impossible, unless a helping hand were held out to him, either along the Nile or by way of Suakin and Berber.[6] To reach Khartum from

---

[1] Of the *Orontes*; transport offr. at Trinkitat and Suakin.

[2] Employed in condensing and storing water at Suakin.

[3] Beachmaster at Trinkitat and Suakin.   [4] Harbour-master at Suakin.

[5] Superitnended condensing and distilling at Suakin. In 1882, this officer at Suez gained distinction by wedging down the safety valve of a dilapidated crane's boiler, in order to hoist two locomotives which otherwise could not have been lifted (Hext: Rep. on Com. and Transp. Serv. in Egypt).

[6] Authorities for the history of the Gordon Relief Expedition: Desps.; Parl. Papers, c. 4280, 4345, and 4392 (1884–85); Colvile, ' Hist. of Sudan Campaign' (1887);

Cairo involved a journey of 1650 miles up a river full of cataracts, and, except at times of flood, unnavigable by any but small craft. To reach Khartum from Suakin entailed a desert march of about 250 miles, of which one section of 52 miles was waterless, and then a voyage or further march of 210 miles up the Nile from Berber. The military authorities in Egypt strongly favoured the Suakin-Berber route, and in this view they were supported by Vice-Admiral Lord John Hay, K.C.B., who had succeeded Lord Alcester as Commander-in-Chief in the Mediterranean, and who sent Captain Robert Henry More Molyneux up the Nile as far as Wady Halfa to survey the course of that stream. On the other hand, General Sir Garnet Wolseley, who was Adjutant-General in London, and who was likely to command the relief force, if one were sent, was as strongly in favour of the all-river route. His experiences during the Red River Expedition in Canada, in 1870, led him to believe that rapid and sure progress could be made by means of specially built whale-boats, where steamers could not be employed. His view was backed up by a rather lame report from three other officers who had served with him in Canada. General Sir F. C. Stephenson, who commanded the British army of occupation in Egypt, was still unconvinced; but, after much delay and hesitation, the authorities in England adopted the opinion of Wolseley.

In the meantime, in May, half a battalion of British troops was moved up to Wady Halfa, and Commander Tynte Ford Hammill was directed to make a survey of the river above that point, with a view to determining the difficulties of the route; while, on the other hand, some preliminary preparations were made for laying down a narrow-gauge railway westward from Suakin. The Nile route, however, was formally decided on on August 26th, and General Stephenson was informed that Sir Garnet Wolseley would command the expedition. Wolseley reached Cairo on September 9th.

On August 12th the construction of the necessary 800 flat-bottomed "whale-boats" had been begun. The first batch of boats reached Wady Halfa on October 14th, and on October 26th the first boats were hauled up the second cataract. Eight steam pinnaces and two stern-wheel paddle-boats were also equipped for the expedition. To assist in the upward navigation, 377 Canadian

Royle, 'Egypt. Camps.'; Corresp. of *Times*; Slatin, 'Fire and Sword in the Sudan'; H. Brackenbury, 'The River Column'; Sir C. W. Wilson, 'From Korti to Khartum'; var. priv. journals, etc.

boatmen ("voyageurs") were engaged. Although most plucky and energetic, they did not give unqualified satisfaction; and it was afterwards regretted that the whole work of water transport was not entrusted to the Naval Brigade. They were, however, very useful when it became necessary to descend the stream.

It should be borne in mind that on April 19th a telegram had been received at Cairo to the effect that Gordon, at the date of its

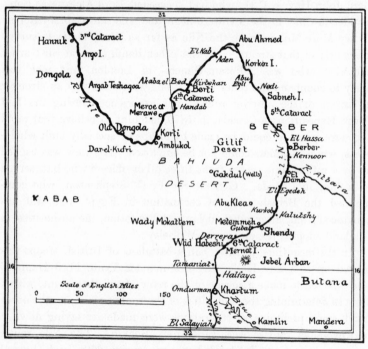

THE NILE FROM DONGOLA TO KHARTUM.[1]

despatch, had provisions for five months, and was already hemmed in. It should also be borne in mind that in the summer the most optimist authorities did not believe that Gordon, even if Khartum were not taken by force or treachery, could hold out beyond the middle of November. These facts indicate how late the work of relief was begun. Gordon actually managed to hold out until January 26th, 1885, when his nearest friends were still some miles from him. The truth is not only that there was fatal delay in starting, but also that the difficulties of the upward passage of the

---

[1] Gubat should be marked below, instead of above Metemmeh.

great river were realised only too late by those who were responsible
for the choice of the route.

The early work of the Navy in connection with this ill-starred
but gallant adventure was confined to surveying and preparing the
channel, and helping the steamers and boats over the cataracts and
through the numerous rapids. Commander Hammill's services at
that period were invaluable, and a tackle invented by him for
hauling boats against a strong stream was especially useful. On
November 3rd, Lord Wolseley in person reached Dongola; and on
the 26th, he appointed his naval A.D.C., Captain Lord Charles
William Delapoer Beresford, to the command of the Naval Brigade
on the Nile. The advance from Dongola of such part of the expeditionary force as was then ready began on December 2nd, and
on December 15th the headquarters of the army were advanced to
Korti; a town lying at the northern end of the chord of a vast and
difficult bend which is made by the river in its descent from Shendi.[1]
By desert, Korti and Shendi are less than 200 miles apart. By
water the distance is more than twice as great. On the bend are
the fourth and fifth cataracts, a multitude of islets and rapids, and
the towns of Abu-Hamed and Berber; but in 1884–85 that particular
stretch of the Nile was practically unknown.

The Naval Brigade,[2] of which Lord Charles Beresford took command, was composed as follows at the beginning of January, 1885 :—

FIRST DIVISION : Lieuts. Alfred Pigott, Rudolph Edward de Lisle, George William
    Tyler,[3] and Robert Archibald James Montgomerie[3]; Sub-Lieut. Edward
    Lionel Munro; Boatswain James Webber, and 51 petty-officers and seamen.
    One Gardner machine-gun.[4]

SECOND DIVISION : Lieuts. Edmund Barker van Koughnet and Richard Poore;
    Sub-Lieuts. Edward Ernest Hardy, and Colin Richard Keppel; Chf. Eng.
    Henry Benbow; Eng. George Sparkes; Surg. Arthur William May, and 50
    petty officers and seamen. One Gardner machine-gun.[4]

NOTE.—Lord Chas. Beresford was borne (Sept. 2, 1884, to July 13, 1885), in the
    Hibernia,[5] flagship at Malta. The other officers and men were borne in
    the *Alexandra*, *Helicon*, *Inflexible*, *Invincible*, *Iris*, *Monarch*, *Superb*, or
    Téméraire, of the Mediterranean fleet.

---

[1] Nearly opposite which is Metemmeh, on the left bank.

[2] This was in addition to various naval detachments employed lower down the
Nile under Capts. Fredk. Geo. Denham Bedford, and Fredk. Ross Boardman.

[3] Joined at Gubat.   [4] Rifle calibre ('45-in.), with five barrels.

[5] This was cancelled in Sept., 1885, and his name was erased from the books of the
Hibernia and transferred to those of the *Alexandra*, so as to enable Lord C.'s service to
count as sea time, though he was not allowed to count it as service in command of a
ship of war. This seems to have been a hardship, looking to the work which he did
in the Soudan, and to the fact that the denial threatened at one time to prevent his
further promotion.

It had at length become painfully clear that, if Gordon was to be saved at all, he must be saved quickly. It was, therefore, decided at Korti to split the relieving force into two columns. One, the desert column, under Colonel Sir Herbert Stewart, was to march overland to Metemmeh, a few miles above Shendi, and there to pick up the steamers which Gordon had promised to send thither from Khartum. The other, the river column, under Maj.-General Earle, was to continue the movement up the Nile valley, and ultimately to join hands with Stewart at Metemmeh. Earle started from Korti on December 28th, accompanied by a small naval detachment. Lord Charles Beresford reached Korti on January 4th from Dal, where he had been engaged in the preliminary work of the expedition. On the following day, Stewart, who had been into the desert to occupy and establish a depôt at Jakdul Wells,[1] 96 miles on the road to Metemmeh, returned to Korti; and, on the 8th, he started again for Metemmeh, accompanied by Beresford and the first division of the naval contingent, the second division, which was following, not having then arrived.

Jakdul was reached once more on January 12th; on the 13th, Colonel Burnaby arrived at the wells with a convoy of grain; and on the 14th the advance was resumed. The column then consisted of part of the Naval Brigade, three 7-pr. screw guns manned by Royal Artillerymen, three troops of the 19th Hussars, the Heavy Camel Regt.,[2] the Guards Camel Regt., the Sussex Regt., and some Mounted Infantry and Royal Engineers, making, with the Transport and Medical Corps, a total of 1581 men, 90 horses, 2880 camels, 340 drivers, and 4 guns.

On the evening of the 16th, the enemy was first discovered, scouts reporting the Arabs to be in large force about four miles ahead, posted to intercept communication with the wells of Abu Klea. A zeriba of thorn bushes was formed, and the column lay within it for the night, the dervishes sniping continually from low hills on the right flank, and increasing their fire at dawn. In the morning it was hoped for some time that the Soudanese would attack the camp; and for fully three hours the whole force stood ready to repel them if they did. As they did not, and as the sniping continued, Stewart decided to fight his way to the wells, leaving, meanwhile, a guard over the baggage in the zeriba. He formed

---

[1] Where Col. Dorward, R.E., with about 400 men, was left in charge.

[2] Including Marines.

square on a clear space 400 yards in advance of the zeriba, placing forty [1] of the Naval Brigade, with the Gardner gun, in the centre of the rear force, but directing Beresford, in case of fighting, to put the gun where it would be most useful. Within the square were camels laden with water, ammunition, etc.

Soon after 9 A.M. on January 17th the square moved off under a very annoying fire from the left flank, and advanced about two miles. Presently, as a low hill was cleared, a line of flags was seen planted along the edge of some high grass, not much more than 400 yards from the left flank of the square, which was thereupon halted in order that its rear might close up. Almost instantly a V-shaped mass of dervishes, estimated to number 6000, sprang from the grass, and, encouraged by about 40 horsemen, charged at a great pace over the intervening ground. Beresford promptly ran his Gardner from the centre of the rear face to a point on the flank, near the left rear corner of the square, and opened fire; and, as the square closed up, he and his men were left just outside it. After firing about forty rounds, he perceived that the gun had rather too much elevation, and ordered " cease fire," in order that the error might be corrected. About thirty rounds more had been fired, with excellent effect, when the gun jammed, owing to the extractor of one of the barrels pulling off the head of a discharged cartridge, and leaving the cylinder in the chamber. The Arabs were then but 200 yards from the detachment. Says Lord Charles :—

"The captain of the gun (Rhodes, Chief Boatswain's Mate) and myself unscrewed the plate to clear the barrel, or take the lock of the jammed barrel out, when the enemy were upon us. Rhodes was killed with a spear. Walter Miller, armourer, I also saw killed with a spear at the same moment on my left. I was knocked down in the rear of the gun, but uninjured, except a small spear scratch on the left hand. The crowd and crush of the enemy was very great at this point, and, as it struggled up, I was carried against the face of the square, which was literally pushed back by sheer weight of numbers about twelve paces from the position of the gun. The crush was so great that at the moment few on either side were killed; but, fortunately, this flank of the square had been forced up a very steep little mound, which enabled the rear rank to open a tremendous fire over the heads of the front rank men. This relieved the pressure, and enabled the front rank to bayonet or shoot those of the enemy nearest them."

None of the Arabs got into the square at that point, which was held by the Mounted Infantry; and very quickly the Gardner and the survivors of its detachment were again within the line. Finding, however, that that particular point was impregnable, the

---

[1] The rest were left in the zeriba.

mass of dervishes surged round the left rear corner, passed along the rear face for a short distance, and then burst in. It was during this brief irruption, for the onslaught was soon repulsed, that Colonel Burnaby was killed. The British fire was too heavy to allow of many getting in, and the few who did get in lived only for a few seconds. Then the gallant tribesmen drew off slowly,

COMMANDER ALFRED PIGOTT.

(*From the picture by Mrs. H. M. Munro.*)

[By permission of the Lords of the Admiralty.]

until they were screened by a nullah and a hillock from the storm of bullets and shells that followed them.

The Naval Brigade, which went into action 40 strong, lost on this desperate occasion 8 killed and 7 wounded, among the former being Commander Alfred Pigott,[1] and Lieutenant de Lisle. The losses of the army, though much less great in proportion, were also

[1] This excellent officer had been promoted a short time before his death, but never knew of his advancement.

serious.   The slaughter of the enemy was enormous, probably
amounting to more than one-fourth of his strength in killed alone.

At 2.30 P.M. the square re-formed, and moved on without further
opposition to Abu Klea wells, which were occupied soon after
5 o'clock.   There the force bivouacked for the night in a defensive
position, suffering terribly from cold, and from lack of provisions,
until the zeriba detachment and the baggage-camels joined on the
following morning.   A fort was built meanwhile for the protection
of the wounded, who were to be left at the wells in charge of a
detachment of the Sussex Regiment.

At 2 P.M. on January 18th the column again marched, and
pursued its tedious way all through the afternoon and following
night, until 6.30 A.M. on the 19th, when the Nile was sighted ahead,
and Metemmeh on the left front.   Colonel Stewart had intended
to strike the river some miles to the westward, but had had reason
to suspect his guide, whom he had put under arrest, and, altering
his direction, had gone too far to the eastward.   Thus, instead of
touching the river at a point where there was no enemy, he
sighted it under the eyes of a large dervish garrison, which lost
no time in opening fire on him.   To give the hungry and weary
men an opportunity of breakfasting, he formed a temporary zeriba.
Unhappily the enemy's practice was very good, and the column
suffered severely, Stewart himself being among those mortally
hit, and Major William Hutcheson Poë,[1] R.M. and Sub-Lieutenant
Munro, R.N., among the wounded.   The Gardner was stationed
where it was conceived that it would be most useful; but it could
effect little, the tribesmen lying in the grass, and showing themselves hardly at all.   Colonel Sir Charles William Wilson, R.E.,
took over the command, and the zeriba was strengthened, two
redoubts being ultimately thrown up to cover it.

About 10 A.M. a square was formed in rear of the zeriba; and
presently it moved away in order to get touch with the river.   The
zeriba, with about 300 men in it, was left under the command of
Lord Charles Beresford, and Colonel Barrow, who put into the
larger redoubt all the sick and wounded, three of the four 7-prs.,
and the Gardner gun, and caused the camels, about 2000 in number,
to lie down outside it.   In the meantime the fire of the dervishes
never ceased.

The advance of the square was covered to some extent by the

[1] C.B. for this service.

fire of the guns and the Gardner, but, nevertheless, it was most fiercely opposed by more than one V-shaped column of dervishes. The tribesmen, however, did not succeed in getting within thirty yards of the British rifles, and at length broke and fled, most of them retiring to Metemmeh. After a two and a half mile march the square reached the Nile; and from 1.20 P.M. onwards the Arabs fired no more at the zeriba and redoubts.[1] On the 20th, leaving a guard at the river, the square returned, and picked up the party from the zeriba, including, of course, the wounded. The reunited force marched forward again at 4 P.M., and at nightfall occupied and encamped in the village of Gubat, a few miles below Metemmeh. By that time some of the horses had had no water for two, and most of the camels no water for five days.

On January 21st, the greater part of the force made a reconnaissance of Metemmeh, Boatswain James Webber having charge of the Gardner in consequence of all the other naval officers who were at the front, Beresford only excepted, having been killed or badly wounded. While the defences of the town were being engaged, Gordon's four little steamers, the *Bordein, Safieh, Tewfikieh,* and *Telahawiyeh,* came down the river from Khartum. They brought word that a body of devishes from Khartum was advancing towards Metemmeh to meet the relief column. The reconnaissance, which otherwise would have ended in a serious attack on the town, was therefore abandoned; and the column, accompanied by the steamers, returned to Gubat, the camp at which place was strengthened. Lord Charles Beresford took the crazy craft in hand with characteristic energy, and, by 3 P.M. on January 22nd, reported them as ready to proceed up the river. He was then so ill as to be unable to walk, so that, unhappily, he was scarcely in a condition to assume charge of them on a service demanding to the full extent every qualification that the best naval officer can possess. As for the other naval officers, all save Webber, as has been said, had been put out of action. Nevertheless, Lord Charles might, and no doubt would, have taken command, and pushed on at once, had it been considered desirable that he should do so, and would have carried out the original plan; which was that he should man two of the steamers from the Naval Brigade, take on board Sir Charles Wilson and fifty men of the Sussex Regt., and steam instantly for Khartum. It was

_____
[1] This action is sometimes spoken of as that of Abu Kru.

deemed impossible to persist with this project; moreover, it was deemed impossible for any of the steamers to start southward at all until the 24th.   In spite of this, however, it was deemed desirable that Lord Charles, with the *Bordein* and the *Telahawiyeh*, should go a few miles down the river to Shendy, into which place he fired a few shells; but no opposition was there met with.

On January 24th, Sir Charles Wilson himself started for Khartum with the *Bordein* and *Telahawiyeh*, 20 British soldiers in red coats, and about 260 Soudanese.   He did not take Lord Charles with him, nor did he supersede the Egyptian masters of the steamers and substitute British officers or petty officers for them.   He merely put an engine-room artificer into each vessel. Colonel Boscawen was left in military charge at Gubat, where only 922 men remained, Colonel the Hon. R. A. J. Talbot, with about 400, having been sent back to Jakdul Wells to bring up provisions and to forward despatches to Lord Wolseley.   The Egyptian soldiers who had come down in the *Bordein*, and who were not trusted, were ordered to garrison an island opposite the British camp, and Lord Charles Beresford, with a detachment of seamen and the Gardner gun, took up his quarters in the *Safieh*, and held himself ready to proceed at short notice to any spot at which his services might be needed.   As for the *Tewfikieh*, to which the wounded Sir Herbert Stewart, then in a hopeless condition,[1] was transferred, she was used as a ferry boat between the camp and the island.   In the meantime, Lord Charles, on the 24th, paid another brief visit to Shendy, where, this time, he was received with a hot fire from the enemy, whom he dispersed.   Daily at 6 A.M., between January 25th and 30th, he weighed, and, with twenty picked marksmen on board, patrolled the river for some miles in each direction, capturing cattle, sheep, goats, fuel and vegetables, raiding villages, and, on one occasion, destroying a strong earthwork.   The *Safieh* was invariably fired at in the course of these little expeditions, especially by parties on the left bank of the river, but the bulletproof shields with which she had been fitted prevented casualties.

Sir Charles Wilson, as might have been expected, met with delay, and finally with disaster.   On the 25th, the *Bordein* grounded.   On the 26th, she grounded again, and twenty-four hours were lost.   At 11 A.M. on the 28th, Khartum was at length sighted, but it was soon seen to be in the hands of the Dervishes.

---

[1] He lingered, however, for several days.

It had, in fact, fallen on the 26th. The steamers reconnoitred a little further up the river,[1] and then, turning round, began their return voyage under a heavy fire, the Soudanese on board evincing grave signs of disaffection. On the 29th, the *Telahawiyeh* was wrecked, and her crew, guns and ammunition had to be transferred to a large nuggar. Emissaries from the Mahdi approached under a flag of truce, chiefly in order to persuade the Egyptian Soudanese troops to surrender. By them a somewhat feeble demand was returned to the effect that a safe conduct should be sent to meet the expedition upon its arrival at Wad-Habeshi, a post some miles lower down, which was held by about 5000 of the enemy. On the 31st, the *Bordein* also was wrecked off the island of Mernat, 30 miles south of Gubat, and a short distance above Wad-Habeshi, and everything in her had to be landed.

With great pluck, Lieutenant E. J. Stuart-Montagu-Wortley, King's Royal Rifles, took a pulling boat and, starting by night, reached Gubat early in the morning of the following day. In his absence steps were taken to render the island defensible.

Part of the second division of the Naval Brigade, under Lieutenant van Koughnet, had by that time joined Lord Charles, who, taking the *Safieh*, and manning her with small detachments from both divisions, and with twenty marksmen from the Mounted Infantry, departed up the river to endeavour to rescue Wilson's party. With him went the two Gardners[2] and two 4-pr. brass mountain guns. The wretched *Safieh* could steam against the stream at the rate of about 2·5 kts. only, so that, even had there been no difficulties in the way of navigation, progress would have been extremely slow.

Early on February 3rd, the *Safieh* sighted the enemy's 3-gun fort at Wad-Habeshi. The captains of the machine guns were warned to direct their fire solely and exclusively at the embrasures, with a view to endeavouring to prevent the gunners there from laying their pieces accurately on the steamer. These directions were so well carried out that although the *Safieh*, owing to her draught of water, had to pass within 80 yards of the work, the guns in the fort could not be fired at her so long as she was beam on. It was only when the steamer had passed the fort about 200 yards, and when the machine guns could no longer fire into the embrasures,

---

[1] As far as the Island of Tuti, at the junction of the Blue Nile with the White.

[2] These were mounted *en échelon* on their own cones on a platform raised above the steamer's bulwarks.

that the enemy managed to put a shot into the crazy vessel's boiler.

Before she lost way the *Safieh* was headed towards the opposite bank, and then, when she was about 500 yards from the work, the anchor was let go, a platform being at once extemporised aft, and one of the Gardners shifted to it.   Rifle fire, even from the twenty picked marksmen, reinforced by fourteen bluejackets, had failed to keep the enemy's guns from being used; but from 7 A.M. to 8.30 P.M., this Gardner imposed silence upon the only gun which would then bear upon the steamer.   Undoubtedly it saved the craft from destruction.   Nearly at the moment of the mishap, Lieutenant van Koughnet was hit in the thigh, and a petty officer was mortally wounded.   Two seamen were badly scalded by the escaping steam, and, in addition, the artificers, and, indeed, everyone in the stoke-hold, had been more or less injured by it.

Beresford communicated with Wilson, and, by strategy, the rescued party was got past the fort in the darkness, the sick and wounded going down in a nuggar, which, though fired at, suffered very little, and the rest marching along the opposite bank.   The enemy was also led to believe that both steamers were being abandoned, the result being that, having moved a gun, fired a few rounds at the *Safieh,* and received no reply, he ceased firing for the night.

The damaged boiler had cooled by 11 A.M.   Chief Engineer Henry Benbow went to work upon it as soon as he could touch it, and, after ten hours of unremitting labour, he succeeded in repairing it.

"Too much credit," says Lord Charles, "cannot be given to this officer, as he had to shape the plate, bore the holes in plate and boiler, and run down the screws and nuts, almost entirely with his own hands, the artificers and everyone in the stokehold having been scalded severely by the explosion when the shot entered the boilers. The plate was 16 inches by 14, so that some idea can be formed of the work entailed upon him."

At 5 A.M. on February 4th, the fires were lighted again, every precaution, however, being taken to get up steam as quietly and unobtrusively as possible.   At 5.50, when day was about to break, but when, happily, all was ready, the Dervishes seem first to have perceived that the *Safieh* had not been deserted.   They burst forth into shouts of rage and brought guns to bear; but, ere they could open fire, Beresford weighed and proceeded up the river, as if steaming for Khartum.   He went only three-quarters of a mile or so, until, finding a place in which he could turn with safety, he put about, steamed back past the fort at his best speed, and used his Gardners and rifles with excellent effect. Below the fort he found the nuggar aground, with the sick and wounded still in her. She was within range of the tribesmen's guns; and at once he sent Sub-Lieutenant Keppel in a boat, with a party of bluejackets, to her assistance, the *Safieh* herself anchoring hard by. It took a long time to lighten and float the craft; and, in the course of the work, young Keppel was wounded. At length both steamer and nuggar were able to move down to the spot at which Sir Charles Wilson, with his party, was awaiting them. All were taken on board, and at 5.45 that afternoon the camp at Gubat was again reached. It had not been attacked.

Nor was it attacked; though undoubtedly it would have been but for the effect produced by the action at Wad-Habeshi. That action saved not only Wilson, but also the entire desert column. The fearful slaughter of his people at Abu Klea and Abu Kru had given the Mahdi a wholesome estimate of the power of British weapons; but his success at Khartum had revived his spirits, and had encouraged him to despatch an overwhelming force of at least 30,000 men against Gubat. Beresford's behaviour caused the commander of this huge army to believe that the British were invincible in or near the water. The man, in consequence, halted or dawdled, his deliberate intention being to wait until the British should quit the neighbourhood of the river. He would then fall upon them in the desert and crush them. But he did not watch them closely enough. When they did move, they started suddenly, and marched more rapidly than he had expected, and he was never able to bring any considerable portion of his army into contact with them. The full value of Beresford's action did not appear at the time. It became evident, however, when, years afterwards, some of the European and other prisoners escaped from the Mahdi's grasp and regained civilisation. Then it was shown that Beresford, Benbow, and their gallant fellows had done even better work than had been supposed.[1]

At Wad-Habeshi, 5400 rounds were fired from the Gardners, 126 from the guns, and 2150 from the rifles. Lord Charles, in his report, gave special praise to Lieutenant van Koughnet, Sub-Lieutenant Keppel, Chief-Engineer Benbow, Boatswain Webber,

---

[1] Wingate to Wolseley, Mar. 18, 1893, enclosing evidence as to effect of Beresford's action.

and Surgeon Arthur William May, and spoke in the highest terms of the behaviour of the whole of his little command. Benbow would have been recommended for the Victoria Cross had Lord Charles not been under the impression that that decoration was not available as a reward for such a service as the gallant officer had performed. Benbow,[1] however, received promotion to the rank of Inspector of Machinery. Another special and exceptional promotion was that of Boatswain Webber to be Chief Boatswain. In 1887, his services were further, and again exceptionally, recompensed, together with those of Gunner Cathie, by promotion to the rank of Lieutenant.

In the interim, the situation of the desert column was quite misunderstood at Korti, where, as Sir G. S. Clarke says, "impossible plans were formed." Happily, the command of the column was given to Major-General Sir Redvers Buller, who left Korti on January 29th, and arrived at Gubat, with six companies of the Royal Irish, on February 11th. Pending his arrival, the steamers were repaired, and, on February 7th, a raid was made with them, and some cattle and goats were captured; but the steamers, especially the *Safieh*, which had been strained by the firing on February 3rd, leaked so badly that they had to return ere the objects of the expedition had been fully accomplished.

Buller decided upon withdrawal to avert disaster. On February 13th, Lord Charles Beresford spiked the guns[2] of the *Safieh* and *Tewfikieh*, and threw them into the river, together with their ammunition. He also disabled the steamers' engines. That night the Naval Brigade bivouacked on shore; and on the following morning the desert column left Gubat on foot, there being no longer any camels available. Abu Klea was reached on the 15th, and the Naval Brigade, with its two Gardners, was ordered into the fort, while the rest of the troops threw up earthworks.[3] Buller then sent forward for reinforcements, camels, and additional ammunition, and, upon these reaching him, proceeded on February 23rd for Jakdul Wells, where he encamped on the 26th. The Naval Brigade and part of the column left Jakdul two days later, and at length resighted Korti without further serious adventures. On the long march from Gubat not a single bluejacket fell out, in spite of the

---

[1] Benbow was also specially complimented by Lord Wolseley.

[2] Brass 4-prs. The Gardners were, of course, preserved and carried off.

[3] At Abu Klea the column was sniped severely at night.

fact that many of the men were shoeless, and that each carried rifle, cutlass, and seventy rounds of ammunition. The Brigade was inspected on March 8th by Lord Wolseley, and was then broken up into detachments and posted at intervals down the river below Korti. Lord Charles Beresford rejoined Lord Wolseley as naval A.D.C., and presently accompanied him to Suakin on a brief visit.

Major-General Earle's river column, which, as has been said, left Korti on December 28th, 1884, encountered great difficulties in making its way up the Nile. On February 10th, 1885, it defeated about 800 Arabs at Kirbekan; but among the 10 British officers and men killed in the action was Earle himself.

Colonel Henry Brackenbury, who thereupon took command, continued the advance until, on February 24th, he was about twenty-six miles below Abu Hamed. There he received orders to retire, and, acting accordingly, he got back to Korti on March 8th. The naval contingent, under Lieutenant William Theobald Bourke, attached to this force, was a very small one, and, in Brackenbury's book, "The River Column," [1] is scarcely mentioned. The work of navigation was done chiefly by the Canadian voyageurs, the bluejackets rendering frequent help, but confining their efforts chiefly to the management of their own craft, and of their single Gardner gun.

In addition to the naval officers whose names have been already mentioned in the text, the following, among others, did duty on the Nile in connection with the futile relief expedition:—

> Capt. Frederick Ross Boardman; Coms. Tynte Ford Hammill,[2] and Julian Alleyne Baker; Lieuts. Charles Tatton Turner,[2] Charles Reeve,[2] William Crawford Reid, and George John Taylor; Sub-Lieut. Francis Hungerford Pollen (Lieut. 4. 2. 85).

Lord Charles Beresford and Captain Boardman were made Companions of the Bath on August 24th, 1885.

So little was the true state of affairs in the Soudan understood by Lord Wolseley, that as late as January 8th, 1885, he demurred to the undertaking of active operations from Suakin, and added, "I am strong enough to relieve Khartum, and believe in being

---

[1] London, 1885.

[2] Promoted, Aug. 17, 1885. A previous batch of promotions, dated Feb. 4, 1885, had included Lieuts. E. B. van Koughnet, and Richard Poore; and Sub-Lieut. Colin R. Keppel, whose names have appeared in the text.

able to send a force, when returning by way of Berber, to Suakin, to open road and crush Osman Digna."[1] Even on February 11th, when Buller was wisely deciding to retreat from Gubat, Wolseley was suggesting that the river column should attack Berber. By that time, however, he was willing that a railway should be made westward from Suakin,[2] and that a subsidiary expedition should enter the desert from the same direction. In a despatch of March 6th,[3] he took a more pessimistic view, admitting that further military operations against Khartum would be impossible until about the end of the summer, when, if he persisted in them, he would require very large reinforcements.

In the meanwhile the War Office had determined to make a serious effort on behalf of the restoration of British prestige in the eastern Soudan. Osman Digna was to be crushed, and the Berber railway was to be constructed. To this end, about 13,000 men, including a Naval Brigade, the battalion of Marines, a brigade from India, and a field battery from New South Wales,[4] were assembled at Suakin in March, under Lieut.-General Sir Gerald Graham.

The Naval Brigade was drawn from the following vessels of Commodore Molyneux's Red Sea division of the Mediterranean fleet, viz. :—

> *Carysfort*, corvette, Captain Walter Stewart; *Dolphin*, sloop, Com. Sydney Marrow Eardley-Wilmot; *Sphinx*, paddle-vessel Commod. R. H. More Molyneux, C.B.; *Condor*, gun-vessel, Com. William Cecil Henry Domville; and *Coquette*, gunboat, Lieut. Fritz Hauch Eden Crowe.

The greater part of the force marched out of Suakin, and occupied Hasheen, on March 20th, when the Royal Marines, under Lieut.-Colonel Albert Henry Ozzard, distinguished themselves, in conjunction with the Berkshire Regiment, by the capture of Dehilbat Hill. On the following day four Gardner guns from the ships were landed, and proceeded with the Naval Brigade to the front on the 22nd.

The Brigade, with the Marines, formed part of a division which left Suakin for Tamai, under Major-General Sir J. McNeill, V.C., with orders to form a half-way zeriba. The column was encumbered by a huge transport, and its advance was impeded by dense bush. At 10.30 A.M. it halted at Tofrik, about six miles out. The

---

[1] Wolseley to Hartington (teleg.).   [2] *Idem.*
[3] Wolseley to Hartington.
[4] Did not land till Mar. 29, and so had no share in the principal actions.

zeriba was to take the shape of three squares *en échelon*, the centre square being the largest; and at the outward corner of each of the small squares was to be a redoubt with two Gardner guns manned by the Naval contingent. The command of the north redoubt was given to Lieutenant Montagu Hamilton March Seymour (*Dolphin*); that of the southern one to Lieutenant Alfred Wyndham Paget (*Carysfort*), Commander Domville having general charge. As for the squares themselves, the northern one was entrusted to the Berkshire Regiment, and the southern one to the Marines, while the large square, which was to contain the stores, etc., was entrusted to the Indian contingent.

Long ere these somewhat elaborate defensive arrangements could be completed, a large body of Arabs attacked, soon after 2.30 P.M. Partly owing to the rapidity of the onslaught, partly to the working detachments being without their arms, and partly to confusion occasioned in the ranks of the 17th Bengal Native Infantry by retiring cavalry riding through them, the northern square was rushed, Lieutenant Seymour and 6 of his bluejackets being killed in the effort to bring their Gardners into the redoubt assigned to them. The Arabs then burst into the centre square; but the gallant Berkshires, standing firm and fighting back to back, cut off the Arabs in the square from those without, and broke the force of the attack. Many of the enemy, however, swept round upon the transport animals, which, in preparation for their return to Suakin, had been collected in rear of the Marines' square; and they succeeded in stampeding the whole train through the zeriba. About half of it was lost. In twenty minutes, however, the rush of the tribesmen was repulsed, at least a thousand of the fanatics remaining dead upon the field. The total British casualties were heavy, though a large proportion of them occurred among camp-followers and other non-combatants. The Naval Brigade, in addition to the seven killed, had Surgeon Matthew Digan and four men wounded.[1] Commander Domville distinguished himself greatly.

Two days later, as a force from Tamai was proceeding in square to meet a convoy from Suakin, about 10,000 Arabs attacked it. They were driven off, and lost about 500 killed, but not until they had captured 100 camels. On that occasion the British casualties, which were happily few in number, included Lieutenant Alfred Edmund Marchant, R.M., wounded. A somewhat similar affair

---

[1] *Times*, Mar. 24 and 25; Royle, and desps.

occurred on March 26th.   On April 2nd, about 7000 men, including
the Naval Brigade, marched to Tesela Hill, and thence next day
towards Tamai.   Having burnt a number of huts in the Khor
Ghob, they returned to Suakin; and on April 6th the Naval
Brigade re-embarked.   A month later, threatenings of trouble
arose on the Afghan border, the consequence being that, on
May 11th, Sir Gerald Graham's army was ordered to withdraw
from Suakin, which thenceforth was left to the protection of a
small Anglo-Indian garrison, and of the men-of-war in harbour.
The withdrawal, and the simultaneous abandonment of the whole
of the Sudan, strengthened both the hands and the prestige of
Osman Digna, who compelled such native tribes as had not
previously submitted to make terms with him.   They also enabled
him to turn his attention to the reduction of the Egyptian garrison
at Kassala, the result being that the town capitulated to the
Mahdists in August.   Mr. Gladstone's government, which had
consented to the evacuation of the Transvaal after Majuba, and
of the Sudan after Khartum, had quitted office in June; but the
abandonment had then gone too far to be arrested.   The work of
reconquest had to be set about afresh, and under better guidance,
in later years.

In connection with the organisation of this second Suakin expedition, most valuable services were rendered by Captain John
Fellowes,[1] as principal transport officer, Commander William
Llewellyn Morrison; Lieutenants Thomas MacGill,[2] Alexander
Milne Gardiner,[2] and William Blewett Fawckner; Paymaster
John William Seccombe ; Chief-Engineer Francis Ford ; and
many other naval officers.   Major Nowell FitzUpton Way,[3] R.M.,
who, as has been said, commanded the Royal Marine battalion
in succession to Lieut.-Colonel Ozzard, from April 3rd onward,
was rewarded with the C.B.

Previous to the arrival of General Graham's expedition, Commodore Robert Henry More Molyneux[4] had been largely responsible
for the defence of Suakin, which, for many months, had been
practically besieged by Osman Digna, and for the security of
which the garrison had been numerically inadequate.   Between
March 26th, 1884, and May 14th, 1885, besides the vessels which
have been mentioned already as having contributed to the Suakin

[1] C.B., Aug. 24, 1885.   [3] Lt. Col., May 17, 1885.
[2] Coms., Aug. 17, 1885.   [4] K.C.B., Nov. 7, 1885, for these services.

Naval Brigade of 1885, the following[1] shared in the arduous work of keeping the Mahdists at a distance:—

> *Albacore,* gunboat, Lieut. Palmer Kingsmill Smythies;[2] *Briton,* corvette, Capt. Rodney Maclaine Lloyd; *Cygnet,* gunboat, Lieut. Alexander Milne Gardiner;[3] *Falcon,* gun-vessel, (1) Com. John Eliot Pringle,[4] (2) Com. John George Jones; *Helicon,* desp.-vessel, Lieut. Alfred Leigh Winsloe;[2] *Humber,* troop and storeship, Com. Arnold John Errington; *Iris,* desp.-vessel, Capt. Ernest Rice; *Myrmidon,* surv.-vessel, Com. Richard Frazer Hoskyn; *Ranger,* gun-vessel, Com. John Pakenham Pipon; *Starling,* gunboat, (1) Lieut. Francis William Sanders;[4] (2) Lieut. James Browning Young; *Tyne,* troop and storeship, (1) Com. Basil Edward Cochrane;[4] (2) Com. William Eveleigh Darwall; *Woodlark,* gun-vessel, Com. William Robert Clutterbuck.

During the period, there were many affairs in which the boats or the guns were engaged, especially at night; and, among the officers, none distinguished themselves more than Lieutenants Palmer Kingsmill Smythies, Francis George Kirby (*Briton*), Hugh Talbot (*Carysfort*), and Montagu Hamilton March Seymour, the last of whom afterwards fell at Tofrik.

While the situation in Egypt, and the almost unchecked ascendancy in the Sudan of the authority of the Mahdi and his lieutenants, were still calling for so much activity on the part of the Navy, one or two interesting, though not very important matters occupied the attention of some of Her Majesty's ships in other quarters.

The hostile action of the French Admiral, Courbet,[5] in China, in 1883–84, was indirectly responsible for the death of a promising young British naval officer. On September 6th, 1884, the gunboat *Zephyr*, Lieutenant Charles Kerr Hope, was proceeding up the River Min, with her colours flying, when, nevertheless, she was mistaken for a French vessel, and fired upon by a Chinese fort. Lieutenant Godfrey Hubbard, who had been promoted less than three months before, was mortally wounded ere the error was discovered, and died on the 13th. The commandant of the fort was promptly disgraced; and the Chinese government behaved so well over this unhappy affair that its good faith could not be impugned. A seaman was wounded on the same occasion, but fortunately recovered.[6]

---

[1] To the crews of which medals were granted.

[2] Promd. June 30, 1885.　　　[3] *Ib.* Aug. 17, 1885.　　　[4] *Ib.* Dec. 31, 1884.

[5] On Aug. 23, 1884, he destroyed a Chinese squadron in the River Min, and bombarded Foochow arsenal.

[6] Desps. and Corr.; Loir, ' L'Escadre de l'Amiral Courbet.'

Elsewhere the *Kingfisher*, sloop, Commander John Harvey Rainier, and the *Frolic*, gun-vessel, Commander Alfred Arthur Chase Parr, were actively employed for brief periods, the *Kingfisher* at Zeila, on the Somali coast, in February, 1885, when she had occasion to land a party to arrest some mutinous native police; and the *Frolic*, on the Gold Coast, on January 31st, 1885, when, by way of reprisals for attacks on British subjects, she landed a party and burnt a town.

The next work of really important character in which the Navy participated was the completion of the conquest of Burmah.

After the second Burmese war and the annexation of the province of Pegu,[1] a revolutionary movement in Upper Burmah placed upon the throne a peaceable prince [2] who proved himself a wise and moderate ruler and cultivated friendly relations with the British. In 1854 he sent a mission to Calcutta, and, in the following year, he received at Amarapoora a British mission headed by Major Phayre, who took with him as his secretary Captain Henry Yule, R.E. This mission failed, however, to negotiate a commercial treaty, which was badly needed. A little later the seat of government was shifted from Amarapoora to Mandalay. In 1862, Phayre, then a Colonel, headed another mission to Burmah, and concluded a rather one-sided commercial treaty, arranging also for a British representative to reside at the capital.

The treaty did not work well, Burmah securing all the advantages, and giving nothing in return. In 1866 a third mission was on the point of departing from India with the object of improving the position of British trade, when an insurrection broke out, and plunged the country into confusion. The king had favoured his brother, whom he had created Crown Prince, at the expense of his sons; and, in August, two of the latter rose, murdered their uncle and one of the ministers, and blockaded their father the King in his palace at Mandalay. Captain (later Sir) Edward Sladen, the British resident, being warned that his position was unsafe, went down to Rangoon; but, after a period of anarchy, the old King suppressed the insurrection, and, at the end of the year, again received Colonel Phayre at the head of a mission. In 1867 Colonel Fytche, who had by that time succeeded Colonel Phayre, concluded an agreement more favourable than that

---

[1] See vol. vi., p. 371, etc.
[2] Known as the Mendoon Prince.

of 1862 ; and thenceforward for many years relations between Burmah and her most powerful neighbour were fairly satisfactory, although, in 1875, they were imperilled by the breaking out of frontier disturbances and internal disorders. In 1878, however, the old King died.

The rightful heir was a personage known as the Myoungan Prince; but the intrigues of an old and unscrupulous Princess named Sinbyumaryin, who had married her daughter Soopyah Lat to Theebaw, one of the King's younger sons, secured Theebaw's proclamation as monarch. Theebaw began his reign by murdering eighty-six of his blood relations. Mr. Shaw, the British resident, protested, but Britain was just then much engaged elsewhere, and failed to take up a firm attitude. Mr. Shaw died at his post, and was succeeded by Colonel Horace Browne, who, unwilling to put up with the treatment accorded to him at Mandalay, presently quitted that capital, and was succeeded by Mr. St. Barbe. By that time, in consequence of British inaction, the Burmese had come to believe that they might do exactly as they pleased ; and eventually not only the resident but also nearly all the European inhabitants had to quit the country. This was in 1880. Theebaw seems to have celebrated the event by carrying out the massacre of five hundred people. It is hardly astonishing that when later he sent an envoy to Simla, asking for a treaty, his advances were coldly received. Subsequently he coquetted with France. Writing to the Indian government in September, 1885, Colonel Sladen said :—

" . . . we have . . . been compelled to withdraw our resident from the capital, and stay further relations with the court, because the condition of things there is so barbarous and insecure, and the attitude of the government so intractable, that we cannot consent on the one hand to countenance massacres and misrule, or on the other to invite insult and risk the lives of our political officers. . . . After refusing the treaty we offered King Theebaw at Simla in 1882, he has thought proper to make political capital out of our forced retirement by forming alliances with European states which have no interests in Burmah, and whose presence on the scene is only intended to encumber our action, and even menace our possessions in British Burmah. As a consequence we already find ourselves in the false and anomalous position of having a powerful ruling state on our borders intriguing against us. . . ."

Colonel Sladen recommended as the only satisfactory remedy for this condition of things that the whole of Upper Burmah should be annexed. Early in October, therefore, an ultimatum was despatched to Theebaw, offering him the alternative of complete submission to British direction, or of war ; and preparations were made for the

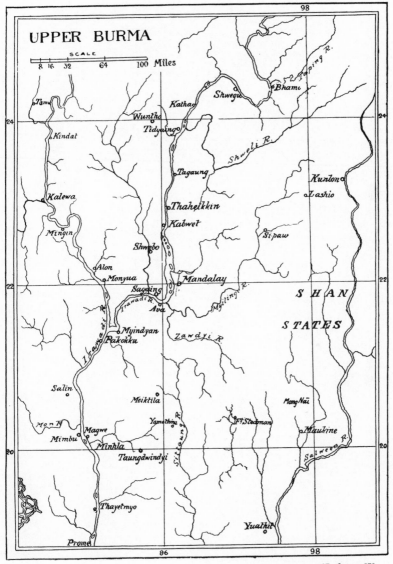

UPPER BURMA

SCALE
8 16 32 64 100 Miles

98

Táma

Kindat

24

Kalewa

Mingin

Alon
Monyua

22

Sagaing

Ava

Myindyan
Pakokku

Salin

Mon R.

Mimbu

Magwe

Minhla

Taungdwindyi

Thayetmyo

Prome

96

Wuntho
Tidyaingo

Katha

Shwegu

Bhamo

Taiping R.

Shweli R.

Tagaung

Thaheikkin

Kabwet

Shwebo

Mandalay

Zawdyi R.

Meiktila

Yamethin

Sittang R.

Sittang R.

Ft. Stedman

Kunlon

Lashio

Sipaw

Myiling R.

S H A N

STATES

Mong Nai

Maukine

Salween R.

Yuathit

98

24

22

20

[To face p. 376.

campaign which, it was then felt, was inevitable. Major-General
H. N. D. Prendergast, V.C., C.B., was nominated to the chief
military command, and, owing to the nature of the country in
which operations were to be carried on, the co-operation of the
Navy was requested, although the point from which the advance
was to begin was, by water, more than two hundred miles from the
sea. On November 13th, 1885, the General received orders to move
upon Mandalay.

The advance upon the capital was naturally made up the river
Irrawaddy, Mandalay being upon that stream, which is navigable
for many miles beyond it, and there being practically no roads from
the British frontier to the heart of Upper Burmah. The town of
Thayetmyo, on the Irrawaddy, a short distance south of the border
line, became the British base, and was a most convenient one, as it
is in immediate water communication with Rangoon, and is, moreover, only fifty or sixty miles north of Prome, which was then the
rail-head. The numerous steamers of the Irrawaddy Flotilla
Company afforded ready means of transport for the military part of
the expedition.

The official conquest of Upper Burmah was little more than a
military promenade, Mandalay being occupied, and Theebaw a
prisoner, a fortnight after the issue of the order to advance, and
there being no fighting of very serious importance during that
period. Nor was there any very extensive employment of naval
force. It was, however, to the co-operation of the Navy with the
Army that the rapidity and comparative bloodlessness of this official
conquest were mainly due. After the official conquest, and the fall
of Theebaw, the Navy proved itself equally valuable in the far more
arduous and wearisome work of repressing the guerillas and dacoits
who sprang up in almost every corner of the land, and for many
months obstructed the general re-establishment of order, and the
effective completion of the conquest. If, therefore, the Navy won
no great glory in Burmah, it at least rendered very substantial
services.

In the middle of October, the only British man-of-war at
Rangoon was the gun-vessel *Woodlark*, Commander William Robert
Clutterbuck. On October 21st, upon reaching Trincomalee from a
cruise, Captain Robert Woodward, of the composite cruiser
Turquoise, received a telegraphic message from the Indian Govern-
ment to the effect that a second man-of-war was needed; and,

proceeding at once, he arrived at Rangoon early on the 27th, and conferred with the Chief Commissioner, with whom it was arranged that the paddle steamer *Irrawaddy*,[1] of the Indian Marine,[2] and the little screw steam-launches *Kathleen* and *Settang*, should be immediately dispatched up the river to the frontier.

Commander Clutterbuck had already prepared these craft, and had armed and manned the *Irrawaddy* and *Settang* from the

CAPTAIN ROBERT WOODWARD, C.B.

Woodlark. Captain Woodward, therefore, placed Lieutenant Frederick Perceval Trench, senior of the *Turquoise*, in command of the *Kathleen*, giving him a suitable crew, and entrusted the three vessels to Commander Clutterbuck, who had his pennant in

---

[1] Mounting two 20-pr. B. and two 9-pr. M. guns.

[2] Capt. John Hext, R.N., Director of the Indian Marine, rendered valuable service throughout the campaign. So also did Commander Alfred Carpenter, R.N., of the Indian Marine Survey. The latter received the D.S.O. for his services. He was much assisted by Lieut. Arthur Channer, R.N.

the *Irrawaddy*, with orders to proceed to Thayetmyo. The flotilla departed on the 28th, and reached its destination some days before the order of November 13th, which authorised the advance into the enemy's country.

In the meantime, Rear-Admiral Sir Frederick William Richards, K.C.B. the naval Commander-in-Chief, who was then at Zanzibar in the *Bacchante*, had instructed Captain Woodward by telegraph to organise a Naval Brigade, and had informed him that twelve 25-pr. guns would be furnished to him by the Indian Government. As these guns arrived in succession from India, they were made ready ; and four of them were sent on to the front on November 11th with the *Turquoise's* contingent of the Brigade, under Lieutenant Frederick Fogarty Fegen. The remaining eight were held back for the *Bacchante's* contingent, which, after the arrival of the flagship on the 19th at Rangoon, proceeded to the front on November 20th, under Commander Charles James Barlow. Woodward had prepared two barges as armed gunboats, mounting in each of them a 64-pdr. muzzle-loader from the *Turquoise*. These barges were fitted out under the superintendence of Carpenter Henry James Lilley, and were supplied with protection consisting of cotton bales and rifle-proof plates. The guns were so mounted at the bows as to admit of their being trained through an arc of 45 degrees. Each barge carried 200 rounds of ammunition for her gun, and two anchors and cables, and, when ready for action, drew 3 feet 9 inches of water. The two gunboats thus improvised left with Lieutenant Fegen on November 11th. With them went also a survey party under Commander Alfred Carpenter, R.N., who was employed at that time in the Marine Survey of British India, and borne for that purpose in the *Bacchante*. Captain Woodward also organised an explosive party, which, under Commander John Durnford, of the sloop *Mariner*, left Rangoon by train on the 13th, and reached Thayetmyo on the day following. In addition, flats, steamers, and launches were selected, made ready, and sent up the river for the use of the contingent. Leaving only the *Bacchante's* contingent to follow him, Captain Woodward himself departed for the front, and overtook the advance on the 17th at Minhla, where he assumed command of the Brigade.

The first hostile movement of the campaign was made on November 14th by Commander Clutterbuck, who, with the *Irrawaddy* and *Kathleen*, undertook a reconnaissance up the river, and, about twenty-eight miles above the Thayetmyo, came upon a Burmese steamer, which he engaged with his machine-guns. She made little or no resistance, and, being captured, was towed down to Thayetmyo, where she was received with cheers by the troops, of whom about 10,000 had been assembled for the expedition. In addition to a number of native Indian regiments and batteries, there were with the force the 2nd battalion of the Liverpool Regiment, the 2nd battalion of the Hampshire Regiment, the 1st battalion of the Royal Welsh Fusiliers, and some Royal Artillery; but there was neither cavalry[1] nor military transport; and the omission to include these obliged the whole expedition to stick to the waterways, and so encouraged the outbreak elsewhere of that dacoity which, after the official conquest of the country had been completed, gave incalculable trouble.

The general advance up the river began almost immediately; and the Burmese forces were encountered on the 17th at Minhla, a town on the right bank, forty-four miles north of Thayetmyo. Close to the town was a fort, but on a knoll on the opposite side of the stream was a far more formidable one, called Gwe-Gyomg-Kamyo, or Kolegone, a work constructed by European engineers, and armed with numerous modern guns. General Prendergast landed troops on each side some miles lower down, and caused them to advance simultaneously by country paths, while, to divert the enemy's attention, the armed steamers engaged the forts in a long-range artillery contest. On the left, or Kolegone bank, the appearance of the troops on a rising ground on the inland side of the fort caused the enemy, who were already demoralised by the fire of the *Irrawaddy* and *Kathleen*, to bolt in confusion. On the Minhla side the advance was pluckily disputed; but at length the fort was carried, and the enemy driven out with slaughter. The Army in these operations lost 5 killed and 31 wounded. The Navy had no casualties.

Off Minhla, on the evening of the 17th, Captain Woodward joined, and took command of the Naval Brigade. On the morning of the following day, he proceeded up the river with the Brigade in the *Irrawaddy*, *Kathleen*, *Palow*,[2] the two gun barges, and the flat *Ngawoon*[3] (having the survey party on board), and was informed by

---

[1] Except a few volunteers from Rangoon.

[2] Steel paddle-vessel, 154 tons, belonging to the Irr. Flot. Co.

[3] Twin-screw vessel, 138 tons, belonging to the Irr. Flot. Co.

a native that 500 Burmese and 4 guns were occupying a fort at
Membo. Steaming thither, he threw a few shell at the supposed
work, and, getting no reply, anchored to await the arrival of the
main body of the expedition, which moved from Minhla on the 19th.
On the 20th, the whole flotilla weighed again, headed by the Naval
Brigade. That night it lay to off Yenan-Gyoung, and, on the night
of the 21st, a little above Yeo-Wah. The Intelligence Department
received news that the enemy intended to make a determined stand
at Pagan; but on the 22nd, when the flotilla advanced, that ruined
city was passed without a shot being fired. Just above it, however,
the flotilla was stopped, while the *Irrawaddy* steamed ahead to
reconnoitre.

She soon returned, reporting the presence of two steamers higher
up, and of large bodies of troops on the left bank; whereupon
Captain Woodward was ordered to move forward with his vessels,
and with the barge *White Swan*, having Royal Artillery on board,
and engage the Burmese, who held a bluff on which were batteries.
The batteries were soon silenced, and the Brigade landed and took
and destroyed their eleven guns. The two steamers, which had
been sunk, were also taken possession of. The *Settang* was left at
Pagan at the service of the garrison which had been landed there;
and at 2.30 P.M. on the 23rd the advance was resumed, the flotilla,
however, anchoring again at dusk.

On the 24th it weighed and proceeded. On nearing the village
of Kaoung-Wah, the leading craft were fired at from a stockade,
which, however, was soon silenced by one of the gun-barges which
was attached to the *Ngawoon*. The *Kathleen* was then sent forward
to ascertain whether the work was still occupied, and, troops being
landed, the stockade was destroyed. Further on, at 4.15 P.M., large
bodies of troops were observed on high ground on Mingyan, and
earthworks were also seen close to the river. The naval craft,
assisted by the Royal Artillery in the *White Swan*, with the launches
Yunan[1] and *Ataran*,[2] and one of the gun-barges, moved up and
engaged, slowly advancing meanwhile. Several little improvised
batteries armed with small guns and filled with riflemen were
successively silenced, the Burmese quitting them, and taking refuge
in the high grass and standing corn in their rear. Near the upper
end of the town the enemy was found much more strongly entrenched,

---

[1] Paddle-vessel, 396 tons, belonging to the Irr. Flot. Cc.
[2] Twin-screw, 140 tons, belonging to the Irr. Flot. Co.

and supported by a respectable battery commanding the river; and, for a time, he held his ground with some pertinacity; nor was it until 6 P.M. that the fire slackened. Indeed, during the whole of the night of the 24th there was intermittent firing, and not until the following morning were the Burmese dislodged and routed. In this affair the Brigade had two bluejackets wounded. A force of troops landed and destroyed the guns, but met with no opposition, and were re-embarked at noon on the 25th, only small detachments being left behind. In the evening the flotilla anchored off Yandaboo, the place of signature of the treaty which ended the war of 1826.

"At daylight on the 26th," says Captain Woodward's report to the General, "a large flat was found to be drifting down on the fleet. She was quickly grappled, towed clear, and anchored. At 7.30 the fleet started, and passed through a line of boats filled with stones prepared for sinking. These boats were cut adrift with but little delay, and the channel cleared. About 4 P.M. a large Burmese government boat was sighted coming down the river, flying a flag of truce."

A launch steamed up unceremoniously to this craft, which is said to have resembled an ancient Greek war-vessel, and, taking her in tow, conducted her to the head-quarter ship, the *Thurreah*. It was the beginning of the end. The boat brought high officers of state, bearing a deprecatory letter from the Burmese prime minister. The officers were sent back with an ultimatum that no offers or proposals could then be accepted, but that if Theebaw should choose to surrender his person, his army, and his capital, the lives and property of himself and his family would be respected, provided always that the European residents in Mandalay should prove to be safe. The ambassadorial boat had been escorted down the river by an armed Burmese steamer, which was boarded from the *Kathleen*, and taken without resistance. That night the flotilla anchored seven miles below Ava.

On the 27th, when the vessels weighed and proceeded, numerous troops were seen on the ramparts of the town; and arrangements were made for storming the defences. Meanwhile, however, another flag of truce appeared, with a message to the effect that Theebaw would surrender; whereupon the General went on board the *Palow*, Captain Woodward's craft, and steamed to the fort. The flotilla presently anchored abreast of the Ava fortifications, and a detachment went ahead in launches to find a passage through a line of sunken obstructions which barred the stream. A clear channel was soon reported.

At that point the steamer *Pulu*,[1] with Rear-Admiral Sir Frederick William Richards, and the *Bacchante's* contingent, arrived and anchored, the naval Commander-in-Chief at once going to the *Palow* to visit General Prendergast. As soon as it appeared that the Burmese no longer purposed to resist, the troops were landed to take over the guns and other arms which were to be surrendered, a brigade being also sent to Sagain fort, on the right bank, for the same purpose. Only about 2500 stand of small-arms seem to have been given up. Probably as many more were carried off by the Burmese. That night the flotilla lay between Ava and Sagain ; and on the 28th it moved up to Mandalay, which was reached, after three hours' steaming, at 9 A.M.

At 1 P.M. the Naval Brigade disembarked, and accompanied the troops to the King's palace, where it took over the custody of the eastern entrance during Colonel Sladen's interview with Theebaw, who agreed formally to surrender on the 29th, when the army made its triumphal entry, and received the monarch and his family. On the 30th the steamer *Tigris*, manned by a naval contingent from H.M. paddle-vessel *Sphinx*, 7, Commander William Llewellyn Morrison, arrived.

At 6.30 P.M. on the 30th, Theebaw, with his suite, was transferred to the *Thurreah* for conveyance to Rangoon ; and on the following morning, escorted by the *Ngawoon*, Lieutenant Godfrey Michell Courage, and one of the Brigade's armed gun-barges, the fallen King departed for Rangoon. After the occupation of Mandalay, further operations were delayed for a time by the difficulties of transport, the prevalence of dacoity near the capital, and an outbreak of cholera among the Madras and Punjab coolies attached to the force. The disease appeared on board the vessels of the flotilla, and, to save them from the scourge, the troops had to be again landed and taken away from the river. In the interim, a party from the Naval Brigade was employed at the palace under the orders of the sorting committee ; the *Irrawaddy*, *Tigris*, and *Kathleen* were detached on various services ; launches patrolled the river for the suppression of dacoity, and the *Bacchante's* contingent was sent to the Chindwin river for the same purpose.[2]

In December a river expedition departed from Mandalay for

---

[1] Steel paddle-vessel, 148 tons, belonging to the Irr. Flot. Co.

[2] Chiefly from Woodward's disps., and Maj. E. C. Browne's 'Coming of the Great Queen' (1888).

Bhamo, a town at the head of the Irrawaddy navigation, and not far from the Chinese frontier.   It consisted of the *Turquoise's* and *Woodlark's* contingents of the Naval Brigade, and troops under Brigadier-General Norman, C.B.,[1] the naval party being in the *Pulu* and two flats; and it left for the north on the 18th.   A search-light, which had been fitted up on the flying-deck of the steamer, and which was used every night, had an extraordinarily intimidating effect upon the natives, who everywhere professed friendship.   Great difficulties of navigation were encountered, owing to the lowness of the river; but Bhamo, or, rather, a point within four miles of it, was reached on December 28th.   Further progress by steamer was impossible.   Theebaw's soldiers were disarmed, and, it being apparent that if they were left on the spot they would turn to dacoity, about 250 of them were sent down to Mandalay.   The Bhamo expedition returned thither without having seen any fighting. It had left garrisons at the principal towns.

So much for the official conquest of Upper Burmah.   The actual reduction of the country to a state of peace and order required a much longer time, necessitated the large reinforcement of the army of occupation, and was not completed until well on in 1887.

For their services in the campaign, Captain Robert Woodward was made a C.B.,[2] Commander Clutterbuck was posted,[3] and Lieutenant Frederick Perceval Trench was made a Commander.[4] After the institution of the Distinguished Service Order in November, 1886, several of the earliest appointments to it were made in respect of services in Burmah in 1885–86.   On January 14th, 1887, Commanders John Durnford, Alfred Carpenter, and Charles James Barlow, and Major Walter Miller Lambert, R.M.A., and on June 18th, 1887, Fleet-Surgeon Thomas d'Arcy Bromlow, and Engineer William Nicklin, were created Companions.

In the subsequent operations against the dacoits, the *Ranger*, 3, Commander John Pakenham Pipon, did long and arduous work which is deserving of remembrance.   Three of his officers, Lieutenants Charles Brownlow Macdonald and Henry Faulconer Aplin, Gunner Thomas Holman, and Pipon himself, patrolled the waters of Upper Burmah in steam launches for a considerable period, and had several skirmishes with dacoits.   Holman won special dis-

---

[1] Though it was accompanied by General Sir H. Prendergast and the headquarters of the army.
[2] May 29, 1886.   [3] March 1, 1886.   [4] Dec. 31, 1885.

tinction by concealing himself and eight seamen in a native boat, which he allowed to drift past the resort of a band of river pirates, who were thus tempted to fire upon him. Returning the fire, he killed five of the enemy, and then landed and destroyed their village, suffering no casualties. For this he was congratulated by General Sir F. S. Roberts, and thanked on the quarter-deck by Rear-Admiral Sir F. W. Richards. Lieutenant Macdonald was, unfortunately, killed in action with dacoits at Shemagar on January 9th, 1887. Lieutenant Aplin, having received an injury to his sight while soldering a tin of gun-cotton, had to be relieved. Commander Pipon was deservedly promoted on January 1st, 1887.

The other naval operations of these and the immediately following years were, for the most part, of but slight importance.

On April 26th, 1886, in consequence of the preparations which were being made by Greece with the obvious object of entering upon a war with Turkey, the representatives of Great Britain, Germany, Austria-Hungary, Russia, and Italy requested the Greek government to reduce its land and sea forces to a peace establishment. Greece refused; whereupon, on May 8th, the five powers declared a blockade of the Greek ports from Cape Malia, at the south of the Morea, to Cape Colonna at the termination of the northern side of the Gulf of Ægina. In the meantime, part of the British Mediterranean fleet had been ordered to Suda Bay, the rendezvous of the squadrons of the allies; and there, as early as April 10th, Vice-Admiral H.R.H. the Duke of Edinburgh, K.G., who was senior officer,[1] and, as such, took charge of the united contingents, found himself in command of the following force:—

	Ironclad Battleships.	Cruisers.	Dispatch-vessels and miscellaneous craft.	Gun-vessels and gunboats.	Torpedo-boats.
Great Britain . . .	5	2	1	7	5
Germany	1				
Austria-Hungary . .	1	1	..	2	6
Russia	1	..	1		
Italy	3	..	1	1	6
Turkey	..	..	..	7	
Total	11	3	3	17	17

[1] Having local rank as Admiral. H.R.H. assumed command in the Mediterranean on Mar. 5, 1886, in succession to Admiral Lord John Hay.

On the declaration of the blockade, the fleet proceeded to the Piræus, and orders were issued for the detention of every vessel under the Greek flag that should attempt to enter or leave the ports on the blockaded littoral. The enforcement of these directions soon had its effect. Greece disarmed; the blockade was raised on June 7th; the vessels which had been detained were liberated; and the allied fleet returned to Suda Bay, where it separated.[1]

On November 23rd, 1886, the Niger Company's steamer *Kuka*, with Consul Hewett on board, arrived at Fernando Po, and reported to the senior officer of the station, Captain George Weightman Hand, of the corvette *Royalist*, who happened to be lying there, that the natives of Patani, a village far up the Niger, had pillaged a factory, and that the Company needed help. Hand sent the gunboat *Wrangler*, Lieutenant Harry Dampier Law, to Bonny, to telegraph for instructions, and, with the *Royalist*, the sloop *Racer*, Commander Arthur George Fullerton, and the paddle-vessel *Alecto*, Lieutenant George Izat, started for the mouth of the Niger, which he reached on the 25th. The Company provided two small steamers, and these, with the *Alecto*, and about 80 bluejackets from the *Royalist* and *Racer*, formed the expedition with which, on December 1st, Hand proceeded about a hundred miles up the stream. He returned on the 10th, having burnt Patani and four hamlets on the Wari branch, destroyed a number of canoes, and driven the troublesome natives into the bush. He met with little or no opposition, and suffered no casualties.[2]

During all these years the slave-trade on the east coast of Africa remained astonishingly active, seeing that steady efforts continued to be made for its repression. Much might be written about the good work done by her Majesty's ships on the station, and by the boats which were detached from them to cruise for suspicious dhows. Indeed, the subject deserves a book to itself. It must suffice here to mention a few episodes of the long war which was thus waged on behalf of human liberty.

In June, 1880, Captain Charles James Brownrigg had been appointed to the *London*, guard-ship at Zanzibar. A most active officer, his activity cost him his life. On December 3rd, 1881, having left his ship in a steam pinnace, with ten men, to inspect

[1] Parl. Papers, 4731, 4732, 4765, 4766 [1886].
[2] Corr. of *N. & M. Record*, Jan. 13 and 20, 1887.

such of his boats as were then cruising off Pemba, he came up with, and ran alongside a dhow which was full of slaves. She flew French colours, but Brownrigg desired to verify her nationality. Perceiving that the British were unprepared, the Arab crew, about five and twenty in number, fired a volley into the pinnace, and then boarded her, killing or wounding the people, or driving them overboard. Brownrigg alone offered serious resistance. He seized a rifle, shot one of his assailants, and, standing in the stern sheets with the clubbed weapon, held out manfully in spite of twenty wounds, two at least of which would have been mortal. Nor did he desist until he fell shot through the heart. Three of his men shared his fate, and three others were wounded. The Arabs allowed the boat to drift; and the survivors of her crew, regaining her, took her back to the *London.* The dhow, then empty, was subsequently captured.[1]

Captain Rodney Maclaine Lloyd, while in command of the corvette *Briton,* between May, 1884, and July, 1887, captured no fewer than ten slave dhows by means of his boats. The sloop *Reindeer,* Commander Henry Briggs Lang, also made several prizes at about the same period, as did the sloop *Kingfisher,* Commander John Harvey Rainier. In 1887, moreover, the country had another sharp reminder that the scoundrels who conducted the abominable traffic were not always willing to be suppressed without hard fighting. In May, Lieutenant Frederick Fogarty Fegen, of the *Turquoise,* Captain Robert Woodward, C.B., was detached from the corvette in her pinnace to cruise for slavers off the island of Pemba, near Zanzibar. On May 30th, with five bluejackets, one Marine, and an interpreter, he was lying at anchor at daylight, when a dhow was sighted. He sent a dinghy, with two men and the interpreter, to board her. The dhow replied to the interpreter's hail with a volley of musketry, the dinghy, and the pinnace's 9-pr. returning the fire. Thereupon the dhow bore down boldly upon the pinnace. Fegen called out, " Prepare to resist boarders! Stand to them, my lads!" and the Arabs in the dhow, about thirteen in number, endeavoured to board. The gallant Lieutenant shot two of them with his revolver, and ran a third through with his sword. An Arab would have speared him, had not an A.B. named Pearson stabbed the man with his cutlass. Fegen was badly wounded in the right arm, but continued to use his revolver with his left. Three of his men were

[1] Hansard (266), 679 : *Times,* 6 and 12 Dec., 1881.

cut down, yet Fegen and one man, though both were injured, maintained the fight, until the dhow, having lost nine of her people, sheered off.   The pinnace and dinghy followed her up most pluckily ; and, a rifle shot killing the slaver's helmsman, the vessel drove ashore and there capsized.   The Arabs on land opened fire in order to cover the retreat of their friends; but they were driven off by some shells from the pinnace's gun, and fifty-three slaves were then rescued from the dhow, twelve others having been drowned.   One British bluejacket was mortally wounded in this most creditable affair, and three others were put temporarily out of action.   Fegen himself had to be invalided home, but enjoyed the satisfaction, on his arrival, of finding that he had been specially promoted [1] for his bravery. [2]

On the same station, the gun-vessel *Ranger*, Commander Samuel Arthur Johnson, was requested in July, 1887, by the Political Agent at Muscat, to proceed to Suweik, on the Batineh coast, in order to protect British subjects and their property.   A rebel chief had seized the local fort, but, upon the *Ranger's* appearance, he assumed a peaceable attitude ; and the threatened British subjects and their goods were taken off without resistance.   This was the extent of Johnson's original orders.   Later it was decided that the rebel chief should be removed; and the *Ranger*, returning, removed him on July 12th, happily without fighting. [3]

On June 24th and 25th in the same year the gunboat *Zephyr*, Lieutenant Charles Kerr Hope, had occasion to punish some piratical Dyaks on the shores of Darvel Bay, North Borneo.   A landing-party destroyed the boats of the freebooters, and a few shells from the ship fired the villages of Bussan Melumtah and Pantow-Pantow. There was very little opposition, nor were there any British casualties. Hope's action was approved by the Admiralty. [4]

In the little military expedition [5] which was undertaken in November, 1887, by Colonel Sir Francis Walker de Winton to punish the rebellious Yonnies, a tribe in the hinterland of Sierra Leone, the Navy bore a small but creditable part, fifteen men of the sloop *Acorn*, Commander William Edward Breeks Atkinson,

---

[1] Com., Aug. 9, 1887.

[2] Woodward's desp.; *Gaz.*; Parl. Papers [5428] Slave Trade, No. 1, 1888.

[3] Corr. of *N. & M. Record*, Aug. 18, 1887.

[4] Accts. and Papers, LII., 1887; *N. & M. Record*, June 16, 1887.

[5] Total force, naval and military, employed: 17 officers, and 278 n. c. officers and men, chiefly of the 1st West Ind. Regt.

accompanying the force, under Lieutenant Francis Alfred Valentine, of that ship. The service was extremely arduous, owing to the density of the forest which had to be traversed, and to the continual fusillade which was kept up by the concealed enemy, whose only projectiles, however, were small shot and rough bits of iron. The total British casualties were about 20 wounded, no one being killed. Robari, the Yonnie stronghold, was reached, shelled, set on fire by rockets, and quickly taken; and the column, after having burnt some other towns, freed several captives, and received the submission of the rebellious chiefs, returned to the coast, the *Acorn's* people re-embarking on January 2nd, 1888. For his behaviour in this brief campaign, Lieutenant Valentine received the D.S.O.[1] His men were later granted the Ashantee medal, with a special clasp.[2] A similar decoration was given to a few officers and men from the sloop *Icarus*, Commander William Martin Annesley, and the gun-vessel *Rifleman*, Lieutenant Charles Golding Prater, who at the same time, and in connection with the same expedition, carried out some useful boat-service in the Rokelle River.[3] Lieutenant Dudley Rawson de Chair, R.N., acted as A.D.C. to Colonel de Winton.

Osman Digna was still troublesome in the neighbourhood of Suakin. On December 17th, 1887, he made an attack on one of the outlying forts; and on March 3rd, 1888, a large body of tribesmen established themselves in an abandoned post, known as Fort Hudson, and thence opened a continuous fire on the place. On the following morning, the guns of the sloop *Dolphin*, Commander George Neville, were turned against them, and the Egyptian troops, assisted by some "friendlies," attacked by land; but the position was very strong, and the attack was confused by a shell from the sloop bursting accidentally among the "friendlies." The force, therefore, was withdrawn. In the following night the enemy also withdrew. On September 17th, another attack was made on the town, the Arabs attempting to cut off the water supply.[4] In consequence of this, military reinforcements were ordered to Suakin. General Sir Francis W. Grenfell, Sirdar of the Egyptian Army,

---

[1] Mar. 9, 1888.

[2] *Gazette*, Apr. 7, 1893.

[3] *A. & N. Gaz.*, Feb. 11; *N. & M. Record*, Jan. 5, 1888; Accts. and Papers, LXXV., 1888.

[4] The sloop *Gannet* failed to shell them out of some of the positions which they subsequently took up. *Daily News*, Sept. 27, 1888.

himself arrived early in November, and additional British troops followed him.

It was determined to attack the Arabs, if possible, by surprise, on December 20th. With this object in view, a preliminary naval demonstration was made off Mersa Kuwai, which lies eight miles to the northward, and was visible from the Dervish camp at Gemaizeh, and the enemy's lines were shelled by the guns in the forts and in the sloop *Racer*, Commander Henry John May. At 6 A.M., the attack was delivered by the troops, assisted by a Naval Brigade under Commander May,[1] Lieutenant Alfred Wyndham Paget,[1] commanding the gunboat *Starling*, and Lieutenants Arthur Horatio Shirley, and Ralph Fearon Ayscough Smith. The Dervish rout was complete; and happily the Anglo-Egyptian loss was small. There were no naval casualties; but Lieutenant Ernest Frederick David, R.M., attached to the Egyptian Army, was among the killed.[2]

Towards the end of 1888, partly in consequence of the revolt of several of the coast towns against German authority, and partly in the interests of the suppression of slavery, a blockade of the Zanzibar littoral was established,[3] under the orders of Rear-Admiral the Hon. Edmund Robert Fremantle, C.B., C.M.G., Commander-in-Chief on the East Indies Station, and in the name of the Sultan of Zanzibar. In this blockade, Germany, France, Italy and Portugal, as well as Great Britain, participated; but, apart from captures of slave dhows —captures which were always to be expected in those waters—the incidents of the blockade were of an uninteresting nature.[4] Two or three captures, which were made just before the blockade was established in December, are worth recalling.

On October 17th, 1888, the steam-cutter of the gun-vessel *Griffon*, Commander John Edric Blaxland, which was cruising under Lieutenant Myles Harry Cooper, sighted a dhow and chased

---

[1] Promoted for this service, Jan. 16, 1889.

[2] Desps.: Royle, p. 462, etc.

[3] Beginning on Dec. 2. It extended from Kipini on the north to the river Rovuma on the south.

[4] The British ships originally concerned were the battleship *Agamemnon*, Capt. Charles Searle Cardale; cruiser *Boadicea* (flag), Capt. the Hon. Assheton Gore Curzon-Howe; cruiser *Garnet*, Capt. Albert Baldwin Jenkings; sloop *Osprey*, Com. Charles Edward Gissing; sloop *Penguin*, Com. George Fowler King Hall; gun-vessel *Algerine*, Com. William Codrington Carnegie Forsyth; and gun-vessel *Griffon*, Com. John Edric Blaxland. Rear-Adm. Deinhard commanded the German contingent, with his flag in the *Leipzig*. For his services on the occasion, Fremantle received the Prussian Order of the Crown, of the 1st class, and Deinhard, the K.C.B.

her, ordering her to lower her sail. The dhow took no notice, and, on the cutter's near approach, opened a sudden and heavy fire on her, wounding Cooper and two seamen, William Ward and Alexander Petty. Cooper directed John Bray, the ship's corporal, to take command and do his best. The five unwounded men in the cutter thereupon continued to fire into the dhow until she drove ashore, the cutter also grounding within a dozen yards of her. The Arabs jumped overboard and fled.

As soon as Bray could refloat his boat, he towed the dhow off; and then, the wounded being in a very serious state, he put two of his men into the prize, and, leaving her, made for the *Griffon* with all speed. Cooper, however, died ere the gun-vessel was reached. Commander Blaxland sent back the steam-cutter in charge of Lieutenant Norman Craig Palmer, and, upon daylight breaking, followed. The dhow, which was found to be armed with a small gun, was taken into Zanzibar.[1]

Another capture was made off Pemba on November 6th by Lieutenant Walter Clifton Slater in the pinnace of the flagship *Boadicea*, Captain the Hon. Assheton Gore Curzon-Howe, after a chase of six hours. The dhow offered resistance, and was not brought to until shots had been fired on both sides; but there were no British casualties. She had forty-one slaves on board.[2] Yet other creditable captures off Pemba, in the same year, were made by Lieutenant Hugh Thomas Hibbert and Boatswain Thomas Job, of the sloop *Penguin*, Commander George Fowler King Hall.

A lamentable event which occurred in the Pacific in 1880 has escaped mention in its chronological place. I have presently to describe a famous triumph of British seamanship and engineering which turned all thoughts to that distant ocean in the spring of 1889; and the occasion seems a fit one for harking back, and prefacing the account of the great hurricane at Samoa with a brief narrative of this other and earlier adventure in the South Sea.

In the summer of 1880, the little sailing schooner *Sandfly* was recommissioned at Sydney by Lieutenant James St. Clair Bower, her old officers and crew going home in the *Raleigh*.

On October 13th, 1880, the schooner anchored at Tezemvoka, in the Solomon Islands, and Bower, with five seamen, left in the whale-boat to survey the east coast of Anuda or Florida Island.

[1] Accts. and Papers, LXXII., 1889.

The boat was expected to return on the 17th, but she did not do so, and, on the 20th, the *Sandfly* proceeded to the east coast of Anuda to make enquiries. She there picked up one of the missing seamen, a man named Savage, who had a terrible tale to tell.

It appeared that at Nogu Island, where the boat had put ashore, the crew had obtained permission to bathe, and had scattered for that purpose. Soon afterwards, crowd of natives had attacked, and had massacred, all those who happened to be near the whaler. Bower and Savage, being at some little distance, had escaped temporarily : but on the following morning the unfortunate Lieutenant had been shot with one of the rifles which had been taken from the boat. Later his body was found, badly mutilated. Savage had hidden, eluded pursuit, swum to an uninhabited islet, made a raft for himself, and attempted to cross to Anuda, but, on the way, had been caught by natives, who, only after some deliberation, had decided not to give him up to Bower's murderers.

The *Sandfly* went to Raita Bay, and sent ashore a boat's crew of eight men, under Sub-Lieutenant Edward Eden Bradford, to punish the offenders, and burn their canoes. On returning, the party was fired at from the bush ; and one seaman was killed, and another wounded. Young Bradford, of whom more was heard later, could do little at that time save recover and bury the bodies of his countrymen, and ascertain with minuteness all the circumstances of the sad affair. Next day the schooner left for Sydney.

Commodore John Crawford Wilson, commanding on the Australian station, at once despatched the corvette *Emerald*, Captain William Henry Maxwell, with Bradford on board, to teach the natives a lesson. The *Sandfly's* boat was given up at Baranago ; but it was found impossible to capture the murderers, though their villages were destroyed. Some time later, Bishop Selwyn persuaded the chief to surrender the offenders, the ringleaders of whom were executed.[1]

A list of the material losses suffered by the fleet during the period under review will be found in the Appendix. Two incidents which, although they did not lead to the actual loss of any of H.M. ships, were within an ace of doing so, occurred in 1889, and must be noticed here.

One incident was of a very dramatic nature. The following terrible telegram reached Washington at the end of March from

[1] *Times*, Jan. 14, 1881; Hansard [257], 722; Parl. Papers, LX. [1881].

Rear-Admiral Lewis A. Kimberly, U.S.N., commanding the American squadron at Samoa :—

" Hurricane at Apia on March 15th. Every vessel in the harbour is ashore, except the English ship *Calliope*, which got to sea. The American ships *Trenton* and *Vandalia* are total losses. The *Nipsic* was beached, with her rudder gone, and may be saved; but the chances are against it. Captain Schoonmaker, 4 officers, and 93 men of the *Vandalia* were lost. The *Nipsic* lost 7 men. The *Trenton's* crew were all saved.

" The German ships *Adler* and *Eber* are total losses. The *Olga* was beached, and may be saved. The German losses number 96."

The men-of-war mentioned in the above telegram were :—

Ships.	Class.	Displ. in Tons.	I.H.P.	Nominal Speed. Kts.	Built. Year.	Screws. No.
Brit. *Calliope*[1] . . .	cruiser	2770	4020	13·75	1884	1
Amer. *Trenton*[2] . . .	cruiser	3900	3100	12·8	1876	1
„ *Vandalia*[3] . .	corvette	2100	1176	10·0	1874	1
„ *Nipsic*[3] . . .	sloop	1375	1375	11·0	1878	1
Germ. *Olga*[2]	corvette	2169	2397	14·0	1880	1
„ *Adler*[2] . . .	{ gun-vessel }	884	724	11·0	1883	1
„ *Eber*[2]	{ gun-vessel }	570	700	12·0	1887	1

[1] Steel, sheathed.   [2] Composite.   [3] Wood.

At the same time a German trading barque and seven coasting vessels were driven ashore at Apia.

The *Calliope* was then commanded by Captain Henry Coey Kane; and her Staff-Engineer was Henry George Bourke, who had as his assistants Engineer William Milton, and Assistant-Engineer James Robert Roffey.

For several days previous to the hurricane the weather had been cloudy and the barometer falling; but no one anticipated the violence of the storm which began on the afternoon of Friday, March 15th. That night the wind blew a gale, and the ships in harbour began to drag their anchors and to be driven ashore, colliding one with another as they went to destruction. The *Vandalia*, for example, drove on to the *Calliope*, carrying away the latter's jib boom ; and the *Olga* also fouled the British cruiser, taking her fore-yard out of her, smashing several of her boats and snapping one of her cables. At about 10 P.M., the *Calliope* had drifted towards the inner reef, was holding by a single anchor only, and was threatened by the *Trenton* and again by the *Olga*.

Kane took the sole course which could avert catastrophe. Calling upon his Engineers for every possible pound of steam, he paid out his single cable so as to enable his ship to clear the *Olga's* stern ; and, when his own stern was within twenty feet of the reef, he ordered full speed ahead, let his cable slip from the locker, and gradually forged his way out in the teeth of the hurricane. He cleared the *Olga*, and slowly passed the labouring American flag-ship *Trenton.* " My anchors are gone, and I am going to sea," shouted Kane. "Good luck to you," returned the gallant Kimberly, while the doomed foreign ships raised a parting cheer. The *Calliope* had a hard struggle, for she was able to make but a knot an hour against the violence of the wind ; but at length she got to sea and safety. Thanks were due, as Kane said in his report, to the admirable order in which the cruiser's engines and boilers had been kept. Had anything gone wrong with them, the *Calliope* must have perished. It was a triumph for the Engineers even more than for the Captain and his executive officers. Bourke[1] was at once promoted.[2]

The other incident was common-place enough.

On March 6th, the battleship *Sultan*, Captain Edward Rice, grounded on an unknown rock in South Comino Channel, Malta, and, on the 14th, in a heavy gale, slipped off the rock and sank. At one time it was feared that her recovery was impossible, but at length Messrs. Baghino and Co. undertook to raise her for £50,000, and on August 27th she was carried into Malta Harbour, where she underwent preliminary repairs. In December she left for Portsmouth, escorted first by the battleship *Téméraire*, Captain Gerard Henry Uctred Noel, and later by the troopship *Tyne*, Commander Walter Somerville Goodridge, and the special service vessel *Seahorse*, Staff-Commander James Roberts Osborn. She made the passage under her own steam at a speed of about seven knots, in charge of Commander Thomas MacGill, and anchored at Spithead on December 22nd. She was subsequently refitted and restored to the service.

The chief naval events of the year following took place within the limits of the East India Station.

In September, 1890, nine German traders in Vitu, a small state on the east coast of Africa, about 230 miles north of Zanzibar, were

---

[1] Fleet-Eng. May 28, 1889.

[2] Reports of Kimberly and Kane; speech of Goschen, May 22 ; teleg. desp. from Auckland to Berlin, Mar. 30; *A. & N. Gaz.*, May 11; *N. & M. Record*, May 16; *Times*, Apr. 1 and May 30, 1889.

murdered, by order, so it was stated, of the Sultan, Fumo Bakari. After communications had taken place between Germany and Great Britain, it was decided that the latter should send a punitive expedition to avenge the crime; and the execution of the business was entrusted to Vice-Admiral the Hon. Sir Edmund Robert Fremantle, who was still Commander-in-Chief on the station, and who, on October 20th, reached Lamu, a Zanzibari port in Vitu,

ADMIRAL THE HON. SIR EDMUND ROBERT FREMANTLE, G.C.B., C.M.G.

(From a photo by J. Hawke.)

with a squadron, and thence despatched an ultimatum to Fumo Bakari, who returned an evasive answer. Among the places at which murders had been committed were Baltia and Mkonumbi, both of which were easily accessible by water from Lamu. On October 24th, therefore, the boats of the flagship *Boadicea*, under Captain the Hon. Assheton Gore Curzon-Howe, of that ship, were sent to Mkonumbi, and those of the *Cossack* and *Brisk*, under Commander John MacKenzie McQuhae, to Baltia; and the villages were burnt, with but slight opposition, the boats returning at night. On the following day, by noon, the ships named in the note below[1] were assembled at Kipini, a port 14 miles from the seat of the Sultan, and at the mouth of the Ozz. Native porters, Indian police in the service of the East African Co., and Zanzibari troops, had been previously engaged for transport duty; and a force of 700 seamen and Royal Marines (with four 7-prs. and four machine guns), besides 100 Indian police, was got ready for a direct advance, while Kau, 20 miles up the Ozz river, and on the flank of the capital, was occupied by Indian police and Zanzibaris, supported by a few boats under Commander Ernest James Fleet (*Boadicea*). That evening a party under Commander Robert Archibald James Montgomerie (*Boadicea*) was pushed about three miles inland, to make a zeriba and a water-depôt. Before midnight the party had to repel a night attack, which cost it three men wounded. Ere daylight on the 26th, the main body landed, over a difficult bar, and by 7 A.M. joined Montgomerie's force; whereupon the general advance began under the Vice-Admiral's direction. Progress was slow, owing to the thick bush and great heat; and at 2 P.M., after a four hours' halt, Commander Alfred Leigh Winsloe (*Brisk*), with 50 bluejackets, was left behind to make another zeriba and depôt. At 4.30 P.M., when the force had halted within striking distance of Vitu in order to make a third zeriba, it was smartly attacked, though the natives were easily driven off. Nothing like Fumo Bakari's whole army, which may have been about 3000 strong, of whom half had firearms, seems to have been engaged. At daylight on the 27th, Gunner William Henry Newman (*Kingfisher*) was left in charge of the last zeriba, and the final advance took place, the enemy soon being encountered in some force, and desultory firing following. The town, as seen from a point about 1200 yards distant, was found to be surrounded, to within about 100 yards, by bush. This bush was shelled and occupied; some Marines, under Lieutenant James Nicholas Lalor, R.M.L.I., with a 7-pr., fired a couple of rounds at the town gate, which was then blown in by a gun-cotton party under Gunner George Alfred Jennings (T.) of the *Boadicea*; and the place was entered with

[1] *Boadicea*, V.-Ad. Hon. Sir E. R. Fremantle, K.C.B., C.M.G., Capt. Hon. A. G. Curzon-Howe; *Turquoise*, Capt. John Wm. Brackenbury, C.B., C.M.G.; *Conquest*, Capt. Wm. Hannam Henderson; *Cossack*, Com. J. M. McQuhae; *Brisk*, Com. A. L. Winsloe; *Kingfisher*, Com. Alexander Milne Gardiner; *Redbreast*, Lieut. Fras. Wm. Keary; *Pigeon*, Hy. Robt. Peel Floyd; *Humber*, Lieut. Jno. Wm. Brown; hired transport *Somali*, Lieut. Ian Mackenzie Fraser; and Brit. Ind. Co.'s ss. *Juba*.

hardly any resistance, the natives being, however, pursued for about three miles, and many of them killed. The town, and Sultan's house, with a large quantity of weapons and ammunition, were burnt; the whole force returned to Kipini on the 28th; and on the 30th the squadron sailed for Mombasa. The total loss sustained was but 12 men wounded; but there were also several cases of sunstroke. Numerous officers were mentioned in the Vice-Admiral's dispatch.[1] Among them was Captain Curzon-Howe, who was rewarded for his services with a C.B. The whole expedition, though of course of no great importance, was a model of good management.

The nature of some of the quieter work done from time to time by the Royal Navy is well illustrated in the following account, taken from the *Times*,[2] of the first passage of a British man-of-war into the Zambesi. The man-of-war in question was the steel twin-screw gunboat *Redbreast*, which then mounted six 4-inch breechloaders, besides two 3-pr. quick-firers, a boat-gun, and two Nordenfelt machine-guns. Previous to the *Redbreast's* visit the only British naval craft which had ever floated on the Zambesi was the little unarmed surveying steamer *Stork*. Writing in October, 1890, the correspondent of the *Times* said :—

"Last year's exploits of Major Serpa Pinto are, of course, fresh in your mind, and no doubt you recollect also that, with a view to guard against the occurrence of similar troubles in the future, the Government determined to place on the Zambesi a couple of light stern-wheel gunboats, and to man them with naval officers and crews. Messrs. Yarrow, of Poplar, built for the purpose the *Mosquito* and *Herald*, vessels drawing less than 18 in. of water; and these, in sections ready for fitting together on the spot, were shipped out in the ss. *Buccaneer*, while men and stores for them proceeded to the mouth of the river in her Majesty's storeship *Humber*, Lieutenant John William Brown. At that period the Zambesi was a private Portuguese waterway, or was regarded as such by the Portuguese; and as it was contemplated that forcible objections might be raised against our intended action, Sir Edmund Robert Fremantle, Commander-in-Chief on the East India Station, collected at Zanzibar a large naval force, with a view to taking and occupying, in case of necessity, all the Portuguese settlements on the coast, and to letting it be plainly seen that, whether the Portuguese liked it or not, we had made up our minds to fly the white ensign on the river. In the meantime, however, the Governments were involved in diplomatic negotiations which were wearisomely protracted until, in August last, the Admiral learnt from home that a treaty had at length been peaceably signed and that Portugal had engaged to allow us to put our stern-wheel gunboats together in the Chinde Mouth of the Zambesi, and to enter the river. On September 2nd a further telegram from home ordered the expedition to act upon this agreement. It had, however, been previously directed, doubtless in order to spare Portuguese susceptibilities, that Sir E. Fremantle himself was not to go, and that the only armed escort for the stern-wheelers was

---

[1] *Gazette*, Jan. 6th, 1891.   [2] *Times*, Dec. 17th, 1890.

to consist of one of the first-class screw gunboats—*Redbreast*, six guns, 805 tons, 1200-horse power, and *Pigeon*, six guns, 755 tons, 1200-horse power. The Admiral selected the *Redbreast*, possibly because her commander, Lieutenant Francis William Keary, has had the advantage of a great deal of surveying experience; and on September 3rd the expedition left Zanzibar, Lieutenant Brown, of the *Humber*, being senior officer. In due course it anchored off the bar at the entrance to the Chinde Mouth, and awaited the tide. This bar is the best of all the Zambesi bars, but there is only a depth of 7 feet of water on it at low-water springs, and the expedition arrived at dead neaps and during a nasty south-east swell. Next morning Lieutenant Keary examined the bar, and, although he was very unfavourably impressed, undertook to lead the way over it. The *Redbreast* drew 13 feet, and the *Humber* 13 feet 4 inches; and it was almost as ticklish a business as going into action, for, had either the *Humber* or the *Buccaneer* taken the ground, she would assuredly have been lost. Happily the passage was made without a scrape; but, to show its difficulty, I may mention that on two subsequent occasions, when the *Pigeon*, a smaller craft than the *Redbreast*, went in to communicate, she struck.

"The passage of the outer bar was, however, a relatively minor matter. Lieutenant Keary had orders from the Admiral to ascertain whether the *Redbreast* could proceed through the Chinde Mouth into the Zambesi proper. If so he was to escort the stern-wheelers and their convoy of canoes laden with stores into the great river, and to see them fairly started. The Chinde Mouth is 18 miles long, and, being almost unknown, had first to be carefully surveyed. Not, therefore, till September 25th was Keary able to report to Vice-Admiral Fremantle that the passage was possible; and even then he had to say that further examination was necessary before anything could be safely attempted. A day or two later, while prosecuting his survey as usual, he was hailed by a Portuguese light-draft gunboat, and politely requested to (*a*) desist, (*b*) return, and (*c*) haul down the British colours. Of course he did not obey the last direction; but he was obliged to desist, and proportionately bound, in spite of the very incomplete and unsatisfactory survey which he had succeeded in making, to endeavour to carry out Sir Edmund Fremantle's wishes, and to take the ship up. The Portuguese gunboat had brought down the Governor of Quilimane, a fire-eating gentleman, who at once began writing protests, issuing orders for the British flag not to be flown, and forbidding the natives to sell food to the expedition. He was willing to admit that the treaty had been signed and that we were acting in accordance with it, but his point was that the waters had not been officially declared free, and that, until they were so declared, they were still closed. While he fumed and protested, the *Mosquito*[1] and *Herald*[2] were quietly completed. When they were evidently ready, the Portuguese gunboat reappeared, and her captain declared plump that his orders were to oppose the advance, and that he should do so, scuttling his ship, if necessary, to block the river, and then lining the banks with rifles. On learning from Lieutenant Brown that the stern-wheelers and the *Redbreast* were going up, no matter what might happen, the Portuguese returned to the Governor in apparently dejected mood. Of course he was in no condition to oppose a vessel of the *Redbreast's* force; but it was within his power to lie in the very middle of the narrow channel, and to calmly say, 'If you wish to pass, take the rest of the river.' In that event there would have been no difficulty about his capture or destruction; but the case would have been deplorable.

"At this juncture the *Pigeon* arrived with despatches from the Vice-Admiral, who was watching Mozambique and the men-of-war there. What the Vice-Admiral's orders were cannot be told; but clearly they decided the business, for early next morning the flotilla started, the *Redbreast* leading, followed in succession by the

---

[1] Lieut. Algernon Hankey Lyons.   [2] Lieut. Henry Joseph Keane.

Herald, James Stephenson (a stern-wheeler belonging to the African Lakes Company), two large lighters, 31 canoes, and the *Mosquito.* For what then happened I venture to think that Lieutenant Keary deserves very great credit. The first twelve miles of the passage were got over without accident; but off Sombo, just as had been apprehended, lay the Portuguese gunboat. Fortunately, she was swung so that the flotilla could just scrape by her. The *Redbreast* made the dash, passing a few feet from her side, and then dropped a stern anchor and signalled to the *Herald* to anchor instantly, the result being that the Portuguese lay between two fires. His game was up, but he fired a blank charge, and, as the *Redbreast* passed, hailed her to bring to. That she did bring to was owing to the facts that the tide would not then serve her any further, that the *Mosquito* was too far astern, and that Keary intended to call on the Governor; but probably the Portuguese captain did not regard the affair in that light. He boarded the *Redbreast*, accompanied Lieutenant Keary ashore, and left him closeted with the Governor, who was ill in bed. The Governor, by all accounts, talked a great deal about outrage and violation of rights, next begged and implored, and finally gave way, and sent orders to the gunboat to offer no further opposition, the advancing force being too powerful. The captain, however, boarded the *Redbreast* again to deliver a written protest of a long and verbose character, and was regaled with a view of a big gun trained upon his ship, and of a deck covered with cartridge-boxes all ready for his entertainment.

" The flotilla weighed soon afterwards, and entered a most difficult and dangerous stretch of navigation. The river was 3 feet lower than had been reckoned on, and the channel was narrower. In some places, where the *Redbreast* had to hug the south bank, the lead showed 14 feet and 15 feet in the port chains, and 11 feet to 13 feet in the starboard. Three miles from the mouth of the Zambesi proper, the flotilla anchored again. The *Redbreast* anchored bow and stern, with 23 feet of water on the port side and only 7 feet on the starboard, and sent on the *Herald*, Keary also going in his steam cutter, to examine the Chinde Bar. The next reach showed 14 feet of water, and, after the ships had weighed anchor, was passed without much difficulty. The one immediately above was even better. In a third, the *Redbreast* took the ground in 10 feet or 11 feet, but was soon got off, and passed on, close under the south bank, with 11 feet on one side of her and 14 feet on the other. The channel was a mere gutter. It was navigation in a ditch. Then came the bar, with the Zambesi beyond, but with the tide falling, and with the *Herald,* which had been sent ahead, out of sight. It was useless to wait for her to return and report, and on went the *Redbreast*; but again she grounded, with 5 feet of water under her starboard forechains, 10 feet under her counter, and 13 feet all along the port side. After all sorts of shifts and exertions she got off backwards, and made another attempt, which was more successful. In 13 feet of water, although she actually drew 13 feet 2 inches, she crossed the bar, and at length anchored safely, with all the convoy, in the river Zambesi, with 24 feet of water under her. For the first time a British man-of-war lay on that great stream. Next morning the *Herald, Mosquito,* and flotilla parted company, the ships cheering and being cheered; and the *Redbreast* was left to return alone as best she might, through a howling gale and a blinding storm of rain. There were the old difficulties and several new ones, but they were promptly overcome, and without mishap the vessel anchored once more near the storeship *Humber*, all hands being happy and proud that the work was done. On October 17th both *Humber* and *Redbreast* rejoined the Admiral at Zanzibar.

" Those on the station who are best able to judge are of opinion that, as a piece of difficult navigation successfully performed in the face of obstacles of more than one kind, the *Redbreast's* exploit takes very high rank." [1]

---

[1] For their services Lieuts. J. W. Brown, on Dec. 31st, 1890, and F. W. Keary, on Jan. 1st, 1891, were made Commanders.

More to the northward, but on the same station, a detachment from the gun-vessel *Ranger*, Commander Samuel Arthur Johnson, had been actively employed very early in the year. The Esa tribe had attacked Bulhar, in Somaliland ; and an expedition consisting of two companies of the 17th Bombay Infantry and 80 native sappers, with a small Naval Brigade under Lieutenant Henry James Langford Clarke, was sent up from the coast to punish the troublesome natives. The Esas made two plucky night attempts against the advancing force, and, on the second occasion, broke into the zeriba and killed or wounded 20 of the troops and sappers. Clarke, however, got his guns to work promptly, and the enemy was driven off. Many cattle were captured, and, in addition, a party of the *Ranger's* seamen and Marines, under Lieutenant Henry Faulconer Aplin, destroyed 150 of the enemy's wells, thus teaching a severe lesson. The expedition suffered great hardship, owing to the heat and lack of water ; and the men of the Naval Brigade returned to their ship barefooted, having literally worn their boots away.[1] For his services Clarke was thanked by the Indian government and by the Admiralty.

On the North America and West Indies station Captain John Harvey Rainier, of the cruiser *Tourmaline*, was able to afford welcome support to the civil power in the repression of some small disturbances which broke out at Tortola, Virgin Islands.

The shocking sacrifice of life which accompanied the loss of the third-class cruiser *Serpent*,[2] off Cape Trece, on the N.E. coast of Spain, on the night of November 10th, 1890, was found to be the result of an error of judgment on the part of those responsible for the navigation of the ship, which ought to have been on a more westerly course. The court-martial, however, added to its verdict the gratifying rider that up to the last both men and officers obeyed orders and maintained good discipline.[3]

After the action at Gemaizeh,[4] the dervishes in the neighbour-hood of Suakin remained fairly quiet for some time ; but towards the end of 1890, when they were in occupation of Handoub, and when Tokar was Osman Digna's headquarters, they showed signs of reviving activity ; whereupon Colonel Holled Smith, who was then governor of the Red Sea Littoral, decided to attack them. On

---

[1] Desps.: *A. & N. Gaz.* Feb. 22, 1890.   [3] *A. & N. Gaz.* 1890, pp. 910, 1014.
[2] *See* Appendix of Ships Lost.   [4] *See* p. 390.

January 27th, 1891, he captured Handoub, after a short engagement, and then sent his force of about 2000 men to Trinkitat by sea, preparatory to an advance on Tokar. In this operation he was much assisted by the officers and men of the sloop *Dolphin*, Commander Horatio Nelson Dudding, and of the gunboat *Sandfly*, Lieutenant Paul Warner Bush; and he was subsequently accompanied on his march inland by Lieutenant Christopher George Francis Maurice Cradock, of the *Dolphin*. The column, having occupied El Teb, moved forward from that place on February 19th, and soon afterwards was attacked at Afafit, where it inflicted a decisive defeat on Osman Digna, who lost 700 men, and fled to Temrin, and ultimately to Kassala.[1]

In August, 1891, the Congressionalist party in Chile completed a successful revolution[2] by the decisive defeat of the Balmacedists at La Placilla. On the 28th, when the victors occupied Valparaiso, many excesses were perpetrated in the town, and it became necessary for the various foreign warships which lay in harbour to land parties as well to protect the consulates and property of the various nationalities as to endeavour to exercise some general restraining influence upon the desperate Balmacedists. Men were put ashore, therefore, under British, American, German and French officers. A body of about 150 British, from the cruiser *Champion*, Captain Frederick St. Clair, and the sloop *Daphne*, Commander Charles Robert Wood, under Lieutenant Reginald Blayney Colmore, of the *Champion*, undertook the guard of the Consulate; and another body, in conjunction with a German force, assumed the duties of police, and rendered very valuable services. When Señor Claudio Vicuña, the Balmacedist president-elect, just before he took to flight, endeavoured to fire upon a crowd of civilians from two machine-guns which he had planted in front of the Intendencia, he was only prevented by the personal intervention of the American and French Rear-Admirals, Parrayon and McCann, and Captain St. Clair, who placed themselves resolutely in front of the muzzles of the pieces. Two days later order was sufficiently restored to allow of the landing-parties being re-embarked. A few months earlier, on February 19th, while trying to arrange an armistice between the belligerent Chileans at Iquiqui, Captain the Hon. Hedworth Lambton, of the *Warspite*, flagship of Rear-Admiral Charles Frederick Hotham, had narrowly escaped

[1] Royle, 487.
[2] For an account of this *see* Laird Clowes: 'Four Modern Naval Campaigns.'

death, one bullet having passed through the bottom, and another through the awning, of his gig as he went ashore to conduct the negotiations.[1]

During the same fratricidal war, the employment of the British sloop *Espiégle*, Captain Arthur Calvert Clarke, at the request of the British Minister to Chile, to carry Balmacedist silver from Chile to Montevideo,[2] was much discussed; and Captain St. Clair, at whose order the treasure was taken on board, incurred in consequence the disapprobation of the Admiralty—a misfortune which, it may be feared, caused his very considerable services to British interests throughout the Chilean struggle to be overlooked at Whitehall.

In the early part of 1891, while the Anglo-French boundary commission was pursuing its labours in the neighbourhood of the Gambia River, the chief, Fodeh Cabbah, resisted the passage of the commission through his territory, and attacked and wounded several Europeans. The *Alecto*, 4, paddle, Lieutenant Frederick Gordon M'Kinstry, was then in the river, and the sloop *Swallow*, Commander Frank Finnis, and the gunboat *Widgeon*, Lieutenant George Latham Blacker Bennett, lay below her, at Bathurst. On March 27th, the craft last named was ordered to join the *Alecto*, and, late in the afternoon, anchored near her off the village of Kansala. The *Alecto* had already inflicted some punishment upon the rebellious chief, who, however, was too strong to be dealt with effectively by her alone. A small landing-party was put ashore early on the 28th, and, on the 30th, the *Swallow* also arrived. On March 31st, and April 1st, additional people, with two 7-pr. guns, were disembarked; and all the rest of the *Swallow's* Marines were landed on the 2nd, reaching the camp at Kaling in the course of the evening. The Governor, and some Royal Engineers, were present with the force. A further advance was made on the 7th, and another on the 11th, when, at Sangajore, a chief appeared with excuses and an apology. The force was therefore withdrawn and re-embarked, after part of it had been absent from the ships for seventeen days, during which period the men had been unable to get out of their clothes.

Unfortunately, Fodeh Cabbah continued to give trouble; and towards the end of 1891, Lieutenant Ian Mackenzie Fraser, commanding the gunboat *Sparrow*, was instructed by Commander Henry Lucius Fanshawe Royle, of the sloop *Racer*, senior officer on the coast,

[1] Private letters; Accts. and Papers, xcv. (1892); and *A. & N. Gaz.*, Oct. 24, 1891.
[2] *Times*, Sept. 4, 1891.

to make inquiries as to the condition of the country, and, if possible, to find out the whereabouts of Fodeh Cabbah, with a view to his capture. Fraser, therefore, obtained the loan of the colonial steam-launch *Lily*, whose movements, as she was often in the river, would be unlikely to excite suspicion, and, taking with him Captain Thomas M. Hawtayne,[1] then Superintendent of Police, went ostensibly on a shooting expedition. Visiting Marigé, he saw Fodeh Cabbah there. He returned and reported; and the Administrator, in consultation with Commander Royle, decided to make a night attack on Marigé as soon as possible, so as to ensure the chief's capture. Men-of-war, with troops, arrived in the river on January 1st, 1892; and, since it was felt that the appearance of these would be quickly reported in the interior, an immediate movement was that day determined on.

In order to mislead Fodeh Cabbah as to the point of attack, Commander Royle embarked at Bathurst in the *Sparrow*, with the Naval Brigade,[2] early on January 2nd, and, arriving at Kansala in the forenoon of the same day, put his people into boats, to be taken up to Bondali by the *Lily*. At Kansala the *Sparrow* was left, both to serve as a base and also to induce the enemy to look for an attack from that direction, if from any. For the same reasons, a hundred men of the 2nd West India Regiment, under Major T. Claridge, were sent up to Kansala in the gunboats *Thrush* and *Widgeon*. Lieutenant Arthur Jabez Loane, commanding the *Thrush*, who was left as senior officer at Kansala, had directions to march to Kaling as soon as possible, destroy Sangajore, and proceed thence to Katemba, to guard the frontier, and to cut off Fodeh Cabbah's retreat, should he endeavour to escape in that direction.

The rest of the brigade arrived at Bondali at 6 P.M. on the 2nd; and Lieutenant Ian Mackenzie Fraser was sent with a force to the

---

[1] N. Staff. Regt.

Details of the Naval Brigade employed in the operations in the Gambia, Jan. 1–5, 1892:—

Racer, Commander Henry Lucius Fanshawe Royle, Lieut. Henry Arthur Beverley Shrubb, Gunner Albert Selley; 53 seamen, 11 Marines, 39 Kroomen.

Thrush, Lieut. Arthur Jabez Loane, Lieut. Herbert Alexander Child, Asst. Paym. Richard Ernest Stanley Sturgess, Gunner John William Renshaw; 20 seamen, 7 Marines, 19 Kroomen.

Widgeon, Lieut. Graham Samuel Philpot Gwynn, Surg. John M'Elwee, M.D., Gunner George Parfitt; 30 seamen, 6 Marines, 19 Kroomen.

Sparrow, Lieut. Ian Mackenzie Fraser, Lieut. Beauchamp St. John Bellairs, Gunner George Salmon; 28 seamen, 7 Marines, 19 Kroomen.

Total: 13 officers, 140 seamen, 33 Marines, 96 Kroomen.

rear of that village, whence he advanced to Marigé, and surrounded it.   As soon as he had made the necessary transport arrangements, Commander Royle also moved to Marigé.   Arriving there at 11 P.M. he found that Fraser had thrown a cordon round the place, and had had an interview with an emissary from Fodeh Cabbah, who was inside, and who had been informed that if he remained quiet during the night he would be left in peace till morning, but that if he endeavoured to get out he would be fired upon.   At 1 A.M. on the 3rd, the chief made a dash for liberty, and, although he lost at least 30 [1] killed, he succeeded in breaking away on horseback.   In the morning the place, which by that time had been abandoned entirely, was entered and searched, and afterwards destroyed, together with two smaller villages.   Four stockaded villages a little further removed were burnt later.   It was reported that Fodeh Cabbah had fled to Medina, just across the boundary.   In the afternoon the force returned to Bondali, where half the Brigade was re-embarked, and sent down to Kansala.   The other half, under Fraser, was left for the night, with orders to burn Bondali before rejoining on the following day.   The first half of the Brigade reached Kansala at 9 P.M. on January 3rd, the second at 6 P.M. on the 4th.

On the 4th Commander Royle recalled Lieutenant Loane, who had taken and destroyed Sangajore, which was then supposed to be the last of Fodeh Cabbah's strongholds inside the British border. On January 5th the whole force returned to Bathurst.   Only one man of the Brigade was wounded. [2]

The retirement of the expedition having left such natives as had been friendly at the mercy of Fodeh Cabbah and his allies, it was deemed advisable by the Administrator to despatch sixty men of the 2nd West India Regiment, and twenty of the Bathurst Police, to Kaling, to inspire confidence among the Jolahs of that neighbourhood and of the Kansala district.   The force was accordingly carried up to Kansala in the *Widgeon* on January 14th, 1892 ; and, on the same evening, it marched to Kaling.   Major Claridge, who was in command of the little post, formed an entrenched camp, and, on the 17th, undertook a small punitive expedition.   On the 19th, he was attacked at Kaling by about three hundred of Fodeh Cabbah's

---

[1] So says the Disp.   An eye-witness puts the number at 13 only.

[2] Royle to Nicholson, Jan. 8th, 1892; to Fraser Llewellyn, Dec. 24th, 1891; Llewellyn to Royle, Jan. 1st, 1892 ; Loane to Royle, Jan. 6th, 1892; Fraser to Royle, Jan. 6th, 1892.

followers, whom he repulsed; but, as he considered that the place was not held in sufficient strength, he sent a request for reinforcements to the senior officer at Kansala. Commander Royle was then absent on duty with the Administrator; but Lieutenant Henry Douglas Wilkin, who was there in command of the *Widgeon*, promptly sent up Lieutenant Gwynn, with twenty-five men from that ship. Wilkin himself was ill with fever, his ship's company was in a bad state of health, and even Gwynn was unwell. Wilkin therefore also sent a steamboat down to the entrance of the pestilential Vintang creek. Below it the *Thrush* was found; and Lieutenant Loane ordered up the *Thrush* to relieve the sickly *Widgeon*, and directed Lieutenant Fraser, of the *Sparrow*, with three officers and thirty men from the *Racer*, to go on to Kaling, where Fraser assumed command.

On the 22nd, Lieutenant Fraser, with part of the garrison, marched out to collect information, and, while absent, learnt that Fodeh Cabbah had passed him, and was hurrying, by way of Kawali and Sangajore, to attack the camp at Kaling. Fraser sent a messenger by another route to warn Major Claridge, and himself rapidly followed the enemy, who, he soon found, had altered his direction, and made towards Gibok or Kambakalli. Late in the afternoon the camp was reached, and found to be safe. On January 24th, Commander Royle, who had returned from his expedition with the Administrator, marched up, and took over the command; and on the 25th, further reinforcements of seamen, Marines, and West India troops were summoned; so that on the 27th the force assembled, and ready for an advance on Medina, consisted of: Naval Brigade, 10 officers and 150 men; West India Regiment, 4 officers and 110 men; Kroomen, 80; and army carriers, 112. These, however, were not collected until after a party of Kroomen and friendlies had been attacked on the 26th, between Kansala and the camp, by some of Fodeh Cabbah's horsemen, and had suffered a loss of 5 killed or mortally wounded. Royle's application for permission to advance upon Medina was refused on political grounds; but Lieutenant Fraser, with part of the Naval Brigade, was sent out, on February 2nd, and, having burnt Kambakalli, and repelled an attack upon his party, re-embarked at Bondali, where, by arrangement, he met the *Alecto*, Lieutenant Frederick William Loane,[1] and the rest of the force.

[1] Apptd. Oct. 28, 1891.

On the following days, Commander Royle captured a few of Fodeh Cabbah's men, and burnt Jaror and Sanding, two of his towns, as well as Jatobar, a place only then for the first time discovered. The expedition afterwards returned to Bathurst.

In addition to the officers already mentioned as having been concerned in the operations, Surgeon Walter Henry Skinner Stalkartt, M.D., of the *Racer*, rendered useful service, and, with Lieutenant Judge D'Arcy, Lieutenant Henry William Simms, and Assistant-Paymaster Arthur Wilson, was noticed in the dispatches.[1]

The expedition was an unsatisfactory one. Either it went too far, or it did not go far enough. The force assembled at Marigé was so small that the men stationed round the village had to be posted at seven or eight paces apart. The cordon, therefore, was far too weak to offer effectual resistance to any really determined attempt on the part of Fodeh Cabbah to escape. Although, moreover, the dispatches do not mention the fact, I have it from eye-witnesses that after the sortie, the darkness and general uncertainty of the situation were such that it was deemed advisable to form the force into a square, and so to keep it standing to its arms during the rest of the night. From this it is evident that, had the enemy taken the initiative, and attacked in force, the position of the British might easily have become precarious in the extreme. The escape of Fodeh Cabbah was also unfortunate, seeing that the French did not properly restrain him when he was upon their side of the boundary line. He should have been followed up, or his immediate extradition should have been obtained. Nevertheless, the Navy, as usual, did its work most creditably. The Admiralty's appreciation of this was expressed in a telegram, which, although apparently it misinterpreted the exact nature of the somewhat scanty results secured, did no more than justice to the individuals most actively concerned. It ran : " Convey to officers and men employed their Lordships' satisfaction with the promptitude, thoroughness, and success with which the expedition against Fodeh Cabbah was carried out."

In 1891 a chief named Carimoo had established himself in a stronghold at Tambi, on the Scarcies River, whence he had raided the natives who were under British protection. He had also fired upon a party of Sierra Leone police in May, 1891. In March,

---

[1] Royle to Admiralty, Feb. 9th, 1892; Claridge to Royle, Jan. 20th; Loane to Royle, Jan. 24th; Wilkin to Sen. Off., Jan. 19th ; Fraser to Royle, Feb. 8th.

1892, being attacked by a small native police-force under Captain Robinson, R.E., Carimoo killed that officer, and repelled his little command. It was necessary to organise a more formidable expedition; and, with that object in view, officers were sent out from England, troops were assembled, and assistance was sought from the sloop *Racer*, Commander Henry Lucius Fanshawe Royle, the special service paddle-vessel, *Alecto*, Lieutenant Frederick William Loane, and the gunboat *Sparrow*, Lieutenant Ian Mackenzie Fraser, all of whom have been mentioned already in connection with operations on the west coast of Africa. The military force, under Colonel Ellis, C.B., included 550 men of the West India Regiment, about 150 frontier police, and about 400 friendly natives; and Maxims, 7-prs., and rockets accompanied it.

Tambi was taken by assault, and destroyed, on April 7th, great numbers of the enemy being killed while endeavouring to escape. On the side of the attack, only 2 men were killed and 6 wounded. After the expeditionary force had been reorganised, another dangerous native stronghold, Toniatuba, was attacked. It was well fortified, and it offered a spirited resistance; but it was captured and destroyed on April 28th, and its chief, Suliman Santa, was killed. The British lost Captain Roberts, of the West India Regiment, killed, and 5 men wounded, one of the wounded belonging to the Naval Brigade.[1] Commander Royle, Lieutenant Fraser, and Lieutenant Henry Douglas Wilkin, of the *Racer* (who commanded the Naval Brigade at the storming of Toniatuba), were awarded the D.S.O.[2] for their good work on this occasion.

In the course of 1893 there were numerous troubles with the natives of East Africa, not only on the Witu coast, where there had been difficulties, as has been shown, in 1890, but also within the confines of the territory of the then existing Imperial British East Africa Company, and, inland, in the neighbourhood of Lake Nyassa and the River Shiré. In every case the services of naval officers and men were employed ere order was restored.

Fumo Omari, successor of that Sultan of Witu who had been chastised by Sir Edmund Robert Fremantle, had grown restless and dangerous. When, in addition, he began to commit outrages, it was decided that his territory should be again attacked. With

---

[1] *Nav. & Mil. Rec.*, Ap. 7, May 5, 12 and 26, 1891: *Times*, June 2, 1892: *A. & N. Gaz.* 1892, p. 265.
[2] Jan. 10, 1893.

that object in view, the third-class cruiser *Blanche*, Captain George Robert Lindley, the sloop *Swallow*, Commander Lewis Dod Sampson, and the gunboat *Sparrow*, Lieutenant Francis George Theodore Cole, proceeded to the estuary, near the head of which lies the town of Mkonumbi, and landed a Naval Brigade, which, being joined by a body of 70 native soldiers, marched into the densely wooded country, led by Lindley in person. After some brisk fighting, Pumwani was taken on August 7th, and Jongeni on August 13th, both places being destroyed. The British loss was one stoker killed, and Lieutenant Maurice Swinfen Fitzmaurice (*Blanche*), and Sub-Lieutenant William Hampton Gervis (*Sparrow*), wounded. Among other officers who, in addition to those already named, were mentioned in the despatches, were Lieutenants Edward Buxton Kiddle, John de Mestre Hutchison, Vincent Barkly Molteno, and Thomas Leslie Thorpe-Doubble, Sub-Lieutenant Murray MacGregor Lockhart, Surgeon Frederick John Lilly, Gunner Charles Higgins, and Boatswain George Henry Kelsey. The expedition, which was accompanied by Mr. James Rennell Rodd,[1] who was then in charge of the Agency at Zanzibar, gained the C.B. for Captain Lindley. In the following October, Fumo Omari having again become troublesome, and having re-fortified Pumwani in defiance of his engagements, it became necessary to make a new expedition into the same district. This was undertaken by a Brigade from the third-class cruiser *Racoon*, Commander Frank Hannam Henderson, the *Blanche*, and the *Swallow*, accompanied by some Zanzibari troops. It is known as the Lamu Forest Expedition, Lamu being close to the point whence the Brigade started inland.[2] Pumwani was again taken, and destroyed.

Further north, and close to the confines of Italian Somaliland, there had been friction earlier in the year. In February during a grand barazza or palaver at Kismayu, between Mr. Todd, the British consular agent, and the native chiefs, the tribesmen made some sort of an attack upon Mr. Todd, who, however, kept them off with his revolver. The gunboat *Widgeon*, Lieutenant William Jabez Scullard, was on the spot, and had landed a party of blue-jackets and Marines to keep guard near the meeting-place. Although, as was stated, a body of 400 Somalis endeavoured to cut off this force

---

[1] Rodd to Rosebery, Aug. 11 and 29; Bedford to Admlty., Aug. 13, 1893.
[2] Henderson to Bedford, Oct. 12, 1893.

from its boats, a few rounds fired from the ship dispersed the enemy, and secured the evacuation of the town.[1] How far the natives really meant mischief is doubtful. It is certain, however, that Scullard's, action was responsible, to some extent, for ill-feeling which led to further complications, although the direct cause of the next trouble seems to have been the unwise stoppage of pay of certain Keriboto levies who, from having served for a time in India, had become known, quite improperly, as " Hyderabad men."

About 60 of these " Hyderabad men," out of a total of 250 employed by the British East Africa Company, mutinied in the summer of 1893, sallied out from Kismayu, attacked and killed one of their officers, Hamilton by name, and seized Turkey Hill Fort, which is on the right bank of the Juba river, and some little way inland from its mouth. The garrison, which fought loyally, and suffered considerable loss, retreated to Kismayu and Fort Golwen. According to some accounts, the mutineers were assisted by disaffected Somalis ; but it seems probable that at Turkey Hill Fort the Somalis did merely jackals' work when the actual attack was over. Certain it is, nevertheless, that very soon afterwards almost all the natives of the district became hostile to the British. Kismayu itself, indeed, was eventually attacked by Somalis, who, however, were driven off.

Not long after the murder of Mr. Hamilton, the third-class cruiser *Blanche* arrived on the spot from Zanzibar. Her Captain, Lindley, had been left behind sick as the result of his exertions in Wituland, and her first Lieutenant, John de Mestre Hutchison, as well as two other officers, though still on board, was incapacitated by illness, so that the command had devolved upon Lieutenant Price Vaughan Lewes.[2] He landed on the beach south of the river's mouth with forty volunteers from the cruiser, and, joined by a body of fifty loyal Keribotos, made a night march and retook Turkey Hill Fort by surprise. He then pushed across to the River Juba, where, below Fort Golwen, the British East Africa Company's shallow-draught stern-wheel steamer *Kenia* was lying, with two Englishmen, who were supposed to be in great danger, in her. Her boiler was repaired under fire, largely by the efforts of Engine-room Artificer G. S. Carey, and Leading-Stoker Alfred White ; and, on the following morning, Lewes steamed up the river, shelled and destroyed the hostile town of Magerada, landed

---

[1] *A. & N. Gaz.* Mar. 11, 1893.   [2] D.S.O. for this service, Dec. 12, 1893.

with thirty men and captured Hajualli after an hour's fighting, and, subsequently crossing the stream, took the village of Hajowen.

The crew of the *Kenia* had afterwards to be withdrawn from her, owing to the weakness of the Company's forces on the spot; but Commander Frank Hannam Henderson, of the *Racoon*, presently rescued about 20,000 rounds of ammunition from the stern-wheeler, as well as 25,000 rupees' worth of goods, and some stores, and conveyed the salvage to Kismayu.[1] He would have done more, had not his further operations been stopped by orders from his superiors, who feared, apparently, to be led into hostilities on a serious scale.

The circumstances attending the first appearance of a British man-of-war in the Zambesi have already been described; and it has been told how the stern-wheel steamers *Mosquito* and *Herald* were put upon the upper waters of that great river. In 1891, a slave-trading chief named Makanjira,[2] whose territory lay on the south-eastern coast of Lake Nyassa, entrapped and killed Captain Cecil Maguire, the commander of the troops in British Central Africa; and it became necessary to punish the marauder, and to assert British supremacy in the neighbourhood of his district. But, since it was felt that nothing decisive could be achieved upon the shores of an inland sea until the control of that sea had first been secured; since the control of Nyassa could not be secured without the assistance of armed steam-vessels; since no craft of that description were, or could be, constructed, upon the lake; and since, moreover, not so much as a boat could pass from the Zambesi, up the Shiré, and so into the Lake, owing to the rapids, preparations for the chastisement of Makanjira were necessarily slow.

From Messrs. Yarrow, of Poplar, the builders of the *Mosquito* and *Herald*, the Admiralty ordered three other craft, which, though smaller than, and differing from, the two first, resembled them in the particular of being capable of being taken to pieces, and so transported overland. One of them, the *Dove*, a paddle-steamer of 20 tons' displacement and 50 I.H.P., was designed for the service of the Upper Shiré, above the rapids. The other two, the *Adventure* and the *Pioneer*, screw steamers of 35 tons' displacement and 80 I.H.P., were designed to do duty upon Lake Nyassa. After

[1] Desps.: priv. letters: *A. & N. Gaz.*, Nov. 25, 1893.
[2] A titular name. Comp. Cæsar, Pharaoh, etc.

having been built, put together, and tried in the Thames, these three little craft were taken to pieces again, and shipped in numerous transverse sections to Chindé, at the Chindé mouth of the Zambesi, where they arrived in October, 1892. Thence, by an arrangement with the German Anti-Slavery Society's expedition, which also was proceeding to the Lake, they were placed in German lighters, and towed up stream by Lieutenant Charles Hope Robertson, who then commanded the *Herald*, and was senior naval officer in the river. By January 20th, 1893, all the materials were at Ishikwawa, 300 miles above Chindé, and immediately below the commencement of the Shiré rapids. Thence, under the management of Lieutenant C. A. Edwards, of the Indian Staff Corps, they were carried in waggons drawn by native porters to Mpimbi, 80 miles further up. Robertson, with six naval artificers, two of Messrs. Yarrow's artificers, and six Indian riveters, also went thither, and, on May 30th, 1893, launched the *Dove*, which hoisted the pennant a few days later. On June 17th, with Robertson in command, she first showed the White Ensign on the Lake. The *Adventure* and *Pioneer* were then put together, and commissioned in a similar manner.

Various circumstances delayed the immediate punishment of Makanjira. In the meantime, on November 8th, 1893, Lieutenant Robertson, then in charge of the *Adventure*, took part in operations against one of Makanjira's allies, Kiwaura, who had seized the town of Kisamba, three miles inland from Kota-Kota. He also assisted, with both the *Pioneer* and the *Adventure*, in an expedition against Makanjira's mother, Kaluunda, a slave-trading chieftainess who ruled on the west coast, about Mount Rifu and Leopard's Bay. On November 14th, the *Pioneer*, Lieutenant Edward Cecil Villiers, covered the landing in Rifu Bay, while the *Adventure*, steaming round a point, took the enemy in flank, and shelled him out of his village there, driving Kaluunda to a mountainous fastness on the north point of Leopard Bay. To succour his mother, Makanjira that night sent over a dhow which, eluding the *Pioneer*, ran herself ashore close under the enemy's stronghold. She was intended to take off Kaluunda and a number of slaves; but, as soon as she was discovered, Villiers steamed in under a brisk fire, and destroyed her. This led to the chieftainess's surrender.

The expedition against Makanjira himself made rendezvous at Monkey Bay, a fiord-like arm on the western side of the Lake, where a depôt belonging to the Admiralty had been established. There flats were borrowed and armed; and at midnight on November 18th, the flotilla, with these in tow, weighed. By dawn next morning it lay off the low-lying shores of Makanjira's territory. The *Adventure* and *Pioneer* shelled the coast for half an hour; and then the troops, Sikhs and native levies, were landed without opposition. An entrenched camp was formed near the enemy's town, upon which the Nordenfelt machine-guns of the gunboats in the bay kept up an occasional fire. On the 20th, after hard fighting, the town, a very large one, was taken and burnt by the troops, but not until part of the attacking party had been surrounded and nearly cut off. Indeed, it might have been annihilated, had not Robertson grasped the situation, and taken the *Adventure* in as close as possible. He worked his Nordenfelts to such good effect that the enemy broke and fled. As soon as the town was in flames, the *Pioneer* steamed off to the northward, where she had the good fortune to find and cut out the only dhow that still remained in the hands of the slavers on the Lake. Unhappily, Makanjira effected his escape into Portuguese territory[1]; and he remained troublesome until the spring of 1894, when, attacking Fort Maguire, he was heavily defeated, and taught so plain a lesson that thereupon he surrendered.

In February, 1893, while the *Dove, Adventure*, and *Pioneer* were still in process of transport up the Shiré in sections, a slave-trading chief named Liwonde attacked an expedition which had entered his district under Captain Johnson, the officer commanding the troops in British Central Africa. The Commissioner, Mr. (afterwards Sir) Harry H. Johnston, collected a small force, and marched against Liwonde's principal village, Malawi, which he took. He then moved to a point on the Upper Shiré where the trading-steamer *Domira* had grounded, while on her way down stream. There he met with very stubborn resistance, and had to fortify himself, though ultimately the *Domira* was got off, whereupon retreat became again possible.

News of the situation reached Blantyre. Without delay, Lieutenant George Shadwell Quartano Carr, of the *Mosquito*, landed twenty-eight of his officers [2] and men, collected ten white volun-

---

[1] Author, in *New Review*, Ap. 1894: desps. of Robertson, and Mr. H. H. Johnston: priv. journs. of Lieut. C. A. Edwards, 35th Sikhs.

[2] Including Surg. Alex. Fleming Harper, of the *Mosquito*.

teers, and a number of natives, and, taking with him a Nordenfelt gun, marched overland at great speed to the relief of the beleaguered Commissioner, being presently followed by Lieutenant Robertson. Mr. Johnston, thus timely reinforced, was able to rout the enemy, and to make a progress through Liwonde's country, with the result that the chief was glad to sue for peace.[1] The work done on this and other occasions in British Central Africa by Lieutenants Robertson and Carr was considered so creditable that each officer was given the C.M.G. on January 3rd, 1895; by which date the protectorate had been rendered comparatively quiet and prosperous. In the interval, Robertson had been made a Commander on January 1st, 1894.

At about the same time, the *Dove, Adventure,* and *Pioneer* were handed over by the Admiralty to the administration of British Central Africa; and the Navy ceased thenceforth to maintain a force on Lake Nyassa.

A few minor operations of the year remain to be noticed.

In April, 1893, owing to an attempt on the part of the authorities to collect arrears of taxes, serious riots broke out in the island of Dominica; and although a party of bluejackets and Marines was landed from the third-class cruiser *Mohawk,* Commander Edward Henry Bayly, to assist the police, order was not re-established until many injuries had been inflicted on both sides, and four of the rioters had been killed. Bayly, who was among the hurt, received the thanks of the Colonial Office and of the Admiralty.[2]

On July 24, in consequence of the refusal of Siam to meet the demands of France for compensation for alleged damage, a blockade of Bangkok was declared by the French Rear-Admiral Humann, who claimed that the measure applied as well to British warships as to merchant vessels, and thereupon ordered the third-class cruiser *Pallas,* Captain Angus MacLeod, and the gun-vessel *Swift,* Commander Francis George Kirby, to proceed outside the limits of the blockade as he defined them. This order was complied with by the British vessels; but, nevertheless, the attitude of some of the French officers was extremely aggressive, and much injustice was done to British traders. On one occasion the French gunboat *Lion,* with her crew at quarters, and her guns bearing on the cruiser,

---

[1] Parl. Paper C. 7031 (1893): desp. of Mar. 19, 1893.
[2] Hansard, xiv., 490.

steamed down in a very provocative manner upon the *Pallas*, which could have blown her out of the water ; and only Captain MacLeod's prudence and coolness averted a most regrettable conflict.　Upon the raising of the blockade, on August 24th, Rear-Admiral Humann obliged the officer commanding the *Lion* to apologise to the Captain of the *Pallas*.[1]

On July 7th, at Samoa, fighting began between the partisans of the ruling chief, Malietoa, and those of his rival, Mataafa, but was stopped by the prompt intervention of the British cruiser *Curaçoa*, Captain Herbert William Sumner Gibson, and the German cruisers *Falke* and *Bussard*, which shelled the rebel position while Malietoa's forces attacked it from the land side.　The result was the surrender of Mataafa, who was conveyed on board the *Curaçoa* to Apia, the capital, the *Bussard* remaining to disarm his followers.[2]　In the course of the previous year, 1892, Captain Gibson had visited the Gardner, Danger, and Nassau Islands, proclaiming a British protectorate over each of those Pacific groups. He had also hoisted the flag in the Ellice Islands, and in those islands of the Solomon group lying within the British sphere of influence.

In the present volume it has not been found possible to devote much space to detailed accounts of such losses as have been occasioned to the fleet by wreck, fire, and other accidents of the sea.　Brief particulars of all losses will be found in the various appendices which are devoted to the subject ; but, had space permitted, it would have been a grateful task to add largely to those meagre notes, and to dwell upon some of the innumerable deeds of heroism which have been performed by officers and men of the Navy when face to face with terrors far more appalling even than those of the most desperate fight with human enemies.　The wreck of the *Birkenhead*, and the burning of the *Bombay*, to mention no other cases, are catastrophes which have enabled British seamen and Marines to display the very highest qualities of discipline, devotion, dignity and manhood.　Unfortunately, the fighting work of the Navy, which is its chief work, puts forward still more pressing claims ; and, as a rule, only when the circumstances of an accident have seemed to have some important connection with the efficiency of the fleet or with the professional capacity of its

---

[1] *Nav. & Mil. Rec.*, Aug. 3 and 10, 1893.

[2] *A. & N. Gaz.*, Sept. 1, 1893 ; *Times*, Oct. 17, 1893 ; and Germ. disps.

leaders has it been deemed permissible to devote more than a few words to the story of the misfortune.

Of accidents of this kind, perhaps the most striking in the whole long history of the Royal Navy was the loss of the *Victoria*.

On June 22nd, 1893, the Mediterranean fleet lay off Beyrout. The Commander-in-Chief, Vice-Admiral Sir George Tryon, K.C.B., flew his flag in the battleship *Victoria*[1]; the second in command, Rear-Admiral Albert Hastings Markham, flew his in the battleship *Camperdown*,[1] his proper flagship, the *Trafalgar*,[1] being under repair at Malta. At 10 A.M. the fleet weighed and left for Tripoli, another Syrian port.

Soon after 2 P.M. Tryon sent for Staff-Commander Thomas Hawkins Smith, who, when he entered the Vice-Admiral's cabin, found Captain the Hon. Maurice Archibald Bourke, of the flag-ship, already there. Tryon said that, in order to bring the fleet into suitable formation for anchoring as he intended, he would form it into two divisions in line ahead, and that, when it should be far enough past the line of bearings for anchoring, he would invert the course of the columns by turning inwards 16 points, leaders together, the rest in succession. He also said that the distance between the columns prior to the inception of this manœuvre should be six cables (1200 yards). It was remarked that, in such a case, the minimum distance between the columns should be eight cables (1600 yards) ; whereupon the Vice-Admiral said : " Yes : it shall be eight cables." Soon afterwards, however, signals were made in the usual manner for the fleet to form columns of divisions in line ahead, the columns to be disposed abeam to port, and to be six cables apart. The Staff-Commander, noticing that the distance was six cables, went to the Flag-Lieutenant, Lord Gillford, and asked him whether there was not a mistake ; and, being shown the order for six cables in Tryon's handwriting, he asked Lord Gillford to make sure before hauling the signal down. The Flag-Lieutenant went to the Vice-Admiral, but was told : " Keep the six cables up."

At 3.27 P.M. the signal to invert the columns by altering course 16 points inwards was hoisted. At that time, it may be explained, the fleet was steaming east by north in two columns, the starboard (1st division) or right hand one of which was led by the *Victoria*, and the port (2nd division), or left hand one, by the *Camperdown*,

---

[1] For particulars, etc. of those ships, see pp. 31 and 32, and the plates facing pp. 48 and 56 in this volume.

those ships being abreast of one another and 1200 yards asunder. The speed was 8·8 knots.

It is curious, and, I think, significant, that Vice-Admiral Fitz-Gerald, in his "Life of Sir George Tryon," does not give particulars of the signal which was actually made; neither does Mr. Thursfield, in the account of the disaster which he contributed to the "Naval Annual" for 1894; neither does the finding of the Court-Martial. It is well, therefore, to give them here.[1] There were, in fact, two separate signals, which, translated from the signal-book, were worded respectively as follows :—

SECOND DIVISION	FIRST DIVISION
16 POINTS TO STARBOARD	16 POINTS TO PORT
IN SUCCESSION	IN SUCCESSION
PRESERVING THE ORDER OF THE FLEET.	PRESERVING THE ORDER OF THE FLEET.

There was nothing in the signals about leaders turning together. The moment for the leaders to begin the evolution in such a case is indicated by the hauling down of the signals. But before the signals can be hauled down they have to be repeated by the other ships and acknowledged. Acknowledgment by the leader of the second division (the *Camperdown*) was on this occasion delayed, owing, as was stated subsequently, to the fact that Rear-Admiral Markham suspected that there must be some mistake, and ordered his Flag-Lieutenant to make an enquiry on the subject by semaphore. Ere, however, the semaphore signal was made, the Commander-in-Chief signalled to ask what the Rear-Admiral was waiting for; and Markham, then jumping to the conclusion that something other than what he had at first imagined must be intended, and placing, as he said, implicit confidence in Tryon, ordered the signal to be acknowledged in the ordinary way. That acknowledgment, of course, meant that the signal was comprehended, and that it could and would be acted upon when the proper moment should arrive. An instant later, at 3.31 P.M., the *Victoria's* two signals were hauled down simultaneously. This indicated that the execution of the two manœuvres was to begin at once, and simultaneously. Accordingly, the helms of the two flagships were put over, and the great vessels began to turn inwards, and towards one another. Tryon stood on the top of the *Victoria's* chart-house, and watched.

---

[1] The signals have been drawn for me, as they were hoisted, by an officer who was present. It is deemed unnecessary to reproduce the flags, etc., that were used.

Staff-Commander Smith, who was by his chief's side then and
until the end, says :—

"As the two ships (*Victoria* and *Camperdown*) neared one another, the port engine
of the *Victoria* was reversed, and, when about 10 points round, both engines were put
'full speed astern,' these directions being given by the Commander-in-Chief.   The two
ships rapidly neared one another, and the *Victoria*, being turned in a smaller circle
than the *Camperdown*, was slightly in advance of the latter, so that the stem of the

VICE-ADMIRAL SIR GEORGE TRYON, K.C.B.

Lost with the *Victoria*, June 22nd, 1893.

(*From a photo by Maull & Fox.*)

Camperdown struck the *Victoria* on the starboard bow, about ten feet abaft the anchor,
at about 3.34 P.M.—the angle between the lines of keel of the two ships being about
six points, or 68°.

" When the collision appeared to be inevitable, the order was given to close water-
tight doors ; and, as the two ships struck, the order was given, ' out collision-mat.'

" The *Camperdown* backed astern ; and exertions were made to get the collision-
mat over the hole ; but the ship settled so quickly by the head that this could not be

done. In the meantime (the Captain having left the top of the chart-house by order of the Commander-in-Chief to see about the water-tight doors) it was thought that the ship, being struck so far forward, would keep afloat for a considerable time; and, being then in deep water (70 to 80 fathoms), it was considered desirable to steer for shallow water—the nearest part of the 5-fathom line bearing about south, distant 4½ miles. The ship's head was turned in that direction, by going astern with the port engine, and ahead with the starboard, so as to clear the *Nile*,[1] the helm being still hard a-starboard. As soon as the ship's head was pointed clear of the *Nile*, both engines were put ahead,[2] and the revolution telegraph put to 38 revolutions, or 7 knots."

The collision-mat could not be got over the hole. Tryon, therefore, had to content himself with ordering all the apertures on the low-lying forward deck to be closed; and men were busily engaged upon that work until, the water rising to their waists, they had to be called in. In the interval the *Victoria's* bows sank steadily deeper and deeper, while the ship took a list to starboard.

"At this time (immediately after the engines had been put 'ahead'), the Commander-in-Chief remarked to the Staff-Commander, 'I think she is going.' The latter replied, 'Yes, sir; I think she is.' The Commander-in-Chief then ordered the signal to be made 'send boats';[3] and, turning round to give these orders to the signalmen, who were on the fore-bridge, abaft the funnels, he saw one of the Midshipmen standing near the standard compass, and said to him, 'Don't stop there, youngster: go to a boat.' These were probably his last words, for, a few moments after this, the ship gave a heavy lurch to starboard, and then turned over almost instantaneously . . ."

Staff-Commander Smith went down with Tryon, but was subsequently saved. His watch had stopped at 3h. 44m. 30s.; so that, in all probability, not more than about ten minutes elapsed between the moment of the collision and that of the *Victoria's* disappearance. During that time, both Smith and Lord Gillford heard the Commander-in-Chief say, "It is entirely my fault." Tryon met his fate calmly and bravely, and, after the ship turned over, was never seen again.

A court-martial to try the surviving officers and men of the *Victoria* assembled in the *Hibernia*, at Malta, on July 17th, and sat until July 27th, Admiral Sir Michael Culme-Seymour presiding, and Captain Alfred Leigh Winsloe acting as prosecutor. Owing to the peculiarities of naval court-martial procedure, Rear-Admiral

---

[1] The second ship of the first division, commanded by Capt. Gerard Henry Uctred Noel. The second ship of the second division was the *Edinburgh*, Capt. John William Brackenbury.

[2] The wisdom of this is questionable, looking to the damaged state of the ship's bows, unless, indeed, the *Victoria* could not go astern.

[3] Several ships had previously begun to get out their boats, but Tryon had forbidden the immediate sending of them, probably fearing lest the sinking of the flagship, while boats were close alongside, would add to the extent of the disaster.

Markham, and his Flag-Captain, Charles Johnstone, of the *Camper-down*, though really on their trial indirectly, enjoyed none of the privileges which are allowed to nominal prisoners.   Markham, however, was present, and was permitted to suggest questions which, by consent of the court, were then put to witnesses.   The essential part of the finding was as follows:—

" . . . the loss of her Majesty's ship *Victoria*, off Tripoli, on the coast of Syria, on the 22nd day of June, 1893, was caused by a collision with her Majesty's ship *Camperdown* : and it is with the deepest sorrow and regret that the Court further finds that this collision was due to an order given by the then Commander-in-Chief, the late Vice-Admiral Sir George Tryon, to the two divisions in which the fleet was formed to turn sixteen points inwards, leaders first, the others in succession, the columns at that time being only six cables apart.

" Secondly : that after the collision had occurred, everything that was possible was done on board her Majesty's ship *Victoria*, and in the squadron generally, both to save life and to save the *Victoria* ; and the Court is of opinion that the order given by the late Vice-Admiral Sir George Tryon to 'annul sending boats, but to hold them in readiness,' was, under the circumstances, a wise one.

" Thirdly : the Court finds that no blame is attributable to Captain the Hon. Maurice Archibald Bourke, or to any other of the surviving officers and ship's company of her Majesty's ship *Victoria*, for the loss of that ship, and doth therefore acquit them accordingly.   The Court desires to record its opinion that the discipline and order maintained on board the *Victoria* to the last by everyone was in the highest degree creditable to all concerned.

" Fourthly : the Court feels strongly that although it is much to be regretted that Rear-Admiral Albert Hastings Markham did not carry out his first intention of semaphoring to the Commander-in-Chief his doubt as to the signal, it would be fatal to the best interests of the service to say he was to blame for carrying out the directions of his Commander-in-Chief present in person."

Some time afterwards, viz., on October 28th, the Admiralty adopted the rather unusual course of reviewing the proceedings and finding in a Minute, which contained the following paragraph :—

" Their Lordships concur in the feeling expressed by the Court that it is much to be regretted that Rear-Admiral A. H. Markham did not carry out his first intention of semaphoring to the Commander-in-Chief his doubts as to the signal; but they deem it necessary to point out that the Rear-Admiral's belief that the Commander-in-Chief would circle round him was not justified by the proper interpretation of the signal. The evidence shows that it was owing to this misconception that the precautions, which mistrust of the order given by the Commander-in-Chief should have prompted, were not at once taken by the Rear-Admiral, and that he did not order Captain Johnstone to reverse the starboard screw, and to close the watertight doors, until after the ships had turned eight points inwards and were end on."[1]

Before the making of any comments on this most terrible disaster, the rendering of a tribute to the magnificent behaviour of the *Victoria's* people in their time of peril must be attended to;

[1] Parl. Paper (1893), including Procs. of C.M., Admlty. Min., and Report of Dir. of Nav. Constr.

for those who survived and those who died behaved equally gloriously. Captain Bourke, in his evidence, said :—

"There was absolutely no panic, no shouting, no rushing aimlessly about. The officers went quietly to their stations, and everything was prepared, and the men were all in their positions, for hoisting out boats or performing any duty that may have been ordered. . . . The men on the forecastle worked with a will until the water was up to their waists ; and it was only when they were ordered aft that they left their work to fall in on the upper deck. . . . In the case of the men working below, I was a witness to their coolness. When the order was passed down for everyone to go on deck, there was no haste or hurry to desert the flat. I can further testify to the men below in the engine-room. In the starboard one, all were in their stations : the engineer officer was there, the artificer, and the stokers. I am sure that those in the port engine-room and the boiler-rooms were equally true to themselves. . . . In all the details of this terrible accident one spot especially stands out, and that is the heroic conduct of those who, to the end, remained below, stolidly yet boldly, at their place of duty. All honour to them especially. The men fallen in on the upper deck also showed the same spirit. . . . When the men were turned about to face the ship's side, it must have passed through the minds of many that to 'look out for one's self' would be the best thing to do. . . . This order to turn about was given apparently about a minute before the end ; and I can hear of not one single instance of any man rushing to the side. . . . Not one was found who had not that control over himself which characterises true discipline and order. It has been shown in evidence that no one jumped from the ship until just as she gave the lurch which ended in her capsizing."

It was all magnificent. Only typical of the general spirit was the attitude of the *Victoria's* much-lamented chaplain, the Rev. Samuel Sheppard Oakley Morris, who stood with the ship's company, and, at the last fearful moment, said coolly and bravely, " Steady, men, steady ! "

The *Camperdown*, it should be added, was herself badly damaged, and was at one time thought to be sinking. Happily, she reached port without serious difficulty.[1]

"The court-martial," says FitzGerald, " did not clear up the point which from the first presented itself as an enigma to the minds of all those who knew Sir George Tryon." Vice-Admiral Fitz-Gerald defines that point as being the question, by what mental powers did Sir George arrive " at the conclusion that six cables apart was a safe distance at which two columns of battleships could be turned inwards, or towards one another ? " I had the honour of knowing Sir George Tryon, and I must admit that the point, or rather the points, on which light seems to be desirable do not occur to me in that shape at all. I cannot believe that, if Tryon *intended* to order the manœuvre which the court-martial supposed him to

[1] FitzGerald : 'Life of V.-Adm. Sir Geo. Tryon': *Naval Annual*, 1894 : Desps. ; and Parl. Paper.

have ordered, he ever did "arrive at the conclusion" that he could attempt it safely with only six cables' distance between the columns. And since he did undoubtedly order and countenance the attempting of some manœuvre when only six cables intervened between the columns, I am inclined to suspect that the manœuvre, as attempted to be carried out, was not the manœuvre which Tryon intended to be performed.

Vice-Admiral FitzGerald himself admits that it cannot be assumed that Tryon purposed to run a risk. Everything that is known of Sir George contradicts that assumption in the most uncompromising manner. Nor can it be supposed that Sir George suddenly went mad. On the other hand, it is on record, not only that Tryon delighted in ordering unexpected and novel manœuvres, which occasionally seemed dangerous until they were actually put into execution, but also that those of his Captains who knew his methods well were accustomed, when there were two or more ways of accomplishing a thing, to anticipate that the Commander-in-Chief would not choose the most obvious or prosaic way. They were prepared for originality and brilliancy, but they could not admit the possibility that Tryon would expose his ships to needless danger.[1]

Now, what was Tryon's object in inverting his columns? It was to bring the fleet into position for anchoring off Tripoli, where the ships were to take up their billets in columns of divisions, with a distance of two cables between the ships in column, and a similar distance between the columns themselves. Intimation of this had been made by signal earlier in the afternoon.

Tryon, Markham, and every Captain in the fleet knew perfectly well that the average tactical diameter of the ships concerned was nearly four cables, or 800 yards[2]; in other words, that the basic diameter of the parabola made by any one of the turning ships must be estimated, for practical purposes, at 800 yards. This being so, the heads of the two columns, being but 1200 yards apart, could not turn simultaneously 16 points inwards—could not countermarch inwards—without cutting one another's courses at some point. If the two ships turned at exactly the same moment, at equal speeds, and on similar parabolas, they would collide. But, even if

---

[1] FitzGerald; 368, 387–390.

[2] The tactical diameter of the *Victoria* herself was only 600 yards; but that of some ships was much more. The accepted tactical diameter for the squadron was 800 yards (4 cables) (FitzGerald, 392).

the distance between the columns had been, as it was suggested it should be, eight cables, or 1600 yards, instead of 1200 yards there would still have been risk of ultimate collision, had the manœuvre been carried out on the lines on which it was attempted; for the ships, upon completing the turn, would have been, if not actually on board of one another, at least so close alongside one another as to be in dangerous proximity. We know that Tryon, after having originally suggested six cables, assented to the distance between the columns being eight cables, and that finally, nevertheless, he ordered the distance to be six cables, in spite of the fact that his attention was called pointedly to the discrepancy. We know, moreover, that eight cables was almost as dangerous a distance as six cables, if the columns were to countermarch according to the supposed plan. We know, too, that Tryon intended the columns to come up to the assigned anchorage at a distance of two cables asunder; so that the most suitable distance apart of the columns previous to the fatal manœuvre (assuming what was attempted to have been what was intended by the Vice-Admiral) would have been not even eight cables, but ten (2000 yards).

There is, I think, but one conclusion to be drawn from all this; namely, that Tryon knew that, for the purposes of the manœuvre which he had in his mind—not necessarily the manœuvre which was attempted—it did not greatly matter whether the initial distance between the columns was six cables or eight cables. If it had greatly mattered, Tryon was the last man in the world to have been careless on the subject, or to have run things too fine.[1]

This conclusion seems to clear the way somewhat; but before I go on to point out what it appears to me to clear the way to, I desire to dwell upon another admitted fact, a fact, however, which has been strangely lost sight of.

The terms of the flag-signal to each division terminated with the direction, "preserving the order of the fleet." Either that direction meant literally and plainly that the order of the fleet in every respect was to be preserved, or it was a direction which, in the circumstances, demanded further elucidation. Tryon did not further elucidate it; wherefore it may be inferred that it was to be accepted literally.

---

[1] The arguments about to be put forth were first advanced by the Author in a letter to the *Times* soon after the catastrophe. He is not aware that they have ever been adequately discussed, though they were cited long afterwards by the *Saturday Review*.

What, then, was the order of the fleet? It was a disposition in columns of divisions in line ahead, the columns disposed abeam to port, with a distance of six cables between the columns. At the head of the first or starboard divisional column was the *Victoria*, followed by the *Nile*, etc.: at the head of the port or second divisional column was the *Camperdown*, followed by the *Edinburgh*, etc. The direction "preserving the order of the fleet" may—I believe, must—have been intended by Tryon to mean that, after the completion of the manœuvre, the *Victoria* was still to head the starboard, and the *Camperdown* still to head the port column, and that the ships following each of the leaders were to follow in the same sequence and manner as before the inception of the manœuvre. It is difficult to perceive what other meaning can be attached to it, in view of the nature of the signals of which it formed part.

If Vice-Admiral Tryon had intended the manœuvre to be carried out as it was unhappily attempted to be performed, surely he would have annulled, added to, or elucidated this significant direction. Surely, too, as I have said before, he would have opened out the columns, not to eight, but to ten cables at least. It does not follow, because others paid no special attention to the direction, that Tryon himself regarded it as of small significance, or was blind to the one principle on which alone it could be literally obeyed. It does not follow, because Markham and some more on the spot had a glimmering but distorted dream of what might be signified, and then abandoned it, that they were not at first very nearly on the right track. It does not even follow, because the Admiralty saw fit to tell Markham that his dream had been entirely erroneous, that their Lordships knew what had been in Tryon's mind. It is certainly strange that the Admiralty did not attempt to explain what was meant by "preserving the order of the fleet," but apparently ignored that direction altogether. I cannot ignore it; for it seems to me, if it be taken in connection with other factors in the situation, to afford a clue to the whole enigma; though I am quite aware that to the ordinary naval mind the direction implies no more than that the body of ships (in this case, a division) to which the signal is made is to preserve its own order. What I feel is that such a direction should have been interpreted by the light of the conditions existing at the moment, and that Tryon probably anticipated that the peculiar conditions would lead his subordinates to attach to the direction the importance which, I suspect, he did.

The two diagrams which follow show with sufficient accuracy (A) the manœuvre which, according to the view of the court-martial and of the Admiralty, Tryon intended that his fleet should perform; and (B) the result of the attempt to perform that impossible manœuvre :—

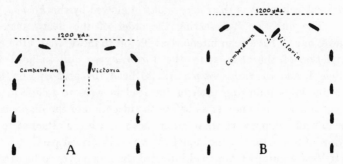

Be it observed that, had it been possible to complete the manœuvre as shown in diagram A, the signals which were made by Tryon would, according to my contention, have been imperfectly carried out, inasmuch as the starboard, or *Victoria's*, column would, have become the port column, and the port, or *Camperdown's*, column would have become the starboard one. Consequently, "the order of the fleet" (which was one of columns of divisions in line ahead, columns disposed abeam to port) would not have been "preserved." On the contrary, the re-arranged columns would have been disposed abeam to starboard, or, in other words, the Commander-in-Chief's ship, instead of leading the starboard column, would have led the port one.

It was possible, however, both implicitly to obey the first part of the signals and to preserve the order of the fleet. How this might have been done is shown in diagram C.

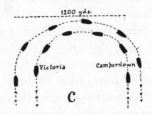

In this diagram, the circle described by the *Victoria* is shown as of larger radius than it need have been, seeing that the *Victoria's*

tactical diameter was 600 yards only. On the other hand, the
circle described by the *Camperdown* is shown as of smaller radius
than it might have been, had it been desirable to take more sea-
room. In fact, here we have a manœuvre which might have been
performed without the remotest danger to any ship concerned;
which would have accomplished Tryon's known and admitted main
object; [1] and which, last but not least, would have fulfilled the final
demands of the signals, in that it would have preserved the order of
the fleet; for in this case, be it noted, the starboard column remains
the starboard one, and the port one remains the port. Another
significant circumstance, to my mind, is that, supposing this
manœuvre to have been contemplated by Tryon, it really did not
matter in the least whether, when they began it, the columns were
six cables or eight cables asunder. At either distance the manœuvre
was perfectly safe and simple.

It is necessary next to enquire whether, so far as is known, the
Commander-in-Chief did anything which was incompatible with this
interpretation of his intentions. I believe that hè did nothing of the
kind. The *Victoria's* helm, from the first, was put as hard over as
possible,[2] so as to make her turning circle as small as it could be
made without reversing the port engine. Only when collision was
imminent was the *Victoria's* port screw reversed, with the object
of allowing the *Camperdown* to pass astern of the flagship, or of
diminishing the angle of incidence. Still later, both engines were
ordered to go at full speed astern. The Commander-in-Chief's ex-
clamation, "It is entirely my fault," determines nothing. Tryon
may have meant merely, "I am to blame for having trusted too
much to the reasoning powers of my subordinates," or "I am to
blame for not having specifically directed the second division to take
the outside circle." I fail to perceive that he must have meant, "I
ordered an impossible manœuvre." For there is a well-recognised
naval custom which dictates that a subordinate shall give precedence
to a Commander-in-Chief, and shall not cross his bows without permission, but shall go under his stern. Rear-Admiral Markham, as
appeared by the evidence at the court-martial, thought, when he
began the manœuvre, that it might be Tryon's intention to circle
outside the second division. Captain Brackenbury, strange to say,

[1] *Viz.*, the inversion of the columns.
[2] It is in evidence that the *Camperdown's* helm, at least at first, was not completely over; yet those in her who believed that the manœuvre in diag. A was to be
attempted must have known that, to attain the object, all possible helm was necessary.

was struck by the same idea. This is what I cannnot understand; and it explains why I have ventured to suggest that Markham and others on the spot seem to have had a glimmering but distorted dream of what might be signified. It greatly astonishes me that, so far as is known, it never occurred to the leader of the second division that by circling outside the first division he might avoid all risk. It astonishes me also that, if Rear-Admiral Markham and Captain Johnstone realised the risk of attempting a countermarch, and expected the Commander-in-Chief to pass outside them, they did not instantly give the *Camperdown* extreme (35 degrees), instead of only 28 degrees of helm, and so make their own ship turn in her smallest circle.

Enough has, I hope, been said to show that, after all, it is not obligatory upon us to believe that Sir George Tryon, had he survived, could not have defended himself. He was condemned unheard. He may have been guilty of criminal negligence; he may even have been smitten with sudden madness; but, on the other hand, there is at least room for the supposition that the manœuvre which he had in his brain was a perfectly safe one, and that his signal might have been reasonably interpreted, and accurately carried out, in such a manner as to obviate all risk of disaster. In any case, the sad episode not only illustrates the extreme unwisdom of attempting to carry out an order which confessedly is not fully understood, but also teaches that, when time permits, a subordinate's duty is to take all such measures as may be possible to enable him to know his chief's mind.

The whole terrible business is so painful a subject to deal with that one passes with a sense of relief to other topics.

Early in 1894 there were new troubles in the Gambia River, and it became necessary to undertake punitive measures against the chief, Fodeh Sillah. Accordingly, Rear-Admiral Frederick George Denham Bedford, C.B., assembled the following vessels of his command, *viz.*, the cruisers *Raleigh* (flag), Captain Edward Harpur Gamble, and *Satellite*, Commander Albert Clinton Allen; the gunboats *Magpie*, Lieutenant Herbert Goodenough King Hall, and *Widgeon*, Lieutenant Hubert Grant-Dalton, and the paddle vessel *Alecto*, Lieutenant Edward Lewis Lang; and it was decided that two columns should advance against the enemy, one landing at Medina Creek. the other moving from British Combo, and both uniting at Birkama.

On February 22nd, in pursuance of this plan, the smaller column, consisting of 50 Marines from the squadron, 50 men of the 1st West India Regiment, and a field-gun, the whole under Lieut.-Colonel Arthur Domville Corbet, R.M., of the *Raleigh*, proceeded as far as Sukutta and destroyed the stockades there, suffering only insignificant loss. On the same day the larger column, under Captain Gamble, who was accompanied by the Rear-Admiral and the Administrator, and who disposed of 200 officers and men, and one field-gun from the ships, disembarked at Medina, and marched in the direction of Birkama. It was found impossible to reach that town; but the force destroyed two stockaded villages on the way thither. On the 23rd it returned to the landing-place; and, while waiting for the tide to rise sufficiently to enable its boats to approach the shore, it was attacked by the enemy, who, protected by thick cover, succeeded in inflicting very severe loss upon it. Lieutenant William Henry Arnold (*Raleigh*), Lieutenant (R.M.) Francis William Archibald Hervey, Sub-Lieutenant Francis Waldemar Theodore Meister (*Magpie*), and ten men were killed; and Captain Gamble, Lieutenants the Hon. Robert Francis Boyle, and Herbert John Savill, Fleet-Surgeon William Rogerson White, Midshipman Arthur Sydney Chambers, Gunner Thomas Berridge, and forty men were wounded, one-fourth of the force being thus put out of action.

The other column, having destroyed Busamballa, entrenched itself, and, though attacked for two hours, beat off the enemy. Corbet was reinforced as quickly as possible; and preparations were begun for dealing with Fodeh Sillah in another way. Commander Charles John Graves Sawle, of the *Raleigh*, took Captain Gamble's place, and, with the squadron, proceeded to Gunjur, which was bombarded on March 6th. A strong body of natives, assembled to resist a disembarkation, was dispersed; a landing was effected on the same day, and, upon the Naval Brigade and troops advancing to the attack, Fodeh Sillah fled.[1]

For their services, Lieutenant Edward Lewis Lang was promoted; Lieut.-Colonel Corbet, R.M., and Fleet-Surgeon White were given the C.B.; and Lieutenant King Hall and Surgeon Walter Bowden (*Raleigh*) were awarded the D.S.O.[2]

The summer of the same year witnessed yet further operations on the west coast of Africa.

[1] Desps., and *A. & N. Gaz.*, 1894, p. 175.   [2] All dated May 26, 1894.

On August 19th, 1894, the acting Consul-General for the Niger Coast Protectorate telegraphed for assistance to St. Paul de Loanda, where the cruiser *Phœbe*, Captain Francis Powell, was lying. She left immediately, and, on the 26th, arrived at the entrance of Brohemie Creek, on the Benin River. She there found the paddle special service vessel, *Alecto*, Lieutenant John George Heugh, and learnt that that craft's steam-cutter had met with a serious reverse. There had already been some trouble, and Heugh, with two Niger Coast Protectorate officers, had been proceeding up Brohemie Creek in the boat, and, encountering an obstruction, had been in the act of turning round when he had been fired at at close quarters by a gun in a masked battery on the bank. The two Protectorate officers had been disabled, the coxswain had been mortally wounded, a leading stoker, Joseph Perkins,[1] had had his foot smashed, and a seaman had been badly hit. Chief-Gunner's Mate Robert H. Crouch[1] had fired a rocket into the battery, and then the cutter, steered by Heugh,[2] and driven by the injured stoker, had steamed back to the *Alecto* in a sinking condition, with her gun dismounted and its shield pierced.

Upon the *Phœbe's* arrival she and the *Alecto* bombarded Nanna's town, near which the outrage had been perpetrated, and began preparations for capturing the masked battery and ultimately for taking the town itself. To this end a force of natives, guarded by seamen, was set to work to make a rough road which should be practicable for guns.

On August 29th a force of 144 officers and men from the *Phœbe*, and 35 from the *Alecto*,[3] with 157 men of the Protectorate troops, preceded by 80 native wood-cutters, advanced in open square formation, accompanied by the *Alecto's* rocket apparatus, a 7-pr. and a Maxim from the *Phœbe*, and a 7-pr. and a Maxim belonging to the Protectorate. From a point near the rear of the battery a few shells were fired into the work, and then the stockade was rushed. Its garrison had fled; but its contents—23 guns of 3-in. and 4-in. calibre, all loaded and primed—were taken, dismounted, and spiked. The advance was continued over very heavy ground, covered in places with soft, stinking mud, and across a deep creek, which had

---

[1] Conspic. Gall. Med. 1894.

[2] D.S.O. for this service, Dec. 21, 1894, and Com. on the same day. Lieut. Godfrey Gore-Brown, of the *Philomel*, received the D.S.O. for his conduct in the final attack.

[3] Under Capt. Powell, and Lieuts Heugh, Murray Thomas Parks, John Dennis Hickley, and John Perceval Shipton.

to be partially filled in with branches ere it could be traversed. Beyond the creek was an open stretch of grass, where the force became exposed to a troublesome fire, and where a bluejacket was hit. Again, beyond, was another creek ; and as it was growing late, it was decided to return to the ships. The retirement was covered by the *Phœbe's* men. Unfortunately the rise of the tide had submerged the branches which had been thrown into the first creek, and it was found impossible to get the *Phœbe's* 7-pr. across. It was, therefore, spiked and thrown into the water. The ships were reached at about 8 P.M.

It was clear that more force was needed, and word to that effect was sent to Rear-Admiral Bedford, C.B.,[1] who arrived upon the scene on September 18th in the cruiser *Philomel*, Captain Charles Campbell. The gunboat *Widgeon*, Lieutenant Hubert Grant-Dalton, followed on the 20th.

On September 25th an attack on Nanna's town[2] was made simultaneously by two detachments. One, under Captain Powell,[3] who was accompanied by the Rear-Admiral, consisted of 136 officers and men from the *Phœbe*, 35 from the *Alecto*, and 50 Royal Marines, with a Maxim, rocket-tubes and a gun-cotton party, besides about 100 of the Protectorate troops. To this detachment the *Widgeon's* people acted as a reserve. The other, under Captain Campbell,[4] consisted of the *Philomel's* people in their boats. Powell's detachment landed at the stockade. Campbell's advanced up the creek and covered the other.

Having landed, Powell made a detour to the right of the previous line of advance, occupied Brohemie without opposition, and was met by Campbell. The expedition destroyed 106 guns, and captured a quantity of stores, many war canoes, and Nanna's personal treasure, amounting to £324 in British money ; but Nanna himself escaped through the swamps. On October 1st the *Phœbe's* 7-pr. was recovered ; and on the same day, after having destroyed the town, the naval portion of the expedition re-embarked.[4]

The other active naval operations of the year were of small importance.

Great Britain had long exercised a nominal protectorate, and,

---

[1] K.C.B. for this service, Dec. 21, 1894.
[2] It had been already shelled on the 19th, etc.
[3] C.B. for this service, Dec. 21, 1894.
[4] Desps.: Accts. and Papers, LXXI. (1895); and journ. of R. U. S. Inst., Feb. 1895.

since 1860, a benevolent though informal guardianship, over the strip of coast land which had been assigned as a reservation to the Mosquito Indians in the republic of Nicaragua. On February 12th, 1894, the republic saw fit to land troops in the Reserve, to occupy Bluefields, the capital, to hoist the Nicaraguan flag, and to arrest the British Vice-Consul, Mr. Hatch, and some of the leading inhabitants. Early on February 25th the cruiser *Cleopatra*, Captain the Hon. Assheton Gore Curzon-Howe, reached the spot from Greytown, with the British Consul, Mr. H. F. Bingham, on board. On the 26th the representative of the Nicaraguan government was informed that the Mosquito flag must be rehoisted, alone, or side by side with that of Nicaragua, and that a written guarantee must be given for the lives of the chief and the other people who had been arrested. In the meantime the cruiser landed a detachment of bluejackets and Marines under Lieutenants Reginald Blayney Colmore, and Sholto Grant Douglas, and Lieutenant William Albert Harris, R.M. The most pressing of the British conditions were eventually complied with.[1] The Indians appeared at the time to be in great terror of their neighbours; but on November 20th, 1894, ostensibly at the desire of those same Indians, the Reserve was formally handed over to Nicaragua, and became part of the province of Zelaya. So terminated the last remnant of a connection with Great Britain which had lasted since 1655.[2]

A somewhat similar affair occurred in July, 1894, on the China Station. Previous to the outbreak of her war with China, Japan landed troops and surrounded Seoul, the capital of Korea. The British Consul-General, happening to go for a walk with his wife and children, and entering the Japanese lines, was rudely sent back by the officer in local charge. Although a formal apology was quickly made, Commander Reginald William Scott Rogers, of the cruiser *Archer*, deemed it wise to land an armed party of thirty men, under Lieutenant Spencer Victor Yorke de Horsey, to protect the Consul-General from further insult. This party was afterwards relieved by a detachment of Marines from the cruiser *Severn*, Captain Reginald Friend Hannam Henderson, C.B., under Lieu-

---

[1] *Times*, Mar. 27 and 29, 1894, and desps.

[2] Great Britain resigned all claim to the coast by the Clayton-Bulwer Treaty, of 1850, and formally ceded the protectorate to Nicaragua by the Treaty of Managua, of 1860; but, till 1894, the Indians continued to be ruled by their own chief, under Nicaraguan suzerainty.

tenant Walter William Frankis, R.M. There was, however, no
more trouble.[1]

A factory at Akassa, belonging to the Royal Niger Company,
having been looted and destroyed by natives of the Brass River
district, Rear-Admiral Sir Frederick George Denham Bedford
conducted a punitive expedition up that stream on February 20th,
1895. His force consisted of a landing party of 150 bluejackets
and Marines from the cruisers *St. George* (flag), Captain William
Carnegie Codrington Forsyth, and *Barrosa*, Commander John
Locke Marx, and the gunboats *Widgeon*, Lieutenant Hubert
Grant-Dalton, and *Thrush*, Lieutenant Henry Loftus Tottenham,
reinforced by 150 of the Protectorate troops. The *Widgeon* and
Thrush began operations by shelling the scrub on the river bank
below Nimbi, the capital of the chief, Koko, who had been responsible for the outrage; and the pinnaces and launches of the squadron,
each with a machine-gun on board, then forced their way through
Tua Creek to Nimbi Creek, and landed their people on Sacrifice
Point. The enemy attacked in war canoes; but, upon three of
these craft being sunk by machine-gun fire, the rest drew off. On
the 21st, the stockades near the shore were blown up. On the
22nd, the two gunboats moved further along the creek, and began
to shell Nimbi itself, while the boats advanced on the town. As
they approached it, a very heavy fire was suddenly opened upon
them from a concealed battery, and several of them were hulled.
Lieutenant George John Taylor, of the flagship, who was in the
leading boat, and two seamen were killed, and five bluejackets, two
native soldiers, and two Kroomen were wounded; but the attack
was pressed home at once, a landing was effected, the stockades
were rushed, and, with little further resistance, Nimbi fell. It was
burnt. On the 24th, the *Barrosa* and *Widgeon* bombarded Fish-
town; and, on the succeeding day, that place was destroyed by a
party from the *Widgeon*, no opposition being offered. Some of the
chiefs who had been concerned in the attack on the Akassa factory
fled, but the majority came in, and made submission.[2] Commander
Marx and Lieutenant Tottenham were promoted on June 30th
following.

A few months later, Rear-Admiral Bedford was succeeded in
command of the Cape and West Africa Station by Rear-Admiral

[1] *Times*, July 24: *Nav. & Mil. Rec.*, Oct. 4, 1894.

[2] *Times*, Feb. 4, 1895; *A. & N. Gaz.*, Mar. 2, 1895: Parl. Pap. 7977 (1896).

Harry Holdsworth Rawson, C.B., who quickly found work awaiting him near the furthest limit of his command. The various operations already described as having been undertaken in British East Africa had failed to teach all the local chiefs the lesson of obedience to the dominant power; and, an ultimatum to M'buruk bin Rashid, chief of M'wele, not having been complied with, it was determined to deal severely with him.

An expeditionary force, consisting of 400 men from the cruisers *St. George* (flag), Captain George Le Clerc Egerton, *Phœbe,* Captain Thomas MacGill, *Racoon*, Commander Powell Cecil Underwood, *Barrosa*, Captain John Locke Marx, and *Blonde*, Commander Henry Marwood Colson Festing, with two Maxims, a 7-pr. gun, and a rocket tube, and accompanied by a body of 60 Soudanese and 50 Askari troops, and by 800 porters, started inland from Mombasa on August 12th, 1895. With it went Rear-Admiral Rawson himself, and staff, General Sir Lloyd William Mathews (R.N. retd.), commanding the Zanzibari army, and Mr. A. H. Hardinge, Consul-General at Zanzibar. After repulsing an attack at Nololo, on August 16th, the expedition arrived before M'wele on August 17th.

When the 7-pr., under Lieutenant Murray Thomas Parks (*Phœbe*), had thrown a few well-directed shells into the strongly stockaded place, part of the force, under Captain MacGill and Commander Underwood, with the two Maxims, made a flanking movement to the left, while the remainder, under the Rear-Admiral, Captain Egerton, and Lieutenant Arthur Henry Christian (*St. George*), moved directly forward to within three hundred yards of the works. A company of the *Racoon's* people, under Lieutenant Cecil Irby Prowse, drew the enemy's fire, and then two companies of the *St. George's* men, under Lieutenants Charles Douglas Carpendale, and William John Frazer, the latter of the Royal Naval Reserve, rushed the stockade in front.

In the meantime, the force under MacGill had come upon another stockade, which was captured by a company from the *Phœbe*, under Lieutenant Francis William Kennedy, and another from the *Barrosa*, under Lieutenant Marcus Rowley Hill. M'buruk escaped, but two of his sons were killed, and two of his standards were taken, one by Lieutenant Frazer, and the other by Lieutenant Walter Henry Cowan, of the *Barrosa*. The British loss was three killed and eleven wounded, among the latter being General Mathews,.

Lieutenant Kennedy, and Midshipman Edward Harry John Grogan, of the *St. George.*[1]

Previous to the setting out of this expedition, a force of seamen and Marines, from the *Racoon* and *Phœbe*, under Commander Underwood, with 150 Soudanese regulars, had landed on July 14th in the Kilifi estuary, and had made a preliminary reconnaissance in search of the enemy. The detachment had been sniped at night, but had not succeeded in getting into close touch with the foe.[2] Still earlier, from June 16th to June 23rd, a force from the gunboat *Magpie*, Lieutenant Henry Venn Wood Elliott, had been landed for the defence of Melindi, when threatened by M'buruk. The sloop *Swallow*, Commander George Lindsay Malcolm Leckie, was also employed on the coast.

Some months later, Aziz, a chief who acted in collusion with M'buruk, attacked and burnt Melindi, the garrison of which had been prematurely withdrawn; whereupon a new expedition was launched against the turbulent natives. This one started inland from Wanga, on the mainland nearly opposite the north end of Pemba Island, having been conveyed there early in February, 1896, by the gunboat *Widgeon*, Lieutenant Edward Duke Hunt. It consisted of Indian troops, under Major G. P. Hatch, and a little Naval Brigade, forty strong, from the gunboats *Widgeon* and *Thrush*, Lieutenant Archibald Peile Stoddart, accompanied by two Maxims and two rocket-tubes. On February 6th, a detachment under Lieutenant Cecil Francis Lacon Watson, of the *Thrush*, attacked and destroyed Bormuz; and, on February 10th, another detachment proceeded to Sega, which, with several neighbouring villages, was similarly dealt with. On February 16th, an advance was made against Moreni, which, when reached and subjected to rocket-fire, was found to have been abandoned. The expedition next went to M'wele, which was captured and occupied on the 20th, the enemy offering but little opposition when a Maxim opened on them. The objects in view having been thus accomplished, the force returned to Wanga, and re-embarked on February 23rd.

In addition to Lieutenants Hunt and Watson, Lieutenant Guy Montagu Marston, and Surgeon Charles Samuel Facey, both of the *Widgeon*, were with the Naval Brigade.[3]

---

[1] *Gazette*, Jan. 22, 1897: *A. & N. Gaz.* (1895), pp. 676, 695, 800.

[2] *A. & N. Gaz.* (1895), 676.

[3] Africa, No. 6 (C. 8274), p. 74: *Times*, Feb. 22, 1896.

In 1895–96 there was still friction with the republic of Nicaragua, where General Zelaya had raised himself to power. An indemnity which had been demanded by Great Britain for the insult to her representative, Mr. Hatch, was not forthcoming; and the unsatisfied claim led in May to the occupation of the port of Corinto, on the Pacific coast, by detachments from part of the Pacific squadron, which was then commanded by Rear-Admiral Henry Frederick Stephenson, C.B., who flew his flag in the first-class cruiser *Royal Arthur*, Captain Frederick Perceval Trench. The incident terminated upon the payment by the republic of an indemnity of fifteen thousand dollars. In the spring of 1896, when President ' Zelaya was contending with a rebellion under General Ortiz, a body of Honduran troops—Honduras being in alliance with Nicaragua—was ordered into Corinto to occupy the place, and, it was alleged, to demand a forced loan from a British banker. The governor represented to the British consul that rioting would probably result, that British property would be endangered, and that he could not hold himself responsible; whereupon a detachment of bluejackets was landed from the cruiser *Comus*, Captain Henry Hart Dyke, under Lieutenants John Scott Luard, and Gerald Thomas Fleetwood Pike. A landing-party was also put ashore from the U.S. cruiser *Alert*, the officers and men of which, as, happily, is usually the case on such occasions, co-operated in the most friendly manner with the British. The consulates and custom-house were occupied, but, upon President Zelaya promising to send Nicaraguan instead of Honduran troops to the town, and to respect foreign property and interests, the detachments were withdrawn on May 4th, after having been three days on shore.[1]

The Ashantee war of 1895–96, which resulted in the dethrone-ment and capture of King Prempeh, was purely a military under-taking; and it was decided from the beginning that no bluejackets were to be employed in it, although Rear-Admiral Rawson held himself prepared to land Marines from his squadron if required. The vessels on the coast at the time were the cruisers *Racoon*, Commander Powell Cecil Underwood, and *Blonde*, Commander Peyton Hoskyns, and the gunboats *Sparrow*, Lieutenant Francis George Theodore Cole, and *Magpie*, Lieutenant Henry Venn Wood Elliott. After Sir Francis Scott's expedition had attained its

[1] *Times*, June 2: *Nav. & Mil. Rec.* July 30, 1896.

objects, in January, 1896, Prempeh and the other most important prisoners embarked at Cape Coast Castle in the *Racoon,* and were conveyed by her to Elmina. Commander William Stokes Rees, of the flagship *St. George,* acted as naval transport officer on the occasion of the disembarkation of the expeditionary force, and received, in consequence, the thanks of the War Office.[1]

The defeat of the raid which was undertaken against the South African Republic by Dr. L. S. Jameson in the last days of 1895 was the occasion of a congratulatory telegram from the German Emperor to President Paul Kruger. The raid was indefensible, and the telegram had no political significance; yet so sensitive was British public opinion to foreign criticism that the Government of the day was induced to order the instant mobilisation of a small Particular Service Squadron. The vessels specially commissioned for the purpose were the battleships *Revenge,* Captain the Hon. Assheton Gore Curzon-Howe (flag of Rear-Admiral Alfred Taylor Dale), and *Royal Oak,* Captain Burges Watson, the first-class cruisers *Gibraltar,* Captain Harry Francis Hughes-Hallett, and *Theseus,* Captain Charles Campbell (2), the second-class cruisers *Charybdis,* Captain John Mackenzie McQuhae, and *Hermione,* Captain Charles Ramsay Arbuthnot, and a flotilla of six torpedo-boat destroyers.[2] The squadron, weakened in the autumn by the detachment from it of several ships to other commands, remained in commission from January 14th to October 21st, 1896, when it was abolished.

During the rebellion in Rhodesia, it was considered desirable to send some British troops to the spot by way of Beira; and arrangements were made accordingly with the Portuguese authorities at that port. The chartered transport *Arab* arrived with the troops off Beira on July 3rd, 1896; but the landing of the expedition would have been almost impossible had not Rear-Admiral Rawson given the co-operation of the naval forces on the spot. Several Maxim machine-guns and some stores were also lent from the ships for the purposes of General Sir F. Carrington's operations.[3]

The punitive measures against M'buruk in 1895–96 had been undertaken in conjunction with the Askari troops of the Sultan of Zanzibar. Within the following twelve months, however, British

---

[1] *A. & N. Gaz.* (1895), pp. 958, 1036 ; (1896), p. 120.
[2] *A. & N. Gaz.,* Jan. 18, 1896.
[3] *A. & N. Gaz.,* 1896, p. 647 : Desp. of Carrington : *Times,* July 13, 1896.

ships of war were obliged to take steps for the repression of rebellion in Zanzibar itself.

The sultanate of Zanzibar had become independent in 1856, under the rule of Sayyid Majid, a son of Sayyid Said, Sultan of Muscat and Zanzibar. The territory originally extended along the African mainland, southward to Tunghi Bay, and northward to Warsheikh. Sayyid Majid had been succeeded in 1870 by his younger brother, Bargash bin Said, under whom the possessions of the sultanate had suffered considerable diminution, Germany, in 1885, enforcing the cession to itself of control over Dar-es-Salam and certain districts inland of it, and securing further advantages in August, 1888, in March of which year Sultan Bargash had been succeeded by his son, Sayyid Khalif. In 1890 fresh arrangements had been made, Germany obtaining possession of the continental coastline from Ruvuma to Wanga, and of the island of Mafia, and the sultanate becoming a British protectorate, and retaining only the islands of Zanzibar and Pemba, a narrow strip of mainland coastline between Wanga and Kipini, the islands of Lamu, Manda and Patta, and the ports and immediate environs of Kismayu, Barawa, Merka, Magdisho, and Warsheikh. Benadir had been leased to Italy. This fresh arrangement was the indirect result of a revolt of some of the coast towns against German rule, and of the international blockade which was instituted for the suppression of slavery along the coast, and in which Great Britain, Germany, Italy, and Portugal took part. The blockade, as has been seen, was enforced for several months in 1888–89, under the direction of the senior British officer, Rear-Admiral the Hon. Edmund Robert Fremantle.[1]

Sultan Sayyid Hamed bin Thwain succeeded his uncle in March, 1893, and died suddenly on August 25th, 1896. As soon as the event was known, Mr. Basil S. Cave, the British acting diplomatic agent, and General Sir Lloyd William Mathews,[2] K.C.M.G., the late Sultan's prime minister, hastened to the palace, and ordered it to be closed; but Sayyid Khalid bin Bargash, a prince of the royal house, who had caused trouble at the accession of Sayyid Hamed bin Thwain, broke into the building with a force of armed men, and assumed so threatening an attitude that Cave and Mathews withdrew. The pretender also forestalled Brigadier-General A. E. H. Raikes, the commander of the regular Zanzibari

---

[1] See p. 390, *antea.*

[2] Sir L. Mathews was a Lieut. R.N. of Mar. 31, 1874, who had retd. June 15, 1881.

troops. In a short time there were about five or six hundred men, with guns, in the palace; while seven hundred regulars, who had deserted, with nine guns, held the square. The insurgents were presently joined by about 2000 Persians, Arabs, Comoro people, Suaheli slaves, and loafers, to whom arms were dealt out.

The British naval force then at Zanzibar consisted of the third-class cruiser *Philomel*, and the gun-vessel *Thrush*. These craft manned and armed their boats, and sent ashore a Brigade of blue-jackets and Marines to hold the English club, which was quite close to the palace prison, and other points of vantage, including the British Agency. The *Thrush* then shifted her anchorage, and steamed to a position abreast of the palace, where she moored, near her sister ship the *Sparrow*, which had come in that morning from the northward. In the course of the forenoon the Zanzibari "man-of-war" *Glasgow*, which, with all the other government craft, had been seized by, or had willingly joined the insurgents, fired a salute in honour of Sayyid Khalid, who sent round to the various consulates to ask for recognition, but was informed that his claims could not be admitted until they should be acknowledged by the British authorities. At sunset, nevertheless, another salute was fired.

On the 26th the deadlock continued. The third-class cruiser *Racoon* arrived from the southward, and was moored abreast of the Custom House. A few hours later, also from the southward, came the first-class cruiser *St. George*, flag-ship of the Cape command; for it should be explained that since the days of the blockade of 1888-89, Zanzibar had ceased to be within the limits of the East India, and had been attached to the Cape of Good Hope station. Eventually the *Racoon* was moored beyond the *Sparrow*, the *Philomel* beyond the *Racoon*, and the *St. George* at one extreme end of the line, the *Thrush* being at the other; thus,—

Ships.	Displ. in Tons.	I.H.P.	Guns.	Commanders.
St. George . . .	7,700	12,000	12	{Rear-Adm. Harry Holdsworth Rawson, C.B. Capt. George Le Clerc Egerton.
Philomel	2,575	7,500	8	Capt. Michael Pelham O'Callaghan.
Racoon	1,770	2,500	6	Com. Powell Cecil Underwood.
Sparrow	805	1,200	6	Lieut. Francis Geo. Theodore Cole.
Thrush	805	1,200	6	Lieut. Archibald Peile Stoddart.

Rear-Admiral Rawson was quickly on shore, whither also re-inforcements of bluejackets and Marines [1] were sent. Messages were despatched to the usurper, and at 7 A.M. on the 27th, he was informed that unless his flag was down by 9 A.M., hostilities would be begun against him. In the meantime all the British ladies and children, and such of the men as desired to be taken off were received on board the men-of-war, which went to quarters; while the foreign ships in harbour, including the German man-of-war *Seeadler*, and the Italian man-of-war *Volturno*, shifted into safe billets, many steaming round to the southward of Shangani Point. The Zanzibari war-ship *Glasgow*,[2] however, cleared for action, and numerous Zanzibari launches and small craft were seen to have guns mounted in their bows, and to be full of armed men.

Two bells sounded on board the *St. George*, but no reply to the ultimatum had been received. Rear-Admiral Rawson waited, never-theless, for the palace clock to strike nine ere he signalled to open fire. The *Thrush* discharged the first gun, and was closely followed by the *Racoon* and *Sparrow*. The guns on shore answered instantly, and soon the *Glasgow*, which lay across the stern of the flagship, also joined in, whereupon she received several shells as well from the *St. George* as from the *Philomel* and *Racoon*. The action had not long continued when a flotilla of dhows was seen to weigh and make sail to the northward. It was believed that some of the leaders of the insurrection effected their escape in these craft.

The *Glasgow* ceased firing after a few minutes. When she began to fire again, a 6-in. shell from the *St. George* silenced her quickly. A Zanzibari launch, the *Chwaka*, had the temerity to approach the *Racoon*, and was sunk by her. Ere twenty minutes had elapsed, the *Glasgow* was seen to be on fire. Nevertheless, after a second period of silence, she fired once more at the *St. George*, which, retaliating with two 6-in. shells, stove in her side near the water line, and put her finally out of action. On shore, the palace was knocked to-pieces, and the old custom house was in flames.

---

[1] Under Maj. Thomas Horatio de Montmorency Roche, and Lieut. FitzStephen John Featherston French, R.M.A.

[2] The *Glasgow* was built by Messrs. Denny, of Dumbarton, and navigated to Zanzibar in 1878 by Capt. Hy. Hand, R.N. On her way she called at Portsmouth to take on board her armament of seven guns, a present from the British Government in acknowledgment of the sacrifices made by the Sultan of Zanzibar for the suppression of the slave trade. She was a single screw composite craft of 180 H.P.N., and fully rigged, measuring 195 ft. long, 30 ft. in beam, and 18 ft. in depth of hold.

At last the pretender's flag was lowered; and at 9·37 the " cease fire " sounded. The *Glasgow* had previously struck, and had hoisted a British flag at the main. She was well on fire; and assistance was then sent to her from the *Philomel*. Nothing, however, could be done for her, and she sank slowly, her decks bursting as she went down.

There was still some firing on shore ; but presently that also died away ; and, an hour or two later, the rightful Sultan, Sayyid Hamoud bin Mohamed bin Said, was proclaimed, and saluted with twenty-one guns from all the war-ships. The pretender had escaped. In the height of the bombardment he had passed through a force of British Marines by whom he and his followers had been disarmed but not recognised. He reached the German consulate,[1] whence he was afterwards deported to German East Africa.

On the Zanzibari side the casualties were very heavy, about 500 people being killed or wounded. One shot from the *Thrush* smashed a gun, and killed the whole of its crew. On the British side the sole casualty was one man, a seaman of the *Thrush*, wounded. It is astonishing that there was not more loss, for the *Thrush* was hit more than a hundred times, and the *Racoon* and *Sparrow* were repeatedly struck, the *St. George* also receiving a few shot.[2]

During the initial, as well as in the later stages of the operations for the reconquest of the Soudan by Sir Herbert Kitchener, the Navy rendered valuable services. In the summer and autumn of 1896, when Dongola was recovered from the Mahdi, four Egyptian stern-wheel gunboats, under the orders of Commanders the Hon. Stanley Cecil James Colville, and Charles Hope Robertson, C.M.G., and Lieutenant David Beatty, with a few non-commissioned officers and men of the Royal Marine Artillery, under Captain Humphrey Oldfield, R.M.A., assisted the advance up the Nile, especially in the action at Hafir, on September 19th, and subsequently. The dervish works at Hafir were shelled very effectively, and a hostile steamer

---

[1] There were present during the bombardment the German warship *Seeadler*, and the Italian warship *Volturno*. Seamen from the *Seeadler* were landed to guard the German consulate. The action of the Germans throughout tended, it must be feared, to obstruct British policy and a peaceable settlement.

[2] Desps.; and Supp. to *Zanzibar Gazette* of Sept. 2, 1896. Letter of Reuter's Corr. of Sept. 2, in the *Times*. Corr. in *Daily Graphic*, Oct. 3.

was sunk, by the gunboats *Tamai*, *Abu Klea*, and *Metemmeh*,[1] which suffered somewhat, and lost two men killed, and Commander Colville and twelve men wounded. A dervish shell actually entered the magazine of the *Abu Klea*, but, happily, failed to explode. After the action, the three boats pushed up to the neighbourhood of Dongola, where, on the 22nd, they were joined by a fifth gunboat, the *Zafir*, under Commander Robertson, who, in the gunboat *El Teb*, which also joined, had grounded, and had been detained in consequence.

Early on the 23rd, Dongola was attacked by land as well as by water, and, after the gunboats had bombarded it, was captured by the army. Upon the defeat and retirement of the dervishes, Colville and Robertson took part in the pursuit as far as Merawe.[2] Colville, who had previously superintended the construction of the gunboats which had proved so useful, was posted,[3] and made a C.B.[4]; Beatty, who had taken command of the flotilla immediately after Colville had been wounded, was rewarded with a D.S.O.[5]

In January, 1897, a peaceful mission of officers in the service of the Niger Coast Protectorate, headed by Mr. J. R. Phillips, then acting Consul-General, was attacked in the bush by the organised forces of the King of Benin, about twelve miles from that city, and all persons except two were massacred. Immediate reprisals were necessary, both to avenge the massacre, and also to prevent the news of an unpunished aggression spreading to the surrounding country, and causing revolts and other violent actions in the adjacent districts.

Rear-Admiral Rawson was instructed to undertake the reduction of Benin City, and, if possible, to capture the King, his generals, and Juju priests. He received the order on January 15th. By February 3rd, the *St. George*, *Philomel*, *Phœbe*, *Widgeon*, *Magpie*, *Alecto*, and *Barrosa*, belonging to the Cape station, and the *Theseus* and *Forte*, from the Mediterranean, had assembled off the Brass and Benin rivers. All stores were landed as soon as possible, and all available Houssas collected at Warrigi, on the Benin river, the main base of the expedition. So as to expose the sailors and Marines for as short a time as possible to the deadly climate of the swamps and

---

[1] *Tamai*, Com. Colville, and Lieut. C. H. de Rougemont, R.A.; *Abu Klea*, Lieut. Beatty; *Metemmeh*, Capt. Oldfield, R.M.A.

[2] Desps. of Kitchener: Royle, 515: *A. & N. Gaz.*, Nov. 7, 1896.

[3] Oct. 31, 1896.   [4] Nov. 17, 1896.   [5] Nov. 18, 1896.

bush of the Benin country, the men were not disembarked from their ships till the carriers had been collected and organised, and everything made ready for the forward march. The general plan of the expedition was to advance the main column, under the personal command of Admiral Rawson, with Captain Egerton, chief of the staff, and Colonel Hamilton in command of the native troops, by the little used Ologbo-Benin route, while a small force, under Captain O'Callaghan, from the *Philomel, Barrosa,* and *Widgeon,*

Ships.	Compt.	Commanders.
St. George . . .	520	{Rear-Adm. Harry Holdsworth Rawson, C.B. {Capt. George Le Clerc Egerton.
Theseus	544	Capt. Charles Campbell (2) C.B.
Forte	320	Capt. Randolph Frank Ollive Foote.
Philomel	190	Capt. Michael Pelham O'Callaghan.
Phœbe	190	Capt. Thomas MacGill.
Widgeon	74	Lieut. Edward Duke Hunt.
Alecto . . ᐧ .	68	Lieut. Charles Edward Pritchard.
Barrosa	159	Com. James Startin.
Magpie	74	Lieut. Henry Venn Wood Elliott.

was sent to Guato, a village on Guato Creek, from which starts the main road to Benin, to deceive the Beni, who would naturally expect the chief attack to come from that direction. A third force, under Captain MacGill, was sent to Sapobar, on the Jamieson river, with men from the *Phœbe, Alecto,* and *Widgeon,* to keep that part of the country employed, and prevent the natives from swelling the main body, and also to attempt to cut off fugitives to the adjoining territory. On February 9th, the hospital ship *Malacca* having arrived with details, the disembarkation of the men began from their ships, into small local steamers, which transported them from the Brass to the Benin river, arriving at Warrigi on the 10th.

On the 11th the main column marched to Ceri, on the banks of Ologbo Creek, two miles below Ologbo. There a reconnaissance showed that both the banks were too rotten and swampy for the men to land anywhere but at Ceri and Ologbo village. Bridging the creek was therefore abandoned, and the whole force had to be taken in detachments two miles up the creek, in a steamboat and two surf-boats, and landed at Ologbo. This was done on the 12th, when

Colonel Hamilton, with a company of Houssas and half a company of bluejackets, effected the first landing. After three hours' firing the enemy retired. News was there received that the attack on Guato had been successful, after two hours' fighting, but that Captain O'Callaghan was waiting for reinforcements before proceeding to destroy Egbene and Ikoro, two towns to the northward and west of Guato. It was also reported that the force under Captain MacGill had met with resistance, but had erected and was holding a stockade, about four miles inland of Sapobar. Rear-Admiral Rawson decided to reinforce the Guato column with a view to holding Guato during the march of the main column, and so necessitate a division of the Beni army, and to leave the existing force at Sapobar to hold the stockade. Those two places were successfully held, with constant fighting, till the end of the expedition, after the fall of Benin City. On the 14th the advance of the main column began; and, after a running fight for two days, a village called Agagi was reached. There the wells, which had been relied on to provide cooking water for the natives, were found to be dry. The Admiral, therefore, immediately revised the column, the second division being left at Ologbo, and all its carriers being employed to carry water for the first division. By such means sufficient carriers were available to carry three days' water supply, at an allowance of two quarts for each white man and Houssa, and one quart for each carrier, cooking included.

On the 17th the march was resumed; and on the 18th, after a running bush fight for five hours, Benin was reached and taken. The town was found to be in the most terrible state from the human sacrifices offered to delay the advance. Seven pits, forty to fifty feet deep, were discovered, with twelve to fifteen bodies in each, the dead and the dying being intermingled. The destruction of houses for the purpose of fortifying the palaver and the King's houses was immediately begun, and preparations were made for withdrawing the sailors and Marines, and leaving the town to the native troops. On Sunday, 21st, however, a roof caught fire, through the carelessness of a native carrier, and in ten minutes the whole town was in a blaze. The ammunition and arms were saved, but all the provisions and kits lost. Happily a fresh supply was received from Agagi the same evening. On the 22nd the sailors commenced the return journey, arriving at Warrigi after a trying march for the sick and wounded, who were carried through the narrow bush paths in hammocks. The whole force was re-embarked by the evening of the 27th, exactly eighteen days after leaving the ships. The naval casualties during the expedition were : Killed in action, 3 officers, Lieutenant Charles Edward Pritchard (*Alecto*), Surgeon Charles James Fyfe (*St. George*), and Captain Gervis Taylor Byrne, R.M.L.I., and 8 men ; wounded in action, 3 officers, Captain O'Callaghan (*Philomel*), Lieutenant Edward Duke Hunt, and Gunner (T.) William Johnston (*Philomel*), and 44 men ; deaths from climate, up to 27th February, 1 officer, Staff-Surgeon Richard Henry Way (*Malacca*), and 4 men. Two officers of the Niger Coast Protectorate Forces were also wounded.[1]

The effects of this short campaign, however, were soon felt more severely by those who had taken part in it. No fewer than 2290 fever cases were attributable to the expedition, and these were practically sustained by the 1200 men landed. The *St. George* landed 338 men, of whom 238, or 71 per cent., were attacked by fever, and who among them endured 443 attacks. The 89 men of the *Phœbe* sustained 337 attacks. The *Forte*, complement 320, had, during the year, 904 cases on her sick list, compared with an average of 230 in ships of her class on the Mediterranean station. The expedition may, nevertheless, be considered as one of the most successful of small punitive undertakings. The organisation, on which the whole success depended, was, thanks to Rear-Admiral Rawson, without a flaw. A force of 1200 men, the majority coming from 3000 to 4000 miles from the Benin country, was collected, equipped, and landed in 29 days, 90 miles from the sea base. It was marched through an unknown country, and on the fifth day, after constant fighting, Benin was taken. In another twelve days the entire force was re-embarked, and the ships were coaled, and ready for further service. The effect of the expedition was, it is needless to say, most salutary on the whole surrounding country.

Among the honours granted by way of reward for the success which had been attained were a K.C.B. to Rear-Admiral Rawson ; C.B.'s to Captains O'Callaghan, MacGill, and Egerton ; C.M.G.'s

---

[1] Bacon : "Benin, the City of Blood" : Rawson's Despatches, especially of Feb. 12th and 22nd.: Corr. of various journals : and accounts of participants. I am much indebted to Capt. R. H. S. Bacon, who served as Intelligence Officer, and who has given me the most interesting statistics concerning the subsequent sickness.

to Captain Foote, and Fleet-Surgeon Michael FitzGerald; and D.S.O.'s to Captain Campbell, Commander Reginald Hugh Spencer Bacon, and Staff-Surgeons James McCardie Martin, and Edgar Ralph Dimsey; with promotion to Commanders James Startin, and William Stokes Rees, and Lieutenants Edward Duke Hunt, Henry Venn Wood Elliott, Stuart Nicholson, Edmund Radcliffe Pears, and Seymour Elphinstone Erskine, all dated May 25th, 1897.

In the year 1896 the Sultan had been induced by the Powers to promise to make certain reforms in the administration of the island of Crete. Soon, however, it became evident that the promise was to be productive of little actual good to the large Christian population, which, in concert with sympathisers in Greece, broke into revolt in January, 1897. In the large towns, and a few isolated garrisons, the Turks, as a rule, held their own; but beyond the range of the Turkish guns most of the country was speedily overrun by armed and organised Christians, strengthened by detachments of Greek regulars, and supported by Greek men-of-war cruising round the coast. Such was the military situation. The diplomatic situation was equally threatening; for the Powers, anxious to help forward the promised reforms, had refused to allow the Sultan to add to the number of his troops in the island, and to employ them in offensive operations against the insurgents. The Powers, in fact, had made themselves responsible, to some extent, for the safety of the Turkish garrisons, while they had also taken under their protection the cause of reform. The position, besides being delicate, was dangerous, seeing that the attitude of Greece was most provocative to Turkey; that Turkey was well able to crush Greece without difficulty; and that any formal conflict between Turkey and Greece might imperil the general peace of Europe.

With a view to bringing the local troubles to an amicable and satisfactory termination, the six Powers, Great Britain, France, Germany, Russia, Italy, and Austria, sent squadrons to the spot in February, 1897; and for nearly two years subsequent to that time, the affairs of Crete were practically managed by the naval officers of the allies, acting at first under the presidency of Vice-Admiral Count Canevaro (Italy), and later under that of Rear-Admiral Edouard Pottier (France), these being the senior flag-officers in Cretan waters. The senior British representative was, first, Rear-Admiral Robert

Hastings Harris,[1] and, afterwards, his successor, Rear-Admiral Gerard Henry Uctred Noel.[2]

Almost immediately after the allied officers had anchored in Canea Roads, a Greek squadron, under the command of Prince George of Greece, arrived with orders to assist the Christians and to harass the Turks. It was warned off at once, and did not reappear. Less decision was displayed in dealing with a Greek military expedition which arrived a little later, under Colonel Vassos. It was unwisely permitted to disembark, although certain storeships which were sent after it were captured. When Vassos attempted to move upon Canea, his further progress was forbidden; and at length, on May 23rd, finding that he was allowed to do nothing, in spite of the fact that by that time war had broken out between Greece and Turkey, he was glad to return to Greece. His men were embarked in Platania Bay by the cruiser *Hawke*, Captain Sir Richard Poore, Bart.

In the interval, to check the advance of an insurgent force from the Akrotiri side, the foreign admirals had landed about 500 men at Canea, above which they hoisted the flags of the six Powers. This took place as early as the middle of February; but, as the landing did not produce the desired effect, the insurgent position was bombarded for about five minutes on February 21st. No one appears to have been injured; yet the " bombardment of Akrotiri " raised an outcry from certain sentimentalists throughout Europe, the result being that although the Christian insurgents eastward of Canea were kept quiet, their compatriots elsewhere in the island grew more aggressive than ever. This was most prejudicial to the settlement of the problem, seeing that the Powers were implicitly pledged to see to the safety of the Turkish garrison. The reply of the admirals was the institution of a strict blockade of the Cretan coasts, and of some of the Greek ports, so as effectually to prevent the insurgents from receiving any further succour from their sympathisers on the mainland.

More active steps had soon to be taken. The Turkish garrison of Candanos, a town about four miles inland, was hard pressed by the insurgents; and on March 7th, an international force of about 500 seamen, under Captain John Harvey Rainier, of the *Rodney*, marched to its relief, and brought it away, together with a great

---

[1] In the *Revenge*, Capt. Reginald Charles Prothero.
[2] From Jan. 12, 1898.

number of Mussulman inhabitants. On its return along a valley to the coast, the force was hustled by the Christians, and some shots were fired on both sides; but the difficult retirement was performed with no loss on the side of the allies, and with but slight casualties among the insurgents. On March 25th an Italian cruiser shelled the insurgents out of a blockhouse which they had captured a few moments earlier on the heights of Melaxa, above Suda Bay; and somewhat later the *Camperdown*, Captain Robert William Craigie, at a range of 5000 yards, using her 13·5-in. guns, dislodged a detachment which was besieging Fort Izzedin, a fine modern work near the entrance to the same bay. To prevent further operations against that fort, Major James Henry Bor, R.M.A., with some Marines from the *Revenge*, was landed to take command of it. These various measures had the desired effect of inducing the insurgents to cease from making organised attacks upon the Turks. The Christians still sniped their opponents as occasion offered; but the action of the admirals put a stop to regular hostilities.

The next effort of the representatives of the Powers was to arrange a *modus vivendi* between the factions while the Turkish garrisons continued in the island. That, however, was found to be impossible, the more so when, early in 1898, Germany and Austria withdrew from the concert, leaving four Powers only to do the work.

The district of Candia, with the towns of Canea and Candia, was the sphere which, by agreement, had been allotted to the special management of Great Britain. The British senior officer, whoever he happened to be at the moment, did what he could in union with the International Council, of which he was a member, and assisted in the keeping of some kind of order on shore; but as the Moslems in the towns were the only people from whom taxes could be collected, and as most of the insurgents remained aloof, the situation was an impossible one. It continued, however, throughout the summer, and might have continued much longer but for a lamentable event which happened in September—an event which, though it involved the loss of gallant British lives, gave freedom at length to Crete.

The council of naval officers had decided to collect a certain proportion of export duties, and to expend the proceeds not for the good of the Turks only, but for the general benefit of the island;

and, with that object in view, they directed that on September 6th the Custom House at Candia should be given up to the British authorities. The moment selected was unfortunate ; for there were but about 130 British troops [1] in the town, the British Commissioner, Sir Herbert Chermside, who had great influence over the Moslem population, was away in England, the Turkish governor, Edhem Pasha, was a fanatic, and the sole British man-of-war on the immediate scene of action was the little torpedo gunboat *Hazard*, Lieutenant Price Vaughan Lewes. Writing a few months after-wards, a distinguished naval officer said :—

> " What occurred will be fresh in everyone's memory—a desperate attack on a small force of British soldiers and sailors by a fanatical and well-armed mob; simultaneous attacks, obviously preconcerted, on the British camp and hospital at the other end of the town; an heroic defence obstinately maintained ; a passive and almost hostile attitude on the part of the Turkish troops and their officers ; followed by the surging of the mob on to an easier prey, the undefended Christian residents and their unfortunate women and children. Incidentally, a naval officer may be permitted to dwell with pride on the gallant conduct of Lieut.-Commander Vaughan Lewes, and his officers and men, which has met with well-deserved recognition from Her Majesty, in the promotion of Commander Vaughan Lewes,[2] and the awards of the Victoria Cross to Doctor Maillard,[3] and the Distinguished Service Order to Lieutenant Nicholson." [4]

Seventeen British lives were sacrificed that day, including those of two leading and two ordinary seamen,[5] a monument to whom has since been placed in the Upper Barracca, at Malta ; and nearly a thousand Christians are supposed to have been massacred. The horrible affair was, however, the death-blow to Turkish authority in the island.

On September 12th, the *Revenge*, which had been absent for a time from Cretan waters, returned, and was presently followed by the battleship *Illustrious*, and the second-class cruiser *Venus*. Rear-Admiral Noel landed at once at Candia, inspected the scene of the attack, and ordered Edhem Pasha to wait upon him on board the flagship on the following morning. Upon complying, the Pasha was told that he must demolish all houses from which fire had been opened on the British camp and hospital, that he must give up to British occupation certain forts and positions, that he must instantly surrender the chief persons who had been responsible

[1] Highland Light Infantry.
[2] Com. Sept. 6, 1898.
[3] Surg. Wm. Job Maillard, R.N. (V.C. Dec. 2, 1898).
[4] Sub-Lieut. Edward Hugh Meredith Nicholson (Lieut. Sept. 30, D.S.O. Dec. 2, 1898).
[5] Wm. Berry, Alb. Champion, Alf. B. Stroud, and Hy. Andrews.

for the rioting and fighting, and that the Moslem population would be disarmed.   After much display of unwillingness, which was corrected by a demonstration on the part of the *Revenge* and *Camperdown*, the demands were all carried out, and a number of offenders were hanged on a conspicuous scaffold.

Soon afterwards a joint note from the Powers summoned the Porte to evacuate Crete within a month.   The evacuation, accordingly, began, and was completed on December 5th, 1898, though not until something little short of actual force had been employed to secure it.   The last Turkish forces were embarked under the superintendence of the officers and men of the *Revenge* and *Empress of India*, and were conveyed to Salonica by the torpedo gunboat *Hussar*.

On December 19th, the four flag-ships of the allied fleets, the French *Bugeaud* (Vice-Admiral Pottier), the Russian *Gerzog Edinburgski* (Rear-Admiral Skrydloff), the Italian *Francesco Morosini*, and the British *Revenge*, proceeded to Milo, where, on the 20th, Prince George of Greece, who had been appointed High Commissioner under the Sultan's suzerainty, left his yacht for the *Bugeaud*,

REAR-ADM. SIR GERARD HENRY UCTRED NOEL, K.C.M.G.

which conveyed him to Suda.   So ended the direct rule of Turkey, which had held the island of Crete since 1669, in face of almost continuous revolts.

In addition to the officers already mentioned as having been specially rewarded for their services, Rear-Admiral Noel was made a K.C.M.G., and Captains Reginald Custance,[1] Harry Tremenheere Grenfell,[2] and Major James Henry Bor, R.M.A., were given the C.M.G. in recognition of the part which they took in the pacification of the long-suffering island.[3]

---

[1] Of the *Barfleur*.   [2] Of the *Trafalgar*.
[3] Desps.: *Times*: *A. & N. Gaz.*: *Nav. & Mil. Rec.*, 1897–98 *passim*: and especially *Unit. Serv. Mag.*, Feb. 1899, pp. 497–510.

The advance southwards for the recovery of the Sudan was renewed in 1897 ; and, as before, the Navy bore some part in it, naval officers commanding the Egyptian stern-wheel gunboats which were employed that year on the Nile in co-operation with the army. These boats, the *Zafir*, Commander Colin Richard Keppel, the *Nasr*, Lieutenant the Hon. Horace Lambert Alexander Hood, and the *Fateh*, Lieutenant David Beatty, D.S.O., surmounted the Fourth Cataract by the end of August, and reached Abu Hamed, which had already been captured by General A. Hunter. Thence they moved to Berber, which was found to be deserted, and which was occupied by the troops on September 5th.

On October 15th the gunboats proceeded to reconnoitre the enemy's position at Metemmeh. At Shendy they opened fire from their quick-firers, howitzers, and Maxims upon the forts, which made a warm reply. The same works were again bombarded on the 16th ; and on November 1st, the reconnaissance was pushed as far as the Sixth Cataract, and valuable information was obtained.

The Nile was falling, and General Sir H. Kitchener decided to keep the gunboats above the impassible rapids at Um Tuir, four miles north of the confluence of the Atbara with the Nile. There they remained during the winter. Towards the end of February, 1898, the Dervishes at Metemmeh crossed the river to Shendy, with the object of uniting with Osman Digna; and Keppel, who by that time had additional gunboats with him, was able to inflict heavy loss upon them during the transit. The united Dervish forces entrenched themselves at Nakheila, on the Atbara, and the Anglo-Egyptian forces took up a position at Ras el Hudi, on the same stream. Meanwhile, the enemy had weakened his garrison at Shendy : and on March 26th, some of the gunboats, with troops on board, attacked that place, and captured it, taking also a large quantity of grain. On April 8th, when Kitchener attacked and defeated Mahmud, the Khalifa's general, on the Atbara, a rocket detachment, which had been landed for service, under Lieutenant Beatty, set the enemy's zeriba on fire in several places, and did excellent work.

The final advance of the Anglo-Egyptian army began in the last week of August along the western bank of the Nile, a force of friendlies marching at the same time along the east bank, and the gunboats moving up the river itself. Commander Keppel's

flotilla at that period consisted of the following, besides five transport steamers :—

Gunboats.	Description.	Guns.	Commanders.
Zafir . .	Stern-wheeler, 128 tons	1 12-pr., 2 6-prs., 1 howitzer, 4 Maxims.	Com. C. R. Keppel, R.N. (senr. off.)
Fateh . .	„ „		Lt. Dav. Beatty, D.S.O., R.N.
Nasr . .	„ „		Lt. Hon. H. L. A. Hood, R.N.
Sheik . .	Single-screw, 140 tons	1 12-pr., 1 howitzer, 4 Maxims.	Lt. John Barnes Sparks, R.N.
Sultan . .	„ „		Lt. Walter Henry Cowan, R.N.
Melik . .	„ „		Capt. W. S. Gordon, R.E.
Tamai . .	Stern-wheeler	1 9-pr., 2 q.-f.	Lt. Hy. FitzRoy Geo. Tal-bot, R.N.
El Teb. .	„		Lt. Cecil Minet Staveley, R.N.
Metemmeh.	„		
Abu Klea .	„	1 22-pr., 2 q.-f.	Lt. A. G. Stevenson, R.E.

Temporarily attached for duty with the above were Capt. Fredk. Manoli Baltazzi
Hobbs, R.M., and Lt. E. O. A. Newcombe, R.E.

The naval detachment included Engineer Edm. Edw. Bond, 3 engine-room
artificers, 3 leading stokers, and 9 non-commissioned officers, R.M.A. (gunnery-
instructors).

On August 28th, misfortune overtook the *Zafir*, which sank
suddenly near Shendy, only two of her Maxims being saved, though,
happily, there was no loss of life. On September 1st, after the
gunboats had cleared the east bank, the howitzers were landed, and
a bombardment of Omdurman was begun. The forts at Khartum
and Tuti island were also shelled from the river. On the day
following, the Dervishes attacked Sir H. Kitchener in great force,
and were repulsed with heavy slaughter, whereupon the army moved
out towards Omdurman, and, though twice attacked most fiercely on
the way, entered it, released the Khalifa's prisoners, and practically
extinguished the power of Mahdism in the Sudan.

Almost immediately afterwards, on September 7th, the arrival
of news that a French force under Captain Marchand, coming from
the west and north, had occupied Fashoda, 600 miles above
Khartum, obliged Sir H. Kitchener to proceed thither. He went
in the post-boat *Dal*, escorted by the *Fateh, Sultan, Nasr*, and
Abu Klea, starting on the 10th, dispersing a small body of Dervishes
on the 15th, and reaching Fashoda four days later. By the exercise

of great tact, he persuaded Marchand to leave the settlement of the questions at issue to the machinery of diplomatism, and contented himself with hoisting the British and Egyptian flags to the south of the French tricolour, with stationing a Sudanese battalion and a gunboat to guard them, and with establishing posts at Sobat and Meshra-er-Rek, on the Bahr el Ghazal. Ultimately it was decided that Marchand had trespassed into a sphere where France had no rights, and on December 11th the gallant captain withdrew by way of Sobat, Abyssinia, and Djibuti.[1]

For their participation in these arduous operations, Commander Keppel was given the C.B.,[2] and Lieutenant Cowan, and Engineer Bond were awarded the D.S.O.[2]

In the operations of the following year, having for their object the capture or destruction of the Khalifa, and ending with the bloody victory at Om Dubreikat on November 25th, 1899, Lieutenant Walter Henry Cowan, D.S.O., commanded the gunboat flotilla, and also accompanied the army as Sir R. Wingate's staff-officer. Among those who served under him on the river were Lieutenants Herbert Lefroy Hunter Fell, Harold Escombe, and William Byron Drury.

Several earlier operations in various parts of the world have yet to be noticed.

In November, 1897, a rebellious chief named Mat Salleh attacked Ambong, in the territory of the British North Borneo Company, and succeeded in burning the Resident's house. In December, an expedition went inland against him, and, on the 13th of the month, shelled his stronghold, but, attempting afterwards to rush it, was repulsed with heavy loss. This man's temporary success encouraged one of his sympathisers, an ex-convict named Si Talleh, to attack the Government station at Limbawang. Being driven off, he fled to a stronghold on the Membakut river, in the territory of the Sultan of Brunei. Operations against him were undertaken in January, 1898, and resulted in the capture of his stockade and the killing or wounding of about forty of his followers, though Si Talleh himself managed for the moment to escape. The co-operation of the gunboats *Plover* and *Swift*, under the orders of Lieutenant Spencer Victor Yorke de Horsey, contributed greatly to the success of the expedition, and to the ultimate seizure of the offender.[3]

---

[1] Desps. : Alford and Sword ; ' The Egyptian Sudan ' (1898): *Times.*
[2] All dated Nov. 15, 1898.   [3] *Times*, Jan. 31, 1898.

During the war between Japan and China in 1894–95, the former Power captured, among other places, Port Arthur on the north and Wei-hai-Wei on the south side of the entrance to the Gulf of Pechili. At the settlement of affairs, after the victory of Japan, the attitude of some of the European Powers deterred the conqueror from profiting to the full by his successes, and from retaining any of his conquests on the mainland. The intervening Powers were France, Germany, and Russia. Each one ultimately secured from China territorial compensation, France getting part of Kiang Hung; Germany, Kiao Chao; and Russia, Port Arthur. Russia's acquisition, though nominally it consisted only of a lease of the place, put her in so favourable a position for coercing China, and for increasing her own naval power in the Far East, that Great Britain, by way of counterpoise, demanded and obtained from China a lease of Wei-hai-Wei for as many years as the Russian occupation of Port Arthur should endure. Upon the evacuation of the port and the neighbouring island of Liu Kun by the Japanese, the British flag was accordingly hoisted on May 24th, 1898, by Captain George Fowler King Hall, of the belted cruiser *Narcissus*; and bluejackets and Marines were landed from the British China squadron to occupy the forts, until regular provision could be made for the garrisoning of them.[1]

On August 31st, 1896, a British protectorate had been proclaimed over part of the hinterland of Sierra Leone, being the territory between 7° and 10° N., and 11° and 13° W.; and subsequently a tax of 5*s*. per hut per annum had been imposed to meet the costs of administration. The imposition of the tax caused great discontent among the ignorant natives; and in February, 1898, it became necessary to send a military force, consisting of a company of the 1st West India Regiment, under Major R. J. Norris, to collect it. The force proceeded by way of the Scarcies River to Rokon, and thence overland to Port Lokko, on the Sierra Leone river, and made that place its base of operations. There was, however, so much opposition that a second company was ordered up, and a request was made by the Governor, Sir Frederick Cardew, that a naval force might convoy it, the intervening district being in a state of great unrest.

The naval force then at Sierra Leone consisted of the second-class cruiser *Fox*, Captain Frank Hannam Henderson, and the

[1] Desps.: and *Times*, May 19, and June 1, 1898.

paddle-vessel *Alecto*, Lieutenant Arthur Fosberry Holmes, which were presently joined by the third-class cruiser *Blonde*, Commander Peyton Hoskyns.

The expedition started on March 5th, the troops being in the Protectorate vessel *Countess of Derby*, and the escort comprising the *Alecto*, and one steam-boat and two pulling boats from the squadron, the *Alecto* towing the boats up Port Lokko Creek as far as Moferri, where the towing was taken over by the *Fox's* steam-cutter, under Lieutenant Frederick Kenrick Colquhoun Gibbons, who was in command. Major Norris and his company were found in laager, sorely pressed; but, after Gibbons had shelled the native position, the enemy drew off. · Provisions for the troops were then brought up from the *Countess of Derby*, and the boats returned.

The rebellion, however, spread; and, on March 29th, two further companies of the West India Regiment and a company of Sierra Leone Artillery were sent into the interior, escorted by the *Alecto* and some Marines. Upon the arrival of the *Blonde*, Captain Henderson, who was senior naval officer, despatched that vessel to the Sherbro river to keep in check the rebels in the neighbourhood of Bonthe, and of Imperri, further up the stream. Commander Hoskyns, who received assistance from the *Alecto* whenever it could be rendered, did most valuable service, and saved the district of Sherbro from being overwhelmed by the Mendi natives. Boat expeditions, organised by him, destroyed Gambia, on the Bum Kittam, and, on May 4th, pushed up the Jong River as far as Bogo, where dreadful massacres had been committed. Hoskyns also helped Lieut.-Colonel Cunningham's force in its advance up the Jong River on May 13th; and the boats at times were under a heavy fire from the banks. Holmes, with people from the *Alecto*, made a reconnaissance to Bendu on May 19th, and on June 11th and 12th rescued a number of Sierra Leone women from the hands of the insurgents on the Bum Kittam.

Another expedition, composed entirely of people from the *Fox*, went up the Bumpe River on May 11th to 14th, and co-operated with the advance of a column under Colonel E. R. P. Woodgate for the relief of Kwalu. The *Fox* herself had gone on May 2nd to Sulima and Mano Salijah, where she had rescued some officials and traders, and had shelled and driven off bodies of rebels. On that occasion, the state of the sea had prevented all the fugitives from being taken off. Those, therefore, who could not be embarked had been marched over the border to Robert Port, in Liberia, protected on their way by the *Fox's* people. Henderson, on his return to Sierra Leone, found that the alarm there had increased during his absence, and that Colonel Woodgate had asked for more ships. The result was the appearance of the first-class cruiser *Blake*, Captain Alfred Leigh Winsloe (on May 14th, when Winsloe became senior officer), and of the third-class cruisers *Phœbe*, Captain Robert Sidney Rolleston, and *Tartar*, Commander John Thirkill White. On July 5th and 6th, Captain Rolleston, with his ship, the *Tartar*, and the *Alecto*, assisted in the landing of two military expeditions which were destined for Shengah and Bumpe respectively; and he was able to lend valuable help on other occasions.[1]

The rising was crushed later in the year by six separate columns of troops under the general direction of Colonel Woodgate. In the final operations the Navy had little share; but, had it not been ready at hand and extremely active at the beginning of the disorders, terrible atrocities must have resulted, and the British colony itself might have been entirely overrun by the rebels.[2]

For their services, Captain Henderson and Commander Hoskyns received the C.M.G. Hoskyns, moreover, was posted on December 31st, 1898, when, also, Lieutenant Holmes was made a commander. In addition to officers who have been already named, the following were among those mentioned in the despatches: Lieutenants William Francis Benwell (*Fox*), Edward Oliver Gladstone (*Alecto*), and Gerald Hubbard Welch (*Blonde*); Sub-Lieutenant Ernest William Denison (*Blonde*); and Engineer William Wesley Hardwick (*Blonde*).

Before proceeding to give any account of the very important events which occupied the attention of the Navy, and, indeed, of the whole Empire, in 1899 and 1900, it will be well to glance at a few minor occurrences which, during those years, necessitated the intervention of commanders of Her Majesty's ships.

Early in 1899 there was a rebellion in Nicaragua, in the repression of which Nicaragua was assisted by the neighbouring republic of Honduras. On February 13th, the second-class cruiser *Intrepid*, Captain John Leslie Burr, C.M.G., anchored off Bluefields to protect British interests, the American warship *Marietta*, Lieutenant-

---

[1] Desps. of Cardew and Woodgate: *Gazette*, Dec. 29, 1899: letters and papers of Henderson: *Times*, Mar. 31, Apr. 9, May 6, etc., 1898.
[2] *Times*, Nov. 15, 1898.

Commander F. M. Symonds, arriving on the 17th in order to look after the still larger interests of the United States.

At Bluefields lay the insurgent steamer *San Jacinto*, a little craft of 150 tons, carrying one 6-pr. Hotchkiss gun. At San Juan de Nicaragua, otherwise known as Greytown, some miles to the southward, lay the Honduran steamer *Tatumbla*, a craft of 400 tons, mounting four guns. Bluefields was in the hands of the insurgents; Greytown in those of the recognised authorities. On February 18th the *San Jacinto* set out with the intention of disembarking a force for an attack on Greytown. She appears to have carried out part of her plan; but on the 23rd, after a brief action, she was captured by the *Tatumbla*. It being then obvious that the insurgent cause was hopeless, and that further rebel activity could lead only to useless bloodshed, the British and American commanders decided to assume control at Bluefields. Accordingly, on the 24th, thirty-two men from the *Intrepid*, under Lieutenants Edward William Elphinstone Wemyss, and Sholto Grant Douglas, and seventeen from the *Marietta*, under Lieutenant F. B. Bassett, U.S.N., were landed to patrol the streets and maintain order. On the following morning the *Tatumbla*, full of troops flushed with victory, and accompanied by her prize, appeared off the town, and demanded its unconditional surrender, under pain of immediate bombardment. Burr pointed out that anything of the sort would be temerarious; and presently the government leader, General Rühling, saw fit to withdraw his ultimatum. Not until Burr and Symonds—who worked in excellent harmony—had disarmed the rebels, and procured for them a guarantee of free pardon, did they hand over the place. This they were able to do on the 26th; and on March 4th, the rebellion having quite flickered out, the *Intrepid* departed for Jamaica.[1]

This was a bloodless triumph for Great Britain and the United States. Elsewhere, in the same year, when bluejackets of the two English-speaking Powers fought side by side, there was, unhappily, serious loss of life.

On August 22nd, 1898, Malietoa Laupepa, King of Samoa, had died. By the final Act of the Conference on the affairs of Samoa, which had been signed at Berlin on June 14th by Great Britain, Germany, and the United States, the Samoans had been given the right to elect a successor " according to the laws and customs of

[1] *Nav. & Mil. Rec.*, Apr. 6, 1899, and priv. letters.

Samoa," but in the event of their not being able to agree, the Chief Justice appointed by the three Powers had been directed to decide.

After heated discussion and the assemblage of armed parties, the candidates had been reduced to two, Malietoa Tanu and Mataafa. Each had a large number of followers who were collected at Mulinuu, the seat of government, and in the municipality of Apia.

CAPTAIN FREDERICK CHARLES DOVETON STURDEE, C.M.G.

(From a photo by Symonds & Co.)

At the latter end of November, the natives not having been able to arrive at a decision, the question had been referred to the Chief Justice. The latter had held a trial of some duration, and on December 31st announced that Malietoa Tanu had been duly elected:

As soon as the decision was known there was great excitement among the followers of Mataafa who were assembled in Mulinuu. They put on their war turbans, painted their faces, and advanced on Apia, taking up positions to attack the Malietoa faction. A party of seamen was landed from the third-class cruiser *Porpoise,* Commander Frederick Charles Doveton Sturdee, to protect the Chief Justice's house in the country; but, when the Chief Justice came into the town on the following day, this party was withdrawn to the Mission house, where the European women and children were collected for safety. Another party was sent to the British Consulate.

Endeavours were made to prevent the natives from fighting, but on the afternoon of January 1st, 1899, hostilities commenced. They ended in the Malietoan side being thoroughly defeated, with some loss. The King was rescued and sent on board the *Porpoise* for safety; and his followers swam or fled in canoes to that ship during the night.

On January 2nd a meeting of the consular and naval Representatives was held, and in view of the situation it was resolved to form a provisional government, consisting of Mataafa and thirteen principal chiefs, to maintain order until instructions should be received from the three Powers. The proceedings of the provisional government gave rise, however, to various difficulties. At the end of February the excitement amongst the natives revived, and the followers of Mataafa, to the number of 4,000, surrounded Apia. At that moment the United States' flag-ship *Philadelphia,* flying the flag of Rear-Admiral Albert Kautz, arrived. Kautz consulted the different officials, and held a meeting; but united action to meet the new danger was not agreed upon. The Rear-Admiral thereupon issued a proclamation calling on the Mataafans to leave the neighbourhood of Apia, and to disperse peacefully to their villages, there to await the decision of the Powers. Instead of obeying, they left Mulinuu (where they were under the guns of the ships), and went into the bush at the back of the town, where they turned Europeans out of their houses, thus obliging them to take refuge in the houses on the beach under the protection of the ships. Remonstrances were sent to Mataafa, calling on him to retire; but these had no effect. Malietoa and many women and children fled to the British Consulate for protection.

Parties from the United States' ship *Philadelphia,* and from her Majesty's ships *Porpoise* and *Royalist,* 12, Commander Arthur Ward Torlesse (which had arrived in February) were landed for the protection of the town; and the British and American Consulates, with the native refugees, were transferred to Mulinuu, whither the Malietoan prisoners who had managed to escape from their opponents also came.

The military situation had become critical. The town is built round the bay, with a few roads and straggling houses at the rear, and the vegetation is very dense. The Consulates were situated round the point with thick bush at the back. They were very isolated, and could be protected from seaward only by the ships' firing into the bush as close as possible to the backs of the houses without striking the latter with fragments of shell. The line to be defended extended for 4,500 yards; the available landing-parties amounted only to 260 men. The Mataafa party had upwards of 4,000 men, armed with about 2,500 rifles of various patterns, many of them modern; and they could have rushed the position at any time, save that they were deterred by fear of the ships' guns. It was considered necessary to re-arm some of the Malietoan natives, but there was little suitable ammunition for them until a supply was received a month later.

On March 14th Rear-Admiral Kautz addressed a further letter to Mataafa, to which no answer was returned. On the contrary, the Mataafans advanced closer.

On the following day Kautz sent two of his officers to Mataafa with an ultimatum, demanding an answer by noon. The letter was received by the chief in charge of the Mataafan outposts, but the officers were turned back. At 12.30 a determined rush was made on the British and American Consulates. Lieutenant Guy Reginald Archer Gaunt, of the *Porpoise*, and Captain Con. M. Perkins, United States' Marines, who were respectively in command, at once stood to arms, but reserved their fire. The Mataafans, finding the garrisons on the alert, retired. A few minutes before 1 P.M. some Mataafan boats were observed manning at Vaiusu, apparently with the intention of attacking Mulinuu, and at about the same time the rush on the Consulates was reported to the Rear-Admiral. He therefore considered it necessary to fire on the approaching boats, and on the Mataafan lines to the rear of the Consulates; and he was accordingly supported by the fire of her Majesty's ships *Porpoise* and *Royalist*. The bombardment continued until 5 P.M. The *Porpoise* also got under weigh and shelled Vaiusu and Vaimoso, destroying the Mataafan villages and several boats.

During the night of March 15th a determined attack was made on the centre of the town by the Mataafans, who temporarily captured a 7-pr. field-piece. This was gallantly rescued by Lieutenant George Ellis Cave (*Porpoise*), and the assailants were driven off. Three bluejackets of her Majesty's ship *Royalist* were killed or mortally injured, and one was wounded, on that occasion.

Repeated attempts were made at night on the Consulates, and in one case the attack was driven well home to the entrenchments which had been thrown up round them; but the assailants were driven off by the guards, assisted by the fire from the ships. There was also at first continual sniping from the bush, both at the Consulates and the ships, during each night. It was necessary to relieve the situation by organising expeditions to drive the enemy out of the municipality, and attacking them wherever possible. They formed their main camp at Vailima round Robert Louis Stevenson's house, and formed camps further back in the bush to retire to, if necessary, besides organising parties to follow up the movements of the ships whenever they went to attack any villages on the sea coast. They had an excellent system of look-outs; and their forts were extremely well-built and hidden in the bush, with about 30 yards cleared in front to allow of the development of rifle-fire. The road and bridges, moreover, were broken down in order to interfere with the movements of guns.

On March 24th H.M.S. *Tauranga*, Captain Leslie Creery Stuart, arrived in Samoan waters with a further supply of 200 rifles and suitable ammunition, she having been summoned from Fiji to reinforce the British and American ships. Stuart became thenceforward senior British naval officer.

The military operations after that date consisted of isolated operations both by land and by sea, conducted for the most part by Commander Sturdee. Expeditions were sent out from the lines at Apia in any direction in which the Mataafans were reported to be in force; and gradually the outposts at the back of the town were extended in order to guard against sudden attack, and to secure as large an area as possible from which to draw food for the friendly natives. A contingent of the latter was regularly organised by Lieutenant Gaunt, and usually formed the attacking column, being supported, however, by an Anglo-American force of bluejackets and Marines. The principal of the land expeditions were as follows:—

On April 1st a combined British and American force numbering

109 men and 150 friendlies, all under the command of Lieutenant Angel Hope Freeman (*Tauranga*), moved out of Apia with a Colt automatic gun, in order to reconnoitre towards Fogalii. It burnt that village, as well as Vailele and Letogo. On its return the force was suddenly attacked in the rear and immediately afterwards on the left and in front. The Colt gun jammed and became useless, and the friendlies bolted. The party being almost entirely surrounded, Lieutenant Freeman ordered a retreat, and the whole force retired to the beach, under cover of fire from the *Royalist*, and then returned to Apia with considerable loss, Lieutenant Freeman, with Lieutenant Philip Vanhorne Lansdale, and Ensign John R. Monaghan, of the *Philadelphia*, and four men, being killed. The gun had to be abandoned, but had been disabled previously by its crew.

On April 13th the native outposts were attacked by the Mataafans, and Lieutenant Gaunt advanced with his native force to assist in repelling the attack. Part of the British landing-party went out under Commander Sturdee to cover Gaunt's force, and, after a fight of more than an hour, the Mataafan party was driven back, leaving four dead on the field.

On April 17th an advance was made on the main position at Vailima by a force consisting of friendlies, Gaunt's brigade, and a party of bluejackets and Marines. Two positions were stormed by Lieutenant Gaunt, and a third, consisting of a large stone work, was attacked; but, as it was too formidable to be stormed without severe loss, and, if captured, could not then have been occupied permanently, the force was withdrawn, and a bombardment undertaken by the ships at 4,800 yards' range. This was very effective, and obliged the position to be evacuated permanently. Gaunt's force lost four killed and seventeen wounded. The enemy's loss was believed to be heavy.

The operations by sea included boat expeditions, covered as a rule by shell fire from an accompanying ship, with the object of destroying Mataafan villages and boats along the coasts. Gaunt's force had several severe fights with the natives defending the different villages.

Meanwhile H.M.S. *Royalist* had been employed in conveying from various parts of the islands to Apia natives of the Malietoan party, and by April 22nd the British and American officers had at their disposal a force of about 2,800 men, of whom 2,000 were armed with rifles ; while Gaunt's force, which had been increased to 700 men, had been regularly organised with five British naval officers. The allies were then in a position to crush the Mataafan party ; but on May 21st intelligence had been received of the appoint- ment by the three Powers concerned of a Joint Commission with power to settle the disputed questions which had arisen in Samoa ; and an arrangement was consequently made in accordance with which certain limits round the town of Apia were laid down, and notice was given to the Mataafans that if they remained outside those limits and awaited the arrival of the Commission in peace, no further action of a hostile nature would be taken against them. Endeavours had been made during the progress of hostilities to induce Mataafa to retire from Apia and await the decision of the Powers, but with no success.

In addition to the officers whose names have been mentioned, five men of the *Royalist* and three of the *Philadelphia* lost their lives during these operations ; and a number of British and Americans were wounded.

Among the rewards conferred for the work thus done in Samoa were the following :—

> Captain Leslie Creery Stuart, C.M.G., January 1st, 1900.
> Commander Frederick Charles Doveton Sturdee, posted June 30th, 1899 ; C.M.G., January 1st, 1900.
> Lieuts. George Ellis Cave, and Guy Reginald Archer Gaunt made Commanders, June 30th, 1901.

In addition, Lieutenants Victor Gellafent Gurner, Richard Harry Parker, and Arthur Welland Lowis, and Staff-Surgeons Henry Bullen Beatty, John Andrews, M.D., and Robert Forbes Bowie did excellent work.

The expenditure of British blood did not, unfortunately, purchase any expansion of the Empire ; for, by an international agreement of November 14th, 1899, Britain, which for many years had had para- mount interests in the Samoan archipelago, abandoned her right to interfere further in the internal affairs of the islands ; of which Upolu and Savaii were handed over to Germany, while Tutuila and the islets east of 171° E. were recognised as belonging to the United States. Moreover, as the result of subsequent arbitration by H.M. the King of Sweden and Norway, it was decided that the action of the British and Americans was without justification, and that Germany, which had supported the claim of Mataafa, was in the right. On the other hand, it is satisfactory to record that, throughout the operations, the British and American officers and men engaged worked together with most cordial good feeling,[1] the Americans repeatedly serving under the orders of British officers, and the American flag-lieutenant being specially told off to assist Commander Sturdee.

In the Persian Gulf there were small disturbances on at least two occasions. On March 3rd, 1899, the paddle-vessel *Sphinx*, Commander Henry Arthur Phillipps, had to land an armed party at Linga to protect British property and interests pending the repression by the Persian authorities of a local revolt; and, at the beginning of August, owing to the enforcement of measures against the spread of plague, there was rioting at Bushire, whither, in consequence, a naval force was dispatched. The withdrawal of the objectionable measures, however, led to the restoration of order, and obviated the necessity for intervention.[2]

In the summer of 1900, during a rebellion at Panama, a bloody conflict took place between the opposing forces in the environs of that town. After the action, the foreign consuls arranged an armistice in order to allow of the numerous wounded being attended to; and the cruiser *Leander*, Captain Frederick Fogarty Fegen, which lay off the port, landed an ambulance party on July 21st, and so rendered valuable service. She also disembarked a detachment of 90 men to protect the foreign consuls in case of need, but, happily, assistance of that kind was not required.[3]

Later in the year, news reached the Foreign Office to the effect that Mr. A. C. W. Jenner, sub-commissioner of the province of Jubaland, in British East Africa, had been treacherously murdered by Ogaden Somalis on November 13th, while at some distance from the coast. Protectorate troops proceeded at once to Kismayu, where a punitive expedition was organised; and the third-class cruiser *Magicienne*, Captain William Blake Fisher, C.B., was also sent thither from Mombasa on the 20th. The Somalis having raided in the neighbourhood, Fisher was requested to assist in the defence of the town; and on December 13th, accordingly, he landed 80 officers and men and some guns, and put Staff-Surgeon George Albert

---

[1] A tablet "In Memory of the brave American and British Sailors who Fought and Fell together at the Samoan Islands in March and April, 1899," has since been erected in St. Peter's Church, Mare Island, California. It bears the names of all who were killed.

[2] *Times*, Aug. 4 and 7, 1899.   [3] *Times*, July 27, 1900.

Dreaper in charge of the hospital. The cruiser's searchlights, which were employed at night, had a powerful effect upon the native mind, and apparently prevented the Somalis from attacking.[1]

The part borne by the Navy in the most considerable war of the long and eventful reign of Queen Victoria is now to be narrated. The extent to which seamen and Marines were employed in this conflict, not a single action of which was fought within many miles of navigable water, affords a remarkable illustration of the adapt-ability of the naval service, and of its extreme value to the Empire in hours of great stress.

It is unnecessary here to go into the well-known history of the causes which, in the autumn of 1899, induced the South African Republic and the Orange Free State to plunge into a war with the British Empire. The costly struggle which followed will ever be remarkable for the chivalrous unanimity with which all parts of that Empire ranged themselves by the side of the mother-land, and identified her cause and her glory with their own. It will also be remarkable for the numerous lessons which it taught to students in the art of war. One of the most pregnant of these lessons was that it was not only desirable, but also practically possible, to employ in land operations, and not merely in sieges, much heavier long-range guns than had been employed previously by any armies in the field. In a word, it was demonstrated that heavy guns could be rendered mobile, even in a difficult country like South Africa—so mobile, indeed, as to be enabled to take part in most of the work of armies.

In spite of its immense military significance, this important development of the functions of artillery would not call for mention in these pages if it had originated with the army. It originated, however, with the Navy; and, moreover, it had so great an in-fluence upon the fortunes of the war, in which also Naval Brigades bore very distinguished parts, that it deserves to be dealt with at some length.

Having despatched an ultimatum which destroyed the last chances for the preservation of peace, the two Republics, on October 12th, crossed the British frontiers at several points. In Natal, the Imperial troops, under Lieut.-General Sir George S. White, V.C., were in great numerical inferiority, and were confined strategically to the defensive. On October 14th, when the first-class cruiser

[1] Parl. Paper (591), 1901.

Terrible, Captain Percy Scott, on her way to China, arrived at the Cape, Ladysmith was already indirectly threatened, and Mafeking and Kimberley, on the western edge of the enemy's country, were still more evidently imperilled. The Boers possessed siege guns, and were in a position to push them to the front from their bases, which were comparatively near at hand ; while the British had only field guns close to the frontier, and had their base 6000 miles from the scene of operations. Captain Scott at once realised that such

CAPTAIN PERCY SCOTT, C.B.

(From a photo by Symonds & Co.)

weapons as even the *Terrible's* 12-pr. 12-cwt. guns would be of value at the menaced points, if only they could be transported thither on mountings which would give them mobility ; for they had better range than the field guns of the army. By the 21st, he had made and tried a mounting, which was found to be fairly satisfactory. It consisted of a log of wood about 14 feet long and 10 or 12 inches square, which had been originally obtained for the construction of a towing target. This, which formed a trail, was

12-PR. 12 CWT. Q.-F. GUN, ON SCOTT'S MOUNTING.

South Africa, 1899 : *China,* 1900.

4 ·7 IN. Q.-F. GUN, FROM THE "TERRIBLE," ON SCOTT'S PLATFORM MOUNTING, AT
LADYSMITH.

mounted on an axle-tree with a pair of ordinary Cape-wagon wheels, and upon it was placed the ship carriage, bolted down and secured, but in such a manner as to admit of its being taken off again and returned to the *Terrible*, if required.[1] Captain Scott's instinct was prophetic. On October 25th, General White telegraphed from Ladysmith to Rear-Admiral Robert Hastings Harris, Commander-in-Chief at the Cape, to know if the Navy could send him some 4·7-in. guns, wherewith to keep the Boer artillery in check. The Rear-Admiral asked Captain Scott if he could design the necessary mounting for such heavy weapons, and get two of the guns ready by the following afternoon. These were platform guns, the mounting consisting of four pieces of timber, 14 feet long by 12 inches square, arranged in the form of a cross. In the centre of the cross was placed the ordinary ship's mounting, bolted through to a plate underneath. Over this the gun-carriage was dropped on to the spindle, and secured by its clip-plate. By great exertions the *Terrible's* people, under their ingenious Captain's superintendence, got the two guns ready by 5 P.M. on the 26th. They were at once put on board the *Powerful*, Captain the Hon. Hedworth Lambton, which, taking also some 12-prs., sailed immediately with them for Durban.

Upon arriving there Lambton lost no time in conveying the guns to Ladysmith, into which he entered with them only just before the investment of the town was completed. Forty-eight hours later, communications were cut; and, for the following 119 days, the garrison, and the Naval Brigade with it, remained beleaguered. Captain Lambton's work will be described later. In the meantime it will be well to follow Captain Scott's further proceedings.

After Ladysmith had been invested, Sir Walter Hely-Hutchinson, Governor of Natal, became naturally anxious concerning the defenceless condition of Durban, and asked the Navy to undertake to hold it. The Rear-Admiral therefore sent the *Terrible* thither; and she arrived on November 6th. The positions were surveyed on the 7th,[2] and on the 8th the town was put into a state of

---

[1] Guns thus mounted, though mobile, were top-heavy, and frequently capsized on broken ground. The heavier guns, mounted a little later, were, on the contrary, wonderfully steady.

[2] Captain Scott, on the 7th, assumed the official commandantship of Durban, which was placed under martial law; and undertook the suppression of espionage, the supervision of traffic up and down the coast, the censorship of private and press corres-

4·7 IN. Q.-F. GUN, ON SCOTT'S IRON MOUNTING.

Showing gun at extreme elevation, South Africa, 1900.

4·7 IN. Q.-F. GUN, ON SCOTT'S IMPROVED MOUNTING.

South Africa, 1899.

2 H 2

security by means of defences covering all the approaches, and protecting the waterworks, etc. In these defences, thanks to the assistance of the townspeople, the local rifle associations, and a corps of mounted gentlemen, every one being loyal and ready with help, there were mounted thirty guns, viz., two 4·7-in.; sixteen 12-prs. of 12 cwt.; two 12-prs. of 8 cwt.; one 9-pr.; two 3-prs.; two Nordenfelts, and four Maxim machine guns. The 4·7-in. guns thus used, and afterwards sent to the front, were on mountings different from those so hurriedly made for Ladysmith. They had double trails, so as to allow of great elevation being given; and they had iron wheels. Each wheel consisted of a plate with a bush for the axle-tree in the centre, with angle-irons in the position of spokes, with an angle-iron flush with the perimeter on each side, and with a tyre shrunk on over all. The trail was secured to a heavy axle-tree, and the carriage bolted on to it. Telescope sights were also fitted.[1] When the *Terrible*, some months later, left South Africa for China, six of these guns were in use, two with Lord Roberts, two with General Buller, and two with General Gatacre. They were easily hauled by a span of oxen, and were sufficiently mobile to accompany any column on the march. In November, the Ladysmith relief column began to advance, and two 4·7-in., and eighteen naval long 12-prs. accompanied it, with a Naval Brigade under Captain Edward Pitcairn Jones, of the *Forte*, and Commander Arthur Henry Limpus, of the *Terrible*.

In those dark days, the Ladysmith garrison could send out news by means of carrier-pigeons, but was able to receive no regular messages from the outer world, until the Navy again went to the assistance of the army. A ship's search-light, with a flashing arrangement, was mounted by Captain Scott on a railway truck, with a locomotive boiler and a dynamo attached; and this, being sent up to Frere, about twenty-three miles from the besieged town, was the means whereby news was thenceforward communicated to Sir George White. When, while the army was

---

pondence and telegrams, the detention of goods intended for the enemy, the maintenance of order, the reception of recruits for the Natal forces, and much more. In addition, as senior naval officer, he anchored the *Terrible*, *Forte*, and *Thetis* in a position to command the Umgeni Valley, and kept the *Philomel* and *Tartar* ready to move and check any effort of the enemy on the Bluff side. Rep. to Hely-Hutchinson, March 14, 1900.

[1] These mountings proved excellent in every respect, and on them the guns were dragged into positions to which, probably, no Boer artillery could have been taken.

4·7 IN. Q.-F. GUN, MOUNTED BY CAPTAIN SCOTT ON A RAILWAY TRUCK.

South Africa, 1899–1900.

6 IN. Q.-F. GUN, ON SCOTT'S MOUNTING.

Trial round, Durban, 1899.

operating in the direction of Spion Kop, General Barton, then at Chieveley, wanted a 4·7-in. gun on a railway truck, Captain Scott put one of his platform mountings, similar to those in Ladysmith, on a low iron trolley, fastened it down with chains, and cut off the ends of the traverse baulks, so as to allow the whole to pass through the tunnels. This mounting was so arranged that the gun could be removed from the truck, and used as a platform gun, if required. It worked exceedingly well, and, when on the truck, could be fired at right angles with the direction of the railway line, without damage to the permanent way, or to the trolley. Three other guns of this description were sent up later, and were employed at the final attack on Pieter's Hill. For this final attack, General Buller wanted still heavier artillery, and, on February 8th, telegraphed to Captain Scott :—

"Have you any 6-in. guns, on carriage that I could move a mile or so across the flat, available in Durban. If you have, telegraph in my name to Admiral, and ask if I may have them for a few days. Utmost importance. If possible I want them Monday the 12th inst., and you to work them."

A 6-in. gun was taken out of the *Terrible*, and, by the morning of the 11th, was mounted, and on its way to the front. The nature of this mounting, which was as efficacious as it was simple, can be seen in the illustration.

Yet again, after the occupation of Ladysmith, General Buller appealed to Captain Scott, this time for a lighter and more mobile mounting for 4·7-in. guns.[1] Four mountings of an improved type were made in consequence. In them, the heavy ship's carriage was removed, and the gun and cradle were placed directly on the trail and axle; steel was used instead of wood, and a single wheel was fitted in the rear, between the trails, to facilitate transport. When extreme elevation, 37°, was required, the rear wheel could be un shipped. These four guns were ultimately turned over to the Royal Artillery.[2]

[1] The names given to some of these are of interest. The 4·7-in. guns in Ladysmith were "Lady Anne" and "Lady Victoria" (the latter being also nick-named "Bloody Mary"); the railway truck gun was "Lady Randolph Churchill"; two of the platform 4·7-in. guns in Natal were "Joseph" and "Josephine"; one of the 4·7-in. guns used on the Modder River was "Joe Chamberlain"; two of the 4·7-in. guns which accompanied Lord Roberts's advance were "Little Bobs" and "Sloper"; the first of the 4·7-in. guns on improved iron mounting, with rear wheel, was "Princess Louis" (after the wife of Capt. Prince Louis of Battenberg, R.N.); and the 6-in. wheeled gun was "Roma."

[2] Chiefly from Procs. of Odd Vols. Society, of Hong Kong, June 13, 1900; Scott to Hely-Hutchinson, Mar. 14, 1900; and priv. corresp.

There can be no question that the resourcefulness thus exhibited by the Navy was of vital assistance to the army in the great operations of the war; and that, without the Navy's help, the campaign must have been even more laborious and costly than it actually was. It is well, therefore, to put on record that the entire credit for designing all these mountings rests with Captain Percy Scott. In carrying out his ideas, he was chiefly assisted by Commander Arthur Henry Limpus, Lieutenant Frederick Charles Ashley Ogilvy, Engineer Francis John Roskruge, and Carpenter James Johns, who were well supported by the carpenters, armourers, engine-room artificers, and blacksmiths of the *Terrible*, and later, by the Foreman of Simon's Bay Dockyard, Mr. Clements, and his staff, and still later by the officials of the locomotive works of the Natal Government Railways. One officer, who was freely mentioned in the press at the time as having assisted in making the designs for the mountings, knew nothing of the plans when they were being carried out, and was merely employed afterwards to take drawings of some of them, in order that further mountings might be built if needed. For this work, Captain Scott was, perhaps inadequately, rewarded with a C.B.[1] He also received grateful acknowledgments from the Colonial Office, and from General Buller, and, in common with the other naval officers employed, the thanks of the Admiralty.

Very early in the campaign, Kimberley, on the western border of the Orange Free State, was invested by the Boers; and a division, under Lieut.-General Lord Methuen, was moved up for its relief along the line of the Buluwayo Railway. A Naval Brigade,[2] under Captain Reginald Charles Prothero, from the *Doris*, *Monarch*, and *Powerful*, at Simon's Bay, joined Methuen on November 22nd, with

---

[1] March 13, 1900.

[2] A Naval Brigade, composed as follows, had been landed on Oct. 20th at Simon's Bay from the *Doris*, *Monarch*, *Terrible*, and *Powerful*, but had been recalled again without seeing any fighting : Com. Alfred Peel Ethelston, Maj. John Hulke Plumbe, R.M., 9 naval officers, 7 Marine officers, 53 bluejackets, 290 Royal Marines, and two 12-pr. 8 cwt. guns on ordinary field mountings. This Brigade reached Stormberg Junction on Oct. 23, but, in consequence of the Boer advance, was withdrawn to Queenstown on Nov. 2. There it handed over its two guns to the Royal Artillery, previous to its departure for East London, where the *Terrible's* contingent embarked to rejoin its ship, and the rest of the Brigade took passage in the *Roslyn Castle* for Simon's Bay. The men rejoined their ships there on Nov. 19 (Jeans, ' Naval Brigades in the South African War,' pp. 1–15). The above Brigade, reinforced, landed again on Nov. 19, and constituted the naval contingent the fortunes of which are followed in the text. The strength of the new Brigade was about 400 all told, half being Marines.

four guns,[1] near Belmont. On the following day the guns assisted in supporting the advance of the Guards' Brigade, during the action at Belmont, cleared the height known as Mont Blanc, and made themselves generally useful. On the following day the division advanced; and on the 25th was fought the battle of Graspan, an action in which the Naval Brigade, although it may have been improperly used and somewhat rashly led, covered itself with glory.

The naval guns and ammunition had been entrained, under the

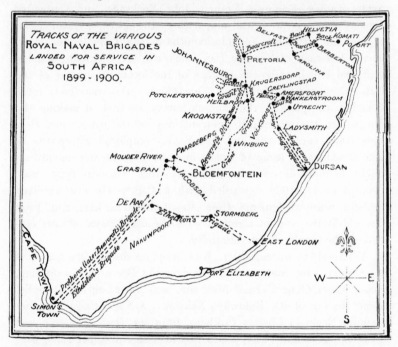

orders of Lieutenant Frederic William Dean,[2] the gun mules being handed over to the army. Dean acted, during the battle, in conjunction with an armoured train full of infantry, on the left of the British advance, but he was able to detrain and employ only two of his four pieces, since he had with him but four half guns' crews.

Lord Methuen's plan was to cover the kopjes in his front with shrapnel, and then to assault them with the 9th brigade, under Lieut.-Colonel C. G. C. Money, C.B. To this force the Naval

---

[1] Four 12-pr. 12-cwt. guns on Scott's mountings.
[2] Promd. Com.

Brigade[1] was attached; and Captain Prothero had been informed
over night that he and his men were to have the honour of leading
the attack. The Naval Brigade, accordingly, paraded at 3 A.M. on
the 25th, and, marching at the head of the column,[2] reached a
point near the left of the Boer position at daylight.

There is nothing in the dispatches to indicate that Prothero
had asked to be allowed to lead. He merely says that he had been
ordered to do so by Lord Methuen ; and it is tolerably apparent
that the Lieut.-General, on his own initiative, stationed the seamen
and Marines in the forefront of the battle, and deliberately entrusted them with the hard work of the day. Whether he did so
as a compliment to the Navy, or from a desire to spare the army,
seems to be immaterial; nor is there any doubt whatsoever that
the seamen and Marines were delighted to find themselves in the
post of honour. Nevertheless, the disposition was an unjustifiable
one ; and attention must here be called to its unwisdom, lest it
should form a precedent when a Naval Brigade is again acting
with a British army in the field. First of all, the Navy was ashore
in South Africa primarily to do work which the army, for various
reasons, could not do. It was there to compensate for lack of
troops, and to provide and work guns more efficient than the army
had at its disposal. But it was certainly not there to do work
which could be more fitly done by the army, when the army happened to be locally in quite sufficient strength to carry on its
legitimate business. Secondly, the Navy has its own duties, from
which it should never be drawn, save at the most urgent need ; and,
that being so, it follows that it is a serious matter deliberately and
unnecessarily to expose a large body of seamen and Marines to
severe loss, seeing that seamen and Marines, unlike ordinary
soldiers, are long-service men, many with scientific training, who
are very expensive products, and who cannot be produced at all
except after long preparation. If Lord Methuen had desired certain
work to be done, and had found that he had no troops which were
capable of doing it, his employment of the Navy to form a storming
party would clearly have been defensible. But it happens that at
Graspan a large force of troops which might have been sent to
attack the kopjes was so little employed that its commanding
officer was able to report at night: "There were no casualties in

---

[1] Except about 50 men who were with Dean and the guns on the railway.
[2] Behind were the Yorkshire Light Infantry, and the Loyal North Lancashires.

my brigade to-day." [1]   And, even in Money's command, there were troops, such as the Northumberland Fusiliers and the Northamptons, which, while the Navy was employed to bear the brunt of a great action, " did not advance until near the conclusion of the engagement." [2]   It is bad policy, and poor economy, to use an expensive tool for work for which it is not made, while a comparatively cheap tool, which has been made for the very purpose, is at hand.   Yet

COMMANDER ALFRED PEEL ETHELSTON.

(*From a photo by West.*)

the Navy was pleased enough, and, as will be seen, did the work with enthusiasm.

When it was supposed that the kopjes had been sufficiently shelled, the seamen and Marines deployed into a single line on the right of the attack, with intervals of four paces between the men, and advanced on the enemy's position, led, in the centre, by Captain Prothero, on the left by Major John Hulke

---

[1] Colvile's desp.   [2] Desp. of Nov. 26th.

Plumbe, R.M.L.I., and on the right by Commander Alfred Peel
Ethelston.[1] Methuen and Money said afterwards that the Brigade
was in too close formation. Be that as it may, the people certainly
suffered terribly. The enemy first opened a heavy front fire at a
range of about 600 yards, and soon supplemented that with a still
heavier cross fire from some broken ground on the left flank of
the advance. In the meantime the kopje to be stormed looked

MAJOR JOHN HULKE PLUMBE, R.M.L.I.
(*From a photograph by Heath and Bullingham.*)

almost inaccessible, and, besides being held in force, it had large
guns on it. Nevertheless, the Brigade advanced steadily by rushes.[2]
Ethelston was killed; but Lieutenant the Hon. Edward Spencer

[1] On the extreme left of the firing line was one company of the Yorkshire Light
Infantry, 85 strong. The rest of the firing line was composed of 55 bluejackets and
190 R.M.A. and R.M.L.I. As supports there were seven companies of the Y.L.I., which
later reinforced the right of the firing line, and, in reserve, the half battalion of Loyal
North Lancashires (Jones, in Jeans's ' Nav. Brigades ').

[2] The steadiness was extraordinary. Says Jones: "It is an extraordinary fact
that, though under fire for the first time, many men, in order to make their aim more

Harry Boyle took his place, and continued to lead the right. Prothero[1] was wounded, and had to be carried unwillingly to the rear; Plumbe fell dead; and the command of the decimated party devolved upon Captain Alfred Edmund Marchant,[2] R.M.L.I. Prothero tells how the fire was so hot that several times he saw a man hit three times before he reached the ground. Yet there was no hesitation from the beginning to the end. Midshipman Cymbeline Alonso Edric Huddart, twice wounded, continued to press cheerfully on until he was mortally hit. Lieutenant Walter Thomas Cresswell Jones,[3] R.M.L.I., though hit in the hip, charged to the top of the hill ere he stopped to have his wound dressed. Captain Guy Senior, R.M.A., fell dead before he gained it. Midshipman William Wood Sillem[4] was stunned when half way up, but recovered himself in time to lead some men to the summit. Others who distinguished themselves were Lieutenant Frederick John Saunders, R.M.L.I., Gunner Ernest Edward Lowe, and Midshipman Thomas Frederick John Livesey Wardle,[5] with Fleet Surgeon James Porter, M.D.[6] And so, at length, the top of the deadly kopje was gained, and Marchant, collecting as many men as possible, advanced with them to the furthest position, driving the Boers thence in full retreat.[7]

During the advance, Dean, with his two guns, co-operated with a battery of Royal Artillery in shelling the enemy's positions from the British left, first at 5000 yards, and later at 4000 and 2800; until, at 8 A.M., he received verbal orders to retire. He was then under a hot shrapnel fire, which cost him 6 men wounded; and, deeming that if he obeyed he would either lose heavily or have to abandon his pieces, he stuck to his post for an hour and a half longer, until the Boers were in retreat. With his detachment

---

accurate, actually lowered their sights frequently as they advanced, disregarding the rule laid down of fixed sights below 500 yards." And again: "Drill books have taught that men should not lie down during the last 500 yards of the attack, because of the supposed impossibility, once they have lain down, of making them rise and face a short-range magazine fire. It is certain, however, that the whole attack would have been swept away if they had remained on their feet continually; and there was no difficulty whatever in making them rise up again. They wanted no leading; they were only too anxious to close with the enemy, and get it over . . . ." (Jeans, p. 30).

[1] C.B., Oct. 21, 1900.   [2] C.B., Oct. 21, 1900.
[3] D.S.O., Oct. 21, 1900.   [4] Noted for promotion.
[5] Noted for promotion.   [6] Dep. Insp., Oct. 21, 1900.
  [7] For an admirable account of the action, see *The Globe and Laurel*, Mar., 1900. It is by Lieut. W. T. C. Jones, R.M.L.I.

Lieutenant George William McOran Campbell, Sub-Lieutenant Richard Foster White, Midshipman Thomas Charles Armstrong, and Surgeon Charles Marsh Beadnell, though the last was formally invalided, did good work; and first-class petty officers T. W. Ashley (*Doris*), and Fuller (*Monarch*), gained favourable notice for the coolness and accuracy with which they laid their guns. The whole loss of the little Naval Brigade that day in the assault was 15 killed and 79 wounded.[1] It did the best part of the business, and suffered more than two-thirds of the casualties. Lord Methuen afterwards paid it a special visit, and complimented it upon its splendid behaviour. Her Majesty, besides expressing to the boy's family her "admiration and pride" at young Huddart's "noble conduct," graciously telegraphed her congratulations to the Brigade on its gallantry, and expressed her regret at its heavy losses.[2]

After the battle of Graspan, Rear-Admiral Harris telegraphed to promote Captain Marchant, who was the senior unwounded officer of the Brigade, to the rank of Major,[3] pending the decision of the Admiralty, and to appoint him to the command until a senior officer should reach the spot. For the first time, consequently, for many years, a Marine officer commanded in the field a Naval Brigade composed of bluejackets as well as of Royal Marines. The Brigade halted for one day at Enslin, and, on November 27th moved on by train to Klokfontein, whence it moved again early on the 28th to take up a position 4800 yards from the banks of the Modder River.

In the early part of the battle of that day the naval guns engaged, and temporarily silenced, two out of several well-concealed guns of the enemy, and then advanced in order to find a position whence they could render more effectual assistance to Lord Methuen's attack, but soon had to retire under a hot fire from the Boer Mausers and Maxims. On the 29th both banks of the river were occupied by the British. During the long halt which ensued, Major Marchant was relieved in the command of the Brigade by

---

[1] Of 5 officers and 190 men engaged the Marines had 2 officers and 9 men killed, and 1 officer and 72 men wounded; a total loss of 44 per cent. The bluejackets had 2 officers and 2 men killed, and 1 officer and 5 men wounded (*see* Jeans, p. 34). The Desps. gave the total loss of the Brigade as 14 killed and 91 wounded, this including, apparently, Dean's 6 wounded. The 3 dead officers were buried at Enslin, east of the siding there. The dead men were buried at the foot of the captured kopje. The Australian Light Horse fenced in the grave.

[2] Desps. in *Gazette* of Jan. 26, 1900, and March 30, 1900; R.-Adm. Harris's telegram of Nov. 26, 1899.

[3] Confirmed Dec. 6, 1899.

Commander Spencer Victor Yorke de Horsey, of the *Monarch*, who himself was superseded a few days later by Captain John Edward Bearcroft, of the *Philomel*, Major Archibald George Brabazon Urmston, R.M., of the *Powerful*, taking over the command of the Marine detachment at about the same time.

Another welcome arrival, while the army lay on the Modder River, was a naval 4·7-in. gun on a Scott's mounting, which had been prepared at Simon's Town, and which promptly began a daily bombardment of the entrenchments which the Boers under Cronje had thrown up on the Magersfontein Hills. It used now common shell and now lyddite. On December 9th, when Lord Methuen made a reconnaissance in force, this gun advanced and shelled the enemy's works, though without much apparent success; and on December 11th, when the bloody battle of Magersfontein was fought, the same weapon rendered what service it was capable of. It could not, however, do the work of the considerable park of heavy artillery which was needed that day, and it failed to keep down the fire of the Boer guns. During the action, and throughout the following night, the four naval 12-prs. and their escort of Marines were south of the river for the protection of the stores there, and of a new deviation bridge which had been constructed. Had the enemy been enterprising, these guns might have been cut off with comparative ease. When, on the morrow, the exhausted army fell back upon them, the enemy's opportunity vanished.[1]

On the 14th all the naval guns were placed in positions north of the Modder, whence they again daily bombarded the Boer entrenchments. A second 4·7-in., which arrived from Simon's Town a little later, was mounted, however, on the south bank, to cover the right rear of the army. A naval searchlight, also sent from Simon's Town, and worked by bluejackets in charge of Midshipman James Menzies,[2] enabled communications by means of flashing signals to be maintained with the beleaguered garrison of Kimberley, where a searchlight was already in use.

In December, 1899, and January, 1900, enteric and other fevers worked havoc with the force on the Modder, and the number of available bluejackets was so reduced by sickness that one of the 4·7-in. guns had to be handed over to the Royal Marine Artillery. Early in February, two additional 4·7's under Commander William

[1] Methuen to Roberts, Feb. 15, 1900.
[2] Died of enteric at Bloemfontein.

Lowther Grant, of the *Doris*,[1] appeared upon the scene, and were presently sent to Enslin, and thence elsewhere; and on February 7th Field-Marshal Lord Roberts[2] reached the camp, and it became evident that the long and dreary period of inaction was drawing to an end. It is remarkable that throughout the war the various Naval Brigades were never so healthy as when they were doing work of exceptional hardship.

Commander Grant, with his two 4·7's, 5 officers and 59 men from the *Doris* and *Barrosa*, besides native drivers and colonial conductors, entered the Orange Free State on February 13th.[3] Lieutenant Dean, with two 12-prs., was also with the head of the invading army.[4] Kimberley was relieved on February 16th ; Cronje had evacuated the Magersfontein lines on the 15th ; and, as soon as these facts were known to Lord Methuen at the Modder, he also advanced, the remaining two 4·7's and two 12-prs. accompanying him, and then marching on Jacobsdal, where, on the 18th, the Brigade picked up Grant again. Dean, meanwhile, was with the force which was pursuing Cronje.

At 9.30 P.M. on the 18th the Brigade, complete again except so far as Dean and his two 12-prs. were concerned, went forward once more and pushed on as rapidly as possible, being incited to make all possible exertions by Lord Roberts's words when he cantered up to it on the following morning. " I have Cronje surrounded," he said, " and want to give you a show."[5] Yet though the men, the weary oxen and the heavy guns, on the 18th and 19th covered twenty-seven miles in twenty-two hours, of which fifteen were actually spent in marching, they did not sight Cronje's laager at Paardeberg until about 11 A.M. on the 20th.

Three of the 4·7's, including both of Grant's, together with a 12-pr., were at once ordered to the north side of the Modder, whence, at 4.30 P.M., they opened on the Boer camp at less than 3000 yards. That afternoon the 4·7's fired thirty-seven rounds of lyddite and common shell, but did not then, nor during the following seven days, provoke any reply. The remaining 4·7, and the three 12-prs. were posted on the south side of the river, only 1300 yards

---

[1] Landed at Port Elizabeth, Jan. 31; joined at the Modder, Feb. 3; sent to Enslin, Feb. 8.

[2] To whom Com. the Hon. Seymour John Fortescue, M.V.O., was attached as naval A.D.C.

[3] With the 9th Division.   [4] With the 6th Division.   [5] Jeans, 65.

from the nearest of the enemy's trenches.[1] The Boers "sniped" these continually during the week, but only succeeded in killing one bluejacket and wounding another. On the 22nd the naval guns on the north were advanced to 2200 yards from the works. Every night the Marines were on trench duty in rear of the guns, to protect them from any interference on the part of a Boer commando which was hovering in the neighbourhood; and they had very arduous and disagreeable work, which, however, they did with their usual cheerfulness. The bluejackets had less to do, and spent most of their nights in comparative comfort.

On the night when the final British advance was made along the river's bed, and when the gallant Canadians sapped close up to the Boer trenches, and decided Cronje to surrender, Surgeon Charles Marsh Beadnell, R.N., of the *Powerful,* was with the Colonials, and, in the morning of the 27th, was the first doctor to enter the laager and to succour the wounded there. After the surrender the Naval Brigade, in common with the rest of the army, "spliced the main brace," and the four guns from the north were, with much difficulty, taken back across the river. Dean's two 12-prs., the carriages of which had been damaged during the pursuit of Cronje, had meantime been ordered away, under Lieutenant William Jarvie Colquhoun, a volunteer from the Victorian Navy, to be repaired. Colquhoun was directed to take them to Simon's Town, but, on his own responsibility, he took them instead to Kimberley, where he got them quickly made good ; and, having thus saved ten days or more, was able to rejoin the Brigade before it moved from the neighbourhood of Paardeberg. This, and other smart work, gained him the D.S.O. at a later date.[2]

Two days, unfortunately, were spent by the bluejackets and Marines close to the filthy laager, the stench from which was appalling. On March 1st the whole army moved to Osfontein, a spot about five miles to the eastward, in order to get away from the decomposing bodies of animals, and to obtain a better water supply. But in the interval the mischief had been done, and the entire force became saturated with the germs of that enteric fever which subsequently cost the lives of so many brave men.

On March 5th, when a further advance to the eastward was imminent, three 12-prs. were sent to join the Highland Brigade on

---

[1] *Gazette,* Feb. 8, 1901.   [2] Oct. 21, 1900.

the north side of the Modder. The fourth—for Colquhoun and his two had not then rejoined—had broken down, and had been returned to be repaired at Simon's Town. On the 6th the four 4·7's were moved to a kopje about 7000 yards from the centre of the Boer position near Poplar Grove, two[1] being placed on the summit, and two on the right shoulder. The getting up of these guns was a most laborious business, and the men were much disappointed on the 7th, when it was evident that the Boers were already retreating. Some of the 4·7's, however, fired a shot or two at the retiring enemy; and the three 12-prs. on the south side of the river were warmly engaged for a time with two Boer guns which were covering the withdrawal. Their crews, however, suffered no loss. The Brigade then marched twelve miles to Poplar Grove, and, owing to the difficulties of the ground and the intense heat, was eight hours on the road. When at length the tired men bivouacked they had been fighting or marching for nearly eighteen hours; and glad were they of the two days' halt which followed.

The advance to Bloemfontein was resumed on March 10th, and in the first twenty-six hours the Brigade covered thirty-four miles. It saw no more fighting ere it reached the capital of the Free State,[2] and, as it moved in rear of the bulk of the Army, its arrival was not reported in time to procure it a place in the ceremonious entry of the city on March 13th. It entered, however, on the 15th, when a bluejacket swarmed up the flagstaff above Government House and reeved halyards by means of which the British flag was hoisted to its place there. Lord Roberts inspected the Brigade on the 21st, and on the 22nd the contingent from the *Powerful* left for England.

For about seven weeks the remainder of the Brigade lay in or near Bloemfontein, suffering severely from enteric fever and dysentery. No fewer than 89 officers and men were taken ill, 49 of that number during the last thirteen days of the halt. But the Brigade was not inactive during the whole of that time. After the Sanna's Post affair the 12-prs. were ordered to the north of the town, and two days later the four 4·7's were placed on a kopje there, known in consequence as Naval Hill. At Naval Hill the men were put into khaki serge and soft felt hats, so that, except for the distinguishing badges on the turned-up hat brims—a foul anchor for the bluejackets and a bugle for the Marines—they were thence-

---

[1] Grant's.

[2] Bearcroft to Harris, Mar. 17, 1900, in *Gazette* of Mar. 12, 1901.

forth dressed much like the rest of the invading force.   On April 18th, the naval guns on the Hill were relieved by four 5-in. naval guns on old Army carriages, manned by the Royal Garrison Artillery; and the Naval Brigade was re-organised in preparation for the further advance.   The seamen, decimated by sickness, were only numerous enough to man the 12-prs. and three of the 4·7's.   The fourth 4·7 was handed over to the Marine Artillerymen, who previously had acted merely as escort.

On the 21st two of the 12-prs. went away, under Commander de Horsey, with a column on a bootless chase of some Boers in the direction of Wepener; and before their return [1] the Brigade was split up as follows :—

> 1. Remaining at Bloemfontein, 2 12-prs.
> 2. Marching east with Com. W. L. Grant, 2 4·7's.
> 3. Marching north with Lord Roberts, 2 4·7's and 4 12-prs.

The detachment which remained at Bloemfontein consisted of the two guns' crews and half a company of Marines,[2] and had no experiences worth recording.

The fortunes of Commander Grant's detachment will be followed later.   It made some noteworthy marches.

The work done by the main body of the Brigade has now to be described.

Lieutenant Eric Percy Coventry Back, with two of the 12-prs., marched from camp on May 1st to join the northward movement; and Captain Bearcroft, with the other two 12-prs., the two 4·7's, and the bulk of the Brigade, followed on the 2nd, reached Karree Siding at 5 P.M. on the 3rd, and picked up Back outside Brandfort at 3 P.M. on the 4th.   Brandfort had been occupied on the previous day by Lord Roberts, after a brief fight.   At Brandfort the Brigade was attached to the 11th Division (Lieut.-General Pole-Carew).   On May 5th the advance was resumed.   In the afternoon the guns came into action against some Boer artillery posted on the north side of the Vet river; but, as the enemy presently retired, there was no general engagement.   On the 6th the Vet river was crossed, and on the 7th and 8th the force halted at Smaldeel.[3]

On the 10th the enemy made as if he would dispute the passage of the Zand river; but, after the 4·7's had fired a few rounds, the

---

[1] On Ap. 29. These guns were in action on the 24th. De Horsey in *Gazette*, Ap. 29.

[2] Under Major A. E. Marchant, R.M., and Lieut. Colquhoun, R.V.N.

[3] *Gazette*, Mar. 12, 1901 : Bearcroft to Harris.

Boers withdrew, fearing to be outflanked. The 12-prs. followed in pursuit, but were unable to get close enough to make themselves useful. On the 12th the army arrived outside Kroonstad, and at 3 P.M. the town was entered by the Brigade, which marched through, and encamped three-quarters of a mile to the north,[1] lying there until the morning of May 22nd. The army then moved forward again, and at 10 A.M. on the 27th the Brigade crossed the Vaal river at Viljoen's Drift, and entered the Transvaal, camping that night beyond Vereeniging.

On May 29th, at the passage of the Klip river, the bluejackets' 4·7-in. gun crossed by the crazy bridge in safety, and, hearing heavy firing ahead, pushed on with all haste. The Marines' 4·7 stuck, one wheel breaking through the roadway and timbers, and delayed the crossing of the 7th and 11th Divisions from 7 till 11.30 A.M. The whole bridge had to be cut away, and a drift made of its remains; but at last, with the aid of 64 oxen and several hundred men, the gun was extricated and the way cleared. The bluejackets' gun, however, did not succeed in getting into action, and, sinking in soft ground during the pursuit, had to remain where it was until daylight. As for the 12-prs., which had also pushed on, they narrowly escaped capture, passing as they did through the suburbs of Johannesburg while that town was still in the hands of the enemy, but safely rejoining the main force in the evening. On the 30th Johannesburg surrendered; and on the afternoon of the 31st the Brigade entered the place and passed before Lord Roberts.[2]

The further advance was begun on June 3rd, and at noon on the 4th Six-Mile Spruit, south-west of Pretoria, was reached. Heavy firing was then in progress ahead. Two miles further, the naval guns mounted a hill, and the two 4·7's were ordered into action, being at once greeted with fire from the enemy's pom-poms. Here Commander de Horsey, who was mounted, was wounded in the foot. On the left front were low hills, on which were several Boer guns : on the right front were two of the Pretoria forts; and about 700 yards ahead was a body of Johannesburg police, firing from behind a stone wall. There were, however, no further casualties in the Brigade, except among the 12-pr. gun mules. One of the forts was hit several times, but it was found afterwards that the work had been already evacuated. When the police had been driven from

---

[1] Bearcroft to Harris, May 16.
[2] Bearcroft to Harris, June 9, 1900.

the stone wall, the 12-prs. moved forward and took cover behind it. At 10 P.M. Pretoria surrendered.[1]

On June 5th the triumphant entry took place.

"It was," writes a participant,[2] "a dirty, dusty crew which represented the Navy at the entry into the capital of the Transvaal. None of us had had the chance of a wash for some time, and among us all there was not a single suit of clothes that even a tramp would have condescended to accept as a gift. Our number was very small. We had lost very many officers and men since the start from Orange River, in action and from sickness, and all that remained at this time at the front were, roughly, a hundred bluejackets and seventy Marines, with ten R.N. and four Marine officers."

The Brigade first encamped two miles outside, to the west, but, three days afterwards, moved to Silverton, eight miles to the east of Pretoria.[3] The Boers made repeated endeavours to reach the spot with shells from their heavy guns ; and, in consequence, on June 11th, with the object of surrounding or driving off the troublesome foe, the battle of Diamond Hill was fought.

The naval guns moved from camp at 2.30 A.M., and proceeded slowly to their assigned position, which they took up at 5.30 A.M., it being very dark. At daylight it was discovered that the ridge on which they were was nearly 11,000 yards from the Boer guns, or 1500 yards more than the extreme range of the pieces as mounted on field-carriages. The guns, therefore, did little on the first day of the fight, but, being advanced about 3000 yards on the second day, were able to shell the enemy's sangars above the railway line, and to prevent a big weapon which the Boers had placed upon a railway truck from becoming troublesome. That day the two 4·7's fired 56 rounds. On the 15th the Brigade was ordered back to the neighbourhood of Koodoospoort,[4] where, and at or near Marks's Farm, it remained until July 22, the guns occasionally firing at the Boer kopjes to the eastward.

During part of that time Lieutenant Back, with two 12-prs., had been detached to the north-east of Pretoria ; but though he was away for a month, and did not rejoin the Brigade until July 26th, he had but few opportunities of shelling the enemy, who was always at long range and probably suffered very little.[5]

[1] Bearcroft to Harris, June 9, 1900.
[2] Account of Lieut. Leslie Orme Wilson, R.M., in Jeans, 129.
[3] Maj. Marchant, R.M.L.I., brought up reserve ammunition from Kroonstad on June 7th. On the same day four bluejackets of the *Tartar*, who had been made prisoners in Natal on Nov. 15, 1899, reported themselves as having escaped.
[4] Bearcroft to Harris, June 17, 1900. Back to Bearcroft, June 16, 1900.
[5] Back to Bearcroft, July 28, 1900.

The advance, when resumed, was by way of Donkershoek and Bronker's Spruit to Bergspruit, where the Brigade lay from July 27th to August 3rd.[1] It subsequently followed the retiring Boers along the line of the Delagoa Bay railway to Middelburg,[2] whence, on August 22nd, it moved to Rietpan, Wonderfontein, and Belfast. The last-named place was held by the Boers in force, their chief position being at Dalmanutha.   Before Belfast, General Buller, coming from Natal, joined hands with Lord Roberts; and, as a result of the conference which was then held, the battle of Belfast was begun on August 26th.

The 4·7's were posted on Monument Hill, one facing due north, and the other (the Marines') facing due east and commanding the railway.   By noon they were heavily engaged with the Boer guns and pom-poms.   In the course of the afternoon the Marines' gun was shifted, and then ordered back again.   Towards evening, Lieutenant Leslie Orme Wilson, R.M., who was in charge of it, was severely wounded.   At night both guns returned to camp; and on the following morning the bluejackets' 4·7 was sent to a point 1200 yards south of the railway station, and subsequently assisted Buller's guns in shelling Bergendal Farm until the British infantry advanced on that post.   This gun was opposed by one of the Boer " long-toms," another of which kept up a duel with the Marines' 4·7. At about 2 P.M. the enemy gave way, whereupon a concentrated fire from all the available artillery was poured into him as long as he was within range.[3]

On the first day of the action Lieutenant Back, with his two 12-prs., had been detached to advance with General Pole-Carew. His experiences shall be narrated presently.

After the occupation of Belfast, the bluejackets' 4·7 was ordered on September 5th to trek southward to Carolina, while the Marines' gun was placed in an entrenched position on Monument Hill, where, in fact, it remained until it was turned over to the army in October.

The bluejackets' gun, otherwise known as 4·7 No. 1, with which went Captain Bearcroft, accompanied General French eastward from Carolina to Barberton.   The column witnessed some fighting on September 10th and 12th, but the naval detachment had very little

---

[1] Bearcroft to Harris, Aug. 2, 1900, in *Gazette* of Mar. 12, 1901.
[2] Bearcroft to Harris, Aug. 18, 1900.
[3] Bearcroft to Harris, Aug. 30, 1900.

part in it. If Bearcroft had been able to get his gun up a certain hill close to Barberton, he could probably have compelled the surrender of about one thousand Boers, who were upon a neighbouring height, but who could not be reached by the guns of the army. The country near Barberton was, indeed, terribly difficult, and ere the town was entered one of the gun wheels broke down so completely that a spare wagon wheel had to be substituted for it until the old wheel could be repaired by the Armourer, Samuel K. Colevill, who displayed great energy and resource.[1] On October 1st this gun and its ammunition were turned over at Barberton to the Royal Artillery; and on the 2nd the Brigade set out by train to return to its ships. It met with several adventures ere it reached Pretoria, the engine breaking down once, the line being twice blown up under it, and a Boer attack having to be repulsed. At Pretoria, Major Urmston, with the crew of the Marines' gun, otherwise known as 4·7 No. 2, joined from Belfast, and Lieutenant Back, with his 12-pr. detachment, joined from Komati Poort. Lord Roberts inspected the reunited Brigade,[2] which then proceeded on its way to Simon's Town, and reached its destination on October 12th.[3]

It has been seen that Lieutenant Back, with two of the *Monarch's* long 12-prs., parted from Captain Bearcroft in the neighbourhood of Belfast on August 26th. Back, who had with him Lieutenant Colquhoun, of the Victorian Navy, Midshipman Andrew Browne Cunningham, and thirty-six men, accompanied the 11th Division[4] which was sent to drive the Boers eastward either into the mountains or across the Portuguese frontier. On the afternoon of the start, when the column was heading north-east, the enemy assailed it with a heavy rifle and pom-pom fire, and the 12-prs. got into action. On the 27th they were again engaged near Machadodorp and assisted in silencing a Boer 6·2-in. gun, but they had to fire forty-one rounds at extreme elevation, and so strained their carriages considerably. Helvetia was reached on the following day and a junction effected with the army of General Buller. The guns, in spite of the difficulties of the route, managed to keep up with the head of the column, and, on one occasion when a Boer

---

[1] Bearcroft to Harris, Sept. 24, 1900, in *Gazette* of Mar. 12, 1901.
[2] Com. Grant's detachment had returned a few days earlier.
[3] Bearcroft to Harris, Oct. 13, 1900.
[4] Guards' and 18th Brigades, under Genl. Pole-Carew.

pom-pom opened suddenly on French's cavalry, were able to silence it promptly, and to drive the enemy's rearguard towards Lydenburg.

On the 29th the Division turned southward again to the railway at Waterval Onder, and shared in the movement which caused the release of a large body of British prisoners at Nooigedacht. During an eight days' halt of the two 12-prs. at Waterval Onder, the strained carriage of one of the guns was replaced by a new mounting sent from Belfast. Armourer's Mate Albert Smithfield, who was with the detachment, made himself invaluable during the whole of his service on shore, and, on one occasion, went even so far as to re-forge a gun axle. The continued efficiency of the guns was largely due to him.[1] In the meantime General Buller turned the enemy on the north, and French harried him on the south, thus securing the flanks of Pole-Carew's advance, which was resumed along the railway on September 11th. Godroan's River was reached on the 13th, and on the 14th the column swerved in a south-easterly direction to Kaapsche Hoek, where it left the 18th Brigade behind it, the Guards being the only infantry remaining with General Pole-Carew. Thence, by way of North Kaap Station and Avoca, where many locomotives and much rolling stock were captured, the column regained the main line of the Delagoa Bay railway at Kaapmuiden Junction. In nine days the naval 12-prs. had covered ninety miles. After a single night's halt they moved on along the Crocodile Valley towards Komati Poort, and bivouacked at Hector Spruit on September 22nd. The whole fifty-four miles between Kaapmuiden and the Portuguese frontier were covered in four days—a wonderful record considering the arduous nature of the country and the badness of the climate. The guns did not come into action again, for the Boers had retired across the border, abandoning among other things the 6·2-in. gun which had been so troublesome on August 27th.

Back and his guns entrained on October 1st to return to the sea. Sometimes getting out and pushing the crazy train and its worn-out engine, the party reached Hector Spruit, where it narrowly escaped extinction in a collision with another train. Not until October 5th did it steam into Pretoria,[2] where, as has been shown, it rejoined Captain Bearcroft.

[1] Back to Bearcroft, Sept. 6, 1900, in *Gazette* of Mar. 12, 1901.
[2] Back to Bearcroft, Oct. 7, 1900.

The only other naval detachment of Bearcroft's Brigade the fortunes of which have to be followed is the detachment which parted company at Bloemfontein, and joined the eastward wing of the northward advance thence. This was Commander William Lowther Grant's detachment, with its two 4·7-in. guns, "Little Bobs" and "Sloper." Its other officers were Lieutenant James Andrew Fergusson (*Barrosa*), Midshipman George Holbrow Lang (*Doris*), and Surgeon Thomas Tendron Jeans,[1] and Gunner James Cannon (*Monarch*).

Grant left the neighbourhood of Bloemfontein on April 23rd and marched due east with his two guns in the wake of the Highland Brigade, taking up a position two days later on Mamena Kop, where he remained until the 30th, when the guns were lowered down again and moved ten miles to Waterval Drift along a bad and narrow road that topped a razor-backed ridge. On May 2nd he joined the 9th Division, under Major-General Sir Henry Colvile, and marched thirteen miles to Fairfield, proceeding thence on the 3rd to Papjei's Vlei. Early on the 4th the enemy was found in position on a steep hill called Baboon Kop on the right front of the advance. The Highland Brigade attacked under cover of a very effective fire from the naval guns, and carried the place with but slight loss. Winberg was reached on the 6th without further fighting,[2] and the detachment halted there until May 22nd, when it resumed the north-eastward march in company with two battalions and the divisional troops of Colvile's command, the rest of the Division[3] being ahead. The strength of the detachment on that day was: officers, 3; seamen and stokers, 50; guns, 2; ammunition, 570 rounds; horses, 7; trek oxen, 290; conductors, 3; natives, 42; wagons, 13; and carts, 3.

On each day from the 22nd to the 25th inclusive some opposition was encountered, but the 4·7's did not get into action. On the 26th, however, the guns opened on a Boer position at 3700 yards' range, and assisted in forcing the enemy to evacuate it. That night the detachment bivouacked north of Lindley. On the 27th the rear-guard was engaged during the greater part of the day's march; and on the 28th the naval guns got into action on the left of the advance, shelling some Boers out of a position on a high ridge, and then

---

[1] Recalled on Apr. 29 to Simon's Town.

[2] Grant to Bearcroft, May 9, in *Gazette* of Mar. 12, 1901.

[3] It was overtaken at Roode Kraal on May 23.

following on to the ridge and again opening on two hostile guns in
the valley beyond it. That day the 9th Division was engaged on
nearly all sides. The 4·7's were in action from 10.30 A.M. until
4.30 P.M., but had to husband their ammunition.[1] At night the
force was practically surrounded, the men were on one-third rations,
and the oxen were showing signs of giving out, while Heilbron, the
immediate objective, was eighteen miles away.

On the 29th, when the Division again advanced, the two 4·7's
were moved alternately, one remaining in position in the rear until
the other had proceeded about three miles, and had found a suitable
spot from which to cover the forward movement of the other. Both
guns were several times in action, and at 10 A.M. both were
simultaneously engaged with three Boer guns on the right flank.
At 7 P.M. the weary force bivouacked at Heilbron, after having
marched 128 miles in eight days, and fought three general actions.[2]

At Heilbron the Royal Engineers dug pits for the two naval
guns, and the bluejackets dug magazines for them. The town was
soon surrounded by the entrenchments of the Boers, who, however,
did not bombard for fear of damaging the place. On June 20th one
of the guns moved out with a force intended to cover the entrance
of a convoy under the escort of Lord Methuen. It opened on a
body of the enemy 9000 yards away and scattered it, but, being too
distant to use shrapnel, did not perhaps cause much loss. The
convoy got in without opposition, bringing supplies which were
greatly needed.[3]

On July 27th the force entrained and evacuated Heilbron, which
was instantly occupied by the Boers. In each train was a Boer of
note, whose presence deterred his friends from firing at it. Krugersdorp, therefore, was reached without accident. Grant remained
there until July 31st, when he was ordered to re-entrain, without
his trek oxen, and to proceed southward to Kopjes Station, where he
arrived on the following morning. A very poor lot of fresh oxen
was there given to him; and on August 2nd he went off to the
north-west with a column which was despatched under General
Hart in the direction of the Vaal River to turn General De Wet out
of a position which he held between Rhebok Kop and Vredefort.
On August 3rd the Boers were found and engaged, one of the 4·7's

---

[1] Number of rounds fired, 43.
[2] Grant to Bearcroft, June 1, in *Gazette* of Mar. 12, 1901.
[3] Grant to Harris, July 1, 1901.

bursting a shrapnel shell right on top of a hostile 15-pr., and putting it out of action. On the night of the 6th De Wet made off along the Zeerust road, and was at once pursued.

Then began one of the most trying experiences of Grant's detachment. A wheel of one of the guns showed signs of weakness almost immediately, but was patched up by means of tools borrowed from the Royal Artillery. A day or two later the wheel required further patching. The ground was difficult, the dust and wind were often terrible, the grass, fired by the enemy, was a source of continual peril, and the marches were long. But for Armourer's-Mate Joseph Tuck, who spent his nights, and indeed almost every minute of every halt, in strengthening the much-tried gun mountings, the 4·7's could not have gone forward. In spite of his exertions, one gun had at last to be sent, in charge of the gunner and seven men, to be overhauled thoroughly at Pretoria. It was absent from the column from August 12th to August 28th. During its absence the other gun gave the Armourer's-Mate more than enough to do, and at length it had to be placed in a wagon, the General, however, consenting to allow this to be done only on the distinct understanding that the heavy piece should be remounted and ready for action within an hour if its services should be needed. By August 22nd, when the column, after many wanderings, entered Krugersdorp, it had marched 265 miles in seventeen days, though it had not succeeded in trapping General De Wet. At Krugersdorp the mounting of the second gun was properly repaired by a local firm. In this remarkable chase the naval detachment lost 61 of its oxen ; but the exertions did no harm to either officers or men, all of whom enjoyed excellent health.[1]

The march was taken up again on August 29th, when, however, the second gun, not being then repaired, had to be left behind with Lieutenant Fergusson, 13 men, 4 wagons, 280 rounds of ammunition, and the necessary natives and oxen. On September 3rd the gun was mounted on the repaired carriage and made ready for firing in seventeen minutes by the unaided exertions of the naval detachment. It was then placed in position on some heights to the north of Krugersdorp, and was thenceforward attached for a time to General Barton's command, though during that period it had no experiences of general interest.

---

[1] Grant to Bearcroft, Aug. 28, 1900; Fergusson to Grant, Aug. 29, 1900.

The other gun, "Little Bobs," with 300 rounds of ammunition, once more accompanied General Hart, in the direction of
Potchefstroom, and, on August 31st, fired a couple of rounds at
short range at some Boers near the Johannesburg waterworks,
which they had that day attacked.   Near Leeuwpoort, on
September 4th, some yeomanry, who were pressed by the enemy,
were relieved, the 4·7 that day firing twenty-four rounds with
excellent effect.   On the 5th the gun was again in action, and fired
fifteen rounds.   Commandant Theron was among the dead Boers
who were subsequently discovered.   On the 9th, after a further
advance, the column was split into two sections with a view to the
surprise of Potchefstroom, the naval gun and its crew being attached
to one of them, and marching thirty-seven miles in the course of
the following night.   The town was taken without resistance, after
the 4·7 had been placed in position to command it.

Thence the column moved on the night of September 11th along
the Ventersdorp road.   Boers were sighted ahead early on the
following morning, and "Little Bobs" fired eleven rounds at them
as they fled.   At Frederickstad the force halted for a week, getting
up supplies from Welverdiend, and 50 rounds of 4·7 ammunition
from Krugersdorp.   While at Frederickstad the naval gun was
twice in action, firing three rounds on the 14th, and thirty-five on
the 17th.   On the latter occasion the enemy brought up a gun
within 4000 yards, and shelled the British transport for some time
until Grant, firing at the flash, got the range, and dropped a lyddite
shell into the midst of the Boers, who thereupon made off.

On the night of the 19th the column marched twelve miles to
Witpootje, and, before getting into camp in the morning, was
engaged.   The gun expended seventeen rounds, and, after breakfast,
moved to the assistance of some yeomanry, who were pressed, while,
later in the day, it helped to turn the Boers out of a comparatively
formidable position, and caused them heavy loss.   In these services
it fired seventy-one rounds.   On the 21st the advance was resumed,
and "Little Bobs" would have been again warmly employed against
a large body of Boers in the open, had not a shell jammed in the
gun after the second round, and so put the weapon out of action
until the enemy was beyond reach.   On the 22nd the column was
once more in action, one, out of the five shots fired by the 4·7, killing or wounding twelve of the foe.   In twenty-five hours the force
marched thirty-seven miles.   On the 25th General Hart returned to

Potchefstroom, which, during his absence, had been re-occupied by the Boers, but which was abandoned as he drew near. Four more marches brought the column back to Krugersdorp on September 30th. In twenty marching days it had covered 310 miles; and during that time "Little Bobs" had fired 187 rounds (22 common shell, 64 shrapnel, and 101 lyddite). Not one man of the naval detachment had fallen out or gone sick while with the Potchefstroom column, in spite of the hardships of the month's work.[1]

On October 2nd both the 4·7 guns were handed over to the Royal Garrison Artillery, and Grant and his people entrained for Simon's Town, where they arrived without adventure on October 7th.[2] It may be said without fear of contradiction that no force, having with it so heavy a gun as a 4·7, had ever before done such splendid marching as Grant's detachment did. From the time of its departure from Bloemfontein it covered 797½ miles in fifty-three marching days, during the whole of which it averaged 15 miles a day. Its most brilliant performance was 37 miles in thirteen hours. The men were always cheerful; and crime, slackness, and neglect of duty were unknown among them. General Hart wrote to Commander Grant:—

"Well assisted by your subordinates, you have overcome serious campaigning difficulties with a ponderous gun which has deservedly become the terror of the enemy."[3]

In his concluding despatch Captain Bearcroft made special mention of:—

Commander S. V. Y. de Horsey; Fleet-Surgeon James Porter; Majors Schofield Patten Peile, and A. E. Marchant, R.M.; Lieutenants Back, Hon. Edward Spencer Harry Boyle, and Edward John Kendall Newman, R.N., and W. J. Colquhoun, R.V.N.; Lieutenant L. O. Wilson, R.M.; Gunners Harry Ball, and Ernest Edward Lowe; and Midshipmen Thos. Fredk. Jno. Livesey Wardle, and Bertram Noel Denison.

The fortunes of the Naval Brigade which went northward from Cape Colony,[4] and of the various fragments which from time to time were detached from it, have now been followed from the day of the first landing at Simon's Bay on October 20th, 1899, down to the return of the last of the officers and men to their ships on October 12th, 1900.

*   *   *   *   *

---

[1] Grant's desp. of Sept. 30, 1900, in *Gazette* of Mar. 12, 1901.
[2] Grant's desp. of Oct. 7, 1900.   [3] Oct. 1, 1900.
[4] During the whole of Lord Roberts's tenure of command in S. Africa, Com. the Hon. Seymour John Fortescue, M.V.O., served as the Field-Marshal's Naval A. d. C.

On the Natal side of the theatre of war Naval Brigades were employed ashore for an equally lengthy period. The history of their exploits has next to be told.

It has been mentioned already that Captain Percy Scott, of the *Terrible,* managed to prepare two 4·7-in. guns on his platform mountings on October 25th and 26th, 1899, and, on the latter day, to put them on board the *Powerful* at Simon's Town for conveyance to Durban, and so to General Sir George White at Ladysmith.

The *Powerful,* Captain the Hon. Hedworth Lambton, was homeward bound *viâ* the Cape from the China Station. Calling at Mauritius, she took on board there half a battalion of the King's Own Yorkshire Light Infantry, and disembarked it in Table Bay on October 13th. On the 20th she landed a detachment which accompanied Commander Ethelstone's Brigade to Stormberg and Queenstown and which afterwards returned to the sea at East London,[1] the *Powerful's* detachment thence rejoining the ship.

In the interval Sir George White's appeal for heavy guns for Ladysmith had reached Rear-Admiral Harris at the Cape, and the *Powerful,* having been filled up with coal, had been despatched with the two badly needed 4·7's. She reached Durban on October 29th. On her passage thither her people constructed wooden field-carriages for three long 12-prs.; crews were told off for all the guns which were to be landed; and two small-arm parties, each of fifty men, were also paraded in khaki ready for disembarkation. The *Powerful's* Brigade[2] landed on the evening of its arrival, and entrained and started for Ladysmith without an instant's unnecessary

---

[1] See note on p. 471, *antea.*

[2] STRENGTH OF THE LADYSMITH NAVAL BRIGADE.

Two 4·7-in. Q. guns on Scott's platform mountings. Three long 12-prs. on improvised field mountings. One 12-pr. 8-cwt. field-gun. Four rifle-calibre Maxim guns. Officers, 17: bluejackets, stokers, engine-room artificers, armourers, cooks, marine servants (3), carpenters, blacksmith, steward's boy, ship's corporal, and sick-berth attendant, 267. The officers were: Capt. the Hon. Hedworth Lambton (C.B., Mar. 13, 1900); Lieuts. Frederick Greville Egerton (mortally wounded and promtd. Nov. 2, 1899), Algernon Walker Heneage (Com., May 2, 1900), Lionel Halsey, and Michael Henry Hodges; Fleet-Paymaster William Hobart Fendall Kay (died of enteric); Surgeon James Grant Fowler; Engineers Edgar Harrold Ellis (Chf. Eng., May 2, 1900), and Charles Cape Sheen (Chf. Eng., May 2, 1900); Gunner William Sims (Lieut., May 2, 1900); and Midshipmen John Richards Middleton, Henry Tresilian Hayes, Robert Cecil Hamilton, Hon. Ian Ludovic Andrew Carnegie, Alick Stokes, and (from the *Terrible*) Edward George Chichester, and Charles Reynolds Sharp. In addition to the above, Lieut. Edward Carey Tyndale-Biscoe (R.N. retd.) and Lieut. Edward Stabb, R.N.R. (died of enteric), joined the Brigade at Ladysmith.

delay, reaching Pietermaritzburg on October 30th at 1 A.M., Estcourt at dawn, and Colenso at 8.30 A.M. The line was clear ahead ; but twenty miles away, around Ladysmith, fighting was in progress ; and, as the two trains pressed onwards, the sound of the guns grew ever louder. The battle of Lombard's Kop was being fought.

As the trains steamed into Ladysmith Station fighting still continued to the eastward, where the British cavalry was at work ; and the 6-in. Boer gun on Pepworth Hill, to the northward, was lazily shelling the town. Within a few minutes the three 12-prs. were unloaded, and sent three miles along the Newcastle road,[1] where they unlimbered on the west side of Limit Hill ; but ere they had time to open against the gun on Pepworth Hill they were ordered to retire. This they did under a very troublesome shell fire from the Boers. The ammunition wagons were sent ahead, and Lieutenant Hodges, with a company of bluejackets, covered the withdrawal. Unfortunately the foremost gun was knocked off its carriage by a bursting projectile, and three of its crew were wounded. A certain amount of panic undoubtedly ensued. The striker was taken out of the gun's breech-block ; attempts were hurriedly made to damage the screw-threads inside the breech aperture by hammering them with stones ; in short, for a few moments, the piece was on the point of being abandoned. Cooler counsels, however, quickly prevailed. The covering company assisted in righting the gun ; a wheel which had been knocked off the carriage was replaced ; a fresh team of oxen was brought up in lieu of the one which had bolted ; and presently the 12-pr. rejoined its two fellows, which by that time had unlimbered and got into action on Gordon Hill.

The two guns, at a range of 6000 and 7000 yards, plied the Pepworth gun with common shell and, excellently sighted by Gunner Sims, quickly put it out of action for the rest of the day. Sir George White was delighted at the practice made, and declared that the Brigade's arrival had saved the situation. No doubt the sudden appearance of long range guns did cause the enemy to desist

---

All the above officers were mentioned in despatches, together with the following petty officers and leading seamen who served as captains of guns : Henry W. C. Lee, Philip T. Sisk, Archibald C. Pratt, Albert G. Withers, and Samuel E. Hemmings, Lee being also specially noted for gallantry. Lambton to Harris, Mar. 12, 1900, enclosing desps. of Jan. 8, Jan. 11, and Feb. 28, in *Gazette* of Mar. 12, 1901.

[1] Each gun, with its wooden trail lashed to the back of a wagon, which served as a limber, was drawn by 16 oxen.

from attempting a raid upon the town. In the meantime, the
8-cwt. 12-pr., which had been taken out beyond Junction Hill by

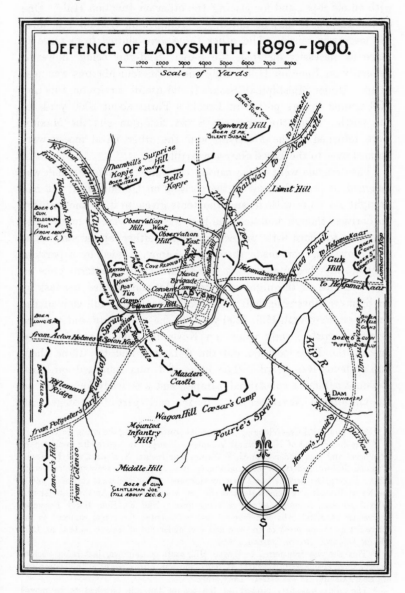

DEFENCE OF LADYSMITH. 1899–1900.

Lieutenant Lionel Halsey, had also retired. Owing to its limited
range it was that day useless. As for the 4·7-in. guns, arrange-

ments were made for mounting one of them on Cove Redoubt,[1] which had hitherto been occupied by the Natal Naval Volunteers [2] with an old 9-pr., and for placing the other on Junction Hill.[3] One of the 12-prs., it may be noted, was retained on Gordon Hill until the siege was raised. The other three were shifted from place to place as necessity dictated, the 8-cwt. field-gun being, however, generally on Junction Hill. Only one of the four Maxims was used at all. Under Midshipman Stokes it did useful service on Junction Hill against snipers posted in Brooks's Farm, about 2000 yards to the north. After the relief the 8-cwt. field-gun and the Maxims were returned to the *Powerful*, and the other naval pieces were handed over to the Royal Garrison Artillery.

The Brigade went under canvas on camping ground which was assigned to it to the rear of the position on Gordon Hill.[4] It had brought no tents with it, and the tents given to it by the military authorities, though doubtless the best available, were in many cases so old as to afford little protection against either rain or sun. The men, however, soon made themselves happy. Aided by a party of Sappers, they began mounting one of the 4·7-in. platform guns on Junction Hill on the night of October 31st and finished the task by daylight on November 2nd. The work was done in full view of the enemy on Pepworth Hill, 6200 yards to the northward, but was not interfered with. Only when, on November 2nd, the 4·7 opened against the Boer position, did the 6-in. gun and the 15-pr. there make themselves heard. The other 4·7 was mounted on Cove Redoubt behind a substantial parapet, and was ready for action on the morning of November 3rd. In the early part of the siege both

---

[1] This gun, "Princess Victoria," retained its position during the entire siege.

[2] The detachment of Natal Naval Volunteers besieged in Ladysmith consisted of 72 officers and men under Com. G. E. Tatum and Lieuts. N. Barrett, and F. Hoare, with one old 9-pr. and two 3-pr. Hotchkiss Q. guns. It entered Ladysmith on Oct. 2, 1899. During the siege it lost 7 men by sickness. After the siege, part of it joined the Naval Brigade at Elandslaagte, and the rest was dismissed. Another detachment, as will be seen, accompanied the relieving force. The Rt. Hon. Harry Escombe, ex-Premier of Natal, who had founded and commanded the corps, returned to the active list at the outbreak of the war, and was under fire at Talana on Oct. 20, 1899 (*Naval Volunteer Record*, Durban, 1900).

[3] This gun was transferred to Wagon Hill, south of the town, just before each of Buller's three unsuccessful attempts at relief, and was finally posted at the eastern end of Cæsar's Camp. It was called "Lady Anne."

[4] The camp was first pitched on the top of the hill, but had to be moved to the rear on Nov. 19th in consequence of the fire from the Boer howitzer on Surprise Hill.

guns fired nearly every day ; but soon the necessity for economising ammunition made itself felt ; and thereafterwards a week sometimes passed without either gun being fired at all. The total supply of ammunition brought into Ladysmith by the Brigade was only the following :—

For 4·7-in. guns:			Small-arm cartridges :		
Common shell	. . .	200 rounds.	For Lee-Metford rifles		39,000 rounds.
Lyddite	. . . .	200 rounds.	For Maxim guns	.	64,000 rounds.
Shrapnel	. . . .	200 rounds.	For revolvers.	. .	5,400 rounds.
For 12-prs. '			Besides 150 rounds of Lee-Metford ammunition carried on each man.		
Common shell	. . .	738 rounds.			
Shrapnel	. . . .	396 rounds.			
Case shot	. . . .	24 rounds.			

The naval gun positions were strengthened continually ; very elaborate systems of wire entanglements were placed in front of them, and carefully protected magazines were dug out hard by. At first the bluejackets did picket duty at night, but, as their numbers were reduced by disease, they were employed almost exclusively in holding the entrenchments and manning the guns. Engineer Charles Cape Sheen rendered the most valuable service to the garrison by supplying it with pure water. He extemporised distillers out of corrugated iron tanks and ordinary water-piping, feeding them with steam from the boiler at the railway repairing shop, and from two locomotive engines ; and thus he provided condensed water for the entire force in Ladysmith from December 11th to January 25th, when no more coal could be given to him. Seeing that the ordinary water supply had been cut off by the enemy, and that the only natural water to be had was the muddy fluid from the Klip River, Mr. Sheen's ingenuity must have been instrumental in limiting the ravages of enteric and dysentery, although those terrible scourges played havoc with the enfeebled and depressed defenders ere the siege was raised. What would have been the result had there been no distillers at all is frightful to contemplate.

Another officer who rendered exceptional service was Fleet-Paymaster Kay, a man of great powers of organisation, foresight, and resource. Towards the end of the siege he acted as Field-Paymaster to the army. Contracting enteric, he, unhappily, died on the voyage home, and was buried at Ascension. But for his exertions as commissariat officer the Brigade would have fared badly indeed.

It is not necessary here to follow all the details of the long and gallant defence of the town. It will suffice to describe only such events as mainly concerned the Naval Brigade.

It has been noted that on November 2nd, the day, by the way, on which the communications [1] of the garrison with the outside world were cut off by the enemy, the 4·7-in. gun on Junction Hill first opened fire on the Boer positions in front of it. Its target was

COMMANDER FREDERICK GREVILLE EGERTON.
(*From a photo by Window & Grove.*)

the "Long Tom" on Pepworth Hill. Immediately after the opening round of a duel which subsequently lasted for two hours, "Long Tom" replied. Its smoke being seen, the people on Junction Hill were ordered under cover, only Lieutenant Egerton and the gun's crew remaining by the British gun. The Boer 6-in. shell came through the embrasure, just touched the upper row of sandbags, and struck Egerton in the legs. "This will put a stop to my

[1] Except by signalling and by occasional runners.

cricket, I am afraid," he said, as they picked him up and laid him in a dhoolie.   On the way down to the hospital he stopped his bearers in order to obtain a light for his cigarette.   That evening he died, conscious almost to the last.   In the interim he had been promoted.

The first considerable action of the siege was on November 9th, the Prince of Wales' birthday, when the Boers began a vigorous artillery fire at dawn, and then attacked both Cæsar's Camp on the south, and Observation Hill on the north.   The two 4·7's did something towards limiting the activity of the enemy's guns ; and at noon, when the attack had practically ceased, all the naval weapons joined in firing a shotted royal salute of twenty-one rounds into the hostile lines.   His Royal Highness's health was drunk in champagne in the mess tent, and a carrier pigeon, which reached Durban safely, was let loose, bearing the 'congratulations of the garrison for transmission to the Prince, who duly acknowledged them.   The only casualty of the day on the side of the Brigade was a wounded sucking-pig.

On Christmas Day Her Majesty the Queen, by way of the heliograph from Weenen, signalled, " Wishing a happy Christmas to her brave soldiers and sailors."   The Boers, less considerate, did not pretermit their usual daily bombardment ; but they did fill a 6-in. shell with plum-pudding, paint " A Merry Xmas " on it, and fire it into Ladysmith.   Such were the humours of the siege.   In the meantime the daily rations per man diminished, until, when things looked blackest, they consisted of a biscuit and a half, and three-quarters of a pound of horseflesh.

The great action of the investment was fought on January 6th, 1900.   It took the form of a desperate Boer attack on, and a still more desperate British defence of, Wagon Hill and Cæsar's Camp, the southernmost of the British works.   Chief Engineer Sheen [1] says :—

"The part played by the Naval Brigade in repelling this fierce attack consisted principally in keeping down the fire of the opposing siege-guns ; but a small party of bluejackets happened to be in the brunt of the fighting, and took a not inglorious part in the successful defence.

"The presence of this small party was due to the fact that, on the night of January 4th, an attempt had been made to shift a 4·7-in. gun from Junction Hill to Wagon Hill . . . to cover the advance of a column intended to effect a junction with Buller's forces in his second attempt to relieve the town.   A heavy thunderstorm, however, had made the ground so soft that the transport of the heavy gun had to be

---

[1] Jeans, ' Naval Brigades in S. A.,' 218.

deferred till next night, when it was successfully accomplished under the occasional glare of a searchlight from Bulwana Hill. The working party consisted, as usual, of a detachment of infantry, larger this time than before, for short rations were beginning to tell on the men's strength, and their lifting power was considerably diminished . . . The string of wagons, with an escort of Gordon Highlanders, arrived at the foot of this hill [1] about 1 A.M.

"Two wagons, one with the great platform beams, the other with tools, etc., were handed up the steep, slippery sides to the rear of the old [2] gun emplacement; and the bluejackets and Highlanders started work with a will, under the persuasive and by this time well-known eloquence of the Gunner,[3] and, in a few minutes had got the platform half way off the wagon, when the harmony of the proceedings was rudely disturbed by a sudden and unexpected splashing and pinging of bullets on the rocks and boulders forming the crest of the hill. . . ."

The Boers, in short, were attacking. On the hill were 13 blue-jackets, 70 of the Gordons, and 30 Royal Engineers, who seized their arms, extended along the summit, and began to fire downward into the darkness. The oxen of the wagons were cut loose and hurried inward; the pickets (Imperial Light Horse) were driven back; and twenty or thirty Boers, all picked marksmen, quickly gained a position on the crest itself, and for many hours defied every attempt to dislodge them.

Gunner Sims took command in an empty gun emplacement on the right of the hill, and made his men fire volleys by half sections, though probably with but little result. He was accompanied and aided by Engineer Sheen. Meanwhile the attack developed on the left of the defence; and soon Cæsar's Camp, and, indeed, the whole of the ridge, was involved. At dawn some Boer 15-prs., which were then on Middle Hill and to the east of it, opened on the British position, the naval 12-pr. "Lady Ellen" at Cæsar's Camp returning the fire at a range of about 4000 yards. It was excellently worked by Midshipman Carnegie, with a crew of three bluejackets and three stokers. As the enemy advanced in greater and greater numbers even the distant naval guns—the 4·7 in Cove Redoubt, under Lieutenant Lionel Halsey, the 12-pr. on Gordon Hill, and another 12-pr. which was then at Leicester Post—were drawn into partici-pating in the action which raged along the whole southern face, from Bulwana Hill on the east to Rifleman's Ridge on the west.

At length the attack seemed to be about to die away, when, soon after 1 P.M., it was renewed with great suddenness and fury against the south-west point of Wagon Hill. The little naval detachment

---

[1] Wagon Hill. The gun, taken from its platform, was placed on one of the wagons.
[2] The gun had been temporarily posted there on a previous occasion.
[3] Mr. William Sims.

there had been relieved at noon by some of the Gordons, and had been having dinner somewhat to the rear of the crest of the hill. Gunner Sims heard a great increase in the firing and a loud shouting; and then he saw some of the defenders from above rushing down on him in a confused mass. He did not lose his head, but extended his thirteen men in skirmishing order, made them fix bayonets, and led them up to the emplacement. There he found Colonel Ian Hamilton at bay with a Boer, and crying out to his men to go back. Back they went very quickly. The panic had been only momentary. Although several Boers had gained the parapet, not one had got further, all who reached it having been shot dead.[1]

In this affair the Brigade had a stoker killed and a bluejacket badly wounded. Soon afterwards Engineer Sheen was slightly hit in the face by a fragment of shell, and Gunner Sims had his rifle blown out of his hands.

An hour or so later, under cover of a storm of rain, the Boers made yet another attack, and were again repulsed; and so the day's fighting ended. It cost the defence 149 killed and 275 wounded. What it cost the enemy is unknown, but 79 of their dead were found within the British lines.

Thenceforward, for nearly two months, there was almost daily bombardment of the town, and ever less and less reply to it. At 1.30 P.M. on February 28th General Hunter rode into the naval camp and told some of the officers that General Buller had just heliographed : "Gave the Boers a thorough beating yesterday, and am sending my cavalry on to ascertain in what direction they are going, as I believe them to be in full retreat."

It was even as Buller had suspected. At 6 P.M. some cavalry under Lord Dundonald entered Ladysmith, and the long-beleaguered town was at length relieved. That afternoon, when the Boers were seen to be removing their 6-in. gun from Bulwana Hill, the seamen gunners, conscious that they need no longer husband their ammunition, did their best to interfere with the operation ; but in the night following the gun was taken away. A week later the remains of the Ladysmith Naval Brigade left for Durban, and thence for Simon's Town and home. Within six weeks of their relief the officers and men were publicly welcomed in London, and were inspected by

[1] *Gazette*, Mar. 12, 1901. Jeans, 220–225.

Queen Victoria at Windsor. The Brigade's loss by wounds and disease was 2 officers and 25 men [1] up to the day of the relief. The total loss was 1 officer and 5 men killed ; 2 officers and 25 men died of disease ; and 1 officer and 4 men wounded. Total, 6 killed ; 27 died of disease ; and 5 wounded. [2]

*   *   *   *   *

It has been mentioned that a Naval Brigade, [3] under Captain Edward Pitcairn Jones, of the *Forte*, and Commander Arthur

CAPT. EDWARD PITCAIRN JONES, C.B., R.N.

Henry Limpus, of the *Terrible*, joined General Sir Redvers Buller [4] in Natal, previous to his first advance for the relief of Ladysmith.

[1] Lambton's desp. of Feb. 28.

[2] A memorial to those of the Brigade who lost their lives in S. Afr. has since been erected in Victoria Park, Portsmouth.

[3] Of 39 officers and 403 men from *Terrible, Forte, Tartar*, and *Philomel*. The officers, other than those of the Natal Naval Volunteers (for whom see note on p. 503), were then, or later, as follows: *Forte*, Capt. Edward Pitcairn Jones (C.B., Oct. 21, 1900); Lieuts. Francis William Melvill (Com., Oct. 21, 1900), and George Percy Edward Hunt (D.S.O., Oct. 21, 1900); Staff-Surg. Frederick John Lilly (Fleet-Surg., Oct. 21, 1900); Actg.-Lieut. John Miles Steel (Lieut., June 30, 1900), and Gunner Edward Holland : *Terrible*, Com. Arthur Henry Limpus (Capt., May 2, 1900); Lieuts. Frederick Charles Ashley Ogilvy (Com., Mar. 9, 1900), Spencer Reginald Strettell Richards, James Stuart Wilde, and George Plunkett England ; Sub-Lieut. Stephen Newcombe; Surgs. Ernest Courtney Lomas (Staff-Surg., Oct. 21, 1900), and Charles Clarke Macmillan (D.S.O., Oct. 21, 1900); Engineers John Frederick Arthur, and Alfred Edward James Murray; Asst.-Eng. Francis John Roskruge (Eng., July 2, 1900); Gunners Joseph Wright, Edwin John Cole, and Edwin Williams; and Mids. Percival Francis Willoughby, Richard Thornton Down, Reginald Becher Caldwell Hutchinson, Austin Charles Ackland, Alwyne Edward Sherrin, Herbert Edward Walter Christian Whyte, George Macgregor Skinner, Gerald Lord Hodson, William Wybrow Hallwright, Herbert Seymour Webb Boldero, and James Andrew Gardiner Troup : *Tartar*, Lieuts. John Edmund Drummond, and Herbert William James (Com., Oct. 21, 1900); and Staff-Surg. John Douglas Hughes : and *Philomel*, Lieuts. Arthur Halsey (Com., Oct. 21, 1900), Charles Richard Newdigate Burne, Archibald Deas, and Francis Alexander Clutterbuck ; Mids. William Rimington Ledgard; and Clerk Walter Thorne Hollins.

[4] To Sir R. Buller, as naval A.d.C., was attached Lieut. Edgar Lees (Com., June 30, 1900).

Early in November a few small detachments of bluejackets had been sent north from Durban—one from the *Tartar* to work a 7-pr. in an armoured train ; another, also from the *Tartar,* under Lieutenant Herbert William James, to defend Pietermaritz-burg with a couple of 12-prs. ; another, from the *Philomel,* under Lieutenant Arthur Halsey, to the same town with two more 12-prs., when James moved forward to Frere ; and yet another, from the *Forte,* under Lieutenant John Miles Steel, to defend the railway at Mooi River. During that period four of the *Tartar's* men were taken prisoners by the Boers, and one was killed, while defending the armoured train on November 15th.

Captain Jones was ordered to proceed with his Brigade to the front on November 26th, and he started that afternoon. On November 29th he reached Frere, where a detachment of the Natal Naval Volunteers [1] reinforced the command, and afterwards formed a welcome addition to the crews of the 4·7-in. guns, of which Jones then had two, besides twelve 12-prs., and eventually eighteen.

Further detachments from the ships joined at Frere, until at length the Brigade attained nearly its full strength.

Early on December 12th, the Brigade, with the two 4·7 and six of the 12-pr. guns, accompanied General Barton towards Chieveley, pitched its camp on Gun Hill, and placed the guns in position under Buller's direction. On the morning of the 13th, fire was opened on the positions and camps of the Boers about Colenso and Hlangwani ; but, the range being great, with a mirage, the work was discon-tinued after two hours and a half's shelling. On the 14th, the guns were moved out to Shooter's Hill, 2000 yards nearer. This reduced the ranges to 5000 and 9000 yards respectively. There was no

---

[1] The detachment of Natal Naval Volunteers serving with the Ladysmith relief force consisted of 52 officers and men under Lieuts. James E. Anderton, and Nicholas William Chiazzari, with three old 9-prs. It proceeded to the front on Sept. 30, 1899. On Oct. 30, Anderton escorted the *Powerful's* Brigade to Ladysmith, but returned at once. On Nov. 3, when ordered to evacuate Fort Wylie, spiking the guns and abandoning ammunition, the detachment disobeyed orders, and carried off everything except a broken gun-carriage. On Dec. 9 the detachment joined Capt. Edward Pitcairn Jones's Naval Brigade, and subsequently took charge of a 4·7-in. gun. On Jan. 16, 1900, Lieut. Chiazzari distinguished himself by working the punt at Potgieter's Drift. On Feb. 19 the two Lieutenants took charge of two 4·7-in. platform guns. After the relief of Ladysmith, Lieut. Anderton and 25 men, with Lieut. Barrett, who had been in Ladysmith, rejoined Capt. Jones. That part of the detachment was dismissed at Durban on June 25, 1900. Chiazzari, who was deservedly awarded the D.S.O. Oct. 21, 1900, was the first Volunteer in the Empire to win that distinction (*Natal Volunteer Record*).

reply; and it is more than probable that little damage was done to the enemy's works. That day the whole of the rest of the army advanced about six miles, from Frere to Chieveley; and orders were issued for the operations which it had been determined to undertake on the following morning, when Buller was to endeavour to force the Tugela at Colenso. Two 12-prs., under Lieutenant Charles Richard Newdigate Burne, were to remain on Shooter's Hill; six 12-prs. were to join Colonel Long, R.A., and act under his orders; and the two 4·7-in. guns, with four 12-prs.,[1] were to move at daylight to a point about 3000 yards from the river, and 800 yards west of the railway. The remaining six naval guns were at that time, two at Frere, two at Estcourt, and two at Mooi river.

At dawn, on the 15th, the detachment with which were the 4·7-in. guns, advanced across the veldt to within about 5000 yards of the entrenched hills on the north of the Tugela, and opened fire at 5.20 A.M., but drew no reply. In the meanwhile, Colonel Long, with the 14th and 66th batteries, R.A., and the six naval 12-prs., under Lieutenants Frederick Charles Ashley Ogilvy, (*Terrible*), Herbert William James (*Tartar*), and Archibald Deas (*Philomel*), was advancing along the east side of the railway, and so got down to some low ground which was cut up with dongas, near the river's bank. The Royal Artillery batteries led, and, at about 6 A.M., took position to open fire, while the naval guns were ordered to their left. Long was then about 1200 yards from the Boers at Fort Wylie, and 450 yards from Colenso station. Suddenly a tremendous fire burst forth from among the trees towards the river, from rifle pits near the river's bank, and from Fort Wylie and its neighbourhood. The gunners and horses of the R.A. batteries were rapidly shot down or driven from their pieces, which were completely silenced within about half an hour. Galloping to his guns, Ogilvy found that the native drivers of four out of his six teams had bolted, and that the oxen belonging to them were almost unmanageable. James, however, succeeded in bringing his two guns into action on the left, against Fort Wylie, and Deas did the same with his two; but the remaining guns, under Gunner Joseph Wright (*Terrible*), were for some time jammed in the drift, and were only extricated and brought into action by the aid of

---

[1] These were under Captain Jones in person.

some artillery horses. Everyone knows how gallant and repeated were the efforts made by the army to recover its two batteries, and how bloody was the almost hopeless struggle, but two of the weapons being saved. The Navy could help only indirectly, by continuing to sweep the Boer positions with lyddite; and, unfortunately, the enemy's guns proved most difficult to make out, being admirably placed. At length, after James [1] had moved his two guns over to the west of the railway to strengthen the force there, Buller was compelled to order a general withdrawal. That was at about 11 A.M. The naval guns were brought out of action one by one, as oxen could be obtained to move them; and it was fully 2 P.M. ere the last of them returned to Shooter's Hill. There was no attempt at pursuit.

In the course of this costly battle of Colenso, the Naval Brigade's work was magnificently done. The *Terribles* extricated their jammed guns and waggons from under a heavy shell and rifle fire with notable coolness. Deas, who had one of his guns capsized, mounted it again without delay and brought it into action; and all hands, including the Natal Naval Volunteers, behaved admirably. Happily, although the loss of the army was very heavy, the Navy had but three men wounded. Among the officers favourably mentioned, in addition to those whose names have been given already, were Surgeon Charles Clarke Macmillan, Midshipmen Herbert Seymour Webb Boldero,[2] and Gerald Lord Hodson,[2] and Clerk Walter Thorne Hollins.

On the 17th, the two 4·7's and the six 12-prs. were moved back from Shooter's Hill to Gun Hill; and Ogilvy's six 12-prs. returned with the bulk of the army to Frere, there to await the reinforcements which were being sent forward under Sir Charles Warren. At Gun Hill, where the main part of the Naval Brigade encamped until January 10th, 1900, the 4·7-in. guns persistently worried the Boers, and occasionally covered reconnaissances. On December 19th, General Buller ordered the guns to cut the road bridge over the Tugela. The range was 7500 yards; and, at first, some difficulty was experienced in doing the work, but at length, thanks largely to the accurate aiming of a 4·7 by its captain, William Bate, one of the spans was severed by means of a lyddite shell. On December 22nd, one of the guns, having begun to show signs

---

[1] Com., Oct. 21st, 1900.   [2] Noted for promotion.

of wear, was dismounted, a fresh gun, obtained from Durban, being mounted in its place within an hour, and the whole operation being done by man power, without sheers or tripods. At about the same time, nine of the *Forte's* and *Philomel's* bluejackets, from the guns at Mooi river and Estcourt, were attached to the balloon section of the army, and afterwards made themselves very useful with it. On January 6th, when the Boers made an attack on Ladysmith, the force went forward in hopes of being able to create a diversion, but scarcely drew the enemy's fire. Yet, upon the whole, the fortnight spent at Gun Hill was extremely monotonous. To fill up the time, some of the men worked up 6000 yards of 6-in. rope into mantlets for use in an armoured train; and some of the officers completed a telescopic survey of the country near them.

On January 9th, Warren's force began to arrive at Frere, whereupon, on the three following days, Captain Jones moved his Brigade away to the British left, and, on the 13th, had his 4·7-in. guns in position on Mount Alice, one of the heights overlooking Potgieter's drift, on the Tugela. Two dummy 4·7's were left, with four of the 12-prs., at Chieveley, and two 12-prs. at Frere; and it was at that time that, as has been already noted, Captain Scott mounted a third 4·7-in. on a railway truck. It is doubtful whether the dummies ever deceived the Boers; but the other guns assisted General Barton in harassing and containing the enemy at Colenso, while the rest of the relieving army entered on that unfortunate part of the campaign which included the operations at Spion Kop.

"It may be gathered," says Lord Roberts, "that the original intention was to cross the river at or near Trichard's drift, and thence, by following the road past Fair View and Acton Homes, to gain the open plain north of Spion Kop, the Boer position in front of Potgieter's drift being too strong to be taken by direct attack. The whole force, less one brigade, was placed under the orders of Sir Charles Warren, who, the day after he had crossed the Tugela, seems to have consulted his general and principal staff-officers, and to have come to the conclusion that the flanking movement . . . was impracticable. . . . He accordingly decided to advance by the more direct road leading north-east and branching off from a point east of Three Tree Hill. The selection of this road necessitated the capture and retention of Spion Kop."

Mount Alice, part of Spearman's Hill, is a plateau about 1000 feet above the river level, commanding a view of the Tugela valley, and of the country between it and Ladysmith. From it the entrenchments at Cæsar's Camp were plainly visible. Immediately below Mount Alice is a second plateau, extending almost to the river, and about 400 feet above it. To the east is Potgieter's drift,

whence the land rises in a wide concave, on the west to the heights
of Spion Kop, and on the east and south-east, towards the Vaal
Krantz ridge.   From the left front of Mount Alice, away to beyond
Colenso, far to the eastward, there was a line of huge defences
covering the undulating, donga-intersected, boulder-strewn slopes
which, towards the river, are for the most part very steep.   The
top of Spion Kop, the highest ground in the vicinity, is about 1500
feet above the river.

On the afternoon of January 16th, part of the army crossed the
river, practically unopposed, at Potgieter's drift, and, by the following
morning, occupied the chain of low kopjes near it.   Eight naval
12-prs., along the edge of the plateau under Mount Alice, assisted in
covering the advance.   Most of the rest of the army crossed at
Trichard's drift, six miles west of Potgieter's.   The advance then
commenced, every yard being stubbornly contested, and Warren's
right being at length apparently arrested.   Spion Kop barred its
way, and the right became, as it were, the pivot on which the attack
wheeled forward.   During this time the naval guns daily assisted in
shelling the Brakfontein position and Spion Kop; and so matters
went on, until the evening of January 23rd, when it was decided to
take and hold Spion Kop.   By 3.30 A.M. on the 24th, the position
was occupied with but slight opposition; and soon afterwards the
naval 12-prs., having left their plateau and crossed Potgieter's drift,
were covering a demonstration against Brakfontein.   As the day
cleared, it was seen that the Boers, beyond the further ridges of the
Kop, were doing terrible execution with rifle and gun fire upon the
troops on the crowded shoulder.   The enemy's guns could not,
however, be seen from Mount Alice; and, soon after noon, James's
two naval 12-prs., besides other reinforcements, were ordered
up, though they could not actually begin the ascent until the
evening, ere which time one of the 4·7's had received instructions
to move at dawn to the westward, to a point whence the Boer
guns could be reached.   The other naval guns were of use in helping
to clear the way for the assault, which was made against the north-
east summit, the conical hill, and the centre summit—all commanding
points whence the Boers were driven.   That night, it looked as if the
worst was over, but before dawn on the 25th, it became known to
the Naval Brigade that the Kop had been evacuated.   James never
reached the top.   This was followed by the withdrawal of Warren's
whole force to the south side of the Tugela.   In the next few days,

six naval 12-prs., with other guns, were put in position on Zwaart Kop, and one of the 4·7's was moved to Signal Hill.

It is useless here to follow in any detail the course of operations in which the Naval Brigade, though constantly of great value, saw little exciting service. Suffice it to say that on February 5th, at the beginning of the movement against Vaal Krantz, the naval guns succeeded in doing some damage to two out of three troublesome Boer pieces on Spion Kop, though the latter could not be seen; that on the 6th, when two of the 12-prs.[1] had been moved to the eastern spur of Zwaart Kop, a lucky shell from the 4·7[2] on Signal Hill blew up the ammunition of a Boer 6-in. gun at a range of 11,500 yards; and that during the retirement on the 8th and 9th, the 4·7-in. guns covered the withdrawal. On the 11th, the naval guns were again back on Gun Hill. On the 12th, Scott's 6-in. gun on field mounting arrived at Chieveley, and three additional 4·7-in. guns on platforms were reported as being on the way up from Durban.[3] Two of the *Terrible's* 12-prs. were at that time attached to a small force stationed at Eshowe, in Zululand, to check Boer incursions in that direction.

On February 13th, orders were given for what proved to be the beginning of the final and successful effort of the indomitable Buller to reach his goal. A move was to be made to the right front. Hussar Hill was to be used as a foothold from which to reach out on the right to Cingolo and Monte Christo, whence Green Hill and Hlangwane could be rendered untenable, and Colenso could be turned. On the morning of the 14th, in consequence, Hussar Hill was seized, four of the naval 12-prs.[4] assisting to occupy it. The 15th witnessed little more than an artillery duel, in which Gun Hill took its share. On the 16th, during which the fire was continued, the 6-in. naval gun was placed on Gun Hill. Cingolo was captured on the 17th. On the 18th the naval guns did specially useful work. The 6-in. on Gun Hill drove away a Boer 6-in. at Bloy's Farm, 18,500 yards distant, and later, with the three 4·7's—one being on the railway truck—silenced a hostile 6-in. which opened on Hussar Hill from the Colenso kopjes. That day the army made itself master of Monte Christo, and everywhere pushed back the enemy upon the river.

On the 19th, two 4·7-in., with other guns, moved to Bloy's

---

[1] Under Lieut. Burne.   [2] Under Lieut. England.
[3] They arrived on Feb. 16th.   [4] Under Lieut. Ogilvy.

Farm, and two 12-prs.[1] to Monte Christo, where, in the course of
the night, the 4·7's joined them. General Barton had previously
occupied Hlangwane. On the following morning it was apparent
that the Boers were all north of the Tugela; and General Barton
entered Colenso, though he subsequently had to evacuate it, only to
retake it later. Thus, on the 21st, Colenso became the rail-head for
British supplies.

More 12-prs. were advanced, and four of them were posted on
Hlangwane. The two 4·7's from Monte Christo were taken down

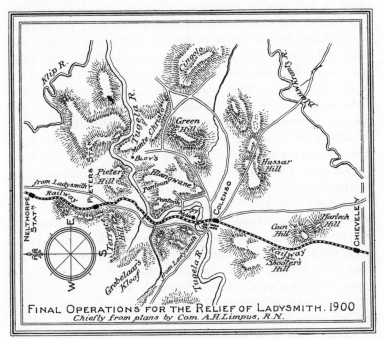

FINAL OPERATIONS FOR THE RELIEF OF LADYSMITH. 1900
Chiefly from plans by Com. A.H.Limpus, R.N.

One inch equals about five miles.

to the river in readiness for crossing by a pontoon which had been
thrown over about a mile north of Fort Wylie; and the advance of
the army continued. On the 22nd, more forces crossed the river;
the two 4·7's, still south of the river, but close to the pontoon,
shelled Terrace, otherwise Hart's, Hill; two 12-prs. took up positions
on the Colenso kopjes; and there was a lively artillery action, the
Boers evidently strengthening, and intending to hold if they could,
the line Grobelaar's Kloof, Terrace Hill, and Pieter's Hill. That

[1] Ogilvy's.

evening, and during the following night, the enemy was very stubborn and determined, and even made counter-attacks.

On the morning of the 23rd, the two 4·7's and two more 12-prs. were brought up among the kopjes; and two 4·7-in. platform guns, with the 6-in. on Gun Hill, assisted in the effort to keep down the hostile fire, four 12-prs. also helping from Hlangwane. The Boers had at least three 45-prs., and a dozen 12- or 15-prs., besides numerous smaller guns and pom-poms, engaged. Towards night, Hart made an assault on Terrace Hill, but was bloodily repulsed.[1] So determined, in fact, was the resistance, and so strong were the positions to be carried, that, though Hart temporarily held a few points which he had gained, he was obliged to abandon most of the advanced ones early on the 24th. These points were reoccupied later; yet further progress in that direction seemed impossible. It was therefore decided to hold the firing line which had been acquired, but to withdraw the reserve battalions and guns south of the river, take up new gun positions to command and enfilade the Boer lines, prolong the British line to the right, and work round the enemy's left flank, thus threatening in succession Pieter's Hill, Railway Hill,[2] and Terrace Hill. Four naval 12-prs.,[3] therefore, were at once sent back to Monte Christo.

February 25th was Sunday, and there was no firing; but the movements begun overnight were continued, and two platform 4·7's from Gun Hill were ordered to Hlangwane, while two wheeled 4·7's joined the 12-prs. on the north spur of Monte Christo, where they were nicely hidden. With General Coke, who held the Colenso kopjes, were two naval 12-prs. The 26th was spent in desultory firing, and in the preparation of a pontoon for effecting a crossing of the Tugela just below the falls.

Early on the 27th the pontoon was thrown across, and a great bombardment of the Boer positions began, the various naval guns making excellent practice. By 9 A.M. the crossing commenced; and by 2.15 P.M. General Barton had taken Pieter's Hill. Three hours later General Kitchener was master of Railway Hill and the adjoining nek, and then, after the further positions had been searched with a redoubled fire from every available gun, was joined by General Norcott, and triumphantly drove the Boers from Terrace Hill,

---

[1] The naval loss on the 23rd was 5 wounded.
[2] Two miles south of Pieter's Station.
[3] Under Lieuts. Melvill and James.

leaving them in possession of but one small knoll of all the hundred that had once barred the road to Ladysmith. It was Majuba Day.

Early on Wednesday, February 28th, the last knoll was taken without the firing of a shot, the bulk of the army crossed the river, and towards evening part of the relieving force entered Ladysmith. On the 29th there was a general advance to Nelthorpe station.[1]

On March 3rd the 4·7's were taken into Ladysmith by train, and the Brigade and the 12-prs. trekked thither and camped beyond the town, two miles to the north-east. The *Terribles* were sent back to their ship at Durban on the 11th and sailed thence in her for China, where they found other active work awaiting them. Such of the guns[2] as remained, and could no longer be manned by the diminished force, were handed over to the army. In the interval her Majesty's gracious thanks to officers and men for their services were received.

*   *   *   *   *

After the relief of Ladysmith, the Naval Brigade then with the Natal Field Force was re-organised under Captain Edward Pitcairn Jones, of the cruiser *Forte*, and thenceforward consisted of 6 officers and 31 men from the *Forte*, 6 officers and 51 men from the *Philomel*, and 2 officers and 31 men from the *Tartar*, with two wheeled 4·7-in. guns, and four 12-prs., two of which had been recently brought up by Lieutenants Steel (*Forte*), and Burne (*Tartar*). The Natal Naval Volunteers had temporarily rejoined their corps. The officers then with the Brigade were :—

Forte. Captain Edward Pitcairn Jones; Lieutenants Francis William Melvill, George Percy Edward Hunt, and John Miles Steel; Staff-Surgeon Frederick John Lilly; and Gunner (T.) Edward Holland (actg.).

Philomel. Lieutenants Arthur Halsey, Archibald Deas; Sub-Lieutenants Charles Richard Newdigate Burne, and Francis Alexander Clutterbuck; Clerk Walter Thorne Hollins; and Midshipman William Rimington Ledgard.

Tartar. Lieutenant Herbert William James; and (but somewhat later) Staff-SurgeonJohn Douglas Hughes.

---

[1] Many of these particulars concerning the relief of Ladysmith are from the rough diary of Capt. A. H. Limpus, R.N., extracts from which were read by him at a meeting at Hong Hong on June 13th, 1900, and later published in the local *Daily Press.* Other details are chiefly from Gen. Clery's Orders, Dec. 14; Gen. Buller's desp. of Dec. 17; Capt. Jones's desp. of Dec. 16; Lieut. Ogilvy's report of the same date; Capt. Jones's desps. of Feb. 8 and 18, and Mar. 2, 1900; Lieut. Burne's letters of Feb. 16; and Fleet-Surg. Lilly's account in Jeans' 'Naval Brigades.'

[2] In the relief operations the 4·7's had fired 4000 and the 12-prs. 12,000 rounds, and some of them showed signs of wear.

About March 14th Lieutenants Halsey and James, with the four 12-prs. moved up to Elandslaagte, where lay the division of General Lyttleton, who was soon afterwards relieved by General Clery ; and on the 19th Captain Jones followed with the 4·7-in. guns, pitching his camp on the 20th half way between Elandslaagte and Sunday's River, below the foot-hills of the Biggarsberg, where the Boers were in force. Nothing of importance happened there until April 10th, when, at 8 A.M., the enemy suddenly opened fire from guns which they had posted across the river at a distance of between 6000 and 7000 yards, making a general attack at the same time. As the Boers were fortunately using black powder, the position of four of their guns was soon detected ; but before the fire could be silenced, the Brigade lost 2 killed, and 4, including Lieutenant Steel, wounded, and had some gun limbers and wagons smashed up. The guns were got into emplacements covering a front of about a mile and a half. The enemy began to draw off at about 4 P.M. ; and at dark the whole British force was also withdrawn to take up a more sheltered position among the Elandslaagte hills. Thereupon the Boers crossed the river, and mounted guns on the British side of it, opening fire from them on April 11th. The command of Sunday's River had been practically abandoned by the British for the moment ; and the Naval Brigade stationed its two 4·7-in. guns on Battle Ridge, two of the 12-prs. on the right flank a mile away, and the other two 12-prs. so as to cover Elandslaagte station, while General Warren's division took up position under Junono's Kop and at Woodcot Farm. On the 14th a welcome reinforcement arrived in the shape of 25 men of the Natal Naval Volunteers, who returned under Lieutenants James E. Anderton and N. Barrett ; for the amount of sickness in camp was becoming very serious, about one-third of the Brigade being temporarily if not permanently useless. On the 16th Clery's division was ordered back to the neighbourhood of Modder Spruit.

On April 20th General Warren was relieved in command of the division by General Hildyard, and proceeded to the Cape. On the 21st the Boers again attacked in force. They had but two guns. With them they quickly picked up the range of the British at 4000 yards ; but their weapons were soon disabled. Lieutenant James, who had been down with enteric since the 18th, was sent with Staff-Surgeon Lilly to the base hospital on the 27th. During all that time there was continual sniping and desultory firing ; and the inactivity and sickness had a very depressing effect, though the seamen, perhaps, stood it better than the rest of the army. On May 8th, at daylight, a small party of Boers attacked the station guard, but was driven off.

Not until May 11th was a move begun with the object of outflanking the enemy in the Biggarsberg. Sunday's River was again crossed; and Hildyard gradually occupied points so as to protect the flank of Sir Redvers Buller's army while it moved round by way of Helpmakaar and Dundee. Lieutenant Halsey, with two 12-prs., crossed on the 13th, Lieutenant Steel with the two others, following at night, and all the guns occupying positions on hills on the other side. By the 16th the entire force had passed the river, the two 4·7-in. guns and a few colonial troops only excepted; and all the country as far as Waschbank was in British hands. On the 17th, the 4·7's traversed the drift, and moved through Wessel's Nek to Waschbank, where the 12-prs. were found. Early on the 18th, the Brigade started with the division, and moved through Glencoe Pass to Glencoe, and thence to Hatting Spruit, where it arrived at midnight, after a magnificent march. It proceeded next for Dannhauser, but was stopped when half way by orders from General Buller, and sent back to Glencoe. On the 23rd, it advanced again to Dannhauser; on the 26th to Ingagane; on the 27th to Newcastle; on the 28th across the Buffalo at Wool's Drift; and on the 29th to a bivouac about three or four miles beyond Utrecht. On the 31st the guns were placed in position before that place, which, however, surrendered in the course of the morning, whereupon the Brigade returned to the bivouac. On June 1st the whole force moved back to the Buffalo, which it crossed on the 2nd. On the 3rd, it reached De Wet's Farm.

On June 6th, at 7 A.M. Captain Jones, in company with General Talbot Coke and half his brigade, a battery of artillery, and the South African Light Horse, quitted the bivouac at De Wet's in order to make a reconnaissance with a view to finding positions for the naval guns on Van Wyk, a high hill facing Botha's Pass, and about 6000 yards from it. On arriving near the hill a considerable rifle fire greeted the column from the enemy on the neighbouring heights; and it became clear that Van Wyk ought to be occupied and held at once, and that the rest of the brigade, and other reinforcements, ought to be brought up. Having selected suitable positions for the guns, Captain Jones started back to find a route by which they might be moved up to the mountain. He fixed upon a very difficult one, and reached camp at about 4 P.M. All that afternoon, there was a brisk fire of both guns and rifles on Van Wyk; and the South African Light Horse had hard work to hold its own until it was reinforced.

Captain Jones was ordered to wait until dark, ere he again proceeded, as the route was much exposed to the Boer fire. At nightfall, Lieutenant Halsey's two 12-prs. were put on a kopje near De Wet's Farm ; and, with the two 4·7's, and the other two 12-prs. under Lieutenant Burne, Jones departed for Van Wyk. It was the weirdest and hardest night trek of the gallant Naval Brigade. The whole country had been set fire to by the Boers, and most of Jones's landmarks were mere blackened masses. Only he, and his aide-de-camp, young Ledgard, had been there before. The latter was sent to guide the 12-prs. which were travelling quicker than the bigger guns ; and Jones himself piloted the 4·7's. The flames roared in the long grass ; the terrified oxen continually broke away from their yokes, and steep hills and deep dongas had to be traversed ; so that it was 4 A.M. on June 7th ere the sheltered drift at the foot of Van Wyk was reached, although the distance covered was only about seven miles. There Captain Jones halted the 4·7's until daylight, but hurried on Burne with the 12-prs. as they were needed by the General at dawn. One of the 12-prs. was consequently able to open on the Boers as soon as the light served. The other was delayed by a broken axle. By using sixty-four oxen to each 4·7, and as many to each ammunition wagon, Jones managed to get his heavy quick-firers into position on Van Wyk in the course of the afternoon. Hildyard characterised the exploit as the record performance of the campaign. The Naval Brigade cordially agreed with the General, until it became necessary to get the guns down again.

By daylight on the 9th the broken carriage of the 12-pr. was repaired [1] ; and all the naval guns were in position for the attack and capture of Botha's Pass on that day. Halsey's 12-prs., with some military guns, were on a nek a mile or two to the right. The action began with a searching fire from all available artillery at the hills of the Drakensberg, above the dongas which led in the direction of the Pass. At 11 A.M., the infantry advanced with three field batteries, General Wynne on the left, General Hamilton on the right, with

---

[1] The other 12-pr. broke its trail on the afternoon of the 8th, when firing at some wandering Boers; but this was also repaired.

cavalry on both flanks, and Coke's brigade holding Van Wyk, and the hills in the rear. The heights were mounted with great rapidity, and with but little opposition, until after the summit had been reached. This, no doubt, was due very largely to the way in which the naval guns had been brought up and handled. The moral effect of the presence of such heavy weapons in totally unexpected places; and the hurling of shell at long range over the heads of the advancing troops, shook the enemy immensely, though, in all probability, not many people were killed. The Boers had had several guns in position on the crest, and had used them; but no sooner did they discover that the British had big guns on Van Wyk than they withdrew their own pieces to safer neighbourhoods. By dusk, the troops were in possession of all the Boer works, and the defenders had gone.

It was a bitterly cold night, and the poor fellows had neither coats nor any other comforts; while the enemy, retiring as usual amid the smoke of their own fires, had burnt all the grass, and so deprived the British cattle of forage. The compensating thought with every one was that at last the Orange Free State had been entered. There was, however, no rest for the Naval Brigade, which, at 8 P.M., was ordered to get its guns down again. There was a dense fog, a fog so impenetrable that a regiment which had been sent to assist in the operation lost itself in the mountains, and did not join company with the bluejackets until seven o'clock on the following morning, when it found them at the bottom. Jones put his entire force on to the drag ropes, and eased down the guns and wagons one at a time, until the passage of the heavy masses wore away the ground, and made it practicable for the bullocks. The men, who had to make eleven journeys up and down, worked magnificently, and without a grumble; and when, at 4 A.M., they had got everything down to the drift to which they had been ordered, they simply dropped where they stood, and slept like the dead till daylight. Then they trekked up over Botha's Pass with General Coke's brigade, and bivouacked that night in the Orange Free State.

On the 11th they moved to Grandsvlei, the guns clearing the hills in front of the troops; and, after an early advance on the 12th, they got into action at about 12.30 P.M. on the hills facing Alleman's Nek, where the enemy, strongly posted, was already shelling the British. The naval guns, speaking generally, undertook the protection of the right attack, where there was very hard fighting, and where most rocky and precipitous hills had to be climbed. As usual, the bluejackets poured in shells just ahead of the advance. The Boers had in action some Maxim guns, which, however, did little damage; and the enemy's gun-fire was overpowered, and the guns themselves were soon withdrawn. By dusk, the Pass and hills were clear, and the Boers in full retreat. In the early hours of the 13th, the Naval Brigade moved on, and took up a position on the Nek. At noon it moved further, and posted its guns at a place whence they were able to shell Zandspruit station, and some retreating burghers. In the evening, bivouacking five miles from Volksrust, the force learnt that Laing's Nek and Majuba had been evacuated, and that General Clery was in possession of them. Thus the great turning movement, begun on May 11th, had attained its object, and, at last, the British had a firm foothold in the Transvaal. On the 14th the Naval Brigade encamped at Volksrust, after a month's most arduous work, and frequent fighting. The people, who had suffered so much from enteric while idle near Elandslaagte, were very well in spite of their hardships.

Captain Jones and his men started again with Hildyard's division on June 16th; but, after Wakkerstroom and Zandspruit had been occupied, a telegram from the Rear-Admiral ordered the *Forte's* contingent back to that ship, which was required for service on the West Coast of Africa. Lieutenant Burne, with his two 12-prs. were therefore left at Zandspruit; and the two 4·7's were turned over to the Army. On June 24th Captain Jones transferred command of the rest of the Brigade to Lieutenant Halsey, who was at Volksrust, and then left for Durban with his own people, and with the detachment of Natal Naval Volunteers.[1]

It may be mentioned here that the Boers seldom or never moved their guns over places half so difficult as were traversed by those of the Naval Brigade. The hostile guns reached their positions from the reverse sides of the hills, where the gradients were often relatively easy. The Naval guns frequently reached places which, in all probability, the Boers would never have attempted to get their guns to by the same route. On the other hand, the Navy would never have experienced the least difficulty in taking its 4·7-in. weapons over any road which was used for the Boer artillery.

---

[1] The above is compiled from notes by Capt. Jones, kindly supplied specially for this work; from the same gallant officer's account in *Jeans*; and from the desps. in *Gazette* of Mar. 12, 1901.

Curious to relate, the bluejackets did not suffer—to the extent of having to fall out—owing to sore feet. As for offences, they were practically unknown. There were two or three cases of leaving camp during the idle time in the earlier days. The culprits were punished by being sent back to their ships; and they regarded that as the severest retribution that could be inflicted on them. Never was there any sign of flinching under fire, although, on three or four occasions, the Brigade was exposed to very heavy shelling. The force behaved magnificently in every way.

After the withdrawal to its ships of the main portion of the Brigade in June there remained on shore on the Natal side one detachment under Lieutenant Charles Richard Newdigate Burne, and another under Lieutenant Arthur Halsey.

Burne's detachment, which came originally from the *Tartar*, was turned over, while it was still serving in Natal, to the *Monarch*, guardship at the Cape. With two 12-prs. it took part in the march to, and occupation of Wakkerstroom, and in the defence of Zand-spruit, and a spirited little action four miles to the north of it. On July 24th, when Burne was disabled by jaundice and Lieutenant Francis Alexander Clutterbuck[1] was in temporary command, the battery was concerned in the attack on Gras Kop. Burne rejoined on July 27th and thereafter remained at Gras Kop, employing his guns for the defence of the position. The guns also covered the right flank of the two British attacks on Comersfoort on July 30th and August 7th, the latter of which was successful. He had with him Midshipman William Rimington Ledgard, of the *Philomel*, whom he detached with one gun, first to Oppermann's Kraal, and subsequently to Paarde Kop. This detachment was withdrawn in October.[2]

Burne was junior to Lieutenant Arthur Halsey, who, though he had only his own men from the *Philomel* under his immediate orders, commanded in effect both detachments. With his two 12-prs. he accompanied a flying column from Zandspruit towards Amersfoort, and was most useful in covering the subsequent retire-ment from before that place. On July 10th he moved by train to Standerton, where his guns were horsed from a field battery, and were thus given a valuable additional mobility. More than once they were engaged in slight skirmishes. On July 24th he proceeded

---

[1] From Lieut. Halsey's battery.
[2] Burne's undated report in *Gazette* of Mar. 12, 1901.

to Greylingstad, and thence, after about a month, returned to Standerton, where he himself remained until he and his men were recalled to their ship. On September 30th, however, he detached one gun under Lieutenant Clutterbuck to Heidelberg to assist in holding that town.[1]

In the third week of October, 1900, the last remnants of Captain Jones's Brigade returned to their ordinary duty. In his final report Lieutenant Halsey, while recommending the services of a number of men, mentions the case of A. Forcey, Armourer's-Mate, who, though wounded in the affair at Sunday's River, assisted a mortally wounded bluejacket to the hospital tent, and then returned to the guns until he was ordered off to have his own wound dressed.

In January, 1901, when Boer raiding parties were still active in the western parts of Cape Colony, the cruiser *Sibylle*, Captain Hugh Pigot Williams, landed bluejackets and guns in Lambert Bay, as a precautionary measure. There was, however, no fighting at that spot. Unfortunately, the cruiser was wrecked there on the 16th of the month. Various other ships, which never landed officers or men, but which did useful work on the coast, will be found mentioned below.

So ended the active intervention of the Royal Navy in the war with the Boer Republics. Many of its guns, however, in the hands of the army, did good service long afterwards against the enemy. The only gun lost by the Navy was a 7-pr., which was in an armoured train and was worked very early in the campaign in Natal by men from the *Tartar*. The train was derailed by the Boers near Frere on November 15th and captured after a plucky defence had been made. In the circumstances the capture was inevitable. Well, therefore, did the Naval Brigades carry out the spirit of Rear-Admiral Harris's injunction when, on October 20th, 1899, he despatched the first of them to the front. "Take care," he said, "of the guns. Knowing the officers and men who have charge of them, I feel sure that neither bluejackets nor Marines will come back without them."

Numerous naval officers were employed during the war, and especially during the earlier part of it, in connection with the transport arrangements. Among those who were so employed were :—

In South Africa, Captains Sir Edward Chichester, Bart., Edmund Barker Van Koughnet (retd.), and Frederick St. Leger Luscombe; Commander Thomas Hadley

---

[1] Halsey to Harris, Oct. 17, 1900.

(retd.); Lieutenants Stewart Ayscough Perry-Ayscough, and Arthur Lingham (retd.);
and Paymaster William Marcus Charles Beresford Whyte; at Liverpool, Captains Charles
Henry Coke, and Francis John Jeffery Eliott (retd.); Commanders Egerton Bagot Byrd
Levett Scrivener (retd.), and William Maitland-Dougall (retd.); and Fleet-Paymaster
William Basset Autridge; at Southampton, Captain William Graham White; Com-
manders William Job Woodman Barnard (retd.), Duncan Macpherson (retd.), Reginald
York Heriz (retd.), and Arthur Cleveland Heathcote (retd.); Lieutenant Charles William
Pleydell Bouverie (retd.); and Fleet-Paymaster Cecil Plomer Walker; in the Thames'
District, Captain Edward Eden Bradford; Commanders John Teesdale Hardinge (retd.),
Charles William Poynder Allen (retd.), and Herbert Moultrie Heathcote (retd.); and
Paymaster George Whitcroft (retd.); and elsewhere, Commanders (retd.) James Nethery
Hill, Henry Edward Bourchier, Harry Dampier Law, Herbert George Paris, and
John Martin; and Lieutenant (retd.) William Henry Callwell.

Special gratuities and medals for South African service were
subsequently granted to officers, seamen, and Royal Marines who
were borne in the following ships during the period noted against
each, and who were either landed for duty or doing duty on
board :—

CLASS.	H.M.S.	COMMANDER.	PERIOD.
Cruiser III. .	*Barracouta* .	Com. Hugh Cotesworth	24–10–1900—31–12–1900.*
,, III. .	*Barrosa* . .	Com. Wm. Fras. Tunnard	11–10–1899—31–12–1900.*
,, III. .	*Blanche* . .	Com. Murray Thos. Parks	†
,, II. .	*Doris* . .{	R.-Ad. Sir Robert Hastings Harris Capt. Reginald Chas. Prothero	} 11–10–1899—31–12–1900.*
Gunboat I. .	*Dwarf* . .	Lieut. Hastings Frank Shakespear	6–11–1899—19–5–1900.
Cruiser III. .	*Fearless* . .	Com. Hy. Robt. Peel Floyd	5–12–1899—23–8–1900.
,, II. .	*Forte* . .{	a. Capt. Edw. Pitcairn Jones, 20–4–99 b. Capt. Robt. Copland Sparkes, 13–8–00	} 11–10–1899—16–8–1900.
,, III. .	*Magicienne* .	Capt. Wm. Blake Fisher	11–10–1899—6–11–1900.
Gunboat I. .	*Magpie* . .	Lieut. Jno. Knox Laird	12–11–1900—31–12–1900.*
B. ship III. .	*Monarch* .{	a. Capt. Robert Dalrymple Barwick Bruce, 26–1–97 b. Capt. Chas. Hy. Bayly, 1–2–00	} 11–10–1899—31–12–1900.*
Cruiser I. . .	*Niobe* . . .	Capt. Alfred Leigh Winsloe	25–11–1899—23–8–1900.
Gunboat I. .	*Partridge* .{	a. Lieut. Allen Thos. Hunt, 4–5–99 b. Lieut. Eustace La Trobe Leatham, 1–9–00	} 11–10–1899—31–12–1900.*
Cruiser III. .	*Pelorus* . .	Capt. Hy, Chas. Bertram Hulbert, 26–1–99	8–12–1899—26–6–1900.
C. Def. ship .	*Penelope* . .	(Tender to *Monarch*)	(As *Monarch*.)
Cruiser III. .	*Philomel* . .	Capt. Jno. Edw. Bearcroft	11–10–1899—31–12–1900.*
,, I. .	*Powerful* . .	Capt. Hon. Hedworth Lambton	11–10–1899—15–3–1900.
,, III. .	*Racoon* . .	Com. Alf. Ern. Alb. Grant	13–1–1900—15–6–1900.
Gunboat I. .	*Redbreast* . .	Lieut. Marcus Rowley Hill	†
Cruiser III. .	*Sappho* . . .	Capt. Cecil Burney	†
,, II. .	*Sibylle* . . .	Capt. Hugh Pigot Williams	†
,, III. .	*Tartar* . .{	a. Com. Fredk. Robt. Wm. Morgan, 29–6–99 b. Com. Robt. Hy. Travers, 18–8–00	} 11–10–1899—2–10–1900, & †
,, I. .	*Terrible* . .	Capt. Percy Moreton Scott	14–10–1899—27–3–1900.
,, II. .	*Thetis* . .	Capt. Wm. Stokes Rees	5–11–1899—31–12–1900.*
Gunboat I. .	*Thrush* . . .	Lieut. Warren Hastings D'Oyly	11–1–1900—4–9–1900.
,, I. .	*Widgeon* .{	a. Lieut. Anthony Fras. Gurney, 1–3–97 b. Lieut. Wyndham Forbes, 5–9–00	} 11–10–1899—31–12–1900.*

* Signifies that these ships' companies remained serving after the end of the year 1900.

† Signifies that these ships' companies began their service (counting for South African medals and gratuities)
after the end of the year 1900.

At the very height of this exhausting war, the Empire was
called upon to exert itself in another quarter of the world; and, as
in South Africa, so in Eastern Asia, the Navy was largely instrumental in protecting British life, property, and interests, at a
moment when sufficient military force for that purpose was not
upon the spot.

Early in 1900, the so-called "Boxer" movement, which had been slowly gathering head for some time, began to assume formidable proportions in China. According to the mouthpieces of the Chinese government, it was a rebellious upheaval of misguided patriots. Events proved that the insurgents were less rebels than unofficial tools, whom it was intended to employ against the foreign element in China, and then reward or disown, as might be convenient. The Boxer movement was, in fact, a movement secretly subventioned by the reactionary majority among the Chinese princes and mandarins in high office, and directed primarily against the Christian missionaries and their families throughout the country, but also, in a more general way, against all foreign residents, Japanese as well as European.

In May the movement became dangerous. Outrages, and even murders, were committed in various directions; the railways, which were managed and worked by Europeans, were obstructed, and in places torn up; and the legations at Peking were threatened. In consequence of the disturbed situation of affairs a considerable international naval force [1] had by that time been assembled in the mouth of the Peiho. From Peking, from Tientsin, and from Taku the reports became daily more and more alarming. The Commander-in-Chief, Vice-Admiral Sir Edward Hobart Seymour, K.C.B., in the first-class battleship *Centurion*, Captain John Rushworth Jellicoe, was, with part of his squadron, at Wei-hai-Wei, where, on May 29th, he learnt that Fengtai, the station next to Peking on the Tientsin-Peking railway, and five stations on the Peking-Hankau line, had been burnt. On the following day he heard direct from the British Minister at Peking that the position there was "extremely grave, the soldiers mutinous, and people very excited," and that European life and property were in danger.

In the interim H.M. sloop *Algerine*, Commander Robert Hathorn Johnston Stewart, which had reached Taku, at the mouth of the Peiho, on May 30th, had promptly disembarked and sent up to Peking a small detachment of Royal Marines. Others were sent up on the same day from the first-class cruiser *Orlando*, Captain James Henry Thomas Burke, and from various foreign vessels, to assist in guarding the legations; with the result that on May 31st, the total number of legation guards of all nationalities that had

---

[1] H.M.S. *Orlando* and *Algerine* and thirteen vessels of other nationalities had arrived by May 30.

been forwarded to the Chinese capital was 337, of whom 79 [1] were British Marines under Captains Bernard Murton Strouts (commanding the Tientsin winter guard), Lewis Stratford Tollemache Halliday (*Orlando*), and Edmund Wray (Wei-hai-Wei detachment). In addition, 104 British seamen and Marines [2] were at Tientsin.

On May 31st, Vice-Admiral Seymour, in the *Centurion*, with the destroyer *Whiting*, Lieutenant Colin MacKenzie, quitted Wei-hai-Wei for the mouth of the Peiho, leaving behind him Rear-Admiral James Andrew Thomas Bruce, in the *Barfleur*, with instructions to send on the *Endymion*,[3] which was expected on the following day, and the destroyer *Fame*.[4] The *Centurion* arrived off Taku [5] on June 1st, and the Vice-Admiral at once telegraphed to the Minister at Peking that, if necessary, he would land and send up 200 more seamen and Marines. The Minister's reply, received on the 2nd, was to the effect that the guards already despatched had entered without opposition, and that affairs were quieter.

On June 3rd, the Commander-in-Chief landed at Tongku, above Taku, and went by train to Tientsin in order to inspect the arrangements which had been made for the guards there, and to collect information. At Tientsin he learnt that several fresh murders and outrages had been committed in various quarters. He returned to Taku by river, in order to obtain a knowledge of it with a view to future action ; and, on the 4th, he sent a field-gun's crew from the *Centurion* to Tientsin, to take the place of ten men from the *Algerine*, who could not be longer spared from that sloop. On the 5th, moreover, he reinforced the *Algerine*, which lay just below Taku, with 100 men from his flagship, so as to have them ready for landing should their services be required ; and on the same day, in the *Centurion*, he had a conference with the senior officers of the seven other nationalities which were represented in the mouth of the river—French, German, American, Russian, Japanese, Austrian, and Italian. Sir Edward, himself, was the senior of the eight, and Rear-Admiral Courejolles, of the French navy,

---

[1] This number includes, however, three naval ratings, viz., Leading Signalman Harry Swannell, Armourer James Thomas, and Sick-berth Attendant R. Fuller, all of whom proved invaluable in Peking. They belonged to the *Orlando*. With the detachment was a Nordenfelt gun.

[2] Under Lieut. Philip Nithsdale Wright (*Orlando*).

[3] Capt. George Astley Callaghan.   [4] Lieut. Roger John Brownlow Keyes.

[5] The anchorage for large ships is thirteen miles below the town, outside a bar.

second. Great unanimity and good-feeling prevailed at the meeting.
It was also on the 5th, that, having heard that British life and
property were in danger at Peitaiho, a few miles south of Shanhaikuan, he ordered thither the *Humber*,[1] storeship, from Wei-
hai-Wei, directing that she should first take on board 25 additional
Royal Marines. The first-class cruiser *Aurora*,[2] which had arrived
at Wei-hai-Wei on the 4th, was, at the same time, ordered to the
Peiho, where she arrived on the 7th.

On the 6th, the guard at Tientsin was reinforced with 50
seamen [3] from the *Centurion*, and 75 Marines ; and a second conference of senior naval officers being held, it was decided that,
in case of communication with Peking being cut off, the way
should be reopened by force. It was on that day that the Austrian
senior officer, Captain von Montalmar, of the *Zenta*, gracefully
requested that such of his men as had been sent on guard service
to Tientsin might be placed under the orders of the senior British
naval officer there.

Previous to the third conference, which was held on June 9th,
news was received that the Boxers intended to attack the foreign
settlements at Tientsin on June 19th, and that a Chinese general
had defeated a body of rebels twenty miles from that town.
At the conference an alarming telegram arrived from the British
Minister, Sir Claud Macdonald. It declared that, unless those
in Peking were speedily relieved, it would be too late ; and
Vice-Admiral Seymour, having read the news to his colleagues,
chivalrously said that for his part he should start at once with
all his available men, and that he hoped that they would co-
operate.

The danger was no imaginary one, such as had been signalled a few
years earlier from Johannesburg in order to bring about the Jameson
Raid. A handful of Europeans, Americans, and Japanese, including
women and children, as well as men, was in the most imminent
and deadly peril at the hands of a riotous soldiery and a lawless
population, who were capable of nameless iniquities. The various
legations [4] in which these unfortunates found temporary refuge were
large and, to some extent, scattered ; and less than 350 Marines

---

[1] Com. Henry Jocelyn Davison.   [2] Capt. Edward Henry Bayly.
[3] Under Lieut. Wyndham Lerrier Bamber. These bluejackets and Marines subsequently joined the Vice-Admiral's column for Peking, a detachment from the *Aurora*,
with a field-gun, taking their place.   [4] See plan *infra*.

were available for the defence of the long lines of walls and of the crazy buildings. The Vice-Admiral's decision has been adversely criticised by many; but Sir Edward would have shown himself unworthy of his nationality, of his manhood, and of his command, had he not leapt as it were instantly in the direction of those who so sorely needed succour, and called upon his fellows to follow him. It was one of the rare occasions where something very like rashness becomes a duty. There seemed to be no other way of rendering help; and any delay promised to have the most fearful consequences. Moreover, Sir Edward then had every right to suppose that he was proceeding not against regular Chinese troops, but only against proscribed rebels. His colleagues, one and all, adopted his view.

That night, 477 officers and men, British, American, Austrian, and Italian, were sent up by river to Tongku, and, being entrained there, reached Tientsin by 7.30 A.M. Thence they steamed off at 9.30 A.M. in the direction of Peking, and at night they halted near Lofa, where the line had been badly damaged. There two other trains joined, bringing additional British, and detachments of Germans, Japanese, Russians, and French; and making, with the crew of a fourth train that joined on the 11th, the total force as follows :—

NATIONALITY.	OFFS.	MEN.	GUNS.	IN COMMAND.
British	68	{640 seam. {213 Mar.	{1 6-pr. Q. 3 9-pr. M. L. 2 45-in. Maxims 6 45-in. Nordenfelts.	{V.-Ad. Sir E. H. Seymour, K.C.B. {Capt. Jno. R. Jellicoe (*Centurion*).
German	23	427	2 Maxims	Capt. von Usedom (*Hertha*).
Russian	7	305	1 field-gun	Capt. Chagkin (*Rossia*).
French	7	151	1 field-gun	Capt. de Marolles (*d'Entrecasteaux*).
U.S. American . .	6	106	{1 13-pr. } {1 Colt. mach.}	Capt. B. H. McCalla (*Newark*).
Italian	2	38	1 Maxim	Lieut. Sirianni (*Calabria*).
Japanese . .	2	52	..	Capt. Mori.
Austrian . . .	1	24	..	Lieut. Prochaska (*Zenta*).
	116	1956	19	

The expedition was thus entirely and exclusively naval, though with it went, as intelligence officer, Mr. Clive Bigham, honorary attaché to the Peking legation; as engineer, Mr. Archibald Currie, C.B., of the Peking-Tientsin railway; and, as interpreter, Mr. C. W. Campbell, British consul for Wuchow.

The line having been repaired, and Lofa occupied by a small garrison,[1] the expedition moved forward on the 11th. At 6 P.M.,

[1] Under Lieut. Horatio Walcott Colomb.

about three miles short of Langfang station, a body of Boxers, who had previously tried to cut off an advanced working party, attacked train No. 1,[1] but was soon repulsed, with a loss of about 35 killed. Progress, owing to the way in which the line had been damaged, was very slow, and Langfang itself was not reached until the morning of June 12th. It was then perceived that the injuries to the permanent way immediately ahead were quite recent; and as the advance of the trains could not be pressed on at once, owing to the condition of the bridges, etc., Lieutenant Arthur Gordon Smith, of the *Aurora*, was despatched with three officers and 44 men, to endeavour to make his way to Anting, thirteen miles further, to seize and hold the railway station there, and to prevent fresh harm being done on the intervening section of line. Smith occupied Anting on the morning of the 13th; but, after having bloodily repelled four attacks, in the last of which 450 Boxers were engaged, he began to fall short of ammunition, and, wisely retiring, rejoined the main body at 2.30 P.M. That afternoon, Major James Robert Johnstone, R.M.L.I., with 60 men, was also sent forward towards Anting. He advanced a few miles, but, near a spot where a full mile of the metals and sleepers had been removed, he was attacked. He drove back the Boxers, who lost about 25 killed; and then, perceiving that the damage which he had been sent to prevent had been already done, he returned to Langfang on the 14th. So far, apparently, there had been no casualties on the side of the allies.

Soon after 10 A.M. on the 14th, the leading train at Langfang was resolutely assaulted by great numbers of Boxers, who approached it with marvellous determination, and were driven off with some difficulty, after about 100 of them had been killed. In this affair five Italians fell. At 5.30 a messenger on a trolly arrived from Lofa to report that the guard there also was being attacked. Seymour himself steamed thither with train No. 2, but arrived to find that the brunt of the fight was over, and that the enemy, harassed in his retreat by the reinforcements, had left behind him about 100 killed. Two guns were taken from the Boxers. On the other hand, two seamen of the *Endymion* were wounded, one mortally.

On the 15th, the trains still remained perforce at Langfang.

[1] Commanded by Capt. McCalla, U.S.N. It contained British (*Centurion*) and American seamen and marines, and a few Austrians.

From the rear it was reported that the line behind Lofa[1] had been broken up by the enemy; and on the 16th, early in the morning, an effort was made to send a train back to Tientsin; but it returned at 3 P.M., with news that the railway was so badly damaged between Lofa and Yungtsun as to be beyond repair with the resources carried by that detachment. Thereupon, at 4 P.M., Vice-Admiral Seymour, with train No. 1, went back to investigate, leaving Nos. 2[2] and 3[3] at Langfang, and No. 4[3] at Lofa. That night he remained between Lofa and Yungtsun, repairing the line, and so working down to the latter place, where he found the station destroyed, and the line beyond, in the direction of Tientsin, a wreck beyond possibility of restoration by his force.

Sir Edward was then face to face with a serious situation. His communications were completely cut; he was rapidly running short of provisions and ammunition; and he could not hope, it was evident, to get much further than Anting by railway. On the 17th, therefore, he sent orders recalling trains Nos. 2, 3, and 4 from Lofa and Langfang; and in the course of the 18th, all three rejoined the Commander-in-Chief at Yungtsun, where Captain von Usedom, I.G.N., senior officer with Nos. 2 and 4, reported that those trains that day had been attacked at Langfang by fully 5000 infantry and cavalry, including imperial Chinese regulars. The enemy had been twice repulsed, losing over 400 killed; but the allies had had 6 killed and 48 wounded. Seymour had previously contemplated the possible failure of the railway advance on Peking, and had endeavoured to send down to Tientsin directions for a concentration of stores and transport junks at Yungtsun, with a view to the establishment there of a base for an advancement by river to Tungchow, and thence, by marching, to the capital; but the messengers had not succeeded in getting through; and, even if they had reached Tientsin, nothing could have been sent thence, owing to the condition of affairs there, and to the siege and bombardment of the place by the Chinese. Of all this Sir Edward was ignorant. He only knew that at Yungtsun there were. no signs either of supplies or of transports; nor did he manage to procure either from the natives in the neighbourhood.

On June 19th, after a further conference of senior officers had

---

[1] On the 15th, in fact, Capt. Burke, from Tientsin, tried to take supplies by train to Lofa, but found the line torn up.

[2] Manned exclusively from *Endymion* and *Aurora*.

[3] Containing mixed nationalities, but no British or Americans.

been held, Yungtsun was evacuated at 3 P.M., the trains [1] being abandoned, and an effort being made to regain Tientsin by marching down the left bank of the river. The Germans had fortunately captured four junks on the 18th from the Boxers, and in those the wounded were embarked and made as comfortable as the circumstances permitted. Progress was slow, owing to the shallowness of the stream in places; and one of the junks, having grounded, could not be got off until a 6-pr. quick-firing gun belonging to the *Centurion* had been thrown overboard to lighten her. That night the force bivouacked only two and a half miles below its previous halting-place. On the 20th the march was resumed, its speed being necessarily regulated by that of the junks, which were found very difficult to manage. At 9.15 A.M., the Chinese opened fire from a village, but were driven on, after some resistance, to the next one, and then again to the next and the next for several miles. Some of the villages had to be carried with the bayonet. In the afternoon, the enemy for the first time employed a 1-pr. quick-firing gun, which, it is true, did comparatively little damage, but was somewhat demoralising, as, firing smokeless powder, its exact whereabouts could not be detected. At 6 P.M., after having made about eight miles that day, the force bivouacked.

The march was again resumed on June 21st,[2] at 7.30 A.M. About an hour later, after the left flank of the head of the advancing column had been reconnoitred by a body of Chinese cavalry, the enemy began a most harassing series of attacks, bringing up a field-gun and a 1-pr. quick-firer. The former, firing black powder, disclosed its position every time it opened fire, and was kept in check by one of the British 9-prs., and by machine-guns; but the opposition steadily increased, and there was continuous fighting until Peitsang, the chief place between Yungtsun and Tientsin, was reached. There, the Chinese position being very strong, the force was halted at 6 P.M., after having done little more than six miles during the day; and it was decided that, as soon as the men should have rested a little, they must make an effort to get through under cover of the night. In the meantime the field and machine-guns were put on board a junk which had been captured on the 20th.

At 1 A.M. on the 22nd, the night march was begun. It was soon seen that the enemy was not to be caught napping, for his signal

---

[1] They were afterwards burnt by the Boxers.

[2] On that day a rumour of the capture of the Taku Forts reached the force.

fires burst out in more than one place; and, when a mile and a half had been covered, a heavy fire was opened on the advanced guard from a village two hundred yards ahead. The Marines, fixing their bayonets, carried that village; but, owing probably to the fire from the place, the junk carrying the guns sank during the fighting, and had to be abandoned, the Maxims only being saved. At 4 A.M. the head of the force arrived opposite what proved to be the imperial Chinese armoury, near Hsiku, on the right bank. Two unarmed Chinese soldiers came out of a house hard by, and seemed friendly and harmless; but no sooner had they returned to cover than a furious fire was opened from both guns and rifles.

"Rifle fire," says Sir Edward, " was directed to a 47mm. Hotchkiss gun at the north corner of the Armoury, and two 10cm. guns on the river front. Some of the men at the guns were killed and others driven from them. Major Johnstone, R.M.L.I., of the *Centurion*, was then sent higher up the river to cross over unobserved, with a party of 100 Marines and seamen, to rush the position at the north corner. There is a village about 150 yards from this, which enabled the attacking force to come up without being seen until they emerged from it, when they charged with a cheer, joined in by those on the other side of the river; and the Chinese in that part of the Armoury fled precipitately. At the same time, lower down the river, a German detachment crossed over and captured two guns (10cm. Krupp) in their front, and subsequently several others. The two detachments then cleared the whole Armoury grounds."

With the Armoury in its possession the expeditionary force was in comparative safety, for, with the aid of the captured guns, the place was defensible, although, so far as was then known, the people had with them but three days' provisions at half allowances. Indeed, a few hours after the Armoury had been taken, it was attacked by a large and determined force, which poured in a heavy shell fire, and was only repulsed at considerable cost. Among the killed was Commander Buchholtz, of the German navy. At 3 P.M. the main body of the allies crossed the river, the position was fully occupied, and the wounded[1] were brought into it.

That evening Sir Edward ordered Captain Richard Osborn Maclean Doig, R.M. (*Endymion*), and Henry Talbot Rickard Lloyd, R.M. (*Aurora*), to take 100 Marines and endeavour, by making a detour to the northward and along the railway in the dark, to reach the foreign settlement at Tientsin, and to communicate the situation of the force to those who might aid it. Mr. Archibald Currie undertook to guide the detachment, which, however, encountered active

[1] There were then 160 wounded, including 71 British. The force had also lost 35 killed, including 14 British.

resistance as soon as it struck the railway, and, after losing four men, had to return.

Early on the 23rd the Armoury was again attacked[1] unsuccessfully; but, in defending it, several fell, including Captain Herbert William Hope Beyts, R.M.A. (*Centurion*).[2] A subsequent search of the buildings led to the welcome discovery of about fifteen tons of rice, besides medical comforts, and immense supplies of guns, arms, ammunition,[3] and war material of the latest pattern. Thus re-equipped, the expedition might have forced its way down to Tientsin, had it but been able to carry its 230 wounded with it. Unfortunately it had no means of transport for them. All it could do was to send out runners with news of its situation, and bombard such strongholds of the enemy as lay within range. One of the native couriers despatched that day ultimately, and after passing through many dangers, managed to reach Tientsin. On the 24th, the Allies again bombarded the positions of the enemy. Very early on the 25th, it was observed that one of these positions below the Armoury was firing towards Tientsin; and at 6 A.M., to the great joy of the expedition, European troops were reported to be in sight. An hour later, a relief column,[4] under the Russian Colonel Shirinski, reached the place, and took the heaviest part of his immediate anxiety from Sir Edward's shoulders.

The Commander-in-Chief had still, however, to provide for the wounded, who were taken back across the river that afternoon, to conduct the force back to Tientsin, and to destroy the Armoury and its immense and valuable stores. This last work was entrusted to Lieutenant Edward George Lowther-Crofton, and acting Torpedo-Gunner Charles Davidge, both of the *Centurion*, who alone remained behind for the purpose, and, after having set everything aflame, crossed the river, mounted ponies, and so rejoined the main body, which had begun its march down the left bank at 3 A.M. on the

---

[1] According to a Chinese deserter, General Nieh attacked the Armoury with no fewer than twenty-five battalions (Seymour's desp.).

[2] The duties of company officer of the flagship's Marines were thenceforth taken over by Engineer George Herbert Cockey.

[3] Including a million rounds for ·303 in. Maxims, which fitted the British rifles, and much Mauser ammunition. The Russians and Japanese, being out of their own ammunition, were thereupon re-armed with Mausers from the Armoury.

[4] It was accompanied by Com. David Beatty, D.S.O., of the *Barfleur*, although he was suffering from two wounds, received on the 19th, which were only partially healed. He was posted Nov. 9, 1900. With him were 600 British. Shirinski had 1000 Russians, and 900 men of other non-British nationalities.

26th, and which reached Tientsin, without further adventure, six hours later. As the Armoury was believed to contain three million pounds' worth of stores, its destruction was no small consideration, seeing that the regular Chinese troops were known by that time to have sided with the Boxers.

The British officers killed or wounded in the course of this expedition were :—

Killed : Captain Herbert William Hope Beyts, R.M.A. (*Centurion*), June 23rd.
Wounded : Captain John Rushworth Jellicoe (*Centurion*), June 21st.
    ,,   Lieutenant Wyndham Lerrier Bamber (*Centurion*), June 21st.
    ,,   Lieutenant Horatio Walcott Colomb[1] (*Endymion*), June 21st.
    ,,   Sub-Lieutenant Lawrence Walter Braithwaite[2] (*Endymion*), June 22nd.
    ,,   Midshipman Charles Dominick Burke (*Centurion*), June 21st.
    ,,   Midshipman Frank O'Brien Wilson (*Centurion*), June 21st.
    ,,   Clerk Augustus Elliott Tabuteau (*Centurion*), June 21st.

The total losses of the expeditionary force between June 10th and June 26th were 2 officers and 63 men killed, and 20 officers and 210 men wounded, or 295 casualties in all; of whom 30 killed and 97 wounded were British. Among the wounded were Captains von Usedom, I.G.N., and (in three places) B. H. McCalla, U.S.N., both of whom rendered most valuable services.

Sir Edward Seymour,[3] who, on June 27th, wrote separate and graceful letters of thanks to the senior officer of each nationality that had thus so loyally co-operated with him, made special mention, in his despatch of the same day to the Admiralty, of :

Captain John Rushworth Jellicoe[4] (*Centurion*); Commander Charles Delabere Granville[5] (*Centurion*), and William Osbert Boothby[6] (*Endymion*); Lieutenants George Murray Kendall Fair, Horatio Walcott Colomb[7] (*Endymion*), Edward George Lowther-Crofton[8] (*Centurion*), and Arthur Gordon Smith (*Aurora*); Midshipman William Beverley Courselles Jones[9] (*Centurion*); acting Gunner Charles Davidge (*Centurion*); Major James Robert Johnstone,[10] R.M.L.I.; Captain Richard Osborn Maclean Doig, R.M.L.I.; Admiral's Secretary Francis Cooke Alton[11]; Assistant-Paymaster Charles John Ehrhardt Rotter[12] (*Centurion*); Fleet-Surgeon Thomas Martyn Sibbald (*Centurion*); Engineer George Herbert Cockey[8, 9] (*Centurion*); Assistant-Engineer Arthur Ernest Cossey[9] (*Aurora*); and Messrs. Clive Bigham, Archibald Currie, C. E., and C. W. Campbell.[13]

Captain Bowman H. McCalla, U.S.N., reporting to his government, also mentioned with gratitude, and recommended for United

---

[1] Subsequently again wounded at Tientsin Arsenal, June 27. Com., Nov. 9, 1900.
[2] Lieut., Nov. 9, 1900.   [3] G.C.B., Nov. 9, 1900.   [4] C.B., Nov. 9, 1900.
[5] Capt., Nov. 9, 1900.   [6] Noted for promotion.   [7] Com., Nov. 9, 1900.
[8] D.S.O., Nov. 9, 1900.   [9] Noted for promotion.
[10] Brev. Lt.-Col., Nov. 9, 1900.   [11] Fleet-Paym., Nov. 9, 1900.
[12] Paymaster, Nov. 9, 1900.   [13] *Gazette*, Oct. 5, 1900.

States' medals, Vice-Admiral Seymour, Captain Jellicoe, Lieutenant Lowther-Crofton, Major Johnstone, R.M.L.I., Fleet-Surgeon Sibbald, and Surgeons Edward Butler Pickthorn (*Centurion*), and Eric Danvers Macnamara (*Endymion*), besides paying eloquent testimony to the high qualities displayed by Sir Edward Seymour, and expressing his personal sense of pleasure at having been asked to serve

[signature]

CAPT. JOHN RUSHWORTH JELLICOE, C.B., R.N.

under him, and to command officers and men of the nationality of so gallant a Commander-in-Chief.   Of McCalla, Sir Edward said :—

" Had he been thoroughly British, he could not have more kindly and loyally stood by me in every way, and carried out any wish I expressed." . . . "Considering the gallant way in which he exposed himself, I am only equally surprised and thankful that he is still alive."

It is because of Captain McCalla's own approved bravery that the following two paragraphs from his despatch specially deserve to be handed down in the Royal Navy.   Dealing with the events of the 21st, he said :—

"Among the many acts of courage during the day was a deed of conspicuous bravery and readiness of resource which reflects credit upon the whole naval profession, and was done by one British bluejacket from the *Centurion*, Edward Turner, and seaman George, from the *Aurora*.[1]   Shortly after the enemy opened fire from the arsenal grounds, one of the junks in which there were British and American wounded drifted across the river, and grounded against the bank occupied by the Chinese. These two bluejackets, forming a part of the guard of the junk, sprang overboard, and, pushing the junk afloat, towed her out of the line of fire, and anchored her securely to the bank; but, unfortunately, not until three of the wounded had been killed."

And of the events of the 23rd, he said :—

" At early dawn a heavy fire was opened upon the enclosure . . . by a force of Chinese who had entered the grounds during the night.   It was an inspiriting sight to witness the promptness and courage with which the line of British Marines, under Major Johnstone, sprang forward, apparently as one man, and drove the enemy over the western rampart and on to the plain beyond."

All the foreign nationalities co-operated very loyally with the British ; but none, perhaps, showed quite the same fraternal spirit as the Americans, though the Germans were second only to them. The experience was unique.   On a purely military expedition, yet

---

[1] George really belonged to the *Orlando*.   He was given the Conspicuous Gallantry Medal in 1901.   Gold medals from the Life-Saving Assoc. of New York, with personal letters of thanks from the Sec. of the U.S. Navy, were subsequently forwarded to Herbert George, A.B. (*Orlando*), and Edward Turner, L.S. (*Centurion*).

without the support of a single soldier, seamen and marines of eight nationalities, European, American, and Asiatic, served together under a British flag-officer for a fortnight.[1]

Sir Edward Seymour, as has been said already, was absolutely right in starting up country for Peking with such force as he could collect. The necessity was terribly pressing. Yet it must be recollected that, by acting as he did, he temporarily crippled the four British vessels from which he drew his officers and men; and that, therefore, except in the face of the very gravest necessity, he would have been wrong; for, after all, a naval commander's first business is, save on such exceptional occasions, to preserve the fighting efficiency of his ships for utilisation afloat, especially when, as was the case in China, there is a reasonable possibility that the ships may be called upon, at a moment's notice, to proceed to sea, or even to go into action in defence of the interests of their countrymen.

[signature]

REAR-ADMIRAL SIR JAMES ANDREW THOMAS BRUCE, K.C.B.
(*Signature as Captain.*)

During Vice-Admiral Seymour's absence, indeed, some of the vessels at the mouth of the Peiho were obliged by circumstances to go into action. According to a British naval officer's letter in the *North China News*, they had not enough men in them to work them properly; and, in consequence, a catastrophe might have easily resulted. At the same time, as will be seen, the resources of the Navy were severely taxed in other ways.

On June 11th, on the day, that is, following Seymour's departure to attempt the relief of the legations, the first-class battleship *Barfleur*, Captain George John Scott Warrender, bearing the flag of Rear-Admiral James Andrew Thomas Bruce, second in command

---

[1] Authorities: Desps. of Seymour, and each of the senior officers: corr. in *Globe* (Aug. 17, 27, 28), *Times, Express, Nav. and Mil. Record*; notes and officers' letters in *Globe and Laurel*; Mids. George Gipps, 'The Fighting in North China'; numerous private letters.

on the station, arrived at the mouth of the Peiho from Wei-hai-Wei, and found there a considerable fleet of British, American, German, Austrian, French, Russian, Japanese, and Italian ships of war. On the night of the 14th, news came down the river to the effect that all the rolling stock on the Peking line had been ordered to be sent up for the purpose of bringing down a Chinese army to Tongku, where, of course, it would sever the communications of the allies with Tientsin. The senior naval officer in the Peiho, the Russian Vice-Admiral Hiltebrandt, at once summoned a council of his colleagues, and, as a result, directions were sent to the captains of ships above the bar to prevent any railway plant from being removed from Tongku, to stop any Chinese army from reaching that place, and, if necessary, to use force and to destroy the Taku Forts. On the following day came the further report that the Chinese were laying down electric mines to block the mouth of the river. On the morning of the 16th, after another council had been held on board the Russian flagship *Rossia*, notice was sent to the Viceroy of Chili at Tientsin, and to the commandant of the Forts, that, looking to the position of the allied forces in the Peiho, and to the situation of the expedition under Seymour, it was purposed, with or without permission, to occupy the Taku Forts at 2 A.M. on the 17th; and orders to that effect were given to the allied commanders above the bar, the senior of whom was Captain Dobrovolski, of the Russian gunboat *Bobr*. The vessels then above the bar were as follows :—

NATIONALITY.	SHIP.	DISPL. TONS.	COMMANDER.	GUNS.
British . . .	*Algerine*, slp.	1050	Com. Robert Hathorn Johnston Stewart	6–25 pr. Q.; 4–3 pr. Q.; 3 Maxims.
„ . . .	*Fame*, destr.	272	Lieut. Roger John Brownlow Keyes	1–12 pr. Q.; 5–6 pr. Q.
„ . . .	*Whiting*, destr.	300	Lieut. Colin MacKenzie	1–12 pr. Q.; 5–6 pr. Q.
Russian . .	*Bobr*, g.b.	950	Capt. Dobrovolski	1–9 in. B.; 1–6 in. B.; 6–9 pr. B.; 5–1 pr. Q.
„ . . .	*Giliak*, g.b.	963	—	(?)
„ . . .	*Korietz*, cruis.	1213	—	2–8 in. B.; 1–6 in. B.; 2–6 pr. Q.; 2–3·9 in.; 4–1 pr.
	Several torpedo-boats.			
German . .	*Iltis*, g.b.	895	Com. Lans	4–3·9 in. Q.; 4–6 pr. Q.; 2 mach.
French . . .	*Lion*, g.b.	473	—	2–5·5 in. B.; 2–3·9 in. B.
Japanese . .	*Atago*, g.b.	614	—	1 8·2 in. B.; 1–4·7 in. B.; 2–1 in. mach.
United States .	*Monocacy*, padd.	1370	Com. F. M. Wise	4–8 in. M.; 2–60 pr. B.; 1–3 pr. how.; 1–12 pr. s. b. how.; 2–3 pr. Q.; 6–1 pr. Q.; 1 mach.

The situation of the forts will be seen from the accompanying plan. They were armed partly with modern 4·7-inch (12 cm.) Krupps and 5-inch Vavaseurs mounted *en barbette* behind ⁻shields, but also with rifled and smooth-bored muzzle-loaders, and they had large garrisons.

It was arranged that the *Monocacy* and *Atago* should remain on guard just below Tongku, and that the fighting, if it became neces-sary, should be done by the other vessels, which, accordingly, were ordered to take up certain assigned stations by 4 A.M. on the 17th. They were reinforced with extra men from the ships lower down, so as to be able to land detachments; and other reinforcements were sent to Tongku. The *Algerine* took up her appointed station soon

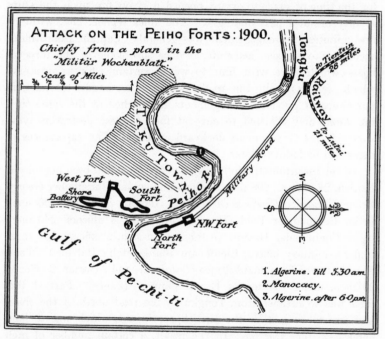

after 8 P.M. on the 16th, lying about a mile above the North-West Fort, and clearing for action, with the *Korietz*, *Giliak*, and *Bobr*, in order above her. Two miles still further up were the *Lion*, and, immediately above her, the *Iltis;* but, soon after the action began, the *Iltis* moved down next to the *Algerine*, and the *Lion* put herself between the *Iltis* and the *Korietz;* so that, at about 2 A.M., and thenceforward till about 4.30 A.M., the order of the line, from below upwards, was *Algerine*, *Iltis*, *Lion*, *Korietz*, *Giliak*, *Bobr*, and, still further up, *Atago* and *Monocacy*. At 4.30 A.M. the *Iltis* dropped down past the *Algerine* to within a third of a mile of the North-

West Fort, there remaining until about 5.30 A.M., when she and the *Algerine*, followed by most of the other vessels, moved to a fresh position nearly due east of the South Fort, and about five hundred yards from it.   It does not appear that the *Giliak* shifted her billet until later, when the firing was practically over. She had a compartment full of water.   One correspondent [1] stated that the *Monocacy*, lying off Tongku, had an 8-inch shell right through her.

After receiving the ultimatum, the Chinese, instead of waiting for the time of grace to expire, opened a heavy fire upon the ships at fifty minutes past midnight.   The allies replied, and, within a few minutes, the engagement was general.   Captain Dobrovolski, according to Russian accounts, at once sent some of the torpedo-boats which were with him to watch certain Chinese cruisers,[2] which were lying in the roads below.   Commander Stewart, in pursuance of previous arrangements, despatched at the same time the *Fame* and *Whiting* to cut out four Chinese destroyers lying alongside the Government dockyard at Taku.   The experiences of these will be followed later.

In the meantime the following landing force had been organised : British, 23 officers, 298 men, under Commander Christopher George Francis Maurice Cradock (*Alacrity*) ; German, 3 officers, 130 men, under Commander Pohl (*Hansa*) ; Japanese, 4 officers, 240 men, under Commander Hattori (*Kasagi*) ; Russian, 2 officers, 157 men, under a military officer, Lieutenant Stankevitch ; Italian, 1 officer, 24 men, under Lieutenant Tanca (*Calabria*); and Austrian, 2 officers, 20 men, under Lieutenant Ernst Stenner [3] (*Zenta*).   Part of this force was to advance from Tongku by the road north of the river, and was to be met by the British contingent, which was to land abreast of the *Algerine*.   In the result, a certain number of men were also thrown ashore by the other vessels engaged, so as to reinforce the Tongku column.   The German and Japanese commanders courteously offered the direction of the operations to

---

[1] *Nav. and Mil. Rec.*, Aug. 9, 1900.   Lieut. W. C. Davidson, U.S.N., says it was a 6-in. projectile.   *Procs. of U.S. Nav. Inst.*, Dec. 1900.

[2] These were ultimately boarded by boats from the allied fleet, and, without resistance being offered, the breech-pieces were removed from the guns, and the charges from the torpedoes.   *Italia Mil. e Marina.*

[3] The *Gazette* of Oct. 5, 1900, owing to slovenly editing, printed this officer's name and ship as " Lieutenant Ernt. Tatniams Quenta."   I am indebted for the real name to Capt. Leopold Ritter von Jedina, of the Imp. Aust.-Hung. Navy.

Commander Cradock ; but it would appear that there was some independent action, seeing that Stankevitch reports that, at a given period, he " invited " Commander Pohl to begin the attack, and that Pohl refused, on the ground that the fire from the forts had not then been sufficiently weakened.

The landing-party from the *Algerine,* including the Italians, who had made rendezvous on board her, was set ashore within about an hour of the opening of the engagement. Meantime, the bombardment was hot. The *Algerine* first directed all those of her 4-inch guns that would bear on the North-West Fort; but, finding that much ammunition was being expended, and that the shooting in the moonlight was not very accurate, Stewart presently continued firing only one 4-inch. The *Iltis,* followed by the *Lion,* dropped down and took up position soon after 1.30 A.M. ; and, at about the same time, the tug *Fa Wan,* which till then had been alongside the *Algerine,* shoved off and went up to Tientsin, with orders and stores. At 2.45 came news from Commander Cradock that he was about to assault the North-West Fort. The ships, therefore, ceased firing at it, continuing to bombard the North and South Forts only ; but, at 3.45, came another message, to the effect that the North-West Fort was practically untouched, and far too strong to be yet attempted ; and, as it was then daylight, it was found possible to do it serious damage within the following hour, the *Algerine* again using all her starboard 4-inch guns against it, and the *Iltis* making excellent practice. By 4.30 A.M. the work had almost ceased to reply.

At 5.30, Stewart, having hoisted a prearranged signal, weighed, and, followed by all the vessels except the *Giliak,* which could not move, passed down the river, engaging the North Fort, which made no return, and the South Fort, which returned a very heavy fire. It was then that most of the casualties occurred. The *Algerine* suffered no worse damage than a steam-cutter hulled at the davits, a few cowls shot through, and some standing and running rigging cut away, and she had only half a dozen people hurt. The *Giliak*[1] had already had 10 killed, and 2 officers and 47 men wounded, one or two shots below the waterline, a small magazine exploded by a shell, and a steam-pipe severed ; but, not moving, suffered no further. The *Iltis* lost her gunner and 7 men killed, and her commander and about 30 men wounded ; the *Lion* had 1 man

---

[1] She had attracted attention to her position by unwisely using her searchlight.

mortally wounded; the *Korietz* had 2 officers and several men killed and wounded; and only the *Bobr* seems to have escaped scot free. The *Iltis* was fought in a most magnificent manner, and excited the admiration of the whole squadron. As for the unfortunate *Giliak*, she had much difficulty in extinguishing a fire which broke out in her, as she had no steam available, and had to work her pumps by hand. Stewart gave warm praise for their behaviour to Lieutenants Arthur Sydney Chambers, George Duncan, and Sydney Robinson.

Having reached the mouth of the river, abreast of the South Fort, at about 6.20 A.M., the ships continued firing, blowing up a magazine at 6.55, and so silencing the work. At 7.10 A.M. the engagement ceased.

As regards the proceedings of the *Fame* and *Whiting*, Lieutenant Keyes says :—

"In compliance with your order of 16th inst., to take H.M.S. *Whiting* under my command and capture the four Imperial Chinese destroyers lying between Taku and Tongku, so as to ensure the safe passage of the *Iltis*, German, and *Lion*, French, gun-vessels at 3 A.M., I beg to report that, having visited the place during the evening with Lieutenant and Commander MacKenzie, of H.M.S. *Whiting*, and found them moored head and stern in single line off the south steep-to bank, with wire hawsers laid out from each bow and quarter; I arranged as follows: That the *Fame* should weigh at 2 A.M., followed by the *Whiting* at a distance of about one and a half cables (the distance between the fourth and second destroyers). Each vessel to tow a whaler, with a boarding party of twelve men, under Lieutenants [Wilfred] Tomkinson [1] (*Fame*), and [John Alfred] Moreton (*Whiting*). That we should pass well out in the stream, to give them the idea we were proceeding up the river, and, when the *Fame's* bow was abreast of No. 4, and the *Whiting's* abreast of No. 2, sheer in and board them over the bow, each whaler boarding the next astern, and each boarding party being covered by a rifle party and the guns.

"When the forts commenced the heavy firing about 0.45, both ships being in a very exposed position, and the necessity of clearing immediate, I directed the *Whiting* to weigh and proceed as arranged. This was effected most successfully. After a slight resistance, and the exchange of a few shots, the crews were driven overboard or below hatches. There were a few killed and wounded; our casualties nil. No damage was done to the prizes. The *Fame's* bow was slightly bent when we closed to board, and the *Whiting* was struck by a projectile of about 4 or 5 in.[2] abreast a coal bunker. This was evidently fired from a mud battery on the bend between Taku and Tongku, which fired in all about thirty shots at us, none of the others striking, though several came very close. I could not reply for fear of striking the Russian gun-vessels lying behind it. There was a good deal of sniping from the dockyard, so I directed all cables of the prizes to be slipped, and proceeded to tow them up

---

[1] The *Gazette* carelessly printed this officer's name as Tomlinson.

[2] MacKenzie says, "one 5-in. shot in the hull just forward of engine-room bulkhead, starboard side, passing through bunker (full), carrying away wing door of boiler, and damaging several tubes and putting No. 4 boiler out of action." But the destroyer was still able to steam.

to Tongku. At this point Mr. Macrae, the Manager of the Tug and Lighter Company, came to my help. I cannot speak too highly of this gentleman's assistance. He took one destroyer off my hands, as did another of the same company's tugs for the *Whiting*. In the former case Mr. Macrae had to use force, with the assistance of one of my men on the Chinese crew, most of whom tried to jump overboard when we came under the fire of the mud battery. In the latter case Mr. Mayne,[1] Midshipman, of the *Barfleur*, was in command of a guard of seamen with a Maxim, and also did very well. So soon as the destroyers were captured the *Iltis* and *Lion* passed. The torpedoes were in the tubes, but war heads were not fitted. Ammunition for Q.F. guns in two destroyers was on deck.

"By 5 A.M. they were securely berthed at Tongku. It was not a good position, owing to shell passing over the bombarding ships, but the best I could find under the circumstances. Fortunately no damage was done.

"Mr. Mayne, Midshipman, in charge of a tug[2] with despatches and stores for Tientsin, informed me that his Chinese crew would not pass a fort 12 miles up the river at Lun Chang;[3] so I proceeded, in company with the *Whiting*, to force a passage if necessary. Finding no opposition, I returned, as directed by you, to Taku."

Two of the captured destroyers were the *Hai Lung* and *Hai Cheng*.

Keyes mentioned with approval the conduct of Lieutenant Wilfred Tomkinson, Gunner George Mascull,[4] and Engineer George Gerald Knight; and MacKenzie reported highly of the behaviour of Lieutenant John Alfred Moreton. Of the prizes, one was given to the Germans, one to the Russians, and one to the French. The one kept by the British was renamed *Taku*, and commissioned by Lieutenant Tomkinson. The *Whiting* was sent to Nagasaki for repairs, and was back in the Peiho on July 9th.

Commander Cradock, who was in charge of the international landing party at the capture of the forts, reported:—

"It was arranged that, after an effective bombardment, the north-west fort should be the first to be attacked; then the north fort (on the same side of the river), and finally the long string of south forts on the other bank. Before the advance it was agreed that half the British should have[5] the firing line, with the Italians on the left, and the Germans and Japanese; and that the other half of the British, with the Russians and Austrians, should form the supports and reserves. . . . At 2.45 A.M., when some 2500 yards from the north face of the fort, the advance commenced, deploying from the right, which flank rested on the river bank. The whole ground 1000 yards this side of the fort was hard mud, but, unfortunately, quite flat, without a vestige of cover. The objective of the British was to force or scale the west gate, and, this done, to endeavour to gain an entrance into the inner fort by means of another gate, the whereabouts of which was not quite clear. To do this they were to advance

---

[1] Ronald Clinton Mayne was noted for promotion.

[2] The *Fa Wan*, which had left the *Algerine* at 1.30 A.M.

[3] MacKenzie calls it Sheng Shing.

[4] This officer was awarded the Conspicuous Service Cross, soon after the institution of that decoration.

[5] The *Gazette* misprints part of this sentence, and my version is conjectural.

in skirmishing order to within 50 yards of the moat on the north face; then close on the right, swing round the corner of the fort along the military road, the right flank leading in loose formation, and seeking what cover the right bank might afford, and charge on the west entrance.

"The advance continued until within 1000 yards of the fort, when I could plainly see that, owing to the darkness, it had suffered little from gun fire, and was practically intact, no guns being silenced. I therefore halted the men, and returned myself to consult the other commanding officers as to continuing. It was at once unanimously agreed that, to take it in its present condition, all its guns being still in action, would entail a serious and unnecessary loss of life; and it was therefore decided to retire slightly for the cover afforded by a bend in the river, and wait until the fort was further reduced.

"It was not until 4.30 A.M., half an hour after dawn, that the heavy ordnance was finally silenced by the ships, although two field guns, which had been previously silenced, now began to play on the attacking party.

"The second formation of attack was different from the first. On the previous retirement the *Alacrity's* and *Endymion's* men had been ordered to remain 300 yards to the front, as an observation party. They were under cover of a small rising, and, shortly before the advance, were joined by the Russians on the left.

"In the firing line were the *Alacrity's* and *Endymion's* on the right, Russians on the left, and Italians, in loose formation, immediately on the right flank, the military road slightly interfering with their getting into line. The *Barfleur's* closed in the rear of the fighting line, reinforcing while the charge was sounded. The foreign forces and the remainder of the British were in close support, the Russians inclining to the left to make their attack on the right rear.

"When the charge was sounded the Japanese doubled up from the supports in column of route along the road, and raced with the British along the intervening 300 yards to the west gate, the two nations scaling the parapet together.

"Part of the British force also gained an entrance through two gun ports, and over a low part of the ramparts to the right of the gates, which were utilised[1] by my officers through the instrumentality of Lieut. Duncan, of H.M.S. *Algerine*, who, from previous observation on shore, had found these weak spots.

"The inner and second gate was forced by rifle fire from the British and Japanese; and, this done, the fort was practically ours. . . . The remaining forts were taken with slight resistance; and after the north fort was captured the British and Germans were each able to turn and work one of the fort's guns on the still active artillery in the south fort across the river."

According to German accounts,[2] although the Russians headed the assault, the muddy nature of the ground enabled the nimbler Japanese to overtake them. The Japanese would then have been first in, had not Commander Hattori been shot down. Owing to this, Commander Pohl was "one of the first" to enter the fort. Dobrovolski says that "he heard afterwards" that the troops who led the attack were Russians and English; and Stankevitch reports that "though the English wavered at first, they finally advanced with the Russians." The Russians also claim[3] that Stankevitch and four of his men were first in, but that, as they

[1] Again the *Gazette* has obvious misprints or omissions, and I have to conjecture.
[2] In *Militär Wochenblatt*.   [3] Dobrovolski.

had no flag, the British flag was the first to be hoisted over the work. Numerous eye-witnesses, however, bear out the substantial truth of Rear-Admiral Bruce's report that—

" The Japanese and British stormed the north-west fort together, and the Japanese commander was, I believe, the first man in, and then assisted Commander Cradock up, when, I much regret to say, the Japanese commander was killed."

The casualties were, happily, not heavy, the British losing only 1 killed and 13 wounded.[1] After the forts had been captured, it was arranged that, so far as possible, one should be occupied by each nation; and, accordingly, the North-West one was occupied by the British, and put into a good defensive state.

Cradock mentioned, as having distinguished themselves, Lieutenants Eric Charrington [2] (*Alacrity*), and Arthur Russell Hulbert [3] (*Endymion*), and Midshipmen Dennis de Courcy Anstruther Herbert [4] (*Orlando*), Lionel Henry Shore [4] (*Barfleur*), and Charles Cabry Dix [4] (*Barfleur*), the last of whom " undoubtedly saved his Lieutenant's life." Surgeon Robley Henry John Browne [5] (*Alacrity*), was praised for his attention to the wounded.

It may be mentioned here that, on June 25th, Captain George John Scott Warrender (*Barfleur*), then in command of the Naval Brigade at Tongku, ordered the destroyer *Fame* to reconnoitre, and if possible destroy all munitions of war in Hsin Cheng fort, up the river. Lieutenant Keyes accordingly embarked Lieutenant George Duncan and twelve men from the *Algerine* at 6 A.M. on the following day, and proceeded. Anchoring the *Fame* off the work, he landed with 32 men, took precautions against surprise, entered the fort without opposition, blew up the magazine, and disabled six 15 cm. (5·9-in.) Krupp breechloaders on recoil mountings, which commanded the river and the Tientsin road. The damage was done by putting a $2\frac{1}{4}$ lb. charge of gun-cotton under the trunnions of each piece, thus shattering and bending the carriage, but not permanently injuring the weapon itself. By the explosion of the magazine, two seamen were unfortunately hurt. Keyes reported that in all probability there were further munitions of war which he had not been able to discover.

---

[1] Some of the wounded, among whom was Asst.-Paym. Herbert James Hargraves, seem to have been hit on board the *Algerine*, seeing that Cradock reported only one killed and six wounded. Compare Bruce of June 17 with Cradock of same date.

[2] D.S.O., Nov. 9, 1900.   [3] Com., Nov. 9, 1900.
[4] Noted for promotion.   [5] Staff Surg., Nov. 9, 1900.

While these operations were in progress, serious events were happening at Tientsin. The course of them is well summarised in a dispatch sent thence on July 8th by Vice-Admiral Seymour.

When the Commander-in-Chief departed on June 10th, to attempt to reach Peking, Captain Edward Henry Bayly (*Aurora*), was left in charge of the British forces at Tientsin. That officer immediately discovered that the Chinese were doing all that lay in their power to prevent trains from being sent forward to Seymour with reinforcements, and to interrupt his communications. Trains were sent through only with difficulty; and on the 14th, the tearing up of sections of the line, and the impossibility of effecting repairs, cut off the expedition from its base. On and after that day, Captain James Henry Thomas Burke (*Orlando*), took command of the Naval Brigade, Captain Bayly remaining Commandant of the settlement. From the 10th to the 16th, Lieutenant Charles Donnison Roper (*Aurora*), with 50 men, was detached from Tientsin to Tongshan to protect British railway servants there. He then withdrew with the Europeans to Peitaho, and there, on the 21st, embarked in the *Humber*, Commander Henry Jocelyn Davison, for Taku.

In the meantime it had become clear that Tientsin was to be attacked. The Chinese in the place shut up their shops and left the European settlements. Very fortunately, 150 British seamen and Marines, under Commander David Beatty, D.S.O. (*Barfleur*), had reached the town on the 11th, and about 1700 Russians, with cavalry and field-guns, on the 13th. On the 15th, some mission-houses in the French settlement and the cathedral in the native city were burnt, and the telegraph wire to Taku was cut. That night a search-light train patrolled the line between Tientsin and Tongku, and 200 Russians occupied the station at Chun Liang Cheng. On the day following the Boxers made the first of their attacks on the settlements and upon the railway station, which was held by the Russians, but were driven off. A repairing train was set to work on the up line. Another train, sent to Tongku, was fired at by the forts near that place, and returned to Tientsin next morning. On the 17th, the repairing train, which had a gun mounted in it, went with a small naval force under Midshipman Henry Crosby Halahan, and defeated about 80 or 90 Chinese troops outside the station. The Russians, assisted by Lieutenant George Bingham Powell (*Aurora*), with a 6-pr., also went out and inflicted losses on the enemy. The Military College, on the river, opposite the British concession, was taken by an allied force under Major Edward Vyvyan Luke, R.M.L.I. (*Barfleur*) :[1] and the buildings and guns found there were destroyed. While these operations were going forward, guns in the native city opened a desultory bombardment of the foreign settlement. It was deemed advisable to attempt to withdraw the Russian force from Chun Liang Cheng station; but a train sent in that direction on the 18th, under Lieutenant Frederick Laurence Field (*Barfleur*), failed to reach the place, owing to the damaged condition of the line, and, after a brisk engagement, returned just in time to help, by a flank attack, in repulsing a Chinese assault upon Tientsin railway station. The Russians there had been hard pressed, but had been succoured by two British companies under Commander Beatty, with a 9-pr. under Lieutenant Philip Nithsdale Wright (*Orlando*).

On June 19th two Chinese field-guns were posted near the railway embankment opposite the British concession, and opened an annoying fire. Commander Beatty, with three companies of seamen, crossed the river, hoping to capture them with a rush; and a body of Russians moved out at the same time to co-operate; but the British were suddenly enfiladed by a large hostile force, which took post behind a mud wall, and poured in so heavy a fire that retreat was necessary. In this affair, 15 of the British were wounded, including Commander Beatty, Lieutenants George Bingham Powell (*Aurora*), and Anselan John Buchanan Stirling (*Barfleur*), and Midshipman Archibald Philip Donaldson (*Barfleur*). The last named was badly hit, and died on July 3rd. The Chinese were, however, obliged by the fire of a 9-pr. on the Bund to remove their two pieces. In directing the fire of this gun from the roof of the consulate, Lieutenant Wright (*Orlando*) was wounded in two places. In the evening, Mr. J. Watts, of the Tientsin Volunteers, undertook, with a guard of three Cossacks, to ride to Taku with dispatches; and, thanks to his pluck, and his great knowledge of the country, he got through in safety. On the two following days, although the bombardment of the Concession continued, only small and unimportant skirmishes took place. On the 22nd, troops were seen afar off advancing from the direction

---

[1] The British contingent lost one killed and four wounded

of Tongku; and on the next day, at about noon, a column of 250 seamen and Royal Marines, 300 Royal Welsh Fusiliers, 40 Royal Engineers, 150 United States' marines, and 23 Italians, reached Tientsin. It had left Tongku three days earlier, under Commander Cradock (*Alacrity*), and had met with but little opposition until near its goal, when it had encountered a heavy fire. An American 3-pr., assisted by a force of about 1200 Russians, which was advancing to Tientsin by another route, checked this, and enabled the detachment to get through. The British lost in the affair 2 killed and 5 wounded. The reinforcing Russians, under Major-General Stessel, camped on the left bank of the river, opposite the settlements.

On the 24th further help arrived in the shape of detachments of the 1st Chinese regiment (from Wei-hai-Wei), and 50 men from the *Terrible*, with one of Scott's 12-prs. The *Terrible* had made the mouth of the Peiho on the 21st, and her services proved to be almost as useful in China [1] as they had previously been in South Africa, for she brought up with her from Hong Kong the Fusiliers and Engineers above mentioned. In the afternoon, the 12-pr., in conjunction with a 6-pr. on the wall, shelled the western arsenal, and set it on fire, causing some explosions.

At the same time, Captain Bayly, of the *Aurora*, made arrangements with the Russian general for the despatch of the force which, as has been seen, relieved Vice-Admiral Seymour at the armoury or arsenal near Hsiku, only five miles distant, whence a native messenger had arrived on the 24th. Of this force, 600 were British. The whole marched soon after midnight, and returned on the 26th. After it had departed, that is to say, on the morning of the 25th, the *Terrible's* 12-pr. was placed on the river bank to shell the gun or guns which, from a position in the native city, had been seriously annoying the settlements. Although the guns could not be seen, their approximate station had been ascertained by carefully watching their flashes at night; and, within a few minutes, they were silenced. This little success allowed the relieving force from Hsiku to return unmolested on the day

---

[1] The *Terrible* disembarked in all 10 officers, 200 men, four 12-pr. 12-cwt. guns on Scott's carriages, and four Maxims, for service in China; and the only British naval guns which reached Peking were hers. Nevertheless, none of her officers was among the recipients of honours for the operations in China.

following.   Up to that date the British casualties at Tientsin
were :—

SHIP.	OFFICERS.		SEAMEN AND MARINES.	
	K.	W.	K.	W.
Barfleur	1[1]	5[2]	1	26
Aurora	..	1	..	1
Endymion . . .	..	..	..	1
Orlando	..	1	4	16
Terrible	..	..	..	..
Alacrity	..	..	..	..

[1] Mids. Donaldson, though he did not actually die till July 3rd.
[2] Including (besides Com. Beatty and Lieut. Stirling) Midshipmen: Valentine Francis Gibbs, George Louis Browne, and Lionel Henry Shore (the last being noted for promotion).

In his despatch dealing with the events of this period, and dated July 8th, Sir Edward Seymour specially noticed the services of Captain Bayly,[1] Commander Beatty,[2] Lieutenants Philip Nithsdale Wright[3] (*Orlando*), Herbert Du Cane Luard[4] (*Barfleur*), and Frederick Laurence Field (*Barfleur*), Major Edward Vyvyan Luke,[5] R.M.L.I. (*Barfleur*), Surgeon John Falconer Hall,[6] M.B. (*Barfleur*), Midshipman George Gipps[7] (*Orlando*), second-class petty officer William J. Christmas[8] (*Barfleur*), Patrick Golden,[8] A.B. (*Barfleur*), and William Parsonage,[8] A.B. (*Aurora*).   Wright was recommended for special immediate promotion ; Christmas, Golden, and Parsonage distinguished themselves by carrying off, under fire, the three officers who were wounded on the 19th.   Golden and Parsonage were themselves wounded in consequence of their gallantry and devotion.

On his return to Tientsin, on June 26th, Seymour found the settlement presenting a very desolate appearance, the railway-station being wrecked, the mud huts or cottages of the labouring— but hostile—Chinese round the settlement burnt, to prevent the enemy from taking cover there ; many of the houses in the settlement closed or unoccupied, the buildings generally more or less injured by shell-fire or by incendiaries, the streets barricaded with bales, and trade entirely suspended.   Most of the women and children had been sent on board ships in the river, but some

[1] C.B., Nov. 9, 1900.
[2] Posted, Nov. 9, 1900.
[3] Com., July 10, 1900.
[4] Com. Nov. 9, 1900.
[5] Brev. Lt.-Col., Nov. 1900.
[6] Staff Surg., Nov. 1900.
[7] Noted for prom.
[8] Conspicuous Gallantry Medal, 1901.

still remained.   Several ladies were doing good work in nursing the wounded.

On the morning of the 27th, the Russian forces began to bombard the large Chinese arsenal two miles E.N.E. of the British concession ; and Seymour, by request, sent out a force of seamen, under Commander Cradock, and of Marines under Major James Robert Johnstone, R.M.L.I., the whole, about 600 strong, being commanded by Captain James Henry Thomas Burke, of the *Orlando*.[1]   This had been asked for as a reserve ; but it was brought into action immediately upon its arrival, and ordered to advance parallel with the left face of the arsenal, the Russians taking the centre and right face.   The British were exposed to a heavy flanking fire ere they could turn and face the arsenal, and then they had to advance under a harassing shrapnel fire ; but, fixing bayonets at a distance of 250 yards, they charged, and quickly drove out the enemy.   The Russians were equally successful on their side.   As the Naval Brigade was no longer required, it returned to Tientsin.[2]   Its casualties were 7 killed, and 21, including 2 officers, wounded.   The arsenal was destroyed.[3]

During all this time, the Legations in Peking were besieged. On the 28th came a message, dated June 24th, from Sir Robert Hart, head of the Chinese Customs, with the anxious words, " Our case is desperate : come at once " ; and on the following day came another, to the same effect ; but nothing could be done, a sufficient relieving force not then being ready to start up country.   Indeed, the Europeans everywhere were still hard pressed.

On July 4th the Chinese opened fire on the settlement from several fresh guns, and, in the afternoon, made an unsuccessful attack on the railway station.   British Marines, under Captain George James Herbert Mullins, R.M., of the *Terrible*, assisted in the defence, as did also a force of seamen under Commander Charles Delabere Granville.   That day two additional 12-prs. were

---

[1] As an example of what may be done with a short-handed ship, it may be mentioned that while the *Orlando*, which had a complement of 486 all told, had no fewer than 362 of these serving ashore and elsewhere, she steamed 900 miles, and brought the Chinese Regiment from Wei-hai-Wei to the Peiho.

[2] The *Endymion's* returned to their ship on July 1.

[3] The Russians ruthlessly destroyed with it a huge quantity of valuable machinery, guns, and scientific instruments.

received from the *Terrible*, and two Krupps (about 9-prs.) from the Taku forts. Up to that time, the Tientsin brigade had had only one 12-pr., two 9-pr. muzzle-loading field guns, and three 6-pr. Hotchkiss guns. An effort was made on the morning of July 6th further to supplement these by cutting out a 1-pr. quick-firer which had been pushed up by the enemy to within short range; but the attempt failed, owing to the gun being on the opposite side of the river, and the nearest bridge being too exposed for men to cross it. At noon, the Allies opened a bombardment of the forts in the native city, and of the western arsenal. The forts were silenced by the 12-prs.; the French guns set fire to the Viceroy's Yamen; and the Japanese guns shelled the arsenal. In the afternoon, Major Bruce, of the 1st Chinese regiment, offered to take out a 9-pr., and silence the 1-pr. quick-firer before mentioned by approaching it along a covered road known to him. Finding this road too narrow for his gun, he unfortunately ventured upon the main road, which was swept by the enemy's fire, and was thus obliged to retreat, with a loss of 2 killed, and 5, including himself, and Midshipman Frank Samuel Drake Esdaile (*Barfleur*), wounded. Young Esdaile died on the fol-lowing day.

The bombardment was renewed on the 7th, it being abso-lutely necessary to do everything possible to keep down the fire of the Chinese guns, which were very troublesome, and very difficult to locate. A reconnaissance by Japanese cavalry to the south-west showed also that the Chinese were endeavouring to work round on that side, in order, probably, to cut the com-munications of the allies by river. A large force was dis-covered near the racecourse, and opened a heavy fire. On the 8th it was decided to make a combined movement with the object of driving off this body; and, accordingly, early on the 9th, the Japanese Brigadier-General Fukushima led out to the southward a number of his own men, with 1000 British (400 naval) under Brigadier-General Dorward, 150 Americans, and 400 Russians.

When well clear of the settlement, the force wheeled to the right, attacked the Chinese near the racecourse, seized some earthworks, and captured four 3-pr. Krupps, and about 50 rifles, and then advanced further in a northerly direction, ultimately entering the western arsenal, which was found to have been evacuated, but which still contained two guns. Beyond the arsenal, and towards the south wall of the city, the troops and seamen were exposed to so heavy a fire that they retired, after burning the arsenal. The British naval loss on this occasion was 1 killed and 3 wounded.

Early on July 11th the Chinese made a more determined attack than ever before upon the railway station, and were not repulsed until they had fought for three hours in the most stubborn manner. The allies lost rather heavily; but the casualties[1] were almost entirely confined to the French and Japanese. Later in the day, opening on the forts in the native city, the *Terrible's* 12-prs., and one of the *Algerine's* 25-pr. (4-in.) quick-firing guns did excellent work, demolishing a pagoda which had been used as a look-out station; but, in spite of repulses and defeats, the number of the enemy seemed to increase. Seymour, writing on July 12th, estimated it at not less than 20,000; while against them were, on the same day, 1420 British, 560 Americans, 400 Germans, 50 Austrians, 2160 French, 40 Italians, 4450 Russians, and 3090 Japanese; total 12,170, a number quite insufficient both to protect the settlement and to take a vigorous offensive. Happily the river remained open, and traffic undisturbed, so that supplies came up freely. In the meantime the Russians were hard at work repairing the railway.

For their services during the period from June 26th to July 11th, Sir Edward Seymour specially mentioned and recommended Lieutenants Thomas Webster Kemp[2] (*Aurora*), John Edmund Drummond (*Terrible*), and Frederick Armand Powlett (*Centurion*), Sub-Lieutenant Edward Coverley Kennedy[3] (*Barfleur*), Signal Boatswain George Ellis (*Centurion*), acting Gunner Joseph Wright (*Terrible*), Midshipman Edward Oliver Brudenel Seymour Osborne[4] (*Centurion*), and Carpenter James Attrill (*Centurion*). Lieutenant Kemp, in addition to other services, had been found particularly useful as interpreter[5] in Russian; Sub-Lieutenant Kennedy had been recommended to the Vice-Admiral by Major Waller, of the

---

[1] The only British naval loss was one Marine killed.

[2] Com., Nov. 9, 1900.

[3] Lieut., Nov. 9, 1900.

[4] Noted for promotion.

[5] There were not, at the time, more than three officers in the service qualified as interpreters in Russian. Kemp was also qualified in Hindustani and Arabic.

United States' marines. The British naval casualties in the same
period were :—

SHIP.	OFFICERS.		SEAMEN AND MARINES.	
	K.	W.	K.	W.
Centurion . . .	..	2	5	12
Barfleur	1	1	1	7
Terrible	..	1	1	10
Aurora	..	..	2	6
Orlando	..	..	1	5
Endymion . . .	..	1	2	4
Alacrity	..	1	..	1
Wei-hai-Wei Detach.⎱ (R.M.) . . . .⎰	..	..	1	2

On the evening of July 11th, the Allies having received reinforcements of American and Japanese troops, the officers and men
of the *Centurion* were sent back to their ship, and Sir Edward
Seymour himself, with his staff, returned to his flagship outside
Taku bar.   The senior British naval officers left ashore were
Captain Bayly, commandant at Tientsin, and Captain Burke, commanding the Naval Brigade.

On July 13th a general attack was made by the allies upon the
Chinese walled city of Tientsin, and its forts. A large force of
Russians, accompanied by some Germans and French, attacked on
the east and north-east ; and the rest of the forces from the settlement marched out by the Taku gate, and began a detour to the
west, in preparation for an assault on the south gate of the city.
At General Dorward's request, Captain Bayly directed all the naval
guns which were in position to bear on the enemy's posts to be
ready to open fire at 4 A.M ; and he arranged to control the
batteries by telephone from the signal tower of Gordon Hall.
Owing to darkness and mist, fire was not actually opened until
4.30, whereupon the Chinese responded by heavily shelling the
settlement.   The British naval guns were admirably handled by
Lieutenants Herbert Du Cane Luard, and John Edmund Drummond.   The fighting lasted continuously until about 1 P.M., after
which the allies contented themselves for the most part with
merely maintaining or improving their positions.   In the night,
most of the defenders abandoned the walled city ; early on the
morning of the 14th, the Japanese blew in the outer southern gate ;
and by 6 A.M. the whole southern part of the place was in the

hands of the allies. Very many junks, and a stern-wheel steamer were captured in the canal to the north ; and, at about noon, the large fort to the north-east was taken by the Japanese, who behaved most bravely throughout. A few hours later, the city was divided into four administrative districts, the north-west portion being assigned to the British.

Captain Burke, who led the Naval Brigade of about 300 blue-jackets and Marines, and marched out at 3.30 A.M. on the 13th, with the mixed force by the Taku gate of the settlement, joined the left attacking column, to support the Japanese in the effort against the south gate of the walled city. He says :—

"After passing the end of a deserted village at 4 A.M. the head of the column turned to the right, in the direction of the western arsenal. The British naval guns on the mud wall now opened fire on the arsenal and city. Soon after the Japanese had reached the plain they deployed, and immediately came in contact with a body of Imperial Chinese troops, whom they soon drove back, with apparently slight loss to themselves. The column then advanced till the bridge leading to the front gate of the western arsenal was reached. This was at about 5 A.M., when a halt was made to permit the Japanese to repair this bridge, which had previously been destroyed by fire on the 9th inst. The Naval Brigade was extended, and ordered to lie down, and maintained this position for some time, when the Chinese small-arm men on the city wall got the range very accurately, and caused many casualties in our ranks, including the deaths of Captain Lloyd, R.M.L.I., H.M.S. *Aurora*, and James Brown, A.B., H.M.S. *Barfleur*. I then moved the Brigade some distance to the right, and it was some little time before the enemy again obtained our range, when their fire was again very destructive.

"At about 7.15 A.M., the Japanese having completed the repair of the bridge, the whole column advanced over it, the Japanese entering the arsenal, and the remainder taking cover under its mud wall. Here we remained without further casualty until noon, when the Japanese had cleared the arsenal and commenced the attack. Shortly after this the American marines joined in the attack, and were reinforced by our ' A ' company of seamen.

"About 1 P.M. our ' B ' company and all our Marines advanced under a heavy fire in support of the Japanese centre, and took cover as supports in a village, and remained there for the rest of the day. At 8 P.M. the remaining two companies of our seamen went out to occupy two large houses on our left, to prevent their occupation by snipers, and, an hour later, were reinforced by 100 French marines. All these men returned to the mud wall shortly after daybreak on the 14th. At 10 P.M. on the 13th our ' A ' company returned from the firing-line, bringing in the American wounded,[1] who were very numerous.

"At 3.45 A.M. on the 14th, the Japanese succeeded in blowing in the outer southern gate of the city, and opened the inner gate and entered, supported by our ' A ' company and Marines. They then occupied this gate. The remaining three companies of our seamen advanced at 5 A.M., entered the city, and cleared the main road and side streets between the south and north gates. Outside the latter were several junks in the canal, which were seized by us."

Captain Burke praised the behaviour of his officers and men ;

[1] Belonging to the 9th regt. U.S. infantry, which lost 23 killed and 32 wounded.

and General Dorward, in a letter to Sir Edward Seymour, declared that the success of the operations was largely due to the manner in which the naval guns were served by Lieutenant John Edmund Drummond. He expressed his appreciation of the gallantry and fine spirit of the seamen and Marines generally, who had been among the first to enter the city, and of the way in which, under a heavy fire, Lieutenant Phillimore and " A " company had suc- coured the hard-pressed United States' 9th regiment.

The naval casualties in these operations were :—

SHIP.	OFFICERS.		SEAMEN AND MARINES.	
	K.	W.	K. OR D. OF WOUNDS.	W.
Barfleur	..	2 [1]	5	15
Aurora	1 [2]	..	..	7
Terrible	..	..	..	9
Orlando	..	..	..	4
Wei-hai-Wei guard, R.M.	..	..	..	1

[1] Major Edward Vyvyan Luke, R.M.L.I., and Lieut. Frederick Laurence Field, R.N. (*Barfleur*).
[2] Capt. Henry Talbot Rickard Lloyd, R.M.L.I.

The Commander-in-Chief specially noticed the behaviour of Lieutenant Valentine Egerton Bagot Phillimore [1] (*Barfleur*), Mid- shipman Basil John Douglas Guy (*Barfleur*), who was subse- quently awarded [2] the Victoria Cross for having coolly attended a wounded man under a very hot fire, and then helped to carry him into shelter, Ernest Whibley,[3] O.S. (*Barfleur*), for helping to carry three men across a fire-swept zone, sick berth steward Thomas Gardner [3] (*Barfleur*), and first-class petty officer James Drew (*Barfleur*). To these names would have been added that of Captain Henry Talbot Rickard Lloyd, R.M.L.I., had he not unfortunately fallen while gallantly doing his duty.

Between July 14th and July 20th the greater part of the Naval Brigade returned to the fleet, Captain Bayly thanking the officers and men very warmly in a letter dated July 20th.

The capture of Tientsin liberated a considerable force of the allies, and, no doubt, taught a valuable lesson to the Chinese. On July 27th, when Lieutenant-General Sir Alfred Gaselee arrived at Tientsin, to take the command of the international forces, there were, consequently, fewer difficulties than there had been in the

[1] D.S.O., Nov. 9, 1900.   [2] Nov. 8, 1900.   [3] Conspic. Gallantry medal.

way of the relief of the legations at Peking, if, perchance, any of the legations still stood. It was known that one at least of the ministers had already met his death, and that some of the legation buildings had been evacuated as untenable; but beyond this, although the most terrible rumours were in circulation, and were very widely believed, in China as well as in Europe and America, there was little certain news of what had occurred.

Gaselee, with 20,100 men of seven nationalities, and 70 guns, moved from Tientsin on August 4th. The British Naval Brigade[1] accompanying him was a comparatively small one, consisting of about 200 bluejackets from the *Centurion, Barfleur, Terrible, Endymion, Aurora, Phœnix,* and *Fame,* with four guns, and about 300 officers and men of the Royal Marine Light Infantry.[2] On the 5th a movement began, having for its object the turning of the Chinese position at Peitsang. This brought on a hot action, which ended in the complete rout of the enemy. On August 6th another battle, with similar results, was fought at Yangtsun; on the 9th there was a cavalry skirmish at Hohsiwu; on the 12th Tungchao was occupied without opposition; and on the 14th, after less fighting than had been expected, Peking was entered; and, to the immense relief of the civilised world, it was discovered that the ministers—with the exception of the murdered German envoy—and most of the members of their staffs, were safe, though on many occasions they had been desperately hard pressed, and, when rescued, were in extreme peril.[3]

The story of the long defence of the legations has been told by Dr. Morrison, correspondent of the *Times,* who was present during the whole of the period. It has been said already that the British guards in Peking, when the siege began, consisted of 79 men,

---

[1] Under Capt. George Astley Callaghan (*Endymion*), Com. Robert Grant Fraser (*Phœnix*), and Lieuts. William Bourchier Sherard Wrey, George Holmes Borrett, Thomas Webster Kemp, Herbert Du Cane Luard, Arthur Russell Hulbert, Roger John Brownlow Keyes, and John Edmund Drummond. The other naval officers were Chaplain the Rev. George Morrow Tichborne, Staff-Surg. John Lloyd Thomas, Surg. John Falconer Hall, Asst.-Paym. Charles John Ehrhardt Rotter, and Mids. Valentine Francis Gibbs, James Andrew Gardiner Troup, Ernest William Leir, Basil Edward Reinold, Godfray Bruce Cargill, Henry John Studholme Brownrigg, and Guy Dalrymple Fanshawe, and actg.-Gunner Joseph Wright.

[2] Under Maj. Edward Vyvyan Luke, Capts. (R.M.) William Albert Harris, George James Herbert Mullins, and John William Dustan, and Lieuts. (R.M.) Charles Lawson Mayhew, Harold Gage Bewes Armstrong, and Charles d'Oyly Harmar.

[3] *Gazette,* Nov. 6th, 1900.

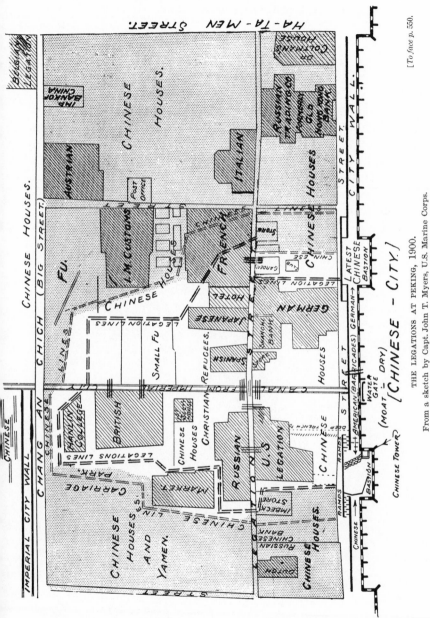

[*To face* p. 550.]

THE LEGATIONS AT PEKING, 1900.

From a sketch by Capt. John T. Myers, U.S. Marine Corps.

(*By permission of the Board of Control, U.S. Naval Institute.*)

namely : a signalman, an armourer, and a sick berth attendant from
the *Orlando*, 27 Marines from the same ship, and 49 Marines
from Wei-hai-Wei, the whole under Captains Bernard Murton
Strouts, Lewis Stratford Tollemache Halliday, and Edmund Wray,
R.M.L.I.   The little force, co-operating with the other legation
guards, and with the volunteers, made a most gallant defence, and,
as Morrison says, " kept up the best traditions of the British Army."
Its casualties were very heavy.   Captain Strouts and 3 men were
killed, or died of their wounds before the arrival of the relief
force, and Captains Halliday [1] and Wray,[2] with 14 men, were
wounded.[3]

As at Graspan in South Africa, so at Peking in China, the Royal
Marines were the chief heroes ; and it is but right, therefore, to
describe with some fulness their share in the gallant defence of the
Legations.   Dr. Morrison's account is generally accessible.   Less
accessible, and certainly quite as interesting, though doubtless of
inferior literary merit, are various accounts which, during 1900 and
1901, were printed in the *Globe and Laurel* (the journal of the
Royal Marines), and which were contributed by officers and men
who had been fighting units of the imprisoned garrison.   They were
written primarily for the information of the authors' comrades, and
not for the public eye ; and for that reason they are doubly valuable.
One of them is by Corporal D. J. Gowney,[4] of the Wei-hai-Wei
detachment.   Another is by Corporal William Gregory,[5] also of the
Wei-hai-Wei detachment.   A third is by Major Halliday, V.C.[6]   I
should transcribe this last, but for the fact that it deals only with
events up to the day when the writer was wounded.   For the same
reason I do not copy Corporal Gregory's narrative.   I reprint, with
a few corrections and verbal alterations, Corporal Gowney's story,
which is in effect a rough diary, and I supplement it with a few
notes derived from other sources.

In his covering letter to the editor of the *Globe and Laurel*,

---

[1] Brev. Maj., Sept. 12, 1900, and later V.C.   [2] Brev. Maj. Nov. 1900.
[3] The official account of the naval operations in China is to be found in the *Gazette*,
Oct. 5 and Nov. 6, 1900.   Much of the additional information given above is taken
from the columns of the *Times, Western Morning News*, and *Globe and Laurel*.   *See*
also ' From Portsmouth to Peking *via* Ladysmith ' (Hongkong, 1901), and Gipps, ' The
Fighting in North China ' (1901).   The contents of numerous private letters from
officers present have also been drawn upon, as well as the official reports of the foreign
officers.
[4] *Globe and Laurel*, Nov., 1900.   [5] *Globe and Laurel*, Dec., 1900.
[6] *Globe and Laurel*, Nov., 1901.

Gowney points out that, with the exception of the three naval ratings already mentioned,[1] and Captain Poole, of the East York-shire Regiment, who was there for instruction in Chinese, the Marines were the only British regular forces in Peking; that all the European non-combatants, about 500 in number, were ultimately concentrated in the British Legation, as being the largest and most defensible; and that in many places the enemy's trenches and barricades were at the close within from forty to a hundred yards of the position. Here is the diary[2] :—

"Tientsin, May 30th, 1900. Arrival of detachments of Royal Marines, the first to arrive being 25 from Wei-hai-Wei, under Capt. E. Wray, the second from H.M.S. *Orlando*, under Capt. L. S. T. Halliday. Both detachments had a rough time of it coming up the Peiho, going aground several times. Each reached Tientsin within an hour or so of midnight. The total force now in Tientsin is 79, the whole under the command of Capt. B. M. Strouts, who, with 25 Marines, has been doing duty in Tientsin since December 3rd last. . . . Arrival of Americans, Japanese, Italians, French, and Russians. Germans and Austrians still to come.

"May 31st. To-day was a very busy one, packing up in preparation to leave barracks at noon: but we were delayed until late in the afternoon on account of the late arrival of the Russian, French, and Italian guards. Entraining at 4 o'clock, and leaving Tientsin station with a hearty send-off from the Europeans, we arrived at Peking about 7 in the evening. After a delay of over an hour and a half, we proceeded on the way to the British Legation, which lay about five miles from the station. We were all glad when we were met by a good cheer from the British Legation staff, for one and all were done up, the streets of Peking being shocking. One minute one is floundering about in refuse heaps, and the next in inches of dust; and the smells from the natives' houses are unbearable. Thousands of Chinese had turned out to see us come in; but no hostile demonstration, such as had been expected, took place on their part. On arrival at the Legation we were split into two parties, one going to the theatre, and the other to the bowling-alley, both being utilised as barracks.

"Peking, June 1st. Arrangements are being made for nursing; and the officers are getting things into ship-shape order. Arrival of German and Austrian guards. Total force of all nationalities: British, 79; Russians, 75; French, 75; Austrians, 60; Germans, 50; Americans, 50; Italians, 50; Japanese, 25; total, 464.

"June 2nd. Orders received that ten men and a N.C.O., Corpl. G. Sheppard, under Capt. Wray, should proceed to the Summer Legation as escort to Miss Armstrong and the British Ambassador's children.

"June 3rd. Departure at 5.15 of escort for the hills, which were reached at 10.15. Several men suspected to be Boxers were seen in the vicinity of the Legation, but offered no force to the party.

"June 5th. Return of escort from the Summer Legation. A force of 35 French and 10 Italians was sent to guard the Cathedral, which lay about two or three miles to the N.W.

"June 6th. Buying up of all provisions from the store keepers by the commissariat officer, Capt. Wray. Council of war, attended by all officers, at the British Legation.

"June 7th. Marine force detailed for defence of the position in case of attack.

"June 8th. Missionaries and refugees coming into the Legation from the outlying

---

[1] See p. 521.

[2] By kind permission of officer editing the *Globe and Laurel*.

missions. Reports that Boxers are growing very hostile. Guard in readiness to proceed to assistance of missionaries.

"June 9th. Burning of the grand stand on the racecourse. The Empress Dowager came into the city from the Summer Palace.

"June 10th. News that Vice-Admiral Seymour had left Tientsin for Peking.

"June 11th. Baggage guard of 22 Marines, under Capt. Halliday, with 30 wagons, proceeded to the station to meet the Vice-Admiral's force. After waiting for an hour or so, news came that the railway line and bridges were destroyed. Learnt that British Summer Legation was burnt down last night. Murder of a member of the Japanese Chancery outside the Yung-Ting-Mên. The last remaining telegraph wire was cut. It was repaired and was open for two hours, but was then again cut.

"June 12th. Reports from different sources that Boxers in great numbers are flocking around the city.[1]

"June 13th. Three hundred Boxers came in at the Ha-ta-Mên this morning, and burnt the Methodist chapel. They were repulsed by French volunteers, who killed and wounded several. Mounting of a picket 12 strong on the north bridge, to intercept any Boxers approaching the Legation.

"June 14th. Capture of a Boxer, with arms and uniform. Every man at his defence post, as there are rumours that an attack is to be made on the Legation. Attack on the Legation by about two or three hundred Boxers, who advanced towards the north bridge with flaming torches and firebrands with the intention of setting fire to the Legation. They were met by our picket under Capt. Halliday,[2] who repulsed them, they leaving four killed and two severely wounded behind them. The remaining wounded were carried off. We had no casualties.

"June 15th. Orders received for 25 Marines, under Capt. Halliday, and a small detachment of Germans, to proceed to the west end of the Ch'ien-Mên to fetch in Christians. On the way a large force of Boxers was met. They were murdering the Christians and pillaging their homes. We immediately opened fire, and inflicted severe loss upon them. On returning, we found that two houses inside the city gate were on fire. Christians refugees are streaming in from all quarters.

"June 16th. Huge fire outside the Ch'ien-Mên, destroying the richest quarter of the Chinese city, and finally setting alight to the outside guard-house of the Ch'ien-Mên itself.

"June 17th. To-day at noon our picket on the north bridge was fired upon by Imperial troops, who had manned the Imperial city wall, and housetops opposite. There were no casualties. An expedition went to the east side of the Legation, the force consisting of 20 British, 9 Americans, and 5 Japanese, under the command of Captain Wray. When it was about a mile out it discovered 40 or 50 Boxers in a temple. They were surrounded by our force, and not a man escaped. The arms were collected and handed over to the British Ambassador. Four shots entered the British Legation. There was a rumour that the relief column had been driven back to Tientsin. Two Boxers were captured on the north bridge. Very heavy rifle firing went on all round, principally from the Austrian and German Legations. Several bodies of soldiers are moving about freely, probably taking up positions to attack us. The Americans and Russians are taking up a defensive position on the west end, and the Germans on the east end of the city wall. This is an important position, as the city wall overlooks all the Legations, and is to be held at any cost. These positions are reinforced every twenty-four hours by the British Marines.

---

[1] On this day the thermometer stood at 103 degrees in the shade (Halliday).

[2] "I fired a volley, which stopped them, except one, who dashed on to the bridge, flourishing an enormous sort of pike, and was shot by Sergt. J. E. Preston when within four feet. Strouts came up with reinforcements. . . . He was charged by a Boxer . . . but shot him" (Halliday).

"June 18th. Defences, barricades, and trenches are being rapidly made. Every man sleeps at his defence post with 140 rounds of ammunition.

"June 19th. There are rumours that China has declared war with the Powers on account of the Taku forts being fired on, and that we are given twenty-four hours in which to clear out. We do not yet know what our reply is. The north bridge picket is withdrawn into the Legation.

"June 20th. The Ambassador's reply to the ultimatum for us to clear out in twenty-four hours is that we must remain here, as we have no transport, etc. All the Europeans are coming into the British Legation, as their own guards cannot protect them in their own Legations, and better work can be done with them all concentrated in one Legation. A strong force of Imperial troops and Boxers was repulsed with heavy loss at the French Legation! The German Ambassador, Baron von Ketteler, was killed, and his secretary severely wounded on the way to the Tsung-li-Yamen.

"June 21st. Constant sniping around the Legation. The Austrian Legation is in flames. By some error all the Legation guards east of the canal came in, but returned almost immediately, and, fortunately, were able to retake their Legations. The French succeeded in killing a lot of Boxers who had got in during their absence. There was very heavy continuous firing all round. The Austrian Legation and the Customs are abandoned. The *Peking Gazette* has the Emperor's declaration of war in it.

"June 22nd. Burning of the Italian and Dutch Legations. Sir Claude Macdonald, British Ambassador, took supreme command of all forces. Tung-fu-Hsuang's troops were reported to be in a temple adjoining our Legation; but, on a party under Captain Halliday proceeding thither, the place was found to be empty. There was an attempt at the south-west corner, which overlooks the Mongol market, to burn the British Legation, to which, however, no damage was done,[1] though thirty houses in the market square were burnt to the ground. Private A. Scadding was killed while on duty on the west wall.

"June 23rd. Heavy continuous firing all round us. There was another daring attempt at the north end of the Legation to fire the buildings. Only slight damage was done, but Hanlin College and some houses adjoining the Legation were completely gutted.

"June 24th. The British Marines made a successful sortie into the Mongol market at 2.30. They succeeded in driving a large body of Imperials and Boxers out of their position, and in causing them heavy loss. Our casualties were two, Captain Halliday,[2] who was in command, being severely wounded in the early part of the charge, and Captain Strouts also having a narrow escape, he having taken command of the force from Captain Halliday. A bullet grazed his neck, wounding him slightly. Our force also succeeded in capturing arms and ammunition, and in destroying the entire north face of the market. Private A. G. Sawyer was severely wounded in this engagement. Private G. Goddard was wounded while walking to his post inside the Legation.

"June 25th. Two Boxers, prisoners, were shot at daybreak. A volunteer company was formed under the command of Captain Strouts.

"June 26th. Lance-Corporal T. R. Allin was wounded while doing duty with the

---

[1] "The ladies all joined in handing buckets, and have all through done wonderfully, and shown great pluck " (Halliday).

[2] "Led a sortie among some ruined houses. Went down a narrow alley, and came upon five men with rifles round the corner of a house. One immediately plugged me in the shoulder, cutting the left brace of my Sam Browne belt in half. I then began to empty my revolver into them. As they were only a yard away, there was no question of missing. I finished four, and the fifth bolted around another corner " (Halliday).

Americans at the barricade.[1] The first issue of horse-flesh was made in the Legation. There was again a hot rifle-fire around us.

"June 27th. Lance-Corporal W. J. Sparkes was severely wounded while acting as look-out in the fort on the west wall. The south-east corner of the Legation was bombarded by artillery, which did considerable damage to the buildings, but no harm to the inmates.

"June 29th. Private C. W. Phillips was killed while proceeding to the guard room. Captain Strouts sounded the general attack on the big bell.

"June 30th. Privates A. J. Tickner and W. Horne were severely wounded with shrapnel while doing duty with the Germans at their barricade on the city wall.

"July 1st. There was a sortie by a mixed force of British, Italians, and French, under command of an Italian officer,[2] to capture a field-gun. It was unsuccessful. The casualties were two Italians killed and their officer severely wounded; three British wounded—Privates S. W. Haden, J. Buckler, and J. Dean—and one French wounded. An attempt was also made by 9 British Marines, 3 Americans, and 2 Russians, under Captain Wray, to erect a barricade on the city wall. It failed, there being too hot a fire from each end of the wall. The British casualties were two— Captain Wray and Private K. King. The Americans lost one. The full losses during the day near the Americans' barricade, and on the ramp, were 11: British, 2 wounded; Americans, 1 killed and 1 wounded; Russians, 1 wounded; and 2 coolies killed and 4 wounded. The coolies were assisting to build barricades. Private J. W. Heap was severely wounded while on duty at the Germans' trenches. The Chinese have advanced their barricade by building zig-zag breastworks to within twenty yards of the Americans' barricade.

"July 3rd. There was a successful attack by a mixed force on the enemy's trenches and barricades.[3] The force consisted of 27 British, 14 Americans, and 15 Russians. The attack started at 2.30 A.M. under Captain Myers, U.S. Marines, and succeeded in driving the enemy from his positions at the point of the bayonet, in occupying the trenches and barricades, and in inflicting severe loss, also capturing banners, arms, and ammunition. Our losses were Corporal William Gregory, severely wounded in the foot, and Private W. T. Woodward; the Americans had two privates killed and Captain Myers severely wounded; and the Russians had two wounded.

"July 5th. The students' quarters were shelled from the wall of the Imperial city.

"July 6th. A messenger who was sent out has returned, reporting that he could not get through, as he was constantly watched.

"July 7th. An old English cannon was discovered which, mounted on an Italian gun-carriage, was fired with good results. The weight of the shot is about 5 lbs. Mitchell, an American gunner, got the gun fixed. It has already received several names, such as "International," "Long Claude," etc. Armourer Thomas, and Mitchell, U.S.M., began making shell for the 1-pr., and ammunition for various rifles. The houses in the Mongol market overlooking our south-west defence were set on fire by our force.

---

[1] "An American sergeant and myself and Lance-Corp. Allin were building a barricade, when the enemy dropped a shell right into the very bag we were placing. It exploded; and it was a great wonder that the three of us were not killed, but we got off with Allin being wounded rather bad about the chest. I got stunned, and was grazed a little about the head" (Gregory).

[2] "The captain lost his head, and set fire to the houses in the rear; and the men retreated pell-mell." Morrison; who says, however, that the force included Germans, Russians, and volunteers, as well as British, Italians, and French, and who does not say that the commander was an Italian.

[3] They were only 25 ft. from the nearest American picket (Morrison).

"July 10th.   The command of the Italian guard at the Fu (Japanese [1] defences) was taken over by Captain Wray, the previous practice having been to employ a roster of officers.

"July 11th.   At noon an attempt was made to send out a messenger by the canal sluice gates.   The Chinese sentries fired on him immediately, but he ran back without being hit.

"July 12th.   Private A. E. Westbrook wounded while on duty with the Japanese at their trenches.   A prisoner who was captured this morning by French marines states that Tung-fu-Hsuang's troops are opposing us on the city wall, and along our lines on the south; that Jung-Lu's are behind the French Legation; that several are killed and wounded every day; and that there are about 3000 of Tung-fu-Hsuang's troops in the city.   Direct attack having failed, and our rifles being better than theirs, it has been decided to starve us out.   The soldiers believe we have several thousand troops under arms here.   The prisoner thought we certainly had over 2000.   To-day the British Marines have done duty at each nationality's barricades and trenches.

"July 13th.   Sergeant J. E. Preston was slightly wounded with a brick while on duty in the Legation.   This occurred while he was assisting Gunner Mitchell, U.S.M., who captured an enemy's banner [2] in the Hanlin, adjoining the Legation.   The French Legation was undermined, and one house blown up, two Frenchmen being killed.

"July 15th.   There was a call for more volunteers to keep watch by day, in order to give the troops a much-needed rest.   Private A. T. Layton severely, and Corporal D. J. Gowney slightly wounded, while on duty at the Japanese defences.

"July 16th.   Captain Strouts [3] killed, and Dr. Morrison wounded.   Both, in company with Colonel Shiba, Japanese military attaché, were visiting the British sentries at the Italian post in the Fu, which is under the command of Captain Wray.   Colonel Shiba also had a narrow escape, a bullet passing through his jacket.   The burial of Captain Strouts was an impressive ceremony, the Tientsin guard, Dr. Poole, and Captain Poole acting as pall-bearers.   The deceased officer is sadly missed by the Marine force.   Private W. Roe wounded while acting as look-out on the fort on the west wall.

"July 17th.   Very quiet.   There are rumours that the enemy is negotiating for a cessation of hostilities.

"July 18th to Aug. 4th.   Negotiations between the Ministers and the Chinese Government.   There was a general interruption of hostilities, with, however, occasional sniping by the enemy on the west of our defences.

"Aug. 5th to 8th.   The enemy is getting very troublesome, especially in the Mongol market which adjoins our western defences.   The market and ruins were occupied by the British under the command of Lieutenant von Strauch, a retired German officer.   There were no casualties.

"Aug. 9th to 11th.   We succeeded in advancing our defences within from twelve to fifteen yards of the enemy in the Mongol market.   This was done to checkmate the enemy.

"Aug. 12th and 13th.   There was a heavy fusilade all round, with several casualties.

"Aug. 14th.   We were hard pressed all round by the enemy, who were reinforced

---

[1] The gallant Japanese had suffered so heavily as to be unable fully to man them (Morrison).   On the previous day, in a panic, the Italians and Austrians in the place had temporarily abandoned it.   British Marines thenceforth took the place of the Austrians.   " It was difficult to keep the southerners at their posts.   They were said to have no lack of spirit, but their *forte* was in attack " (Morrison).

[2] Flying "from a sandbag shelter in the carriage walk, over the very wall of the British Legation" (Morrison).

[3] Born May 27, 1870; educd. at Aldenham; entd. service 1888; lieut. 1889; captain 1897.   "He was struck in the upper part of the left thigh by an expanding bullet, and died an hour after being brought into the hospital, to the grief of the entire community.   He was always cool and self-reliant, and never spared himself, while always considerate for his men " (Morrison).   Strouts had been chief-of-staff to Sir C. Macdonald.

by Chinese retreating before the allied forces advancing to our relief. Heavy cannon-
ading and Maxim fire were heard away to the south-east. At length the relief forces
arrived, the first man to enter the Legation being a private of the Sikhs. The General
and staff followed. The enthusiasm was tremendous. The Naval Brigade, with guns,
remained at the Temple of Heaven, a couple of miles south of the Tartar city.

Aug. 15th. Arrival of the Marine battalion, 250 strong, under the command of
Major Edward Vyvyan Luke, the other officers being Captains William Albert Harris,
and John William Dustan, and Lieutenants Charles Lawson Mayhew, Harold Gage
Bewes Armstrong,[1] and Charles d'Oyly Harmar. Fifty Marines, under Captain James
Herbert Mullins, had remained at Matou."

The defence of the Legations at Peking was a fine exploit; and
the Royal Marines, who were the soul of it, behaved on the occasion
in such a manner as to be worthy of their glorious reputation.
They can be given no higher praise. The little British guard of 79
all told lost, killed and wounded, 20 of its number. Graspan
showed, it is true, a much higher proportion of casualties among the
Marines engaged; but even the fierce brief fight at Graspan did not
try the metal of officers and men as those two and a half months in
Peking did, nor afford so fine an opportunity for the display of the
finest of all military qualities, steadfastness and resource.

In recognition of the good work done by the Marine guard at
Peking the Admiralty subsequently directed that six months' service
should be counted, in the case of the officers, towards qualification
for retiring allowances, and, in the case of the non-commissioned
officers and men, towards the completion of limited engagements,
and towards qualification for good conduct badges and pensions.

A parliamentary paper issued in 1901 showed the total strength
of the British Naval forces landed in China in 1900, and the
casualties incurred, to have been as follows :—

		Number Landed		Total Deaths		Total Wounded	
	—	Officers.	Men.	Officers.	Men.	Officers.	Men.
Royal Navy	Executive.	124	1,090	3	37	10	147
	Engineer	8	296	..	8	..	27
	Civil	22	109	..	2	1	3
Royal Marine Artillery		12	69	3	3	2	6
Royal Marine Light Infantry . . .		1	476	1	33	..	73
Totals		167	2,040	7	83	13	256

[1] Capt. Nov. 9, 1900, for his services.

These statistics embrace only the officers and men actually dis-embarked, and do not include casualties on board ship at the bombardment of the Taku Forts.

It should be added that on October 1st the Admiralty des-patched to Sir Edward Seymour a long letter,[1] full of generous appreciation of the services of the Commander-in-Chief, Rear-Admiral Bruce, and the officers, seamen, and Royal Marines engaged in the first ineffectual march towards Peking, the capture of the Taku forts and of the Chinese destroyers, and the operations at Tientsin. The same letter transmitted the thanks of the Secretary of State for Foreign Affairs. A G.C.B. awarded to Vice-Admiral Seymour; a K.C.M.G. to Rear-Admiral Bruce; C.B.'s to Captains Bayly, Burke, Callaghan, and Jellicoe; D.S.O.'s to Lieutenants Lowther-Crofton, Charrington, Mackenzie, and Phillimore, and Engineer George Herbert Cockey; and V.C.'s to Midshipman Guy, and Major Halliday, together with numerous pro-motions, most of which have been already chronicled in the notes, afforded further evidence of the high estimation with which the work of the Royal Navy in China was regarded by Her Majesty's advisers. The services and gallantry of petty officers, seamen, and private Marines were not, however, as adequately recognised, owing largely to the existence of regulations preventing the granting of the D.S.O. to other than officers. The medal for Conspicuous Gallantry, conferred in several instances, was almost inadequate for some of the services rendered.[2] Seeing how important it is, under the conditions of modern warfare, to encourage self-reliance, initiative, resource, and, of course, gallantry in all ranks, it is to be regretted that better provision had not then been made for rewarding and honouring the display of such qualities on the lower deck.

After the relief of Peking, the war in China assumed a more distinctively military character, and, as troops from various quarters arrived upon the scene of action and were placed under the supreme command of Field-Marshal Count von Waldersee, the naval detachments were withdrawn as rapidly as possible to their ships. The Navy continued to do most useful work by guarding threatened towns along the coast, removing refugees, and pre-

---

[1] *Gazette*, 1900, p. 6115.

[2] It was to meet part of this difficulty that the Conspicuous Service Cross was afterwards instituted (O. in C. of June 15th, 1901). The Conspicuous Gallantry Medal is awarded under O. in C. of July 7th, 1874, and Feb. 22, 1896.

1900. *THE " PIGMY " AT SHANHAIKUAN.* 559

venting the Imperial Chinese fleet from taking any part in the struggle with the Powers; but practically it saw no more fighting.[1] During the entire campaign it lost no ship, except the shallow-draught river gunboat *Sandpiper*, which, commanded by Lieutenant Henry Cecil Carr, foundered in a typhoon at Hong Kong.[2] The crew, with the exception of one man, was saved by the devotion of the people of the destroyer *Otter*, Commander Henry Douglas Wilkin, D.S.O.

One almost comic episode enlivened the comparative monotony of the work of the Navy during the concluding months of the year. On September 29th, at a conference of the allied admirals at Taku, it was decided to occupy the Chinese forts at Shanhaikuan, the point at which the Great Wall touches the sea. That night, at eleven o'clock, the little gunboat *Pigmy*, 6, Lieutenant John Frederick Ernest Green,[3] left the Peiho by order of Vice-Admiral Seymour, carrying with her as passengers Sir Walter Hillier, a political officer, and Colonel Charles Herbert Powell, 1st Goorkhas, a member of Count von Waldersee's staff. The *Pigmy's* proper complement was 73 all told, and her largest gun was a 4-in. breech-loader. It is clear, therefore, that the capture and occupation of the forts, which were large and powerful, was not intended to be her mission. She went, in fact, mainly to reconnoitre, in preparation for the arrival of the big ships of various nationalities which followed her.

At noon on the 30th the gunboat reached Shanhaikuan. Green, Hillier, and Powell, finding that everything looked peaceful, went ashore, and had an interview with the Chinese general commanding the forts. That officer proved to be unexpectedly courteous and amenable. He had no desire to fight; he was perfectly willing to withdraw at once; he was even anxious to depart as quickly as possible. It would have been dangerous, of course, to leave such extensive and well-armed works unguarded. Lieutenant Green therefore returned on board, and directed Lieutenant Harold

---

[1] In November, 1900, however, the gunboat *Plover*, 6, Lieutenant Carlton Valentine de Mornay Cowper, was despatched from Wei-hai-Wei to release some junks which had been captured by pirates at the Bourchier Islands. She chased one of the pirate craft to the Yalu river, and there took her. At Wumaton Island she subsequently landed a party which, after some struggle, made prisoners of seven of the freebooters, who were afterwards executed, and killed three more in action.

[2] She was afterwards raised.

[3] Com. for his services.

Douglas Briggs to disembark with eighteen men[1] and occupy the place.

Meantime, Russian troops were advancing overland to take possession of the forts. They arrived in the course of the day, demanded admission to the railway station and works, were politely refused by the officer in charge, who professed that he had no orders to admit them, and at last pitched their camp on the beach. Conscious of the growing difficulty of the situation Lieutenant Green, leaving his little garrison on shore, returned with all speed to Taku for further instructions. In his absence the huge Russian armoured cruiser *Rurik*, a vessel with a complement of nearly 800, reached Shanhaikuan. The *Pigmy*, reinforced with fifty bluejackets, was promptly sent back, and arrived at night to find the *Rurik* landing her people by searchlight. The Russians, however, had not been admitted to the works, nor were they admitted until after the appearance on the scene, some hours later, of the British Commander-in-Chief, in the *Centurion*, with numerous other vessels of the different Powers. It was then arranged that the railway station and the sea fort should fly the allied flags, and, as for the other forts, that they should be apportioned out at the rate of one to each one or two nationalities.[2] Not until then were the *Pigmy's* men relieved from a situation which, but for the good temper of all concerned, might easily have brought about regrettable results. Shanhaikuan subsequently became a great landing-place for stores for the international troops.

The war in South Africa had led to a general rallying of the British Empire round the mother country, and to the despatch to the scene of hostilities of a succession of military contingents from all the self-governing states owing allegiance to the Crown, as well as from many of the smaller colonies. The fighting in China gave occasion for a more modest, yet scarcely less significant, demonstration of the unity of the Empire. On August 9th, 1900, the steamer *Salamis* left Sydney for China, having on board a number[3] of officers and men of the New South Wales Naval Defence Force under Commander Edward Richard Connor[4] (retired navigating Lieu-

---

[1] This allowed an officer and six men to the railway station, and two bluejackets to each of the six forts, one at least of which mounted 40 guns.

[2] *North China Daily Mail* in *N. and M. Record*, Jan. 10, 1901; and private letters from *Endymion*, *Centurion*, and *Dido*.

[3] New South Wales, 300; Victoria, 200 (Procs. in Parl., Aug. 6, 1900).

[4] C.M.G. Nov. 29, 1900.

tenant, R.N.), and of the New South Wales Naval Artillery
Volunteers, under Lieutenant M. A. Roberts of that corps (the
whole being under Lieutenant Alexander Gillespie, R.N., who
commanded with the temporary rank of Captain), and also of
the Victorian Naval Defence Force, under Commander F. Tickell,[1]
Victorian Navy. At the same time South Australia sent the twin-
screw gunboat *Protector* to Chinese waters.[2]

[1] C.M.G. Nov. 29, 1900.

[2] Gratuities in respect of services rendered in China in 1900 were subsequently
granted to the officers and men of the following ships : *Alacrity*, Com. Christopher
Geo. Fras. Maurice Cradock; *Algerine*, (1) Com. Robt. Hathorn Johnston Stewart,
(2) Com. Edw. Duke Hunt; *Arethusa*, Capt. Jas. Startin; *Aurora*, Capt. Edw. Hy.
Bayly; *Barfleur* (flag of R.-Ad. Bruce), Capt. Geo. Jno. Scott Warrender; *Bona-
venture*, Capt. Chas. Jno. Graves-Sawle; *Centurion* (flag of V.-Ad. Seymour), Capt.
Jno. Rushworth Jellicoe; *Daphne*, Com. Chas. Wm. Winnington-Ingram; *Dido*,
Capt. Philip Fras. Tillard; *Endymion*, Capt. Geo. Astley Callaghan; *Esk*, Lieut. Wm.
Fredk. Blunt; *Fame*, (1) Lieut. Roger Jno. Brownlow Keyes, (2) Lieut. Chas.
Playdell Mansel; *Goliath*, Capt. Lewis Edm. Wintz; *Hart*, Lieut. Jno. Garnet
Armstrong; *Hermione*, Capt. Robt. Stevenson Dalton Cumming; *Humber*, Com. Hy.
Jocelyn Davison; *Isis*, Capt. Geo. Morris Henderson; *Linnet*, Com. Wm. Wyatt
Smythe; *Marathon*, Capt. Jno. Geo. Mostyn Field; *Orlando*, Capt. Jas. Hy. Thos.
Burke; *Peacock*, Lieut. Chas. Penrose Rushton Coode; *Pigmy*, Lieut. Jno. Fredk. Ern.
Green; *Pique*, Capt. Harry Campbell Reynolds; *Plover*, Lieut. Carlton Valentine de
Mornay Cowper; *Redpole*, Lieut. Chas. Fredk. Corbett; *Rosario*, Com. Claude Arth.
Wm. Hamilton ; *Snipe*, Lieut. Arth. Hugh Oldham; *Terrible*, Capt. Percy Moreton
Scott; *Undaunted*, Capt. Arth. Calvert Clarke ; *Wallaroo*, Capt. Fras. Chas. Methuen
Noel; *Waterwitch*, Lieut. Wm. Owen Lyne ; *Whiting*, Lieut. Colin MacKenzie; *Wood-
cock*, Lieut. Hugh Dudley Richards Watson; and *Woodlark*, Lieut. Hy. Eilbeck
Hillman.

KHEDIVE'S BRONZE STAR, EGYPT, 1882, 1884, ETC.
(Gun-metal, worn on a blue ribbon.)

CHAPTER XLVIII.

VOYAGES AND DISCOVERIES, 1857–1900.

SIR CLEMENTS R. MARKHAM, K.C.B., F.R.S.

The Search for Franklin—McClintock's success—The Hydrographers—The voyage of the *Challenger*—Nares and Markham to the Arctic—The modern surveying service.

BADGE OF THE DISTINGUISHED
SERVICE ORDER.

(Obverse.)

Instituted Sept. 6th, 1886.

Ribbon : red, edged with blue.   To be worn on the left breast.

SOON after the peace with Russia the news came that Dr. Rae, servant of the Hudson's Bay Company, had bought some silver spoons and forks, and a few other articles which had belonged to officers of Sir John Franklin's expedition, from a party of Eskimos. Their story was that the last survivors had died on a cape and an island near the estuary of the Back River. This was the very spot which the authorities had declined to search during the previous ten years, in spite of Dr. King's representations and entreaties. Their duty was now clear. An expedition must be sent to examine the shores of King William Island and ascertain the fate of Sir John Franklin and his gallant followers. What the Admiralty did do was very different. They hurriedly paid the reward of £10,000, offered to anyone who discovered the fate of Franklin, to Dr. Rae in order to close the subject. They refused to send an expedition. In other words, the Government declined to lift a finger to discover the fate of those officers and men who, owing to Admiralty blunders, had perished in the service of their country. This refusal was in spite of the entreaties of Lady Franklin, and of all the leading scientific men in the country. Then Lady Franklin nobly came forward to spend her last shilling rather than that this disgrace should be incurred. The steamer

Fox was purchased, and a small private expedition was equipped, almost entirely at her own expense. There could be no question as to the best man to command it. Captain Francis Leopold McClintock accepted the honourable post. Lieutenant William Robert Hobson went with him, and Allen Young,[1] an officer of the mercantile marine, gave not only his services, but also a large subscription towards the expenses of the expedition.

McClintock sailed in the spring of 1857. He was unfortunate in crossing Melville Bay. He was beset in the ice of the middle pack, and drifted southward down Baffin's Bay and Davis Strait throughout the winter. At length, during a gale of wind, the ice broke up, and, amidst fearful dangers from the heaving masses, the *Fox* was released from her long imprisonment. Most men would have sought a friendly port for rest and refreshment. Not so McClintock. He at once turned her head northwards. In the season of 1858 he was more fortunate. He succeeded in reaching a bay down Prince Regent's Inlet, which was sufficiently near to his work, and which he made his winter quarters for 1858–59.

The sledge-travelling commenced in the spring of 1859. He was to examine the whole coast of King William Island, and to visit Montreal Island at the mouth of the Great Fish River. Hobson was to search the north coast of King William Island, and Allen Young was to complete the discovery of Prince of Wales Island, by uniting the furthest points of Brown and Sherard Osborn. McClintock went down the east side of King William Island and reached Montreal Island, finding various traces. After rounding Cape Herschel he came upon a most pathetic object. It was the skeleton of a young steward who had fallen down to die as he struggled onwards. Then he came to the boat, containing two skeletons and many articles belonging to officers of Franklin's expedition. The most important vestiges had already been discovered by Hobson. For a second time McClintock trod this classic, almost sacred ground round Cape Victory before returning to his ship. The great discovery was the document signed by Crozier and FitzJames, which finally revealed the fate of Franklin and his devoted followers.

McClintock brought back the *Fox* to England in the autumn of 1859, amidst the plaudits of his countrymen. The Admiralty

---

[1] Born 1830; Lieut. R.N.R. 1862; comd. *Pandora* in Arctic Exped. 1875–76; Kt. 1877; C.B.; retd. com. R.N.R. 1886.

then recognised his services, and the Queen conferred upon him the honour of knighthood. Thus closed this famous episode in the history of our Navy. The despatch of Sir John Franklin's expedition and the work of the expeditions to ascertain his fate covered a period of fourteen years. It was a period when many officers and men were receiving a training and gaining experiences which were afterwards of great advantage to the service.

The Navy lost two of the best friends it ever had when Sir John Barrow retired in 1845, and Sir Francis Beaufort in 1855. Neither long survived his retirement. The former died in 1849, the latter in 1857. It is said that good men's places are easily filled. Both these eminent men are still missed.

Captain John Washington[1] succeeded Sir Francis Beaufort as Hydrographer. In 1836, he had made a journey to Morocco, and he had written a valuable account of it; he had been for several years Secretary of the Royal Geographical Society; and his surveying services had been chiefly on the English coast, in command of the *Shearwater* and *Blazer*. Washington died at his post in 1864. In his time Captain Henry Mangles Denham, in the *Herald*, was carrying on surveys in the Fiji Islands and other parts of the Pacific from 1852 to 1859; while Arthur Lukis Mansell,[2] the worthy successor of Graves and Spratt, executed the Syrian survey in the *Tartarus* and *Firefly*, and in 1864 continued his excellent work in the Ionian Islands and on the coast of Albania. Two other valuable surveying officers, Captains William Louis Sheringham, and George Augustus Bedford, were much employed on the coasts of England and Scotland; but Bedford was also on the west coast of Africa, and in the Gulf of St. Lawrence. In 1862 he succeeded Mr. Michael Walker as Assistant Hydrographer, and was afterwards Superintendent of Charts at the Admiralty.

Captain George Henry Richards,[3] who became Hydrographer in 1864, had served in the *Sulphur* and *Samarang* with Belcher, in the *Philomel* with Sulivan, and in the *Acheron* with Stokes. He was Commander of the *Assistance* in the Arctic regions from 1852 to 1854, and afterwards conducted a survey of the coasts of Vancouver's Island in the *Plumper*. It is to the credit of Sir George Henry Richards that, at least on one occasion, he followed success-

[1] Entd. Navy 1812; Lieut. Jan. 1, 1821: Com. Aug. 14, 1833; Capt. Mar. 16, 1842.

[2] Com. Sept. 29th, 1855; Capt. Jan. 1st, 1865; retd. Mar. 7th, 1866.

[3] *See* List of Flag-Officers.

fully in the footsteps of Sir Francis Beaufort. It was mainly
due to him that the *Challenger* was commissioned in 1872, properly
equipped, and despatched on a scientific expedition round the
world. The command was given to Captain George Strong Nares,[1]
who had served with McClintock and Mecham in the Arctic regions,
and since done good service as a surveyor. With him was associated
a civilian scientific staff under Charles Wyville Thomson,[2] with
which the naval officers always worked in perfect harmony. In 1875
Nares was recalled to command an Arctic expedition, and was
succeeded by Captain Frank Tourle Thomson. The *Challenger* expedition has justly acquired a world-wide reputation for the immense
extent and value of its researches, more especially those connected
with deep sounding and dredging, and the scientific examination of
the great ocean beds. It has occupied many years to work up the
numerous collections ; and the twenty volumes of the results of the
Challenger expedition, brought out under the auspices of Sir John
Murray,[3] are the monument to one more peace-victory gained by the
British Navy for the good of the whole civilised world.

During Sir George Henry Richards's term of office the revision of
the survey of Magellan's Strait was undertaken by Captain Richard
Charles Mayne, in the *Nassau*. For three years, 1866–69, that
officer, who had served with Richards in the *Plumper*, conducted
surveys from Punta Arenas to Cape Virgins, and from Cape Pilar
to Port Famine. He also examined 255 miles of the channels
from the Gulf of Peñas to Magellan's Strait. Mayne was the
author of ' Practical Notes on Marine Surveying.'

The renewal of Arctic exploration became an important question,
both for geography and for the Navy, as soon as the *Fox* returned.
The loss of Sir John Barrow was then deeply felt. The long hard
fight had to be fought without the aid of Sir Francis Beaufort.
But Sherard Osborn was a host in himself. During his Arctic
service, and long before, Sherard Osborn had been deeply impressed
with the importance, indeed the necessity, of expeditions of discovery and research for the welfare of the Navy in time of peace.
" Do not keep us for ever crossing topgallant yards and cleaning
brass work ! " he exclaimed. How much greater is the need now,

Born 1831; Capt. 1869; K.C.B. 1876; retd. Capt. Apr. 24, 1886; retd. r.-adm.
1887; retd. v.-adm. 1892.

Born 1830; served with dredging expeds. of *Lightning* and *Porcupine*, 1868–69;
prof. of nat. hist. at Edinburgh, 1870–81; Kt.; died 1882.

[3] Born 1841; biologist; K.C.B. 1898.

when there are no longer topgallant yards to cross ! Osborn read
a paper before the Royal Geographical Society in 1864, advocating
the renewal of polar research, which created a deep impression
throughout the country. He was a man who was not to be beaten.
He read another paper in 1867, and continued his advocacy in every
shape and form, undaunted by fruitless interviews with First Lords,
or by any other form of obstruction. At length his perseverance
was rewarded. In the autumn of 1874 Mr. D'Israeli announced
the intention of the Government to despatch an Arctic expedition,
"to encourage that spirit of enterprise which had ever distinguished
the English people."

An old sloop, the *Alert,* was selected, and a whaler, purchased
for the service and strengthened for ice navigation, was re-named
Discovery. The command was entrusted to Captain Nares, of the
Challenger, with Albert Hastings Markham as Commander; and
Captain Henry Frederick Stephenson commanded the *Discovery.*
Officers of great promise were appointed to the two vessels, such as
Beaumont,[1] Aldrich,[2] Parr,[3] May,[4] Wyatt Rawson,[5] and Egerton.[6]
The route selected was Smith Sound, at the head of Baffin's Bay.
The Royal Geographical Society, through which body Sherard
Osborn had conducted his propaganda, had always advocated
the exploration of the polar region for scientific purposes, and
not a foolish rush to the pole. But the instructions drawn up
by the Admiralty contained the fatal order to go as far north as
possible.

The expedition sailed in May 1875, and proceeded up Smith
Sound, the difficulties of the navigation being overcome by Nares's
consummate seamanship. The *Discovery* was left to winter in
Lady Franklin Bay, and the *Alert* pressed northward to encounter
the impenetrable polar pack, seen at other points by Parry,
McClintock, Mecham, McClure, and Collinson. Nares was forced
to winter on an open coast and at the edge of this pack, the most
northern winter quarters ever formed. Some very gallant work
was done during the autumn travelling, and the two young officers,

---

[1] Lewis Anthony Beaumont, 1st Lieut. of *Discovery*; see list of Flag-Officers.

[2] Pelham Aldrich, 1st Lieut. of *Alert*; see list of Flag-Officers.

[3] Alfred Arthur Chase Parr, 2nd Lieut. of *Alert*; R.-Adm. May 24, 1901.

[4] William Henry May, 4th Lieut. of *Alert*; R.-Adm. Mar. 28, 1901.

[5] Wyatt Rawson, 3rd Lieut. of *Discovery*; mort. wounded at Tel-el-Kebir; promd.
Com.; died Sept. 21, 1882.

[6] George Le Clerc Egerton, Sub-Lieut. of *Alert*; Capt. Jan. 1, 1893.

Rawson and Egerton, distinguished themselves in the very early spring by opening communications between the two ships. But the seeds of scurvy had been sown during the long winter, and broke out soon after the spring travelling commenced. The fatal Admiralty order to press northwards under all circumstances also hampered the operations. But all was done that brave men could do. Markham and Parr pushed northwards over the polar pack, dragging heavy boats which obliged them to make three journeys over the same ground, where the ice was broken up into endless ridges of hummocks. Never had so hard a service been performed. The party reached the highest northern point up to that time attained by man. Aldrich explored the coastline to the east, Beaumont to the west, and the naturalists were indefatigable in their several departments. But the disease that had broken out so unexpectedly was a great hindrance to the work. The expedition, however, returned in the autumn of 1876, with the loss of only two men, and with an exceptionally rich harvest of scientific results.

Sir George Henry Richards had retired from the post in 1874, and was succeeded as Hydrographer by Frederick John O. Evans, C.B.,[1] who had held the post of Superintendent of the Compass Department during the previous ten years. He held office until 1884, when he was succeeded by Captain William James Lloyd Wharton,[2] well known for his excellent work on the east coast of Africa.

On the return of the *Alert* she was sent to Magellan's Strait to complete the work of King, FitzRoy, and Mayne, again under the command of Sir George Nares, who was relieved by Captain John Fiot Lee Pearse Maclear to finish the commission. The ordinary surveying service has since kept seven or eight small vessels employed, two for the British Isles, two for the Mediterranean, three for Australia and the Pacific, one in China, and one in the West Indies. But much valuable scientific work, including deep-sea soundings, is done by the surveying vessels, in addition to surveys of coasts and harbours. There are two Captains, four Commanders, and about thirty Lieutenants and Sub-Lieutenants employed on board the surveying vessels.

The results of the British naval surveys during the nineteenth century have been that the whole world is supplied with

---

[1] Master, R.N. Nov. 23, 1841; retd. as captain June 5, 1872; subsequently K.C.B.
[2] Born Mar. 2, 1843; retd. as r.-adm. Jan. 1, 95, but remained Hydrog.; K.C.B. 1897.

admirably engraved charts, constantly corrected and brought up to date, and supplied with sailing directions.

A contemplation of the work of naval expeditions since the time of Byron cannot fail to force the conviction that this is legitimate work for the Navy in time of peace. At the end of the century there appeared to be a tendency to abandon this glorious position; to seek no more for peace victories for our Navy; to give place to other nations in the work of discovery. But it only needs a more thorough study of the history of the Navy, and a more clear appreciation of her needs, in order that a public opinion may be formed which will restore us to the position we held at the time when Barrow and Beaufort could make their influence felt. For success in war it is not only ships that we need, but also trained officers and men, who have acquired confidence and experience in the course of special service, in addition to a knowledge of the ordinary routine of mastless steamships.

BADGE OF THE DISTINGUISHED SERVICE ORDER.
Reverse.
(*See p.* 562.)

APPENDIX A. TO CHAPTERS XLVI.–XLVIII.

LIST OF FLAG-OFFICERS PROMOTED FROM THE BEGINNING OF 1857 TO THE END OF THE REIGN OF QUEEN VICTORIA (ACTIVE LIST ONLY).

(In continuation of the List in Vol. VI, pp. 538–544.)

NAME (with honours, title, etc., at date of promotion to Flag-rank, honours and titles subsequently acquired being within brackets).	BORN.	LIEUT.	COM-MANDER.	CAPTAIN.	REAR-ADMIRAL.	VICE-ADMIRAL.	ADMIRAL.	ADMIRAL OF THE FLEET.	REMARKS. Rank attained only on or after retirement is indicated in small letters.	DIED.
Joseph Nias, C.B. (K.C.B. 67)		26-12-1820	11-11-1827	8-7-1835	14-2-1857	12-9-1863			{ Retd. V.-A. 1866; retd. a. 18-10-1867 . }	1879
Henry John Codrington, C.B. (K.C.B. 67)	17-10-1808	12-6-1829	20-10-1831	20-1-1836	19-3-1857	24-9-1863	18-10-1867	22-1-1877		4-8-1877
John M'Dougall (3) (K.C.B. 62)	1790	3-1-1810	9-2-1820	16-8-1836	12-5-1857	3-11-1863				12-4-1865
Michael Quin		16-7-1812	5-10-1824	10-1-1837	14-5-1857	14-11-1863				1870
Sir Thomas Maitland, Kt., C.B. (suc. as Earl of Lauderdale, 62; K.C.B. 65; G.C.B. 73)	3-2-1803	16-5-1823	30-4-1827	10-1-1837	18-6-1857	30-11-1863			{ Retd. V.-A. 27-3-1864; retd. a. 8-4-1868 . }	1-9-1878
Robert Smart, K.H. (K.C.B. 65)	9-1796	11-9-1820	21-4-1828	10-1-1837	9-7-1857	3-12-1863	15-1-1869		{ Retd. A. 3-2-1873; retd. a. f. 27-12-1877 . }	10-9-1874
George Rodney Mundy (C.B. 59; K.C.B. 62; G.C.B. 77)	19-4-1805	4-2-1826	25-8-1828	10-1-1837	30-7-1857	15-12-1863	26-5-1869		{ Retd. A. 19-4-1875; retd. a. f. 27-12-1877 . }	23-12-1884
Hon. Henry Keppel, C.B. (K.C.B. 57; G.C.B. 71)	14-6-1809	29-1-1829	30-1-1833	5-12-1837	22-8-1857	11-1-1864	3-7-1869	5-8-1877	Retd. A. F. 14-6-1879.	
John Jervis Tucker		20-9-1822	15-1-1827	28-6-1838	10-9-1857	9-2-1864			{ Retd. V.A. 19-10-1864; retd. a. 10-9-1869 . }	1886
John Kingcome (K.C.B. 65)		1-7-1815	8-1-1828	28-6-1838	10-9-1857	5-3-1864			{ Retd. V.-A. 1-4-1866; retd. a. 10-9-1869 . }	1871
Frederick Bullock		22-1-1812	26-8-1829	28-6-1838	2-10-1857	28-3-1864			{ Retd. V.-A. 11-11-1864; retd. a. 10-9-1869 . }	1871
John Elphinstone Erskine	13-7-1806	2-1-1826	24-12-1829	28-6-1838	4-11-1857	15-6-1864	10-9-1869		Retd. A. 13-7-1876.	6-1887
James Hope, C.B. (K.C.B. 60; G.C.B. 65)	8-3-1808	9-3-1827	26-2-1830	28-6-1838	19-11-1857	16-9-1864	21-1-1870		{ Retd. A. 8-3-1878; retd. a. f. 15-6-1879 . }	9-6-1881
Horatio Thomas Austin, C.B. (K.C.B. 65)	7-1796	9-9-1822	26-5-1831	28-6-1838	28-11-1857	20-10-1864				1865
William Ramsay, C.B. (K.C.B. 69)		8-9-1821	15-8-1831	28-6-1838	8-12-1857	12-11-1864			{ Retd. V.-A. 7-1866; retd. a. 27-2-1870 . }	1871
Sir Baldwin Wake Walker (1), Bart., K.C.B.	1803	6-4-1820	15-7-1834	24-11-1838	5-1-1858	10-2-1865	27-2-1870		Retd. A. 1-4-1870 .	12-2-1876
Alexander Milne (civ. K.C.B. 58; G.C.B. 71)	10-11-1806	8-9-1827	25-11-1830	30-1-1839	20-1-1858	13-4-1865	1-4-1870		{ Retd. A. 10-11-1876; retd. a. f. 10-6-1881 . }	29-12-1896
Lord Clarence Edward Paget, C.B. (K.C.B. 69; G.C.B. 80)	17-6-1811	14-5-1831	25-9-1834	26-3-1839	4-2-1858	24-4-1865	1-4-1870		Retd. A. 18-6-1876 .	22-3-1895
Richard Laird Warren		1-1-1829	24-12-1833	9-5-1839	13-2-1858	5-5-1865	1-4-1870			29-7-1875
George Elliot (4) (K.C.B. 77)	1812	12-11-1834	15-1-1838	3-6-1840	24-2-1858	12-9-1865	1-4-1870		Retd. A. 26-9-1878 .	13-12-1901

LIST OF FLAG-OFFICERS—continued.

Name (with honours, title, etc., at date of promotion to Flag-rank; honours and titles subsequently acquired being within brackets).	Born.	Lieut.	Commander.	Captain.	Rear-Admiral.	Vice-Admiral.	Admiral.	Admiral of the Fleet.	Remarks. Rank attained only on or after retirement is indicated in small letters.	Died.
Hon. Frederick Thomas Pelham, C.B.	2-8-1808	22-2-1830	22-9-1835	3-7-1840	6-3-1858	—	—	—		21-6-1861
Sydney Colpoys Dacres, C.B. (K.C.B. 67; G.C.B. 71)	1805	5-5-1827	28-8-1834	1-8-1840	25-6-1858	17-11-1865	1-4-1870	—	1875	8-3-1884
John Shepherd (2)		2-2-1813	28-8-1828	26-10-1846	24-11-1858	—	—	—	Retd. A.	2-4-1863
Thomas Henderson	6-1795	2-2-1830	12-2-1834	4-11-1840	18-12-1858	—	—	—		10-4-1865
Lewis Tobias Jones, C.B. (K.C.B. 61; G.C.B. 73)	24-12-1797	29-8-1822	28-6-1833	4-11-1840	17-6-1859	2-12-1865	—	—	{ Retd. V.-A. 1-4-1870; retd. a. 14-7-1871 . }	11-10-1895
Robert Fanshawe Stopford	19-12-1811	24-12-1830	28-6-1838	4-11-1840	2-5-1860	2-4-1866	—	—	{ Retd. V.-A. 25-1-1871; retd. a. 14-7-1871 . }	4-1-1891
Robert Spencer Robinson (civ. K.C.B. 68)	6-1-1809	27-9-1830	28-6-1838	5-11-1840	9-6-1860	2-4-1866	—	—	{ Retd. V.-A. 1-4-1870; retd. a. 14-7-1871 . }	27-7-1889
Thomas Matthew Charles Symonds, C.B. (K.C.B. 67; G.C.B. 80)	15-7-1813	5-11-1832	21-10-1837	22-2-1841	1-11-1860	2-4-1866	14-7-1871	15-6-1879	Retd. A. F. 15-7-1883 .	14-11-1894
Thomas Leeke Massie	1805	11-11-1827	28-6-1838	17-3-1841	7-11-1860	—	—	—	{ Retd. R. A. 1-4-1866; retd. v.-a. 2-4-1866; retd. a. 20-10-1872 . }	ob.
Sir Edward Belcher, Kt., C.B. (K.C.B. 67)	1793	21-7-1818	16-3-1829	6-5-1841	11-2-1861	2-4-1866	—	—	{ Retd. V.-A. 1866; retd. a. 20-10-1872 . }	18-3-1877
James John Stopford	17-4-1817	5-10-1837	18-2-1840	14-5-1841	4-6-1861	—	—	—	retd. v.-a. 2-4-1866 .	12-5-1868
Woodford John Williams	1809	25-6-1828	28-6-1838	2-6-1841	22-6-1861	2-4-1866	—	—	{ Retd. V.-A. 1-4-1870; retd. a. 20-10-1872 . }	19-12-1892
Augustus Leopold Kuper, C.B. (K.C.B. 64; G.C.B. 69)	16-8-1809	26-2-1830	27-7-1839	8-6-1841	29-7-1861	6-4-1866	20-10-1872	—	Retd. A. 1876	28-10-1885
Charles Eden, C.B. (K.C.B. 73)	3-7-1808	11-2-1832	17-11-1834	11-8-1841	5-8-1861	6-4-1866	—	—	{ Retd. V.-A. 1-4-1870; retd. a. 8-2-1873 . }	7-3-1878
Hon. Charles Gilbert John Brydone Elliot, C.B. (K.C.B. 81)	12-12-1818	27-6-1838	16-7-1840	16-8-1841	5-8-1861	6-4-1866	8-2-1873	1-12-1881	Retd. a. f. 12-12-1888	1895
Hon. Joseph Denman	23-6-1810	9-3-1831	7-8-1835	23-8-1841	15-1-1862	—	—	—	{ Retd. R.-A. 1-4-1866; retd. v.-a. 20-11-1866 . }	26-11-1874
George St. Vincent King, C.B. (K.C.B. 73; suc. as Bart., and assumed name of Duckworth-King)	15-7-1809	15-1-1830	8-8-1834	28-8-1841	4-4-1862	20-3-1867	20-4-1875	—	Retd. A. 1877	18-8-1891
Edward Pellew Halsted		28-1-1829	6-12-1836	15-4-1842	12-4-1862	24-5-1867	—	—	{ Retd. V.-A. 1-4-1870; retd. R.-A. 1-4-1866 . }	1873
George Goldsmith, C.B.		8-8-1828	6-5-1841	16-9-1842	19-5-1862	—	—	—	{ Retd. R.-A. 1-4-1870; retd. v.-a. 18-10-1867 . }	ob.
Charles Frederick	7-5-1797	20-4-1818	6-5-1829	23-12-1842	20-5-1862	18-10-1867	—	—	{ Retd. V.-A. 1-4-1870; retd. a. 18-3-1869 ; retd. a. 30-7-1875 }	23-12-1875

Name									Retirement	Died
Henry Kellett, C.B. (K.C.B. 69)	2-11-1806	15-9-1828	6-5-1841	23-12-1842	16-6-1862	8-4-1868	—	—	Retd. V.-A. 1871; Retd. V.-A. 1-4-1870; retd. a. 30-7-1875	1-3-1875
William Henry Anderson Morshead, C.B.	1811	21-9-1832	8-6-1841	23-12-1842	4-10-1862	15-1-1869	—	—	Retd. V.-A. 1871; retd. a. 30-7-1875	12-2-1886
Richard Collinson, C.B. (K.C.B. 75)	1811	23-3-1835	8-6-1841	23-12-1842	10-11-1862	17-3-1869	—	—	Retd. V.-A. 1871; retd. a. 30-7-1875	12-9-1883
George Ramsay, C.B. (suc. as 12th Earl of Dalhousie)	26-4-1806	30-4-1827	10-1-1837	20-3-1843	22-11-1862	17-3-1869	—	—	Retd. V.-A. 1878; retd. a. 30-7-1875	20-7-1880
Hastings Reginald Yelverton (*formerly* H. R. Henry), C.B. (K.C.B. 69; G.C.B. 75)	3-1808	18-12-1830	9-1-1839	5-9-1843	30-1-1863	26-5-1869	30-7-1875	—	Retd. A. 1878	23-7-1878
John Adams	—	16-2-1815	10-1-1837	18-12-1843	6-2-1863	—	—	—	Retd. R.-A. 1-4-1866	17-12-1866
George Henry Seymour, C.B.	1818	27-6-1838	28-1-1842	24-5-1844	23-3-1863	1869	—	—		25-7-1869
Frederick Hutton	1801	17-5-1825	28-6-1838	3-7-1844	1-4-1863	—	—	—		6-3-1866
William Hutcheon Hall, C.B. (K.C.B. 67)	—	8-6-1841	10-6-1843	22-10-1844	3-4-1863	—	—	—	Retd. R.-A. 1-4-1866; retd. v.-a. 26-7-1869; retd. a. 11-12-1875	25-6-1878
George Greville Wellesley, C.B. (K.C.B. 80; G.C.B. 87)	2-8-1814	22-4-1838	16-4-1842	2-12-1844	3-4-1863	26-7-1869	11-12-1875	—	Retd. A. 2-8-1879	6-4-1901
Hon. George Fowler Hastings, C.B.	28-11-1813	7-1-1832	30-6-1838	31-1-1845	27-4-1863	10-9-1869	—	—		21-3-1876
Hon. Swynfen Thomas Carnegie, C.B.	8-3-1813	21-4-1832	28-6-1838	10-6-1845	27-4-1863	21-1-1870	—	—		29-11-1879
Henry Lyster	18-11-1807	10-1-1824	23-11-1841	30-6-1845	26-6-1863	—	—	—		1864
Frederick Warden, C.B.	26-7-1814	18-9-1828	6-6-1838	24-7-1845	12-9-1863	—	—	—		11-11-1869
Arthur Lowe	27-11-1814	15-8-1835	28-8-1841	30-8-1845	24-9-1863	27-2-1870	18-6-1876	—	Retd. V.-A. 1-4-1870; retd. a. 18-6-1876	*ob.*
Edward Gennys Fanshawe (C.B. 71; K.C.B. 81; G.C.B. 87)	13-12-1803	17-4-1827	4-5-1836	7-9-1845	3-11-1863	1-4-1870	—	—	Retd. A. 27-11-1879	10-3-1894
Claude Henry Mason Buckle, C.B. (K.C.B. 75)	30-5-1811	18-10-1837	21-12-1841	6-11-1845	14-11-1863	1-4-1870	—	—	Retd. V.-A. 29-5-1873; r.-a. 22-1-1877	31-7-1889
Hon. Thomas Baillie (3)	9-8-1815	30-10-1835	4-11-1840	13-11-1845	30-11-1863	1-4-1870	—	—	Retd. R.-A. 1-4-1870; retd. v.-a. 1-4-1870; retd. a. 22-1-1877	8-3-1895
George Giffard, C.B. (K.C.B. 75)	22-4-1815	2-1-1837	26-8-1841	26-12-1845	3-12-1863	1-4-1870	—	—	Retd. R.-A. 1-4-1870; retd. v.-a. 1-4-1870; retd. a. 22-1-1877	1899
Sir Frederick William Erskine Nicolson, Bart., C.B.	—	—	—	12-5-1846	15-12-1863	1-4-1870	—	—	Retd. R.-A. 1-4-1870; retd. a. 22-1-1877	
Hon. James Robert Drummond, C.B. (K.C.B. 73; G.C.B. 80)	15-9-1812	27-12-1832	9-6-1838	8-6-1846	11-1-1864	2-6-1870	22-1-1877	—	Retd. V.-A. 1-1-1874; retd. a. 22-1-1877	7-10-1895
John Lort Stokes	—	10-1-1837	16-8-1841	4-7-1846	9-2-1864	—	—	—	Retd. A. 16-9-1877	1885
Henry Mangles Denham (Kt. 66)	28-8-1800	26-12-1822	20-3-1835	17-8-1846	5-3-1864	—	—	—	Retd. R.-A. 1-4-1870; retd. v.-a. 14-7-1871; retd. a. 1-8-1877	3-7-1887
Arthur Forbes	—	11-3-1828	27-12-1838	27-8-1846	28-3-1864	—	—	—	Retd. R.-A. 1-4-1866; retd. v.-a. 14-7-1871; retd. a. 1-8-1877	20-3-1891

LIST OF FLAG-OFFICERS—continued.

Name (with honours, title, etc., at date of promotion to Flag-rank; honours and titles subsequently acquired being within brackets).	Born.	Lieut.	Commander.	Captain.	Rear-Admiral.	Vice-Admiral.	Admiral.	Admiral of the Fleet.	Remarks. (Rank attained only on or after retirement is indicated in small letters.)	Died.
Harry Edmund Edgell, C.B.	1809	3-6-1828	10-1-1837	9-11-1846	15-6-1864				Retd. R.-A. 1-4-1866; retd. v.-a. 14-7-1871.	1876
Frederick Henry Hastings Glasse, C.B.	11-4-1806	20-2-1826	28-6-1838	9-11-1846	16-9-1864				Retd. R.-A. 1-4-1870; retd. v.-a. 14-7-1871.	1884
Charles Gepp Robinson	3-12-1805	30-9-1826	28-6-1838	9-11-1846	20-10-1864				retd. a. 1-8-1877.	31-10-1875
George Thomas Gordon		6-5-1829	1-8-1840	9-11-1846	28-10-1864				Retd. R.-A. 1-4-1870; retd. v.-a. 14-7-1871.	ob.
Erasmus Ommanney (C.B. 67; Kt. 77)	22-5-1814	10-12-1835	9-10-1840	9-11-1846	12-11-1864	14-7-1871			Retd. V.-A. 1-1-1875; retd. a. 1-8-1877.	
Douglas Curry	15-8-1811	12-6-1829	4-11-1840	9-11-1846	10-2-1865					15-9-1869
George William Douglas O'Callaghan (C.B. 67)		6-6-1834	11-8-1841	30-11-1846	11-4-1865				retd. a. 1-8-1877.	28-12-1900
Charles Wise		24-12-1833	23-12-1842	28-2-1847	13-4-1865				Retd. R.-A. 1-4-1866; retd. v.-a. 1-10-1871.	1877
Thomas Pickering Thompson	1810	5-6-1834	23-11-1841	25-6-1847	24-4-1865				Retd. R.-A. 1-4-1870; retd. v.-a. 1-10-1871.	5-3-1892
Wallace Houston		3-3-1832	7-5-1842	23-7-1847	5-5-1865				Retd. R.-A. 1-4-1870; retd. v.-o. 1-10-1871.	17-5-1891
William John Cavendish Clifford, C.B. (suc. as 2nd Bart. 77)	12-10-1814	7-5-1838	7-3-1842	18-8-1847	12-9-1865	1-10-1871			Retd. V.-A. 1872; retd. a. 1-8-1877.	11-4-1882
Thomas Fisher (2)		28-12-1833	23-11-1841	11-10-1847	17-11-1865				Retd. R.-A. 1-4-1866; retd. v.-a. 2-11-1871.	6-6-1891
Thomas Harvey (2)	12-8-1810	24-12-1829	6-11-1840	31-1-1848	2-12-1865				retd. a. 1-8-1877.	8-4-1868
William Loring, C.B. (K.C.B. 75)	31-10-1811	26-2-1836	27-8-1841	31-1-1848	7-3-1866	2-11-1871	1-8-1877		Retd. A. 23-11-1881.	4-1-1895
Sir William Legge George Hoste, Bart.	19-3-1818	27-6-1838	5-11-1843	15-2-1848	2-4-1866					10-9-1868
John Fulford	16-2-1809	29-7-1831	4-11-1840	1-5-1848	2-4-1866				Retd. R.-A. 1-4-1870; retd. v.-a. 7-5-1872; retd. a. 5-8-1877.	ob.
Alfred Phillipps Ryder (K.C.B. 84)	27-11-1820	2-7-1841	15-1-1846	2-5-1848	2-4-1866	7-5-1872	5-8-1877		Retd. A. 27-10-1884.	30-4-1888
Henry Chads (K.C.B. 87)	1819	14-6-1841	31-1-1845	5-6-1848	2-4-1866	20-10-1872	16-9-1877	29-4-1885		
Francis Scott, C.B.		11-2-1835	2-7-1841	12-8-1848	2-4-1866	8-3-1873			Retd. V.-A. 1873	1-6-1875
Sir Adolphus Slade, K.C.B.		27-11-1827	23-11-1841	10-1-1849	2-4-1866				Retd. R.-A. 1867; retd. v.-a. 6-4-1873.	13-11-1877

Name									Retirement	Died
Arthur Farquhar (2) (K.C.B. 86) . . .	1815	4-11-1840	2-12-1844	27-10-1849	2-4-1866	6-4-1873	9-3-1878	—	Retd. A. 9-1-1880 .	14-1-1903
Edwin Clayton Tennyson D'Eyncourt (C.B. 73) . . .	1813	21-2-1837	8-6-1841	1-11-1849	2-4-1866			—	{ Retd. R.-A. 1-4-1870; retd. v.-a. 30-4-1873; retd. a. 21-3-1878 }	
Thomas Henry Mason (C.B. 75) . . .	1811	21-7-1837	8-6-1841	1-11-1849	2-4-1866			—	{ Retd. R.-A. 1-4-1870; retd. v.-a. 30-4-1873; retd. a. 21-3-1878 }	20-2-1900
Sidney Grenfell (C.B. 67) . . .		20-5-1833	5-11-1840	15-1-1850	6-4-1866			—	{ Retd. R.-A. 1-4-1870; retd. v.-a. 30-4-1873; retd. a. 21-3-1878 }	ob.
Richard Strode Hewlett, C.B. . . .		10-1-1837	23-9-1845	15-1-1850	6-4-1866			—	{ Retd. R.-A. 1-4-1870; retd. v.-n. 30-4-1873; retd. a. 21-3-1878 }	3-4-1875
Sir John Charles Dalrymple Hay, Bart. (C.B. 69; K.C.B. 85).	11-2-1821	6-2-1845	28-8-1846	20-1-1850	6-4-1866			—	{ Retd. R.-A. 1-4-1870; retd. v.-a. 30-4-1872; retd. a. 21-3-1878 }	
James Horsford Cockburn . . .		5-11-1840	24-4-1846	7-4-1850	6-4-1866			—	{ Retd. R.-A. 1-4-1870; retd. v.-a. 30-4-1873; retd. a. 21-3-1878 }	10-2-1872
James Willcox, C.B. . . .		23-11-1841	9-11-1846	10-4-1850	6-4-1866			—	{ Retd. R.-A. 1-4-1870; retd. v.-a. 30-4-1873; retd. a. 21-3-1878 }	1877
Hugh Dunlop, C.B. . . .		8-2-1828	12-8-1842	3-8-1850	6-4-1866			—	Retd. A. 18-1-1886 .	15-4-1887
Astley Cooper Key, C.B. (K.C.B. 73; G.C.B. 82) .	1821	22-12-1842	18-11-1845	11-10-1850	20-11-1866			—	{ Retd. R.-A. 1-4-1870; retd. v.-a. 29-5-1873; retd. a. 26-9-1878 }	3-3-1888
Frederick Byng Montresor . . .	1811	30-7-1835	12-1-1843	29-4-1851	20-3-1867			—	Retd. A. 9-6-1882 .	15-12-1897
Charles Farrel Hillyar (C.B. 69; K.C.B. 87) .	1817	24-3-1842	15-5-1848	20-2-1852	24-5-1867			—	{ Retd. R.-A. 1-4-1870; retd. v.-a. 25-8-1873; retd. a. 15-6-1879 }	14-12-1889
Thomas Hope (2). . . .	10-7-1810	6-7-1832	23-11-1841	27-3-1852	31-5-1867			—	{ Retd. R.-A. 1-4-1870; retd. a. 15-6-1879 }	31-8-1867
Edward Southwell Sotheby, C.B. (K.C.B. 75) . .	14-5-1813	3-10-1835	30-10-1841	6-9-1852	1-9-1867			—	{ Retd. R.-A. 1-4-1870; retd. v.-a. 25-8-1873; retd. a. 15-6-1879 }	6-1-1902
Michael De Courcy (3), C.B. . . .	8-5-1811	28-6-1838	12-2-1842	6-9-1852	18-10-1867			—	{ Retd. R.-A. 1-4-1870; retd. v.-a. 25-8-1873; retd. a. 15-6-1879 }	22-10-1881
John Walter Tarleton, C.B. (K.C.B. 73).		22-9-1835	9-11-1846	27-9-1852	8-4-1868			—	{ Retd. V.-A. ; retd. a. 15-6-1879 }	25-9-1880
Lord Frederick Herbert Kerr . . .	30-9-1818	21-10-1840	3-7-1846	10-12-1852	9-4-1868			—	{ Retd. R.-A. 1-4-1870; retd. v.-a. 1-1-1874; retd. a. 15-6-1879 }	15-1-1896
Edmund Heathcote . . .		10-1-1840	13-6-1849	15-12-1852	1-1-1869			—	{ Retd. V.-A. 1877; retd. a. 15-6-1879 }	24-10-1881
Geoffrey Thomas Phipps Hornby (K.C.B. 78; G.C.B. 85).	20-2-1825	15-6-1844	12-1-1850	18-12-1852	1-1-1869	1-1-1875	15-6-1879	1-5-1888	Retd. A. F. 20-2-1895 .	3-3-1895
Charles Frederick Alexander Shadwell, C.B. (K.C.B. 73)	1814	28-6-1838	27-6-1846	25-2-1853	15-1-1869	20-4-1875		—	{ Retd. V.-A. 1879; retd. a. 2-8-1879 . }	1-3-1886

LIST OF FLAG-OFFICERS—*continued.*

NAME (with honours, title, etc., at date of promotion to Flag-rank, honours and titles subsequently acquired being within brackets).	BORN.	LIEUT.	COMMANDER.	CAPTAIN.	REAR-ADMIRAL.	VICE-ADMIRAL.	ADMIRAL.	ADMIRAL OF THE FLEET.	REMARKS. *Rank attained only on or after retirement is indicated in small letters.*	DIED.
William King Hall, C.B. (K.C.B. 71)	1816	28-7-1841	21-3-1848	6-6-1853	17-3-1869	30-7-1875	2-8-1879	—	Retd. A. 1881	29-7-1886
Thomas Wilson (2), C.B.	1811	9-5-1839	20-9-1843	12-8-1853	17-3-1869	11-12-1875	27-11-1879	—	Retd. R.-A. 1-4-1870; retd. v.-a. 11-12-1875; retd. a. 27-11-1879 .	11-10-1894
Edward Augustus Inglefield, C.B. (K.C.B. 87)	27-3-1820	21-9-1842	18-11-1845	7-10-1853	26-5-1869	11-12-1875	27-11-1879	—	Retd. A. 27-3-1885 .	5-9-1894
William Edmonstone, C.B. (suc. as 4th Bart. 71)	29-1-1810	23-2-1829	23-11-1841	20-10-1853	3-7-1869			—	Retd. R.-A. 1-4-1870; retd. v.-a. 22-3-1876; retd. a. 9-1-1880 .	18-2-1888
James Francis Ballard Wainwright	26-4-1820	22-12-1841	21-12-1849	2-11-1853	26-7-1869			—		4-1872
James Newburgh Strange	2-10-1812	23-2-1838	30-3-1842	10-1-1854	10-9-1869	— —		—	Retd. R.-A. 1-4-1870; retd. v.-a. 22-3-1876; retd. a. 9-1-1880 .	1-11-1894
James Charles Prevost		10-12-1835	22-10-1844	17-4-1854	16-9-1869			—	Retd. R.-A. 1-4-1870; retd. v.-a. 22-3-1876; retd. a. 9-1-1880 .	1891
Sir William Saltonstall Wiseman (2), Bart., K.C.B.	4-8-1814	28-6-1838	7-2-1846	17-4-1854	12-11-1869			—	Retd. R.-A. 1-4-1870 .	14-7-1874
James Aylmer Dorset Paynter	1817	23-11-1841	8-7-1846	17-4-1854	21-1-1870			—	Retd. R.-A. 1-4-1870	17-12-1876
Arthur Cumming, C.B. (K.C.B. 87)		28-9-1840	9-11-1846	19-4-1854	27-2-1870	22-3-1876	9-1-1880	—	Retd. A. 6-5-1882	17-2-1893
Arthur Parry Eardley Wilmot, C.B.	24-4-1815	3-7-1840	26-9-1847	29-4-1854	1-4-1870	18-6-1876		—	Retd. R.-A. 18-6-1873; retd. v.-a. 18-6-1876 .	3-4-1886
Robert Coote (C.B. 73)	1-6-1823	25-9-1843	25-6-1847	29-4-1854	1-4-1870	18-6-1876	3-1-1881	—	Retd. A. 1-6-1885 .	ob.
William Houston Stewart, C.B. (K.C.B. 77; G.C.B. 87)	9-1823	26-9-1842	19-5-1848	9-7-1854	1-4-1870	12-11-1876*	23-11-1881	—	Retd. A. 31-3-1885 .	13-11-1901
Hon. Arthur Auckland Leopold Pedro Cochrane, C.B. (K.C.B. 89)	24-10-1821	12-4-1845	12-4-1851	29-8-1854	1-4-1870	12-11-1876	1-12-1881	—	Retd. A. 22-6-1886 .	
Frederick Archibald Campbell		11-5-1837	27-4-1851	13-9-1854	1-4-1870			—		1874
Frederick Beauchamp Paget Seymour, C.B. (K.C.B. 77; G.C.B. 81; cr. Lord Alcester, 82)	12-4-1821	7-3-1842	5-6-1847	19-10-1854	1-4-1870	31-12-1876	6-5-1882	—	Retd. A. 12-4-1886 .	30-3-1895
Hon. John Welbore Sunderland Spencer	12-3-1816	23-11-1841	12-10-1857	19-10-1854	1-4-1870			—	Retd. R.-A. 20-12-1871; retd. v.-a. 22-1-1877 .	17-10-1888
Reginald John James George Macdonald (K.C.S.I. 77; K.C.B. 87)	1820	14-12-1842	20-1-1848	19-10-1854	1-4-1870	22-1-1877	9-6-1882	—	Retd. A. 7-7-1884 .	ob.
George Henry Richards (civ. C.B. 71; Kt. 77; K.C.B. 86)	1-1820	12-7-1842	18-11-1845	21-10-1854	2-6-1870			—	Retd. R.-A. . . retd. v.-a. 5-8-1877 .	14-11-1896
Sir Francis Leopold M'Clintock, Kt. (K.C.B. 91)	1819	29-7-1845	11-10-1851	21-10-1854	1-10-1871	5-8-1877	7-7-1884	—	Retd. A. 8-7-1884 .	

* Promotion suspended during part of tenure of Controllership of the Navy, 1876-77.

Name		22-12-1840	3-8-1847	13-11-1854	20-12-1871	—	—	15-12-1888	Retd.	ob.
Sir Leopold George Heath, K.C.B.	1817	22-12-1840	3-8-1847	13-11-1854	20-12-1871	—	—	—	{Retd. R.-A. 12-2-1873; retd. v.-a. 16-9-1877.}	
Henry Schank Hillyar, C.B.	1819	23-12-1842	25-2-1853	13-11-1854	11-2-1872	—	—	—		3-8-1893
George Granville Randolph, C.B. (K.C.B. 97)		27-6-1838	9-11-1846	18-11-1854	24-4-1872	16-9-1877	—	—	{Retd. V.-A. 26-7-1881; retd. a. 8-7-1884.}	
Lord John Hay (3), C.B. (K.C.B. 81; G.C.B. 86)	23-8-1827	19-12-1846	28-8-1851	27-11-1854	7-5-1872	1-12-1877	8-7-1884	15-12-1888	Retd. A. F. 23-8-1897.	
George Hancock	1819	1-7-1844	24-1-1850	19-1-1855	20-10-1872	—	—	—		20-9-1876
Hon. Francis Egerton	15-9-1824	4-5-1846	30-1-1850	1-2-1855	8-2-1873	—	—	—	{Retd. R.-A. 14-11-1875; retd. v.-a. 9-3-1878; retd. a. 27-10-1884.}	15-12-1895
Edward Bridges Rice (C.B. 81; K.C.B. 87)	30-10-1819	5-8-1844	7-4-1850	24-2-1855	12-4-1873	9-3-1878	27-10-1884	—	{Retd. V.-A. retd. a. 30-10-1884.}	19-10-1902
Thomas Miller	1819	22-7-1844	23-8-1847	16-5-1855	6-4-1873	21-3-1878	—	—	{Retd. V.-A. retd. a. 30-10-1884.}	ob.
Hon. George Disney Keane, C.B.	26-9-1817	26-12-1840	9-11-1846	9-7-1855	30-4-1873	—	—	—	{Retd. R.-A. 27-9-1877; retd. v.-a. 21-3-1878; retd. a. 30-10-1884.}	19-10-1891
Sherard Osborn, C.B.	1822	4-5-1846	30-10-1852	18-8-1855	29-5-1873	21-3-1878	—	—		6-5-1875
Rowley Lambert, C.B.	22-4-1828	23-4-1848	25-2-1853	29-9-1855	25-8-1873	—	—	—		22-7-1880
Augustus Phillimore (K.C.B. 87)	24-5-1822	7-9-1845	28-4-1852	10-10-1855	1-1-1874	30-1-1879	30-10-1884	—	Retd. A. 24-5-1887.	ob. 27-2-1878
William Charles Chamberlain	21-4-1818	4-11-1840	22-10-1844	21-2-1856	19-1-1874	—	—	—		
George Ommanney Willes, C.B. (K.C.B. 84; G.C.B. 92)	19-6-1823	11-12-1844	17-4-1854	10-5-1856	11-6-1874	1-2-1879	27-3-1885	—	Retd. A. 19-6-1888.	18-2-1901
William Garnham Luard, C.B. (K.C.B. 97)	1820	6-5-1841	29-9-1850	11-3-1857	1-1-1875	15-6-1879	31-3-1885	—	Retd. A. 7-4-1885.	10-12-1893
John Corbett, C.B. (K.C.B. 86)	15-7-1822	4-5-1846	20-2-1852	10-8-1857	20-4-1875	2-8-1879	7-4-1885	—	Retd. A. 15-7-1887.	6-10-1901
Edward Winterton Turnour, C.B.	1821	20-9-1843	20-9-1855	10-8-1857	25-4-1875	9-9-1879	—	—	{Retd. V.-A. 20-1-1880; retd. a. 29-4-1885.}	
Algernon Frederick Rous de Horsey	27-7-1827	26-7-1846	10-6-1853	7-9-1857	7-9-1875	27-11-1879	29-4-1885	—	Retd. A. 25-7-1892.	
Henry Boys (2)	1824	9-2-1846	14-5-1853	17-10-1857	30-7-1875	9-1-1880	1-6-1885	—	Retd. R.-A. 1-7-1885.	
Robert Jenkins, C.B.	22-1-1825	27-3-1846	3-5-1853	30-12-1857	4-11-1875	—	—	—	{Retd. R.-A. 1-1-1880; retd. v.-a. 20-1-1880.}	22-8-1894
William Montagu Dowell, C.B. (K.C.B. 82; G.C.B. 94)	2-8-1825	25-10-1847	13-11-1854	26-12-1858	11-12-1875	20-1-1880	1-7-1885	—	Retd. A. 2-8-1890.	
Arthur William Acland Hood, C.B. (K.C.B. 85; G.C.B. 89; cr. Lord Hood of Avalon, 92)	14-7-1824	9-1-1846	27-11-1854	26-2-1858	22-3-1876	23-7-1880	18-1-1886	—	Retd. A. 14-7-1889.	16-11-1901
Charles Fellowes, C.B.	1824	29-6-1846	26-1-1855	26-2-1859	18-6-1876	31-12-1880	1886	—		1886
Charles Wake.	23-10-1824	5-8-1846	3-2-1855	23-6-1859	21-9-1876	3-1-1881	—	—	{Retd. V.-A. 19-1-1881; retd. a. 12-4-1886.}	26-3-1890
Sir John Edmund Commerell, V.C., K.C.B. (G.C.B. 87)	13-1-1829	3-12-1848	29-9-1855	18-7-1859	12-11-1876	19-1-1881	12-4-1886	14-2-1892	Retd. A. F. 12-1-1899.	21-5-1901

LIST OF FLAG-OFFICERS—*continued.*

Name (with honours, title, etc., at date of promotion to Flag-rank, honours and titles subsequently acquired being within brackets).	Born.	Lieut.	Com- mander.	Captain.	Rear- Admiral.	Vice- Admiral.	Admiral.	Admiral of the Fleet.	Remarks. *Rank attained only on or after retirement is indicated in small letters.*	Died.
Richard James, Lord Gifford (C.B. 77; suc. as 4th Earl of Clanwilliam, 79; K.C.M.G. 82; K.C.B. 87; G.C.B. 95).	3-10-1832	12-9-1852	26-2-1858	22-7-1859	31-12-1876	26-7-1881	22-6-1886	20-2-1895		
Hon. Fitzgerald Algernon Charles Foley.	5-9-1823	15-1-1846	7-9-1855	6-8-1860	31-12-1876	23-11-1881	24-6-1887		Retd. A. 7-6-1887	
H.S.H. Ernest Leopold Victor Charles Auguste Joseph Emich, Prince of Leiningen, civ. G.C.B. (mil. G.C.B. 87; G.C.V.O.)	9-11-1830	2-5-1855	10-8-1857	25-10-1860	31-12-1876	1-12-1881	7-6-1887		Retd. A. 9-11-1895	
Frederick Henry Stirling	1829	29-5-1848	25-3-1854	19-11-1860	22-1-1877					ob. 13-2-1880
Charles Webley Hope	1826	11-5-1848	2-8-1854	15-5-1861	1-8-1877	31-12-1881				28-5-1888
William Gore Jones, C.B.		6-11-1848	13-11-1854	20-8-1861	5-8-1877	6-5-1882				ob.
Hon. Henry Carr Glyn, C.B., C.S.I.		7-2-1852	15-1-1855	20-8-1861	16-9-1877	9-6-1882			Retd. V.-A. 18-10-1887	
Richard Vesey Hamilton, C.B. (K.C.B. 87; G.C.B. 95)	28-5-1829	11-10-1851	10-8-1857	27-1-1862	27-9-1877	17-2-1884	18-10-1887		Retd. A. 28-5-1894	
Charles Lodowick Darley Waddilove	13-5-1828	10-9-1849	3-2-1855	15-4-1862	31-12-1877	1-4-1884	1-5-1888		Retd. A. 13-5-1893 .	17-10-1896
John Dobree M'Crea.		2-9-1830	10-5-1856	15-4-1862	31-12-1877					ob.
Leveson Eliot Henry Somerset.	29-8-1829	24-10-1851	10-5-1856	15-4-1862	28-2-1878	7-7-1884	19-6-1888		Retd. A. 1891	7-2-1900
John Eglinton Montgomerie, C.B.	23-12-1825	1-1-1848	23-7-1855	24-11-1862	9-3-1878				{ Retd. R.-A. 8-4-1880; retd. v.-a. 8-7-1884; } retd. a. 15-12-1888	10-9-1902
Sir William Nathan Wrighte Hewett, V.C., K.C.B. (K.C.S.I. 83)	12-8-1834	26-10-1854	13-9-1858	24-11-1862	21-3-1878	8-7-1884				13-5-1888
Algernon McLennan Lyons (K.C.B. 89; G.C.B. 97)	30-8-1833	28-6-1854	9-8-1858	1-12-1862	26-9-1878	27-10-1884	15-12-1888	23-8-1897		
H.R.H. Prince Alfred Ernest Albert, Duke of Edinburgh, K.G., K.T., G.C.S.I., G.C.M.G.	6-8-1844	(see below)		(see 23-2-1866)	30-12-1878*	30-11-1882*	18-10-1887*	3-6-1893*		30-7-1900
Thomas Brandreth	6-8-1825	23-12-1845	5-2-1858	9-5-1863	31-12-1878	30-10-1884	14-7-1889		Retd. A. 1890	10-12-1894
Thomas Bridgeman Lethbridge	28-10-1828	16-10-1848	7-9-1857	19-9-1863	31-12-1878	27-3-1885	2-8-1890		Retd. A. 1890	30-12-1892
Francis William Sullivan, C.B., C.M.G. (K.C.B. 79)	31-5-1834	22-2-1856	28-6-1859	9-11-1863	31-12-1878	31-3-1885	5-8-1890		Retd. A. 25-2-1892	
Edward Hardinge, C.B.	19-5-1830	25-2-1852	10-5-1856	12-12-1863	30-1-1879	7-4-1885			{ Retd. V.-A.; retd. a. 6-8-1890 }	2-5-1894
William Graham, C.B. (K.C.B. 87)	10-9-1826	26-3-1849	26-2-1858	12-12-1863	1-2-1879	29-4-1885	6-8-1890		Retd. A. 10-9-1891	
Anthony Hiley Hoskins, C.B. (K.C.B. 82; G.C.B. 93)	1-9-1828	26-3-1849	26-2-1858	12-12-1863	15-6-1879	1-6-1885	20-6-1891		Retd. A. 1-9-1893	
Nowell Salmon, V.C., C.B. (K.C.B. 87; G.C.B. 97)	20-2-1835	5-1-1856	22-3-1858	12-12-1863	2-8-1879	1-7-1885	10-9-1891	13-1-1899		21-6-1901

* Special promotions.

Name									Remarks	Died
John Clark Soady	7-6-1832	9-4-1851	9-12-1858	12-12-1863	9-9-1879	24-11-1885	—		Retd. V.-A. 26-11-1885	7-3-1889
Edward Henry Howard	16-9-1832	7-1-1853	7-5-1857	16-2-1864	27-11-1879	26-11-1885	—		Retd. V.-A. 29-11-1889	18-1-1890
John Kennedy Erskine Baird (K.C.B. 90)		28-12-1854	3-7-1857	16-2-1864	31-12-1879	18-1-1886	14-2-1892		Retd. A. 16-9-1897	
Charles Thomas Curme	2-8-1827	4-3-1848	26-2-1858	16-2-1864	1-1-1880	9-3-1886	—		Retd. A.	19-2-1892
George Willes Watson (K.C.B. 91)	5-4-1827	8-3-1849	9-8-1858	16-2-1864	9-1-1880	12-4-1886	25-2-1892		{ Retd. V.-A. 4-1-1891 ; retd. a. 5-4-1892 }	26-4-1897
Henry Dennis Hickley	11-12-1826	24-8-1847	26-8-1858	16-2-1864	20-1-1880	22-6-1886	—		{ Retd. R.-A. 6-4-1887 ; retd. v.-a. 24-5-1887 ; retd. a. 5-4-1892 }	
Frederick Anstruther Herbert	1827	11-11-1848	18-11-1858	16-2-1864	14-2-1880	—	—		Retd. A. 25-10-1888	
Henry Bouchier Phillimore, C.B.	25-10-1833	28-6-1854	25-3-1863	14-7-1864	8-4-1880	24-5-1887	—		Retd. A. 9-12-1894	3-7-1893
Hon. William John Ward	9-12-1829	24-6-1850	26-2-1858	25-7-1864	23-7-1880	7-1-1887	5-4-1892		{ Retd. V.-A. 29-1-1891 ; retd. a. 26-7-1892 }	11-1900
Henry Rushworth Wratislaw	29-8-1832	3-2-1855	22-3-1858	25-7-1864	31-12-1880	15-7-1887	—			
William Henry Whyte	24-1-1829	11-5-1849	1-4-1858	25-7-1864	3-1-1881	18-10-1887	25-7-1892		Retd. A. 9-8-1892	5-11-1896
Henry Duncan Grant, C.B.	12-10-1834	31-10-1855	18-6-1858	30-9-1864	19-1-1881	6-1-1888	9-8-1892		{ Retd. V.-A. 8-11-1888 ; retd. a. 13-5-1893 }	
John Moresby	15-3-1830	2-7-1851	11-12-1858	21-11-1864	26-7-1881	1-5-1888	—			1885
John Crawford Wilson		31-10-1855	30-1-1861	17-2-1865	23-11-1881	—	—		{ Retd. R.-A. 3-4-1888 ; retd. v.-a. 14-5-1888 ; retd. a. 13-5-1893 }	
Sholto Douglas, C.B.		31-10-1855	28-4-1858	1-3-1865	1-12-1881	—	—		{ Retd. V.-A. 30-8-1890 ; retd. a. 13-5-1893 }	
William Henry Edye	30-8-1830	25-2-1853	6-8-1860	11-9-1865	31-12-1881	14-5-1888	—		{ Retd. R.-A. 7-7-1885 ; retd. v.-a. 19-6-1888 . }	4-5-1889
Arthur Thomas Thrupp	1828	25-2-1852	17-9-1858	16-12-1865	31-12-1881	—	—			
Sir Michael Culme-Seymour, Bart. (K.C.B. 93; G.C.B. 97)	13-3-1836	25-5-1857	6-6-1859	16-12-1865	6-5-1882	19-6-1888	13-5-1893	—	{ Retd. A. 13-3-1901 ; V.-A. of U.K. 1901 }	
Sir Frederick William Richards, K.C.B. (G.C.B. 95)	30-11-1833	31-10-1855	9-2-1860	6-2-1866	9-6-1882	—	—	29-11-1898*		
H.R.H. the Duke of Edinburgh (see also above)	6-8-1844	24-2-1863	†	23-2-1866	(see 30-12-1878)	(see 30-11-1882)	(see 18-10-1887)	(see 3-6-1893)		30-7-1900
Ralph Peter Cator		19-8-1850	17-9-1858	11-4-1866	31-12-1882	—	—		{ Retd. R.-A. 27-12-1886 ; retd. v.-a. 18-11-1888 ; retd. a. 28-5-1894 }	
Hon. Walter Cecil Carpenter (previously Talbot)	27-3-1834	2-9-1854	16-6-1859	11-4-1866	31-12-1882	8-11-1888	28-5-1894		Retd. A. 11-3-1896	
Theodore Morton Jones	1828	20-1-1849	22-8-1859	11-4-1866	31-12-1882	—	—		{ Retd. R.-A. 8-1-1883 ; retd. v.-a. 15-12-1888 }	26-8-1895
Robert Gordon Douglas	7-6-1829	3-5-1853	3-7-1860	11-4-1866	8-1-1883	15-12-1888	—		{ Retd. V.-A. 7-6-1894 ; retd. a. 9-12-1894 }	
Charles Trelawney Jago		23-10-1849	6-8-1860	11-4-1866	20-3-1883	—	—		{ Retd. R.-A. 27-12-1886 ; retd. v.-a. 4-7-1889 . }	11-1891

* Special promotion (additional).   † Promoted from Lieutenant to Post-Captain.

LIST OF FLAG-OFFICERS—continued.

Name (with honours, title, etc., at date of promotion to Flag-rank, honours and titles subsequently acquired being within brackets).	Born.	Lieut.	Commander.	Captain.	Rear-Admiral.	Vice-Admiral.	Admiral.	Admiral of the Fleet.	Remarks. Rank attained only on or after retirement is indicated in small letters.	Died.
William Samuel Brown (later W. S. Greive).	2-1-1831	28-2-1854	11-9-1860	11-4-1866	17-2-1884	14-7-1889	—	—	Retd. V.-A. 1889	29-10-1891
George Tryon, C.B. (K.C.B. 87)	4-1-1832	21-10-1854	25-10-1860	11-4-1866	1-4-1884	13-8-1889	9-12-1894	—		22-6-1893
Algernon Charles Fleeschi Heneage (K.C.B. 92)	19-3-1833	8-3-1854	10-1-1861	26-6-1866	7-7-1884	29-11-1889	—	—	Retd. A. 19-3-1898	
Sir Walter James Hunt-Grubbe, K.C.B. (G.C.B. 99).	23-2-1832	23-5-1854	23-3-1861	5-7-1866	8-7-1884	2-8-1890	20-2-1895	—	Retd. A. 23-2-1897	
Charles John Rowley	26-12-1832	21-12-1852	9-7-1861	5-7-1866	27-10-1884	5-8-1890	9-11-1895	—		ob.
Richard Wells (K.C.B. 96).	3-2-1833	3-2-1855	12-12-1863	6-7-1866	30-10-1884	6-8-1890	11-3-1896	—	Retd. A. 26-12-1897	
Thomas le Hunte Ward, C.B.	4-8-1830	22-10-1853	31-1-1861	15-4-1867	27-3-1885	—	—	—	{ Retd. R.-A. 4-8-1890; retd. v.-a. 30-8-1890; retd. a. 9-11-1896 }	
William Arthur, C.B.	1830	8-3-1854	1-4-1861	15-4-1867	31-3-1885	—	—	—		15-11-1886
Hon. Edmund Robert Fremantle, C.B., C.M.G. (K.C.B. 89; G.C.B. 99).	15-6-1836	14-1-1857	9-7-1861	15-4-1867	7-4-1885	30-8-1890	10-10-1896	—	{ Retd. A. 15-6-1901; R.-A. of U.K. 1901 }	
John Ommanney Hopkins (K.C.B. 92; G.C.B. 99)	13-7-1834	23-10-1854	24-11-1862	14-9-1867	29-4-1885	4-1-1891	9-11-1896	—	Retd. A. 13-7-1899	
St. George Caulfield D'Arcy-Irvine, C.B.	23-5-1833	9-11-1854	29-1-1863	25-10-1867	1-6-1885	29-1-1891	23-2-1897	—	Retd. A. 10-5-1897	
Henry Fairfax, C.B. (K.C.B. 96).	21-1-1837	25-8-1858	4-11-1862	3-4-1868	1-7-1885	20-6-1891	10-5-1897	—		20-3-1900
William Elrington Gordon.	20-5-1831	22-10-1853	20-8-1861	16-4-1868	5-7-1885	—	—	—	{ Retd. R.-A. 20-5-1891; retd. v.-a. 10-9-1891. }	1897
Alfred John Chatfield (C.B. 87)	27-8-1832	6-3-1854	16-4-1862	16-4-1868	1-1-1886	—	—	—	{ Retd. R.-A. 27-8-1891; retd. v.-a. 10-9-1891; retd. a. 23-8-1897 }	
Thomas Barnardiston	4-12-1833	3-2-1855	24-6-1862	14-8-1868	1-1-1886	10-9-1891	—	—	{ Retd. V.-A. 28-12-1891; retd. a. 23-8-1897 }	
Lindesay Brine	5-11-1834	27-11-1854	24-6-1862	16-10-1868	1-1-1886	28-12-1891	—	—	{ Retd. V.-A. 5-11-1894; retd. a. 23-8-1897 }	
James Elphinstone Erskine (K.C.B. 97).	2-12-1838	28-6-1859	4-8-1862	4-11-1868	18-1-1886	14-2-1892	23-8-1897	—		
George Lydiard Sulivan.	26-3-1832	26-9-1853	28-10-1862	1-6-1869	9-3-1886	20-2-1892	—	—	{ Retd. V.-A. 26-3-1892; retd. a. 16-9-1897 }	
William Codrington, C.B.	21-2-1832	31-10-1855	29-7-1864	1-6-1869	12-4-1886	25-2-1892	16-9-1897	—		29-7-1888
Henry Frederick Nicholson, C.B. (K.C.B. 97).	24-10-1835	17-12-1857	11-4-1866	20-7-1869	22-6-1886	—	—	—	Retd. A. 11-12-1897	
Alexander Buller, C.B. (K.C.B. 96)	30-6-1835	10-4-1855	10-6-1863	10-12-1869	1-1-1887	26-3-1892	11-12-1897	—	Retd. A. 30-6-1899	
Loftus Francis Jones	19-7-1836	25-5-1857	4-10-1861	4-4-1870	1-1-1887	5-4-1892	26-12-1897	—	Retd. A. 26-10-1899	
George Stanley Bosanquet	18-4-1835	22-9-1855	9-11-1863	4-4-1870	1-1-1887	25-7-1892	—	—	{ Retd. V.-A. 10-3-1894; retd. a. 19-3-1898 }	
William Henry Cuming.	26-5-1832	6-8-1855	21-11-1864	4-4-1870	6-4-1887	—	—	—	{ Retd. R.-A. 10-6-1887; retd. v.-a. 9-8-1892. }	8-5-1896

Name								Retired	
Francis Mowbray Prattent	19-5-1833	14-5-1853	24-11-1862	19-5-1870	24-5-1887	9-8-1892	—	Retd. V.-A. 6-9-1892	31-10-1892
Edward Kelly	26-4-1836	3-6-1856	1-3-1865	22-10-1870	10-6-1887	5-10-1892	—		16-1-1892
Frederick Charles Bryan Robinson	3-4-1836	4-4-1855	30-9-1863	24-7-1871	7-7-1887				18-1-1896
Edward Stanley Adeane, C.M.G.	7-12-1836	25-2-1858	8-9-1864	24-7-1871	1-1-1888	13-5-1893	19-3-1898	Retd. A. 7-12-1901	18-10-1902
Richard Edward Tracey (K.C.B. 98)	24-1-1837	28-6-1859	19-4-1865	29-12-1871	1-1-1888	23-6-1893	29-11-1898	Retd. A. 24-1-1902	
Charles Frederick Hotham (K.C.B. 95)	10-3-1813	17-2-1863	19-4-1865	29-12-1871	6-1-1888	1-9-1893	13-1-1899		
Lord Charles Thomas Montague Douglas Scott, C.B. (K.C.B. 97)	20-10-1839	19-7-1859	12-9-1865	6-2-1872	3-4-1888	10-3-1894	30-6-1899		
Sir Robert Henry More Molyneux, K.C.B.	6-8-1838	28-6-1850	18-12-1865	6-2-1872	1-5-1888	29-5-1894	13-7-1899		
Robert O'Brien FitzRoy, C.B.	2-4-1839	5-9-1859	13-2-1866	6-2-1872	14-5-1888	7-6-1894			7-5-1896
Nathaniel Bowden-Smith (K.C.B. 97)	21-1-1838	19-5-1859	26-6-1866	29-5-1872	19-6-1888	5-11-1894	26-10-1899		
James George Mead	4-3-1834	8-1-1855	16-12-1865	29-11-1872	1-1-1889	9-12-1894	—	{ Retd. R.-A. 4-3-1894; retd. v.-a. 9-12-1894	
William Henry Maxwell	13-6-1840	13-1-1860	6-6-1866	29-11-1872	1-1-1889		—	{ Retd. V.-A. 25-6-1895; retd. a. 21-3-1900	
Lord Walter Talbot Kerr (K.C.B. 96)	28-9-1839	5-9-1859	3-4-1868	30-11-1872	1-1-1889	20-2-1895	[21-3-1900]	Retd. A. 24-5-1901	
George Digby Morant (K.C.B. 1901)	8-8-1837	15-5-1858	6-2-1866	13-2-1873	1-1-1889	20-6-1895	[13-3-1901]		
Edward Hobart Seymour (K.C.B. 97; G.C.B. 1900)	3-4-1840	11-2-1860	5-3-1866	13-2-1873	14-7-1889	9-11-1895	[24-5-1901]		
Henry Craven St. John	5-1-1837	10-8-1857	12-4-1866	18-9-1873	13-8-1889	19-1-1896	[15-6-1901]	Retd. A. 16-6-1901	
William Robert Kennedy (K.C.B. 97)	14-3-1838	8-12-1857	18-7-1867	20-6-1874	29-11-1889	11-3-1896	[16-6-1901]	Retd. A. 1900	
John Arbuthnot Fisher, C.B. (K.C.B. 94)	25-1-1841	4-11-1860	2-8-1869	30-10-1874	2-8-1890	8-5-1896	[2-11-1901]		
Henry Frederick Stephenson, C.B. (K.C.B. 97)	7-6-1842	7-6-1861	26-4-1868	6-1-1875	4-8-1890	10-10-1896	[7-12-1901]	{ Retd. R.-A. 29-9-1894; retd. v.-a. 23-2-1897	
Charles George Fane (K.C.B. 1901)	14-11-1837	19-5-1859	16-10-1868	9-8-1875	5-8-1890	9-11-1896		{ Retd. R.-A. 24-12-1894; retd. v.-a. 23-2-1897	
John Frederick George Grant	30-11-1835	14-1-1857	6-3-1867	6-9-1875	6-8-1890				
Henry Foster Cleveland	28-4-1837	14-1-1857	3-4-1868	26-11-1875	30-8-1890		—		
Compton Edward Domvile (K.C.B. 98)	10-10-1842	28-10-1862	2-9-1868	27-3-1876	4-1-1891	23-2-1897	[25-1-1902]	Retd. R.-A. 1895	6-12-1896
Francis Durrant, C.M.G.	24-6-1837	26-11-1859	29-12-1869	15-5-1876	29-1-1891				
Frederick George Denham Bedford, C.B. (K.C.B. 94)	28-12-1838	26-11-1859	29-12-1871	15-5-1876	20-5-1891	10-5-1897			
John Fiot Lee Pearse Maclear	27-6-1838	19-5-1859	14-8-1868	13-10-1876	20-6-1891				
Albert Hastings Markham	1-11-1841	3-4-1862	29-11-1872	3-11-1876	1-8-1891	23-8-1897		{ Retd. R.-A. 21-8-1891; retd. v.-a. 23-8-1897	25-4-1893
Samuel Long	5-1-1840	24-4-1860	3-4-1868	12-12-1876	7-9-1891				
Alfred Taylor Dale	26-9-1840	16-4-1860	4-4-1870	31-12-1876	10-9-1891	16-9-1897			
Claude Edward Buckle	7-2-1839	26-6-1859	18-6-1866	22-1-1877	1-1-1892	11-12-1897			ob. 1900
Richard Duckworth-King	16-7-1840	8-2-1860	5-8-1867	16-2-1877	17-1-1892	26-12-1897			
Harry Holdsworth Rawson, C.B. (K.C.B. 97)	5-11-1843	10-5-1863	7-9-1871	4-6-1877	14-2-1892	19-3-1898	—	Retd. V.-A.	

LIST OF FLAG-OFFICERS—*continued.*

Name (with honours, title, etc., at date of promotion to Flag-rank, honours and titles subsequently acquired being within brackets).	Born.	Lieut.	Commander.	Captain.	Rear-Admiral.	Vice-Admiral.	Admiral.	Admiral of the Fleet.	Remarks. Rank attained only on or after retirement is indicated in small letters.	Died.
Robert Hornby Boyle	11-10-1840	31-8-1861	20-1-1868	25-8-1877	20-2-1892					13-6-1892
Cyprian Arthur George Bridge (K.C.B. 99)	15-3-1839	28-6-1859	15-2-1869	17-9-1877	25-2-1892	29-11-1898				
Edmund Charles Drummond	4-8-1841	11-5-1862	11-10-1867	31-12-1877	26-3-1892	21-12-1898				
Charles Searle Cardale	21-4-1841	31-8-1861	14-8-1868	9-1-1878	5-4-1892	13-1-1899	—	—	Retd. V.-A. 3-3-1900	
Edmund John Church	14-2-1842	16-4-1861	8-12-1868	9-1-1878	1-1-1893	30-6-1899	—	—	Retd. V.-A. 11-7-1899	
Walter Stewart, C.B.	13-7-1841	10-12-1861	13-5-1869	9-1-1878	1-1-1893	—	—	—		26-10-1896
John Reginald Thomas Fullerton (civ.) C.B.; K.C.V.O. 96; G.C.V.O. 1901)	10-8-1840	13-3-1861	6-2-1872	10-1-1878	1-1-1893	11-7-1899	—	—	Retd. V.-A.	
Charles Barstow Theobald	5-8-1843	5-10-1863	16-11-1863	23-3-1878	1-1-1893	—	—	—	{ Retd. R.-A. 5-8-1893; retd. v.-a. 13-7-1899	
Henry St. Leger Bury Palliser	22-6-1839	26-11-1859	15-2-1869	25-3-1878	26-4-1893	—	—	—	{ Retd. R.-A. 22-6-1899; retd. v.-a. 13-7-1899	
Ernest Rice	24-2-1840	9-2-1860	22-10-1870	25-3-1878	13-5-1893	13-7-1899	—	—		
Frederick Samuel Vander-Meulen	20-11-1839	18-7-1859	4-4-1870	25-3-1878	23-6-1893	26-10-1899	—	—	Retd. V.-A. 20-11-1899	
Hilary Gustavus Andoe, C.B.	19-2-1841	13-3-1861	6-2-1872	25-3-1878	1-1-1894	20-11-1899	—	—	Retd. V.-A. 1901	
Armand Temple Powlett	17-5-1841	8-8-1860	4-4-1870	31-12-1878	1-1-1894	3-3-1900	—	—	Retd. V.-A. 1901	
Alexander Plantagenet Hastings, C.B.	31-10-1844	3-8-1865	19-7-1870	31-12-1878	1-1-1894	21-3-1900	—	—	Retd. V.-A. 28-3-1901	
Rodney Maclaine Lloyd, C.B.	3-7-1841	31-8-1861	9-8-1870	4-2-1879	4-4-1894	10-8-1900				
Francis Starkie Clayton	19-7-1839	18-7-1859	4-4-1870	27-2-1879	10-3-1894	—	—	—	{ Retd. R.-A. 19-7-1899; retd. v.-a. 1-1-1901	
Arthur Hildebrand Alington	10-10-1839	26-11-1859	4-4-1870	31-10-1879	28-5-1894	—	—	—	{ Retd. R.-A. 13-1-1899; retd. v.-a. 1-1-1901	
Henry John Carr	6-7-1839	11-2-1860	29-12-1871	31-10-1879	7-6-1894	—	—	—	{ Retd. R.-A. 6-7-1899; retd. v.-a. 1-1-1901	
Charles Lister Oxley	17-10-1841	7-11-1861	6-2-1872	31-10-1879	1-1-1895	1-1-1901				
Robert Hastings Harris (K.C.M.G. 98; K.C.B. 1900)	12-10-1843	18-3-1863	22-6-1870	9-12-1879	1-1-1895	[19-2-1901]				
Hugo Lewis Pearson	30-6-1843	14-9-1863	6-2-1872	9-12-1879	1-1-1895	[13-2-1901]				
John Fellowes, C.B.	1-4-1843	24-3-1863	19-9-1873	29-1-1880	1-1-1895	[17-3-1901]				
Charles Cooper Penrose Fitzgerald	27-3-1838	24-7-1871	24-7-1871	19-3-1880	1-1-1895	[13-3-1901]				
Arthur Knyvet Wilson, V.C., C.B.	4-3-1842	11-12-1861	18-9-1873	20-4-1880	20-6-1895	[28-3-1901]				
Archibald Lucius Douglas	3-2-1842	23-5-1862	1-5-1872	19-6-1880	9-11-1895	[24-5-1901]				
William Home Chisholme St. Clair	9-9-1841	20-12-1860	4-12-1868	31-7-1880	1-1-1896	[16-6-1901]			Retd. V.-A. 9-9-1901	
Atwell Peregrine Macleod Lake	11-4-1842	8-4-1863	31-12-1875	3-1-1881	11-3-1896	[9-9-1901]				
Gerard Henry Uctred Noel (K.C.M.G. 98)	5-3-1845	21-4-1866	31-3-1874	11-1-1881	8-5-1896	[2-11-1901]				
John Williar Brackenbury, C.B. C.M.G.	30-11-1842	15-3-1865	18-3-1876	8-4-1881	10-10-1896	[7-12-1901]				
Thomas Sturges Jackson (Kt. 1902)	6-3-1842	22-3-1864	1-11-1873	14-10-1881	20-10-1896	[24-1-1902]				
Richard Horace Hamond	17-1-1843	9-11-1864	13-2-1873	31-12-1881	9-11-1896				Retd. R.-A. 31-3-1898	

Name							
Arthur Dalrymple Fanshawe	2-4-1847	21-9-1868	5-1-1874	31-12-1881	23-2-1897	[24-1-1902]	
Day Hort Bosanquet	22-3-1843	28-11-1863	1-9-1874	30-6-1882	10-5-1897		
Lewis Anthony Beaumont (K.C.M.G. 1901)	19-5-1847	23-8-1867	3-11-1876	30-6-1882	23-8-1897		10-8-1901
Lord Charles William Delapoer Beresford, C.B.	10-2-1846	21-9-1868	2-11-1875	11-7-1882	16-9-1897		
Albert Baldwin Jenkings	2-3-1846	15-9-1867	31-3-1877	11-7-1882	11-12-1897		
Henry Coey Kane, C.B.	12-1843	31-8-1864	22-1-1877	18-11-1882	26-12-1897		Retd. R.-A. 1899
Frederick Ross Boardman, C.B.	6-1843	9-11-1864	24-9-1873	31-12-1882	19-3-1898		
James Andrew Thomas Bruce (K.C.M.G. 1900)	15-7-1846	13-2-1866	1-10-1874	29-6-1883	31-3-1898		Retd. R.-A. 1899
Henry Rose	10-2-1844	31-8-1864	31-12-1875	29-6-1883	29-11-1898		
Pelham Aldrich	8-12-1844	11-9-1866	3-11-1876	29-6-1883	21-12-1898		
Swinton Colthurst Holland	8-2-1844	12-9-1865	25-3-1878	9-4-1884	13-1-1899		
Ernest Neville Rolfe, C.B.	11-8-1847	20-12-1871	30-8-1879	20-5-1884	13-1-1899		
Arthur William Moore, C.B., C.M.G.	30-7-1847	19-5-1870	31-12-1881	27-6-1884	13-1-1899		
Andrew Kennedy Bickford, C.M.G.	16-7-1844	25-1-1866	31-12-1878	31-12-1884	22-6-1899		
William Alison Dyke Acland (suc. as 2nd Bart.)	18-12-1847	21-9-1868	31-3-1879	1-1-1885	30-6-1899		Retd. R.-A. 1901
William Frederick Stanley Mann	21-6-1846	6-7-1867	15-5-1876	30-6-1885	6-7-1899		
John Hugh Bainbridge	31-5-1845	28-6-1866	18-8-1876	30-6-1885	11-7-1899		
Charles Carter Drury	27-8-1846	5-8-1868	1-5-1878	30-6-1885	13-7-1899		21-9-1902
Edmund Frederick Jeffreys	1-10-1846	29-4-1867	4-2-1879	30-6-1885	19-7-1899		
Reginald Neville Custance (C.M.G. 1900)	20-9-1847	6-2-1868	31-3-1878	31-12-1885	1-8-1899		
Burges Watson (C.V.O. 99).	24-9-1846	5-9-1866	3-7-1879	31-12-1885	25-8-1899		
John Robert Ebenezer Pattisson	10-12-1844	21-1-1867	3-7-1879	1-1-1886	26-10-1899		
William Hannam Henderson	20-6-1845	11-9-1866	31-12-1879	1-1-1886	20-11-1899		
James Iacon Hammet, C.M.G.	15-5-1848	29-7-1869	23-6-1880	1-1-1886	1-1-1900		
Harry Tremenheere Grenfell, C.M.G.	9-3-1845	16-3-1866	22-6-1876	4-2-1886	3-3-1900		
Sir Baldwin Wake Walker (2), Bart., C.M.G.	24-9-1846	18-2-1868	31-7-1880	4-2-1886	21-3-1900		
Robert William Craigie	25-7-1849	3-9-1872	16-11-1879	30-6-1886	10-8-1900		
Wilmot Hawkworth Fawkes	22-12-1846	19-11-1867	19-3-1880	30-6-1886	1-1-1901		
H.R.H. Prince George Frederick Ernest Albert, Duke of York, K.G., K.T., K.P., etc. (Duke of Cornwall; G.C.M.G.; Prince of Wales, 1901)	3-6-1865	8-10-1885	24-8-1891	2-1-1893	1-1-1901*		

HONORARY FLAG OFFICERS.

Name							
H.R.H. Albert Edward, Prince of Wales, K.G., K.T., K.P., G.C.B., etc. (now)	9-11-1841			18-7-1887			Suc. to the Throne 22-1-1901
H.M. King Edward (VI.)							
H.I.M. William II., German Emperor and King of Prussia, K.G., etc.	27-1-1859			2-8-1889			
H.R.H. Prince Albert William Henry of Prussia, K.G., etc.	14-8-1862		[13-9-1901]		5-2-1901		

* Special promotion.

APPENDIX B. TO CHAPTERS XLVI.–XLVIII.

LIST OF H.M. SHIPS TAKEN, DESTROYED, BURNT, FOUNDERED OR WRECKED BETWEEN THE END OF THE YEAR 1856, AND THE DEATH OF QUEEN VICTORIA, JAN. 22ND, 1901.

(*From Command Paper, No. 176, of 1891; supplemented from other sources, and by information kindly supplied by direction of the Rt. Hon. the Earl of Selborne, First Lord of the Admiralty.*)

YEAR.	DATE.	H. M. SHIP.	GUNS.	DISPL. TONS. [* Old measurement.]	H.P.I. [* Nom.]	COMMANDER. [* Lost his life on the occasion.]	REMARKS.
1857	Ap. 14	*Raleigh*, frig. . .	50	*1,939	—	Commod. Hon. Hy. Keppel, C.B. / Com. Edw. Winterton Turnour.	Wrecked near Macao. All saved.
1857	July 10	{*Transit*, screw iron trooper . . .}	—	*2,587	*400	..	Wrecked in the Strait of Banca.
1859	?	*Sappho*, brig sloop.	12	*428	—	Com. Fairfax Moresby (2).*	Supposed foundered on Australian Station. All lost.
1859	Feb. 8	*Wizard*, brig sloop	6	*231	—	Lt. Alf. Prowse Hasler Helby.	Wrecked on Seal Rock, Berehaven. All saved.
1859	Feb. 26	*Jaseur*, scr. g. b. .	2	*301	*80	Lt. John Binney Scott.	Wrecked on Baxo Nuevo, W. Ind. All saved.
1859	May 9	*Heron*, brig sloop .	12	*482	—	Com. Wm. Henderson Truscott.	Foundered between Ascension and Sierra Leone. 25 saved.
1859	June 25	*Lee*, scr. g. b. . .	2	*299	*80	Lt. Wm. Hy. Jones.	Sunk in action with the Pei-ho forts.
1859	June 25	*Plover*, scr. g. b. .	2	*235	*60	R.-Ad. Jas. Hope, C.B. / Lt. Wm. Hector Rason.*	Abandoned under fire of the Pei-ho forts.
1859	June 28	*Cormorant*, scr. g. b.	4	*675	*200	Com. Armine Wodehouse.	Sunk by fire from the Pei-ho forts.
1860	—	{*Assistance*, scr. st. ship . . . .}	—	*1,820	*400	Com. Chas. Jno. Balfour (1).	Wrecked off Hong-Kong.
1860	Oct. 21	{*Perseverance*, scr. iron trp. ship}	2	*1,967	*360	Com. Ed. Roche Power.	Wrecked off Mayo, C. de Verdes. All saved.
1861	Aug.	*Driver*, padd. . .	6	*1,056	*280	Com. Horatio Nelson (2).	Wrecked on Mariguana I.
1861	?	*Camilla*, brig sloop	16	*549	—	Com. Geo. Twisleton Colvile.*	Supposed foundered on China station. All lost.
1861	Dec. 29	{*Conqueror*, scr. wood line-of-battle s. .}	101	*3,265	*800	Capt. Ed. Southwell Sotheby, C.B.	Wrecked on Rum Key.
1863	Feb. 5	*Orpheus*, scr. . .	21	*1,706	*400	Commod. Wm. Farquharson Burnett, C.B.* / Com. Robt. Heron Burton.*	Wrecked off Manukau, N.Z.
1863	Dec. 23	*Lively*, scr. g. b. .	2	*254	*60	Lt. Wm. Walsh.	Wrecked off the Dutch coast.

Year.	Date.	H.M. Ship.	Guns.	Displ. Tons. [* Old measure-ment.]	H.P.I. [* Nom.]	Commander. [* Lost his life on the occasion.]	Remarks.
1864	Ap. 3	*Magpie,* scr. g. b. .	2	*236	*60	Lt. Geo. Robt. Bell.	Wrecked in Galway Bay.
1864	Nov. 4	*Racehorse,* scr. g. v.	4	*695	*200	Com. Chas. Rd. Fox Boxer.	Wrecked near Chefoo. Few saved.
1864	Dec. 14	*Bombay,* scr. wood line-of-battle shp.	67	*2,782	*400	R.-Ad. Hon. Chas. Gilbert Jno. Bry-done Elliot, C.B. Capt. Colin And. Campbell.	Burnt off Montevideo.
1865	Oct. 23	*Bulldog,* padd. . .	6	*1,124	*500	Capt. Chas. Wake.	Destroyed to prevent capture, at C. Haytien.
1866	July 10	*Amazon,* scr. . .	4	*1,081	*300	Com. Jas. Ed. Hunter.	Sunk by collision with s.s. *Osprey,* off the Start.
1866	Oct.	*Griffon,* scr. g. v. .	5	*425	*80	Com. Duncan Geo. Davidson.	Stranded after colli-sion with H.M.S. *Pandora,* off Little Popo.
1867	(?)	*Osprey,* scr. g. v. .	4	*682	*200	Com. Wm. Menzies.	Wrecked on coast of S. Africa.
1868	Sept. 24	*Rattler,* scr. . .	17	*952	*200	Com. Hy. Fredk. Stephenson.	Wrecked on China station.
1868	Nov. 15	*Gnat,* twn. scr. g. v.	2	*464	*120	Com. Chas. Barstow Theobald.	Wrecked off Balabac I., China.
1869	Mar. 29	*Ferret,* brig sloop .	8	*385	—	Lt. Hilary Mansell Carré.	Wrecked off Dover. All saved.
1870	May 9	*Slaney,* scr. g. v. .	1	*301	*80	Lt. Wm. Fras: Leoline Elwyn.	Wrecked on the Paracels, China.
1870	Sept. 5	*Trinculo,* scr. g. b. .	2	*273	*60	Lt. Hon. Fras. Geo. Crofton.	Wrecked off Gibral-tar. Only 2 lost.
1870	Sept. 7	*Captain,*[1] iron turret battleship. . .	6	*4,272 / 6,950	*900	Capt. Hugh Talbot Burgoyne, V.C.*	Capsized off Finis-terre. Only 18 saved.
1870	Dec. 15	*Psyche,* padd. d. v.	2	*835	*250	Lt. John Fellowes.	Wrecked on Pt. Mechini, Catania.
1871	June 19	*Megæra,* scr. iron st. ship .	6	*1,395	*350	Capt. Arth. Thos. Thrupp.	Beached at St. Paul's I.
1874	May 21	*Niobe,* scr. . . .	4	*1,083	*300	Com. David Boyle.	Wrecked off Mique-lon I.
1875	Sept. 1	*Vanguard,* iron central battery battleship . .	14	*3,774 / 6,010	*800 5,312	Capt. Rich. Dawkins.	Accidentally rammed by H.M.S. *Iron Duke* off the Kish Bank, and sank. No life lost.
1878	Mar. 24	*Eurydice,*[2] training frigate. . . .	4	*921 / 1,014	—	Capt. Marcus Aug. Stanley Hare.*	Capsized off the I. of Wight. Only 2 saved.
1878	Oct. 31	*Fanny,* c. g. cruiser	—	*153	—	Chf. Offr. Joseph Greet.*	Run down off the Tuskar, by s.s. *Helvetia:* 17 lost.
1880	Mar. (?)	*Atalanta,*[3] training frigate. . . .	4	*923	—	Capt. Francis Stirling.*	Never heard of after having left Ber-muda on Jan. 31st. All hands, 280, lost.

[1] With the *Captain,* in addition to Capt. Burgoyne, there perished her designer, Capt. Cowper Phipps Coles ; Com. Richd. Sheepshanks ; Lieuts. Chas. Giffard, Fras. Bennett Renshaw, Richd. Ponsonby Purdon, Robt. Fry Castle, and Ed. Wm. Fredk. Boxer ; Capt. (R.M.A.) Rich. Archd. Gorges ; Lieut. (R.M.) Jno. Alex. Armstrong Eckford ; Chaplain and Nav. Inst. Rev. Edm. Sheppard Powles ; Staff-Com. Robt. Jno. Corsillis Grant ; Paym. Julian Alex. Messum ; Asst.-Payms. Richd. Cornish, and Arnold West ; Chf.-Eng. Geo. Rock ; St.-Surg. Mat. Burton, M.D. ; Surg. Robt. Purves ; Actg. Asst.-Surg. Jno. Ryan ; Engineers W. C. Moreton, P. Baldwin, G. H. Barnes, J. H. Willis, and F. Pursell ; Lt. Nordenfelt, of the Swed. Navy ; two Greek mids. ; a son of Adm. Sir Baldwin Wake Walker ; a son of Mr. Childers, then First Lord ; a son of Lord Northbrook ; and other officers. The total loss was 472.

[2] There perished with the *Eurydice,* in addition to Capt. Hare, Lieuts. Francis Hope Tabor, Charles Vernon Strange, William Edward Black, and Stanley Alfred Brooke Burney ; Staff.-Surg. James Leech Whitney ; Paym. Frank Pittman ; Sub-Lieuts. Hon. Edward Robert Gifford, Herbert Sayres Edmunds, Walter Stuart Smith, and Sydney Granville Randolph.; Surg. Robert Murdoch ; Gunner Frederick Allen ; Boatswains William Brewer and Joseph Warren ; and Asst.-Clerk William Lamont. The total loss of life was about 300. A few military passengers were on board.

[3] Among the officers who, with Capt. Fras. Stirling, perished in the *Atalanta* were Lieuts. Fredk. Arth. Blackett, Arth. Dove, and Philip Evan Fisher ; Nav.-Lieut. Wm. Hy. Stephens ; Chaplain the Rev. Robt. Nimmo ; Paym. John Ashton ; Gunner Wm. Silk ; Boatswains Fredk. Standish, and Rich. Clancy, etc.

Year.	Date.	H.M. Ship.	Guns.	Displ. Tons. [* Old measurement.]	H.P.I. [* Nom.]	Commander. [* Lost his life on the occasion.]	Remarks.
1881	Ap. 26	*Doterel*, comp. sc. sloop	6	1,137	900	Com. Rich. Evans.	Sank off Sandy Pt. owing to an accidental explosion on board: 143 lives being lost.
1882	Sept. 12	*Phœnix*, comp. sc. sloop	6	1,130	1,130	Com. Hubert Hy. Grenfell.	Wrecked of P. Edward's I. No lives lost.
1883	June 7	*Lively*, padd. disp. v.	2	985	1,460	Com. Alf. Arth. Chase Parr.	Wrecked off Stornoway. No lives lost.
1884	Sept. 22	*Wasp*, comp. sc. g. b.	4	465	470	Lieut. Jno. Dundas Nicholls.*	Wrecked off Tory Island: 52 lives lost.
1887	Sept.	*Wasp*, comp. sc. g. b.	6	670	1,000	Lieut. Bryan Jno. Huthwaite Adamson.*	Never heard of after having left Singapore, Sept. 10. All hands, 80, lost.
1889	Sept. 16	*Lily*, sc. g. vessel .	3	720	830	Com. Gerald Walter Russell.	Wrecked off Labrador: 7 lives lost.
1890	Oct.	*No. 62* (1st class) torpedo-boat). .	—	75	700	..	Lost while in tow of H.M.S. *Buzzard* in a gale, N. Amer. station.
1890	Nov. 10	*Serpent*,[1] 3rd cl. cr.	6	1,770	4,500	Com. Harry Leith Ross.*	Wrecked off N. coast of Spain: 173 lives lost; 3 saved.
1892	Aug. 8	*No. 75* (1st class) torpedo-boat). .	—	75	700	Actg. Sub-Lieut. Arth. Wm. Craig.	Sank after collision with t. b. No. 77 off the Maidens. No one lost.
1893	June 22	*Victoria*,[2] battleship	15	10,470	14,000	V.-Ad. Sir Geo. Tryon, K.C.B.* Capt. Hon. Maur. Archib. Bourke.	Sank after being rammed by H.M.S. *Camperdown*, off Tripoli, Syria. C.-in-Chf., 21 officers and 350 men lost.
1898	July 29	*No. 28* (1st class) torpedo-boat). .	—	60	600	Lieut. Hon. Edw. Spencer Harry Boyle.	Stranded in Kalk Bay. Badly damaged. Used in Dec. 1898 as a target by Cape Squadron, and sunk.
1900	Nov. 27	*Hind*, coastguard cutter	—	130	—	Chf. Off. John McDonald.	Wrecked on Shipwash Sands.
1901	Jan. 16	*Sibylle*, 2nd cl. cr. .	8	3,400	9,000	Capt. Hugh Pigot Williams.	Wrecked in Lambert's Bay, S. Afr.

[1] The officers lost in the *Serpent* were:—Com. Harry Leith Ross; Lieuts. Guy Alwine John Greville, Peter Noel Richards, and Torquill MacLeod; Paym. James William Dixon; Chf.-Eng. John James Robins; Asst.-Engs. William Piercy Edwards and Frederick Victor Head; Staff-Surg. William Masters Rae; Gunner Frank Holsgrove, and Boatswain Thomas Hicks.

[2] In addition to Sir Geo. Tryon, the following officers perished with the ship:—Lieut. Philip Harvey Munro; Chaplain the Rev. Saml. Sheppard Oakley Morris; Fleet-Paym. Valentine Dyer J. Rickcord; Fleet-Eng. Felix Foreman; Eng. Fredk. Geo. Harding; Asst.-Engs. Hy. Chas. Deadman, Wm. Ernest Hatherly, and Wm. Rowland Seaton; Gunner Wm. Howell; Boatswain Wm. Barnard; Carpenter Philip Hy. Beall; Mids. Leslie Inglis, Arth. Chas. Grieve, Ayscough Guy Hawksworth Fawkes, Herb. Marsden Lanyon, Walter E. Henley, Harold W. Gambier, and Lawrence J. P. Scarlett; Naval-Cadet Fraser S. Stooks; Clerk to Sec. Hy. Ross Allen; and Asst.-Clerk Arth. Darley Savage.

PUBLISHER'S NOTE

In the original edition the four photogravure plates and twenty-five full-page illustrations faced the text pages as listed on pages xiii–xiv. In this edition these illustrations are collected on the following pages in the order in which they appeared in the first edition. The original position indicators have been retained.

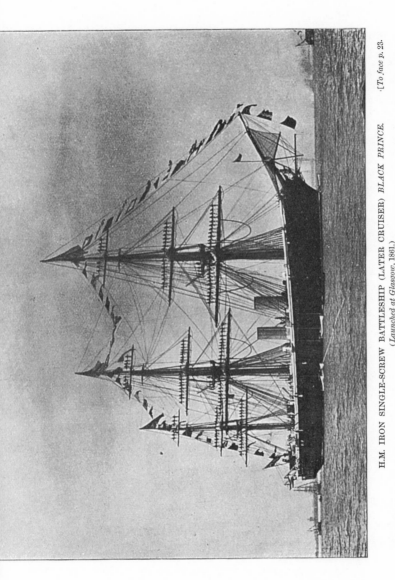

H.M. IRON SINGLE-SCREW BATTLESHIP (LATER CRUISER) *BLACK PRINCE.*   [*To face p.* 23.

(*Launched at Glasgow,* 1861.)

Displacement, 9210 tons; length, 380 ft. 2 in.; beam, 58 ft. 4 in.; mean draught, 26 ft. 10 in.; I.H.P. 4000; speed, 12·5 knots.
Engines by Messrs. Penn.

Protection, for 200 ft. over battery, 4·5 in. iron, backed by 18 in. teak; bulkheads, 4 in. No armour at ends.
Original armament, 10 12-ton M.; 16 6½-ton M., etc. Later armament, 22 6½-ton (7 in.) M.; 2 6-in. B.; 4 3-pr. Q.; 8 boat guns;
7 machine guns; torpedo-tubes, 2.

[In 1900 this ship served as a training vessel for boys at Queenstown.]

[*To face p.* 34.

H.M. TWIN SCREW, STEEL, BARBETTE BATTLESHIP *GLORY.*

(*Launched at Birkenhead, 1899.*)

Length, 390 ft.; beam, 74 ft.; mean draught, 26 ft.; displ, 12,950 tons; I.H.P., 13,500; speed, 18·25 kts.
Two sets of vertical triple-expansion engines by Lairds. Belleville boilers.
Armour: partial Harveyed nickel steel belt, 6 in.; bulkheads, 12 in.; barbettes, 12 to 6 in.; casemates, 5 in.
Armament: 4 12-in. 46-ton B.; 12 6-in. Q.; 10 12-pr. Q.; 2 12-pr. field; 6 3-pr. Q.; 8 ·45-in Maxims; torpedo-tubes, 4.
Complement, 750.

[*To face p.* 38.]

H.M. TURBINE, STEEL TORPEDO-BOAT DESTROYER *VIPER*.

(*Built at Hebburn,* 1900.)

Length, 210 ft. ; beam, 21 ft. ; mean draught, 8 ft. 2 in. ; displ, 325 tons ; I.H.P. 10,000 ; speed, 36·58 kts.

Armament : 1 12-pr. Q. ; 5 6-pr. Q. ; 2 18-in. torpedo tubes.

H.M. STEEL TWIN-SCREW TORPEDO-RAM *POLYPHEMUS*.

(*Launched at Chatham*, 1881.)

Displacement, 2640 tons; length, 240 ft.; beam, 40 ft.; mean draught, 20 ft.; I.H.P. 5500; speed, 17·8 kts.
Horizontal engines by Humphrys and Tennant. Boilers, 8; furnaces, 16.
Protection: steel deck, 2–3 in. Armament: 6 6-pr. Q.; 2 machine guns; torpedo-tubes, 5. Complement, 142.

[*To face p.* 40.

H.M. STEEL TWIN-SCREW TORPEDO DEPÔT SHIP *VULCAN.*

(*Launched at Portsmouth, 1889.*)

Displacement, 6620 tons ; length, 350 ft. ; beam, 58 ft. ; mean draught, 23 ft. ; I.H.P. 12,000 ; speed, 20 kts. Engines by Humphrys and Tennant.

Protection: steel deck, 2·5–5 in.   Armament : 8 4·7 in. Q. ; 12 3-pr. Q. ; 1 boat-gun ; 16 machine guns. Carrying on deck, 6 60-ft. torpedo-boats ; 2 countermining launches and 4 other steam-boats.   Complement, 432.

[*To face p.* 42.

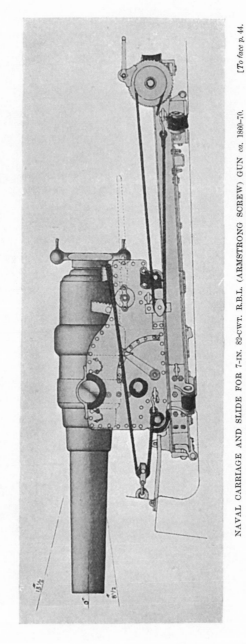

NAVAL CARRIAGE AND SLIDE FOR 7-IN. 82-CWT. R.B.L. (ARMSTRONG SCREW) GUN *ca.* 1860–70.

From drawings specially supplied by Sir W. G. Armstrong, Whitworth & Co., Ltd.

[*To face p.* 44.]

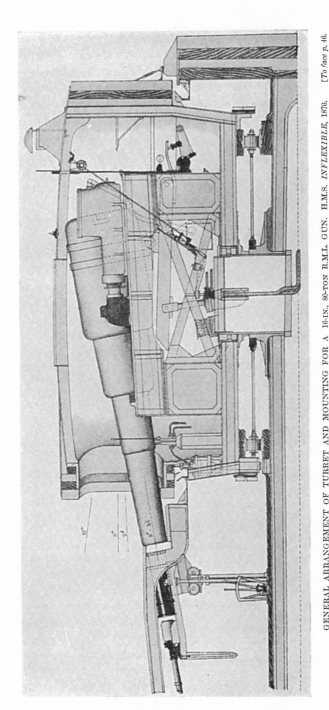

GENERAL ARRANGEMENT OF TURRET AND MOUNTING FOR A 16-IN., 80-TON R.M.L. GUN. H.M.S. *INFLEXIBLE*, 1876. [*To face p.* 46.

(*From a drawing specially supplied by Sir W. G. Armstrong, Whitworth & Co., Ltd.*)

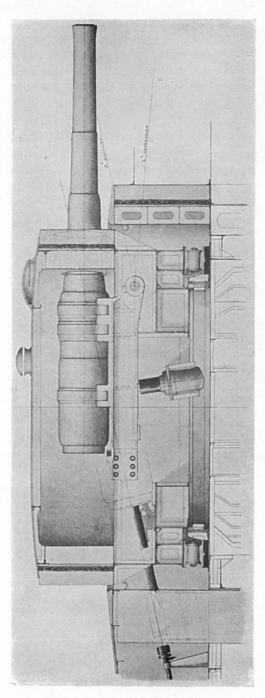

SECTION THROUGH BATTERY AND TURRET.

H.M.S. *VICTORIA* (1887).

Showing one of the pair of 16·25-in. 111-TON B.L. guns, behind 18-in. armour.

(*From a drawing; specially supplied by Sir W. G. Armstrong, Whitworth & Co., Ltd.*)

[*To face p.* 48.]

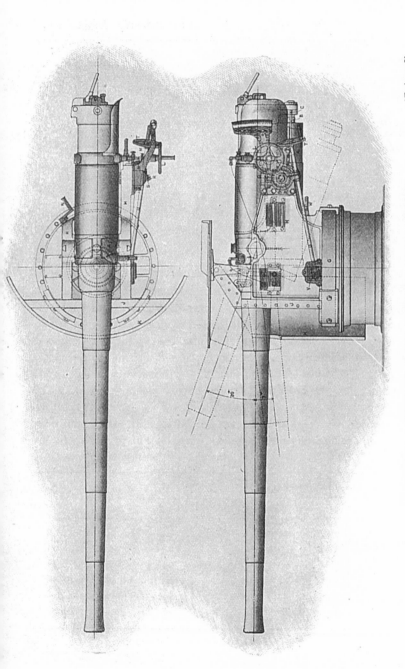

[*To face p.* 50.

A 4·724-IN. (120 MM.) QUICK-FIRING GUN ON CENTRE PIVOT MOUNTING.

(Last years of the XIXth Century.)

(*From a drawing specially supplied by Sir W. G. Armstrong, Whitworth & Co., Ltd.*)

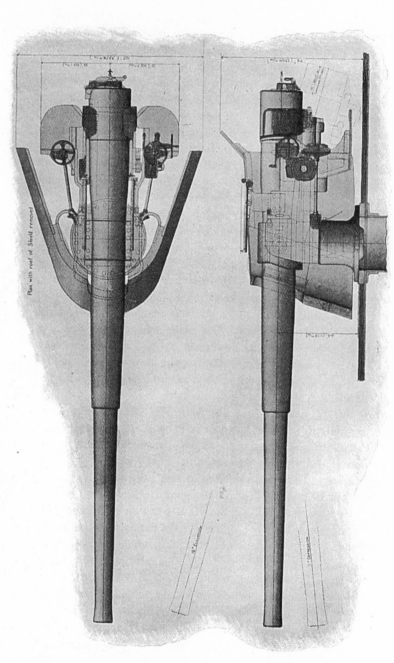

[*To face p.* 52.]

Plan with roof of Shield removed

A 6-IN. (152 MM.) 45-CALIBRE QUICK-FIRING GUN, ON UPPER-DECK MOUNTING.

(Last years of the XIXth Century.)

(*From a drawing specially supplied by Sir W. G. Armstrong, Whitworth & Co., Ltd.*)

H.M. TRAINING BRIG *NAUTILUS.*
(*Built at Pembroke,* 1879.)

Displacement, 501 tons; length, 105 ft.; beam, 33 ft. 6 in.; mean draught, 13 ft. 2 in.   Built of wood.

[*To face p.* 62.

H.R.H. PRINCE GEORGE FREDERICK ERNEST ALBERT, OF WALES, K.G., K.T.,
K.P., G.C.V.O., P.C., DUKE OF YORK, ETC., REAR-ADMIRAL, A.D.C.,
COLONEL-IN-CHIEF, ROYAL MARINES.

(From a photo by Lafayette, taken when H.R.H. was a Captain.)

[*To face p.* 83.

Admiral Sir Michael Seymour (2) G.C.B.

Vice-Admiral of the United Kingdom.

From the engraved portrait by F. Holl, Senr, after A. de Salome.

Walter L. Colls, 96. Sc.

Calcutta's barge.   Keppel's galley.   *Calcutta's pinnace.*

[To face p. 104.

THE ACTION IN FATSHAN CREEK, JUNE 1st, 1857.

(From a chromolithograph after O. Brierly, kindly lent by Adm. Sir W. R. Kennedy, K.C.B.)

NOTE TO THE ABOVE BY SIR W. R. KENNEDY. "The graphic picture of this event, painted by Mr. Brierly from description, though correct in most details, is misleading, inasmuch as two boats are depicted close to the Commodore's galley, one flying the white ensign, the other the blue, which would seem to imply that one boat was the *Calcutta's*, the other the *Raleigh's*. This mistake may be perhaps excused, seeing that Brierly was not present; . . . but, as a matter of fact, the two boats almost touching the Commodore's galley at the moment were . . . the *Calcutta's* barge, with Lieutenant Culme-Seymour . . . in charge, and my pinnace" (*Calcutta's*) "under Lieutenant Robert James Wynniatt, I being forward working the gun."

ATTACK ON THE TAKU FORTS, 20TH MAY, 1858.

(After a picture by Bedwell.)

[*To face p.* 118.

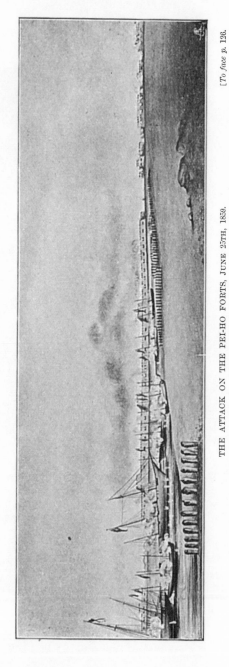

THE ATTACK ON THE PEI-HO FORTS, JUNE 25TH, 1859.

[*From a sketch made on the spot by Lieutenant (later Admiral Sir) George Digby Morant.*]

[*To face p.* 126.]

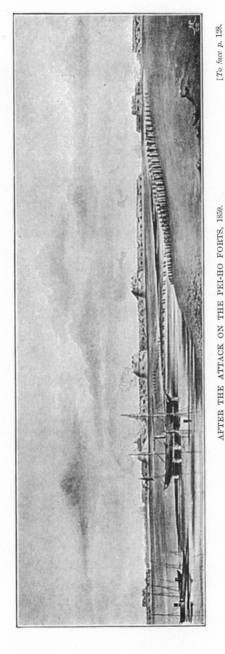

AFTER THE ATTACK ON THE PEI-HO FORTS, 1859.

[*From a sketch made on the spot by Lieutenant (later Admiral Sir) George Digby Morant.*]

[*To face p.* 128.]

[To face p. 162.

H.M. SINGLE-SCREW, IRON, ARMOURED SHIP *AGINCOURT.*

(*Launched at Birkenhead,* 1865.)

Length, 400 ft. ; beam, 59 ft. 4½ in. ; mean draught, 27 ft. 9 in. ; displ, 10,600 tons ; I.H.P. 4000 ; speed, 13·2.kts.
Horizontal common return connecting-rod engines by Maudslay.
Armour : complete 5½ in. iron belt to upper deck, except at bows ; 4½ in. forward bulkhead.   Conning-tower, 5½ in.
Original armament : 10 12½ ton M.: 16 6¼ ton M.   Complement, 710.

H.M. PADDLE, WOODEN ROYAL YACHT *VICTORIA AND ALBERT.*
(Built at Pembroke, 1855.)

Length, 300 ft.; beam, 40 ft. 3¾ in.; mean draught, 16 ft. 11 in.; displ., 2470 tons; I.H.P., 2980; speed, 15·7 kts.
Complement, 151.

[*To face p.* 217.

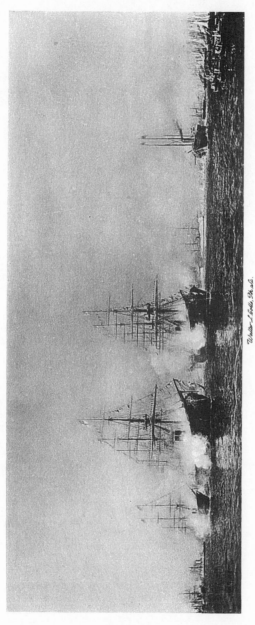

Waterlow & Sons. Ph. Sc.

The Jubilee Review at Spithead:

July 23rd 1887.

From the picture painted by Sir O. W. Brierly for her late Majesty, Queen Victoria.

By gracious permission of H. M. the King.

[*To face p.* 330.

H.M. IRON TWIN-SCREW CENTRAL-BATTERY BATTLESHIP *ALEXANDRA.*

(*Launched at Chatham, 1875; reconstructed, 1890, and so shown in the picture.*)

Displacement, 9490 tons; length, 325 ft.; beam, 63 ft. 8 in.; mean draught, 26 ft. 6 in.; I.H.P. 7000; speed, 14 kts.
Engines by Humphrys and Tennant.

Protection: complete iron belt, 10 ft. 6 in. deep, and 6–12 in. thick; over battery, 8–12 in.; bulkheads, 5–8 in.; deck, 2 in.
Armament, see p. 324. (After 1880): 4 9·2 in. B.; 8 10-in. M.; 6 4-in. B.; 4 6-pr. Q.; 6 3-pr. Q.; 3 boat-guns; 16 mach.; torpedo-tubes, 4.
Complement, 680.

[To face p. 332.

H.M. TWIN-SCREW, IRON, TURRET BATTLESHIP *INFLEXIBLE.*

(*Built at Portsmouth,* 1876.)

Length, 320 ft.; beam, 75 ft.; mean draught, 26 ft. 4 in.; displ. 11,880 tons; I.H.P. 6500; speed, 12·6 kts.
Armour: belt and central citadel (partial), 16-24 in. iron; turrets, 17 in. compound.
Armament, see p. 324. (In 1900): 4 16-in. M.; 8 4·7 in. B.; 4 6-pr. Q.; 2 3-pr. Q.; 2 field; torpedo-tubes, 4.
Complement, 470.

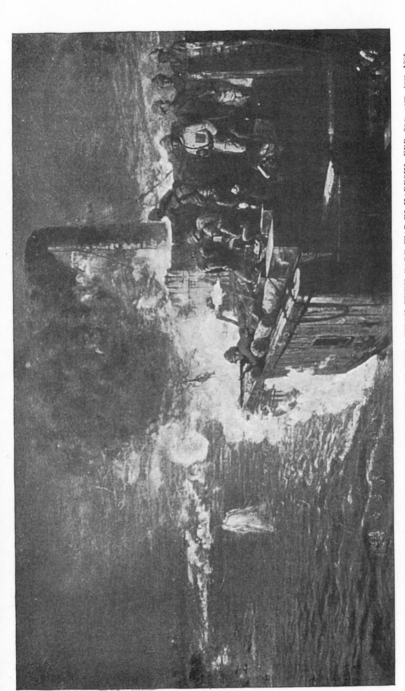

THE *SAFIEH*, CAPTAIN LORD CHARLES W. D. BERESFORD, IN THE ACTION WITH FORT WAD-EL-HABESHI, FEB. 3RD AND 4TH, 1885.

(*From a picture in the possession of Rear-Admiral Lord Charles Beresford, C.B.*)

[*To face p. 306.*

H.M. SINGLE-SCREW, STEEL AND IRON, SHEATHED CRUISER *CALLIOPE*.

(Launched at Portsmouth, 1884.)

[*To face p.* 394.

Length, 235 ft. ; beam, 44 ft. 6 in. ; mean draught, 19 ft. 11 in. ; displ., 2770 tons ; I.H.P., 4000 ; speed, 14·6 kts.   Engines by Messrs. Rennie.   Armament : 4 6-in. B. ; 12 5-in. B. ; 2 field ; 9 mach.   Complement, 291.

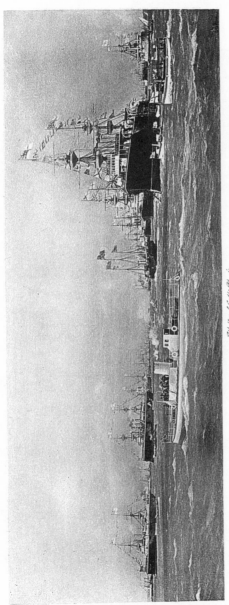

Walter Crisk Photo.

The Diamond Jubilee Review at Spithead.

June 26th 1897.

From the picture painted by Eduardo de Martino for her late Majesty, Queen Victoria.

By gracious permission of H. M. the King.

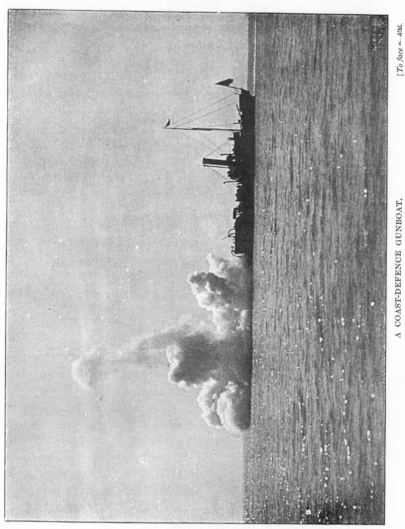

A COAST-DEFENCE GUNBOAT.

(*Type of a number built 1870–73.*)

Displacement, 254 tons; I.H.P. 110; speed about 7·5 knots. Original armament, 1 10-in. muzzle-loader.

H.M. STEEL TWIN-SCREW TORPEDO GUNBOAT (TORPEDO-BOAT CATCHER) *RATTLESNAKE.*

(Launched by Messrs. Laird, at Birkenhead, 1886.)

[*To face p.* 440.

Displacement, 550 tons; length, 200 ft.; beam, 23 ft.; mean draught, 9 ft.; I.H.P. 2700; speed, 18·5 kts.
Vertical triple-expansion engines by Messrs. Laird.
Armament: 1 4-in. B.; 6 3-pr. Q.; torpedo tubes, 4.

[*To face p.* 464.]

H.M. TWIN SCREW, STEEL, SHEATHED CRUISER *TERRIBLE*,

Sister ship to the *Powerful.*

(*Built at Clydebank*, 1895.)

Length, 538 ft. over all ; beam, 71 feet ; mean draught, 27 ft. ; displ. 14,200 tons ; I.H.P., 25,000 ; speed, 22 kts.
Armament : 2 9·2-in. B. ; 12 6-in. Q. ; 16 12-pr. Q. ; 2 12-pr. field ; 12 3-pr. Q. ; 9 ·45-in. Maxims ; 4 torpedo-tubes.

Vice-Admiral Sir Edward Hobart Seymour, G.C.B.

After a photograph by Maull & Fox.

INDEX.

VOLUME VII.

So far as possible, the rank ascribed to executive officers is that to which they had attained upon leaving the Navy, or, if still serving, upon the conclusion of the period covered by this History. Retired rank is not noticed.

2 R 2

Seymour, V.-Adm. George Henry, 157, 571
Seymour, Adm. Sir Michael (2), 85, 88, 93–97, 101, 102, 104, 106 n.[1], 110, 116, 119 n.[3], 122, 138; quoted, 100, 106, 107, 117; cited, 119 n.[2], 122
Seymour, Lieut. Montagu Hamilton March, 372, 374
Shadwell, V.-Adm. Sir Charles Frederick Alexander, 88, 126, 127, 129, 130, 269, 270, 573
Shah, 38, 286 and n.[1], 287, 288 n.[2], 307
Shakespear, Lieut. Hastings Frank, 519
Shakespeare's Head tavern, 75
Sha-lui-tien, 123
Shameen Forts, 95
Shamrock, 150
Shanghai, 132, 157–160, 162–165, 171, 221
Shanhaikuan, 559, 560
Shanks, Paym. Hemsley Hardy, 208
Shannon, Carpenter William, 331 n.[1], 332
Shannon, 26, 28, 31, 53, 110, 138, 142, 143; Brigade of, in India, 142, 143
Shark's Point, 285
Sharp, Mids. Charles Reynolds, 493 n.[2]
Sharpe, Capt. Philip Ruffle, 228
Sharpshooter, 38, 40
Shaw, Mr. (agent of Lond. Miss. Soc.), 348
Shaw, Mr. (Resd. in Burmah), 376
Shaw, Dept. Insp.-Genl. Doyle Money, 135, 346
Shaw-Lefevre, the Rt. Hon. George John, Sec. of Admlty, 2
Shearman, Asst.-Eng. John George, 144, 145
Shearwater, 564
Sheen, Chf. Eng. Charles Cape, 493 n.[2], 497, 500, 501
Sheepshanks, Com. Richard, 583 n.[1]
Sheerness :—
    Dockyard Superintendents at, 7
    Gunnery school at, 70
Sheik, 450
Shendy, 365
Shepherd, R.-Adm. John (2), 7, 570
Sheppard (R.M.), Corpl. G., 552
Shepstone, Sir Theophilus, 303 n.[1], 315 n.[1]
Sheringham, Capt. William Louis, 564
Sherrin, Mids. Alwyne Edward, 502 n.[3]
Shiba, Col., 556
Shimadzu Sabura, 193, 194
Shipton, Lieut. John Perceval, 428 n.[3]
Shipwrecked Fishermen and Mariners' Royal Benevolent Society, 74
Shiré River, 407, 410, 412
Shirinski, Col., 528 and n.[4]
Shirley, Com. Arthur Horatio, 390
Shone, Asst.-Surg. William James, 144
Shore, Mids. Lionel Henry, 539 and n.[4], 543
Shousing, 172
Shrubb, Lieut. Henry Arthur Beverley, 403 n.[2]
Siam, 84, 413, 414

Sibbald, Fleet-Surg. Thomas Martyn, 288, 529, 530
Sibylle, 94, 95, 102, 106 n.[1], 114 n.[1], 518, 519, 584
Sierra Leone, 151, 388, 406, 452–454
Signalling :—
    Commercial Code of, 64
    Military masts used for, 63
    Night, 64 and n., 65
    School of, 70
Sikhs, 145, 147
Sikukuni, Chief, 303 n.[1]
Silk, Gunner William, 583 n.[3]
Sillem, Mids. William Wood, 476 and n.[4]
Simmonds, Seaman, 147
Simms, Lieut. Henry William, 406
Simonoseki, 195, 203–208
Simoon, 135 n.[3], 253 and n., 256, 258 nn.[2 4], 262
Sims, Lieut. William, 493 n.[2], 494, 500 and n.[3], 501
Sinbyumaryin, Princess, 376
Sinclair, Cons., 161, 221
Sinde, 224 n.[1]
Singleton, Capt. Uvedale Corbet, 272
Sin-ho, 133, 134
Sinkat, 350, 351, 353
Sir Charles Forbes, 102, 107
Sir George Grey (Jap.), 197
Sir Hugh Rose, 224 n.[1]
Sirianni, Lieut. 523
Sirius, 38, 283
Sisk, Philip T. (pet. off.), 494 n.
Sitka, 310
Skinner, Mids. George Macgregor, 502 n.[3]
Skrydloff, R.-Adm., 448
Slade, R.-Adm. Sir Adolphus, 76 and n.[3], 572
Sladen, Col. Sir Edward, 375, 376, 383
Slaney, 117–119, 136, 221, 583
Slater, Lieut. Walter Clifton, 391
" Slave-Catching in the Indian Ocean," cited, 225
Slaver, waterlogged, from Fiji, 232
Slavers, encounters with :—
    Africa, East, 136, 189, 226, 234, 263, 264, 279, 289, 312, 386–388
    Africa, West, 152, 187–189, 210
    Arabian Gulf, 224
    Bahrein, 225
    Mozambique, 314
    Persian Gulf, 233
    West Indies, 137
    Zanzibar, 310 and n.[2], 390, 391
Slight, Capt. Julian Foulston, 114 n.[1], 120 and n.[1]
Sloper, Seaman David, 275
Small-arms, improvements in, 50
Small-pox, 306; in slavers, 233
Smart, Adm. Sir Robert, 7, 86, 89, 569
Smith, Lieut. Arthur Gordon, 524, 529
Smith, Navg.-Lieut. Edmond Carter, 277
Smith, Capt. Frederick Harrison, 136, 188